W9-AWS-179

WORKING AMERICANS

1880–2006

Volume VII: Social Movements

WORKING AMERICANS
1880–2006

Volume VII: Social Movements

by Scott Derks

A Universal Reference Book

Grey House
Publishing

PUBLISHER:	Leslie Mackenzie
EDITORIAL DIRECTOR:	Laura Mars-Proietti
EDITORIAL ASSISTANT:	Jane Murphy
MARKETING DIRECTOR:	Jessica Moody
AUTHOR:	Scott Derks
CONTRIBUTORS:	Jim Copening, Josh Chilton, Tony Smith
ASSISTANT to the author:	Brian Stanley
COPYEDITOR:	Elaine Alibrandi
COMPOSITION & DESIGN:	ATLIS Graphics

A Universal Reference Book
Grey House Publishing, Inc.
185 Millerton Road
Millerton, NY 12546
518.789.8700
FAX 518.789.0545
www.greyhouse.com
e-mail: books @greyhouse.com

Publisher's Cataloging-In-Publication Data
(Prepared by the Donohue Group, Inc.)

Derks, Scott.
  Working Americans, 1800–2006 / by Scott Derks.

  v.   ; cm.

Title varies.
"A universal reference book."
Includes bibliographical references and indexes.
Contents: v.1. The working class—v. 2. The middle class—v. 3. The upper class—v. 4. Their children.—v. 5. At war.—v. 6. Women at work – v. 7. Social movements.
  ISBN: 1-891482-81-5 (v. 1)
  ISBN: 1-891482-72-6 (v. 2)
  ISBN: 1-930956-38-X (v.3)
  ISBN: 1-59327-024-1 (v. 5)
  ISBN: 978-1-59237-101-3 (v. 7)
  ISBN: 1-59327-101-9 (v. 7)

1.   1. Working class—United States—History—19th century.   2. Working class—United States—History—20th century.   3. Labor—United States—History—19th century.   4. Labor—United States—History—20th century.   5. Occupations—United States—History—19th century.   6. Occupations—United States—History—20th century.   7. Social classes—United States—History—19th century.   8. Social classes—United States—History—20th century.   9. United States—Economic conditions.   I. Title.

HD8066   .D47 2000
105.5/0973/0904

First edition published 2006
Printed in the USA

ISBN 10: 1-59237-101-9
ISBN 13: 1-978-1-59237-101-3

Preface

This book is the seventh in a series examining the social and economic lives of working Americans. In this volume, the focus is on the men and women who initiated or participated in social movements. These people include those willing to participate in a silent Negro protest march against lynching, a physician who violated the law and strictures of his community to offer birth control information, a mother's feverish attempts to ban action comics and a businessman willing to raise money to aid the post-World War Jewish refugees of Poland.

The first volume, *Working Americans: 1880–1999: The Working Class,* explores the struggles of the working class through the eyes and wallets of three dozen families. Employing pictures, stories, statistics and advertisements of the period, it studies their jobs, wages, family life, expenditures and hobbies throughout the decades. The second and third volumes, *The Middle Class* and *The Upper Class,* capture the struggles and joys of families possessing progressively greater wealth and their roles in transforming the economy of America from 1880 to 1999. The fourth volume, *Their Children,* builds upon the social and economic issues explored previously by examining the lives of children across the entire spectrum of economic status. This volume addresses parents, child labor, education, peer pressure, food, fads and fun. *Volume V* examines the life-changing elements of war and discusses how enlisted personnel, officers and civilians handled the stress, exhilaration, boredom and brutality of America's various wars, conflicts or incursions. *Volume VI: Women at Work* celebrates the contributions of women, chronicling both the progress and the roadblocks along the way. This volume highlights the critical role of women on the frontlines of change.

Working Americans VII: Social Movements explores the various ways America's men and women—of all ages—felt called upon to challenge accepted convention, whether the issue was cigarette smoking in 1901 or fighting the construction of a massive hydroelectric dam in 1956. This study of grassroots American protest highlights topics championed by America's conservatives, liberals and the deeply concerned. Some acted out of gratitude, like the young man who supported the Orphan Train, or anger, such as the ex-soldier who conducted guerilla warfare demonstrations for Vietnam Veterans Against the War. Some wanted better labor conditions, less kissing in silent films, more attention to the environment or fewer prayers in school. Not all of those who are profiled were successful or happy with the consequences of their protest, such as the man from Guatemala who tried to improve his working conditions in a poultry plant, or the young woman who protested against nuclear weapons. But like the woman who was scorned for writing a polite letter to the editor to condemn tight-fitting corsets, they all took a stand. Some of the issues transcend the decades, while some, like the prohibition of plume hunting to supply the hat industry, seem happily anachronistic.

As in the previous volumes, each story is unique, as each of us is unique: the Southern white woman who took up the cause of the Scottsboro boys, the fight to aid the despised Japanese Americans during World War II, a teenager's determination to ban the Beatles and a Native American's resolve to bring pride to his community through protest. During this journey we will discover a full-time pro-life advocate, a teenaged boy who staged a labor strike for children and a Depression-era farmer who led a land revolt to save a neighbor's farm. Each has a story to tell.

All of the profiles are modeled on real people and events, although, as in the previous books in this series, the names have been changed and some details added based on statistics, the then-current popularity of an idea, or writings of the time. Otherwise, every effort has been made to profile accurately the individual's early life, education and work experiences. To ensure that each profile reflects the feeling of its subject, diaries, letters, biographies, interviews and magazine articles were consulted and used. In some cases the person profiled represents national trends and feelings, but mostly, they represent themselves. Ultimately, it is the people, events and actions of working Americans—along with their investments, spending decisions, time commitments, jobs and passions—that shape society in our changing world.

Scott Derks

Introduction

Working Americans 1880–2006 Volume VII: Social Movements, is the seventh volume in an open-ended series. Like its predecessors, *Social Movements* profiles the lives of Americans—how they lived, how they worked, how they thought—decade by decade. The previous volumes focused primarily on economic status. This volume focuses on Americans, from all walks of life, who fought for something they believed in—for themselves, their family, the human race.

Social Movements takes you:

- Into the home of three young girls whose mother fights for a woman's right to not wear restrictive metal corsets in 1896;
- Into the office of a physician who risks public scorn by promoting birth control rather than risk the lives of his young patients who find themselves continuously pregnant in 1921;
- Into the high school of a 15-year-old who leads a Ban the Beatles campaign after John Lennon compared his group's popularity to that of God in 1966;
- Onto a football field where a star football player fights for rights for the disabled after being paralyzed in a car accident in 1992;
- Into a community divided by the right to pray in school in 2000;
- Onto a basketball court where a coach fights for equal opportunities for his female players in 2004.

Arranged in 11 decade-long chapters, this newest *Working Americans* volume includes three individual **Profiles** per chapter, with four in the expanded last chapter. The opening sections highlight the individual's work, home and community, followed by historical and economic information of the time. **Historical Snapshots** chronicle major milestones; **Timelines** pinpoint the progress of the social issue profiled; and a variety of **News Features** put the topic in context. These common elements, as well as specialized data, such as **Selected Prices,** punctuate each chapter and act as statistical comparisons between decades, as well as between Americans of different socioeconomic backgrounds. The 34 men and women profiled in this volume represent a wide range of ages, social backgrounds, ethnicity, and professions.

The social issues you'll read about are not all social movements in the strictest sense of the words. They are, however, all stories of social improvements, from the point of view of those willing to take a stand. From trying to contain the flu epidemic in 1919, to the fight to make America alcohol free in 1937, to the struggle against the conservation of the Spotted White Owl in 1986, this volume covers 10 major topics, from Censorship to Religion, with dozens of variations. The Table of Contents following this Introduction provides a detailed list of topics.

Working Americans 1880–2006 Volume VII: Social Movements is so much more, however, than simply a list of social issues in America. It's a window into how Americans think, act, react and get motivated. Fighting for change is the American way, from immigrants struggling to find work, to same sex couples struggling for the right to marry. The right to protest is one of the distinguishing factors that sets this country apart from many others around the world.

Like the other six volumes in this series, *Working Americans 1880–2006 Volume VII: Social Movements* is a compilation of original research—personal diaries, school files, family histories—combined with government statistics, commercial advertisements and news features. The text is presented in bulleted format. There are hundreds of supportive graphics—photographs, advertisements, magazine covers, even campaign buttons.

Like the earlier volumes in this *Working Americans* series, *Volume VII* is a "point in time" book, designed to illustrate the reality of that particular time. Some activists were successful and some were not. Many of the fights portrayed in this volume are still being fought. As issues are resolved, there are dozens more waiting for their champion. This is America.

Praise for earlier volumes—

"the volume succeeds at presenting various cultural, regional, economic and age-related points of view . . . [it is] visually appealing [and] certainly a worthwhile purchase. . ."

Feminist Collections

". . . easy reading that will help younger students come to an understanding of the lives and situations of American women."

ARBA

"The volume 'promises to enhance our understanding of the growth and development of the working class over more than a century.' It capably fulfills this promise . . . recommended for all types of libraries."

ARBA

"[the author] adds to the genre of social history known as 'history from the bottom up,' which examines the lives of ordinary people . . . Recommended for all colleges and university library collections."

Choice

"this volume engages and informs, contributing significantly and meaningfully to the historiography of the working class in America . . . a compelling and well-organized contribution for those interested in social history and the complexities of working Americans."

Library Journal

"these interesting, unique compilations of economic and social facts, figures, and graphs will support multiple research needs. They will engage and enlighten patrons in high school, public, and academic library collections."

Booklist

This is no dull statistical compilation of economic history. It is a very interesting, readable account of life in the United States for the worker or laborer. It would be very useful for undergraduate students researching laborers or working and social conditions.

Journal of Business & Finance Librarianship

TABLE OF CONTENTS

Dedicated to my mentors who focused me at different stages of my life: *Mary Long, Bill & Weenie Daniel, Bob Miller, Joe Workman, Dick Workman, Louie Koester, Jim McColl, Ed Dolby, Jim Morris, Austin & Carol Watson*

ACKNOWLEDGEMENTS

It is always an honor to work with smart, motivated people. The author wishes to thank and recognize the superb research and writing assistance provided by newcomers Jim Copening and Josh Chilton as well as veterans of this series, Brian Stanley, Tony Smith, Marshall Derks, Erika DePaz, Hal Stallworth, Elizabeth Derks and Lucia Derks. Thanks to Harry Allen and Sharon Cargill for their inspiration, fascinating conversation and photographs. Also, a tip of the hat to librarians nationwide, especially those affiliated with Wake Forest University and the Blue Ridge Regional Library. And, as with the previous books in this series, thanks must be lavished on grammar gymnast Elaine Alibrandi for her Olympic performance and Laura Mars-Proietti for her gentle coaching and strong support.

1880–1899

The 20 years leading to the twentieth century were shaped by major change: the movement of people from farm to factory, the rapid expansion of wage labor, the explosive growth of cities and massive immigration. Nearly everywhere the economic and social life of working people was changing. Beneath the glitter and exuberant wealth of the Gilded Age swirled an ocean of discontent yearning for the gold-laden streets of America promised to millions of immigrants. Health for commoners was primitive, and infectious disease was rampant in crowded cities. Children of the working class routinely left school in their teens to work beside their parents, the middle class was small, and college was largely an institution reserved for the elite and wealthy men of America. Farmers, merchants and small-town artisans found themselves increasingly dependent on market forces and huge concentrations of power unprecedented in American history. The new emerging capitalistic order was quickly producing a continent where only a few were very rich and many were very poor. Child labor laws were largely nonexistent, and on-the-job injuries were common, even expected. It was an economy on a roll with few rudders or regulations—an economy ripe for unrest, reform and new ideas.

The rapid expansion of railroads opened up the nation to new industries, new markets and the formation of monopolistic trusts that catapulted a handful of corporations into positions of unprecedented power and wealth. This expanding technology also triggered the movement of workers from farm to factory, the rapid expansion of wage labor, and the explosive growth of cities. Farmers, merchants and small-town artisans found themselves increasingly dependent on regional and national market forces. The shift in the concentrations of power was unprecedented in American history. At the same time, professionally trained workers were reshaping America's economy alongside business managers or entrepreneurs eager to capture their piece of the American pie.

Across America the economy—along with its work force—was running away from the land. Before the Civil War, the United States was overwhelmingly an agricultural nation. By the end of the century, non-agricultural occupations employed nearly two thirds of the workers. As important, two of every three Americans came to rely on wages instead of self-employment as farmers or artisans. At the same time, industrial growth began to center around cities, where wealth accumulated for a few who understood how to harness and use railroads, create new consumer markets, and manage a ready supply of cheap, trainable labor. Jobs, offering steady wages and the promise of a better life for workers' children, drew people from the farms into the cities, which grew at twice the rate of the nation as a whole. A modern, industrially based work force emerged from the traditional farmlands, led by men skilled at managing others and the complicated flow of materials required to keep a factory operating. This led to an increasing demand for attorneys, bankers, and physicians to handle the complexity of the emerging urban economy. In 1890, newspaper editor Horace Greeley remarked, "We cannot all live in cities, yet nearly all seem determined to do so."

The new cities of America were home to great wealth and poverty—both produced by the massive migrations and influx of immigrants willing to work at any price. It was a time symbolized by Andrew Carnegie's steel mills, John D. Rockefeller's organization of the Standard Oil monopoly, and the manufacture of Alexander Graham Bell's wonderful invention, the telephone. By 1894, the United States had become the world's leading industrial power, producing more than England, France, and Germany—its three largest competitors—combined. For much of this period, the nation's industrial energy focused on the need for railroads requiring large quantities of labor, iron, steel, stone, and lumber. In 1883, nine tenths of the nation's entire production of steel went into rails. The most important invention of the period—in an era of tremendous change and innovation—may have been the Bessemer converter, which transformed pig iron into steel at a relatively low cost, increasing steel output 10 times from 1877 to 1892.

The greatest economic event during the last two decades of the nineteenth century was the great wave of immigration that swept America. It is believed to be the largest worldwide population movement in human history, bringing more than 10 million people to the United States to fill the expanding need for workers. In the 1880s alone, 5.25 million immigrants arrived, more than in the first six decades of the nineteenth century. This wave was dominated by Irish, German, and English workers. Scandinavia, Italy, and China sent scores of eager workers, normally men, to fill the expanding labor needs of the United States. To attract this much-needed labor force, railroad and steamship companies advertised throughout Europe and China the glories of American life. To an economically depressed world, it was a welcome call.

Despite all the signs of economic growth and prosperity, America's late-nineteenth-century economy was profoundly unstable. Industrial expansion was undercut by a depression from 1882 to 1885, followed in 1893 by a five-year-long economic collapse that devastated rural and urban communities across America. As a result, job security for workers just climbing onto the industrial stage was often fleeting. Few wage earners found full-time work for the entire year. The unevenness in the economy was caused both by the level of change under way and irresponsible speculation, but more generally to the stubborn adherence of the federal government to a highly inflexible gold standard as the basis of value for currency.

Between the very wealthy and the very poor emerged a new middle stratum, whose appearance was one of the distinctive features of late-nineteenth-century America. The new middle class fueled the purchase of one million light bulbs a year by 1890, even though the first electric light was only 11 years old. It was the middle class, too, that flocked to buy Royal Baking Powder, (which was easier to use and faster than yeast) and supported the emergence and spread of department stores that were sprouting up across the nation.

1894 Profile

Child Welfare: The Orphan Train

Otis Sandusky used his experience as a foundling on an Orphan Train to make the experience smoother and less frightening for other orphans arriving in Dysart, Iowa.

Life at Home

- Otis Sandusky liked to think of himself as a crusader for children, although he would never actually say that out loud.
- However, since he started acting as a part-time agent for the Children's Aid Society, he felt as though he was rescuing children from a life of crime or worse.
- After all, he came out okay after being shipped into the healthy air of the Midwest; why shouldn't more homeless children be saved from urban blight?
- Otis Sandusky was named after his adoptive father when he was three years old after a five-day ride on the Orphan Train; it was his first real name.
- Until he was adopted, he had simply been called "Baby Boy" by the Sisters of Mercy, who operated the Foundling Asylum and coordinated adoptions through the Children's Aid Society.
- The first recorded appearance of Baby Boy Otis was as a day-old baby abandoned in a basket provided by the Founding Asylum of New York City.
- The note pinned to his shirt and probably written by his mother said simply, "Care for my baby boy. I can't."
- The unnamed child was one of seven children left at the Foundling Asylum that week.
- At three years old, he was placed on an Orphan Train with 39 other two- and three-year-olds for adoption in the West.

Three-year-old Otis Sandusky rode the Orphan Train all the way from New York City to Iowa.

Big Otis Sandusky needed sons to help him on the family farm.

- When the Orphan Train stopped at a depot station in Indiana, Baby Boy Otis and the other children—a wriggling mass of tired, hungry, cold toddlers from the streets of New York—were lined up on the platform.
- Otis began to cry.
- The nine families who had gathered to adopt a child all passed him by without a look.
- Within an hour, 11 children had been picked out by the farm families, loaded into horse-drawn wagons, and taken to their new homes.
- The children who were not picked were marched back onto the train for inspection at the next designated depot station in Illinois or Iowa or Texas.
- Baby Boy Otis cried at the next stop, and the next.
- When the train stopped in Dysart, Iowa, the Orphan Train was down to six children—five girls and Baby Boy Otis, who couldn't stop crying.
- That's where the Sandusky family found a child and Otis got a name, a home, and a future.

- Baby Boy Otis was named after Otis and Celestine's first child, who had died of cholera.
- Baby Boy's new father Big Otis was not sure this tiny, red-faced crybaby would be much of a farm hand, but over time he became pleasantly surprised.
- At the constant urging—nagging, really—of Celestine, the Sanduskys formally adopted Otis on his fifth birthday, the age of the first Otis Sandusky when he died.
- Over time, the Sanduskys would adopt three more Orphan Train children, two boys and then a girl named Pearl.
- When Otis turned 17, he began helping out whenever an Orphan Train came near, serving as agent, scout, and recruiter for adoptive families in Iowa.
- Otis was even made a member of the screening committee that included the town doctor, clergyman, newspaper editor, store owner, and a teacher—all men, of course.
- The committee helped to select potential parents for the children.
- He was even talked into telling his personal story in church to encourage other families to adopt, while his little brothers made faces at him from the balcony.
- His little sister, who was very polite and attentive, simply smiled throughout the talk.
- Otis's primary job was farm work, especially in the planting and harvesting times, but he cherished his designation as agent, which brought with it extra cash and the chance to see children who had started life just as he had.

Otis and Celestine Sandusky lost their first son to cholera.

Life at Work

- Father Anton Erdman, pastor of the St. Benedict's Catholic Church in Sexton, Iowa, and "Little" Otis Sandusky were both at the depot when the Orphan Train arrived in Dysart on a wintry day in 1894 with a baker's dozen of very young children.
- By long tradition and habit, all the frightened children would have been unceremoniously herded off the train and ushered into the town hall to be adopted by anyone who would have them—if Otis had not spoken up.
- The children who were not selected by a family would be put back on the train to try again in another town along the route: a terrible feeling for scared, homesick little children, Otis knew.
- For decades, this ceremony had been taking place.
- Since 1857, the Children's Aid Society had transferred 26,000 homeless, abused, or unwanted children from the urban squalor of New York City to a healthy environment in the countryside.
- This time, however, within minutes of their arrival, the children were loaded into Father Erdman's surrey for a ride to the rectory of St. Benedict.
- It was there, insisted Otis, that families could meet the frightened orphans and more easily decide to take them home.
- The church felt more like a home than did a train station, and besides, it was warmer out of the blistering winter that chapped the children's faces and elicited runny noses.
- For days the children had been in the care of only the conductor and one agent; most of the children possessed only the clothes they wore.
- Many thought they had been placed on the train to be sent away because they did something wrong.
- Nuns had sewn the names of the children in the dress or shirt they wore, their only identification or connection with their New York City homes.
- Most had no birth certificate or anyone to speak for their past.
- Many had been baptized as Catholics regardless of their birth mother's religion.
- The children were not even aware that they had dirty, coal-streaked faces when they greeted their prospective parents.
- Otis tried to clean up the children; the sickly and those who were crying were picked last in this rough land of hard work and bitter cold.
- But for all his scrubbing and good intentions, Otis only upset the sensitive ones even more.
- Then, in trooped the couples, most of whom had requested a child, often designating gender and eye or hair color.
- The Orphan Train had not stopped in 13 months, and many families were eager for a chance to adopt.
- Several of the women had been at the church service in which Otis spoke about his early life aboard the Orphan Train.
- He hated it when the women would mention the "crybaby" part and vowed not to mention that again.
- Thanks to a country fiddler who was sympathetic to the Orphan Train children, the church felt festive, just as Otis had hoped.
- Slowly, the farmers and their wives walked from child to child, and attempted in an instant to make a lifetime decision.
- Most of the couples already had children, but wanted more.
- Childbirth was a dangerous experience on the prairie, and farmers could always use another hand.

Children on the Orphan Trains often had no birth certificate or anyone to speak for their past.

- One by one, the children were selected and asked to stand beside their new parents.
- But when the church party was over, one little blond boy remained.
- The Merrills had planned to adopt only one of the 13 children, but after Father Schemel talked quietly with Elmer Merrill, they ended up with two children.
- To Otis's great relief, all of the children had been adopted.

Life in the Community: Dysart, Iowa

- The Children's Aid of New York and the Foundling Hospital required no legal adoption process, but adopting families had to promise to provide the children with some schooling and report to the institution about the child on a yearly basis.
- Children were taken on trains in groups of 10 to 40, under the supervision of at least one "western" agent, to selected stops along the route.
- Railroads were the least expensive way to move children westward from the poverty of inner city homes, orphanages, poorhouses, and sometimes right from the streets.
- In the open air of the West and Midwest, it was believed, solid, God-fearing homes could be found for the children.
- The Sisters of Mercy worked tirelessly to save lives and help both the young, unwed mothers and unwanted children, but rarely gathered information on the parents of the child.
- Often, a child was left at the Foundling Hospital with no information given; the baby was simply placed in a basket on a turntable which a sister inside the building would turn to bring the baby in without the adult ever being seen.
- This device encouraged people to save the baby while remaining anonymous.
- As the program developed, the sisters requested that the unwed pregnant women stay at the Foundling Hospital to have their babies and then nurse theirs plus another one for a time.
- At the end of the agreed-upon time, the mothers could leave with no further restrictions placed on them.
- The goal was to bond mother and child so the mothers would seek a way to keep their children.
- While at the Foundling, many women were taught a craft or skill that would help them find work and raise their children, with a little help.
- The women learned safe and sanitary cooking and housekeeping methods.
- As a result of exceptionally high immigration into America's port cities, the problem of homeless or abused children grew rapidly.
- Children as young as six years old worked to help support the family when food became scarce.
- Because it was not a priority, job safety was unregulated, and many men were killed in accidents at work.
- This left women and children to make their own living as best they could, even though few jobs were open to women with children.
- Infectious diseases from living in unsanitary quarters led to the early deaths of overworked mothers.

MRS. WINSLOW'S SOOTHING SYRUP, FOR CHILDREN TEETHING.

Wherever these Receipt Books are distributed, Mrs. Winslow's Soothing Syrup will be found at some Store in the vicinity.

Mrs. Winslow's Soothing Syrup.

This valuable preparation has been used with never-failing success in thousands of cases.

It not only relieves the child from pain, but invigorates the stomach and bowels, corrects acidity, and gives tone and vigor to the whole system.

It will almost instantly relieve griping in the bowels.

We believe it the best and surest remedy in the world, in all cases of

Dysentery and Diarrhœa in Children,

whether it arises from teething or from any other cause.

Look well for the genuine article, with fac-simile of *CURTIS & PERKINS, New York*, on the outside wrapper, without which none is genuine.

Mrs. Winslow's Soothing Syrup is sold by all Druggists throughout the United States.

- In nearly all the East Coast port cities, orphanages were rapidly built to care for as many children as could possibly be taken.
- To place the children, priests and ministers throughout the Midwest and the West would make an announcement to the congregation, asking for volunteers to take the children.
- Couples signed up for a male or female child, specifying the hair and eye color they preferred.
- The priest would then notify the Children's Aid Society or the Foundling that the community could take a specific number of children with blond hair and blue eyes; brown hair and brown eyes; black hair and blue eyes; or a certain darkness of skin.
- One such request was for a boy with red hair because the farmer had five red-haired daughters and no sons.
- Everyone agreed that if a family got a child who "fit in," the child and the community would be better served.
- Based on the rules, boys over 16 years of age were to be retained as members of the family for one year, after which a mutual arrangement would be made concerning their future.
- Parties taking these boys agreed to write to the Society at least once a year, or to have the boys do so.
- If for any reason the child had to be removed from the household, the Children's Aid Society did it at their own expense.
- Most children began their new lives legally classified as indentured; thus, they were ineligible to inherit unless the family adopted them or a will specified that they were to be given an inheritance.

HISTORICAL SNAPSHOT
1894

- Approximately 12,000 New York City tailors struck to protest the existence of sweatshops
- The first Sunday newspaper color comic section was published in the *New York World*
- Antique-collecting became popular, supported by numerous genealogy-minded societies
- A well-meaning group of Anglophiles called the America Acclimatization Society began importing English birds mentioned in Shakespeare, including nightingales, thrushes and starlings, for release in America
- Overproduction forced farm prices to fall; wheat that sold for $1.05 a bushel in 1870 now sold for $0.49 a bushel
- The first Greek newspaper in America was published as the *New York Atlantis*
- New York Governor Roswell P. Flower signed the nation's first dog-licensing law; the license fee was $2.00
- Hockey's first Stanley Cup championship game was played between the Montreal Amateur Athletic Association and the Ottawa Capitals
- Thomas Edison publicly demonstrated the kinetoscope, a peephole viewer in which developed film moved continuously under a magnifying glass
- Workers at the Pullman Palace Car Company in Illinois went on strike to protest a wage reduction; President Grover Cleveland ordered federal troops onto the trains to insure the delivery of mail
- Labor Day was established as a holiday for federal employees
- Congress established the Bureau of Immigration
- Congress passed a bill imposing a 2 percent tax on incomes over $4,000, which was ruled unconstitutional by the U.S. Supreme Court
- The United States Government began keeping records on the weather
- Astronomer Percival Lowell built a private observatory in Flagstaff, Arizona, and began his observations of Mars
- The Regents of the University of Michigan declared that "Henceforth in the selection of professors and instructors and other assistants in instruction in the University, no discrimination will be made in selection between men and women"
- French Baron Pierre de Coubertin proposed an international Olympics competition to be held every four years in a different nation to encourage international peace and cooperation
- The *Edison Kinetoscopic Record of a Sneeze* was released in movie theaters

Selected Prices, 1894

Automobile, Winton Motor Carriage $1,000.00

Coffee, 11 Pounds, Parched $1.00

Diapers, Six $0.05

Dinner Set, Porcelain, 100 Pieces $14.00

Gloves $0.50

Hotel Room, Columbia, South Carolina $2.50

Lactated Baby Food $0.25

Linoleum, Yard $0.80

Tuition, Columbia Female College, per Year $200.00

Typewriter $25.00

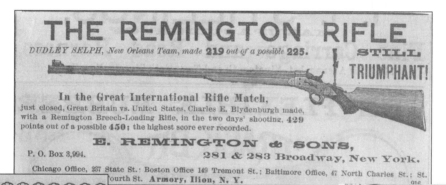

Announcement,
The Algona Courier
(Iowa), 1894

Father Schemel Bancroft (Iowa) has of late found good homes for 10 children which were sent him from an orphan asylum in New York which shelters 2,000 waifs. Father Eckert of Wesley has also found good homes for several and we understand that in the vicinity of the Prairie Church fifteen of the homeless children have of late been placed in comfortable homes. One day last week a number of the little waifs from the same place arrived in Algona over the Northwestern Road. All have been placed with good families. . . .

Letters Left on Babies by Their Mothers, New York Foundling Hospital:

December 1, 1875
Dear Sister,

Alone and deserted, I need to put my little one with you for a time. I would willingly work and take care of her but no one will have me and her too. All say they would take me if she was 2 or 3 years old, so not knowing what to do with her and not being able to pay her board, I bring her to you knowing you will be as kind to her as to the many others who are under your care, and I will get work and try hard to be able to relieve you of the care when I can take her to work with me. She is only three weeks old and I have not had her christened or anything. No one knows how awful it is to separate from their child but a mother, but, I trust you will be kind and the only consolation I have is if I am spared and nothing prevents and I lead an honest life that the father of us all will permit us to be united.

—A Mother
continued

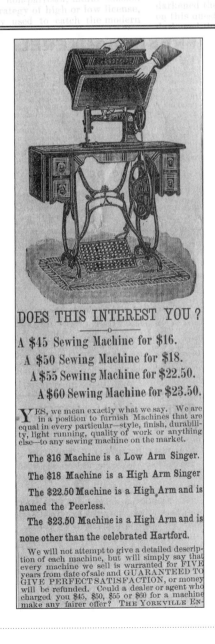

Letters . . . *(continued)*

Most Holy Redeemer Church

Dear Sisters,

By the love of God be so kind as to take this poor orphan child in and if she should die, please to bury her for me and I will be very happy. You must not think that I have neglected her. I have worked very hard to pay her board but I can't afford to bury her. So, by the love of God, take this little child in. May God Bless you all for your kindness to all the little sufferers. This little child has suffered since she was born and I have paid debts but I have not paid all but I shall. My husband is dead and I have nobody to help me. Be kind to my little lamb. May the great God receive her into Heaven where she will be loved by God.

This two Dollars is to have this child christened Willie. Do not be afraid of the sores on its face; it is nothing but a ringworm. You'll remember this badge. [Cloth badge included that reads, "General Grant our Next President"]

St. Patrick's Church Rectory

263 Mulberry Street

July 1870

To the Sisters of the House,

Necessity compels me to part with my darling boy. I leave him, hoping and trusting that you will take good care of him. Will you let some good nurse take charge of him and will you try to find some kind hearted lady to adopt him and love him as her own while he is young that he may never know but what she is his own mother? It would break my heart to have him grow up without a mother to love and care for him. God only knows the bitter anguish of my heart in parting with this little dear, still if it costs me my life I am obliged to give him up.

He is just from the breast, he has been sick with his bowels, they have not been right for a long time. I have cried and worried over him so much that I think my milk hurt him. I think a change of milk with good care will make him well soon. I got these things thinking I could keep him but as I can not they may be of use to you. I shall always take an interest in this Institution.

He is 4 weeks old. Will you please to remember his given name and if he is adopted, request that they will not change his name; so that at some future day, if that name should be asked for, you will be able to tell what became of him or where he is. Perhaps you will think me very particular, but if any mother will take it home to her own heart and think how she would feel to have her dear little boy torn from her breast, I think they would excuse me.

This is the last time I can speak of him as mine, and if in years to come if I could hear that he had a home and kind friends, I could die in peace. On the other hand, if I should never hear, it would haunt the day of my death. Please excuse all that you think is not right but for God's sake remember the last request of a heart broken mother.

Orphan Train Timeline

1853
Charles Lorring Brace and a group of businessmen formed the Children's Aid Society of New York City and developed the concept of "free-home-placing-out" to aid homeless and neglected children.

1854
The first group of children went to Dowagiac, Michigan.

1869
The Foundling Asylum of the Sisters of Charity was formed to care for babies abandoned in the wake of the Civil War.

1870
Within months of opening, the Foundling Asylum was caring for 123 babies as well as providing a refuge for unwed mothers.

The rapidly developing railroads ran from New York to Omaha, Nebraska, expanding the reach of the Orphan Train.

1872
The Sisters of Charity began construction on a large, attractive, well-equipped facility devoted to the special needs of children.

The United States Supreme Court invalidated the restrictive immigration laws passed by the states.

1882
Congress passed its first general immigration statute.

1892
Ellis Island, located in New York Harbor, opened as property of the United States Bureau of Immigration.

"Children's Day at the Circus, More Than Five Thousand of Them Have an Afternoon of Pleasure," *The New York Times*, April 13, 1894:

Yesterday was a great day for the children of the institutions of the city, when more than 5,000 of the youngsters attended Barnum & Bailey's great show, at Madison Square Garden. Great was the rejoicing of the children when they saw the elephants, the lions, tigers, and all sorts of animals from the four quarters of the globe.

The masterful doings of the men, women, and horses in the circus rings were likewise a wonder to the little visitors, who have infrequent experiences in the amusement world. They cheered lustily at the brilliant equestrian and acrobatic feats of the performers. The following is a partial list of the institutions represented at the show: St. Joseph's Asylum, Children's Aid Society, Avenue B School, New-York Infant Asylum, Children's Fold, Hebrew Sheltering Guardian, Neighborhood Guild, Protestant Half Orphans' Asylum, Duane Industrial School, Asylum of the Sacred Heart, St. Barnabas, Charities and Correction, Phelps School, Sisters of Mercy, God's Providence and St. Barnabas, Hospital for Cripples, Dominican Convent of Our Lady of the Rosary, Mission of the Immaculate Virgin, Protestant Episcopal Orphan Asylum, Italian Mission, Hebrew Institute, West Side Italian School, Industrial School of United Hebrews, Lady Deborah's Mission, St. Michael's Home, Home industrial School, St. Monica's Little Mother's Aid, University Settlement, and St. Vincent's Orphan Asylum.

"Festivities for Foundlings, Six Hundred Little Ones Have Turkey and Cranberry Sauce," *The New York Times,* November 30, 1984:

The New-York Foundling Hospital, at Sixty-eighth Street and Lexington Avenue, was the scene yesterday of joyful festivities, which will long dwell in the memories of the 600 little tots who are tenderly cared for in that institution.

For weeks they had heard tales of roast turkey and cranberry sauce, until they even dreamed of the feast to come. Promptly at 12 o'clock the doors of the long playroom were thrown open, and the tables were quickly surrounded by 300 mothers and the older children.

In addition to this, the seven nurseries, each of which is 90 feet long and 30 feet wide, were fitted with tables, and at these were placed the 600 babies and "run-arounds," the latter being the children old enough to get into mischief.

Sister Irene, who is at the head of the hospital staff, and her 34 assistants, all decked out in their pretty costumes of blue with white aprons, white sleeves, and white Swiss cap, managed the dinner in perfect style.

"We do not often give them turkey," said one of the sisters, "because roast beef is more wholesome, and there is danger with the bones in eating fowl." The sisters were constantly called upon yesterday to extract stray turkey bones from little throats.

"Our children," continued the sister, "range in ages from one day to six years, the great majority of them being under two years old. They receive a training here that is intended to fit them for adoption by the best families. Since the founding of the hospital 24 years ago, we have cared for 26,000 infants, 10,000 of whom have been placed in permanent homes.

"Five thousand needy and homeless mothers have also shared the charitable shelter of the Foundling Hospital, and our outdoor department gives constant employment to 1,100 respectable women, who nurse the little foundlings in their own homes."

"Poverty Is Expensive," *The Yorkville Enquirer,* Yorkville, South Carolina, October 26, 1892:

"There is nothing so expensive as poverty," says a Washington housewife. It seems paradoxical to put it so, but no poor man can afford not to be a few dollars ahead in the world. The extreme case is that of the very poor, who must pay for coal double the price charged the rich, because they have to get it by the bushel or scuttle full, and so with everything else.

The poor woman must pay $50 for a sewing machine on installments, though she could buy it for $35 cash down. Her lack of the ready cash costs her $15, that is, whereas it is the poor who ought to get everything cheaper; they have always to pay enormously more than the rich for the same things, merely because they are poor.

In extremity they must seek the pawnbroker, who again preys upon their slender resources because they have so little. Credit for anything always costs money, and the poor are those who must pay for it. "Our means are very moderate and the only reason that we get along so comfortably as we do is that we never owe for anything.

"Years ago we were always in debt, and the struggle was severe to get along, without counting the distress and annoyance incidental to owing tradesmen money. Finally, we found out what the matter was, and got square with the world through a long effort of self-denial. Our income is no greater now than it was then, but it produces at least one-third more because we have no bills. Depend upon it; a poor man cannot afford to be somewhat ahead of the world, otherwise the world will very soon get so far ahead of him that life will be a burden."

1896 PROFILE

WOMEN'S HEALTH: THE ANTI-CORSET CAMPAIGN

Cora Gaillard, the wife of a doctor in Bridgeport, Connecticut, and a mother of three daughters, was concerned about the health risks associated with wearing corsets.

Life at Home

- Cora Gaillard had heard about the attacks for years on the wearing of corsets.
- At times it seemed that every bellicose speaker who could spell "M.D." had a reason to condemn the sturdy undergarment, revered for its ability to fashion an hourglass figure.
- Some doctors blamed tightly-laced corsets for weak stomach muscles in girls, fainting spells, numbness of the legs, and even infertility.
- Others emphasized the impact on the respiratory system of women, which was widely understood to be different from that of men.
- And cartoonists and stereographic card manufacturers loved to show sisters pulling the lacing so tight on one another that a foot braced on the back was often required.
- The conversion of Cora Gaillard began with her three teenage daughters and was supported by her husband, a medical doctor in Bridgeport, Connecticut.
- After several years of hearing complaints from her husband's patients, Cora was convinced the corset made the marriage bed uncomfortable and generally led to reduced sexual relations between husband and wife.

Cora Gaillard suspected that corsets were damaging to women's health.

- Fashion dictated, and vanity decided, that corsets must create continuous and severe constriction.
- Even waists that naturally measured 25 inches could be cinched back to 19 inches when a French-designed back-fastening corset with a long steel busk down the front was worn.
- As a teenager, Cora remembered well the sacrifices she had made to achieve a waist smaller than her age using a modern steam-moulded, spoon busk corset with enough boning and cording to create a perfect hourglass shape.
- But whenever she rebelled against the confining garment, her mother invariably reminded her that wearing a corset was "the hallmark of virtue" and that "an uncorseted woman reeked of license."

- But Cora now had another motivation: healthy teenage children, nearing a marriageable age, and the production of numerous healthy grandchildren.
- She was also concerned that fainting, poor circulation, and lethargy in women were all a result of tightly laced corsets.
- Cora began dressing her girls in corsets when each reached the age of nine.
- The two oldest, Florence and Lucca, willingly accepted the confining strictures as a symbol of growing up.
- The youngest, Carolina the tomboy, hated corsets and more than once abandoned the undergarment behind the rose bush hedge.
- Maybe it was a sign: The two oldest girls had been named for the Italian hometowns of their great-grandparents, Florence and Lucca, to honor the first Proiettis to come to America.
- They were conservative, hardworking, and religious.
- Carolina had been named for the home state of her paternal grandmother, who was from the undisciplined city of Charleston, South Carolina, where liquor drinking, horse races, and cock fights were practiced openly, even on Sundays.
- Despite her tussles with the untamed spirit of Carolina, Cora was convinced that tight corsets deformed young women, restricted their movement, and limited their ability to produce healthy children.
- Although Cora believed it was prudent for herself to continue wearing a corset, she bought bust girdles for her daughters so they could make full use of their lungs, and maybe avoid the many complaints so common to corset-wearing women.

The Gaillard's three daughters wore modified corsets to avoid common ailments brought on by the garment.

Life at Work

- For most of her married life, Cora Gaillard had assisted in her husband's medical practice; she was nurse, office manager, counselor, and substitute doctor.
- Despite her husband's fancy diplomas and advanced education, Cora was convinced that she knew as much about medicine as he did, especially when it came to women's health.
- Day after day she cared for women who were in pain because of the clothing they wore, while men all agreed that women just liked to complain.
- That's why she wrote that letter to the editor that had stirred up so much trouble.
- She had not shown it to her husband first because she knew he would object and be no help at all.

- However, she hadn't expected this much of a reaction.
- Now, what was done was done, and she was going to accept the Bridgeport Women's Club's invitation to speak about corsets the following month.
- Besides, someone needed to speak out about how fashion, vanity, tradition, and the preferences of men affected women's health.
- Cora was riled up about long skirts that dragged the ground collecting all manner of filth, the tendency of women to faint because of excessive constriction, and the disgusting way that tight corsets rearranged vital organs and prevented women from doing normal house tasks because they could not bend over.
- And she hadn't even addressed the burden of multiple petticoats that hung off the waist or the tyranny of tight garters that cut off circulation to the legs.
- Cora had even read somewhere that Susan B. Anthony had said, "I can see no business avocation in which woman in her present dress can possibly earn equal wages with man."
- But Cora was in enough trouble with her husband without quoting the words of a feminist; that would court accusations that she supported both equality and free love like the radicals.
- Already she was being accused of trying to de-sex women now that she was older and had stopped having children.
- Cora even heard herself compared to Washington's Dr. Mary E. Walker, who had advocated that men and women were so similar in anatomy that the sexes should dress identically.
- All because of one letter to the editor.
- Cora encountered criticism from every corner—including her embarrassed daughters—that she wanted the sexes to be equal when all she wanted was good health for women.
- What was so radical about one-piece flannel underwear in place of a confining corset, and a skirt four inches off the floor so women could walk without stumbling?
- Besides, it was obvious that the freedom offered by the modern bicycle was going to propel changes in courting, dress, and women's health.
- Her girls were going to be part of the future no matter what anyone said, even if the oldest girls were not speaking to her and Carolina insisted on sitting separately at church.

Life in the Community: Bridgeport, Connecticut

- The city of Bridgeport, Connecticut, had long seen itself as a business town that was proud of its manufacturing tradition, including gun cartridges, brass goods, and corsets.
- Warnco, a renowned manufacturer of corsets, relocated to Bridgeport in 1876, and Cora's husband treated many of its workers.
- Many in the community were proud of the notoriety Warnco was receiving for its Redfern satin corset, designed in Paris.
- To many, Cora's corset protest was bad for the future of the community.
- Secretly, she believed that any town that would elect P. T. Barnum as its mayor should not take itself so seriously.
- Beginning in the 1830s, the invention of the metal eyelet and its use in corsets allowed greater force to be exerted when lacing tightly.
- About the same time, the medical attacks on corsets began, especially as more women attempted to attain the wasp-like figure then in vogue.
- Corsets were commonly worn 14 hours per day; some women also employed night-stays to ensure that the waist was retrained to the smaller size.
- Complaints associated with tight lacing included nervous disorders, hysterical fits of crying and insomnia, constipation, indigestion, headache, backache, curvature of the spine, respiratory problems and fainting, apoplexy, apathy, stupidity, soured temper, lack of appetite, starvation, displacement of the liver, effects on the secretion of bile, anemia, chlorosis, interposes, neurasthenia, hernia, imperfect circulation, dyspepsia, nausea, vomiting, pressure on the breast, inflamed nipples, displacement of the uterus, and lack of sexual desire.
- Elizabeth Stuart Phelps was unequivocal about the corset in 1874: "Make a bonfire of the cruel steels that have lorded over your thorax and abdomen for so many years and heave a sigh of relief, for your emancipation, I assure you, from this moment has begun."

- Doctors, too, railed that the contraption was harmful, documenting that corsets put up to 80 pounds of pressure on every square inch of a woman's torso, squeezing her rib cage in, while pressing on her internal organs.
- However, the medical community was far from united: While some said tight lacing reduced fertility, others claimed that the weaker sex needed corsets to support their frail bodies.
- According to outspoken feminist Frances Willard, "Niggardly waists and niggardly brains go together. A ligature around the vital organs at the smallest diameter of the womanly figure means an impoverished blood supply to the brain, and may explain why women scream when they see a mouse."
- Yet, a flood of advertisements pitched a corset for every activity, including leisure, sleeping, riding, bicycling, as well as pregnancy and nursing corsets.
- By the 1890s, more than 400 brands were being manufactured as they became more affordable and accessible to the working class women.

HISTORICAL SNAPSHOT
1896

- "Yellow journalism" was named after the color comic figure featuring the Yellow Kid that ran in the Hearst *New York Journal* and the Pulitzer *New York World*
- Theodore Herzl called for a Jewish homeland in Palestine
- Legendary lawman Wyatt Earp refereed a heavyweight title fight between Bob Fitzsimmons and Tom Sharkey
- F. W. Rueckheim & Brother of Chicago received a trademark for the candy treat "Cracker Jack"
- The United States Army took over the operation of Yellowstone National Park
- The Anchor Brewing Company was founded in San Francisco
- An advertisement appeared in *Horseless Age,* the first automotive trade journal, for the Duryea Motor Wagon Company
- Swedish chemist Svante Arrhennius explained the "greenhouse effect," predicting that the planet would gradually become warmer
- American physician Franz Pfaff discovered that the oily residue in poison oak was responsible for the painful rash
- Utah was admitted to the Union as the forty-fifth state
- Dr. Henry Louis Smith at Davidson, North Carolina, produced the first x-ray photo in the United States to reveal a bullet in a dead man's hand
- Civil War photographer Matthew B. Brady died in the charity ward of a New York hospital at age 73
- U.S. Marines landed in Nicaragua to protect U.S. citizens in the wake of a revolution
- The first modern Olympic Games, with eight nations participating, formally opened in Athens, Greece, after a lapse of 1,500 years
- The Vitascope system for projecting movies onto a screen was demonstrated in New York City
- The United States Supreme Court ruled 7 to 1 in *Plessy v. Ferguson* and endorsed the concept of "separate but equal" racial segregation
- The Dow Jones Industrial Average was first published by Charles H. Dow using an index of 12 industrial companies
- William Jennings Bryan propelled himself to presidential candidacy when he stood before the Democratic Convention and made his famous "Cross of Gold" speech
- Booker T. Washington became the first African American to receive an honorary degree from Howard University

Selected Prices, 1896

Corset	$1.25
Hair Remover	$1.00
Horse Muzzle	$2.50
House, Four-Room Cottage	$1,800.00
Rifle, Remmington	$30.00
Shirt, Man's	$1.50
Theater Ticket, *Comic Elephants*	$0.40
Tuition, Columbia Female College, Year	$200.00
Typewriter	$25.00
Writing Paper, Linen, 72 Sheets	$0.75

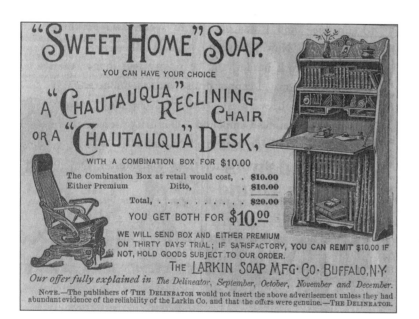

Timeline of Corsets and Ladies' Undergarments

Early 1700s

Corsets were a must for bourgeois and noble women in Europe, eager to separate themselves from the popular classes, who could not afford the specialized garment.

Working class women adopted a "little corset" which laced up the front, rather than the back, and was more affordable.

Mid-1700s

An anti-corset campaign raged across Europe by doctors concerned that corsets deformed women's bodies.

Frenchman Jacques Bonnaud wrote a pamphlet about the effect of corsets on women entitled, "The Degradation of the Human Race Through the Use of the Whalebone Corset: A Work in Which One Demonstrates That It Is to Go Against the Laws of Nature, To Increase Depopulation and Bastardize Man, So to Speak, When One Submits Him to Torture from the First Moments of His Existence, Under the Pretext of Forming Him."

Corset manufacturers asserted that corset-wearing city girls had better bodies than country girls because of the corset.

1795

Following the French revolution, the corset was exiled temporarily.

1804

The corset reappeared in France in support of the empire waist style that emphasized a high waist to accentuate a woman's breasts.

1830s

Swiss industrialist Jean Werly built the first corset factory to mass produce affordable corsets.

Corset advertisements began appearing in European magazines, while expensive American magazines such as *Godey's Lady's Book* would not show them for another 30 years.

continued

Timeline . . . *(continued)*

1840s

New-style corsets emerged, made from white twill cotton that used vertical rows of whalebone shaped to the natural body.

1850s

Major innovations in undergarment production included eyelet holes strengthened with metal rings, while India rubber and elastic were alternatives to whalebone.

Women corset-makers began to dominate in England, France, and Germany, all of which supplied the United States market.

1860

The number of corsetières working in Paris totaled 3,772, while stay manufacturing in London employed 10,000 workers.

1868

Britain produced three million corsets a year for its own use and imported two million more corsets from France and Germany.

1874

Mary J. Safford-Blake, M.D., lectured against the immovable bondage of the corset, while Carolina E. Hastings called the corset "an instrument of human torture" and blamed the deterioration of the thoracic muscles on its wearing.

1880

The popularity of ready-to-wear corsets encouraged manufacturers to expand the line of corsets using different varieties of materials, colors, sizes, and fits; brightly colored corsets also became more acceptable.

1881

The New York Times predicted that all women would be wearing trousers within two or three years.

1886

Bustles returned and in a more exaggerated form than before; they sometimes jutted out at right angles from the center back of the body.

Steel strips were attached to the insides of dresses to exaggerate the backward curve of the bustle.

1890s

To promote better health, Dr Gustave Jaeger marketed a range of woolen underwear including "Sanitary Woolen Corsets" for women.

Manufacturers interested in selling health-supporting corsets advertised the electric corset, to emphasize the metallic composition of the garment.

1896

The Sears, Roebuck catalogue featured 20 types of corsets; the most popular was Dr. Warner's Health Corset, which featured straps over the shoulders and light boning.

Stages of a Corset in the Life of a Woman, by French Corset Specialist Violette:

At 10 a girl puts on her first brassiere—a light underbodice reaching down to the waist.

At 18, for her debut in the world, she dons a batiste corset with supple stays.

When she marries, it is time for the nuptial corset with very firm stays.

"Fresh Censure of the Corset, Prominent Medical Testimony Against Any Use of Stays," *The New York Times*, February 12, 1893:

An Englishwoman's periodical is carrying on a crusade against tight lacing. In this evil, a serious obstacle is the Pharisaical element. As in temperance, it is the "moderate drinker" who is the most hard to reform, and in religion, the "moral man" most difficult to convert, so of corsets it is the woman who "does not lace" who perhaps is chiefly responsible for a failure to abolish entirely the use of stays. She wears them, oh, yes, but "so loose they cannot possibly do any harm." And her abhorrence of wasp waists equals that of the most active reformer. These lukewarm impediments will do well to read what an English medical expert says about any use of the corset:

"This apparatus is, per se, an unscientific appliance, and many women suffer from its use who do not in any way 'pull in.' Strip a man to the waist and you will see no markings of the skin; similarly examine the waist of a woman who has been wearing a corset however loosely applied, and the skin is found marked by pressure, pinched up, and corrugated. While the skirts are suspended from the waist, some protection from pressure in the way afforded by the corset, even if modified, is necessary, and it seems, therefore, that the fundamental error of dress in women is suspension from the waist, entailing pressure on important organs, instead of from the shoulders, as in men."

The corset should be discarded; but if it must be retained...it should be made without whalebone or steel springs, and should be held up by a band over the shoulder. . . . Nothing ought to interfere with the action of the abdominal muscles and the diaphragm.

—Lecture by Arvilla B. Haynes, M.D., 1874

"Narcotics and Improper Dress," *The New York Times;* October 14, 1897:

First in importance, because of its widespread character and of the profound mischief which it works in the human organism, must be mentioned the narcotic habit. Whatever may be the particular poison to which the individual may be addicted, whether alcohol, tobacco, opium, cocaine, tea or coffee, chloral, absinthe, or hasheesh, the vice is one and the same. The recent studies of Andriesen, Tuke, Hodge, and others have shown how these drugs destroy man, soul and body, by producing degeneration of the delicate fibres by means of which nerve cells communicate with one another, thus isolating the individual units of the cerebrum, and so destroying memory, coordination, will, and judgment, and wrecking the individual physically, mentally, and morally.

Next in the category of destructive forces, I must enumerate the slavery to conventional dress.

A careful study of this subject has convinced me that, aside from the liquor and tobacco habits, there is no deteriorating force which deals such destructive blows against the constitution of the race as the wrong, unphysiological customs in dress which prevail among civilized American women.

Scarcely a woman can be found who has reached the age of 25 or 30, and who has worn the conventional dress, who is not suffering from dislocation of the stomach, the kidneys, the bowels, or some other important internal organ. The present outlook is, however, somewhat hopeful. The bicycle has forever delivered women from the thralldom of long skirts, and gives encouragement that the necessity for breathing capacity may yet banish the corset and its accompanying tight bands.

74. Reveries.

"Bicycling and Its Attire," *The Delineator*, April 1896:

Bicycling is an evolution. For several years merely a branch of athletics, indulged in as a pastime by the ultra, it has developed into a serious factor in fin de siècle progress. Its merits are many and its pleasures incalculable. No other mode of travel, save, perhaps horseback riding, is capable of giving such thorough enjoyment as the wheel, so exhilarating is the ease and rapidity of its motion, and none is more conductive to health and symmetrical bodily development. Many for whom outdoor exercises have heretofore possessed no attraction and whose habits were sluggish for the lack of them, are fascinated by the wheel, claiming it is without rival, its influence being felt mentally as well as physically. Distances are rapidly and easily covered; varied prospects are successfully presented, and new ideas and trains of thought are engendered.

The hygienic value of wheeling appeals to every admirer of vigorous and healthy manhood and womanhood. While certain muscles are brought more into action than others, all are benefited by the exercise. The power of the respiratory organs is strengthened by the large quantities of pure air taken into the lungs, creating a more perfect oxygenation of the blood and invigorating the entire system, a tonic far pleasanter than any yet compounded by chemist. Physicians now generally concede the value of the wheel in the treatment of invalids and convalescents able to take a form of exercise requiring so much physical exertion. . . .

The best dress for wheeling is still a mooted question, opinion being divided between the short skirt and the bloomer costume. Whichever is adopted, it should be as light in weight as possible and so fashioned that it will in no wise hamper the movements of the rider. In long full skirts there lurks danger; they become easily entangled in the chain or pedals and thus bring about disaster. Wool sweaters with large sleeves are fashionable, but are objected to by some on the score of their snug fit, which sharply defines the figure. They absorb perspiration, however, and are for that reason particularly desirable for warm weather wear. Fashion provides numerous other waists as smart as they are convenient. If a corset is insisted upon (the rider will be far more comfortable without one), a short, lightly boned affair that ends above the hips and is made without steels in front, should be chosen.

"Her Point of View," *The New York Times,* February 25, 1894:

The dress reform symposiums which have been held at the Madison Square Garden through the week have evidently driven the wedge of sensible dress a little further in. It is still apparently a case of St. Anthony preaching to the fishes,

> "Much delighted were they,
> But preferred the old way."

But in point of fact there is a large class of women who are convinced that they are miserably clothed, and who are only waiting for custom to pave the way for a change in their garments.

It is a melancholy truth that men who rail at women's slavery to fashion and foolish notions of dress are among the chief obstacles in the way. They talk and inveigh, but when it comes to the women's—their women's—acting, they prove the stumbling blocks. When physicians who urge their patients to doff corsets, wear untrammeling gowns and broad-soled boots, are not able or willing to insist that their wives and daughters shall reap the benefits of this advice, it militates against its usefulness. And the lay husbands and fathers are no better. "You women are geese to dress as you do," is a kind of stock phrase with them, but they are tremendously tenacious that their womenkind shall be counted in with the flock.

"Nice woman, that Mrs. So-and-So," a man says, "but a little odd, you know. Affects thick waists, short skirts, and that sort of thing." And the same man will look over his wife's gown and comment, with a little mournful philosophy: "My dear, I'm afraid you're growing stout. Where is that slender sylph I married?"

Men have got a distinct office in this dress reform movement. They have got to accord their individual support as well as to indulge in abstract theorizing. A happy destiny has emancipated them in a great degree. But they did not achieve this greatness; it was thrust upon them. There is abundant evidence to prove that men are as devoted to dress and custom as women, have about as many vanities concerning their personal appearance, and are as willing, many of them, to sacrifice personal comfort to accomplish them.

Aside from the men, however, it is of course undeniable that woman is her own worst foe in the matter. She is learning though, slowly, but surely, and her emancipation is not far away.

Conservative women do not look for or desire the radical changes that are offered by many reformers. A skirt that clears the ankles is a sensible and convenient length, possessing for walking all the advantages that one of knee length does. Many women wear the former now and are unnoticed.

The chief points that should be insisted upon are the suspension of the garments from the shoulders, the doing away of stiff boning and heavy cumbersome trimmings and methods of cut. This Mrs. Jenness Miller and others have shown that it is possible to accomplish, and yet accommodate the gown in general features to the prevailing mode. Nor is a variety of fabric and design to be frowned upon. It must follow that different tastes and purses will dictate different choosings.

Any reform must come gradually. The physical culture movement is doing its work, even though the women lace themselves into corsets after their hour of exercise. Pretty soon the operation will be too difficult and the corset will be discarded. Many corset-wearing mothers are keeping them from their growing daughters. This is the way for the work to go on, slowly and without a startling innovation. It will not be done in a day or a month or a year, but 50 years from now women will study with amazement the fashion plates of today and wonder that their sisters could have lived in such clothing.

"What Women May Wear, Not Corsets, of All Things, Said Mrs. M. S. Lawrence,"
The New York Times; May 22, 1895:

A large and interested audience of girls was gathered in the Teachers College, at Morningside Heights, yesterday afternoon, when Mrs. Margaret Stanton Lawrence, the physical director of the college, gave a lecture upon dress, with all the necessary illustrative accompaniments.

A skeleton, revealed by the open door of a little portable closet, rattled his bones rather cheerfully than otherwise against the narrow walls of his abiding place. The Venus of Milo, hanging complacently by the side of an abnormally ugly specimen of the wasp-waisted woman, the interior of the human structure in various natural and unnatural conditions on charts, and the figure of the modern woman, as she appears occasionally in a comparatively healthy condition, were exhibited.

There was to be seen a bicycle gown, a part of a rainy day dress, and sundry mysterious packages which revealed in time the few hygienic garments the woman who considers herself properly clad wears beneath her gowns, bicycle or otherwise.

The lecture was particularly intended for the mothers of the college girls, but owing to the weather they did not appear. Mrs. Elizabeth Cady Stanton, Mrs. Lawrence's mother, was the guest of honor, and was heartily applauded by the girls as she came into the room with her daughter.

The corset is the bête noire against which Mrs. Lawrence contends with every principle of theory and practice, and it was the basis of all her remarks yesterday. The organs contained in the thorax were illustrated by a cheerful-looking artificial set of cheese cloths made to measurement by Dr. Eliza Mosher of Brooklyn, under whom Mrs. Lawrence studied. The heart was a dainty pincushion affair of red and blue, and other bodily organs were represented in a like manner. The lungs were such a commodious breathing apparatus that every girl present wondered if it could be possible that there was space enough in her chest to contain such an amount of delicate mechanism.

"I have been asked," said Mrs. Lawrence, "if the various organs were colored in this way, but they are not. The colors merely indicate the different organs.

"The development of women is most important, for it depends upon their condition whether those who come after will be well or ill able to stand the tremendous strain that comes upon the people of the nineteenth and twentieth centuries.

"It is because of the corset that one of the toasts at all medical dinners is, 'Woman, God's Best Gift to Man and the Support of the Doctors.' The corsets are pretty machines, often trimmed with gay ribbon and lace, but the loosest corset causes a pressure of 40 pounds on the most sensitive part of the body, and a tight corset a pressure equal to 70 or 80 pounds. 'Armorsides, warranted not to break,' I have seen on some of the corset advertisements, and it is a very good name, I think."

continued

"What Women May Wear, Not Corsets, of All Things . . ." *(continued)*

Then Mrs. Lawrence showed her pretty cheesecloth organs in their proper places and how they all suffered from pressure upon any one of them. It was about this time that a gentle ripple of laughter started at one side of the room, and gradually spread over it. It was only an innocent and unsuspecting young man, who with notebook in hand had mistakenly wandered into a woman's dress convocation.

"Has that man gone?" said Mrs. Lawrence, as she made her way back to the charts. He had gone very quickly, and every one laughed again.

"A man and a woman breathe exactly alike when properly dressed," went on Mrs. Lawrence. "It is necessary to have plenty of oxygen, and that is only obtained by deep breathing. Dr. Austin Flint says that after they are grown, women do not breathe as men do, but that is not so. He has experimented with fashionable women only. Dr. Mosher has made experiments with men. Without a corset, breathing is low down, and with a corset, merely in the chest.

No. 31R322 $11.50

No. 31R321 $11.00

No. 31R323 $10.50

No. 31R324 $13.50

LADIES' TAILOR MADE SUITS.

We furnish these in sizes from 32 to 42 inches around the bust and from 38 to 44 inches in skirt length; the average length of waist in back is 16 inches and the length of inside sleeve '8½ to 19 inches; these are regular measurements; sizes different than these must be made to order, in which case we charge 20 per cent above the regular price. **If for some reason you have to** return a suit to us, never return skirt or jacket alone; return both and we will be pleased to exchange the suit; parts of suits will not be accepted.

No. 31R321 LADIES' TAILOR MADE SUIT. Made of all wool Venetian cloth, coat shaped collar and lapels, fly front, yoke effect, finished with tailor made flaps of the same material; tailor made straps on the back seams; bell sleeves trimmed with straps; jacket lined throughout with romain lining; skirt tailor made with graduated flounce stitched several times, lined with black glazed lining and interlined at the bottom, bound with velvet. An exceptionally pretty suit. Colors, a new shade of gray, or castor. Price.. **$11.00**

No. 31R322 LADIES' TAILOR MADE SUIT. Consisting of a jacket and a rainy day skirt; coat collar and lapels on jacket faced with black peau de soie; double breasted dip front; back reaches only to the waist; velvet collar; bell sleeves; jacket is lined throughout with black satin; tailor made skirt, stitched twelve times around the bottom; silk band around the waist; inverted plait in the back. We can furnish in black or blue wool mixed melton cloth with narrow, invisible white stripes. Price..... **$11.50**

No. 31R323 LADIES' STYLISH BLOUSE SUIT. Consisting of blouse and skirt, made of all wool cheviot serge. The blouse is made with a rolling collar, large lapels and revers, as shown in illustration; trimmed with satin straps; bell sleeves trimmed like the jacket; satin strap trimming in back of jacket, which reaches to the waist only. The jacket is lined throughout with black satin. Tailor made skirt with graduated flounce, trimmed with two rows of satin strap trimmings above the flounce; glazed lining and interlining in the flounce, velvet binding. Colors, black, blue or brown. Price.. **$10.50**

No. 31R324 LADIES' TAILOR MADE SUIT. Consisting of jacket and skirt, made of all wool Venetian cloth. Jacket has coat shaped collar and lapels, single breasted, can be worn as a blouse or buttoned; neatly trimmed with three satin straps reaching from the waist in front all around the shoulders to the waist in back; belt all around the blouse trimmed with satin straps; similar trimmings on the cuffs. The jacket is lined throughout with a good quality of satin lining. The skirt is strictly tailor made, has a graduated flounce, has four rows of satin strap trimmings; glazed lining, interlining at the bottom, velvet binding. Colors, black, royal blue or castor. Price.. **$13.50**

No. 31R325 LADIES' TAILOR MADE SUIT. Consisting of jacket and skirt, made of all wool Venetian cloth. Eton effect jacket, which can be worn open as well; neatly trimmed with satin around the coat shaped collar and lapels and all around the waist; similar trimming on both sides of the front as well as on the back of the jacket, which reaches to the waist only; fancy cuffs, trimmed to match the suit. Jacket lined throughout with black silk lining. The skirt is tailor made, with graduated flounce, trimmed with satin straps stitched around the bottom; has a drop skirt made of black glazed lining. They are the newest things shown for the coming season. Colors, black, castor or blue. Price.. **$13.75**

No. 31R326 LADIES' TAILOR MADE SUIT. Consisting of jacket and skirt. The jacket is made full moire, shaped collar, new shaped lapels, dipped front, yoke effect, stitched and finished with straps of same material from yoke to the bottom of the jacket; strap trimming on the back of the jacket, which reaches to the waist only; several rows of stitching all around the jacket; jacket lined all through with taffeta silk; cuffs made of black moire or watered silk. The skirt is well tailor made, has a graduated flounce, trimmed with strips made of the same material and stitched several times; finished with small, silk covered buttons; is lined throughout with black glazed lining and interlined around the bottom; velvet binding, and silk ribbon around the waist. Colors, black, blue or castor. Price.. **$16.50**

1898 News Feature

"The Child's Dearest Playmate," *The Ladies' Home Journal*, June 1898:

There is no inconsistency at once so glaring, and no sight so pathetic, as a child dressed so primly that it is afraid to play in the dirt for fear of soiling its clothes. It is like an umbrella which is never taken out in the rain. There are undoubtedly occasions and times for children to be "dressed up." But when a child is, as so many are, "dressed up" from early morning until bedtime, and has constantly ringing in his ears the injunction not to soil its clothes, it would seem as if a more unnatural state of things could scarcely exist. A child is happiest when at play, and generally, the dirtier it is the happier it is. And why should it be otherwise? We of an older growth are happiest when we are closest to dear old Mother Earth. What greater joy is there than the throwing of one's self upon the grass in summer and lying at full length upon the bosom of the earth? So the child's happiest moments are those which are spent in digging in the sand at the seashore or the dirt of the garden. And as the child is happiest, so is its pleasure the healthiest.

Just as at last Christmas time this magazine made a plea for the absolute freedom of children on that holiday, so with the season now at hand, pleas for permission for the children to have freer and closer acquaintance with their dearest playmate: the earth. Of course, the playmate is not clean; it is not conducive to keeping the little skirts white or the miniature trousers without rents. But then, what playmate is there which has so much to give to the child? What playmate is so absorbing or so infinite of resource? It is a child's cheapest playmate. Its only cost may be paid with soap and water and the mother's needle. It is the only rival to the doctor, and his most effective one. With the simple exercise of a little prudent oversight, the soil never did a child any harm. The little socks may wear out, the little dresses may appear to the sharpest eyes as though they never had been white, but on the cheeks of the child and in the sparkle of its eyes are seen what the earth has given in return to the little digger of its soil. Far richer is what it gives than what it takes away.

The time is short enough before the child tires of its playmate. Only a few years lie between the wonderful fortress of sand and the conventional home of mortar. No happier period, no freer time, no healthier moment ever comes to a human being than when as a child it stands in proud contemplation of its house of sand. We never get so close to Mother Earth again, we are never so natural. Let the children, therefore, know well the soil. Let every possible moment be spent upon it and in it. If the family purse cannot stand the laundry stain, let the little frocks and trousers be adapted to the soil. Far better are dollars spent on children's clothes than pennies given to doctors. The sturdiest, happiest children are those who practically live out-of-doors. Let them romp, then: let them play: let them dig, and the more they grovel in the cool, health-giving soil, the more content let us, as parents, be. The closer we keep our children to Nature, to Mother Earth, the wiser are we as parents and the healthier are our children.

Let them have their little gardens, let them build their homes of sand.

Every hour of such play brings them health, every romp makes sturdy their little limbs, every breath of leaf and soil makes finest fibre, every moment gives pure and healthful delight. The soil is the child's best friend.

1898 Profile

Child Labor: The Children's Jacket Makers' Strike

At only 15 years old, Harry Gladstone went from poor immigrant to labor leader, organizing the boys and girls in the clothing trade to fight for better wages and working conditions.

Life at Home

- Harry Gladstone's first impression of America was formed at the Immigration Station at Castle Island, New York.
- There, five-year-old Harry was examined, poked, and peered at by an officious man who spoke no Yiddish and didn't appear to like those who did.
- It was one of Harry's earliest memories.
- In 1888, Harry, his sisters, and parents were part of a flood of Jewish immigrants seeking opportunity in America.
- The family fled Poland when the wave of attacks against Jews in the Pale of Settlement had accelerated; the family was desperate when they located help from the Alliance Israelite Universelle, which provided clothing, medical care, and enough money for passage to America.
- Steerage accommodations were Spartan but cheap; Harry's father said often, "Don't complain if you are still alive."
- Two-thirds of the ocean liners which carried immigrants docked in New York Harbor.
- To five-year-old Harry Gladstone, most of the world's "tired and poor" were unloaded the day he arrived.
- In accordance with dictates to keep undesirables from entering the United States, every new immigrant was thoroughly

Young Harry Gladstone organized working children to fight for better wages.

examined with the often-stated threat that the ill or unemployable would be sent back to Europe.

- Tired, scared, and enormously wary of people in uniforms, Harry was driven to be extra friendly.
- No one responded to a single comment he made, no matter how hard he tried.
- Then, a woman attached to the Hebrew Immigrant Aid Society stepped forward to translate Yiddish into English.
- The immigration officer became no more friendly, but at least he stopped staring at Harry in a mean way.
- By the time Harry's family arrived in New York City, "all the gold had already been raked from the streets," his father said.
- The promise of instant prosperity dissipated; noise, people, poverty, and problems were everywhere.
- To support the family, Harry's father became a fruit peddler, pushing a handcart up and down the streets of New York City.
- On the Lower East Side alone, 150,000 peddlers sold their wares.
- Harry's father knew he could make more money if he left the city, but travel was costly and the risks high.
- When he struck out to explore Pennsylvania and the opportunities that lay west, he promised to return soon.

Harry's parents soon realized that job opportunities for immigrants in America were limited.

Like Harry, many poor immigrant children would have to give up school for work in the factories.

- That day was the last time he saw his father, the last day he attended school, the last time he considered himself a child.
- Harry Gladstone went to work to support his family when he was nine.
- At first he stayed in the peddler's game, like his father.
- But the real money was in clothing, the needlecrafts, if a man was willing to work long enough hours.
- Ready-to-wear clothing had been growing in popularity, made possible by new, heavy sewing machines, steam presses, and millions of immigrants willing to work 16 hours a day sewing garments.
- It didn't take Harry long to figure out the cards were stacked in favor of the factory owners; few workers got ahead.
- Men earned between $6.00 and $10.00 a week, women and girls between $4.00 and $5.00.
- The factory owners employed skilled cutters who cut out the garments, then sent the bundles of cuttings to the contractors, who hired workers to do the basting, sewing, pressing, and finishing.
- A garment was usually made by a team of three: the machine operator, the baster, and the finisher.

Life at Work
- The past week had been the most exhilarating of Harry Gladstone's young life.
- He was only 15 and now the leader of a labor union that defeated the bosses.
- And to make life sweeter, the strike settlement was signed at the same hour as the peace protocol was approved by the representatives of the United States and Spain.

The union Harry founded had 75 members, both boys and girls.

- A month ago he was just Harry Gladstone, a machine tender or basting puller in a jacketmaker's sweatshop.
- Now he is being triumphantly called the "boy agitator of the East Side" by the New
- York newspapers.
- Having arrived in New York 10 years earlier, Harry was only able to spend three years in the Chrystie Street Grammar School before he was needed to help support the family.
- Thanks to a quick mind and hard work, he spoke English fluently enough, and even preferred that tongue to his native Yiddish when addressing the boys, whom he is fond of referring to as his "fellow workmen."
- His prominence in the children's jacketmakers' strike was due to the initiative he took in organizing the boys and girls in the trade.
- The union he founded to fight the needlecraft bosses had 75 members, both boys and girls.
- The youngest boy was 12 years old; he was unsure of the youngest girl's age because girls wouldn't tell their correct ages.
- The strike was over wages and the way they were measured.
- The average machine tender or turner made $2.00 to $3.00 a week.
- "While the operators are working on them jackets we must keep turning the sleeves and flaps and the collars," Harry said. "Sometimes three or four operators commence to holler at us, so that we get mixed up and nearly go crazy trying to attend to them all.
- But the bosses don't care, he paid us the same."
- The children's jacketmaker's strike demanded that they be paid $1.00 per machine and that the work day be limited to nine hours, down from 12.

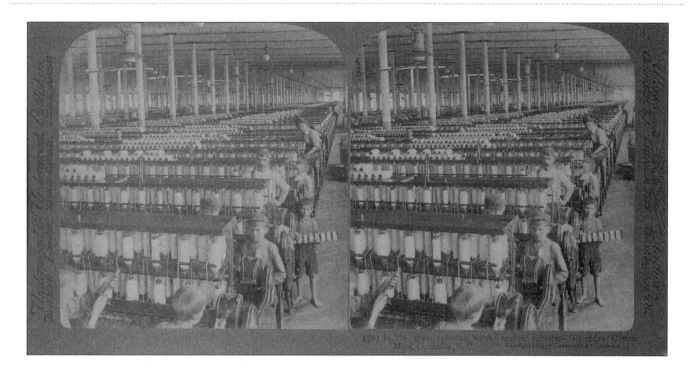

(20) In the great spinning room—600,000 spindles—Olympian Cotton Mills, Columbia, S. C.

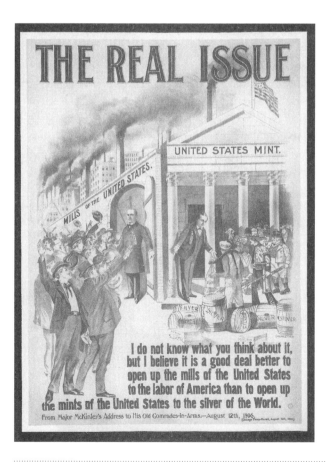

THE REAL ISSUE

MILLS OF THE UNITED STATES.

UNITED STATES MINT.

I do not know what you think about it, but I believe it is a good deal better to open up the mills of the United States to the labor of America than to open up the mints of the United States to the silver of the World.

From Major McKinley's Address to His Old Comrades-in-Arms.—August 12th, 1896.

- When the strike ended, Harry wanted to continue making speeches.
- The workers were not much interested; it was time to tend to bread-and-butter issues like feeding their families.
- Throughout the strike, Harry believed it was his job to help hold the union together by telling them to "think about your poor fathers and mothers you have got to support."
- Harry also reminded his fellow workers that they could be attending school and getting an education if the bosses did not demand 14- to 15-hour days "in a pest-hole, pulling bastings, turning collars and sleeves, and running around as if they were crazy."
- Harry firmly believed in the philosophy, "If you don't look out for yourselves, who will?"
- Besides, these are children, he said to reporters, who were being asked to work long hours, who "have not had time to grow up, to get strength for work," and must spend their "dearest days in the sweatshop."
- To his fellow strikers, Harry said, "The only way to get good wages is to stick together, so let us be true to our union."

Life in the Community: Lower East Side, New York City

- The growing economy of America attracted millions of eager newcomers after the Civil War.
- Twelve million people boarded ships to come to America between 1865 and 1900.
- About half were Germans and Irish, and nearly a million were British, many of whom had industrial experience.
- The number of machinists exploded from 55,000 in 1870 to nearly 300,000 thirty years later.
- The expansion of machine-made manufacturing allowed the country's industrial output to outstrip that of England by 1885.
- During the 1880s, American steamship and railroad agents combed southeastern Europe to entice workers with promises of abundance and opportunity around every corner.
- As the nineteenth century came to a close, immigrants continued to pour into America; the largest single group, next to the Italians, was the Jews from Eastern Europe.
- They came from Rumania and the Austrian province of Galicia, but especially from the Jewish Pale of Settlement in Poland, part of the Russian empire, to escape the violent pogroms there.
- Most found abundance in lesser quantities than had been reported.
- Often entire families were forced to work to make ends meet.
- Most re-formed themselves into ethnic communities based upon old customs, religions, and language.
- Although the many nationalities mingled at work, intermarriage was rare.
- At their houses of worship, immigrants found religious leaders who knew the familiar liturgy, the language, and news from their communities back home.
- To further strengthen ethnic ties, fraternal associations were created that provided mutual insurance against illness or took charge of the body when someone in the community died.
- Yet, the union movement often reached across ethnic lines to create unity.
- The expanded size of factories and the cost of machinery concentrated the power into fewer hands, making the employer more powerful and determined to control costs—including wages.
- The continuing flood of immigrants made wage increases difficult.
- Within the clothing industry, union organization was impacted by the number of tailors who worked beside their wives and daughters in tiny apartments.
- Approximately 18,000 tailors worked in New York City alone in the 1890s.
- Most were themselves employed by fellow tailors who cut cloth from the manufacturing firms for distribution.
- Tailors were paid by the piece and often worked 12-hour days in poorly lit rooms.
- By the last decade of the 1800s, unions and strikes were proliferating, even though the workers themselves often doubted the union's ability to help them.
- The labor union movement was further bolstered when skilled workers such as locomotive engineers and craftsmen embraced it.
- During the depression of 1893-1897, unemployment topped 16 percent.
- Long hours and unpredictable unpaid layoffs were the rule, and safety and working conditions were largely unregulated.

- The upper class and the emerging middle class of America discounted demands for better living conditions.
- Most industrial towns financed their municipal improvements by levies on the residents who would benefit directly from them; thus, working class areas were excluded from sewer systems, decent water supplies, lighting, and paved roads.
- Children of workers tended to drop out of school earlier to aid the family, often jeopardizing the next generation's opportunity for prosperity.

[Form 21-1901]   1–55   STATE OF NEW YORK   Book 1 Page 363
Department of Labor
Bureau of Factory Inspection
ALBANY,   FEB 17 1905

DEAR Gentlemen

Please inform this Department whether the following requirements specified in the notification sent you 11–3–04, have been complied with:

Guard all set screws on collars of shafting.

Yours respectfully,

Jno. M. MacAllin
Commissioner of Labor.

John Williams
First Deputy Commissioner of Labor.

PLEASE RETURN THIS CARD WITH REPLY.   a7679

HISTORICAL SNAPSHOT
1898

- America boasted more than 300 bicycle manufacturing companies
- Uneeda Biscuit Company was created
- J.P. Stevens & Company was founded in New York
- The production of motorcars reach 1,000 annually
- The racist "grandfather clause" marched across the South, ushering in widespread use of Jim Crow laws and restricting most blacks from voting
- Pepsi-Cola was introduced in New Bern, North Carolina, by pharmacist Caleb Bradham
- Bricklayers were paid $3.41 per day and worked a 48-hour week; marble cutters made $4.22 per day
- The consolidation of Greater New York City was created through the merger of Brooklyn and Manhattan
- Henry James published "The Turn of the Screw"
- The Travelers Insurance Company of Hartford, Connecticut, issued the first automobile insurance policy which cost $11.25 to purchase $5,000 in liability coverage
- The Supreme Court ruled that a child born in the United States to Chinese immigrants was a U.S. citizen, and therefore could not be deported under the Chinese Exclusion Act
- Postcards were first authorized by the Post Office
- The song "Happy Birthday to You," composed by sisters Mildred and Patty Hill, was coming into common use
- Toothpaste in collapsible metal tubes was becoming widely available
- The battleship *Maine* was destroyed in Havana harbor, Cuba, killing 260 of its crew, triggering the Spanish-American, War
- Admiral George Dewey's fleet attacked Spain's holdings in Manila Bay, the Philippines conquering the nation for America
- Wesson Oil was introduced
- The trolley replaced horse-drawn cars in Boston
- *The New York Times* dropped its price from three cents to one cent a copy, tripling circulation
- The boll weevil began its destructive spread through the cotton fields of the South
- Cellophane was invented by Charles F. Cross and Edward J. Bevan
- The Union Carbide Company was formed
- H.G. Wells published the classic "War of the Worlds," about an invasion of Earth by Martians
- The northern California Mount Tamalpais and Muir Woods railroad was featured in the first documentary film made in the San Francisco Bay Area
- Buddy Bolden, cornetist and New Orleans brass band leader, was an early practitioner of what would later be called jazz
- Giraud Foster used the money earned from the invention of closure snaps for clothing to build a $2.5 million estate on 400 acres in Lee, Massachusetts
- America's first forestry school was founded in the Pisgah National Forest in North Carolina
- A telephone excise tax was created to help finance the Spanish-American War

Selected Prices, 1898

Bicycle Skirt	$2.50
Blush, for Lips and Face	$1.00
Dinner, New York City	$1.25
Doilies, Nine Linen	$0.10
Fountain Pen	$4.00
Pesticide, Mosquito, Six Wafers	$0.10
Piano, Steinway Upright	$200.00
Sarsparilla, Bottle	1.00
Shirt, Man's	$1.50
Watch, Woman's	$5.00

MELLIN'S FOOD

1898

"WE ARE ADVERTISED BY OUR LOVING FRIENDS."

MARTiN WESLEY GRAY.

In all cases where an infant must be artificially fed, MELLIN'S FOOD is earnestly recommended. MELLIN'S FOOD will make cow's milk agree with your baby.

MRS. GRAY, of 3105 Columbus Ave., Minneapolis, Minn., writes:

My baby is a MELLIN'S FOOD baby; he has had nothing else, and is jolly and happy all day long.

Write to us (a postal will do) and we will send you a sample of Mellin's Food free of expense.

DOLIBER-GOODALE COMPANY, BOSTON, MASS.

1789--PAST AND PRESENT.--1897.

Pears' binds the men and maids to-day
With those a hundred years away;

And so long as fair white hands, a bright, clear complexion, and a soft,
healthy skin continue to add to beauty and attractiveness, so long will

Pears' Soap

continue to hold its place in the good opinion of women who wish to be
beautiful and attractive. Its purity is proverbial; so also is that of Pears'
Shaving Stick, which may be used on the tenderest and most sensitive skin,
and is renowned as the best Shaving Soap in the world.

20 International Awards—Be sure you get the genuine.

"A View of the Pullman Strike," *The Wall Street Journal,* July 5, 1894:

An executive officer of one of the corporations which had considerable trouble during the last year with the labor element, said Tuesday: "I believe that this Pullman boycott will be a good thing for the people. It is bound to terminate in the complete defeat of the strikers. And such being the case, it is better to have it in a radical form than to have sporadic cases from month to month and year to year. The discontent of labor has become more and more assertive month by month since last summer. It can be liked to poison in the human system, and it is better (to carry out the simile) that the poison cause prostration and be thrown off by Nature through a fit of sickness than to remain in the system, manifesting its deadly effect for an unlimited time."

How the Other Half Lives, by Jacob A. Riis, 1890:

Turning the corner into Hester Street, we stumble upon a nest of cloakmakers in the busy season. Six months of the year the cloakmaker is idle, or nearly so. Now is his harvest. Seventy-five cents a cloak, all complete, is the price in this shop. The cloak is of cheap plush, and might sell for eight or nine dollars over the store counter.

Seven dollars is the weekly wages of this man with wife and two children, and $9.50 rent to pay per month. A boarder pays about a third of it. There was a time when he made $10.00 a week and thought himself rich. But wages have come down fearfully in the last two years. Think of it: "come down" to this.

The other cloakmakers aver that they can make as much as $12.00 a week, when they are employed, by taking their work home and sewing till midnight. One exhibits his account-book with a Ludlow Street sweater. It shows that he and his partner, working on first-class garments for a Broadway house in the four busiest weeks of the season, made together from $15.15 to $19.20 a week by striving from 6 a.m. to 11 p.m., that is to say, from $7.58 to $9.60 each.

The sweater in this work probably made as much as 50 percent, at least on their labor. Not far away is a factory in a rear yard where the factory inspector reports teams of tailors making men's coats at an average of $0.27 a coat, all complete except buttons and buttonholes.

"Plight of the Tailors," by Ray Stannard Baker, *McClure's Magazine*, December 1904:

Each year crowds of foreign immigrants poured into the East Side. They were poor, ignorant, and they had been oppressed; they knew nothing of American life, though they expected much; they found at once that living here, rent, food, and fuel were far more expensive than in their old homes. Their first necessity, therefore, was work, no matter what, to furnish them with the necessities of life.

There are not many things that an unskilled foreigner, knowing no English, can do, but almost any man or women can sew. And thus flourished the sweatshop, the home of the "task system" where men, women and children worked together in unhealthful, often diseased, and sometimes immoral surroundings. Nowhere in the world at any time, probably, were men and women worked as they were in the sweatshop, the lowest paid, most degrading of American employment. The sweatshop employer ground all the work he could from every man, woman, and child under him.

It was no uncommon thing in these sweatshops for men to sit bent over a sewing machine continuously from 11 to 15 hours a day in July weather, operating a sewing machine by foot-power, and so often driven that they could not stop for lunch. The seasonal character of the work meant demoralizing toil for a few months in the year and a no less demoralizing idleness for the remainder of the time.

Copyright 1903, by B. KUPPENHEIMER & Co. Chicago

Labor History Timeline

1840

President Martin Van Buren signed an executive order that established a 10-hour workday without a decrease in pay.

1842

The Massachusetts Supreme Court ruled that unions were legal organizations and had the right to organize and strike.

1849

The carpenters in San Francisco and Sacramento struck for a pay of $16 a day, and agreed to $14 a day.

1851

Two railroad strikers were killed and others injured by the state militia in Portgage, New York.

1860

In Lynn, Massachusetts, 800 women operatives and 4,000 workmen marched during a shoemaker's strike.

The Union movement comprised two million members.

1866

The National Labor Union was formed by printers, machinists, and stonecutters.

1867

Massachusetts established the first factory inspections focused on safety standards.

1869

The Knights of Labor was formed.

1874

Unemployed workers were beaten in New York's Tompkins Square Park by a detachment of mounted police who charged into the crowd, striking men, women, and children indiscriminately with billy clubs.

1877

U.S. railroad workers began strikes to protest wage cuts that halted the movement of U.S. railroads and resulted in federal troops being called out to force an end to the nationwide strike.

Ten protesting miners were hanged in Pennsylvania.

A general strike called by members of the Chicago German Furniture Workers Union resulted in battles with federal troops, who killed 30 workers and wounded over 100.

1881

Samuel Gompers established the Federation of Trades and Labor Unions.

1882

Thirty thousand workers marched in the first Labor Day parade in New York City "to show the strength and esprit de corps of the trade and labor organizations."

1884

The Federation of Organized Trades and Labor unions passed a resolution demanding that "8 hours shall constitute a legal day's work."

Timeline . . . *(continued)*

1886

Two hundred thousand workers nationwide went on strike to demand the universal adoption of the eight-hour day.

The size and influence of the Knights of Labor grew as hundreds of thousands of American workers joined.

About 16,000 workers, dominated by Poles, walked off their jobs in Milwaukee, Wisconsin, angrily denouncing the 10-hour workday; as protesters chanted for the eight-hour day, the militia fired into the crowd, killing seven.

The Haymarket Riot in Chicago erupted, the origin of international May Day observances.

1887

The Louisiana militia shot 35 unarmed Black sugar workers striking to gain a dollar-per-day wage, and lynched two strike leaders.

Congress passed labor relations acts pertaining to arbitration rights of railroad workers.

1890

New York garment workers won the right to unionize after a seven-month strike.

Los Angeles Times owner locked out striking typographers and declared war on the labor movement.

The Sherman Anti-trust Act passed to combat industrial abuses.

1892

The homestead strike at the Carnegie steel mill in Homestead, Pennsylvania, resulted in the deaths of seven Pinkerton guards and 11 strikers.

Striking miners in Coeur D'Alene, Idaho, dynamited the Frisco Mill, leaving it in ruins.

1893

The Pullman Palace Car Company strike resulted in the burning of seven buildings within the 1892 World's Columbian Exposition in Chicago's Jackson Park; 14,000 federal and state troops were required to put down the strike, which was sparked by a reduction in wages.

Congress passed legislation requiring safety equipment on railroad engines.

1894

Attempting to break a strike, federal troops killed 34 American Railway Union members, who were led by Eugene Debs against the Pullman Company in the Chicago area.

The American Federation of Labor called for the organization of women into trade unions.

1896

The state militia was sent to Leadville, Colorado, to break a miner's strike.

1897

Nineteen unarmed striking coal miners and mine workers were killed and 36 wounded by a posse in the Lattimer Massacre for refusing to disperse near Hazleton, Pennsylvania.

1898

The Erdman Act, which made it a criminal offense for railroads to dismiss employees based on their union activities, was declared invalid by the United States Supreme Court.

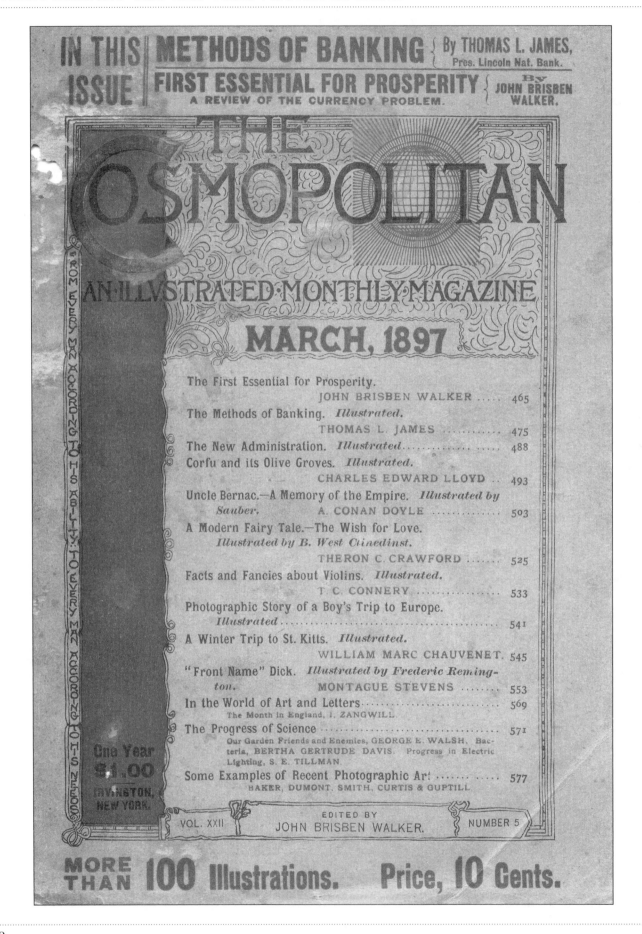

"Troubles of Ladies' Tailors," *The New York Times,* June 13, 1898:

Ladies' tailoring is becoming an important branch of industry in this city, and the 1,500 and odd union ladies' tailors are complaining that their employers have taken advantage of the dull season to try and break up their organization.

In this trade, the men have been encroaching upon the domain of the female dressmaker, and men's tailor-made suits have, it is said, been steadily becoming more fashionable, and many men who were formally employed in the male tailor's trade have become ladies' tailors because they can earn more money. They earn between $18 and $20 per week.

With the return of the summer, the dull season for ladies' tailors begins. Fashionable girls and women hurry off to the summer resorts, where, the men say, gauze and muslin and other light clothing are the general rule, and the women are not so particular as to the exact fit of these outdoor summer garments as they are about their city dresses. Consequently, the demand for fine dresses has greatly fallen off, and that for fashionable evening dresses does not cut much of a figure.

The men say that the employers have taken advantage of all this, and are urging them to sign statements that they will not join any union while in their employ, and if they are already members of unions, to state that fact.

"Thomas & Co. Close Down," *The New York Times,* February 6, 1898:

As a result of the strike among the employees, the firm of Thomas & Co., shoe manufacturers at Hewes and South Fifth Streets, Brooklyn, yesterday shut down its large plant, and it is not known how long it will be closed.

There were nearly 500 employees, among them Dennis Ward. He is regarded by the union men as a "scab." They requested the superintendent, Charles Turner, to discharge him. The superintendent refused, and on Tuesday, 250 men went on strike. Two days later the strikers were joined by 100 more employees. It was said that the shutdown was necessary because the boilers needed an overhauling.

The strikers denied this last night, and said the firm could not go on with work while the strike is in progress. The strikers declare they will not yield until Ward is discharged. The firm, it is said, will not discharge Ward, but would not object should he voluntarily withdraw.

"Small Riot of Shop Girls," *The New York Times,* January 22, 1898:

There was a small riot of shop girls in Sixth Avenue last night, resulting from the arrest of one of their escorts.

A large number of young men have been in the habit of gathering about the employees' entrance of the Siegel-Cooper Company's store in the evening at the time for the hundreds of girls who are employed there to leave and go to their homes. The authorities of the store instructed Detective Bernard and Special Policeman John Leonard, whom they employ, to disperse the gathering.

Last evening, the young men as they assembled were warned to keep away. They defied the officers and maintained that they had the right to stand or walk in the street as long as they were peaceful. George Wallun of 410 East Twenty-third Street, who said he was in the habit of calling to escort a young woman to whom he is engaged, mounted a box and proceeded to make a speech. Bernard arrested him, and Leonard was leading him away when the girls began to swarm out like hornets. They surrounded the policeman and the prisoner and made Leonard's face burn with their sarcasms.

The young woman for whom Wallun had called fainted when she heard he was under arrest. She was promptly carried away by her friends, but the incident increased the indignation of the other girls who gathered 500 strong on the sidewalk and said they would strike if the order against escorts was not rescinded.

1900–1909

The dawning of the new century gave every evidence that America was the fulfillment of the New World's promise of economic and political freedom. And reform was in the air. Labor unions gained membership; the regulation of milk and meat products captured the public's attention; cities focused on the creation of parks and child welfare began to receive national attention. At the same time, the number of inventions spawned by the power of electricity was revolutionary. Americans were eager to compete on the world stage by inventing a better automobile, more efficient factories or clean, inexpensive window-glass. A rotating kiln manufactured in 1899 unleashed large quantities of cheap, standardized cement, just in time for a nation ready to leave behind the bicycle fad and fall madly in love with the automobile. In the midst of this spirit of innovation, ever changing America was willing to protect its abundant birds or consider the benefits of the eight-hour work day, while also leading the world in productivity, exceeding the empires of France and Britain combined.

In the eyes of the world, America was the land of opportunity. Millions of immigrants flooded the United States, often finding work in the new factories of the New World—many managed by men who came two generations before from countries like England or Germany or Wales. When Theodore Roosevelt proudly proclaimed in 1902, "The typical American is accumulating money more rapidly than any other man on earth," he described accurately both the joy of newcomers and the prosperity of the emerging middle class. Elevated by their education, profession, inventiveness, or capital, the managerial class found numerous opportunities to flourish in the rapidly changing world of a new economy.

At the beginning of the century, the 1900 U.S. population, comprising 45 states, stood as 76 million, an increase of 21 percent since 1890; 10.6 million residents were foreign-born and more were coming every day. The number of immigrants in the first decade of the twentieth century was double the number for the previous decade, exceeding one million annually in four of the 10 years, the highest level in U.S. history. Business and industry were convinced that unrestricted immigration was the fuel that drove the growth of American industry. Labor was equally certain that the influx of foreigners continually undermined the economic status of native workers and kept wages low.

The change in productivity and consumerism came with a price: the character of American life. Manufacturing plants drew people from the country into the cities. The traditional farm patterns were disrupted by the lure of urban life. Ministers complained that lifelong churchgoers who moved to the city often found less time and fewer social pressures to attend worship regularly. Between 1900 and 1920, urban population increased by 80 percent compared to just over 12 percent for rural areas. During the same time, the non-farming work force went from 783,000 to 2.2 million. Unlike farmers, these workers drew a regular paycheck, and spent it.

With this movement of people, technology, and ideas, nationalism took on a new meaning in America. Railroad expansion in the middle of the nineteenth century had made it possible to move goods quickly and efficiently throughout the country. As a result, commerce, which had been based largely on local production of goods for local consumption, found new markets. Ambitious merchants expanded their businesses by appealing to broader markets.

In 1900, America claimed 58 businesses with more than one retail outlet called "chain stores"; by 1910, that number had more than tripled, and by 1920, the total had risen to 808. The number of clothing chains alone rose from seven to 125 during the period. Department stores such as R.H.Macy in New York and Marshall Field in Chicago offered vast arrays of merchandise along with free services and the opportunity to "shop" without purchasing. Ready-made clothing drove down prices, but also promoted fashion booms that reduced the class distinction of dress. In rural America, the mail order catalogs of Sears, Roebuck and Company reached deep into the pocket of the common man and made dreaming and consuming more feasible.

All was not well, however. A brew of labor struggles, political unrest, and tragic factory accidents demonstrated the excesses of industrial capitalism so worshipped in the Gilded Age. The labor-reform movements of the 1880s and 1890s culminated in the newly formed American Federation of Labor as the chief labor advocate. By 1904, 18 years after it was founded, the AFL claimed 1.676 million of 2.07 million total union members nationwide. The reforms of the labor movement called for an eight-hour workday, child-labor regulation, and cooperatives of owners and workers. The progressive bent of the times also focused attention on factory safety, tainted food and drugs, political corruption, and unchecked economic monopolies. At the same time, progress was not being made by all. For black Americans, many of the gains of reconstruction were being wiped away by regressive Jim Crow laws, particularly in the South. Cherished voting privileges were being systematically taken away. When President Roosevelt asked renowned black educator Booker T. Washington to dine at the White House, the invitation sparked deadly riots. Although less visible, the systematic repression of the Chinese was well under way on the West Coast.

1901 PROFILE

ANTI-SMOKING CAMPAIGN: ANTI-CIGARET LEAGUE OF AMERICA

Wife and mother Ella Louise Scouras dedicated herself to a cause: to stop the epidemic of cigarette smoking by focusing on the youth of Chicago.

Life at Home

- Ella Louise Scouras was determined to stop cigarette smoking in its tracks.
- With two children of her own, she knew how the devil "drink" and its sister "smoke" loved to lurk in the shadows, just waiting to slip into the back door of the unsuspecting or the weak.
- In the previous year alone, 4.4 billion cigarettes were consumed, but that number was falling, thanks to the work of the Anti-Cigaret League based in Chicago.
- If her husband would permit it, Ella Louise would make saving Chicago's youth from cigarettes her full-time work, although she admitted that she was freer to make her own decisions than were most women.
- Her American-thinking husband let her come and go pretty much as she pleased.
- When Illinois native Lucy Page Gaston launched a war on cigarette smoking, focused on the city's newsboys and shop boys, Ella Louise had both a champion and a cause.
- Thirty-six-year-old Ella Louise had enjoyed a comfortable life as the wife of a Chicago road commissioner who earned more than $2,400 a year in good times and bad.
- Unlike most factory workers, he was paid year 'round and was never laid off.
- According to a report on employment, the average Illinois family earned $756.63 annually, including wages of the husband, wife, working children, and income from boarders.

Ella Louise Scouras fought to eliminate smoking among Chicago's youth.

- In addition, the income of most factory workers suffered from periodic, unpaid lay-offs, allowing most of them to earn wages only 42 weeks a year.
- Without question, Ella Louise knew she was far better off than her Greek immigrant grandparents who brought the family to Chicago two decades earlier.
- Her grandfather, like most immigrants, spoke little English when he arrived, but was not afraid of hard work—even in the smelly, dangerous stockyards.
- He believed in loving his family, earning his wages, drinking his share, and dressing well—sometimes in that order.
- Mrs. Scouras, as her husband invariably called her, felt both fortunate for herself and desperate to help others, especially now that her children were in school most of the day and the Welsh nanny was available when they returned home.
- She also knew that as the wife of a road commissioner who carried enormous responsibility, she must not get her priorities confused.
- Home and her husband's well-being came first.
- That included watching out for her son, who told everyone that he was going to become a famous baseball player for the White Sox, and a daughter who loved to ride her new bicycle.
- But Ella Louise never let her husband's burden stray far from her thoughts.
- At the time, Chicago had 2,790 miles of streets, of which 1,206 miles were "improved."
- The paving materials used to improve roads varied: cedar block, 749 miles; macadam (crushed stone), 387 miles; asphalt, 100 miles; brick, 49 miles; and granite block, 29 miles.
- And no one could agree on what was best.
- Much of the wood block paving was prone to rotting and did not stand up well to heavy steel such as wheeled wagon traffic.
- Asphalt was smooth, but provided poor footing for horses in the winter.
- The legion of bicyclists hated macadam; motorists disliked brick.
- The other 1,500 miles, found predominately in the poorer and outlying areas, were unpaved and often turned muddy and impassable when it rained.
- Then, there was the question of whether the streets should be lighted at night.
- Although street lighting had long been in use in Chicago, some people still equated street lighting at night with immoral activity.
- Every day, Ella Louise's husband George had to make hundreds of tough decisions concerning which neighborhood got a road or sidewalk and which did not.
- When one community won, another lost; the loser always claimed the fix was in and a bribe was involved, a very insulting accusation, Ella Louise felt.
- Despite all the corruption she heard about in municipal Chicago, she was sure that none had walked through her door.
- George was wrestling mostly with the future of sidewalks.
- Alongside the 2,790 miles of streets were 5,889 miles of sidewalks.
- Most of Chicago's sidewalks were made of wood, 4,490 miles in all; concrete sidewalks comprised 1,076 miles, and stone, 286 miles.
- Changing from wood to concrete was expensive and often upset shopkeepers, but the maintenance of wood was astronomical.
- And because George and Ella Louise were members of a local cycling club that rode on Sunday afternoons, they received lots of advice.
- Riding together was one of their great pleasures; bike riding was adventurous and liberating.

George and Ella Louise Scouras were active members of a local cycling club.

- Her other passion was movie watching.
- Ella Louise simply could not abide the atmosphere created within the hundreds of nickel-shops where short movies were shown.
- They were noisy, smoky, and filled with the wrong sort of people.
- So to watch moving pictures—especially focused on exotic travel—Ella Louise talked George into ordering the Edison kinetoscope so they could watch movies such as *Around the World in Eighty Minutes.*

Life at Work
- Ella Louise Scouras first met Lucy Page Gaston when they both attended a Women's Christian Temperance Union rally in downtown Chicago four years earlier.
- As though it were her right and her place, Lucy spoke eloquently about the ruination brought about by alcohol; Ella Louise listened in rapt attention.
- Imagine the courage it must have taken to stand up and speak out, she thought, especially in front of a group of cigar-smoking men.
- Spinster and former schoolteacher Lucy Page Gaston was from the tee-totaling town of Harvey, Illinois, where the Gaston family had moved in 1893.
- At an early age, Lucy became active in temperance affairs, which then evolved into her special mission of saving boys from the evils of tobacco, especially cigarettes.
- Ella Louise fully understood that the fight to stop men from spending all the family money on drink had been a struggle for Christian-minded women for more than 60 years.
- Yet saloons in Chicago were both legal and numerous, numbering approximately 8,000.
- To Ella Louise's way of thinking, a city's issuing liquor licenses was the same as sanctioning drunkenness.
- Even worse, not one single restriction existed to stop Sunday drinking.

- When the two women met, the campaign to stop men from drinking had become an exhausting, uphill battle even with all the power of the nationwide Women's Christian Temperance Union and the Anti-Saloon League.
- But the nasty habit of cigarette smoking was new and seemingly everywhere in the streets of Chicago.
- According to Lucy Gaston, cigarette smoking was an evil that could be stopped if action was taken immediately, especially so if the focus was on the youth of Chicago.

- As a key aid and assistant to Lucy, Ella Louise was able to meet people, organize protests, and type recruitment letters.
- Ella Louise loved to help write (mostly edit) the articles used in the National Anti-Cigaret League's broadside, *The Boy.*
- The publication emphasized the perils of "smoker's face" caused by the chemical "furfural" ingested during the process of cigarette smoking.
- Furfural, Lucy had learned through scientific reading, was formed in the combustion process from glycerin, used as a moistening agent in tobacco products.
- Ella Louise's writing explained the science of smoking, but she especially enjoyed helping to write the stories that linked immoral and heinous criminal behavior to cigarette users ranging from incorrigible youths to adult murderers.

- Even her own children, good Greek Orthodox, churchgoing youths raised in a good home, were constantly clamoring for the giveaway cards in cigarette boxes: exotic animals, scantily clad actresses, flags of the world.
- There was always something more to collect.

- And the worst part was the willingness of her own brother—a pharmacist no less—to sell cigarettes and push the collector card books on anyone willing to buy.
- Anyone who put animal pictures in cigarette boxes was clearly attempting to lure more children into the filthy habit.
- Chewing tobacco was bad—her father carried plug tobacco in his pocket every day of his adult life—but smoking was worse.
- Luckily there was a way to recover from smoker's face.

- According to the research done by Miss Gaston, smoker's face and its related ailments could be healed with a weak solution of silver nitrite after every meal for three days running, especially when combined with eating a bland diet and taking plenty of warm baths.
- Ella Louise was amazed at Lucy's energy and willingness to stand up to businessmen and call their product "coffin nails" straight to their faces.
- Already the nation was paying attention.
- In 1898, Congress had pushed up taxes on the cigarette 200 percent as a way to pay for the Spanish-American War, a tax which boosted the cost of a ten-for-a-nickel pack of cigarettes by 20 percent.

- In 1899, the Anti-Cigaret League held its first convention in Chicago, attended by 100 boys.
- Some of the boys came from Sunday schools, but many were ragamuffins from the street, bolstered by Lucy's best supporters—newsboys who worked the streets and their friends the shop boys.
- Four Chicago businesses had totally banned their 1,100 employees from smoking.
- Giant retailer Montgomery Ward said it was convinced that the smell of nicotine was not only offensive to customers, but that cigarettes would "stunt growth, befog the memory, and prevent an alert intellect."
- Foremen at Montgomery Ward had even been assigned the task of spying on employees in their homes to make sure they didn't smoke on their off-duty hours.
- Ella Louise was proud to tell anyone who would listen that Iowa, Tennessee, and North Dakota had outlawed the sale of cigarettes, thanks to the work of Gastonites and their allies.

- In addition, a dozen states were considering legislation to ban the sale of cigarettes or their use in the workplace.
- Cigarette production was 4.9 billion units in 1897, but by 1901, fewer than 3.5 billion were produced.

Life in the Community: Chicago, Illinois

- Ella Louise Scouras was convinced that Chicago was the greatest city in America, due to the hard work of the mayor and the Chicago Road Commission.
- Often she marveled at the engineering know-how that allowed the City of Chicago to reverse the flow of the Chicago River as a way to dispose of city wastewater.
- At the turn of the new century, Chicago boasted 1.6 million pedestrians, approximately 50,000 horse-drawn vehicles, 377 registered automobiles, and dozens of riding horses.
- Chicago was the center of bicycle manufacturing, thanks to the Schwinn Bicycle Company, established in 1895.
- Schwinn made the modern safety bicycle that was replacing the high wheel or "ordinary" bicycle.
- Some bicycles were used for business and commuting, but an explosion of interest had been shown by middle- and upper-class young adults for exploring the countryside.

- The fast vehicles—electric streetcars, light carriages, and automobiles—had top speeds of about 20 miles per hour, but a pace of this sort was often impossible, illegal, and reckless.
- Chicago was served by a 500-mile network of streetcars that charged $0.05 per ride, but did not provide transfers; riders paid every time they boarded.
- The "L" or elevated railroad also charged $0.05, and the streetcars and "L" provided 260 million rides each year, or about 160 rides annually for each Chicago resident.
- The busiest streets were those with streetcar lines.
- In addition to the many pedestrians and streetcars, slow moving wagons would take advantage of the steel rails; a horse could pull a wagon much easier along the rails than over other pavements.
- Other problems such as a broken cable or an obstruction on the tracks could stop an entire streetcar line for a prolonged period of time.
- Only the wealthy could afford the expense and inconvenience of buggies and carriages, and the stabling, feeding, and care of horses.
- Most of the horse-drawn vehicles were wagons used to deliver freight from the railroads, docks, and warehouses.
- Urban working-class horses were often imported from farms toward the end of their lives and worked the same 60-hour weeks as their owners.
- Many horses returned to the same crowded tenement districts as their human counterparts and occupied crowded stables on the rear of the lots, or even in basements.
- Many of the 377 automobiles were basically wagons with an electric, gasoline, or steam motor, and a steering wheel or tiller attached.
- There were only 21 automobiles used for business purposes; most were owned by wealthy eccentrics and trendsetters.
- The private cars were hand-built, expensive, and usually required a chauffeur to drive and maintain them.
- According to the 1900 census, approximately one-third of Chicago's 1.7 million residents were foreign-born and recent immigrants.
- The city's 354,000 families mostly rented; only 86,000 families lived in homes they owned.
- The average rent paid in the poor districts was $8-$10 per month, bath and heat not included.
- Toilets were either shared indoor water closets, or two-hole outhouses underneath the sidewalk or stairs; a bath cost $0.25, although the city would provide a laborer a public bath for free.
- The lodging hotels favored by single men with steady employment charged between $0.25 and $0.50 a night and featured a bathroom down the hall and separate rooms for each lodger.
- The cheapest hotels provided floor space shared among hundreds of other men for $0.02.
- For $0.05, a mattress was provided.
- Older houses in the more fashionable neighborhoods rented for $25-$60 per month.
- Apartments for the upper class along the fashionable boulevards could be rented for $100-$300 per month.
- Select Lakeshore Drive palaces went for $1,000 per month, and featured conveniences such as bathtubs and flush toilets; a few even had new electric lights, telephones, and steam heat.

282 SEARS, ROEBUCK & CO., Cheapest Supply House on Earth, Chicago. CATALOGUE No. III.

OUR ACME WONDER JUVENILES.

OUR $10.75 BICYCLE. NEW 1902 MODEL.

FOR BOYS FROM 7 TO 12 YEARS OF AGE.

AT $10.75 we offer the highest grade Boys' Bicycle made, the equal of bicycles that others sell at double the price. Our $10.75 price is based on the actual cost of material and labor, with but our one small percentage of profit added, the lowest price ever quoted on a

Strictly High Grade Guaranteed Bicycle for Boys.

$10.75

No. 19R69
Select Size and
Order by Number.

EQUIPMENT. These bicycles, made especially for boys from 7 to 12 years of age, carry the highest grade equipment, including the same tire that we use on our highest grade adults' wheels, the celebrated Seroco single tube pneumatic tire, covered by the regular association 30 days' guarantee, a tire that with care will last many seasons.

TEN DAYS' TRIAL OFFER. While we require you to send cash with your order, we give you the privilege of a ten days' trial of the bicycle, during which time if you have any reason to feel dissatisfied with your purchase, simply return the bicycle to us and we will immediately return your money including transportation charges.

OUR GUARANTEE. Every bicycle is covered by our binding guarantee, covering every piece and part that enters into the wheel. We guarantee the material perfect, and if not so the wheel can be returned to us at once and your money will be cheerfully refunded.

DESCRIPTION.

TWO SIZES—Be careful in ordering. The small size, for boys from 7 to 9 years of age, has a 16-inch frame, the wheels being 24 inches; specify Catalogue No. 19R69. The large size, for boys 10 to 12 years old, has an 18-inch frame with 26-inch wheels, and should be ordered from Catalogue No. 19R71.
TIRES—The celebrated Seroco single tube.
PEDALS—Ball bearing rat trap.
CHAIN—High grade ⅜-inch chain.
HANDLE BAR—High grade raised steel handle bar, full nickel plated, full finished, complete with leather grips.

From the above illustration, engraved by our artist from a photograph, you can form a very good idea of the appearance of this handsome new 1902 Model $10.75 Bicycle for Boys.

NOTE—The 16-inch frame is for boys from 7 to 9 years of age. The 18-inch frame is for boys from 10 to 12 years of age.

SADDLE—Special high grade Juvenile saddle.
GEAR—Every wheel geared to 60 inches.
HANGER—We use the very latest 1902 style Juvenile hanger, the strongest, best finished and nicest hanger used on a boys' wheel.

SPROCKETS—We use handsome sprockets, latest 1902 style, both front and rear; highly finished, heavily nickel plated and polished; assorted designs. At our special $10.75 price, we include a fine leather tool bag, complete with wrench, oiler, pump and tire repair outfit.

ENAMEL—Frames are enameled either maroon or black; elegantly finished. All usual bright parts are highly nickeled.

No. 19R69 Boys' bicycle, 16-inch frame with 24-inch wheels, for boys 7 to 9 years of age.......... **$10.75** | No. 19R71 Boys' bicycle, 18-inch frame with 26-inch wheels, for boys 10 to 12 years of age.......... **$10.75**

OUR $10.75 NEW 1902 MODEL DROP FRAME GIRLS' BICYCLE

FOR GIRLS FROM 7 TO 12 YEARS OF AGE.

THIS SPECIAL $10.75 BICYCLE is the highest grade bicycle made for girls. Made of the highest grade material, by skilled mechanics, equipped with the highest grade equipment, including the celebrated single tube guaranteed Seroco tire, and offered at our special $10.75 price, at a price based on the actual cost of material and labor, with but our one small percentage of profit added.

THIS IS THE EXACT SAME BICYCLE as our special $10.75 boys' wheel, with the exception of the girls' style of drop curved frame.

YOU WILL NOTE we furnish these wheels with 16-inch frame for girls from 7 to 9 years of age, 18-inch frame for girls from 10 to 12 years of age. The price is the same. In ordering be sure to note the different size frames to accommodate the different ages.

UNDERSTAND, every bicycle is covered by a binding guarantee as to quality of material and workmanship. Every pair of tires is covered by our regular guarantee.

..DESCRIPTION..

This bicycle is exactly the same as the boys' bicycle, with the exception of the drop curved frame. The frames are 16 or 18 inches high, made from highest grade tubing, nicely enameled, nicely finished, made extra strong in every part. The wheels are 24 or 26 inches in diameter, strictly high grade. We use high grade, full finished spokes, non-warpable hickory rims. Hubs are strictly high grade, drawn from bar steel, full finished, heavily nickel plated, ball bearing throughout, with ball retainers.
TIRES—Tires are the celebrated Seroco single tube pneumatic tires, fully guaranteed. Tires come complete with quick tire repair outfit.
SADDLE—We use a special high grade Juvenile saddle.
HANDLE BAR—We furnish a strictly high grade steel, raised handle bar, heavily nickel plated, highly finished, complete with leather grips.
BEARINGS—We use strictly high grade bearings, drawn from bar steel, full finished, accurately gauged and adjusted, tempered to a straw color, highly finished and fully guaranteed.

$10.75

No. 19R74
Select Size and
Order by Number.

TEN DAYS' TRIAL OFFER. While we require you to send cash with your order, we give you the privilege of a ten days' trial of the bicycle, during which time, if you have any reason to feel dissatisfied with your purchase, simply return the bicycle to us and we will immediately return your money, including transportation charges.

From the above illustration, engraved by our artist from a photograph, you can form some idea of the appearance of our handsome new model, $10.75 bicycle, the 1902 wheel, but you must see, examine and compare this bicycle with bicycles offered by other houses at greatly advanced prices to appreciate the extraordinary value we are offering.

CHAIN—We use a high grade ⅜-inch chain, the best chain used on any juvenile wheel.
PEDALS—We use high grade combination pedals, full ball bearing, heavily nickel plated and highly finished.
HANGER—We use the very latest 1902 hanger.
SPROCKETS—Sprockets are the latest style for 1902, made from the very best steel, highly polished, heavily nickel plated and beautifully finished, assorted designs.

GEAR—Geared to 60 inches.
EQUIPMENT—You get in this wheel the very highest grade equipment, the same high grade equipment that goes on our highest grade ladies' wheel, including the very best Seroco tires, finest nickel plated handle bars, ball bearing pedals, extra quality saddle, tool bag, quick repair outfit, wrench and oiler.
ENAMEL—Enameled in either black or maroon, as desired, handsomely finished, all usual parts heavily nickel plated on copper.

No. 19R74 Girls' 16-inch drop frame bicycles, with 24-inch wheels, for girls 7 to 9 years of age.......... **$10.75** | No. 19R78 Girls' 18-inch drop frame bicycle, with 26-inch wheels, for girls 10 to 12 years of age.......... **$10.75**

HISTORICAL SNAPSHOT
1901

- North Carolina proposed a literacy amendment for voting to diminish the role of the Black vote
- The Spindletop oil field produced 80,000 barrels a day, making the United States the world's premier supplier of petroleum
- When William McKinley became the third American president to be assassinated in 35 years, Vice President Theodore Roosevelt took office
- Jergens lotion, automobile licenses, Cadillac, Mercedes, motor-driven bicycles, instant coffee, Clicquot Club ginger ale, Quaker oats, and synthetic dye all made their first appearance
- In the art world, Mary Cassatt completed her painting, *The Oval Mirror,* Frederic Remington sculpted *The Cheyenne,* and the Chicago museums featured 49 works by John Twachtman
- Businessman Andrew Carnegie donated $5.2 million to the New York Public Library for its first branch offices
- South Dakota made school attendance mandatory for children aged 8 to 14
- Forty-two cereal makers were located in Battle Creek, Michigan
- Russian pogroms drove many Jews to emigrate to America
- The construction of freight tunnels in Chicago was begun to carry telephone and telegraph wires and cables
- Popular songs included "Ain't Dat a Shame?," "Way Down in Old Indiana" and "Rip Van Winkle Was a Lucky Man"
- *The Settlement Cookbook* including the words, "the way to a man's heart is through his stomach" was published by a Milwaukee woman working with immigrants
- The widows of four Revolutionary War soldiers were still alive and drawing pensions
- In *The World of Graft,* Josiah Flynt exposed bribe-taking in New York, Boston, and Chicago
- In baseball, new rules mandated that the catcher stand behind home plate at all times and not catch the first two strikes on a bounce
- For women, fashion demanded that hair was puffed, padded, and piled high under hats to emphasize the "S" curve of the mature bust and hips
- The giraffe was discovered in Africa by Europeans
- Popular movies included *A Trip Around the Pan-American Exposition, Execution of Czolgosz, New York in a Blizzard,* and *The Conquest of Air*
- Booker T. Washington wrote *Up from Slavery,* Mark Twain published *To a Person Sitting in Darkness* and John Muir wrote *Our National Parks*
- President Theodore Roosevelt was widely criticized for inviting Black educator Booker T. Washington to dine with him at the White House
- The "five civilized tribes," including the Cherokee, Creek, Choctaw, Chicasaw, and Seminole, were granted United States citizenship

Selected Prices, 1901

Adding Machine	$10.00
Alarm Clock	$2.50
Automobile, Two-Passenger	$1,900.00
Bedroom Suite, Hardwood	$21.00
Butter, Pound	$0.28
Camera, Delmar Folding	$3.75
Eyeglasses	$2.50
Motor Bicycle	$200.00
Rubber Teething Ring	$0.10
Whiskey, Gallon	$3.50

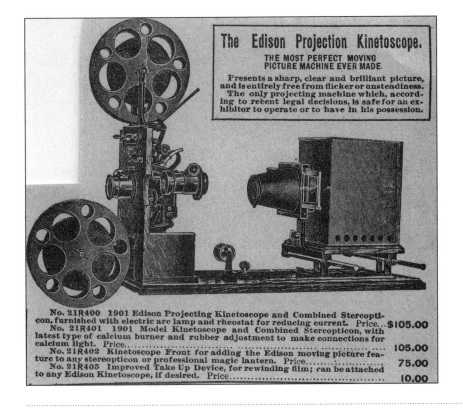

SEARS, ROEBUCK & CO., Cheapest Supply House on Earth, Chicago. CATALOGUE No. 111. 373

OUR NEW ACME MODEL SURREY, $58.90.

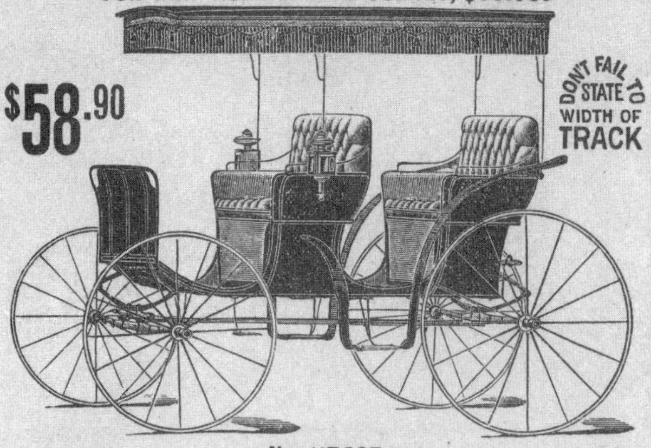
$58.90
DON'T FAIL TO STATE WIDTH OF TRACK

No. 11R627

GENERAL DESCRIPTION.

BODY—5 feet 10 inches long, 26 inches wide. High seat panels, high solid phaeton spring backs of seats with round corners.

GEAR—Axles, $1\frac{1}{16}$-inch, double collar, fantail, swaged, made of selected axle steel. Full sweep elliptic springs, four-plate front, five-plate rear. Double reaches, ironed full length, full back circle fifth wheel. Quick shifting shaft coupler.

WHEELS—Sarven's patent wheels, full bolted between each spoke. Front wheel 38 inches high, rear wheel 42 inches high, 1-inch tread.

UPHOLSTERING—Upholstered in 14-ounce English dark green body cloth, padded, lined, seat ends latest style diamond piped patent biscuit tufting.

TOP—Full canopy top, trimmed throughout with a good fringe, with full length side and back curtains, oil burning lamps.

PAINTING—Body painted dark green with nonpareil green pillars. Gear is painted dark coach or Brewster green, handsomely trimmed.

TRACK—Narrow, 4 feet 8 inches; or wide, 5 feet 2 inches, as desired.

No. 11R627 Price, fitted with best steel tires.......... $58.90
Price, fitted with 1-inch best Goodyear rubber tires.......... 74.40

EXTRAS.

Full leather cushion, leather backs and seat linings.......... $3.50
Pole in place of shafts.......... 1.50
Both pole and shafts.......... 3.50

Weight, crated, about 750 pounds.

Shipped from Brighton, Ohio, or Kalamazoo, Mich. Customer pays freight.

OUR ACME MODEL $63.90 CUT UNDER CANOPY TOP SURREY.

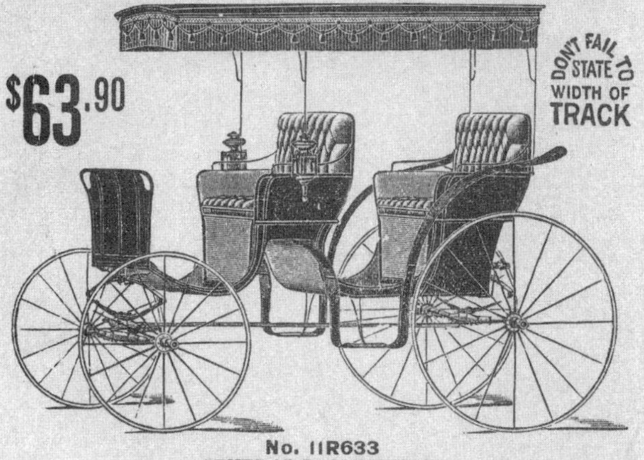
$63.90
DON'T FAIL TO STATE WIDTH OF TRACK

No. 11R633

GENERAL DESCRIPTION.

BODY—Body is good size, 5 feet 10 inches long, 26 inches wide on the bottom. Iron seat rods run down through the sills. Seats are made with extra high seat panels, full rounded, as illustrated.

GEAR—Heavy Anderson surrey gear, $1\frac{1}{16}$-inch double collar, fantail, steel axles, swaged and finished. Full oil tempered elliptic springs, four-plate front and five-plate rear; a heavy single surrey reach, heavily ironed full length and full bolted; Robinson full back circle fifth wheel; kingbolt in rear of axle. Quick shifting coupler.

UPHOLSTERING—Cushions and backs trimmed in 14-ounce English wool faced green body cloth, biscuit tufted cushions with diamond and pipe pattern back, as illustrated. Seat ends are padded and lined, soft coil springs in backs and cushions, full worsted carpet, heavy enameled leather dash.

TOP—A good, strong, substantial canopy top. Four steel standards, full braced and well built. Top is trimmed with a good quality head fringe, top lined with good quality lining, furnished complete with full length side and back curtains. Oil burning lamps.

WHEELS—Sarven's patent; full bolted between each spoke. Front wheel 34 inches high, rear wheel 42 inches high; 1-inch tread, tired with a heavy, round edge, full crimped steel tire.

PAINTING—The body is painted dark green, with nonpareil green pillars and black moldings, giving it a very beautiful, yet modestly rich effect. Gear is painted dark Brewster green, handsomely striped and trimmed.

TRACK—Narrow, 4 feet 8 inches; or wide, 5 feet 2 inches, as desired.

No. 11R633 Price, fitted with best steel tires.......... $63.90
Price, fitted with 1-inch best Goodyear rubber tires.......... 79.40

EXTRAS.

Pole in place of shafts.......... 1.50
Both pole and shafts.......... 3.50
Heavy leather cushions and back in place of cloth.......... 3.50

Weight, crated, about 825 pounds.

Shipped from Brighton, Ohio, or Kalamazoo, Mich. Customer pays freight.

OUR ACME MODEL $64.90 EXTENSION TOP SURREY.

$64.90
DON'T FAIL TO STATE WIDTH OF TRACK

No. 11R639

GENERAL DESCRIPTION.

BODY—5 feet 10 inches long by 26 inches wide on bottom. The seats are high solid phaeton seats, heavy high rounded panels, extra high rounded panel backs.

WHEELS—The wheels are Sarven's patent with heavy steel bands. They are 1-inch, tired with heavy steel tires, rounded and crimped. Front wheel is 38 inches high and rear wheel 42 inches high.

GEAR—Anderson surrey gear, built heavy, strong and firm, and well finished. The axles are $1\frac{1}{16}$-inch double collar, fantail, swaged. Extra heavy, elliptic end springs, four-plate in front and five-plate in rear; full circle Robinson fifth wheel, with kingbolt in rear of axle. Quick shifting shaft coupler.

UPHOLSTERING—Cushions and backs trimmed in 14-ounce English wool faced green body cloth, padded and lined seat ends. Soft coil springs in cushions and backs. Oil burning lamps.

PAINTING—Dark coach green body with nonpareil pillars, black molding. Gear, dark green, handsomely striped.

TOP—Leather quarter extension top. The quarters and stays are extra deep and extra long and cut from genuine heavy buffed leather.

TRACK—Narrow, 4 feet 8 inches; or wide, 5 feet 2 inches, as desired.

No. 11R639 Price, fitted with best steel tires.......... $64.90
Price, fitted with $\frac{7}{8}$-inch best Goodyear rubber tires.......... 78.35
Price, fitted with 1-inch best Goodyear rubber tires.......... 80.40

EXTRAS.

Leather cushions and backs in place of cloth.......... 4.00
Pole complete in place of shafts.......... 1.50
Both pole and shafts.......... 3.50

Weight about 800 pounds.

Shipped from Brighton, Ohio, or Kalamazoo, Mich.

OUR NEW ACME MODEL CUT UNDER EXTENSION TOP SURREY.

$69.95
DON'T FAIL TO STATE WIDTH OF TRACK

No. 11R645

GENERAL DESCRIPTION.

BODY—Latest style cut under extension body. Body is good size, 5 feet 10 inches long by 26 inches wide on the bottom. The seats are heavy high paneled surrey seats, full rounded.

GEAR—This gear is built on a $1\frac{1}{16}$-inch double collar, fantail, swaged axle. One long cut under surrey reach, heavily ironed full length; full circle fifth wheel. End springs, four-plate in front and five-plate in rear; kingbolt in rear of axle. Quick shifting shaft coupler.

WHEELS—They are 1-inch tread; Sarven's patent, with heavy steel bands; The tires are extra heavy, rounded edge, full crimp steel tires, full bolted. The front wheel is 34 inches high, rear wheel 42 inches high.

UPHOLSTERING—Upholstered in a 14-ounce English wool faced dark green body cloth. Seat ends full padded and full lined, soft coil springs in back and cushions. Oil burning lamps.

TOP—Extra high, extra wide and extra deep extension leather quarter top. Quarters and stays cut extra large and from genuine leather.

PAINTING—This body is painted a dark green with black pillars; the gear is a dark Brewster green, neatly striped.

TRACK—Narrow, 4 feet 8 inches, or wide, 5 feet 2 inches, as desired.

No. 11R645 Price, fitted with best steel tires.......... $69.95
Price, fitted with $\frac{7}{8}$-inch best Goodyear rubber tires.......... 83.40
Price, fitted with 1-inch best Goodyear rubber tires.......... 85.45

EXTRAS.

Leather cushions and backs in place of cloth.......... $4.00
Pole complete in place of shafts.......... 1.50
Both pole and shaft.......... 3.50

Weight, crated, about 825 pounds.

Shipped from Brighton, Ohio, or Kalamazoo, Mich.

Salaries in Chicago, 1900:

The Chicago Budget for 1900 listed the following public sector annual wages:

- Janitors (male), $720; (female), $540
- Coal passers, $720-$780
- Firefighters, $840-$1,134
- Patrolmen, $1,000; police matrons, $720
- Laborers, $600
- Stenographer (female), $900; male clerks, $900-$1200
- Mayor, $10,000
- Department heads, $3,000-$6,000

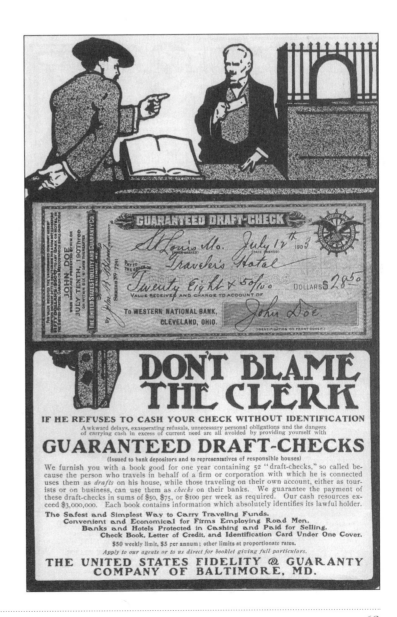

Smoking Timeline

1880

The first cigarette machine patent was issued.

1881

James Buchanan "Buck" Duke began manufacturing cigarettes in Durham, North Carolina.

1883

Congress eliminated the Civil War excise tax on cigars imposed in 1862.

1884

Buck Duke took his tobacco business national by forming a cartel that eventually became the American Tobacco Company.

Buck Duke began using cigarette manufacturing machines; his company alone produced 744 million cigarettes, more than the combined national total in 1883.

1886

A patent was issued for a machine to manufacture plug tobacco.

"Cameo" brand cigarettes were created to attract women smokers.

1887

Buck Duke slashed cigarette prices, sparking a price war.

1889

Buck Duke spent $800,000 in billboard and newspaper advertising.

The five leading cigarette firms were combined.

1890

The Women's Christian Temperance Movement published "Narcotics" that discussed the evils of numerous drugs including tobacco and cocaine.

Chewing tobacco consumption in the U.S. was three pounds per capita.

"Tobacco" appeared in the *US Pharmacopoeia*, an official government listing of drugs.

Twenty-six states and territories outlawed the sale of cigarettes to minors.

The American Tobacco Company was formed.

1892

Congress received a petition to prohibit the manufacture, importation, and sale of cigarettes.

Book matches were invented.

1893

Washington State's ban on the sale and use of cigarettes was overturned on constitutional grounds as a restraint of trade.

1895

Admiral cigarettes produced the first known motion picture commercial.

1896

Smoking was banned in the House of Representatives, but chewing was still allowed.

continued

Timeline . . . *(continued)*

1898

Congress raised taxes on cigarettes 200 percent at the start of the Spanish-American War.

The Tennessee Supreme Court upheld a total ban on cigarettes, ruling "their use is always harmful."

1899

Lucy Page Gaston founded the Chicago Anti-Cigaret League.

The U.S. Senate Finance Committee rolled back the wartime excise tax on cigarettes.

The Pall Mall brand was introduced by Butler & Butler Tobacco Co.

1900

Washington, Iowa, Tennessee, and North Dakota all outlawed the sale of cigarettes.

For the year, 4.4 billion cigarettes were sold.

Price competition and the anti-cigarette movement pushed many smaller companies out of business.

Buck Duke's companies controlled nine out of 10 cigarettes sold in America.

The U.S. Supreme Court upheld Tennessee's ban on cigarette sales.

R.J. Reynolds reluctantly merged his company into Duke's Tobacco Trust.

Approximately 300,000 cigar brands were on the market.

1901

Strong anti-cigarette activity was recorded in 43 of the 45 states, with only Wyoming and Louisiana having no organized campaign.

Duke combined his Continental Tobacco and American Tobacco companies into Consolidated Tobacco.

Duke's Consolidated bought the British Ogden tobacco firm in order to enter the British market.

Consumption topped 3.5 billion cigarettes and six billion cigars; four in five American men smoked at least one cigar a day.

The Sears, Roebuck and Company catalogue advertised a "Sure Cure for the Tobacco Habit."

"Anti-Cigaret War Commences, Convention Called by Miss Gaston Attended by about 100 Boys—Approved by Judge Burke," *Chicago Daily Tribune*, April 2, 1899:

Boys from the streets and boys from Sunday schools, newsboys, ragged youngsters, who soon departed, boys from business establishments and boys from children's homes, constituted the first anti-cigaret convention, which was held yesterday in Willard Hall, where Miss Lucy Page Gaston opened her anti-cigaret campaign. The number of boys, about 100, did not realize the best expectation of the promoters of the convention, but they announced that the meetings will be held each month, with hopes of larger audiences. The newsboys won the prize for the largest attendance, their presence augmented by the presence of the Daily News Band.

The principal speaker at the convention was to have been Judge Edmund Burke. He was unable to attend, but he sent his speech in a letter to Miss Gaston, and it was read to the boys by Miss Elizabeth Burdick. After approving the effort to check the spread of the cigarette habit among boys, Judge Burke's letter said:

"You act upon the theory adopted by all teachers of youth, if the early years are guarded and spent in purity, manhood is safe and liberty of choice will not be a curse but the highest blessing. There is no mother or father of whatever creed or race but will bid you Godspeed.

"Great is the danger. While presiding in the criminal court last year an unbroken procession of boys, from Monday to Saturday, week after week, month after month, passes before me. Almost every boy is found to be addicted to the cigaret habit. It seems to demoralize him, to take away his moral fiber, and to make him an easy prey to other vices. I cannot believe that our laws and times would tolerate for a single moment the cigaret evil if the desolation that it works could be fully realized."

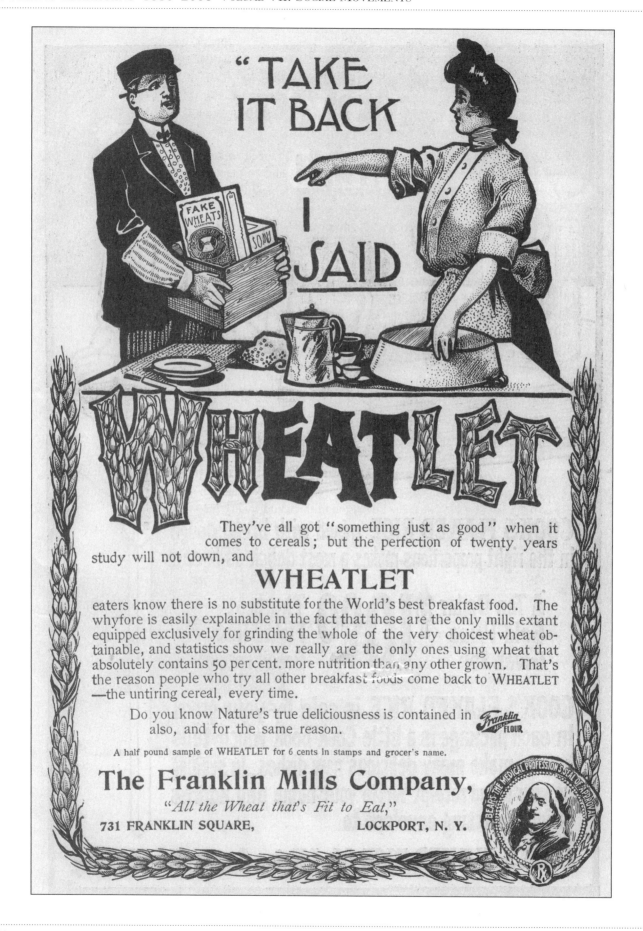

"Pin-Swallowing Woman May Have Appendicitis," *Chicago Daily Tribune*, May 12, 1901:

As a result of swallowing pins while at work on the hats in the millinery department of Marshall Field & Co., Miss Winifred Voss was taken to her house in Austin yesterday, being too ill to continue her work. She suffered acute pains, and the opinion of the doctors who attended her is that the pins may have caused appendicitis.

This termination of Miss Voss' pin-eating days comes after several weeks' experience in swallowing the small bits of metal. It was during the stress of spring trimming that Miss Voss swallowed her first pin, but after that she began to swallow so many, not because she wanted to but because they would slip down, that her associates no longer marveled. Until yesterday they suggested fields of remarkable promise in the line of mysterious feats as being open to young women.

After a while the pins began to reappear, coming from her body and arms. One came out of the wrist, another out of the forearms, and several out of her back. The girl reined in health and strength, however, and never missed a day at her work until yesterday.

"Mayor Harrison Hints at Having Fourth Term," *Chicago Daily Tribune*, May 12, 1901:

Mayor Harrison hinted broadly at a meeting of old-time Chicago wheelmen last night that he might want to run for mayor a fourth time. At the meeting, which was held at the Chicago Athletic club, the Mayor said he had ridden into office on a bicycle.

"I think I have done a good deal for wheelmen in Chicago," said the Mayor, "and I am going to do more for them, because I may want to run for Mayor again. I am not one of the oldest cyclists in the city, but I am still in the ring. Some years ago, when I didn't dare ride a high wheel, I contented myself with spinning around on a tricycle. I am not one of those who are giving up the wheel for the automobile. In fact, I long prided myself that I never had ridden in one. A few days ago, however, when I was in Washington, I got into an automatic 'bus' without knowing what sort of vehicle it was, and I am now without my distinction."

The banquet was attended by many of the early bicyclists, who met to toast old bicycle clubs which long have been defunct. Edward F. Brown and Burley B. Ayers, said to be the first men in Chicago to ride the high wheel, were present.

"[It is] the rudest thing . . . a man throwing his smoke into the face of women and children as they pass up and down the street. Have you a right to throw in my mouth what you puff out of yours? That foul smoke and breath! And you would like to be called a gentleman."
—Letter to the Editor,
The Smasher's Mail, March 23, 1901

1904 Profile

Public Health/Food Additives:
Pure Food and Drug Act

Farm boy Jim Rosser was proud to be a member of the Poison Squad, whose human experiments were exposing the dangers of food additives, especially in meat.

Life at Home

- Jim Rosser was proud of his association with the Poison Squad, even around people who made fun of his work.
- Thanks to his sacrifices, Congress would soon pass the Pure Food and Drug Act, designed to eliminate harmful additives, regulate patent medicine, and raise the quality of food distributed across America.
- Like many of the Poison Squad volunteers, Jim also served as a clerk for the Grain Division of the Department of Agriculture.
- Two years earlier, when he was told he could have a free place to sleep and free food so the Chemistry Division could test for poison preservatives, he jumped at the chance.
- Jim was 19, six foot two, and always hungry.
- Unlike most volunteers, he stayed a member of the Poison Squad for 24 months, despite headaches, indigestion, and occasionally a spontaneous loss of supper.
- After all, the hygienic table studies underway were not only designed to test commonly used meat preservatives like formaldehyde, but they were also the initiators of legislation to gain purity in food.
- Congress was clearly listening.
- For years, those in the patent medicine industry had spent heavily to block legislation; advertising in newspapers across the nation, they unabashedly used their economic clout to eliminate stories that condemned their practices.
- In addition, both the meat and dairy industries were outraged over possible regulation of their products.

Jim Rosser risked his health as a member of the Poison Squad.

- But Jim knew that chemist Dr. Harvey W. Wiley was incorruptible.
- When Jim signed on, he was just looking for a few free meals.
- So what if he occasionally got sick from eating tainted food? A free meal was a free meal.
- Not that the first few months weren't rough.
- Dr. Wiley, who wanted to find the limits of the men, discovered during the first month that not all stomachs were created equal.
- Two men quit after a month, six at the end of the first year.
- Some of the guys who hated the constant headaches, stomach upset, and nausea had left the boarding house in the middle of the night and never returned.
- However, Jim was a farm boy from Iowa, raised with an iron gut.
- Congress authorized the tests on humans in 1902 by appropriating funds for an investigation on whether preservatives should be used or not, and if so, which ones and in what quantities.
- Jim was astounded by the number of people reading the newspaper reports of the Poison Squad.
- To many, he was a hero standing up against bad food and corruption in the food industry.
- Jim even talked to *The Washington Post* reporter George Rothwell Brown himself, although secretly, in case it upset Dr. Wiley.
- None of the volunteers were actually named in the articles, but Jim could tell who else was leaking information.
- Most of the time it sounded like the chief cook, so Dr. Wiley must have thought the publicity was okay.

- But Jim was glad that his mother in Iowa had not seen the often used designation "Poison Squad," created by the Washington newspapers.
- She had been opposed to her only son leaving the farm.
- Her boy moving to a city as big as Washington was bad enough, but his being a human guinea pig would terrify her.
- Only two decades prior, scientists had discovered the diabolical role of microbes in the human body.
- Advertisements on the city's streetcars read, "A diller, a dollar, a chemical scholar, What makes you grow so thin? Because the civil service has put the borax in."

- More to the point, the newspapers were now fixated on the need for pure milk legislation and the increasing role of the federal government in health issues.
- Even popular Royal Baking Powder was touting its product as pure.
- When the *Post* dreamed up the fake story that Jim and the other test subjects "had blossomed out with a bright pink complexion that would make a society belle sick with envy," Dr. Wiley got thousands of letters from young women begging for the secret formula.
- Dr. Wiley, chief of the Bureau of Chemistry in the U.S. Agricultural Department, had been viewed as unorthodox by his professional colleagues for decades.
- Early in his career, while a professor at Purdue, Dr. Wiley was called before the trustees because they were "deeply grieved" at his conduct.
- Dr. Wiley had committed the sin of being too familiar with his students by "putting on a uniform and playing baseball"; even worse, he discredited "the dignity of a professor" by buying a bicycle.
- "Imagine my feelings," one trustee said, "on seeing one of our professors dressed up like a monkey and astride a cartwheel riding along our streets."
- But few questioned his single-minded devotion to knowledge and scientific study.
- "I arrive at my conclusions by experimentation, when experimentation can be used at all," Dr. Wiley said. "I believe in tying it on the dog."
- Dr. Wiley rejected the idea that disease caused moral failing; he believed good public policy would lead to good public health.

Life at Work

- Dr. Wiley took command of the Division of Chemistry in 1883, the same year that Robert Koch discovered the germ of cholera and its transmission by water and food.
- At the start of the tests in 1902, the *Post* reported "the United States government will open, for the first time in history, a scientific boardinghouse, under the direction of Prof. Wiley."
- Dr. Wiley believed these were the most extensive experiments on human beings conducted anywhere in the world.
- "Twelve young clerks, vigorous and voracious, have volunteered to become boarders free of charge, in the interest of science. They will eat food treated with various chemicals to prove whether or not borax and formaldehyde are injurious," the *Post* reported.
- Government clerks were the preferred volunteers because they had passed the civil service exam and shown themselves to have a "reputation for sobriety and reliability."
- Included among the volunteers was a Yale graduate known for his speed in the 100-yard dash.
- Jim Rosser quickly learned that he only had to endure the chemical-laden meals half the time.
- Every two weeks he was part of the control team, who did not have to see borax, salicylic acid, formaldehyde, or copper salts liberally sprinkled on their meals.
- Initially, Jim had watched incredulously as borax was added three times a day at the "hygienic table" where the Poison Squad took their meals.

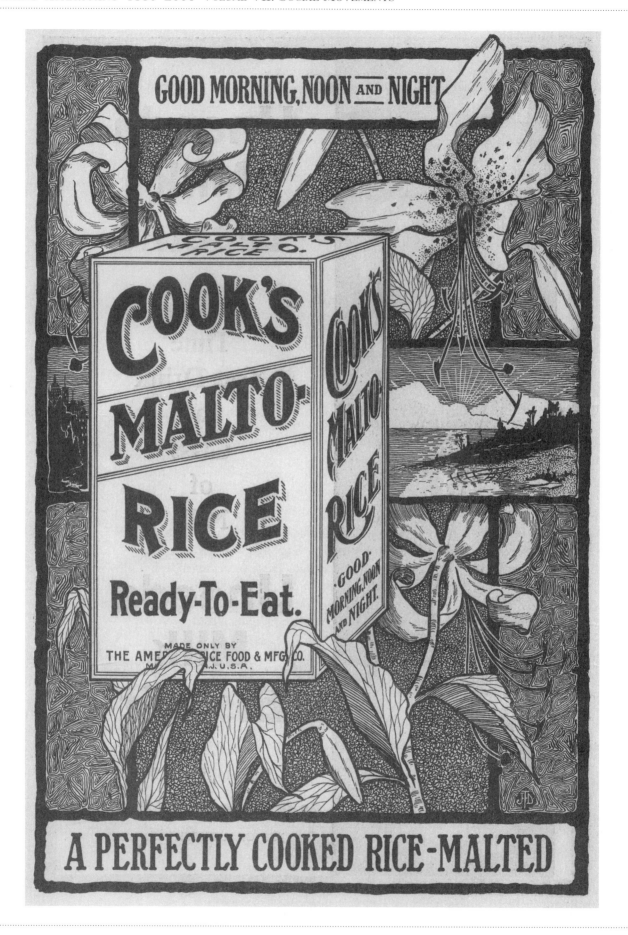

- Dr. Wiley said that he picked borax as the first test food because it was the most important of the commonly used preservatives.
- The second round of testing involved salicylic acid and a double dose of Dr. Wiley's firmly held belief that the human race was becoming hairless and toothless because of increased intellectuality and the prevalence of "ready-chewed" health foods.
- "The loss of tail, hair, teeth are all steps forward toward human perfection," Dr. Wiley said. "Man's brain is growing, and takes nutriment from the hair, which falls out, and consequently is growing less abundant year by year. Now, you take a woman. Woman still has long hair, but that's because woman is still a savage. Notice how fond she is of gaudy colors. Her brain hasn't the capacity of a man's."
- To be part of the Poison Squad, Jim had to agree to abstain from any food and drink not prepared by the scientists in charge of the experimental meals.
- Worst of all was not the mild headache caused by borax or the indigestion resulting from benzoic acid or formaldehyde, but the examination after each meal.
- Dr. Wiley required that the dozen Poison Squad subjects be stripped and weighed after every meal so that their physical condition could be determined.
- Jim then took and recorded his temperature and "speed of pulse."
- Efforts were even made to collect Jim's sweat to determine if any preservative was eliminated by the body through perspiration.

- After each meal, Jim was required to carry a satchel at all times with containers for his urine and his feces.
- Jim had to return the contents of the satchel to the chemists every day.
- He did not like to discuss that part of the experiment.
- Once a week, Jim was examined by physicians from the Public Health and Marine Hospital.
- Despite the hardship, Jim loved the companionship of the Poison Squad.
- With all the publicity, they felt compelled to make up songs and stage skits.
- While visiting a minstrel show, Jim and his friends howled with laughter when the performers sang a Poison Squad ditty called "They'll Never Look the Same."
- "If ever you should visit the Smithsonian Institute/Look out that Professor Wiley doesn't make you a recruit/He's got a lot of fellows there that tell him how they feel/ They take a batch of poison every time they eat a meal./For breakfast they get cyanide of liver, coffin shaped,/For dinner, undertaker's pie, all trimmed with crepe;/For supper, arsenic fritters, fried in appetizing shade,/And late at night they get a prussic acid lemonade./They may get over it, but they will never look the same."
- Recently, in the spirit of mischief, one of Jim's bunk mates dropped 10 grains of quinine into another boarder's coffee, which took effect as the unsuspecting victim was on a theater date.
- Enough to say the date and the evening went badly for all concerned.
- The cooks tried a variety of ways to test the preservatives.
- Initially, borax was added to the butter, which Jim hated.
- Then the chemists tried adding the preservative to milk, meat, and coffee.
- Jim and his buddies began avoiding milk, meat, and coffee.
- Dr. Wiley had put the test chemical in a capsule that everyone would swallow during the meal.
- During some meals, the pill-swallowing became a community ritual; at others, it was the subject of great mirth and laughter.

- For many meals, Dr. Wiley took his place beside the men and consumed the test preservative himself.
- The worst part of the experiment was the holiday season.
- At Christmastime, Jim had to decline invitations to parties and dinners.
- The gloom was so pervasive, according to Jim, even the Ping-Pong game scheduled for Christmas day had been postponed.
- Christmas dinner included apple sauce, borax, soup, turkey, more borax, canned string beans, sweet potatoes, white potatoes, borax, chipped beef, cream gravy, cranberry sauce, celery, pickles, borax, rice pudding, milk, bread and butter, tea, coffee, and a little borax.
- Jim loved to tell friends while making his right eye twitch and his mouth sag that he has never been healthier in his life.
- The stomach pains, headaches, and discomfort resulted in Dr. Wiley's declaring that both boric acid and borax created disturbances of digestion and should be banned as food preservatives.

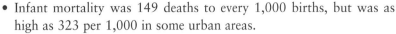

Life in the Community: Washington, DC

- Washington was abuzz with the newest controversy: Was milk safe to drink?
- Many came to believe that infant deaths triggered by "summer" diarrhea were caused by unprocessed milk.

- Infant mortality was 149 deaths to every 1,000 births, but was as high as 323 per 1,000 in some urban areas.
- Unsafe milk was only one of many food scares that had rocketed through the city, propelled by real sickness, bad science, and rampant rumors.
- The experiments of Dr. Harvey Wiley were designed to separate scientific fact on food safety from recurrent food scares.
- Little truth in advertising existed; "Pure Vermont maple syrup" often was little more than colored and flavored Iowa corn syrup.
- At the same time, manufacturers argued that certain preservatives, such as sulfur, were indispensable in processing wine or raisins.
- The public was growing increasingly skeptical and fearful of all types of toxic substances found in foods.
- Dr. Wiley first asked Congress for funds in 1899 during Senate food adulteration hearings, and was awarded funding three years later.
- When the experiments began, the purity of food had been long promoted by women's groups and health organizations—a point Dr. Wiley rarely acknowledged.
- The public's attention was particularly drawn to the healthy food issue during the Spanish-American War after soldiers complained about "embalmed beef" so saturated in chemicals as to be inedible.
- The Spanish-American War was America's first military venture overseas.
- Problems of transport were complex and inspection was totally inadequate, according to reports.
- In December 1898, Nelson A. Miles, the commanding general of the army, made a public charge that refrigerated beef supplied to the army had been "embalmed" with harmful preservative chemicals.

- Miles also criticized the canned boiled beef that the troops universally reviled for its poor quality, tastelessness, and often nauseatingly spoiled condition.
- Numerous cases of deadly food poisoning resulted among the American troops in Cuba.
- Official inquiries found no evidence of harmful chemicals in either type of beef, but concluded that use of the easily spoiled canned beef in the tropics was a serious mistake.
- The need for reform was obvious, and ordering procedures were upgraded, the first school for military cooks was established, better cooking utensils and mess gear were developed, and campfires were replaced by field ranges.

HISTORICAL SNAPSHOT
1904

- The United States Supreme Court decided that Puerto Ricans were not aliens and could enter the U.S. freely, but stopped short of awarding them citizenship
- Pope Pius X banned low-cut dresses in the presence of churchmen
- The first athletic letters were given to the University of Chicago football team
- Enrico Caruso was paid $4,000 for recording 10 songs for Victor Records
- The American occupation of Cuba following the Spanish-American War ended
- A fire in Baltimore raged for about 30 hours and destroyed more than 1,500 buildings over 80 blocks
- Giacomo Puccini's opera *Madame Butterfly* was poorly received during its world premiere at La Scala
- America acquired control of the Panama Canal Zone for $10 million and began construction of the canal
- The first color photograph was published in the *London Daily Illustrated Mirror*
- The American Academy of Arts and Letters was founded
- The St. Louis World's Fair, commemorating the centennial of the Louisiana Purchase, opened a year late and popularized the hamburger, Dr. Pepper, iced tea, and ice cream cones
- Andrew Carnegie donated $1.5 million to build a peace palace
- Blind-deaf student Helen Keller graduated with honors from Radcliffe College
- Construction of Grand Central Station began in New York City
- Inventor Wilbur Wright made the first controlled half-circle while in flight
- A New York City police officer ordered a female passenger in an automobile on Fifth Avenue to stop smoking a cigarette
- George Bernard Shaw's *How He Lied to Her Husband* premiered in New York City
- On the first day of the New York City subway's opening, 350,000 people rode the 9.1 miles of tracks
- Sigmund Freud's book *The Interpretation of Dreams* was published
- In St. Louis, Missouri, police tried a new investigation method called fingerprinting
- Harvard Stadium became the first stadium built specifically for football
- Incumbent Theodore Roosevelt was elected president of the United States, defeating Judge Alton B. Parker of New York
- King C. Gillette patented his Gillette razor blade
- Farmers in Georgia burned two million bales of cotton to prop up falling prices
- Artist Claude Monet painted *Water Lilies*

THE SCRIBNER SUMMER FICTION

THOMAS NELSON PAGE

BRED IN THE BONE

"Seven splendid stories."—*Newark Daily Advertiser.*
"All are in Mr. Page's best vein."—*Washington Star.*
Illustrated, $1.50

EDITH WHARTON

THE DESCENT OF MAN

"Firmly puts her upon a pedestal as the foremost literary artist of America."—*Pittsburg Gazette.* 12mo, $1.50

JAMES B. CONNOLLY
Author of "Out of Gloucester."

THE SEINERS

"If you love the tales where men do things and where they glory in reckless daring for the very love of it, do not fail to read 'The Seiners.'"—*Brooklyn Eagle.* $1.50

HENRY SETON MERRIMAN

TOMASO'S FORTUNE

"Told with the verve of the true story-teller."—*Pittsburg Gazette.*
"He never wrote a better book."—*New York Tribune.* 12mo, $1.50

MARY TAPPAN WRIGHT

THE TEST

"The situations are powerful and controlled."—*The Dial.*
"Intense human interest holds one to the last paragraph."—*St. Louis Globe-Democrat.* 12mo, $1.50

A. T. QUILLER-COUCH

FORT AMITY

"Must be classed among the best of modern historical novels."—*Newark Daily Advertiser.* 12mo, $1.50

FRANCES POWELL

THE BY-WAYS OF BRAITHE

"A clever tale of mystery and crime . . . handled with that feeling for things eerie and unexpected which is perhaps Miss Powell's most salient gift."—*New York Tribune.* 12mo, $1.50

BEATRIX DEMAREST LLOYD

THE PASTIME OF ETERNITY

"A love story of absorbing interest."—*Boston Herald.*
"There is quality and distinction."—*N. Y. Evg. Post.* 12mo, $1.50

HAROLD STEELE MACKAYE

THE PANCHRONICON

"This is an irresistibly funny book."—*The Outlook.*
"Jules Verne outdone."—*N. Y. Evening Post.* 12mo, $1.50

W. A. FRASER

BRAVE HEARTS

"Like the thoroughbreds he writes about, Mr. Fraser's narrative is always full of action."—*New York Evening Sun.* 12mo, $1.50

ANNA A. ROGERS

PEACE AND THE VICES

"As fascinating a heroine as Dell Talty has not danced her way across the pages of contemporary fiction in a long while."—*Boston Transcript.* 12mo, $1.50

A. E. THOMAS

CYNTHIA'S REBELLION

"Plenty of humor and much spirit."—*Philadelphia Press.*
"Unusually entertaining."—*The Outlook.* 12mo, $1.50

CHARLES SCRIBNER'S SONS, NEW YORK

Selected Prices, 1904

Baby Walker	$1.80
Beer, 12 Pints	$1.50
Camera, Kodak	$50.00
Clock, Grandfather	$30.00
Petticoat	$1.39
Refrigerator	$16.50
Saddle	$19.90
Sheep Shears	$1.04
Stereoscopic Viewer	$0.28
Tooth Cleanser, Tube	$0.25

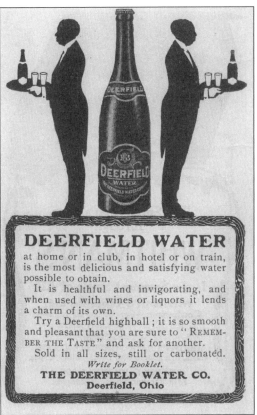

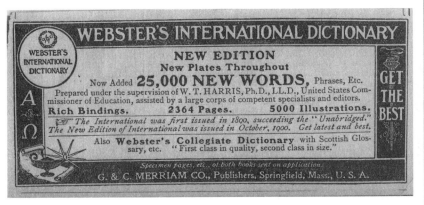

"The Song of the Poison Squad"

O we're the merriest herd of hulks
that ever the world has seen;
We don't shy off from your rough
on rats or even from Paris green:
We're on the hunt for a toxic dope
That's certain to kill, sans fail.
But 'tis a tricky, elusive thing and
knows we are on its trail;
For all the things that could kill
we've downed in many a gruesome wad,
And still we're gaining a pound a day,
for we are the Pizen Squad.
On prussic acid we break our fast;
we lunch on a morphine stew;
We dine with a matchhead consomme,
drink carbolic acid brew;
Corrosive sublimate tones us up
like laudanum ketchup rare,
While tyro-toxicon condiments
are wholesome as mountain air.
Thus all the "deadlies" we double-dare
to put us beneath the sod;
We're death-immunes and we're proud as proud
Hooray for the Pizen Squad!
—S. W. Gillilan

Timeline of Food and Drug Laws

1820

Eleven physicians established the U.S. Pharmacopeia, the first compendium of standard drugs for the United States.

1848

The Drug Importation Act was passed by Congress requiring U.S. Customs Service inspections to stop entry of adulterated drugs from overseas.

1862

President Lincoln appointed chemist Charles M. Wetherill to serve in the new Department of Agriculture. This was the beginning of the Bureau of Chemistry, the predecessor of the Food and Drug Administration.

1880

U.S. Department of Agriculture chief chemist Peter Collier recommended passage of a national food and drug law, following his own food adulteration investigations. The bill was defeated, but during the next 25 years, more than 100 food and drug bills were introduced in Congress.

1883

Dr. Harvey W. Wiley became chief chemist, expanding the Bureau of Chemistry's food adulteration studies. Campaigning for a federal law, Dr. Wiley was called the "Crusading Chemist" and "Father of the Pure Food and Drugs Act."

1897

The Tea Importation Act was passed, providing for Customs inspection of all tea entering U.S. ports, at the expense of the importers.

1898

The Association of Official Agricultural Chemists (now AOAC International) established a Committee on Food Standards headed by Dr. Wiley.

The states began incorporating these standards into their food statutes.

1902

The Biologics Control Act was passed to ensure purity and safety of serums, vaccines, and similar products used to prevent or treat diseases in humans.

Congress appropriated $5,000 to the Bureau of Chemistry to study chemical preservatives and colors and their effects on digestion and health. The studies drew widespread attention to the problem of food adulteration and increased public support for passage of a federal food and drug law.

1906

The original Food and Drugs Act was passed by Congress on June 30 and signed by President Theodore Roosevelt. It prohibited interstate commerce in misbranded and adulterated foods, drinks, and drugs.

The Meat Inspection Act was passed the same day, aided by shocking disclosures of unsanitary conditions in meat-packing plants, the use of poisonous preservatives and dyes in foods, and cure-all claims for worthless and dangerous patent medicines.

"Advocate of Can Washing, Bacteriologist at Experiment Station Upholds the Maggot Theory," *The Washington Post*, April 12, 1903:

The Commissioners have received from C. F. Donne, dairyman and bacteriologist of the Maryland Agricultural Station, a letter relative to the ruling of the Washington health authorities requiring the city milk dealers to wash cans before returning them to the farmers.

He says he has investigated the matter and knows that maggots get into unwashed cans. He says the practice will not force a hardship on the dealers.

"Boarders Turn Pink, Peculiar Effect of Food Served to Dr. Wiley's Guests," *The Washington Post*, April 12, 1903:

Science is playing some pranks with Dr. Wiley. The use of borax, formaldehyde and other meat preservatives on the class of subjects of chemical research at the Bureau of Chemistry has produced results of the most astounding character and now everyone connected with the Bureau is anxious to write a pamphlet about it.

Where Dr. Wiley looked for convincing proof of the harmlessness of drugs on American meats for export, he has so far looked in vain, and when about a week ago the complexions of his dozen or so poison-pill patients underwent a remarkable change, he, scientifically speaking, threw up the sponge. The borax, acid, and whatnot mixed in their food have worked a change in the complexion of the 14 government clerks quite inexplicable even to the scientific mind, and the experts of the department are floundering around badly in their efforts to fathom the mystery.

The change in the complexion of the chemical scholars has not been of an alarming character. On the contrary, each of the young men undergoing a heroic course of treatment has blossomed out with a bright pink complexion that would make a society belle sick with envy. As a result, chemicals of all kinds at the bureau have jumped 100 points above par. The boarders no longer object to eating any quantity of scientific mixtures. There is something in it for them now, and they are, in consequence, the most clamorous beef eaters in Washington.

"Now It Is Tubed Food, Collapsible Inclosure to Replace the Present Tins," *The Washington Post*, October 31, 1904:

The preservation of food by the "tinning" or "canning" process has played a greater role than many know in modern civilization, and especially in warfare. It has made, or its absence has unmade, many campaigns, and the extension of work in undeveloped countries has often been made possible only through it. But it is possible that in many ways, for a number of preparations, the collapsible tube will supplant the tin can and glass jar.

Heretofore, the tubes have been used only for toilet preparations, tooth pastes, mucilage, etc., but it is now proposed to extend their uses to food. A company has been formed to sell ice cream put up in this way, and one can see many advantages gained by the adaptation to other things. Condensed milk, cream, butter, cheese, jellies, marmalades, gravies, and even meats in tubes may soon become common articles in households, and especially those pestered by the servant-girl problem. Careful attention, of course, is demanded as to the material of which the tubes are made and the possible corrosive or poisonous action of the contained articles upon them. . . .

But what shall the word-maker and namer say? He can "wire" his telegrams, "phone" his orders, but instead of "tinned," will he ask the grocer to send him a "tubed" or "collapsible" lunch?

"Open World's Market," *The Washington Post*, March 4, 1898:

That the enactment of pure food laws is the desire of the American people was sufficiently demonstrated yesterday in the course of the discussion of the Brosius bill, before the pure food congress. . . .In every congree since the Forty-eighth, a bill of this character has been considered, but never has there been one so comprehensive or embodying the vital principles of American commerce so thoroughly. . . .

Yesterday morning's session of the Pure Food Congress was opened with an interesting address on "Food Adulteration" by Prof. H. W. Wiley, chief chemist of the Department of Agriculture, which was listened to with great attention by the delegates, and was later the subject of much favorable comment. . . .

Chairman Trimble, of the Committee on Credentials, reported 155 accredited delegates in attendance, representing 24 states and Territories, various departments of the government, and the National Confectioners' Association, National Millers' Association, Wholesale Druggist Association, Brewers' Association, American Pharmaceutical Association, Bookkeepers' Union, National Creamery and Butter Association, the farming industry, and numerous state and local associations.

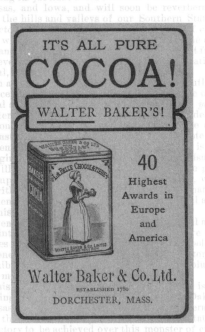

IT'S ALL PURE
COCOA!
WALTER BAKER'S!
40 Highest Awards in Europe and America
Walter Baker & Co. Ltd.
ESTABLISHED 1780
DORCHESTER, MASS.

1905 Profile

Animal Conservation: Plume Hunting

Jake Hebert, a reformed plume hunter, found himself hunting the hunters as he patrolled mangrove swamps and intricate estuaries trying to save exotic and beautiful birds from extinction.

Life at Home

- Born in Chicago in 1870, Jake Hebert was relocated to South Florida as a boy of six.
- His father had celebrated the nation's centennial by moving the family from a major urban center comprising schools, churches, and restaurants to a land populated by panthers, snakes, alligators, and mosquitoes.
- It was an abrupt change.
- Schooling became sporadic as teachers came and went from America's newest frontier.
- Much of Jake's education came during long days of hunting.
- He rarely told anyone that his ancestors had come to America on the second voyage of the *Mayflower*; it seemed an incongruous thing to say in the mosquito-laden swamps of Florida.
- Some neighbors claimed Florida was "the new wild west" where men could be men and enforcing the law was a dangerous occupation.
- His great-grandfather had been in law enforcement; his grandfather was an accomplished surveyor, and his father worked for the emerging postal service.
- Jake was eager to become involved in law enforcement, even in the unruly world of south Florida.

Jake Herbert was eager to work in law enforcement.

Florida was seen as "the new wild west".

- In his mid-thirties with a wife and child to feed, he was especially glad for a regular job paying $35 a month via the American Ornithologists' Union, particularly since he was a reformed plume hunter.
- The time was long past, Jake believed, to stop the destruction of the bird rookeries; within just a few years of aggressive hunting, the insatiable demands of the hat industry had wiped out most of the area's rosette spoonbills, snowy egrets, and flamingos.
- Flamingoes had even been eliminated from the town of Flamingo, Florida, named for the elegant pink bird.
- The real problem was not just the hunters, but the big city hat buyers.
- They were the ones, Jake preached often and loudly, who turned delicate bird feathers into objects of fashion and made them worth their weight in gold and more.
- Without them, birds would be safe from bullets and could stay off the tops of ladies' heads.
- By the turn of the twentieth century, the mass killing of egrets and other plume birds for feathers to adorn women's hats was a serious concern among the nation's growing cadre of environmentalists, especially those who belonged to the Audubon Society, a conservation organization founded in 1886.
- In 1901, at the urging of Audubon Society leaders and the American Ornithologists' Union, the Florida legislature enacted a bird protection law that provided for the hiring of local game wardens.
- Jake was one of the first wardens selected.

Life at Work

- For three years, Jake had matched wits and sometimes weapons fire with an array of plume hunters and other nefarious characters, some of whom were strangers, but most of whom were friends or acquaintances.
- Some had even been hunting partners in another time.
- Now as a warden, he fully understood that any time he caught a poacher in the act, he was confronting a threatened man who had a gun in his hand.
- He also knew that most South Florida citizens believed that the state law was another unnecessary intrusion on their lives and should not be enforced.
- After all, this was a land that offered few ways to make a large living; depending on the species and the buyers, some birds would fetch $10 each or more.
- A good morning in a well-stocked rookery could be worth $250.
- From the beginning, Jake knew that a major part of his job was education, especially during the off-season from April to January.
- Weeks were spent patrolling the coastal waters in a sailboat and talking to alligator hunters or posting No Bird Poaching signs at rookeries.
- He even visited the leadership of the Seminole and Miccosukee Indians, although they rarely plume hunted extensively for resale to the high-fashion hat market.
- Some hunters he talked with agreed to stop killing birds because of the law; some simply did not wish to be caught, fined, and jailed.
- Some only "pot" hunted, shooting curlews or cormorants or roseate spoonbills for food year 'round.
- The hardcore hunters, who killed hundreds of birds on each outing, didn't care what Jake had to say, and told him so.
- Most of the locals were full-time farmers and part-time hunters, but a few plume hunters from the Ten Thousand Islands, who contracted with feather firms in New York, traveled widely to fill the orders of the hat industry.
- Early on, Jake was determined to stop the destruction of the great white heron, which stood three feet tall, and the magnificent snowy egret, known as the heron with the golden slippers.

Jake would spend weeks patrolling for hunters and posting signs at rookeries.

- Totally clothed in white feathers, snowy egrets often congregated in huge groups, completely covering a mangrove island in a sea of white.
- But stopping locals from plundering the landscape was only one part of the problem; every winter when the threat of ferocious swarms of mosquitoes abated, wealthy northern sportsmen traveled south for another bird trophy.
- Jake's bosses, safely ensconced in the New York offices, were particularly anxious for him to arrest people who shot wildlife from tour boats.
- The widely advertised practice had been popular for 25 years, and they wanted it stopped.
- The plume hunting season was short—from January 15 to around April 15—when the birds' plumage was at its finest.
- Jake's work required long hours spent in the distant swamps to deter hunters from shooting out an entire rookery in one morning.
- After months of vigilance and time away from his family, Jake would lose the battle to save the birds in a single day.
- And the birds were not the only ones targeted; Jake's wife often feared for his life, with good reason.

Life in the Community: South Florida

- Since the 1870s, rising economic prosperity and the growth of an urban middle class had provided opportunities to purchase nonessentials.
- Emulating the fashionable elite, men selected fedoras with feather trim and women adorned their hair, hats, and dresses with "aigrettes" (sprays) of breeding plumage taken from a variety of birds.
- As a result, women's hats became larger, hat ornamentation became more lavish, and the feather trade expanded its enterprise to include marketing the remains of some 64 species of native birds.
- Herons were favored, along with the plentiful, widely distributed, and delicately plumed snowy egret.
- These birds had evolved extravagant breeding plumage to attract their mates.
- The feathers, apparently, had such a similar effect on nineteenth-century men that the supply began to disappear.
- So extensive was the decoupling of egrets and their skins that egrets were adopted as the symbol of the bird preservation movement.
- The inventories of one commercial sales room in London in 1902 showed sales of 1,608 packages of herons' plumes.
- One showroom represented 48,240 ounces, requiring four birds per ounce of plumes, or 192,960 herons, to fill the inventory.

Genuine Parisian Style.

$5.75

No. 39R155 Elegant Parisian Gainsborough effect dress hat with semi-tam crown. A very elegant hat for stylish dressers. The entire wire frame is covered with white silk mull and overlaid with a black spangled net. The black and white combination of trimming is very stylish and much desired this season. The semi-tam crown is covered with an exceptionally pretty imported spangled crown. Over the brim and beneath the crown is a fold of black silk velvet, same extending to the back in a large bow and falling over the brim where it is caught on the bandeau. A large black Amazon real ostrich plume of very fine quality and six black satin roses complete the trimming of this richly millinered hat. Well worth $10.00. Can be ordered trimmed as described only. Price, each................$5.75

GREAT SALE OF REAL OSTRICH FEATHER PLUMES AND TIPS.

Fine Demi-Plumes, 33 Cents and Upward

ALL OUR...

TIPS AND PLUMES, are made of THE HARD, GLOSSY OSTRICH STOCK

We do not handle the poor, fluffy goods.

No. 39R315 Our special 9-inch Demi-Plume, made from real ostrich feathers. Excellent quality and warranted to give perfect satisfaction. Black only. Price, each....33c

No. 39R317 A very full 10-inch Demi-Plume, made from extra quality real ostrich feathers. Fine fiber and handsome curl. Very rich and glossy in appearance. Colors, black, cream or white. Always state color desired. Price, each................ 49c

No. 39R319 Real Ostrich Feather Demi-Plumes, 11 inches long, very heavy and plump, with fine soft curl. Exceptionally handsome. Fine fiber and glossy finish. Colors, black, cream or white. Always state color desired. Price, each................75c

No. 39R321 Real Ostrich Demi-Plumes. These are the next grade better than above. Fine selected stock. Length, 12 inches. Black, white or cream. Good $1.25 value. Price, each................87c

No. 39R323 Fine Ostrich Demi-Plume, 13-inch. Made of fine selected stock, hard finish, long and glossy fibers. Colors, black, cream or white. Price, each................$1.10

No. 39R325 Finest Quality Real Ostrich Feather Demi-Plume, 14 inches long, full and heavy, with exceptionally fine curl, glossy and beautiful. In fact, these are the richest and finest appearing plumes we have ever imported. Colors, black, cream or white. Price, each................$1.33

No. 39R327 Our Highest Grade and Best Quality Genuine Ostrich Feather Demi-Plume, made of glossy, hard fiber, ostrich stock, a rich, glossy black, fine curl, very handsome and plump, length full 15 inches. Colors, black, cream or white. Price, each................$1.62

- Killing the mature birds that were caring for their young caused the destruction of two to three times that number of young or eggs.
- In 1903, the price offered to plume hunters was $32 per ounce, which made the plumes worth about twice their weight in gold.
- At that time, the millinery trade employed 83,000 people, or one of every 1,000 Americans.
- The industry leaders resisted criticism of exploitation and carefully explained that the bulk of feather collection was limited to shed plumes found scattered on the ground within rookeries.
- "Dead plumes" brought only one-fifth the price of the live, unblemished, little-worn ones.
- To counteract the charges of cruelty, the industry circulated claims that most feather trim was either artificial or produced on foreign farms that exported molted feathers.
- Plume hunting was not the exclusive problem of Florida; seabirds of the Atlantic coast as well as birds of the West Coast—terns, grebes, white pelicans, and albatrosses—were all hunted for their feathers.
- By the turn of the twentieth century, plume hunters were killing as many as five million birds each year.
- The first stance of preservationists was to enact laws to prevent the killing, possession, sale, and importation of plume birds and ornamental feathers.
- Around this goal, they disseminated their information through numerous periodicals, including *Bird Lore* and *Audubon Magazine*.
- The real impact began when the Audubon Society and other conservation organizations offered public lectures on such topics as "Woman as a Bird Enemy" and erected Audubon-approved millinery displays.
- The Audubon Society also created regulatory committees to audit the millinery sold in key areas.
- As a result, more women came to recognize their role in the plume hunting issue.

Historical Snapshot
1905

- Undertaker A. B. Stroenger invented the dial telephone
- Congress discontinued the coinage of gold dollars, ending a practice begun in 1849
- Actor Fatty Arbuckle endorsed Murad, the first celebrity testimonial of a brand of cigarettes
- Japan and Russia agreed to peace talks brokered by President Theodore Roosevelt
- The world's first theater geared exclusively for motion pictures opened in Pittsburgh, Pennsylvania
- The radical labor union, the International Workers of the World, was founded in Chicago
- *McClure's* published "The Railroads on Trial," which called for additional government regulation
- A race riot in Atlanta, Georgia, killed 10 blacks and two whites
- The average American farmer cultivated 12 acres of land
- Orville Wright piloted a flight that lasted 33 minutes and covered 21 miles
- Former President Grover Cleveland wrote in *Ladies' Home Journal* that he was opposed to women voters, saying, "We all know how much further women go than men in their social rivalries and jealousies . . . sensible and responsible women do not want to vote."
- George Bernard Shaw's *Mrs. Warren's Profession* premiered in New York City and was banned by censors
- Russian Orthodox Father George Gapon led a procession in St. Petersburg of some 200,000 that ignited the Revolution of 1905
- Congress granted statehood to Oklahoma, leaving New Mexico and Arizona as the only remaining territories
- The five Tribes of the Indian Territory proposed the creation of the state of Sequoyah
- The Rotary Club was founded in Chicago
- Elastic rubber began to replace whalebone and lace in women's corsets
- Archeologists unearthed the royal tombs of Yua and Tua in Egypt
- Royal Crown Cola, Palmolive Soap, Vick's VapoRub, the Staten Island ferry, and the entertainment trade publication *Variety* all made their first appearance
- Governor Frank Steunenberg of Idaho was killed by an assassin's bomb; three leaders of the Western Federation of Miners in Colorado were charged
- U.S. auto production increased from 2,500 annually in 1899 to 25,000
- Women in nonagricultural jobs doubled in 10 years to 4.3 million, as clerical work with emerging typewriter technology required higher skills and offered better pay
- Congress debated whether patent medicines should be required to list their ingredients, which included cocaine, morphine, and alcohol

Selected Prices, 1905

Corset	$1.00
Cuff Links, Solid Gold	$2.00
Dining Table, Oak	$11.25
Fire Insurance, $500	$4.50
Harness, Horse	$8.95
Shoes, Women's	$3.00
Snake Fight Ticket	$2.00
Trunk	$6.88
Washing Machine	$6.38
Water Heater	$198.00

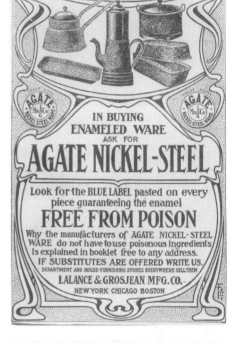

The unwritten rules of conduct in southwest Florida's Ten Thousand Island Region, *Man in the Everglades*, 1927:

Suspect every man.
Ask no questions.
Settle your own quarrels.
Never steal from an islander.
Stick by him, even if you do not know him.
Shoot quick, when your secret is in danger.
Cover your kill.

Plume Hunting Timeline

1877
South Florida hunters were paid $0.25 per bird plume

1880
Florida steamboat tour operators attracted tourists with advertisements extolling the excitement of shooting alligators and shore birds from the comfort of the boat's deck

1884
Paris hat makers paid Florida hunters $0.50 per brown pelican skin, $0.25 for sea swallows and terns, $10.00 each for great white herons, and $25.00 for flamingo skins

1886
Big game hunter and *Forest and Stream* magazine editor George Grinnell created the Audubon Society to protect and preserve birds

Science magazine reported that five million birds were being killed annually to support current hat fashions

Ornithologist Frank Chapman reported that feathers from 160 different birds could be found on the hats of fashionable women in New York City

1887
Thirty-nine thousand *Forest and Stream* readers joined the newly formed Audubon Society

1889
The Audubon Society folded under the weight of its success and the demands of publishing *Forest and Stream*

continued

Timeline . . . *(continued)*

1890

Key West was Florida's largest city, claiming a census of 18,940

1891

Florida passed but failed to enforce poaching laws

1892

The Sierra Club was founded with 182 charter members, led by John Muir

1896

The Audubon Society was revived by Boston socialite Mrs. Augustus Hemenway to stop the slaughter of birds for their plumes

1899

Naturalist Frank Chapman financed and launched *Bird Lore,* a bimonthly magazine that bore the motto: "A bird in the bush is worth two in the hand"

1900

The Federal Lacey Act outlawed the interstate transport of animals killed in violation of state law

The millinery industry employed 83,000 workers, mostly women

1901

Florida passed stricter poaching laws

The Audubon Society hired its own game wardens, known as swamp rats, to stop plume hunting

1903

President Theodore Roosevelt created the Pelican Island National Wildlife Refuge in Florida as a sanctuary for sea birds threatened by plume hunters; this was the first time the federal government had set aside land for the benefit of wildlife

President Theodore Roosevelt visited Yosemite with John Muir of the Sierra Club

1905

Under President Theodore Roosevelt's leadership, the individual states began stricter enforcement of game laws, including limits and the length of hunting seasons

Audubon bird warden Guy Bradley was killed in the line of duty near Flamingo, Florida

Representatives of 35 state Audubon organizations were incorporated as the National Association of Audubon Societies for the Protection of Wild Birds and Animals

"Raleigh (Dyess) used to tell me how they'd kill the plume birds in the 'Glades. He was a plume bird hunter back in 1905 and along in there and they'd kill them by the thousands down there and bring them out, and like he said, they'd skin them out and put paper backing on them to hold them in shape, and they'd ship them to New York where they put them on the women's hats for decoration. He said he saw it go from where you could kill hundreds of them in a day to where you couldn't find any of them; they just got scarce.

—Joe P. Brown at Immokalee, Florida

Eye-witness account of an unpaid agent of the National Association of Audubon Societies camping in south Florida, dated February 27, 1912, published in *Bird Lore*:

I spent two days and nights camped here, and made three counts of the egrets as they came in to roost or left in the morning. The first time I saw 522, the next 534, and the last evening counted 541.

This is the scene where we shortly found that the plumers were shooting them, and the last night, as I was counting, shooting commenced on the other side of the Cypress, at least a mile from camp, and we counted 123 shots. Evidently, four men with shotguns were shooting them at their roost, which is two miles from where they will nest.

We waded over a mile, waist deep, to find the camp of the hunters, and found it just deserted, the fire still burning, and showing that four men had just departed on horseback.

I trust you can prevail on some of the patrons and humane people to put a stop to this. It can be done easily with a little money, and, as there must be 600 birds that will begin nesting in two weeks, if unprotected there will not be a single bird left.

I can get a man to watch it, a good man who lives in the woods and knows all the plume-hunters, and who will put a stop to it if you can raise enough money to engage him. We can get him deputized here also, and he will then tell all the hunters he is a warden to guard the Big Cypress until the birds leave.

The gun, fishline, net, and the ocean beach were the sources from which we obtained our food and whatever else we needed. In fact, if a Florida cracker was not a good hunter, he was worthless in all other ways.

—Florida Cracker Charlie Pierce, 1890s

"Birds and Bonnets," Letter to the Editor from ornithologist Frank Chapman in *Forest and Stream* listing the 39 native species of dead birds he saw on 542 fashionable hats during two walks in Manhattan, New York, in February 1886:

BIRD SPECIES	NUMBER OF HATS SEEN	BIRD SPECIES	NUMBER OF HATS SEEN
Grebe	7	Blue Jay	5
Green-backed Heron	1	Eastern Bluebird	3
Virginia Rail	1	American Robin	4
Greater Yellowlegs	1	Northern Shrike	1
Sanderling	5	Brown Thrasher	1
Laughing Gull	1	Bohemian Waxwing	1
Common Tern	21	Cedar Waxwing	23
Black Tern	1	Blackburnian Warbler	1
Ruffed Grouse	2	Blackpoll Warbler	3
Greater Prairie Chicken	1	Wilson's Warbler	3
Northern Bobwhite	16	Tree Sparrow	2
California Quail	2	White-throated Sparrow	1
Mourning Dove	1	Snow Bunting	15
Northern Saw-whet Owl	1	Bobolink	1
Northern Flicker	21	Meadowlark	2
Red-headed Woodpecker	2	Common Grackle	5
Pleated Woodpecker	1	Northern Oriole	9
Eastern Kingbird	1	Scarlet Tanager	3
Scissor-tailed Flycatcher	1	Pine Grosbeak	1
Tree Swallow	1		

"900 Birds Brought to Port," *Fort Myers Press* (Florida), February 27, 1890:

Capt. Cuthbert and mate, Will Henderson, bird hunters of high renown, sailed into our port one day last week on Capt Cuthbert's schooner with something over 900 bird plumes, having been out some six weeks. This is what we call a good haul. Mr. W. R. Washburn, the lively bird plume dealer of this city, purchased the whole lot.

"Cruel Treatment of Birds Demanded by Dame Fashion," by Lynds Jones, *Birds and Nature Magazine*, November 1900:

All of my readers probably know in a general way that Dame Fashion is responsible for the destruction of the lives of many birds, but they may not know to what extent this is true.

Why do we say that any cruel treatment of the birds is chargeable to fashion? It can hardly be necessary to remind ourselves that there is in almost every boy's nature a touch of the savage instincts which find expression in the desire to kill something. Traces of this instinct do not entirely disappear with the development into manhood, but show themselves there in the love of hunting and fishing. Let these remnants of savagery be appealed to by the promise of gain, and they are immediately fanned into flame in the natures of those persons who are naturally more strongly drawn to this primitive occupation of men. In short, place before the professional hunter an easy means of profiting by his skill as a hunter, and in far too many instances he will smother any humane instincts which he may have for the sake of the gain. It is the demands of fashion for plumes and feathers for hat trimmings which place before these hunters the temptation to kill. Have we not a right, therefore, to place the blame at the door of Fashion?

But what are the practices which we call cruel? In the first place, it is cruelty to cause the destruction of life without good and sufficient reason. Unnecessary sacrifice of life is cruelty. Certainly no one will say that it is necessary to trim hats with feathers. Fashion decrees that feathers must be worn, and presto! feathers are worn. In the second place, it is cruel to kill birds who are feeding young ones in the nest, leaving them to starvation. Yet this is just what has happened and does happen every year. Plume hunters are no respecters of times and seasons. With them there are no closed seasons. The birds which they are after gather in large rookeries during the nesting season and are therefore much easier to capture then than at other times.

Most of the herons and similar plume-bearing birds are hunted and killed for the plumes alone, or at most, for a very small part of the whole plumage. The part wanted is taken and the rest left to waste, while the bird's body is never used for anything. If nothing worse, it is an unpardonable waste. In Florida alone, whole rookeries of herons and ibises numbering hundreds and even thousands of individuals have been wholly destroyed.

Now the insatiable plume hunter, in his effort to supply the demands of a no less insatiable fashion, is pursuing the unfortunate birds into the vastnesses of Mexico and South America. There is but one way to stop this work of extermination, and that is to take away the demand. This remedy lies wholly in the hands of women. Unless they are willing to take a firm stand against the use of feathers for purposes of ornament, the birds are doomed. This may seem like a strong statement, but a little reflection will prove it true. When the birds which are now hunted for plumes and feathers are gone, there will be a modification of the

continued

"Cruel Treatment of Birds Demanded by Dame Fashion . . ." *(continued)*

demand to include birds of different plumage, just as the aigrette is giving place to the quill. After the quill and the long-pointed wing will come the shorter wing, and after that the plumage of the small birds, and the cycle of destruction will be complete.

Someone may ask why it is that the birds are so foolish as to allow the hunter to kill hundreds in a single day from one rookery. Why don't they leave the region when the shooting begins? The plume hunter has learned cunning; he no longer uses a shotgun, but a small caliber rifle, or a wholly noiseless air gun. The rifle makes no more noise than the snapping of a twig, and will therefore not frighten the birds. By remaining concealed, the hunter may kill every bird that is within range. Since each bird is worth from $0.25 to $5.00, according to the kind, a single day's work (or slaughter) is profitable. The temptation is certainly great, and becomes almost irresistible to him who loves hunting for its own sake.

The most cruel part of the whole business I have already stated, but it will bear repeating. It is the killing of the breeding birds before the young are able to care for themselves. There is abundant evidence that the breeding time is the favorite time for hunting among plume hunters, because then the old birds are more easy to kill, and because then the plumage is the most perfect, for then the wedding garments are put on.

It should not be an impossible task to stop this whole cruel business. But laws will not do it without a wholesome public sentiment behind it. Women are notably foremost in all good works, and many of them are doing nobly in this work, but it is painfully evident that many are not. Let us make "a long pull and a strong pull and a pull all together," and then we shall drag this growing evil back and down forever.

The man who shoots birds with a gun adds nothing to our knowledge. But the man who shoots birds with a camera places us in closer relations with their habits and he brings results that add greatly to general knowledge. It's all very well to say that the man with the gun brings back specimens, but the various species are pretty generally known as to plumage and structure. The pictures, however, appeal to and interest many to whom a mere verbal explanation of habits of nesting and feeding would be both unattractive and unintelligible.

—Frank M. Chapman's comments before the Linnaean Society, New York, October 14, 1900

Diary entries of Florida bird warden Guy Bradley, 1903:

Jan. 24-25—Visited Alligator Lake and its rookery. Found wood Ibises getting ready to lay, also plenty of egrets feeding in the marsh. Narrowly escaped being bitten by a large cotton-mouthed moccasin.

Jan. 26-27—Visited Sandy Key and East Cape Sable, also egret and duck feeding grounds. Found signs of hunters but no one there; posted warning notices.

Jan. 29—Heard a lot of shooting out in the Bay; went out in a small boat and tried to catch a boat that was leaving one of the cormorant rookeries but the wind sprang up and they got away.

1907 NEWS FEATURE

"The Automobile in America," by John Farson, *The Making of America, Volume IV,* 1907:

For a comprehensive grasp of the automobile in the United States, a few lines are full of suggestion: In the last census year, the government took no cognizance of the business in its reports, though there are 75,000 machines of all types now in use in this country. There are more than 100 manufactories producing these machines in the United States, the automobiles averaging $1,200 apiece. The output of these factories in the last year approached $50 million in value, while nearly $6 million worth of foreign machines were imported, averaging close to $6,000 each. And as a feature of the rapid growth of the automobile mechanism, it may be recalled that the steam automobile, built in 1892, is treasured in Akron, Ohio, as one of the ancient vehicles out of which, in 13 years, the mile-a-minute carriage and the 10-ton truck have evolved. . . .

To-day the manufacture of automobiles is the second most important industry in France, while in the United States, it must be anticipated that their manufacture is to make a formidable subject for the census reports of 1910. Already the steel makers of the world are making concessions to the needs of builders and are turning out a quality of steel that shall serve the purpose of one industry. More than 100 manufactories are making accessories designed for the American automobile, from lamps to goggles and caps. While, as to the states, counties, cities, and towns that are making laws and ordinances for the regulating of the machines and drivers, they are legion. In this respect there has been a good deal of prejudice on the one side of the general public, and on the side of the owners and drivers a good deal of lawlessness and disregard for the rights of the road. With the growth of the industry as it is promising, and with the utilizing of the machine through every field of vehicle transportation, both prejudice and lawlessness must surrender to sanity in the situation.

The American west is the seat of the industry on this side of the Atlantic, nearly 50 percent of the machines produced coming from Michigan, in the vicinity of Detroit. With Michigan in the lead, the other states in their order are Ohio, Wisconsin, Massachusetts, New York, Indiana, Pennsylvania, Connecticut, Illinois, and Missouri. . . . Six hundred cars were imported from France, Italy, Germany, England, Belgium, and Switzerland in the last year, each paying a duty of 45 percent ad valorem. New York, which has more of these imported machines than any state in the union, leads with a total of 17,000 automobiles of all makes, sizes, and purposes, while in 1901 there were only 901 machines registered. Massachusetts, with probably 9,000 machines, takes second place in numbers.

In the city of New York, the automobile has come into more universal use, perhaps, than in any other city of the world. It has 600 cabs, scores of express wagons, a swift machine for the head of the fire department, the great touring coaches, the heaviest trucks, and on down to the lightest and easiest small runabout. Chicago and Buffalo, New York, are rapidly gaining on New York, however, as the utility of the auto in the business world is becoming more generally recognized.

At the present time, the manner in which the automobile is taking place in the great draying centers of the cities, throwing the horse out of the race and lending economy of space and cleanliness to congested streets, is one of the most striking features of its prospects. Two things in the past have been handicaps to the business automobile. In the first place, the demands for the passenger vehicles have been clamorous enough to keep the attention of most of the builders to that line of machines. And, on the other hand, the necessity for a standard automobile mechanism for heavy work at draying has been slow at developing results. Changes and improvements in the passenger machines have been following one another so rapidly that to standardize the dray has seemed superfluous. Yet it is in the coming machine which shall release the dray horse that the trade must look for great stimulus. . . .

As tabulated by this English concern, the showing of the horse against the motor is interesting to any student of the traction problem in city or country. One of the sharp discrepancies in the motor truck cost is the fact that its operators received $170 more than did the operators of the two vans, horse-drawn, and in the motor machine the entry of $350 to the account of depreciation seems more than enough as compared with the $250 for the horse outfits.

In detail, however, the comparisons of cost are

Steam five-ton truck, $1,903.00

Drivers' wages, $455.00
Carrier's wages, $338.00
Repairs to truck, $224.75
Oil for truck, $83.20
Coal for boilers, $245.00
Insurance on truck, $59.50
Interest on first cost, $125.00
Depreciation of values, $350.00
Incidentals, $22.55

Total operating cost, $1,903.00

Against this motor truck, the cost of two vans, the seven horses, and the two drivers necessary are as follows, the first cost of horses and vans being $2,000, as against the $2,500 for the steam truck.

Seven horses and two vans, $1,902.00

Wages, two drivers, $624.00
Food for horses, $1,355.00
Shoeing horses, $153.00
Veterinary's services, $42.60
Repairs, vans, and harness, $55.75
Interest on first cost, $102.50
Depreciation, horses and vans, $250.00
Incidentals, $16.50

Total costs, $2,599.35

Virtually the automobile business, as it stands to-day, has been built up in the last five years. A machine that is two years old this summer is likely to be a back number to the point of the well-to-do owner trying to get rid of it at a fair figure. Because of the difficulty of reaching the automobile limitations, the builders of the machines have been handicapped and the builders and the workers in the industry have suffered.

At the present time, the lack of a tire that shall compare in stability and strength with the rest of a well-built machine is the one great drawback to the automobile. In the past, this expense annually, for tires alone, has been such that the person of ordinary means would not be able to run an automobile out of his salary were the machine presented to him without charge.

Perhaps the merchandise truck and dray have the best equipment of tires at the present time. In many cases, the tires are solid rubber and may not be punctured. Some of them have worked well with a steel tire under almost any condition of the roads. But it is the belief of the automobile manufacturer that a tire finally is to be evolved which will give to the passenger machine the absolutely necessary, easy springing sweep and swing that characterizes riding in the automobile, and that at the same time this tire material will embody the lasting qualities that must mark the rest of the mechanism.

When this shall be accomplished, the automotive industry in the United States, as elsewhere in the world, will have come in for its greatest single impulse.

1910–1919

As the second decade of the century began, the economy was strong and optimism was high, especially among the newly emerging middle class—the beneficiaries of improved technology, a stable economy and the unregulated, often unsafe labor of the working class. Jobs were available to everyone; America enjoyed full employment, yet hours remained long and jobs were dangerous. Child, female and immigrant exploitation remained, despite a rising level of progressive debate regarding the plight of the underclass. Women banded together for full suffrage and against alcohol. Worker-inspired unions battled for better working conditions and minorities of various origins, colors and faiths attempted to find their voice in the midst of a dramatically changing world. Divorce was on the rise, consuming one in 12 marriages. The discovery of "salvarsan 606" the miracle treatment for syphilis, was hailed as both a lifesaver and an enticement to sin. At the same time, the emerging middle class was proving that it was capable of carrying a greater load of managerial decisions, freeing factory owners and stockholders to travel, experiment, and study ways to cure the ills of the poor. Millions of dollars were poured into libraries, parks and literacy classes designed to uplift the immigrant masses flooding American shores. The United States was prospering and, at the same time, the country's elite were re-evaluating America's role as an emerging world power which no longer looked to Britain for approval.

Immigration continued at a pace of one million annually in the first four years of the decade. Between 1910 and 1913, some 11 million immigrants—an all-time record—entered the United States. The wages of unskilled workers fell, but the number of jobs expanded dramatically. Manufacturing employment rose by 3.3 million, or close to six percent in a year during the period. At the same time, earnings of skilled workers rose substantially and resulted in a backlash focused on protecting American workers' jobs. As a result, a series of anti-immigration laws was passed culminating in 1917 with permanent bars to the free flow of immigrants into the United States. From the beginning of World War I until 1919, the number of immigrants fell sharply while the war effort was demanding more and more workers. As a result, wages for low-skilled work rose rapidly, forcing the managerial class—often represented by the middle class—to find new and more streamlined ways to get the jobs done—often by employing less labor or more technology.

In the midst of these dynamics, the Progressive Movement, largely a product of the rising middle class, began to shape the decade raising questions about work safety, the rights of individuals, the need for clean air and fewer work hours. It was a people's movement that grasped the immediate impact of linking the media to its cause. The results were significant and widespread. South Carolina prohibited the employment of children under 12 in mines, factories, and textile mills; Delaware began to frame employer's liability laws; the direct election of U.S. senators was approved; and nationwide communities argued loudly over the right and ability of women to vote and the need and lawfulness of alcohol consumption.

During the decade, motorized tractors changed the lives of farmers, and electricity extended the day of urban dwellers. Powered trolley cars, vacuum cleaners, hair dryers, and electric ranges moved onto the modern scene. Wireless communications bridged San Francisco to New York and New York to Paris; in 1915, the Bell system alone operated six million telephones, which were considered essential in most middle class homes as the decade drew to a close. As the sale of parlor pianos hit a new high, more than two billion copies of sheet music were sold as ragtime neared its peak. Thousands of Bibles were placed in hotel bedrooms by the Gideon Organization of Christian Commercial Travelers, reflecting both the emerging role of the traveling "drummer" or salesman and the evangelical nature of the Progressive Movement.

Yet in the midst of blazing prosperity, the nation was changing too rapidly for many—demographically, economically, and morally. Divorce was on the rise. The discovery of a treatment for syphilis was met with pros and cons. As the technology and sophistication of silent movies improved yearly, the Missouri Christian Endeavor Society tried to ban films that included any kissing. At the same time, the rapidly expanding economy, largely without government regulation, began producing marked inequities of wealth—affluence for the few and hardship for the many. The average salary of $750 a year was rising, but not fast enough for many.

But one of the biggest stories was America's unabashed love affair with the automobile. By 1916, the Model T cost less than half its 1908 price, and nearly everyone dreamed of owning a car. Movies were also maturing during the period, growing rapidly as an essential entertainment for the poor. Some 25 percent of the population, including many newly arrived immigrants, went weekly to the nickelodeon to marvel at the exploits of Charlie Chaplin, Mary Pickford, and Douglas Fairbanks, Sr.—each drawing big salaries in the silent days of movies.

The second half of the decade was marked by the Great War, later to be known as the First World War. Worldwide, it cost more than nine million lives and swept away four empires—the German, the Austro-Hungarian, the Russian, and the Ottoman—and with them the traditional aristocratic style of leadership in Europe. It bled the treasuries of Europe dry and brought the United States forward as the richest country in the world.

When the war broke out in Europe, American exports were required to support the Allied war effort, driving the well-oiled American industrial engine into high gear. Then, when America's intervention in 1917 required the drafting of two million men, women were given their first taste of economic independence. Millions stepped forward to produce the materials needed by a nation. As a result, when the men came back from Europe, America was a changed place for both the well-traveled soldier and the newly trained female worker. Each had acquired an expanded view of the world. Yet women possessed full suffrage in only Wyoming, Colorado, Utah and Idaho.

The war forced Americans to confront one more important transformation. The United States had become a full participant in the world economy; tariffs on imported goods were reduced and exports reached all-time highs in 1919, further stimulating the American economy.

1912 Profile

Suffrage: The Kansas Campaign

Flora Nance worked tirelessly for women's suffrage in Kansas, never shying away from difficult tasks such as lobbying politicians, fundraising, or appealing to legislators' wives for support.

Life at Home

- Flora Nance was concerned and excited about another run at Kansas suffrage.
- For most of the state's pioneering history, women had stood shoulder to shoulder with men on the farm.
- If they pulled their weight on the farm, they should have the right to vote in all elections.
- So when Flora received a letter from Mrs. Catharine Hoffman announcing plans to make another appeal to the state legislature beginning in 1912, Flora was ready to help.
- Her role, she was told, was to talk—a job she was born to do, she believed—and that included conversing with male politicians who considered themselves important.
- Her other skill was organization.
- Many farm wives, left in solitude most of the day, were shy and afraid to take a leadership role.
- Not Flora Nance.
- Possessing a quick laugh and unlimited energy, Flora was organized, focused, and ready to accept any challenge.
- Besides, she felt her long friendship with Quaker Governor Roscoe Stubbs and his long history of friendliness toward the women's suffrage issue gave the women of Kansas an opportunity for success.
- But there was much to do and very little time.

Flora Nance worked tirelessly for women's suffrage in Kansas.

- The first task was some politics at home convincing her husband that her traveling the state to campaign for suffrage was good for the family with money tight and both the children and the horses needing tending.
- The teenagers were old enough to care themselves and the horses, too; children these days were becoming too soft anyway, and a little responsibility wouldn't hurt anyone.
- But her husband Jay took more convincing.
- It wasn't that he didn't want her to work for suffrage; he simply did not want her to leave.

SUFFRAGETTE SERIES N° 11.

EVERYBODY
WORKS BUT
MOTHER:
SHE'S A
SUFFRAGETTE

I WANT TO VOTE, BUT
MY·WIFE·WONT·LET·ME

COPYRIGHTED. 1909 BY DUNSTON-WEILER LITHOGRAPH CO.

- For most of their married life, they had awakened together and talked in the morning; Jay was not eager to see that change.
- But after a day of not speaking, Jay told Flora, "This is work only women can do. Do your best."
- The Kansas Equal Suffrage Association held its annual meeting in Topeka on May 16, 1911, followed by a meeting of the board on July 10.
- Then the president submitted a plan, largely created by Flora at her kitchen table, for the complete organization of the state.
- The plan named district presidents, who were to create in each county an organization similar to that of the state.
- County officers were then responsible for keeping in touch with every precinct in their county.
- This meant that every woman in the state would have a voice.
- Organization, education, and publicity became the watchwords.
- The chairwoman of the membership committee then devised a plan for enrolling every woman as a member of the Suffrage Association, as a sympathizer, or as opposed to the cause.
- Membership in the Association was set at $0.50.
- The board agreed that public speakers for other associations or occasions might be requested to speak for suffrage, but suffrage speakers must not put any other "creed, doctrine, or ism" into their speeches.
- Flora knew from previous campaigns that ladylike decorum worked better than shouting when convincing men about the vote.

Life at Work

- The first goal of the 1912 Kansas Suffrage campaign and Flora Nance's first challenge was convincing the legislature to approve a referendum on suffrage.
- A referendum would give the men of the state the right to determine if Kansas women could vote in national elections.
- Since 1861, women had been voters, but only in local contests.
- Thanks to months of preparation, the session began successfully.

- On January 13, 1912, a resolution was introduced in the House providing for the submission to the people of an equal suffrage amendment to the Kansas constitution.
- Flora and her legion of women swung into action.
- First, every legislator was asked by each member of the women's committee to vote for suffrage, giving the sense of a true groundswell of support.
- They also recruited the votes of the legislators' wives, knowing the private views of the spouses could have important public impact.
- Flora also made sure that all dinners, receptions, and teas given for the members' wives included the subject of women's suffrage.
- Within a month, the amendment resolution passed both the House and Senate by a large majority and was signed by Governor Stubbs.
- Flora believed that organization and the support of the legislators' wives carried the day.
- After two tries over 50 years, the issue of suffrage was to be settled during the general election of 1912.
- Phase two of the campaign was underway.
- At the first Women's Association meeting following the legislative approval of the referendum, the Department of Education chairwoman unveiled a threefold plan: The distribution of literature, the endorsement of suffrage by educational bodies, and essay contests in public schools.
- Flora was immediately intrigued by the idea of a children's essay contest on suffrage.
- Clearly it was an excellent chance to make converts of the parents, by involving farm women who help with the homework.
- Under the plan, the essays were entered for county prizes; the county winners entered the district contests, and the winners in the districts competed for the state prize.
- Debates between the schools were to be arranged, also.
- Mrs. C. A. Hoffman, chairwoman of the press department, furnished suffrage articles to the many state newspapers, thus reaching the remotest parts of the state.
- But Flora quickly realized the women would need to tackle the problem of finances.
- Politicians had told the women that they would need at least $30,000 to conduct a statewide campaign.
- The suffragists knew that they would never be able to raise that amount, having no favors or patronage to bestow, if successful, in return for financial aid.
- Starting with $140 in the treasury, they set to work to raise the money, pledging from $25 to $200 each.
- Throughout the campaign, money kept coming in driblets as local organizations held bazaars, food sales, ice cream festivals, suffrage teas, or some suffragist sold a bit of fancy work or made a gift of money.
- Many of the county-seat towns put on the play, *How the Vote Was Won.*
- Minstrel and picture shows were also popular ways of raising funds.
- Some farm women donated hens to the cause, and self-denial weeks were observed.
- One lucrative source instituted by Flora's committee was the sale of balloons.

Farm women helped raise money for the cause by organizing bazaars or selling fancywork.

- Two-and-a-half feet in circumference when blown up, the balloons were bright orange and lettered with "Votes for Women" or "Votes for Mother."
- They were sold on the streets, at picnics, fairs, parties, and other gatherings.
- June 29, 1912, was even set aside as "Balloon Day," and all profits from the sale of these balloons were given to state headquarters.
- Over $500 was raised.
- Orders for "Votes for Women" balloons came from all parts of the United States, as did financial aid.
- Women's groups and progressives in Nebraska, Florida, Arkansas, California, Missouri, Kentucky, and Pennsylvania all sent contributions.
- Chadron, Nebraska, sent a check for $16.85, the proceeds of a food sale for the Kansas campaign.
- Emma DeVoe of Tacoma, Washington, sent cookbooks to be sold at $1.00 each.
- The National Suffrage Association gave generously, $2,200 in total.
- All together, a little less than $16,000 was raised, mostly from Kansas events.
- But still, the campaign was constantly strapped for cash.
- As Flora learned daily, organizing 105 counties and educating 400,000 people was expensive.
- Only the stenographers in the state headquarters received compensation; everyone else was a volunteer.
- Speakers and organizers from outside the state donated their time.
- Traveling expenses were met by collections taken at meetings; lodging for traveling speakers was usually provided by resident suffragists.
- An extremely hot summer was followed by a bitter winter; women worked in 110 degree heat and 20 below zero, but the biggest problem was not opposition, but apathy.
  - The district president reported "stupendous apathy among the women," and "suffrage is worse than lukewarm here."
  - The head of the Wichita district reported, "I find politicians who have frivolous or intellectually inferior wives are not in favor of suffrage."
  - Flora remembered the need for good organization and avoided the mistakes in the campaign of 1894; to keep the campaign on a nonpartisan basis, she steered clear of political alliances.
  - However, the women didn't shrink from an opportunity to tell the suffrage story.
  - When they attended political meetings, the speakers usually received polite notes passed to them asking that they speak a word for the suffrage amendment.
  - Suffragists were frequently given a place on the program at political meetings of both parties.
  - While the women avoided affiliation with political parties, they did seek the endorsement of other organizations in the state.
  - To counter charges that women did not want the right to vote, all state organizations of women, comprising more than 60,000 persons, were asked to endorse the suffrage amendment.
  - The amendment was endorsed by a variety of organizations in the state, including the Teachers Association, State Federation of Labor, State Grange, State Board of Agriculture, Conference of Churches, G. A. R., Editorial Association, and State Temperance Union.
  - In her appeal to the men to cooperate in the woman's "struggle for political liberty," the Association preached that the interests of the sexes were insepa-

Suffragists frequently spoke at political meetings for the suffrage amendment.

rable; that women had ever stood by men in promoting a good cause; and that men had never failed to help other men in their struggles for liberty.

- They especially appealed for help with " people whom women cannot approach, and places where women do not congregate, and in these places you could be of valuable service, that is in barber shops, hotel lobbies, all kinds of shops, on the streets, and at public meetings for men."
- This appeal worked well in many communities.
- But when former president and current Progressive candidate Theodore Roosevelt toured the state seeking votes, he avoided the issue of women's suffrage.
- A speaking tour by Miss Jane Addams of Hull-House produced enthusiastic crowds among both men and women wherever she went.
- The appearance of the Chicago-based social reformer created extensive publicity for the suffrage cause.
- During her one-week visit, she gave several speeches each day, including a talk to the Armour packing plant workers in Kansas City.
- At the request of the Kansas Suffrage Association, the Armour superintendent turned out all 1,000 of its workingmen for the speech, who took off their hats and cheered when Miss Adams completed her talk.
- When Miss Addams was presented with an armful of American beauty roses, Flora began to sense victory for the first time.

Flora and her activists were confronted at every turn by men who declared that women had no desire to vote.

- Flora and her activists quickly learned that it was cheaper and easier to go where the crowds were instead of waiting at a church or hall for the crowds to come to them.
- This was done by attending chautauquas, county fairs, old settlers' reunions, teachers' institutes—wherever there was a gathering.
- They also planned picnics, parades, concerts, rallies, etc.
- Chautauquas were particularly good places for campaigning since they were held in many counties, lasted for a week or more, and drew unusually large crowds.
- Despite Flora's quick mind and superb planning, the women were still confronted at every turn by cigar-chomping men who declared that the women had no desire to vote, that men should not permit their women to mingle in the dirty pool of politics, and that the women they talked with preferred to remain upon the pedestal where gentlemen had placed them.
- But the women pressed on and distributed thousands of leaflets and other materials at all gatherings, at schools, and on rural mailboxes.
- The suffragists were also urged to watch the candidates running for office putting up their pleas for votes on telegraph poles, trees and fences, so the women could plaster "Votes for Women" alongside.
- Eventually the whole state was to be placarded so that no farmer could ride to town without seeing the words many times.

- A number of counties organized automobile teams to go into the small towns to hold street meetings.
- One automobile campaign trip included the same route covered by the Rev. Olympia Brown Willis and other suffrage workers in the campaign of 1867, when they often rode in ox-teams or on Indian ponies, and spent the nights in dugouts or sod houses.
- Another automotive trip covered over 1,000 miles, included 40 towns and reached 10,000 people.
- In October, the Association appealed to the clergy of Kansas to reciprocate woman's helpfulness in the church by preaching a sermon October 13 on the subject, "Woman and Her Place in the World's Work."
- As the November vote drew near, Flora Nance frantically wrote letters to bolster her tired network of suffragists.
- House-to-house canvasses were made in doubtful districts.
- On election day, hundreds of women worked at the polls all day, and sat up far into the night for the returns.
- The vote was close: 175,246 votes for the amendment and 159,197 against.
- Flora was elated and exhausted, and ready to return to farming.
- A crop failure in 1912 had put the Nance family in debt again.

Life in the Community: Kansas

- While much of the East continued to argue over suffrage, Kansas women were expressing their opinion at the polls.
- Starting in 1861, women were able to vote in school board elections.
- The Kansas Equal Suffrage Association, formed in 1884, generated enough interest that in 1887, the legislature gave women the right to vote in municipal elections.
- By 1910, many Kansas women believed the time had arrived for universal suffrage, the privilege of voting in statewide and national elections.
- Despite the successes, it had been a road littered with disappointments.

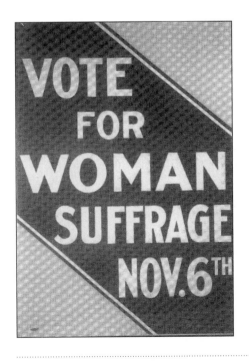

- When Kansas became a state in 1861, suffragist Clarina I. H. Nichols lobbied delegates to delete the word "male" from the franchise clause in the new state constitution.
- The larger effort failed but resulted in the granting of school board suffrage.
- After the end of the Civil War, the Kansas Impartial Suffrage Association launched a statewide referendum campaign hoping to fan the flames of "universal suffrage" for both blacks and women.
- The result in 1867 was the nation's first popular referendum on women's suffrage and defeat by a wide margin.
- Blame for the defeat was placed on women's apathy, anti-liquor crusaders, and radical outside agitators.
- The rise of the Populist movement brought the suffrage movement back to life in the 1880s and early 1890s, when grassroots rural protest erupted against wealthy railroad monopolies, high-priced grain storage, and unstable prices for farm goods.
- Struggling farm families began to embrace women's suffrage to bring about economic and political justice.
- The victory of women's suffrage at the ballot box in neighboring Colorado in 1893 spurred a second Kansas referendum campaign in 1894.
- Populist speakers addressed large crowds in Grange halls and schoolhouses in every corner of the state.
- The popular weekly newspaper *The Farmer's Wife* brought the movement into every farmhouse in Kansas.
- But the campaign to give Kansas women the right to vote in all elections became entangled with internal and external political bickering, and the referendum was defeated at the polls for the second time.
- Fresh energy and more prosperous times spurred a third attempt to enact women's right to vote in 1912.
- The political climate had changed, and rural support for suffrage was strong.
- More than 100 petitions containing 25,000 names were gathered in 1911.
- As in the past, the liquor industry, fearing the power of women at the polls, raised more than $1 million for an anti-suffrage campaign, even though Kansas had outlawed saloons 32 years earlier.
- In turn, suffrage organizers had learned that stridency offends men and rethought their approach.
- "We were never spectacular. . . . We tried to put our enemies to sleep and arouse our friends to action. . . . We did not fight for suffrage, we worked for it," one supporter wrote.
- In 1912, Kansas became the eighth suffrage state.
- Women had achieved the vote in Colorado in 1893, followed by Utah (1896), Idaho (1896), Washington (1910), California (1911), Arizona (1912), Oregon (1912), Kansas (1912), Illinois (1913), Nevada (1914), and Montana (1914).

HISTORICAL SNAPSHOT
1912

- AT&T engineers produced the vacuum tube, creating the possibility of transcontinental phone service
- The United States Government forced DuPont to give up a major part of its explosives business
- The Hearst Corporation acquired *Harper's Bazaar* fashion magazine, *Motor Boating* and *Sailing* magazine
- Standard Oil established America's first gas station in Cincinnati
- The synthetic resin PVC, polyvinyl chloride, was first produced
- German scientist Alfred Wegener theorized that the continents had drifted to their present positions from the breakup of a single primeval supercontinent which he called Pangaea
- Scientists came to believe that dietary deficiencies in substances named "vitamins" might cause such diseases as beriberi, rickets, and pellagra
- The 25,000-acre National Elk Refuge was established outside of Jackson Hole, Wyoming
- Charles Franklin Kettering, president of Delco, introduced the electric-starter on the 1912 Cadillac
- German psychologist William Stern introduced the term "intelligence quotient" or "IQ"
- New Mexico and Arizona became the forty-seventh and forty-eighth states
- The world's first flying-boat airplane, designed by Glenn Curtiss, made its maiden flight
- New U.S. football rules shortened the field to 100 yards, touchdowns became six points instead of five, four downs were allowed instead of three, and the kickoff was moved from midfield to the 40 yard line
- Juliette Gordon Low organized the Girl Guides, the first Girl Scouts troop in America, in Savannah, Georgia
- Three thousand twenty cherry blossom trees, a gift from Japan, were planted on the Potomac River in Washington, DC
- The 66,000-ton *RMS Titanic* left on its maiden voyage with 2,223 passengers and crew aboard

Selected Prices, 1912

Apartment, New York City, Three-Room, Month $55.00
Bicycle $15.95
Face Powder, per Box $0.50
False Teeth, per Set $5.00
Linoleum, Inlaid, per Yard $2.35
Nightgown, Children's $0.22
Ocean Liner Fare, New York to Rotterdam $50.00
Piano, Steinway, Baby Grand $2,000.00
Toupee $21.65
Water Pistol $0.21

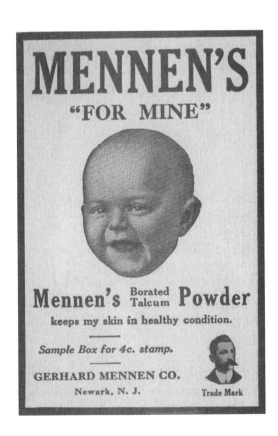

MENNEN'S

"FOR MINE"

Mennen's Borated Talcum Powder

keeps my skin in healthy condition.

Sample Box for 4c. stamp.

GERHARD MENNEN CO.

Newark, N. J.

Trade Mark

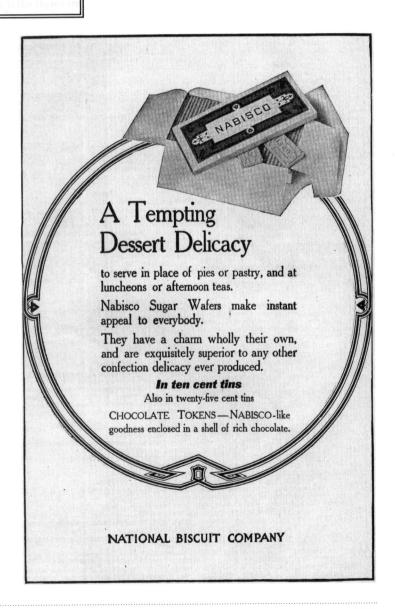

A Tempting
Dessert Delicacy

to serve in place of pies or pastry, and at luncheons or afternoon teas.

Nabisco Sugar Wafers make instant appeal to everybody.

They have a charm wholly their own, and are exquisitely superior to any other confection delicacy ever produced.

In ten cent tins

Also in twenty-five cent tins

CHOCOLATE TOKENS—NABISCO-like goodness enclosed in a shell of rich chocolate.

NATIONAL BISCUIT COMPANY

National and Kansas Suffrage Timeline

1829

Author Frances Wright traveled the United States on a paid lecture tour advocating more control over divorce and birth control and attacking organized religion for the secondary role it assigned women.

1838

Sarah Grimké published *Letters on the Equality of the Sexes and the Condition of Women.*

1840

The World Anti-Slavery Convention was held in London, where women, including abolitionists Lucretia Mott and Elizabeth Cady Stanton, were barred from participating.

1848

The first women's rights convention in Seneca Falls, New York, attracted 300, including Amelia Bloomer, Charlotte Woodward, and Frederick Douglass.

1850

The first National Women's Rights Convention was held in Worcester, Massachusetts, attended by Paulina Wright Davis, Frederick Douglass, Abby Kelly Foster, William Lloyd Garrison, Lucy Stone, and Sojourner Truth.

1851

Sojourner Truth delivered her "Ain't I a Woman?" speech at a women's rights convention in Akron, Ohio.

The second National Women's Rights Convention was held in Worcester, Massachusetts.

Westminster Review published John Stuart Mill's article, "On the Enfranchisement of Women," actually written by his companion, Harriet Hardy Taylor.

1852

Newspaper editor Clara Howard Nichols addressed the Vermont Senate on the topic of women's property rights.

Harriet Beecher Stowe's *Uncle Tom's Cabin* was published.

1853

The World's Temperance Convention was held in New York City at which women delegates, including Susan B. Anthony, were not allowed to speak.

1854

The Massachusetts legislature granted property rights to women.

1855

Prominent suffragists Lucy Stone and Henry Blackwell were married in a ceremony that eliminated the vow of obedience.

1861

Kansas gained statehood.

Suffragist Clarina I. H. Nichols lobbied to delete the word male from the franchise clause of the new Kansas state constitution.

1866

The Eleventh National Women's Rights Convention was held in New York City; suffragists and the American Anti-Slavery Association merged into a new organization named the American Equal Rights Association.

continued

Timeline . . . *(continued)*

1867

The Kansas Impartial Suffrage Association was formed; suffragists were defeated on the fall ballot.

At the American Equal Rights Association annual meeting, opinions were divided sharply on supporting the enfranchisement of black men before women.

1868

Elizabeth Cady Stanton and Susan B. Anthony begin publishing *The Revolution*, a weekly newspaper devoted to suffrage and other progressive causes.

1869

The territory of Wyoming was the first to grant unrestricted suffrage to women.

Arguments over the Fifteenth Amendment led to a split in the movement.

Elizabeth Cady Stanton and Susan B. Anthony formed the National Woman Suffrage Association, which allowed only female membership and advocates for woman suffrage above all other issues.

Lucy Stone formed the American Woman Suffrage Association, which supported the Fifteenth Amendment and invited men to join.

1870

The American Woman Suffrage Association began publishing the *Woman's Journal*.

The Fifteenth Amendment was ratified; women who went to the polls to test the amendment were turned away.

The Utah territory enfranchised women.

1872

The Dakota territory legislature voted down a suffrage proposal by one vote.

1874

The Women's Christian Temperance Union was founded.

The U.S. Supreme Court ruled that the Fourteenth Amendment did not grant women the right to vote.

Michigan's male voters voted down women's suffrage.

1875

Women in Michigan and Minnesota gained the right to vote in school board elections.

1878

California Senator A. A. Sargent introduced a federal amendment to grant women the right to vote.

1882

Suffrage was defeated in both Nebraska and Indiana.

1883

The women of the Washington territory were granted full voting rights.

1887

The U.S. Supreme Court struck down a law that enfranchised women in the Washington territory.

Kansas women won the right to vote in municipal elections.

Rhode Island voted down a referendum on women's suffrage.

1890

The National and American Associations merged to form the National American Woman Suffrage Association, with Elizabeth Cady Stanton as the new organization's first president.

continued

Timeline . . . *(continued)*

1893

Colorado men made their state the second in which women had the right to vote.

1894

The Kansas suffrage referendum was defeated.

1895

The National American Woman Suffrage Association formally condemned Elizabeth Cady Stanton's *The Woman's Bible,* a critique of Christianity.

The New York State Association Opposed to Woman Suffrage was formed.

1896

The National American Woman Suffrage Association launched an aggressive, but losing suffrage campaign in California.

Idaho enfranchised women by severing the suffrage issue from the eastern movement and Prohibition.

Utah became a state, and Utah women regained the right to vote.

1897

The National Suffrage Bulletin, edited by Carrie Chapman Catt, was launched.

1900

Susan B. Anthony retired as the president of the National American Woman Suffrage Association and recommended Carrie Chapman Catt as her successor.

1902

An international gathering of women from 10 nations met in Washington, DC, to plan an international effort for suffrage.

New Hampshire's men voted down a women's suffrage referendum.

1904

Dissidents from the International Council of Women formed the International Woman Suffrage Alliance.

Dr. Anna Howard Shaw became president of the National American Woman Suffrage Association.

1906

Elizabeth Cady Stanton's daughter, Harriot Stanton Blatch, formed the Equality League of Self-Supporting Women to reach out to working class women.

1909

The Women's Trade Union League coordinated a large strike by 20,000 women workers in New York's garment district; wealthy women supported the strike with a purchasing boycott.

1910

A grassroots campaign in Washington State achieved full enfranchisement for women.

The Women's Political Union organized a large-scale suffrage parade in New York City.

1911

California women won full voting rights.

continued

Timeline . . . *(continued)*

1912

Alaska's territorial legislature enfranchised women.

Male Kansas voters approved full woman's suffrage.

Oregon's grassroots suffrage campaign resulted in full voting rights for women.

The Arizona territory obtained statehood and women won the right to vote.

Presidential candidates courted the female vote for the first time.

I have sold two dozen eggs, 10 pounds of butter, one peck of crab apples, and engaged two pecks more. This goes to the suffrage fund.

—Letter by Mrs. C. W. (Lizzie) Smith, Stockton, Kansas, 1911

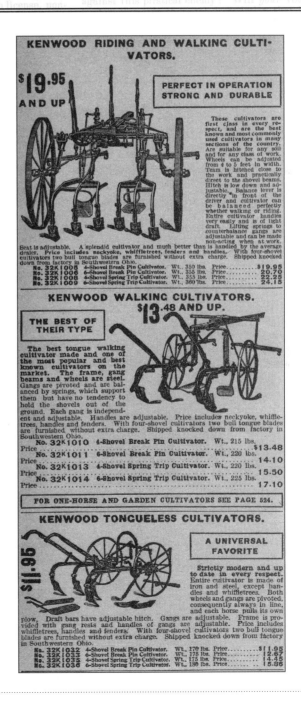

What Eight Million Women Want, by Rheta Childe Dorr, 1910:

Not only in the United States, but in every constitutional country in the world, the movement towards admitting women to full political equality with men is gathering strength. In half a dozen countries women are already completely enfranchised. In England the opposition is seeking terms of surrender. In the United States the stoutest enemy of the movement acknowledges that woman suffrage is ultimately inevitable. The voting strength of the world is about to be doubled, and the new element is absolutely an unknown quantity. Does anyone question that this is the most important political fact the modern world has ever faced?

I have asked you to consider three facts, but in reality they are but three manifestations of one fact, to my mind the most important human fact society has yet encountered. Women have ceased to exist as a subsidiary class in the community. They are no longer wholly dependent, economically, intellectually, and spiritually, on a ruling class of men. They look on life with the eyes of reasoning adults, where once they regarded it as trusting children. Women now form a new social group, separate, and to a degree homogeneous. Already they have evolved a group opinion and a group ideal.

And this brings me to my reason for believing that society will soon be compelled to make a serious survey of the opinions and ideals of women. As far as these have found collective expressions, it is evident that they differ very radically from accepted opinions and ideals of men. As a matter of fact, it is inevitable that this should be so. Back of the differences between the masculine and the feminine ideal lie centuries of different habits, different duties, different ambitions, different opportunities, different rewards.

Women, since society became an organized body, have been engaged in the rearing, as well as the bearing of children. They have made the home, they have cared for the sick, ministered to the aged, and given to the poor. The universal destiny of the mass of women trained them to feed and clothe, to invent, manufacture, build, repair, contrive, conserve, economize. They lived lives of constant service, within the narrow confines of a home. Their labor was given to those they loved, and the reward they looked for was purely a spiritual reward.

A thousand generations of service, unpaid, loving, intimate, must have left the strongest kind of a mental habit in its wake. Women, when they emerged from the seclusion of their homes and began to mingle in the world procession; when they were thrown on their own financial responsibility; found themselves willy-nilly in the ranks of the producers, the wage earners; when the enlightenment of education was no longer denied them; when their responsibilities ceased to be entirely domestic and became somewhat social; when, in a word, women began to think, they naturally thought in human terms. They couldn't have thought otherwise if they had tried.

ENLIST AS LOCAL AGENT
for the Fast-Working, Fast-Selling
Oliver Typewriter!

The battle lines of the Oliver Typewriter forces are forming for another campaign of conquest. The triumphs of 1910—the most brilliant ever achieved by a great sales organization—have served to inspire to more mighty deeds in the coming year.

The roll-call of the Oliver Sales Organization shows over 15,000 men **under arms**—the most magnificent body of trained salesmen in the world.

This Sales Force, great as it is, can not cope with the tremendous increase in business which the popularity of the Oliver Typewriter has created.

Resident Agents Wanted in Every Town and Village

This advertisement is a call for reinforcements,—to enable the Oliver Sales Force to extend its skirmish lines to all sections of the country.

The central idea of our selling system is to have—**everywhere**—a vigilant agent of the Oliver Typewriter constantly **on the ground.** Whether that agent devotes part or all of his time to the sale of the Oliver Typewriter is left to his own discretion.

Teachers, tradesmen, doctors, ministers, lawyers, stenographers, telegraph operators, printers, mechanics—men and women in a multitude of different occupations—can succeed as Local Agents for the Oliver Typewriter. If you have the **will** to take up this work, **we will point out the way.**

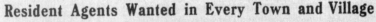

The OLIVER Typewriter
The Standard Visible Writer

The Oliver Typewriter has been breaking records since the day it was placed on the market. **Efficiency** records, **speed** records, endurance records—it has won them in quick succession. It sets the swiftest pace in sales by giving unparalleled **service**.

With **several hundred less parts** than other standard typewriters, its **simplicity, strength, ease of operation, versatility and convenience** are correspondingly **increased**.

"17-Cents-a-Day" Plan
a Wonderful Aid to Agents

This machine, with all of its advantages, all of its time and labor-saving devices, the Local Agent can buy—**and sell**—for Seventeen-Cents-a-Day.

The Oliver Typewriter No. 5—the newest model—the $100 machine—equipped with a brilliant array of new devices and conveniences, actually offered for **pennies**!

This irresistible offer enables the Local Agent to succeed **right from the word "go**!"

Write for Inspiring Book,
"The Rise of the Local Agent"

Read the life stories of men who rose from the Local

Agency ranks to positions of great importance in the Oliver Organization—How one Local Agent is to-day the Typewriter King of Mexico. (Mexican Government reports show that more Oliver Typewriters are imported than all other typewriters combined.)

These inspiring stories will open your eyes to the **big opportunities still open** for ambitious men to carry the Oliver flag, fight for new records and reap the rewards of success.

Send a personal letter to-day while the **Call for Volunteers** is ringing in your ears.

Address Agency Department

THE OLIVER TYPEWRITER CO., 223 Oliver Typewriter Bldg., Chicago

The Crisis, W. E. B. Du Bois, October 1911:

Every argument for Negro suffrage is an argument for women's suffrage; every argument for women's suffrage is an argument for Negro suffrage; both are great moments in democracy. There should be on the part of Negroes absolutely no hesitation whenever and wherever responsible human beings are without voice in their government. The man of Negro blood who hesitates to do them justice is false to his race, his ideals, and his country.

"The Lack in Women's Lives," *The Youth's Companion*, March 1909:

A writer in the *Atlantic Monthly* agrees with the general opinion that the masculine half of mankind has considerably the best of life, but adds that the question, Which of woman's alleged disadvantages has operated the most seriously against her? is one of individual opinion.

For myself, she writes, living as I have done in a village of small size and few diversions, the thing I have resented most, hated most, has been and is now, that it is not possible, that it has never been possible, for me to hike with my menfolk to the village store, or to the shoemaker's shop, or to the railing of the old creek bridge, every evening of my life, *and talk*.

Take these menfolk of mine! In the pauses of gossip and of yarns, old and new, they have more or less thoroughly exploited, take it the year round, every event of importance that has occurred on the face of the earth during their entire lives; and echoes of the past and portents of the future have not been lacking.

Here they have forged their beliefs, and here they have nerved themselves to action. No wonder that I have envied them! Nothing like it ever came into the life of any woman since the world began.

It couldn't, you know; there has not been time. Things at home had to be looked after even if the menfolk did become patriots and heroes.

The babies had to be born and reared and fed; the food had to be prepared, the dishes washed, the clothes made and mended, the house looked after, and all the other odd jobs done that nobody wanted to do. This, you will admit, has taken time, lots of time, all the time of nineteen-twentieths of all the women who have ever lived, someone says. And although I am the last to suggest that it has turned out so badly, either for the woman or the race she has reared, I must yet insist that, as a rule, it has been dull for the woman.

Excerpts from the Kansas Suffrage Association bulletin describing field work in summer, 1912:

I have been traveling for seven weeks in the Seventh District, have gone over 200 miles overland, made many speeches in towns and school houses, and I trust have many converts to my credit.

—Mrs. Lillian Mitchner

A suffrage parade and open air meeting at Holton, June 22nd, was a great success. I have spoken nine times within five days in Jackson County, in all to 800 or 900 people. Now for Troy, Hiawatha, Sabetha, and Seneca.

—Dr. Helen Brewster Owens

Mrs. Baldwin will speak for us on the Fourth. On July first we give a playlet in the airdome. This will be repeated in the surrounding towns in Johnson County. Merchants, grocers, and laundry men, one day in the week, put a suffrage leaflet into each package sent out. A suffragist stays in each store on that day to assist.

—Mrs. Angeline Allison

We left a rainbow flyer and Congressional speech in every mail box between Topeka and Lawrence. We decorated the car with balloons before we started and at every house, we tooted our horn and when the people came running out, we gave them literature.

—Mrs. C. Charles Clark, Rosedale, State Chairman of Finance

House to House Canvass well under way in Riley County, 600 members. Enrolled 58 members after a talk to the Institute June 25th. . . . In two blocks canvassed only one opposed.

—Mrs. Matie Kimball, President, Fifth District

Douglas County is wide awake. North Lawrence has practically completed the canvass. Very few are opposed. Miss Laurenia Shaw and her lieutenants are working among the teachers in the Institute. She is driving all over the county organizing the school districts. We expect soon to give the play *How the Vote Was Won*.

—Dr. Alberta Corbin

"Women's Equity Union, Want Seats on Ferryboats, All Complain of Rules Barring Women from Restaurants after 6 p.m., Resolutions Adopted with Enthusiasm," *The New York Times*, February 10, 1898:

If civil rights cannot be obtained by women through the ballot, they are to have them through organizations by way of the Civic and Political Equality Union of the City of New York, which held its first open meeting at the Tuxedo yesterday afternoon.

The union is not a political organization. That was plainly stated by the President Mrs. Lillie Devereaux Blake, who presided, but there are certain rights which it believes women should have and certain offices she should hold for the general benefit of all women. . . .

There are as many women as men in the metropolis, it was stated, and in some respects . . . women to be of greater importance, representing home and motherhood.

Therefore, the union asks that suitably qualified women be appointed on the Boards of Health and Education, and to the Department of Street Cleaning, that there be no discrimination in the pay of men and women in the city's employ doing equal work; that women students and physicians have equal access, on equal terms with men, in the city hospital, and that women in charge of the city, as patients, paupers, or criminals, be allowed to have a woman physician if they so desire; that women be protected in their civil rights in being entitled to food or shelter in any house of public entertainment by day or night, if they are as respectable as men claiming the same privileges, and, lastly, that provision shall be made for seats in all public conveyances, and that on ferryboats rules shall be enforced to secure seats for women in the portions of the boats nominally reserved for them.

"What we ask in beginning this work," said Miss Harriette Keyser, Chairman of the Industrial Committee of the union, "is that women work shoulder to shoulder; we must put down in our souls that a wrong done to one woman is a wrong done to every woman. We are working for men as well as women when we work for equal wages. The low wages of women are an injury to men, and through them they frequently lose the positions."

The subject of seats in public conveyances, particularly in ferry boats, received much attention. Every woman had a grievance to relate about women who had gone to restaurants or hotels after 6 o'clock and been turned away.

Letter written by Susan B. Anthony to Judge Samuel N. Wood of Kansas, April 21, 1867:

The fact here at the east is, that we cannot meet expenses. Neither the Radical republicans or Old Abolitionists, nor yet the Democrats open their purses, pulpits, or presses to our movement. I think all of them are really glad to have us work but none of them have the courage or the conscience to openly and earnestly and religiously take sides with us.

But no matter, we must work on with such forces as we have at command.

Please make your best and wisest statement of work to be done in Kansas. We will make the strongest possible appeal to get the means to help you make Kansas the first state to give Universal Suffrage.

1917 PROFILE

CIVIL RIGHTS: ANTI-LYNCHING SILENT PROTEST PARADE

Twenty-two-year-old Etta Graham, who had never been south of Coney Island, heard stories all of her life about how colored people were treated down South, and wanted to make a difference.

Life at Home

- Etta Graham, who was born and raised in Harlem, was used to hearing about the injustices suffered by colored people in the South.
- Relatives and neighbors who had escaped the oppression of the South often told stories about beatings and lynchings and humiliations.
- Some had left their homes in Marion, South Carolina, or Tupelo, Mississippi, with little more than the clothes on their backs.
- Etta was proud to live in Harlem, New York, where Negroes had a future.
- For more than a decade, her father had operated a successful store, selling groceries, carriage supplies, and hardware.
- Etta grew up in a spacious five-room apartment above the store and learned early that it took hard work to get ahead.
- Although she had sometimes objected to the discipline of work, she respected her parents and the life they had built.
- But life in Harlem was changing.
- Every day, Southern blacks with little education and less money were arriving in the city and looking for work.
- Most arrived knowing someone who would put them up, but poor people could only care for poorer people for so long.
- Twice, cousins from Mississippi had come to Harlem seeking work, and twice her father had faced the painful task of putting them out when the stay lasted too long.
- Work was plentiful to the skilled, but elusive to those with a third-grade education and experience only in row farming.

Etta Graham worked for civil rights for colored people who lived in the south.

- They deserved better, Etta knew, but felt helpless until the idea of protesting the humiliating conditions of the South was announced at church.
- Everyone was already talking about the riots in East St. Louis, Illinois, where 40 Negroes were killed in mob violence and 6,000 black families were driven from their homes.
- The conflict was over jobs; hungry Negroes eager for any job were willing to work for lower wages than whites, igniting a race riot.
- In Etta's mind, a race riot was the same as an individual lynching; both involved white people taking the law into their own hands.
  - Maybe that was why she was so captivated by the minister's call for a mass demonstration.
  - The plan was brilliant in its simplicity: a silent protest parade of Negroes through the heart of Manhattan to condemn the injustice of racism, Jim Crow laws, and most of all, lynching.
  - No shouting, no fighting, no words—only protest signs.
  - Etta was intrigued by the boldness of the plan even as she fretted over how white New York might react.
  - Would white troublemakers try to disrupt the silent protest? Could Harlem's Negroes contain themselves and not say a word? Would anybody have the courage to show up on a Saturday afternoon after working all morning?
  - Fear troubled Etta's sleep all week.

"Great Results from Hard Beginnings"

BOARD OF NATIONAL MISSIONS
Of the Presbyterian Church in the U. S. A.
DIVISION OF MISSIONS FOR COLORED PEOPLE
507-511 Bessemer Building
Pittsburgh, Pa.

Life at Work

- Marching on a Saturday meant that she would have to ask permission from her father, but even that was worth the risk.
- The National Association for the Advancement of Colored People had organized the event through New York's black churches in response to the riots in East St. Louis, Illinois.
- They envisioned it as the nation's largest organized demonstration by black Americans in U.S. history.
- By 1 p.m. on a warm Saturday in July, everyone had assembled at Fifty-ninth and Fifth.
- The ministers had decided that the 800 assembled children would lead the parade.
- They were followed by several thousand Negro women, who created a sea of white with their finest Sunday outfits.
- The third section of the silent march was composed of men.
- Along the parade route, another 20,000 Negroes stood in solidarity.
- The silence was profound.
- Before the march of 8,000 people was on the move, Etta's heart was pounding; what if the police attacked the parade? What if riots broke out?
- Marching for her race was frightening and exciting at the same time.
- Banners were everywhere.
- One woman displayed a banner showing a Negro woman kneeling before President Woodrow Wilson, appealing for him to bring democracy to America before carrying it to Europe.
- Etta thought it spoke volumes to a nation at war, but the police quickly declared it objectionable and organizers were forced to withdraw it.

- At the head of the march, a banner read, "Your Hands Are Full of Blood," referring to the racial violence in East St. Louis.
- Etta was proud to hold one end of a sign reading, "We Are Maligned as Lazy, and Murdered When We Work," which also referred to the cause of the East St. Louis riots: white resentment over black employment.
- In her heart, she knew that she would not be there but for the urging of her pastor, Rev. Charles D. Martin.
- Rev. Martin, like black preachers across New York, had called upon congregations to fight against lynching with a silent protest march up Fifth Avenue, a place Etta had only been once before.
- In all, more than 100 ministers, black civic clubs, and fraternal organizations called upon their members to join the protest.
- Rev. Martin talked about the hundreds of lynchings in the South, and the Jim Crow laws that prevented blacks from voting and using parks, libraries, and public transportation.
- But most of all, he discussed the daily humiliations suffered by every Southern Negro, and then asserted, "We must march because we deem it to be a *crime to be silent* in the face of such barbaric acts."
- She knew from talking to her Southern cousins that she could not change the South, but she could add her voice, even a silent one, to protest injustice.
- Suddenly, just before the march began, her whole body grew calm; only after her fear began to dissipate did she begin to realize that she was not marching as a member of a church, but as the representative of a whole race of people.
- So in silence she marched until she reached Twenty-third Street and the parade dispersed, when some of the protestors permitted themselves a few cheers.

Life in the Community: Harlem, New York

- The settlement of Harlem dated to 1658 and the founding of New York as a Dutch Colony.
- Initially, the land was populated by farmers.
- By the 1830s, the role of farming was diminishing when a railroad line was built linking Harlem with Manhattan's Park Avenue, spurring development.
- As New York City's population grew in the 1880s and transportation became more efficient, the development of Harlem became inevitable.
- Speculators built quality row houses for upper and middle class purchasers.
- In the 1890s, most of the buyers in Harlem were American-born white Protestants with first-generation immigrant servants from Ireland, Germany, and Sweden.
- The building boom abated in 1893 during the national recession, but resumed at a torrid pace by 1897.
- The development of Harlem into a predominately black community began in the early days of the twentieth century when an oversupply of housing stock led landlords to begin advertising for African American tenants.
- A typical sign read, "Apartments to Let. 3 or 4 Rooms with Improvements For Respectable Colored Families Only."
- By 1914, 50,000 blacks lived in Harlem.
- Many of the newcomers arrived from the South where Jim Crow laws, the sharecropper system, and lynching made life unbearable.
- Many found greater tolerance in Harlem, but little opportunity for economic advancement, which was one of the reasons the National Association for the Advancement of Colored People (NAACP) thought that a silent Negro protest against lynching would be a success.

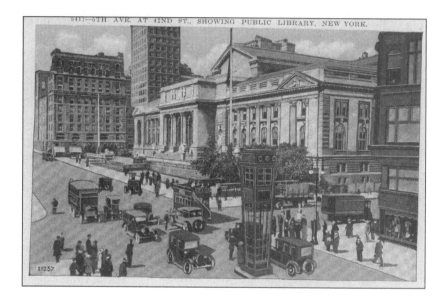

With improved transportation to various parts of Manhattan, the development of Harlem was inevitable.

- During the late 1800s, the lynching of black people in the Southern and border states became an institutionalized way to terrorize.
- Lynching was conceived and carried out more or less spontaneously by a mob who publicly murdered individuals suspected of a crime.
- Most of the lynchings were by hanging or shooting, or both.
- Many involved burning at the stake, maiming, dismemberment, castration, and other brutal methods of physical torture.
- White southerners publicly declared that Negroes could only be controlled by fear.
- *The Chicago Tribune* first began to take systematic account of lynching in 1892.
- That same year, the Tuskegee Institute began to collect and tabulate lynching statistics.
- Beginning in 1912, the NAACP kept an independent record of lynching.
- Lynching peaked in 1892, when 230 persons were lynched; 161 were black and 69 were whites.
- The Southern states accounted for nine-tenths of the lynching.
- Mississippi had the highest incidence of lynching in the nation.
- Most black men were lynched for the crimes of raping white women and murder.
- The racist myth of Negroes' uncontrollable desire to rape white women acquired a strategic position in the defense of the lynching practice.
- Lynching occurred most commonly in the smaller towns and isolated rural communities of the South where people were poor, often illiterate, and lacked power in the community.
- The people who comprised lynch mobs were usually small land holders, tenant farmers, and common laborers whose economic status was very similar to that of the blacks.
- Many Southern politicians and officials supported "lynch-law," and came to power on a platform of race prejudice.
- Because of the tight hold on the courts by local public opinion, lynchers were rarely indicted by a grand jury or sentenced.
- A study of 100 lynchings found that at least one-half were carried out with police officers participating.
- W. E. B. DuBois summed up white motivation, saying "The white South feared—more than Negro dishonesty, ignorance, and incompetency—Negro honesty, knowledge, and efficiency."
- The NAACP was instrumental in awakening the nation to the urgency of stopping lynching.

HISTORICAL SNAPSHOT
1917

- As part of America's entrance into World War I, the United States Army opened its first all-black school for officer training in Des Moines, Iowa
- Clarence Birdseye discovered how to quick-freeze food to retain its freshness
- T. S. Eliot published *Prufrock and Other Observations*, Sinclair Lewis wrote *The Innocents*, and Irving Bacheller's book *The Light in the Clearing* achieved bestseller status
- Congress authorized the sale of War Certificates and liberty loans to support World War I
- C. G. Jung published *Psychology of the Unconscious*; Freud published *Introduction to Psychoanalysis*
- Oscar Micheaux produced and directed the silent film, *The Homesteader*, the first film to be produced and directed by an African American
- Courses in the German language were outlawed as part of the war effort
- Electric voting machines, a Jewish navy chaplain, electric food mixers, and *The Grumps* cartoon all made their first appearance
- Thomas Gainsborough's painting *Blue Boy* sold for $38,800
- The United States Supreme Court ruled that a Louisville, Kentucky law forbidding blacks and whites from living in the same neighborhood was unconstitutional
- A vaccine against Rocky Mountain spotted fever was developed
- Hit songs included, "Go Down Moses," "Goodbye Broadway, Hello France," "Nobody Knows de Trouble I've Seen," and "Hail, Hail, the Gang's All Here"
- The New York Philharmonic celebrated its seventy-fifth anniversary
- Six hundred blacks were commissioned as officers as America entered World War I
- Race riots broke out in East St. Louis, Illinois, stemming from white resentment over the employment of blacks in a local factory; at least 40 blacks were killed during the riots.
- A conflict erupted between black soldiers and white civilians in Houston, Texas; two blacks and 17 whites were killed in the violence
- Emmett J. Scott was made special assistant to the Secretary of War, where he worked for nondiscrimination in the Selective Service Act
- Silent movie premieres included *The Woman God Forgot* directed by Cecil B. DeMille; *Easy Street* and *The Immigrant*, both starring Charlie Chaplin; and *Les Misérables*, directed by Frank Lloyd

Selected Prices, 1917

Bloomers, Woman's	$0.90
Coat, Man's Camel Hair and Wool	$4.85
Deodorant Cream	$0.25
Ice Cream Maker	$3.00
Phonograph	$6.95
Rum, Bacardi, Fifth	$3.20
Telephone Call, Three Minutes, New York to San Francisco	$20.70
Telephone, with Batteries	$11.25
Toilet Paper, Large Roll	$0.07
Vacuum Cleaner	$24.50

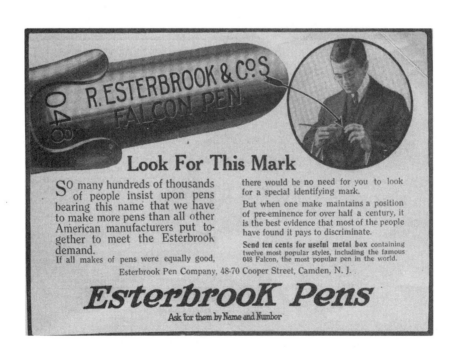

"Open your mouth and shut your eyes,
And I'll give you something to make you wise."

Painted by Edward V. Brewer for Cream of Wheat Co.   Copyright 1917 by Cream of Wheat Co.

"Afro-American Gathering, President McKinley Called Upon to Punish Murderers of Postmaster Baker," *The Washington Post*, March 1, 1898:

Chicago, Feb. 28—Two thousand Afro-Americans, at a mass-meeting held here to-night, entered solemn protests against the recent assassination of Postmaster Frazier B. Baker and his infant child, at Lake City, S.C., and memorialized President McKinley and Congress to take prompt action to punish the murderers. The resolutions adopted recite that effective steps should be taken to put a stop to lynching and proper protection afforded to every citizen, without regard to color.

Among the speakers was Mrs. Ida B. Wells-Barnett, of the Anti-Lynching League.

"The South Carolina Honor," Letter to the Editor from Francis J. Grimke, Pastor, Fifteenth Street Presbyterian Church, *The Washington Post*, March 3, 1898:

I desire to thank you for your two splendid editorials on the recent lynching in Lake City, S.C., and in doing this I feel sure that I express the sentiments of every colored person in the country. Nothing could be stronger, nothing could be more humane and patriotic than your noble utterances. It is only by such plain, outspoken denunciation of wrong that such barbarities, such blots upon our civilization, are to be prevented.

Lynching Timeline

1900

Congressman George White of Pennsylvania, the sole remaining African American in Congress, introduced a bill making lynching a federal crime; "To cheapen Negro life is to cheapen all life. The first murder paves the way for the second until crime ceases to be abhorrent."

Congressman George White's bill was defeated soundly by a majority in Congress.

Three days of racial violence rampaged through New York City's theater district.

1901

African American Congressman George H. White gave up his seat in the U.S. House of Representatives; no blacks were elected to Congress for the next 28 years.

President Theodore Roosevelt invited Booker T. Washington to dine with him at the White House, making Washington the first black American to receive such an invitation.

One hundred and five black Americans were lynched.

1902

Eighty-five black Americans were lynched.

1903

W. E. B. DuBois' book, *The Souls of Black Folk*, was published, which called for action on behalf of the rights of blacks.

Eighty-four black Americans were lynched.

1904

Educator Mary McCleod Bethune founded a college in Daytona Beach, Florida, known today as Bethune-Cookman College.

Seventy-six black Americans were known to have been lynched.

1905

African American intellectuals and activists, led by W. E. B. DuBois and William Monroe Trotter, began the Niagara Movement, which renounced Booker T. Washington's accommodation policies set forth in his "Atlanta Compromise" speech 10 years earlier.

Fifty-seven black Americans were known to have been lynched.

1906

Black troops in Brownsville, Texas, rioted against segregation; President Theodore Roosevelt discharged three companies of black soldiers involved in the riot.

During a race riot in Atlanta, Georgia, 10 blacks and two whites were killed.

Sixty-two black Americans were lynched.

1908

An unrecorded number of men and women were killed and wounded in a race riot in Springfield, Illinois.

William Howard Taft was elected president.

Eighty-nine black Americans were lynched.

continued

Timeline . . . *(continued)*

1909

The National Association for the Advancement of Colored People (NAACP) was formed on February 12, the centennial of the birth of Lincoln, to promote use of the courts to restore the legal rights of black Americans.

Sixty-nine black Americans were lynched.

1910

The Census of 1910 showed a national population of 93,402,151, of which 9,827,763, or 10.7 percent, were black.

The first issue appeared of *Crisis*, a publication sponsored by the NAACP and edited by W. E. B. DuBois.

Baltimore approved the first city ordinance designating the boundaries of black and white neighborhoods.

Sixty-seven black Americans were lynched.

1911

The National Urban League was organized to help African Americans secure equal employment.

Sixty black Americans were known to have been lynched.

1912

Woodrow Wilson was elected president.

James Weldon Johnson published *The Autobiography of an Ex-Colored Man.*

Sixty-one black Americans were known to have been lynched.

1913

The fiftieth anniversary of the Emancipation Proclamation was celebrated.

Former slave, abolitionist, and freedom fighter Harriet Tubman died.

The Wilson administration began government-wide segregation of work places, rest rooms, and lunch rooms.

Fifty-one black Americans were lynched.

1914

World War I began in Europe.

Fifty-one black Americans were lynched.

1915

Renowned African American spokesman Booker T. Washington died.

Fifty-six black Americans were lynched.

1916

The NAACP launched an anti-lynching crusade.

Fifty black Americans were lynched.

1917

America entered World War I; 370,000 African Americans served in military service.

A bloody race riot erupted in East St. Louis, Illinois, resulting in the deaths of 40 people; 6,000 others were driven from their homes.

Thousands of African Americans marched down Manhattan's Fifth Avenue on July 28 to protest lynching, race riots, and the denial of rights.

continued

Timeline . . . *(continued)*

1917

Riots erupted in Houston, Texas, between black soldiers and white citizens; two blacks and 11 whites were killed; 18 black soldiers were hanged for participation in the riot.

Three thousand men, women, and children camped out overnight in a field to witness an announced lynching in Memphis, Tennessee.

The U.S. Supreme Court struck down the Louisville, Kentucky ordinance mandating segregated neighborhoods, voiding segregation laws in Baltimore, Maryland; Dallas, Texas; Greensboro, North Carolina; Louisville, Kentucky; Norfolk, Virginia; Oklahoma City, Oklahoma; Richmond, Virginia; Roanoke, Virginia; and St. Louis, Missouri.

Thirty-six black Americans were lynched.

"Why Do We March?" Leaflet distributed by black Boy Scouts during the Silent March, July 28, 1917:

We march because by the Grace of God and the force of truth, the dangerous, hampering walls of prejudice and inhuman injustice must fall.

We march because we want to make impossible a repetition of Waco, Memphis, and East St. Louis the conscience of the country, and to bring the murderers of our brothers, sisters, and innocent children to justice.

We march because we deem it a crime to be silent in the face of such barbaric acts.

We march because we are thoroughly opposed to Jim-Crow Cars, Segregation, Discrimination, disenfranchisement, LYNCHING, and the host of evils that are forced on us. It is time that the spirit of Christ should be manifested in the making and execution of laws.

We march because we want our children to live in a better land and enjoy fairer conditions than fallen to our lot.

We march in memory of our butchered dead, the massacre of honest toilers who were removing the reproach of laziness and thriftlessness hurled at the entire race. They died to prove our worthiness to live. They live in spite of death shadowing us and ours. We prosper in the face of the most unwarranted and illegal oppression.

We march because the growing consciousness and solidarity of race, coupled with sorrow and discrimination, have made us one; a union that may never be dissolved in spite of shallow-brained agitators, scheming pundits, and political tricksters who secure a fleeting popularity and uncertain financial support by promoting the disunion of a people who ought to consider themselves one.

WINTON SIX

What Will People Say?

WHAT impression will your new car make? Will you have to do the the talking, and explain to your friends why you bought it? Or will your car speak for itself?

If your new car is a Winton Six, designed and finished to your personal taste, it will command respect and win admiration wherever you drive. It will be good to look at, delightful to ride in, and gratifying to own. The Winton Six is never mistaken for any of the look-alike makes.

The Winton Six is mechanically excellent, of course: it holds the world's lowest repair expense record. And you may write your own guarantee. Consider us at your service.

TWO SIZES
33 - - - $2285
48 - - - $3500

Full information on request. Individual designs gladly submitted.

THE WINTON COMPANY
103 Berea Road   Cleveland

**Signs carried during the
Silent March up Fifth Avenue:**

MOTHER, DO LYNCHERS GO TO HEAVEN?

MAKE AMERICA SAFE FOR DEMOCRACY

INDIA IS ABOLISHING CASTE, IS AMERICA ADOPTING IT?

"Fair Play for the Negro," Letter to the Editor by James E. Shepard, President, National Training School, *The New York Times*, July 7, 1917:

To the Editor of *The New York Times:*

The increasing lynchings of a helpless people both North and South, in many instances for trivial things, are having depressing effects on people who love their country and who are loyal and true to the flag. The courts of the land are in control of the whites, so there is never an excuse for a lynching. All crimes should be justly and severely punished and there need be no fear that any a Negro criminal or supposed criminal will ever escape.

The Negro is asking for a right to live and to hope. I appeal to the righteous sense of the Anglo-Saxon and ask the aid of your great paper to stir up sentiment against lynching, the murder of helpless women and children, and the burning of human beings. The spirit of the Anglo-Saxon is for fair play and that the strong do not unnecessarily oppress the weak. Please arouse this dormant spirit and cause America to awaken so that we work side by side to help make the world a better place in which people can live.

"Federal Agents Assert They Have Evidence of Plot to Incite Negroes," *The New York Times*, April 7, 1917:

BIRMINGHAM, Ala.—With the arrest of a white man and a Negro here late yesterday, federal agents, who have the two men in custody, have announced they have evidence of a movement by German agents to incite Negroes in the South. These agents, the federal authorities say, have worked particularly in Alabama, Louisiana, Georgia, the Carolinas, and Mississippi. Posing as Bible salesmen and ministers of the gospel, federal agents declare, they have urged the Negroes to migrate to Mexico, telling them that special trains will carry them there April 15.

A Negro arrested by federal authorities yesterday at the Birmingham railway station is accused of having made speeches to fellow members of his race, in which he urged them to denounce this government and turn their efforts in behalf of Germany.

"$100,000 for Negro Babies," *The New York Times,* March 20, 1917:

A number of men who had luncheon yesterday at Delmonico's at the invitation of George Foster Peabody, Jacob C. Klinck, Clinton L. Rossiter, Lawrence Smith Butler, and L. Hollingsworth Wood started a campaign to raise $100,000 for equipping the Howard Orphanage at Kings Park., L.I., to care for the dependent children of Negro families who have emigrated from the South in the last year. The meeting was occasioned by the conditions among the Negroes now in this part of the country who answered the call of high wages and came North unprepared for cold weather and incapable of meeting the requirements of living conditions here despite the wages they received.

William J. Doherty, Deputy Commissioner of Charities, said that 150,000 Negroes left the South and came North in 1916, and that suffering was widespread among them. He predicted that 250,000 would come in 1917 if the present wages continued, and pointed out that private agencies were needed to care for the Negroes because the laws prevented public institutions of the city and state from taking charge of persons who had lived in New York for a year.

The New York Age, July 29, 1917:

They marched without uttering one word or making a single gesticulation and protested in respectful silence against the reign of mob law, segregation, "Jim Crowism," and many other indignities to which the race is unnecessarily subjected in the United States.

"The South Blamed for Negro Exodus, Lynching a Big Factor," *The New York Times,* July 2, 1917:

A mass meeting of New York Negroes to discuss the problems created by the wholesale migration from the South in the last year, held yesterday afternoon in the Abyssinian Baptist Church, 240 West 40th Street, showed plainly that Northern Negroes are watching the exodus of their people with deep interest and approval, and that they believe the reason for it is not higher wages in the North, but treatment in the South to which they object. The church was packed to the doors, and the speakers were freely applauded.

Several of the speakers alluded to the extent of Negro migration from the South in the past year. Mr. Powell estimated that 350,000 Negroes had left Georgia, Alabama, Florida, and other Southern states within 10 months, and he placed the economic loss to that region, due to their departure, at $200 million.

In Ocala, Fla., he said, the Rev. A. L. James, a Negro clergyman, found his flock so depleted that he gave up his parish and came to New York. Arriving in Harlem, within two days, he found 12

continued

"The South Blamed for Negro Exodus, Lynching a Big Factor . . ." *(continued)*

families from his flock, and was busy reestablishing his church here.

"This migration," said the Rev. Clayton Powell, pastor of the church, "differs from all others in that it has no visible leader. To say that the Negro is coming North for higher wages is grossly to misinterpret the spirit of the exodus. The Negroes are leaving the South because life to them has been made miserable and unbearable.

"They are tired of being kept out of public parks and libraries, of being deprived of equal educational opportunities for their children, for which they are taxed, of reading signs, "Negroes and dogs not admitted." The men are tired of disenfranchisement, the women are tired of the insults of the white hoodlum, and the race is sick of seeing mobs mutilate and burn unconvicted Negro men. These migrating thousands are not seeking money, but manhood rights. All the people coming here are not poor. If the 350,000 Negroes who have recently left the South were offered $5 a day and free transportation back, not 10 percent of them would return in a whole year. If they were assured that these horrible injustices would be removed, especially the hellish institution of lynching, 80 percent of them would return almost as quickly as they came away."

Fred Moore, editor of *The New York Age*, the Negroes' organ, pointed out that in New York you could see white and Negro children going home from school side by side, under the protection of the same policeman. "There is no race friction in the North," he said. "Who is responsible for race friction in the South? How can white people in the South expect the black people to respect them when they are always drawing the color line? Can the white South expect the black South to stay there forever under these conditions?

"We have been patriotic. We have been faithful. We wanted to fight for our country, but the man in the White House drew the color line on us. The South is in the saddle in Washington. But unless *The New York Times* and the other Northern papers that have spoken for us cry out now to the South and tell them where they are heading, it will be too late for them to save themselves. We have been patient. We have never taught our children to hate the white man, but right now the Southern white child is taught in his own home to hate, not only the Negro, but the Northern white man who wants to give the Negro the square deal. The only people who can stop this emigration are the white people of the South, and they can only stop it in one way: by putting an end to lynching and injustice to our race."

The Talented Tenth, by W. E. B. DuBois, 1903:

The Negro race, like all races, is going to be saved by its exceptional men. The problem of education, then, among Negroes must first of all deal with the Talented Tenth; it is the problem of developing the Best of this race that they may guide the Mass away from the contamination and death of the Worst, in their own and other races. Now the training of men is a difficult and intricate task. Its technique is a matter for educational experts, but its object is the vision of seers. If we make money the object of man-training, we shall develop money-makers but not necessarily men; if we make technical skill the object of education, we may possess artisans but not, in nature, men. Men we shall have only as we make manhood the object of the work of the schools—intelligence, broad sympathy, knowledge of what the world was and is, and of the relation of men to it—this is the curriculum of that Higher Education which must underlie true life. On this foundation we may build bread winning, skill of hand, and quickness of brain, with never a fear lest the child and man mistake the means of living for the object of life.

1913 News Feature

"A Strike and Its Remedies, the Conditions Rebelled Against," *The Outlook*, February 1, 1913:

There is now going on in the city of New York a complicated strike of certain women wage-workers (entirely apart from the strike of workers on men's garments, which involves many thousands, chiefly of men workers), the progress of which will have an important bearing upon many aspects of labor and social legislation. The strike here considered is really three strikes of those who are known in organized labor circles as the "International Ladies' Garment Workers." One is the white goods workers' strike; the second the wrapper and kimono makers' strike; and the third the shirt-waist makers' strike. The shirt-waist strikers, who form one of the three parties in the present general strike in the ladies' garment trade, constitute the same organization that struck a year ago, and about half of the individual waist workers now striking were in the former strike.

What are the reasons for this second strike? What are the abuses or injustices or discomforts to which these garment workers object? What is it they hope to accomplish? What is the attitude of the employers?

One of the strike leaders, a woman of education and independent means who has taken up the work from a profound sense of the need of social justice in the treatment of women wage-workers, has answered these questions for *Outlook* as follows:

"We call it, as far as the wrapper and kimono and white goods workers' strikes are concerned, the strike of children and young girls. It is true that the 14-year age law is not often broken, but I myself have talked with hundreds of girls who have given their age as 15 or 16 and have been at work two or three years. The conditions which have led them to organize are: An uncertain wage; the breaking of the 54-hour law for women (and the nine hours a day for six days a week which the law allows is a tremendously long time for girls of 15 or 16 to be working); the unsanitary conditions of many of the shops; the lack of fire protection; a great discrimination in the giving out of the work, which leads to petty tyrannies and jealousies and special animosities against any of the girls who endeavor to better the conditions. Girls of superior intelligence or executive ability who try to organize complaints are specially sought out and punished in a hundred vague ways upon which it is hard to put one's finger. If such a leader among the girls is at all firm in standing for a raise in wages or against lowering wages, she is immediately discriminated against. She is given work which pays the least, or kept waiting for work, or absolutely dismissed for inadequate reasons, and has no appeal. In spite of the 54-hour law, over and over again in some of the shops these girls are worked from eight o'clock in the morning until eight o'clock at night. In the larger shops the girls do not come in direct contact with the employers, who are often unaware of the rude and obscene language which is used by the bosses, foremen, or examiners towards the girls. The girls who are operators on machines have to pay for their machines themselves out of their wages. I have known of cases where a girl operator had to pay as high as 60 dollars for her machine. Here is a typical example from our records: Sarah A., in this country six months; age 18; earns five dollars per week; works from 7 a.m. to 8 p.m.; has paid $27.00 for her machine; parents in this country, also two brothers and a sister; the brothers' age 27 and 21 years; both working on street as street peddlers. If this girl is discharged from the shop in which she works, it may be very difficult, perhaps impossible, for her to get the machine for which she has paid, or any return on her payments.

"Last week Mr. (Theodore) Roosevelt (former U.S. president and contributing editor to *The Outlook*) made a visit to the district of the strike. Here is the story of one of the girls whom he saw and cross-questioned. She is 17 years old, earning $6.00 a week and supporting her mother and two younger children. She is buying her machine, paying for it a certain rate per week, the weekly installment being deducted from her wages. In order to make her little wage go as far as possible she has been walking to and fro from work to save car-fare. On Sunday she has to do all of her own washing, and very often the washing of the others of the family. Her wages are usually paid only once in two weeks, and are sometimes even then held back, so she has to do what she calls 'lend' money (she means borrow money) or get credit at the butcher shop or grocery store, and 'it makes the shopkeepers very cross' with her. She was always 'in trouble with the store,' she said. She is typical of other little girls who, from the age of 14 and 15, are working away the entire sunshine period of their lives in these dark, prison-like factories, and are carrying burdens that are too heavy even for grown people—worrying about the rest, worrying where food and clothing are to come from. This particular little girl is a Spanish Jewess; she is bent and narrow-shouldered, and she shows that her tender muscles are already being warped out of shape. She is a typical working-girl. You can tell her anywhere.

"In some of the shops the work is done by sections. After a girl gets through basting the lace on a garment she is making, she has to take it to be stitched, and she must have a tag to authorize the stitcher to stitch it for her. In one case that I personally know, the man who supplies this tag was so habitually insulting and obscene in his language to a young girl that she could not stand it, and she found that, by paying a penny to a man who did the stitching, he would stitch it for her without a tag. She preferred to pay a penny of her small wages rather than to submit to insult.

"At present the only means of redress that these girls have is to go from shop to shop seeking some improvement. This accounts for what appears to be a sort of restlessness. They will say, 'Mother, I think if I try this shop things may be better,' and they change and change, and it is always the same. I am asked why the 54-hour law now in existence does not protect these girls from the overwork I mentioned. If they knew about the law, could speak the language, could find out where the proper official was, could make their complaints and wait their turns, redress might be possible. But there are not enough factory inspectors to visit all these factory shops and investigate individual complaints. What is needed, and what the strikers are working for, is an organization in each shop with a grievance board and a chairman who can on their behalf appeal either to the employers or the proper official.

"There are many employers of garment workers in New York City who are encouraging us in every possible way to perfect the organization of unions and to establish these grievance boards, realizing that this establishment of general standards will be of great benefit to them as well as to the workers, and that it will also protect them from the unfair competition of employers who are less scrupulous or less decent. As the employers may be divided into two groups of the scrupulous and unscrupulous, so may the workers also be divided. There are some of the workers against whom, because of ignorance or low moral standards, the better workers need to be protected by a good organization.

"The pathetic situation of some of these workers and their childish groping for improvement, and their inability, because of their life and surroundings, to understand how to better themselves or to appreciate the real spirit of this great movement, is illustrated by an incident that happened during Colonel Roosevelt's visit. One little girl, an Orthodox Jewess, when questioned by the Colonel as to what she hoped to win by the strike, said that as she thought it was wrong to work on Saturday (her Sabbath), she could only make $3.33 a week, and she hoped that after the strike they would let her work on Sunday instead of Saturday so she could make more money, as her mother needed it. The amount she hoped to make per week by this great improvement was $4.00!

"I want to lay emphasis on an important phase of this particular strike. In the form of agreement which we are striving to establish in the shirt-waist makers' strike—the so-called protocol of peace—there is a provision by which the rank and file of the workers as well as the rank and file of the employers in the trade shall 'be brought into court and disciplined for any breaches of faith.' Thus, it is the endeavor of the strike leaders and their advisers to raise the social and economic condition of the whole body, and to subject the workers themselves as well as the employers to discipline. This is not merely—as has sometimes been the case in strikes—a class struggle. It is a social struggle."

1919 Profile

Public Health/Flu Epidemic:
Controlling the Influenza Outbreak

Doctor Edwin Bernard, who always trusted in medicine, felt helpless and discouraged in trying to apply his knowledge to the influenza pandemic.

Life at Home
- This has been the most difficult year of 56-year-old Doctor Edwin Bernard's life.
- When the influenza epidemic hit his hometown of Richmond, Virginia, he never dreamed that hundreds would die within days of taking ill.
- In the last months of 1918, Dr. Bernard attended dozens of funerals of friends and patients for whom he could do little.
- He'd had to post hundreds of signs reading, INFLUENZA All Persons Excepting Physicians and Nurses Are Forbidden UNDER PENALTY OF LAW from Entering or Leaving This House, Without Written Permission from the BOARD OF HEALTH.
- In only four months, the epidemic left an indelible mark on the world.
- Even though Congress had approved a special $1 million fund to enable the U.S. Public Health Service to recruit physicians and nurses to deal with the growing epidemic, nothing slowed the death toll.
- With World War I in full swing, the nation's medical corps were already strained before the epidemic swept through.
- Most frustrating of all, the influenza epidemic of 1918 affected the young and the healthy.
- In the past, the flu season had laid many low but killed only the very young, the very old, or the very sick.
- As health professional Victor Vaughan had said, "This infection, like war, kills the young, vigorous, robust adults. . . . The husky male either made a speedy and rather abrupt recovery or was likely to die."

Dr. Edwin Bernard did his best to control the influenza epidemic.

Holidays were difficult for the hundreds of families affected by the epidemic.

- For Dr. Bernard, the month of October was the saddest and most frightening of his life.
- Not only was he around disease-stricken patients every day, but his 19-year-old son was in the military, where the epidemic was most pronounced.
- It was in the middle of October that he made three decisions: never again to prate about the great achievements of medical science; to humbly admit his ignorance in this case; and finally, to find a way to be better prepared next time.
- Day after day, he visited the makeshift hospital configured at John Marshall High School, where he saw hundreds of sick.
- Every bed was full, but still more patients crowded in, their faces of a bluish hue, and their coughing yielding bloody sputum.
- On his watch, 555 people had died.
- An estimated 675,000 Americans died during the influenza pandemic—more than had died in the Great War.

Of the U.S. soldiers who died in Europe, half of them fell to the influenza virus.

- Of the U.S. soldiers who died in Europe, half of them fell to the influenza virus.
- Worldwide, between 20 million and 40 million people died, making it the most devastating epidemic in recorded world history.
- Known as "Spanish Flu" or "La Grippe," the influenza of 1918-1919 infected one-fifth of the world's population and 28 percent of Americans.
- But in its earliest stages, influenza spreading among men living in close quarters did not particularly alarm public health officials, especially with the war going on.

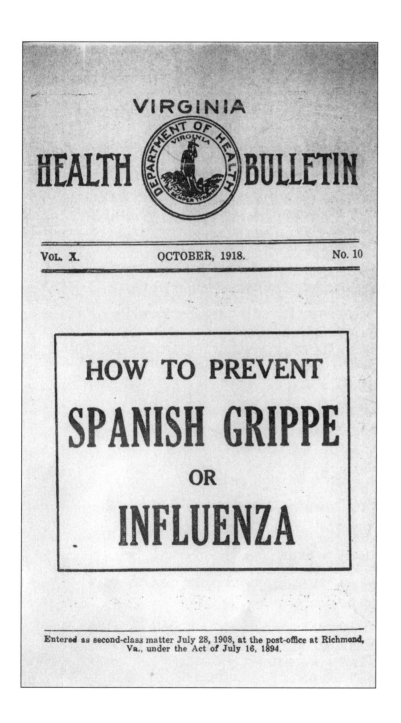

How to Save Yourself and Others From Influenza

(Advice Offered by the Virginia State Board of Health)

The germs of influenza are in the fresh secretions
of the nose and mouth.

Do not attend crowds or large gatherings indoors or outdoors.

Avoid people who are coughing or sneezing.

Keep your mouth shut.

Keep three feet from person talking, or wear a mask made of four layers of gauze to cover the nose and mouth, and tied with tape behind the head.

Always wear a mask when with a patient.

Don't put into your mouth fingers, pencils or other things that don't belong there.

Don't use cup used by others without thoroughly washing it.

When you cough or sneeze, cover your nose or mouth with a handkerchief, or turn your face to the floor.

Wash your hands before eating.

Avoid getting hungry, tired or cold.

Sleep and work in rooms filled with fresh air, but keep the body warm.

Eat plenty of simple, nourishing food and avoid alcoholic drinks.

If you get influenza, go immediately to bed to ward off pneumonia, and stay in bed several days after fever subsides to avoid weakness following grippe.

Life at Work

- It was impossible to escape from the illness.
- Even President Woodrow Wilson suffered from the flu in early 1919 while negotiating the Treaty of Versailles to end World War I.
- Those lucky enough to avoid infection had to deal with the public health ordinances to restrain the spread of the disease: total cleanliness and the wearing of protective face masks, no coughing or spitting, and no gathering in groups.
- Dr. Bernard was at the forefront of a campaign to distribute gauze masks to be worn in public.
- Despite the objections of his wife, he wore the mask even at home and in bed.
- He also sent boxes of the masks to his son, who was stationed at a military base on the West Coast.
- At Dr. Bernard's insistence, Richmond's stores did not hold sales, and funerals were limited to 15 minutes.
- The Virginia State Fair was ordered to close one day after opening.
- Pharmacies were encouraged to remain open at night.
- Even so, the month of October was the worst.
- Bodies piled up in hospitals, converted schools, and morgues.
- The horse-drawn ambulances were too slow and the automobile ambulances too few.
- Then Virginia was confronted with a shortage of coffins, morticians, and gravediggers.
- Lumber yard owners were persuaded to build wooden boxes which were stained black.
- Neighbors complained when the hammering from the lumber yards went on well past midnight.
- At the same time, everyone was looking to the doctors and scientists to create a magic shot capable of ridding the world of the terrible illness.
- During his first shift at the converted John Marshall High School, where 1,000 patients were housed, Dr. Bernard discovered that patients were being given whisky to make them feel better.
- He immediately put a stop to that foolishness.
- He knew that better solutions must be found before the next flu outbreak wiped out an entire generation of young people.
- The influenza pandemic circled the globe, in part because of the mass movements of men in armies and aboard ships in World War I.
- During the summer and fall of 1918, more than one million American soldiers crisscrossed the Atlantic ocean.
- Early health campaigns employed the rhetoric of war to fight the microscopic enemy.

John Marshall High School was converted to a makeshift hospital for 1,000 influenza patients.

- Health studies were made in certain localized regions, looking at the climate, the weather, and the racial composition of cities.
- Humidity was linked to more severe epidemics as it "fosters the dissemination of the bacteria."
- Yet, the origins of the influenza variant were still unknown.
- Speculation was rampant and varied: American swine to Chinese immigrants, to calculated germ warfare perfected by the hated "Huns" of Germany.

Rapid spread of the influenza virus was blamed on the mass movement of men in armies and aboard ships in World War I.

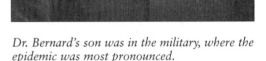

Dr. Bernard's son was in the military, where the epidemic was most pronounced.

- Dr. Bernard had determined that his job was to prevent the spread of the illness.
- He had drafted a city ordinance to outlaw the common drinking cups used in most factories, but more was needed.
- His next target was the common towel used by dozens of workers each week.
- Ventilation in public buildings also needed to be studied.
- There were so many questions: Why were healthy young people the primary victims, and why did some die so quickly while others recovered?
- Like medical scientists across the nation, Dr. Bernard wanted to understand what had caused the flu, how it had spread, and how to stop it if it happened again.

Life in the Community: Richmond, Virginia
- Lacking reliable medical defenses against influenza, Dr. Bernard spent the earliest phase of the outbreak looking for preventative measures.
- Educating the public about an illness that was largely a mystery was a priority.
- But communication was a problem; public gatherings were discouraged and face-to-face meetings avoided.

- The telephone system was overwhelmed by too many distraught callers.
- With the help of government officials, Dr. Bernard worked with the Red Cross, the Post Office, and the Federal Railroad Administration to adorn Virginia and the nation with posters.
- U.S. Surgeon General Rupert Blue ordered the printing and distribution of pamphlets with titles like, "Spanish Influenza," "Three-Day-Fever," and "The Flu."
- The Colgate company pitched in with advertisements that detailed 12 steps to prevent influenza; the recommendations included "chew food carefully and avoid tight clothes and shoes."
- Physical exhaustion was discouraged.
- The Committee of the American Public Health Association advocated legislation to prohibit public coughing and sneezing.
- Washing hands before every meal and paying special attention to general hygiene were encouraged, along with exposure to fresh air.
- Physicians advised rinsing the mouth with everything from chlorinated soda to a mixture of sodium bicarbonate and boric acid.
- Still, whole sectors of the population were left in the dark.
- Rural farm families in southern Virginia relied on folk remedies to fend off or cure the flu.
- These mothers insisted that their children stuff salt up their noses or wear goose grease poultices around their necks.
- In other parts of the country, onions were a potential savior.
- A four-year-old girl from Portland, Oregon, was said to have recovered fully from the flu after her mother dosed her with onion syrup and buried her from head-to-toe for three days in glistening raw onions.
- Still others swore by a shovelful of hot coals sprinkled with sulfur or brown sugar, which filled every room with a noxious blue-green smoke.
- In Sacramento, California, the streets were flushed with foul-smelling sheep dip.
- Clearly, doing anything to fend off influenza was better than sitting idly by, waiting to become sick.
- The influenza virus was profoundly virulent, with a mortality rate of 2.5 percent compared to that of the previous influenza epidemics, which was less than 0.1 percent.
- Many people stricken with the illness died rapid deaths.
- Four women were reported to have played bridge together late into the night; three of them died from influenza by morning.
- Stories circulated of people on their way to work who suddenly developed the flu and died within hours.
- One physician reported that patients with seemingly ordinary influenza would rapidly "develop the most vicious type of pneumonia that has ever been seen," and later, when cyanosis appeared in the patients, it was "simply a struggle for air" until they suffocated.
- The name Spanish Flu came from the early affliction and large mortalities in Spain, where it killed millions in May 1918.

Residents of Richmond were encouraged to stay indoors to avoid contact with infected individuals.

In some cases, only medical students were left to care for the sick.

- It first arrived in Boston in September of 1918 through the port busy with war shipments of machinery and supplies.
- The virus killed almost 2,000 in October of 1918 alone.
- On November 11, 1918, Americans assembling to celebrate the end of the war triggered a resurgence.
- Hospital facilities and staff were taxed to the limit caring for mustard gas victims and those otherwise wounded in the war.
- In some cases, only the medical students were left to care for the sick; in Virginia, third- and fourth-year classes were closed and the students assigned jobs as interns or nurses.

HISTORICAL SNAPSHOT
1919

- Nebraska, Wyoming, and Missouri became the thirty-sixth, thirty-seventh, and thirty-eighth states to ratify prohibition, which went into effect a year later
- The first Miss America, a married mother of two children, was crowned in New York City
- The Chicago White Sox intentionally threw the baseball World Series to satisfy gamblers
- The U.S. Senate and House of Representatives passed the Volstead Prohibition Enforcement Bill to ban the sale or consumption of alcoholic beverages
- Radio Corporation of America (RCA) was created
- The United Parcel Service was incorporated in Oakland, California
- The American Legion was organized in Paris and incorporated by an Act of Congress
- Oregon introduced the first state tax on gasoline at $0.01 per gallon, to be used for road construction
- Congress established Grand Canyon National Park in Arizona
- Boeing flew the first U.S. international airmail from Vancouver, British Columbia, to Seattle, Washington
- Six thousand American men were reported to have married French women
- Les Irvin was the first to jump from an airplane using an Army Air Corp parachute
- The first U.S. air passenger service began
- The first transatlantic flight was accomplished in a U.S. Navy seaplane
- *The New York Daily News*, America's first tabloid, was first published
- The Treaty of Versailles was signed in France, ending the First World War
- Federal troops were required to control race riots in Chicago
- Carnegie Steel's founder, industrialist and philanthropist Andrew Carnegie, died, having given away more than $350 million and funded the building of 2,509 public libraries
- Most of Boston's 1,500-member police force went on strike
- Steel workers at Gary, Indiana, went on strike for 110 days in an unsuccessful attempt to force U.S. Steel to recognize their union
- President Woodrow Wilson collapsed in Pueblo, Colorado, while on a grueling railroad tour of America to sway public opinion in favor of his version of the Treaty of Versailles

Selected Prices, 1919

Bed and Mattress	$19.95
Children's Shoes, White Oxfords	$1.45
Cigarettes, Murad	$0.15
Electric Radiator	$5.75
Hair Color	$0.25
House, Five-Room	$4,200.00
Magazine, *Vanity Fair*	$0.25
Milk, Quart	$0.12
Trolley Fare, Crosstown, Boston	$0.05
Typewriter, Corona	$50.00

"Missouri Congressman Is Victim of the Influenza," *Washington Post*, October 17, 1918:

St. Louis, Oct. 16—Representative Jacob E. Meeker died here this morning of influenza after his marriage at midnight last night to his private secretary.

Representative Meeker, Republican, had served two terms in the House of Representatives from the Tenth (St. Louis) district. He was re-nominated in the August primary and was here in the interest of his re-election when he became seriously ill. He was removed to a hospital last Monday.

His marriage at midnight to Mrs. Alice Redmon, his secretary, followed an announcement by his physician that he could not recover. He was divorced from his first wife and leaves four children.

He was born in Fountain County, Ind., October 7, 1878, attended school in Florida, was graduated from Union Christian College in Merom, Ind., in Theological Seminary. He was also formerly pastor of the Compton Hill Congregational Church here, but later was graduated from a law school and took up the practice of law.

The funeral will be held at Attica, Md., Tuesday.

After receiving news of the death of Representative Meeker of Missouri, the House adjourned yesterday afternoon, and Speaker Clark appointed a committee to attend Mr. Meeker's funeral.

Mr. Meeker was one of the most forceful speakers in the House, and his enmity to the cause of prohibition and to the activity of the Anti-Saloon League caused him to participate in some of the most notable debates which the House has had during the present session of Congress. Educated for the ministry and serving for the time as pastor of the Congregational Church in St. Louis, Mr. Meeker gave up the ministry for politics, and was elected to Congress to succeed Richard Bartholdt.

"The Marshallite Yearbook," published by the senior class of John Marshall High School, which was converted into a hospital during the flu outbreak of 1918:

Literary Society

Like all other school activities, the Literary Society fell victim to the "flu" last fall. But when "King Flu" had been conquered and the regular routine of the school was restored, the great necessity of something to relieve the tension of school work was realized by both students and teachers.

Senior French Society

That same old enemy, the "flu," apparently in league with the Kaiser, could not prevent the Senior French Society from supporting its little French orphans, although regular meetings of the Society had to be discontinued.

Athletics 1918-1919

Notwithstanding the fact that athletics of 1918-19 were greatly handicapped by the "flu" epidemic, John Marshall succeeded in fighting both the deadly "flu" and her school rivals, to a successful finish.

The football team started to work in full blast as soon as school was organized in September. Coach Jones was just getting his team into shape when the army of "flu" germs added Richmond to its list of captured cities. The team was disbanded, and John Marshall High School was immediately turned into a hospital as the last stand against the invaders.

"An Enforced Vacation," an editorial, *The John Marshall Record*, Richmond, Virginia, 1919:

Little did we think, when leaving school on Friday, October 4, that ere we returned, John Marshall High School would be transformed into John Marshall Hospital. So distressing was the epidemic of Spanish influenza in Richmond, that during a period of four weeks, the very rooms of our daily recitations were the scenes of intense suffering, pain, and even death. One night changed everything. The work of removing desks, benches, etc., from the rooms and replacing them with beds, tables, and hospital equipment took place on Monday, October 7. That week was to be very different from any in the history of our school. Instead of the excitement and bustle of school life, the corridors witnessed the grave, anxious faces of trained nurses, physicians, and their many assistants, as they hurriedly tip-toed from room to room. The school wore indeed a grim aspect. . . .

Those four weeks came as a most unexpected vacation to us, but our time was not spent in idleness. Many of us unfortunately had the influenza, generally cognomened the "flu": others succeeded in obtaining temporary positions. Some of our teachers, and even a few pupils, lent a helping hand to the nurses in charge of the hospital. Day and night they labored over the suffering, watching by their bedsides, ministering to their wants, forgetting themselves in eagerness to serve others. Here we should not forget to make mention of the services of our esteemed principal and of our teachers. . . .

"Prophylactic Inoculations against Influenza," Alex G. Brown, Jr., *Virginia Medical Monthly*, 1919:

The need for prophylactic inoculation of a serum or vaccine against influenza and its deadly complication, pneumonitis, is the most urgent of the hour. If the current reports are true, six million people in the world have died of influenza since the epidemic began. Three hundred and fifty thousand people in the United States of America have died of it within the last four months. Certainly no scourge or plague has equaled it in mortality in the same period of time, while probably no disease has ever before in the history of the world shown the worldwide and countless frequency of incidence. The professional and scientific world stands all but overwhelmed by it and apparently powerless to forestall a repetition of it within the present winter or in succeeding years.

The public health officials as well as private practitioners, no doubt, feel the need of some measure or agent which may be used at least in the presence of cases of influenza (or in epidemics) to protect exposed persons from "taking" the influenza. It is not so easy a matter to undertake inoculation of the population in general, even granted that such a serum or vaccine be found. But were it known that there is obtainable a safe prophylactic vaccine or serum, no greater boon could befall the people than to be able to resort to it when exposed to influenza or even when precaution seems to demand its use. So every probable vaccine or serum, guaranteeing no deleterious or harmful effects when used, based upon fairly sound reason and scientific procedure, which may be offered by scientific workers, should receive hearty reception and a just and fair trial.

William Harvey said truly, in his Dedication, in his famous monograph on the circulation of the blood, "all we know is still infinitely less than still remains unknown." Certainly in the face of appearance of a disease, which has swept over the world in a few months leaving millions of its population dead in its wake, Science and scientific men must feel the weakness and insufficiency of scientific knowledge and power.

No note of disapproval should be sounded which would halt or retard the investigation and research for some specific serum or vaccine. In fact, every real investigator should be welcomed with his vaccine or his serum, if produced along recognized scientific lines. Was not Jenner's first experiment in vaccination, by inoculating a boy of eight years with cowpox, and, after his recovery, with smallpox, without his showing any symptoms of smallpox, received by the medical profession with disapproval, and was it not so with the beginning of many of the great advances in medicine? Was not the typhoid vaccination, which, evidently, has done so much to wipe out the incidence of this disease in military camps, all too slow in reaching general adoption by the profession?

Influenza Timeline 1918

March
At Fort Riley, Kansas, an army private reported to the camp hospital complaining of fever, sore throat, and headache; by noon, the camp's hospital had dealt with over 100 ill soldiers, and by week's end, 500 soldiers were sick.

July
Public health officials in Philadelphia issued a bulletin concerning "Spanish influenza."

August
Sailors stationed on board the Receiving Ship at Commonwealth Pier in Boston began reporting to sickbay with the usual symptoms of the grippe; over 60 sailors were reported ill.

September
Dr. Victor Vaughan, Acting Surgeon General of the Army, went to Camp Devens near Boston where "I saw hundreds of young stalwart men in uniform coming into the wards of the hospital. Every bed was full; yet others crowded in. The faces wore a bluish cast; a cough brought up the blood-stained sputum. In the morning, the dead bodies are stacked about the morgue like cordwood."

The Massachusetts Department of Health alerted area newspapers that an epidemic was underway.

U.S. Surgeon General Rupert Blue of the United States Public Health Service dispatched advice to the press on how to handle the influenza epidemic, prescribing bed rest, good food, salts of quinine, and aspirin for the sick.

Lt. Col. Philip Doane, head of the Health and Sanitation Section of the Emergency Fleet Corporation, fueled the rumors that the Germans were to blame for the deadly influenza by saying, "It would be quite easy for one of these German agents to turn loose Spanish influenza germs in a theater or some other place where large numbers of persons are assembled. The Germans have started epidemics in Europe, and there is no reason why they should be particularly gentle with America."

Chicagoan Edward Wagner fell ill in San Francisco, ending speculation among city public health officials that the flu would not even reach the West Coast.

In Philadelphia, after 200,000 people gathered for a Fourth Liberty Loan Drive, the city was confronted by epidemic conditions that required churches, schools, and theaters to close.

Royal Copeland, the Health Commissioner of New York City, announced, "The city is in no danger of an epidemic. No need for our people to worry."

October 2
The *Richmond Virginian* newspaper announced on its front page that the Spanish flu was heading toward Virginia.

Boston registered 202 deaths from influenza; the city canceled its Liberty Bond parades and sporting events, while churches closed and the stock market was put on half-days.

October 3
Petersburg, Virginia, reported 2,000 flu cases; Norfolk, Virginia, closed its schools and the public was warned to avoid hotels, restaurants, and pool halls.

continued

Timeline . . . (continued)

October 4

Obituaries published in the *Richmond Virginian* began listing influenza or pneumonia as the cause of death.

October 5

Portsmouth, Virginia, after experiencing more than 1,000 cases of flu, closed schools, theaters, and dance halls.

October 6

Philadelphia recorded 289 influenza-related deaths in a single day.

October 7

After all the beds in Richmond, Virginia hospitals were filled, John Marshall High School was opened as a hospital to care for the overflow white patients.

Eight hundred fifty-one New Yorkers died of influenza in a single day; in Philadelphia, the city's death rate for one single week was 700 times higher than normal.

The crime rate in Chicago was down 43 percent.

October 8

Health officials closed down the Virginia State Fair; telephone lines were jammed by excessive calling.

October 9

Richmond health officials reported 3,500 cases of the flu.

Reports grew of outbreaks in Southwest Virginia; medical students from the Medical College of Virginia were dispatched to the rural areas of the state where doctors were few.

October 10

The head of Richmond's emergency flu work was stricken.

Weekend parties, spitting in public, and neighborly visits were banned.

October 14

Officials reported 15,000 cases in Richmond, and 200,000 statewide.

The death toll in Richmond reached 800.

October 18

Richmond health officials predicted the end of the epidemic.

October 19

Dr. C. Y. White announced in Philadelphia that he had developed a vaccine to prevent influenza; more than 10,000 complete series of inoculations were delivered to the Philadelphia Board of Health.

October 24

Richmond reported a death rate of 88 people per 1,000.

October 31

Despite the objections of doctors, the schools, churches, and theaters were reopened.

October 1918 turned out to be the deadliest month in the nation's history, as 195,000 died from the deadly virus.

November

The official toll in Richmond, Virginia, stood at 10,571 cases and 555 deaths.

To celebrate the end of World War I, 30,000 San Franciscans took to the streets to celebrate; most wore a face mask.

continued

Timeline . . . *(continued)*

November

On November 21, when sirens signaled to San Franciscans that it was safe—and legal—to remove their protective face masks, 2,122 of its citizens had died of influenza.

December

The death toll in Virginia reached 6,000.

Five thousand new cases of influenza were reported in San Francisco.

"'Flu' Crisis Past; Only 7 Die in Day, Closing of Public Meeting Places Not Necessary, Says Doctor Fowler," *Washington Post*, December 20, 1918:

The crest of the recurring Spanish Influenza epidemic in Washington has been reached and there will be no necessity of closing churches, theaters, schools, and other public meeting places. That is the belief of Dr. W. C. Fowler, health officer of the District.

Yesterday's reports of the new cases gave tangible proof of the subsidence of the disease here, as elsewhere. For the 24-hour period ended at noon there were 235 new cases reported. This was a decrease of 127 from the preceding period, and only nine were recorded afterward.

The total number of deaths for the 24 hours was seven, a decrease of nine. This was regarded as one of the best indications that the virulence of the malady was not severe and that there would be no renewal of the epidemic in serious proportions.

Dr. Fowler said last night that constant care must be taken to safeguard the public. He said that he was gratified with the manner in which the citizens cooperated in maintaining precautions already prescribed. His belief was that the danger was past.

SAVE YOURSELF

FROM

DIPHTHERIA	SPANISH GRIPPE	TUBERCULOSIS
SCARLET FEVER	INFLUENZA	MEASLES
SORE THROAT	BAD COLDS	WHOOPING COUGH
MUMPS	MENINGITIS	PNEUMONIA

Follow Two Simple Rules

Which Will Protect You and Others.

RULE 1

Don't put in your mouth fingers, pencils, or anything else that does not belong there, nor use a common drinking cup.

RULE 2

Whenever you cough or sneeze, bow your head or put a handkerchief over your mouth and nose.

The Germs of these Diseases are spread through the secretions of the mouth and nose of sick people and carriers.

"'Flu' Has Now Spread to All Sections of Nation," *Washington Post,* October 10, 1918:

Influenza now has spread to practically every part of the country. Reports yesterday to the Public-Health Service showed the disease is epidemic in many Western and Pacific coast states as well as in almost all regions east of the Mississippi River. It is epidemic at three places in Arizona, in Maryland, in many parts of Arkansas, in Louisiana, Missouri, Mississippi, Nebraska, North Carolina, North Dakota, Ohio, South Dakota, Tennessee, Texas, Vermont, Washington, West Virginia, and many other states. In Mississippi amusement places over the state have been ordered closed and all public gatherings prohibited. Schools have been ordered closed and public gatherings prohibited at Seattle, Bremerton, Pasco, Presser, Sultan, and Port Angeles, Washington.

The disease is reported from many parts of California, while in Texas the malady has been reported from 77 counties with the number of cases varying from 1 to 4,000 in each county. A slight decrease is noted in the number of cases reported in Massachusetts.

The epidemic continues in New Jersey and the public health service announced that a physician has been placed in charge at Perth Amboy in cooperation with the state and local health authorities. Aid was especially needed at this point, it was said, because of the recent explosion.

Camp Funston, Kansas, reported 1,430 new influenza cases yesterday, while Camp Custer, Michigan, reported 1,000, and Camp Taylor, Kentucky, 607. The highest number of pneumonia cases, 370, was reported at Camp Meade, while Camp Custer had 275 new cases and Camp Grant, Illinois, 201.

Medical Report, Richmond, Virginia, 1918:

On admission, most of the early cases were blue as huckleberries. Most of them died. Nearly all were coughing up liquid blood and continued conscious until a short time before death. Another type of case became totally unconscious hours or even days before the end, restless in their coma, with head thrown back, mouth half open, a ghastly pallor of the cyanosed face, purple lips and ears a dreadful sight.

American Medical Association final edition of 1918:

The year 1918 has gone: a year momentous as the termination of the most cruel war in the annals of the human race; a year which marked the end, at least for a time, of man's destruction of man; unfortunately a year in which developed a most fatal infectious disease, causing the death of hundreds of thousands of human beings. Medical science for four and one-half years devoted itself to putting men on the firing line and keeping them there. Now it must turn with its whole might to combating the greatest enemy of all—infectious disease.

Rope-skipping rhyme, 1918:

I had a little bird,
Its name was Enza.
I opened the window,
And in-flu-enza

1920–1929

The decade following the Great War was marked by a new nationalism symbolized by frenzied consumerism. By the early 1920s, urban Americans had begun to define themselves—for their neighbors and for the world—in terms of what they owned. The car was becoming ubiquitous, zooming from 4,000 registered vehicles at the dawn of the century to 1.9 million 20 years later. Radios and telephones were introduced into millions of homes and some young women felt free to dress as they pleased, wear make-up and help select the nation's leaders, thanks to the Nineteenth Amendment allowing women's suffrage. This freedom also brought a reaction: decency societies were formed, membership in the Ku Klux Klan grew and immigration was largely stilled. Simultaneously, aggressive new advertising methods began and were successful. Americans bought and America boomed. With expanded wages and buying power came increased leisure time for recreation, travel and even self-improvement. Although infectious disease was still a killer, an increased emphasis on sanitation, air circulation and early treatment was beginning to chase some of the most feared diseases from the nation's ghettoes.

Following the Great War, America enjoyed a period of great expansion and expectation. The attitude of many Americans was expressed in President Calvin Coolidge's famous remark, "The chief business of the American people is business." The role of the federal government remained small during this period and federal expenditures actually declined following the war effort. Harry Donaldson's song "How Ya Gonna Keep 'Em Down on the Farm after They've Seen Paree?" described another basic shift in American society. The 1920 census reported that more than 509 percent of the population—54 million people—lived in urban areas. The move to the cities was the result of changed expectations, increased industrialization, and migration of millions of Southern blacks to the urban North.

The availability of electricity expanded the universe to goods that could be manufactured and sold. The expanded use of radios, electric lights, telephones, and powered vacuum cleaners was possible for the first time, and they quickly became essential household items. Construction boomed as—for the first time—half of all Americans now lived in urban areas. Industry, too, benefited from the wider use of electric power. At the turn of the century, electricity ran only five percent of all machinery, and by 1925, 73 percent. Large-scale electric power also made possible electrolytic processes in the rapidly developing heavy chemical industry. With increasing sophistication came higher costs; wages for skilled workers continued to rise during the 1920s, putting further distance between the blue-collar worker and the emerging middle class.

Following the war years, women who had worked in men's jobs in the late 'teens usually remained in the work force, although at lower wages. Women, now allowed to vote nationally, were also encouraged to consider college and options other than marriage. Average family earnings increased slightly during the first half of the period, while prices and hours worked actually declined. The 48-hour week became standard, providing more leisure time. At least 40 million people went to the movies each week, and college football became a national obsession.

Unlike previous decades, national prosperity was not fueled by the cheap labor of new immigrants, but by increased factory efficiencies, innovation, and more sophisticated methods of managing time and materials. Starting in the 'teens, the flow of new immigrants began to slow, culminating in the restrictive immigration legislation of 1924 when new workers from Europe were reduced to a trickle. The efforts were largely designed to protect the wages of American workers— many of whom were only one generation from their native land. As a result, wages for unskilled labor remained stable; union membership declined and strikes, on average, decreased. American exports more than doubled during the decade and heavy imports of European goods virtually halted, a reversal of the Progressive Movement's flirtation with free trade.

These national shifts were not without powerful resistance. A bill was proposed in Utah to imprison any woman who wore her skirt higher than three inches above her ankle. Cigarette consumption reached 43 billion annually, despite smoking being illegal in 14 states and the threat of expulsion from college if caught with a cigarette. The Hays Commission, limiting sexual material in silent films, was created to prevent "loose" morals, and the membership of the KKK expanded to repress Catholics, Jews, open immigration, makeup on women, and the prospect of unrelenting change.

The decade ushered in Trojan contraceptives, the Pitney Bowes postage meter, the Baby Ruth candy bar, Wise potato chips, Drano, self-winding watches, State Farm Mutual auto insurance, Kleenex, and the Macy's Thanksgiving Day Parade down Central Park West in New York. Despite a growing middle class, the share of disposable income going to the top five percent of the population continued to increase. Fifty percent of the people, by one estimate, still lived in poverty. Coal and textile workers, Southern farmers, unorganized labor, single women, the elderly, and most blacks were excluded from the economic giddiness of the period.

In 1929, America appeared to be in an era of unending prosperity. U.S. goods and services reached all-time highs. Industrial production rose 50 percent during the decade as the concepts of mass production were refined and broadly applied. The sale of electrical appliances from radios to refrigerators skyrocketed. Consumers were able to purchase newly produced goods through the extended use of credit. Debt accumulated. By 1930, personal debt had increased to one-third of personal wealth. The nightmare on Wall Street in October 1929 brought an end to the economic festivities, setting the stage for a more proactive government and an increasingly cautious worker.

1921 Profile

Reproductive Rights: Distribution of Birth Control Literature

The issue of birth control came with the territory for Dr. Henry Boekholt, whose frightened patients begged him to teach them about birth control.

Life at Home

- Henry Boekholt never viewed himself as a radical or an activist.
- He didn't even like to speak in public.
- He was what he was—a simple country doctor who loved to care for the people of his community.
- Since he was a small boy, he had known he would follow in his father's and grandfather's footsteps and become a doctor.
- In Hopatcong, New Jersey, there had been a Dr. Boekholt as far back as anyone could remember.
- Like others in the town, his Dutch ancestors helped settle the area, established the Dutch Reform Church, and shared their love of winter activities such as ice skating and sleigh riding.
- When he married a fourth-generation German 23 years earlier, she was the first non-Hollander in the family since the Boekholts came to America in 1755.
- After the first three years of marriage, he knew she had won family approval when his grandmother pulled him aside and said, "She works like a Dutch woman."
- Everyone in the community had sought help from him at some stage of their lives.
- Now the town was divided concerning his fitness as a doctor.
- The trouble began when he started talking about birth control to some of his patients, mostly farm women who begged for contraceptive information.
- At 48, Henry had seen it all, but increasingly he was troubled by tragedies he could not even describe to his father.

Dr. Boekholt fought for women's right to birth control.

- The women under his care who died in childbirth always haunted his sleep, especially those who were ill-prepared or simply exhausted by too many births.
- He knew that in a country community, birth control was considered to be unnatural.
- Some others believed birth control to be degrading to mental health, and injurious to both the husband and wife in their physical interactions.
- In medical school, he had been taught that married couples who used birth control were being selfish in choosing to limit their family size.
- Moreover, they were choosing to enjoy sexual pleasure over domestic fulfillment.
- For 30 years, he had lived by that doctrine; after all, it was his job to treat his patients' illnesses, not tell them how to live their lives.

Dr. Boekholt's daughter considered herself a modern woman.

- It was hard enough to get his wife and three children to pay attention to his wishes, especially his 16-year-old daughter, who was striving to be a "modern" woman.
- But when a 33-year-old woman who had almost died during the birth of her fifth child begged for help, he listened.
- She was terrified of becoming pregnant again, but she knew that her husband would not agree to using male contraceptives.
- For days he wondered if teaching her preventive, self-help techniques was acceptable.
- His father and grandfather learned from hard-earned experience that self-help medicine was not the mission of doctors.
- Besides, Henry was still unsure that birth control was an appropriate topic to discuss; who was he to tell women when they had borne "enough" children?
- Since 1873, a federal law known as the Comstock Act had forbidden the distribution of birth control information as an "obscene" act.
- Dozens of arrests had been made in enforcing the law, although the courts appeared to say that the distribution of birth control information was permitted for professionals such as doctors.
- To make matters more confusing, the world of birth control was dominated by radical feminists like Margaret Sanger, who were always getting arrested, and self-taught midwives, who preached practices straight out of the Middle Ages.
- And there was always the loud and dominating voice of the Catholic Church, which condemned any limitation on the size of the family.
- Henry no longer believed that birth control was a straight path to sterility, amnesia, and insanity, and had to admit that the Birth Control League's pamphlet on the female contraceptive method was the best he had ever seen.
- But jumping into the complex world of women's reproductive rights meant wallowing in the non-professional world of the lower classes, a place he did not wish to go.
- And intuitively he knew that once he opened the door to birth control, its neighbor was sure to be abortion, a topic he clearly did not wish to broach.

Life at Work

- The 33-year-old woman's name was Hilda.
- She was exhausted from raising stair-step children and convinced she would die in childbirth if she became pregnant again.
- Complications had made childbirth difficult last time, resulting in hemorrhaging, swelling, depression; too little money for food and too little time to care for the other children had not helped.
- Henry Boekholt was not convinced that this anemic, frightened mother of five would survive another pregnancy, either.
- The experience became very personal when Hilda said, "Your wife knows how to stop the babies; why can't I?"
- And he knew she was not alone in her fears.
- Statistically, the United States ranked seventeenth in the world in the care and treatment it provided to women in childbirth.
- According to the Children's Bureau of the Department of Child Labor, 23,000 women had died in childbirth in the United States the year before.
- Every year, 250,000 babies under the age of one year died in the United States.
- This level of mortality for both mothers and babies had been called "startling and disgraceful" by the U.S. House Committee on Interstate and Foreign Commerce, which had investigated the issue.
- Its report said that the majority of women could be saved if the federal government would aid the state and local authorities in giving instruction and treatment to these women before and after birth.
- Dr. J. Whitridge Williams, obstetrician in chief at John Hopkins University, Baltimore, told *The New York Times* that at least 75 percent of the women who died in childbirth could be saved.
- Henry earnestly believed that half of the women he had lost could have been helped with birth control information, better prenatal care, and more family support.
- Apparently, among many of his patients, the creating of a child took two, but the raising only one.
- Studies showed that 80 percent of the women in rural areas like his received no training or care before the birth of a child.
- Many did not have trained care during the period of confinement following childbirth.
- Yet, every time a politician approached the subject of increased funding for maternity care, he was branded as socialistic.
- During 1921, Congress had taken the first steps toward better care of women of child-bearing age, with a $1.4 million allocation to work with individual states to promote the "care of maternity and infancy," including infant hygiene.
- The original request was $4 million from the Children's Bureau.
- National organizations such as the General Federation of Women's Clubs, the Council of Jewish Women, the Continental Congress of the Daughters of the American Revolution, the National Organization for Public Health Nurses, as well as the governors of 34 states had endorsed the educational effort for women and their children.
- In a report to Congress, the House Interstate and Foreign Commerce Committee said, "During the past 20 years, the typhoid rate has been reduced more than 50 percent, the tuberculosis rate has been remarkably reduced, the diphtheria rate has been reduced more than one-half, smallpox has been nearly wiped out, but there has been no reduction in maternal deaths."

Many children were born to mothers who were terrified to go through another pregnancy.

- According to the report, "nearly one-half of infant deaths occur within six weeks of birth and are due chiefly to the condition of the mother and lack of proper care and attention during and following confinement."
- The real problem, Henry believed, was that many physicians still believed birth control to be unnatural and possibly a threat to the race, and that populating the world was an obligation, not a choice.
- So Henry invited Hilda back to his office and explained the reproductive cycle of women and when sexual relations with her husband were safest, told her that female contraceptive devices existed, and gave her a booklet published by a birth control information group.
- He did not anticipate Hilda telling everyone in her neighborhood about the life-saving information he had provided to her.
- Within days, dozens of women of child-bearing age wanted additional information; within a month, he was visited by the town leaders who demanded that he stop "promoting birth control."
- The community did not want a reputation of harboring a radical doctor who would keep people from locating there.
- Henry was stunned by their reaction.
- Then he became angry that the men of Hopatcong, New Jersey, would decide for him and his women patients how he should practice medicine.
- He even grew more determined when he was denounced by name from the pulpit.
- Truly he had crossed a line and there was no going back.

Life in the Community: Hopatcong, New Jersey

- Hopatcong, New Jersey, was settled by Europeans starting in the early 1700s on land traditionally occupied by the Nariticong clan of the Delaware Indian nation, who lived on the shores of Lake Hopatcong.
- In the 1820s, the Morris Company dug a canal that linked the inland community to the Delaware River and thus to prosperity.
- By 1866, the Morris Canal carried almost a million tons of freight, including coal and iron ore.
- In the 1880s, the Central Railroad of New Jersey doomed the slower canal business.
- Hundreds of residents took jobs in the Lake Hopatcong Ice Industry, providing ice blocks to homes as far away as New York City.
- In the 1890s, the community saw the blossoming of Lake Hopatcong as a summer resort, where the wealthy would rent large furnished houses—called cottages—on the water's edge.
- Over time 40 hotels and rooming houses became clustered around the lake, which lured both the wealthy of New York and dozens of vaudeville stars in the summer when most theaters were closed.
- But change hovered over the community following the Great War.
- Agricultural prices were depressed; the Morris Canal was being shut down, and everyday women were wearing make-up and sometimes skirts that didn't reach the floor.
- At the same time, the next phase of the post-suffrage movement was transitioning from voting rights to reproductive rights.
- The idea of a woman's right to control her own body, and especially to control her own reproduction and sexuality, was a radical concept when introduced half a decade earlier.

- Many critics interpreted sexual control to include sexual freedom resulting in both promiscuity and the destruction of morality.
- The movement not only worked to educate women about existing birth control methods, but it also popularized the belief that meaningful freedom for modern women included the right to decide whether they would become mothers, and when.
- During the 1920s, the movement became more professionally directed and less political as the issues of medical health and population control took precedence.
- This transition legitimized the movement while placing sex education and birth control in the background.

For women of the Lake Hopatcong resort community, the post-suffrage movement was transitioning from voting rights to reproductive rights.

HISTORICAL SNAPSHOT
1921

- Congress overrode President Wilson's veto, reactivating the War Finance Corps to aid struggling farmers
- The U.S. Navy ordered the sale of 125 flying boats to encourage commercial aviation
- Milk drivers on strike dumped thousands of gallons of milk on New York City streets
- The Tomb of the Unknown Soldier was dedicated
- The movie *The Sheik*, starring Rudolph Valentino, was released
- The Cherokee Indians asked the U.S. Supreme Court to review their claim to one million acres of land in Texas
- New York City discussed ways to vary work hours to avoid long traffic jams
- The first successful helium dirigible made a test flight in Portsmouth, Virginia
- President Harding freed socialist Eugene Debs and 23 other political prisoners
- Sears, Roebuck President Julius Rosenwald pledged $20 million of his personal fortune to help Sears through hard times
- J. D. Rockefeller pledged $1 million for the relief of Europe's destitute
- Albert Einstein proposed the possibility of measuring the universe
- Airmail service opened between New York and San Francisco
- The U.S. Red Cross reported that 20,000 children died annually in auto accidents
- Warren G. Harding was sworn in as America's twenty-ninth president
- The National Association of the Moving Picture Industry announced its intention to censor U.S. movies
- Junior Achievement, created to encourage business skills in young people, was incorporated
- West Virginia imposed the first state sales tax
- Congress passed the Emergency Quota Act, which established national quotas for immigrants entering the United States
- Race riots erupted in Tulsa, Oklahoma, with 85 people killed
- U.S. Army Air Service pilots bombed the captured German battleship *Ostfriesland* to demonstrate the effectiveness of aerial bombing on warships
- Italian anarchists Nicola Sacco and Bartolomeo Vanzetti were convicted for the May 5, 1920 killing of a paymaster and guard at a shoe factory in South Braintree, Massachusetts
- Adolf Hitler became the president of the National Socialist German Workers' Party
- Franklin D. Roosevelt was stricken with polio at age 39 while at his summer home on the Canadian island of Campobello
- The United States, which had never ratified the Versailles Treaty ending World War I, finally signed a peace treaty with Germany
- The baseball World Series was broadcast on radio for the first time

Selected Prices, 1921

Alarm Clock	$2.50
Bathing Suit, Men's	$5.00
Bathtub	$29.95
Carpet Sweeper, Bissell	$5.00
Corselet and Brassiere	$3.00
Crib	$17.50
Hair Remover, Neet	$0.50
Hat, Women's Silk	$13.75
Motor Yacht	$20,000
Permanent Wave Hairstyle	$15.00

"Humiliating? Well, rather!
—and then I got my Philco!"

Philadelphia Storage Battery Company
Philadelphia

PHILCO DIAMOND GRID **BATTERIES**

There's good health
in this hearty soup!

Luncheon
Dinner
Supper

21 kinds   12 cents a can

Campbell's SOUPS

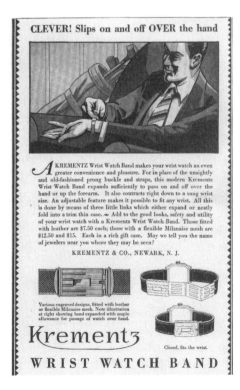

CLEVER! Slips on and off OVER the hand

KREMENTZ & CO., NEWARK, N. J.

Krementz
WRIST WATCH BAND

Women's Rights Timeline

1873

To prohibit the distribution of birth control literature, Congress passed the Comstock Law, officially called the *Act for the Suppression of Trade in, and Circulation of, Obscene Literature and Articles of Immoral Use.*

1900

Two-thirds of all divorce cases were initiated by the wife.

1903

The National Women's Trade Union League was established to advocate for improved wages and working conditions for women.

Marie Curie was awarded the Nobel Prize for physics for her discovery of radioactivity.

1908

The Portia Law School in Boston offered women the opportunity to attend classes in the evening.

1909

Twenty thousand women garment workers struck in New York for better wages and working conditions, forcing over 300 shops to eventually sign union contracts.

1911

American mountain climber Annie Smith Peck ascended Mount Coropuna in Peru at the age of 61; at the summit, she unfurled a banner reading "Votes for Women."

1912

In Atlanta, Georgia, Juliette Gordon Low founded the first American group of Girl Guides, later renamed the Girl Scouts of the USA, to promote self-reliance and resourcefulness.

1913

Alice Paul and Lucy Burns formed the Congressional Union to work toward the passage of a federal amendment to give women the vote.

1914

Margaret Sanger was arrested for publishing information about birth control in her new magazine *Woman Rebel*, which the Post Office banned from the mails.

The Amateur Athletic Union in the United States allowed women for the first time to register for swimming events.

1915

Radical Emma Goldman lectured on "the right of the child not to be born."

1916

Margaret Sanger opened the first U.S. birth control clinic in Brooklyn, New York, which was shut down after 10 days.

1917

Margaret Sanger was tried for disseminating birth control information.

As part of the war effort, women moved into heavy industry jobs in mining, chemical manufacturing, automobile and railway plants, as well as running street cars, conducting trains, directing traffic, and delivering the mail.

Jeannette Rankin of Montana became the first woman elected to the U.S. Congress.

continued

Timeline . . . *(continued)*

1919

Congress passed the federal woman suffrage amendment, originally proposed in 1878, and sent it to the states for ratification.

Barbara Armstrong became the first woman appointed to a tenure-track position at an accredited law school at the University of California at Berkeley.

1920

The Women's Bureau of the Department of Labor was formed to collect information about women in the workforce and safeguard good working conditions for women.

The Nineteenth Amendment to the Constitution granting women the right to vote was signed into law by Secretary of State Bainbridge Colby.

Margaret Sanger published *Woman and the New Race.*

1921

Margaret Sanger organized the American Birth Control League.

Writer Edith Wharton won the Pulitzer Prize for fiction.

FRIGIDAIRE
THE CHOICE OF THE MAJORITY

A new sense of security comes with the use of Frigidaire, the automatic refrigerator. It is the trusted safeguard of baby's health. For Frigidaire eliminates all doubt as to the preservation of food. Milk and cream stay sweet for days. Meats and vegetables keep fresh and wholesome. Pure ice cubes, desserts and salads are frozen as you wish. Visit the nearest Frigidaire display room. Get the facts about low prices and -¦- -¦- convenient terms. Frigidaire Corporation, Dayton, Ohio -¦- -¦-

★ **FRIGIDAIRE** ★
PRODUCT OF GENERAL MOTORS

"Saving Young Mothers," *The New York Times,* August 28, 1921:

It is a startling and disgraceful fact that in this enlightened age and in this prosperous time, more women between the ages of 15 and 45 lose their lives from conditions related to childbirth than any other cause except tuberculosis. If this year it should occur that by some pestilence, such as smallpox, 25,000 persons should die, there would be no holding on the part of the Government to avert the disaster. Yet it is practically certain that 25,000 mothers will lose their lives from causes arising out of motherhood, although we know that at least one-half of these could be saved by advice, care and timely help.

"First Birth Control Clinic to Open Here," *The New York Times*, November 13, 1921:

A birth control clinic, the first in the United States, will be opened in the city next Wednesday, according to an announcement made last night by Mrs. Margaret Sanger at a dinner at the Hotel Plaza in connection with the first American Birth Control Conference, of which Mrs. Sanger is Chairman. . . .

The clinic is at 317 East Tenth Street, where four rooms on the ground floor have been leased for a year. A staff of 40 physicians has been selected, of whom 30 will be in regular attendance and 10 who will act in an advisory capacity. "The little clinic is practically ready to open within the next few days," said Mrs. Sanger.

"The next question will be that of establishing similar clinics in the cities of the various other states of the nation. . . ."

Mrs. Sanger did not give further details in regard to the new clinic, but from Mrs. Anne Kennedy, a member of the committee that arranged the conference, it was learned that the backers of the institution have no fear of the police. "Under a decision of the Court of Appeals," explained Mrs. Kennedy, "Mrs. Sanger was found to have been entirely within the law. The clinic will afford an opportunity to women suffering from a disease, such as tuberculosis, to inform themselves." Mrs. Kennedy further explained that a large staff of doctors was necessary because the plan of those backing the project is to make the clinic immediately a first-class institution for research.

"Birth Control Raid Made by Police on Archbishop's Order," *The New York Times*, November 15, 1921:

The police suppression of the birth control meeting at the Town Hall Sunday night, which culminated in the arrest of two of the speakers after they refused to leave the stage, was brought about at the insistence of Archbishop Patrick J. Hayes of this Roman Catholic Archdiocese.

The first complaint about the meeting, it was admitted yesterday at the archiepiscopal residence in Madison Avenue, was made at the archbishop's direction to Police Headquarters by telephone some time before the meeting, and Msgr. Joseph P. Dineen, the archbishop's secretary, went to the Town Hall before the meeting to meet Police Captain Thomas Donohue of the West Forty-seventh Street Station. Captain Donohue, it was learned, did not know why he had been sent to Town Hall until he met the monsignor there.

Mrs. Margaret Sanger and Mary Winsor, who were arrested at the meeting when they attempted to speak, by the order of Captain Donohue, were discharged yesterday by Magistrate Joseph E. Corrigan for lack of evidence....

The first American Birth Control Conference, which had arranged Sunday's meeting as part of a three-day conference, announced last night that the meeting would be held on Friday night at Bryant Hall, Forty-second and Sixth Avenue. The subject will be "Birth Control: Is It Moral?" and the speakers will be Mrs. Sanger and Harold Cox, a former member of the British Parliament, who had come here from England to speak at the Town Hall.

When Msgr. Dineen was told by reporters yesterday that persons who had attended the meeting had recognized him, he said: "I was present from the start. The archbishop had received an invitation from Mrs. Margaret Sanger to attend the meeting and I went there as his representative. The archbishop is delighted and pleased at the action of the police, as am I, because it was no meeting to be held publicly and without restrictions.

"I need not tell you what the attitude of the Catholic Church is toward so-called birth control. What particularly aroused me, when I entered the hall, was the presence there of four children. I think anyone will admit that a meeting of that character is no place for growing children.

"Decent and clean-minded people of the Catholic Church would not discuss a subject such as birth control in public before children or at all. The police had been informed in advance of the character of the meeting. They were told that this subject—this plan which attacks the very foundation of human society—was again being dragged before the public in a public hall. The presence of these four children at least was a reason for police action."

"Is the New Woman a Traitor to the Race?," a book review of *The Trend of the Race* by Samuel S. Holmes, *The New York Times*, August 28, 1921:

Is the New Woman a traitor to the race? Is this modern development of the status of woman making her a destructive factor, injuring and undermining its very fabric? According to the author of this book, who is a lifelong student of biology and of evolutionary development and is now professor of zoology in the University of California, the question is one which needs very serious consideration. . . .

Getting together a variety of statistics which deal with the biological results of the higher education of woman, her growing economic independence and the wide range of activities from which she can now select her career, Professor Holmes scans all these closely and finds as the result that 50 percent of college women remain unmarried, that the date of marriage among educated women and among those who are economically independent tends to grow later and later and their families smaller and smaller. Here are his conclusions on the biological results of collegiate education for women:

It may be said that about 50 percent of college women remain unmarried. It is apparently true that women of superior intellect and force of character are those who, whether college women or not, are pretty apt to be selected for spinsterhood. They are more likely to win positions which permit them to enjoy the comforts and many of the luxuries of life; they develop other interests which often distract from the appeal of matrimony. In some cases they lose a certain feminine charm, a misfortune that arouses a deep-seated recoil in the opposite sex. There can be no doubt that the race is losing a vast wealth of material for motherhood of the best and most efficient type. Many of the women who are nowadays most prone to sacrifice motherhood to a "career" are just the ones upon whom the obligation of motherhood should rest with the greatest weight. It may be seriously doubted if the growing independence of women, despite its many advantages, is an unmixed blessing. Thus far it has worked to deteriorate the race in the interests of social advancement, a process which is bound to be disastrous in the long run.

"When motherhood becomes the fruit of a deep yearning, not the result of ignorance or accident, its children will become the foundation of a new race."

—Margaret Higgins Sanger, 1920

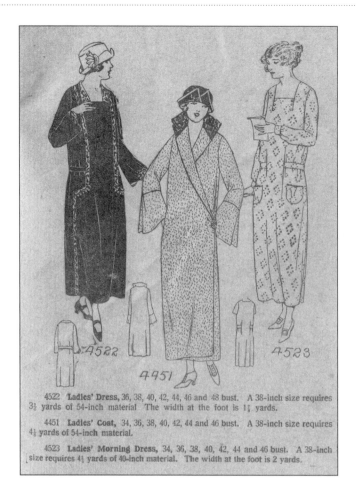

4522 **Ladies' Dress,** 36, 38, 40, 42, 44, 46 and 48 bust. A 38-inch size requires 3½ yards of 54-inch material The width at the foot is 1⅝ yards.

4451 **Ladies' Coat,** 34, 36, 38, 40, 42, 44 and 46 bust. A 38-inch size requires 4⅜ yards of 54-inch material.

4523 **Ladies' Morning Dress,** 34, 36, 38, 40, 42, 44 and 46 bust. A 38-inch size requires 4⅝ yards of 40-inch material. The width at the foot is 2 yards.

"Eugenics Uphold Control of Birth," *The New York Times*, September 27, 1921:

Birth control to prevent the transmission of disease and constitutional defects and the birth of too many children in families of small income where the latest-born are likely to be neglected, was urged by speakers yesterday at the Second International Congress of Eugenics in the American Museum of Natural History. Others deplored the failure of college-bred women to raise more children.

The subject of birth control has been kept in the background, but among the scientists who met yesterday, speaker after speaker attacked the laws forbidding physicians to impart information on this subject, and urged family limitation where economic or other circumstances meant that additional children would have to grow up in sickness or squalor.

Dr. Harriette A. Dilla of Smith College was applauded when she mildly reproached the medical profession for submitting passively to laws of this kind. She said that the denial of scientific information resulted in crimes and tragedies where women, turned away by medical men, resorted to expenditures suggested by despair.

Dr. Irving Fisher of Yale, who was presiding, said that care had been taken to avoid identifying the congress with "protagonists of birth control," but that the subject was one which could not be ignored.

"I think that without question," he said, "birth control is today the great new factor affecting the future character of the human race. Birth control has in its power the determination of the human race."

1923 PROFILE

IMMIGRANT REFORM: AMERICA FOR AMERICANS

Joseph Stellini was certain that if U.S. immigration was not curtailed, Americans like him would be put out of business; his major concern was that immigrants entering the United States could not communicate in English.

Life at Home

- Ever since the Great War ended five years earlier, Joseph Stellini had been on constant alert.
- He knew from experience that the anarchists of Europe would never sleep until America was destroyed and men like him—a small businessman and Rotarian—were put out of business and living behind bars.
- Joseph understood that he had a responsibility to protect America from attack by foreigners, especially immigrants who refused to learn the English language.
- The problem in his own state of New Mexico was bad enough; a recent story in a national magazine said the New Mexico House spent one-fifth of its $7,287.50 personnel budget on translators and interpreters.
- That meant that some of the duly elected members of the Lower House in New Mexico could not transact their legislative business in English.
- What was even worse was how the state's Compact was being violated.
- The Compact under which New Mexico was admitted to the Union specifically required that elected officials "read, write, speak and understand the English language sufficiently well to conduct the duties of the office without the aid of an interpreter."
- Joseph knew in his heart that if he had to hire interpreters to sell tires at his garage, he would go broke.

Joseph Stellini fought against immigrants who refused to learn English.

- His Italian father came to America as a merchant, worked hard and bought a horse stable when carriages were fashionable.
- He was successful because he learned English and became a real American, moving west and creating a business that was capable of putting shoes on horses and tires on cars.
- That tire supply store became one the largest in Santa Fe, serving customers as far away as Farmington, New Mexico.
- A lifelong bachelor, Joseph allowed himself two drinks with friends at the end of the workday, after which he went straight home to handle business, paperwork such as inventory and bookkeeping, and payroll.
- Employing nine men was a big responsibility.
- "A man is not a man," he liked to tell friends "until he has met the pressure of making a payroll week after week."

Life at Work

- Two years earlier, Joseph embarked on a crusade to protect America from anarchists and to make sure the country was preserved for Americans.
- That kind of goal required organization, cooperation and commitment.
- He formed a small group of like-minded businessmen that could mushroom into an army of "right-thinking" citizens prepared to speak out against unfettered immigration.
- The first step was to organize the store owners of Santa Fe based around something simple: No service to anyone who didn't speak English well enough to be understood.
- At Eve's Eats, where the successful merchants of the downtown district gathered six days a week, Joseph threw the idea on the table.
- There was an immediate response: For long enough, America had accepted the world's "tired and poor yearning to be free"; maybe now that the U.S. had fought the Great War and saved Europe from German domination, it was time to take care of Americans.
- After all, they couldn't just let everyone in, or soon there would be no jobs for Americans, especially if the immigrants were willing to work for hardly anything.
- So everyone, except Bill Hammond, who had married a Mexican girl, agreed to put up "Only English Spoken Here" signs in their places of business.
- Joseph told his fellow businessmen they would not lose any business because good Americans would buy more and foreign-speaking immigrants would have a powerful incentive to learn English faster.
- Step two was to organize the service clubs into a single voice dedicated to keeping anarchists away from America's shores.
- Screening out of the lame and criminal should happen on the other side of the ocean, *before* they got to America, so a letter-writing campaign to Congress was organized.
- Nearly everyone agreed that immigration restrictions were necessary, so after Joseph made an impassioned plea for help during a regular luncheon meeting of the city's five key civic clubs, they all agreed to appoint someone to write a letter to their U.S. senators and congressmen demanding stricter immigration laws.
- As a third step, Joseph wanted to put real teeth into the enforcement of immigration laws.
- America needed to protect its borders with a manned patrol if unwanted foreigners, anarchists, communists and illegal immigrants were to be stopped from entering the U.S.

THE

WORLD'S WORK

DEC. 1923   35 CENTS

The Immigration Peril
What The Aliens Are Doing to Us
The March of Events

Published by   DOUBLEDAY, PAGE & CO.   Garden City, N. Y.

During the first 15 years of the 20th century, over 13 million people immigrated to the United States.

- Joseph and his friends began patrolling the land around Santa Fe to keep it free from immigrants coming across the Mexican border.
- Laws alone, he believed, were only a first step; an enlightened, English-speaking citizenry willing to accept responsibility for the implementation of those laws was the political glue that made a democracy function.

Life in the Community: Santa Fe, New Mexico

- The U.S. Census in 1920 placed New Mexico's population at 350,000, of whom half were of Mexican-Spanish stock.
- Joseph believed that most of these immigrants had done a poor job of joining the political life of the democracy that nurtured them.
- Likewise, he had an enormous fear that the 14 million foreign whites who lived in America could easily threaten his way of life.
- The 1920s laws restricting immigration marked a significant change in American policy.
- During the first 15 years of the twentieth century, over 13 million people had come to the United States before America's open door was closed by the dangers and conflicts associated with World War I.
- For some time, public sentiment against unrestricted immigration had been growing.
- Especially among the emerging urban middle class, Americans no longer thought of themselves as having a great internal empire to settle.
- This sentiment expressed itself in a series of measures leading up to the Immigration Quota Laws approved in 1924 aimed at limiting the annual number of immigrants to 150,000, who were proportioned by nationality based on the number of their countrymen and women already in the United States in 1920.
- These laws reduced the stream of immigrants arriving from southern and eastern Europe.
- By drastically limiting immigrant numbers, America curbed one of the great population movements of world history, a process at least two centuries old.
- As immigration slowed to a mere trickle, a small but significant movement of Americans to Europe also was taking place.
- Writers and intellectuals from the United States became dissatisfied with America as a home for art and thought and emigrated to Europe, chiefly to Paris.

The 1924 Immigration Quota laws were aimed at limiting immigrants by nationality.

HISTORICAL SNAPSHOT
1923

- President Warren G. Harding became the first chief executive to file an income tax report
- In a Ku Klux Klan surprise attack on a black residential area of Rosewood, Florida, at least six blacks and two whites died and almost every building in the town was burned
- The U.S. Senate debated the benefits of peyote for the American Indian
- The United States withdrew its last troops from Germany
- Bessie Smith made her first recording: "Down Hearted Blues"
- The burial chamber of King Tutankhamen was unsealed in Egypt
- The first issue of the weekly periodical *TIME* appeared on newsstands
- Montana and Nevada passed the country's first old-age pension grants, which allocated $25 per month
- President Harding died in office
- The Clean Book League of Boston was formed to judge the appropriateness of modern literature, including D. H. Lawrence's *Women in Love*
- The first U.S. dance marathon was held in New York City
- Films featuring sound were shown to a paying audience at the Rialto Theater in New York City
- Insulin became generally available for diabetics
- The Disney Company was founded
- A self-winding watch was patented in Switzerland
- The Teapot Dome scandal resulted in the bribery conviction of Harry F. Sinclair of Mammoth Oil, and Secretary of the Interior Albert B. Fall, the first cabinet member in American history to go to prison
- The play *Runnin' Wild*, which featured a dance known as the Charleston, opened on Broadway
- Goodyear Tire and Rubber Company bought the rights to manufacture Zeppelin dirigibles
- Col. Jacob Schick patented the first electric shaver
- Hyperinflation racked Germany and devalued the Deuschmark so much that 4.2 trillion marks were worth only $1.00
- Adolf Hitler launched his first attempt to seize power with a failed coup in Munich, Germany; while in prison he wrote *Mein Kampf*, subtitled *Four-and-a-Half Years of Struggle against Lies, Stupidity, and Cowardice*
- Nationwide, $250 million was invested in the construction of 300 hotels to accommodate a population in love with the automobile
- Hertz-Drive-Ur-Self, Pan American World Airlines, Welch's grape jelly, the Milky Way candy bar, Sanka coffee and DuPont cellophane all made their first appearance
- Oklahoma Governor Jack Walton was ousted by the state senate for advocating anti-Ku Klux Klan measures

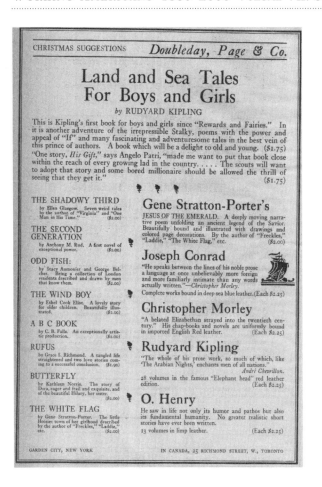

Selected Prices, 1923

Bathtub	$29.95
Cigarette Case, Sterling Silver	$11.72
Coat, Woman's Wool	$12.75
Gas Grill	$15.00
Hat Box	$5.00
Metal Bed, Mattress and Spring	$26.95
Pocket Watch	$63.50
Radio	$14.50
Shirt, Man's	$2.75
Stationery, 24 Sheets and Envelopes	$1.50

L.C.Smith

Ball Bearing THROUGHOUT

L.C. Smith & Bros.

A S long as the typewriter is operated by human hands, errors will occasionally creep into the work it does. One of the many exclusive features of the L.C. Smith Typewriter is the ease and neatness with which corrections can be made.

L.C. SMITH & BROS. TYPEWRITER CO., SYRACUSE, N.Y.—SOLD EVERYWHERE

Swifter — Silenter — STURDIER

A gift that will be treasured always

Modern time is measured from the first Christmas. How appropriate, then, for a Christmas gift is that modern timekeeper, the Hamilton Watch.

From the pocket watch and the strap watch of the business man to the daintiest timepiece that graces a lady's wrist, all Hamiltons have true beauty of design. They also have that accuracy of performance which has earned for the Hamilton its reputation as the watch of railroad accuracy.

HAMILTON WATCH COMPANY, Lancaster, Pa., U.S.A.

Hamilton Watch

"The Watch of Railroad Accuracy"

Hamilton Watches may be had in 14K or filled green or white gold—plain or engraved. $45 and $42 upward.

Just what I wanted—A Kodak

Autographic Kodaks $6.50 up
At your dealer's

Eastman Kodak Company, Rochester, N.Y. *The Kodak City*

U.S. Immigration Timeline

1790

The federal government established a two-year residency requirement for immigrants wishing to become U.S. citizens.

1808

Congress banned the importation of slaves, most of whom were from Africa.

1815

The first great wave of immigration began; five million immigrants came to America between 1815 and 1860.

1818

Liverpool, England, became the most popular port of departure for Irish and British immigrants.

1819

Ships' captains and others were required to keep and submit manifests of immigrants entering the United States.

1820

The U.S. population was 9.6 million; 151,000 new immigrants arrived in America.

1825

Great Britain decreed that it was overpopulated and repealed its laws prohibiting emigration.

Large Norwegian emigration to America began.

1830

Congress passed the Removal Act, which forced Native Americans to settle in Indian Territory west of the Mississippi River.

1846

Crop failures in Europe force tens of thousands of the world's poor to seek refuge in the United States.

The potato famine in Ireland triggered a massive Irish emigration to the United States.

1848

German political refugees emigrated following a political revolution.

1849

The California gold rush ignited mass migration of immigrants from China.

1850

More than 500,000 Irish immigrants had entered the United States in the previous five years.

1860

Poland's economic and political conditions prompted immigrants to move to the United States.

1862

The Homestead Act encouraged naturalization by granting U.S. citizens title to 160 acres.

1864

Congress legalized the importation of contract laborers.

1875

Convicts, prostitutes, and Chinese contract laborers known as "coolies" were barred from entry into the United States.

continued

Timeline . . . *(continued)*

1880

The U.S. population was 50,155,783.

Italy's troubled economy and political climate ignited a migration to America.

1882

Russian anti-Semitic May Laws spurred a dramatic rise in Jewish emigration to the United States.

The federal government firmly established its authority over immigration: Chinese immigration was curtailed; ex-convicts, lunatics, idiots, and those unable to take care of themselves were excluded from entry to the United States.

For the first time, a tax was levied on newly arriving immigrants.

1885

Congress reversed an earlier federal law legalizing the trade in contract labor.

1890

New York was home to as many Germans as Hamburg, Germany.

More than 5.2 million immigrants had entered the country the previous decade.

1891

Congress added health qualifications to immigration restrictions to exclude persons with contagious diseases from entry to the United States.

1892

Ellis Island replaced Castle Garden as America's largest point of entry for immigrants.

1894-1896

To escape Moslem massacres, Armenian Christians emigrated to America.

1897

The wooden buildings on Ellis Island burned to the ground.

1900

The U.S. population was 75,994,575.

More than 3,687,000 immigrants had come to America during the previous decade.

The Ellis Island receiving station reopened with brick and ironwork structures.

Congress established a government in Puerto Rico and granted U.S. citizenship to its island residents.

1903

Epileptics, professional beggars, and anarchists were excluded from entry.

1907

Imbeciles, the feeble-minded, tuberculars, persons with physical or mental defects, and persons under age 16 without parents were excluded from entry to the United States.

An informal agreement between governments clarified the conditions of Japanese immigration to the United States.

1910

The Mexican Revolution spurred thousands of Mexicans to enter the United States seeking employment.

continued

Timeline . . . *(continued)*

1911

Mexicans were exempted from immigrant head taxes to encourage immigration and solve a labor shortage in the Southwest.

1913

California's Alien Land Law declared that immigrants ineligible for citizenship were also ineligible to own agricultural land.

1915

The U.S. Supreme Court ruled that first-generation Japanese were ineligible for citizenship and could not apply for naturalization.

1917

As America entered World War I, anti-German sentiment forced the name change of schools, banks, streets, towns and foods.

All immigrants 16 years of age or older were required to demonstrate their ability to read a 40-word passage in their native language.

Asian immigration was virtually banned.

1914-1918

World War I halted mass migration to the United States.

1921

An annual immigration ceiling was set at 350,000.

Nationality quotas which restricted the flow of immigrants coming from eastern and southern Europe were instituted that limited admissions to 3 percent of each nationality's representation in the 1910 census.

The level of immigration declined.

1924

The National Origins Act reduced the annual immigration ceiling even further, to 165,000.

A revised quota system reduced admissions to 2 percent of each nationality's representation based on the 1890 census.

The U.S. Border Patrol was created.

"The Immigration Dilemma," Letter to the Editor, by Sidney L. Gulick, *The New York Times*, May 10, 1920:

The article on "Our Immigration Dilemma" in the *Sunday Times* on May 2 is not only interesting but unusually full of information. It states the dilemma effectively. Moreover, it urges a highly important suggestion—"the organization of the labor market,"—a step essential to the attainment of a stable and contented social order.

Still, the writer leaves the dilemma where he found it. Suppose the labor market is completely and effectively organized. What would be our attitude toward immigration? Would we then advocate its suspension, as the American Federation of Labor and the American Legion urge? Or would we seek rather to promote the largest possible immigration, as the Interracial Council urges, in the hope of cutting down the high cost of living?

Is it not clear that even a well-organized labor market will still leave us both needing and fearing immigration? Without any new immigration of men who are willing to do the rough manual work on roads, railroads and farms, and in subways, mines and forests, it looks as though the physical basis of our American life would crumble. A serious catastrophe threatens our entire social structure. It is becoming top-heavy. Adequate food, transportation and raw materials are essential if as a nation we are to be kept prosperous, contented and busy. We certainly need immigration.

Yet, on the other hand, the danger of a mighty flood from Europe is immediately before us. None can measure it. The situation in Europe may in two or three years become such that every man and woman will want to get away and come to our shores. An immigration of two or three million a year or even more is by no means unthinkable. Could we take them in and employ them, keeping our own people happy, peaceful and oc-cupied? Could a perfected "organization of the labor market" at all control the situation, so long as immigration is uncontrolled?

The real solution for "Our Immigration Dilemma" is to be found in the "regulation of immigration." We should admit to our shores only so many as we have reason from experience to believe we can wholly Americanize and steadily employ. Each people should be studied and dealt with separately. Only so many should be admitted from each separate people as our developing experience with immigrants of that people shows us is wise. On coming in, do they settle as a rule in the cities, in already congested areas? Or do they go into new regions—into the country? Do they or do they not show themselves eager and able to learn English and to enter wholesomely into our life and share our institutions? Or do they wish to import their diverse political ideas and to upset our institutions and our government? Do they as a rule go into occupations already overcrowded and tend to force down wages and living conditions? Or do they move out into areas where they can secure American standards of wages and will adopt American ideals of life?

Different peoples respond differently to their opportunities here. In the light of our growing knowledge of their response and in the light also of our need for and of our capacity to give them steady employment on an American standard of life, should not their immigration here be regulated? These are the principles advocated by the National Committee for Constructive Immigration Legislation. It advocates neither complete suspension of immigration nor the continuance of the present policy of free immigration. It strikes a medium course and urges the regulation of immigration.

"Coping with Anarchists, Old Law Strengthened by Congress Left Most Immigration Problems Unsolved," *The New York Times*, June 13, 1920:

Immigration was left under wartime regulation by the adjournment of Congress. Problems which the war revealed as hinging on immigration in one way or another were the subject of many hearings by the Immigration Committee of the House, but the shaping of an immigration policy on the lessons set for will be a task for the next session.

Aside from the resolution extending until April 1921—the wartime control of passports—the only piece of legislation of importance bearing on the immigration question was the passage of the bill for the exclusion and expulsion of aliens of anarchist and similar classes. Here a weakness of the old law is remedied, and it is expected to facilitate the getting rid of dangerous aliens.

Under the old law there were two main difficulties: One was to prove that the accused, granting that he was guilty, was a member of an organization suspected of teaching anarchy, and the other that this organization did actually advocate anarchy. As most anarchists deny that they are such, accomplishing their propaganda in secret, most of the cases when brought to trial turned on whether or not it can be established that the accused belonged to an anarchistic organization. Under the law which now goes into effect, specific ways to establish this proof are provided to overcome the previous difficulties, and sabotage is for the first time definitely included as proof of anarchistic belief. . . .

Thus, having in possession, for the purpose of distribution, anarchist literature will by the new statute be proof of guilt. . . .

In framing the new immigration law, the question will come up whether the United States shall provide agents to check out immigrants before they leave Europe with the aim of weeding out anarchists there. Another question that comes up concerns the creation of some system for the registration of immigrants in the years following their entry into the country. The purpose here would be not only to follow up any dangerous aliens, but on the basis of what was learned to devise means to prevent the congregation of aliens in large undigested masses.

53 inches of Turkish cigarette satisfaction
The new size PALL MALLS — *20 for* 30¢

*Try them tonight
for your Luxury Hour*

-that easy chair hour
when every man feels
entitled to life's best

PALL MALL *Specials
New size–plain ends only*
20 for 30¢

*No change in size or price
of* PALL MALL *Regulars*
[*cork tip*]

It is rare indeed that the best things in life can be purchased on a purely bulk value basis. *Superiority usually comes in small packages.* Yet here is the world's finest cigarette, a blend of the rarest and richest Turkish tobaccos, now offered to you at a price that makes it a great *quantity* value as well as a *quality* delight. The *new size* Pall Mall, in the special new package, twenty 2⅝-inch cigarettes at 30c. 53 inches of superlative Turkish cigarette satisfaction. *The new specials come in plain ends only.*

20 *for* 30¢
WEST OF THE ROCKIES 20 *for* 35¢

"The Immigration Peril," by Gino Speranza, *The World's Work*, December 1923:

. . . The basis of the tragedy has its roots in the popular notion or assumption that American institutions are so inherently excellent they fit all peoples. This assumption has been industriously, and at times insidiously encouraged by New Stock "intellectuals." These blatant "friends of freedom" lightly preach that government of and by the people is something that anyone can have and enjoy irrespective of character, intelligence, or special political training and antecedents. These theorists utterly forget that the Constitution of the United States was framed by men of Anglo-Saxon origin for their own government, and it presupposes the long political evolution to which that race has been subjected in the motherland during eight or nine centuries. It presupposes the Anglo-Saxon virtues of fair play. To impose free institutions upon a people which does not possess them is to endanger the social order and bring free institutions into unmerited reproach.

Try to visualize the invasion of "potential American citizens" in a *single year* of "liberal" immigration policy; there rushed in enough Austro-Hungarians to populate 27 towns the size of Portsmouth, N.H.; enough Poles and Jews from Old Russia to fill 18 more towns the size of Lawrence, Kansas; enough Italians to give us a new city of the size of Indianapolis, Indiana, besides four German cities of 10,000 each, six of Scandinavians, one of French, one of Greeks, six of English, five of Irish and nearly two of Scotch and Welch. The balance of that single year's inpouring (merely considering Europe) gave us Belgians, Dutch, Portuguese, Romanians, Swiss, and European Turks to populate six cities of the size of the New Mexican town of Raton, without counting the Serbians, Bulgarians, Montenegrins, and Spaniards. Even under the "Quota Immigration Law," which some assail as being too drastic, there were injected into the fabric of the Republic in 1922 twice as many non-American-minded potential citizens as there are "natives" in New Mexico today, with the added handicap that this mass of cultural alienage represented not one, but 39 different races, nations, and cultures!

Is it unfair to stigmatize as "unreasoning" even a sincere faith which believes that by a mere legal formality after a five-year residence and the simplest of tests, these racial blocks can be transmuted into reliable and useful forces of American democratic self-government? Is it unfair to charge as thoughtless an optimism which assumes that the children of these heterogeneous invaders, born this side of Ellis Island (some, perhaps a week after parents' landing!) can be, on attaining maturity, politically minded as American democrats in any but the most narrow, legalistic sense? Is it an incitement to "race-hatred," as the demagogic race-vote-getters tell you? Or is it not rather an appeal to reason to urge upon the American people the necessity for the serious study of the effects of these huge blocks of racial votes upon American political life?

New Mexico Timeline

1841

Soldiers from Texas invaded New Mexico and claimed all land east of the Rio Grande.

1846

The Mexican-American War began; the United States annexed New Mexico.

1848

The Treaty of Guadalupe Hidalgo ended the Mexican-American War.

1850

New Mexico (which included present-day Arizona, southern Colorado, southern Utah, and southern Nevada) was designated a territory but was denied statehood.

1854

The Gadsden Purchase from Mexico added 45,000 square miles to the territory.

1861

Confederate soldiers invaded New Mexico from Texas.

The Territory of Colorado was created; New Mexico lost its extreme northernmost section to the new territory.

1862

After the Battles of Velarde and Glorieta Pass were fought, the Confederate occupation of New Mexico ended.

1863-1868

Navajo and Apache tribes were relocated to Bosque Redondo; thousands died of disease and starvation.

1863

New Mexico was partitioned in half, and the territory of Arizona was created.

1878

The railroad arrived in New Mexico, opening full-scale trade and migration from the East and Midwest.

1881

Sheriff Pat Garrett shot Billy the Kid in Fort Sumner, New Mexico.

1886

Geronimo surrendered, ending Indian hostilities in the Southwest.

1898

Thomas Edison created the first movie filmed in New Mexico: *Indian Day School*.

1906

The people of New Mexico and Arizona voted on joint statehood; New Mexico voted in favor, Arizona against.

1912

New Mexico was admitted to the Union as the forty-seventh state.

1922

Secretary of State Soledad Chacon and Superintendent of Public Instruction Isabel Eckles were elected as the first women to hold statewide office.

1923

Oil was discovered on the Navajo Reservation.

1928 Profile

Censorship: Purity for Silent Films

Carla Mufson was convinced that impressionable young people should be shielded from the vile thoughts that emitted from Hollywood, so she monitored movies for the Woman's Christian Temperance Union in an effort to edit the films' content.

Life at Home

- The last of 11 children, Carla Mufson almost died at birth.
- Barely breathing when she emerged from the womb, she was set aside while the doctors concentrated on saving the life of her 38-year-old mother.
- From that day forward, everyone agreed, Carla was serious, determined and headstrong.
- Early on she decided that a quality education was more valuable than a farmer-husband, who might harbor a love of intoxicating drink like her father.
- So, despite much discouragement and little support at home, Carla finished 11 years of school, then one year in a secretarial college.
- Although she had never unchained her secret dream of holding a four-year degree from a large university, she remained easy to work with, even on those days when she was convinced that she was smarter than most of the men at the County Bank, where she had worked for 20 years.
- At 48, she knew that attending more college was an opportunity that had passed for her.
- So she spent several afternoons each week counseling scores of promising young girls to pursue a degree in something other than an MRS.
- She had come to believe that even in the liberated 1920s, men still sang most of the songs and women were still expected to hum along in unison.

Carla Mufson monitored movies for the Women's Christian Temperance Union.

Carla and her 10 siblings grew up in the family home in Topeka, Kansas.

Many young women were counseled by Carla to pursue college careers.

- It was while working with the smartest girls in Topeka, Kansas, that she discovered the power of moving picture shows for good and for evil.
- Several very well-raised, bright young ladies would skip tea and conversation to view the latest movie.
- At first, Carla consented to attend the movies as a way to understand this rudeness.
- Her first film experience was *Safety Last,* a wild comedy featuring Harold Lloyd, a lovable country hick with an ingratiating smile and large black glasses.
- Because it was a six-reeler, Carla had enough time to calm her nerves in a darkened room full of strangers and grow accustomed to the flashing titles, organ music, and even the comical plot.
- Halfway through, she realized that she had laughed herself silly.
- What a marvelous experience! How intoxicating an influence on the souls of impressionable girls, she thought!
- That was four years earlier.
- Since then she had feasted on the scenes in *The Hunchback of Notre Dame,* was horrified by the murder of Trina in the movie *Greed,* reveled in the comedy of Charlie Chaplin's *The Gold Rush* and walked indignantly out of a dozen others.
- She was convinced that immoral content in movies should be edited out before young people could see it.
- Besides, if movies in general were not controlled, their romanticized thirst for blood would soon get us into another Great War.
- Many of the patrons she saw in the movies were working class people whose emotions, she felt, were more easily inflamed and who shouldn't be wasting their money anyway.
- After she presented herself to the Woman's Christian Temperance Union and stated her goals, the women there were more than happy for her to monitor movies that came to town.
- They gave her a list of movie guidelines issued by the movie industry, knowing that right-thinking people understood that these rules were just the beginning.
- As a result, Carla began to watch three movies each week, but never with the young ladies she had sworn to protect.
- What would she do and what would her young girls think if an unmarried couple engaged in a passionate embrace?
- It would just be too embarrassing.
- Everyone knew, thanks to the new science, that film images moved straight from the eyes to the brain without interpretation or conscious reflection.
- People simply couldn't help their reactions to movies.

- This was why, in addition to her monitoring activities, she sought out the movie house managers when they came to the bank.
- Someone needed to tell them that morality was more important than money.

Life at Work

- Carla had seen enough movies to know that the alarm bells could not be rung loudly enough, especially with movies like *The Wind*.
- She sat watching it in a darkened theater, surrounded by men and women she had never met, whose voices were stirred to a fevered pitch by an unmarried couple in a kissing embrace that lasted forever.
- Moreover, she was astonished that actress Lillian Gish would act that way, especially when she was driven to commit the sin of murder within the harsh landscape of Texas.
- Without a doubt, the film was capable of unleashing ungovernable spirits among the youth and must be edited if it was to be shown in Kansas again.
- The ladies of The Woman's Christian Temperance Union had been lobbying to restrict the violence and immorality of films for years; obviously, more needed to be done.
- It was a big job; since 1912 nearly 10,000 films had been produced.
- In the 1890s, the Woman's Christian Temperance Union had become interested in the monitoring of movies at the dawn of the fledgling industry.
- Their first goal was the creation of pure motion pictures useful for educational and moral reform, followed quickly by the establishment of an appropriate environment within the nickelodeons and picture palaces.
- They even got an agreement from Thomas Edison that his movie studio would not promote drinking scenes.

Harry Landgon and Joan Crawford in TRAMP, TRAMP, TRAMP, *1926.*

- Mostly, they had to settle for modifying the content of immoral or wrongheaded films distributed in their region.

Lars Hanson and Lillian Gish in THE WIND, *1928.*

- Many fretted that movies were taking the place of the mother as the primary teacher of young children.
- This fear had been vindicated many times.
- After the 1910 Johnson-Jeffries heavyweight fight, in which black boxer Jack Johnson defeated the "Great White Hope," champion Jim Jeffries, race riots erupted all over the United States.
- Immediately, the WCTU noted that "unwonted elation among the more ignorant negroes" caused poor whites to become violent.
- They petitioned Congress to ban films of prize fights; officials in nine states and in scores of racially mixed cities quickly barred prize-fight films.
- By 1912, a federal law banned films featuring a prize fight.
- In 1915 the U.S. Supreme Court ruled that motion pictures could be regulated because they were not art, but instead were created only to make money; thus, the First Amendment did not apply.
- Kansas created a Board of Review shortly thereafter.
- The WCTU also worked community by community in an attempt to convince theater owners not to show unwholesome movies, especially on Sundays, when many children where there.
- In 1922, as a direct result of the reformers' work, the Motion Picture Producers and Distributors Association hired Will Hays, a former Postmaster General, to regulate itself.
- After a short period of elation, the WCTU was soon disappointed because he would not meet their level of purity.
- Many came to believe that the $150,000 annual salary paid to Will Hays was a down payment on his soul.
- In 1925 the National WCTU disbanded the Department of Purity in Literature and Art and formed a Motion Picture Department to get censorship laws passed.
- That's when Carla Mufson became involved in screening movies.
- Though at first it was intimidating to say a movie needed changes, she knew that her work had an impact in both Topeka and a five-state region.
- Because of the high cost of changing movie prints, one state's demand for change often resulted in the distribution of the edited version to the entire region.
- In Kansas, the film reviewers often deleted drinking scenes from movies, making the Kansas WCTU a powerful voice for censorship.
- These deletions also included scenes of white women in physical danger at the hands of villainous, leering Chinamen, German spies, and Mexican assaulters.
- Chastity was paramount and views of miscegenation were to be avoided, as were scenes of black men looking at a woman's figure.
- Nationally, the WCTU was focused on federal regulation, especially when movies with sound were being advertised.
- Without a doubt, every decent woman in America knew that the movie moguls would try to make more money by adding dirty words to their films.
- Movies filled with debauchery were destroying America's image abroad, said President-Elect Herbert Hoover after a Uruguayan editor told him that American movies were a "main obstacle to the proper understanding and esteem between the United States

and the South American countries" because they showed only "cabaret life, the sins of society and crime."

- After all the horrors of World War I, every tool, including movies, should be marshaled toward the cause of international alliances to prevent another devastating war.

Life in the Community: Topeka, Kansas

- The Kansas State Board of Review took an active role in monitoring the moral content of films, forcing movie makers to adapt the film state by state, based on the sensitivities of the state boards.
- After watching the 1920 film *The House of Blindness*, the Kansas board of review demanded that the pivotal scene in which Dora was forced to drink poison be removed.
- As a result, that section of the film wound up on the cutting room floor, although it was untouched in other states.
- Kansas was not alone in its attempt to control the potentially "debasing" new medium; Virginia, Maryland, New York, Pennsylvania and Ohio, as well as approximately 50 cities, had also created boards to review and censor movies.
- Approval guidelines included the review of subtitles, spoken dialogue, songs, other words or sounds, folders, posters and advertising materials to make sure they were "moral and proper."

Al Jolson in THE JAZZ SINGER, *1927.*

The Kansas State Board of Review had the power to remove movie scenes that "corrupted morals."

- When the board viewed films, it was looking for moving picture shows that were "cruel, obscene, indecent or immoral, or such as tend to debase and corrupt morals."
- All films to be shown in the state had to be first passed by a board of three censors.
- This board had the power to remove any scenes that corrupted morals.
- The board also could ban films completely.
- After being reviewed and edited, the film was tagged with a unique serial number that allowed it to be distributed for public showing.
- Penalties for showing unauthorized films ranged from a substantial fine to 30 days in the county jail.
- The State Board of Review met with substantial resistance from the motion picture industry, which was forced to pay for both the initial review and any subsequent edits.
- Motion picture companies spent significant sums lobbying legislators and trying to influence local elections.
- Some movie houses even recruited and then promoted anti-censorship candidates on the big screen itself.
- The first rating system was started in Chicago in 1914, when an official restricted attendance to the movie *The Scarlet Letter* to only persons over the age of 21.
- Even though women in the community supported its showing, the official frankly admitted that he did not know how to explain to his 15-year-old daughter the meaning of the scarlet "A," which was so central to the plot.
- Afterward, movies restricted to those over 21 were issued "pink permits."

Gloria Swanson in QUEEN KELLY, *1928.*

HISTORICAL SNAPSHOT
1928

- The German dirigible *Graf Zeppelin* landed in Lakehurst, New Jersey, on its first commercial flight across the Atlantic
- Future President Herbert Hoover promoted the concept of the "American system of rugged individualism" in a speech at New York's Madison Square Garden
- Three car mergers took place: Chrysler and Dodge; Studebaker and Pierce-Arrow; and Chandler and Cleveland
- The Boston Garden officially opened
- The first successful sound-synchronized animated cartoon, Walt Disney's *Steamboat Willie* starring Mickey Mouse, premiered
- The first issue of *Time* magazine was published, featuring Japanese Emperor Hirohito on its cover
- Peanut butter cracker sandwiches, Rice Krispies, Philco radios, quartz clocks and the Oxford English Dictionary all made their first appearance
- North Carolina Governor O. Max Gardner blamed women's diet fads for the drop in farm prices
- *Bolero* by Maurice Ravel made its debut in Paris
- George Gershwin's musical work *An American in Paris* premiered at Carnegie Hall in New York
- The clip-on tie was created
- Real wages, adjusted for inflation, had increased 33 percent since 1914
- Nationalist Chiang Kai-shek captured Peking, China, from the communists and gained United States recognition
- Aviator Amelia Earhart became the first woman to fly across the Atlantic Ocean from Newfoundland to Wales in about 21 hours
- The first all-talking movie feature, *The Lights of New York,* was released
- Fifteen nations signed the Kellogg-Briand Peace Pact, developed by French Foreign Minister Aristide Briand and U.S. Secretary of State Frank Kellogg; also known as the Pact of Paris, it outlawed war and called for the settlement of disputes through arbitration
- Actress Katharine Hepburn made her stage debut in *The Czarina*
- Scottish bacteriologist Alexander Fleming discovered the curative properties of the mold penicillin
- *My Weekly Reader* magazine made its debut
- Ruth Snyder became the first woman to die in the electric chair

In its first show to feature a black artist, the New Gallery of New York exhibited works byArchibald Motley

- Bell Labs created a way to end the fluttering of the television image
- President Calvin Coolidge gave the Congressional Medal of Honor to aviator Charles Lindbergh

Selected Prices, 1928

Airplane, Single-Engine	$2,000.00
Automobile, Packard Convertible	$4,150.00
Baby's Play Suit	$0.59
Chauffer's Outfit	$78.00
Comforter, Lamb's Wool Filling	$21.00
Hot Water Heater	$55.00
Luggage, Set of Five	$26.95
Maternity Corset	$6.95
Toothpaste, Listerine	$0.25
Tuition and Board at Cornell University, per Year	$1,400.00

Film Industry Timeline

1889

Thomas Edison was commissioned to build the first motion-picture camera, named Kinetograph.

1894

The Edison Corporation established the first motion picture studio, nicknamed the Black Maria, a slang expression for a police van.

The first Kinetoscope parlor opened at 1155 Broadway in New York City, where spectators were charged $0.25 to watch films.

1895

In France, Auguste and Louis Lumière invented the Cinématograph, a combination camera and projector.

1896

The Edison Corporation produced *The Kiss*, the first film ever made of a couple kissing; the short 20-second film, with a close-up of a kiss, was denounced as shocking and pornographic by some early moviegoers and caused the Roman Catholic Church to call for censorship.

1901

With the arrival of electricity, Broadway set out white lights stretching from 13th to 46th Streets in New York City, inspiring the nickname "the Great White Way."

1903

Edison Corporation's Edwin S. Porter directed the first Western, *The Great Train Robbery*, which lasted 12 minutes.

The courts ruled that a film did not have to be copyrighted frame-by-frame, but rather that it could be covered in its entirety by one copyright submission.

1904

The 35 mm film width, and a projection speed of 16 frames per second, were accepted as an industry standard.

1905

In Pittsburgh, the first movie theater opened, named a nickelodeon after the cost of admission, a nickel, and the Greek word for theater, "odeon."

1906

The Keith organization began converting vaudeville theatres into motion picture houses and encouraged parents to send their children there after school was over.

1907

The Saturday Evening Post reported that daily attendance at nickelodeons exceeded two million nationwide.

The Chicago Daily Tribune denounced nickelodeons as firetraps and tawdry corrupters of children.

The first film makers arrived in Los Angeles, which offered a favorable climate and a variety of natural scenery.

Bell and Howell developed a film projection system.

1908

About 9,000 nickelodeons were open across the country.

1909

The New York Times published the first movie review, a report on D. W. Griffith's *Pippa Passes*.

The New York Times coined the term "stars" for prominent movie actors.

continued

Timeline . . . *(continued)*

1909

The Motion Picture Patents Company (MPPC) was formed and became a holding company for all of the patents belonging to the film producers who were members.

The MPPC agreed to submit its films to the Board of Censorship, which had been established by the People's Institute of New York City to head off state and local censorship efforts.

1910

Thomas Edison introduced his kinetophone, which made talkies a reality more than a decade later.

The first movie stunt featured a man jumping from a burning balloon into the Hudson River.

1911

Pennsylvania became the first state to pass a film censorship law.

Credits began to appear at the beginning of motion pictures.

1912

Photoplay debuted, the first magazine for movie fans.

Motion pictures began to move out of nickelodeons and into real theaters as movies became longer, more expensive and featured more stars.

1913

America's first feature-length film dealing with sex was *Traffic in Souls,* a "photo-drama" exposé of white slavery at the turn of the century in New York City.

1914

Charlie Chaplin played the role of the Little Tramp, his most famous character.

Winsor McCay released *Gertie the Dinosaur,* the first animated cartoon.

1915

D. W. Griffith released *The Birth of a Nation,* which introduced the movie techniques of the narrative close-up and the flashback; the film ignited controversy over its depiction of the Civil War and Reconstruction era.

The Bell & Howell 2709 movie camera allowed directors to film close-ups without physically moving the camera.

The Board of Censorship became The National Board of Review.

Movie sex goddess Theda Bara's role as a worldly, predatory woman who stole a married man away from his wife and child in *A Fool There Was* earned her the title of "the wickedest woman in the world."

A Free Ride, the earliest-known silent stag or pornographic film, was released.

1916

Charlie Chaplin signed on with Mutual Studios for an unprecedented $10,000 a week.

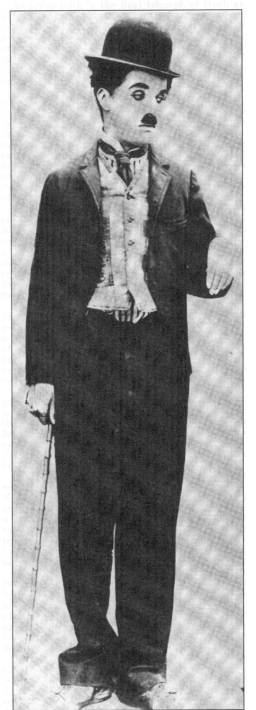

continued

Timeline . . . (continued)

1917

The Lincoln Motion Picture Company, the first African-American-owned studio, was founded.

1919

Charlie Chaplin, D. W. Griffith, Douglas Fairbanks Sr., and Mary Pickford established United Artists in an attempt to control their own work.

Felix the Cat first appeared.

Cecil B. DeMille's film *Male and Female* included a semi-nude scene of actress Gloria Swanson disrobing in preparation for a lavish bath in a sunken tub.

1920

Actress Yvonne Gardelle appeared naked during a Garden of Eden prologue sequence in *The Tree of Knowledge*.

1921

The Sheik, starring Rudolph Valentino, was released.

Charlie Chaplin produced *The Kid*, which featured Jackie Coogan.

Comedian Roscoe "Fatty" Arbuckle was arrested for the alleged rape and murder of 25-year-old actress Virginia Rappe during a wild party in San Francisco, reinforcing the public's image of Hollywood as scandalous.

1922

Hollywood censored itself by creating the Motion Picture Producers and Distributors of America (MPPDA).

Movie director William Desmond Taylor was found murdered in Los Angeles with a bullet in his back; dozens of potential starlets were suspects.

1923

German shepherd Rin Tin Tin became film's first canine star.

Cecil B. DeMille's first version of *The Ten Commandments* featured the largest set ever constructed in movie history up to that time; the "City of the Pharoah" was 120 feet tall and 720 feet wide, with massive Egyptian statuary weighing one million pounds.

The Hollywood sign, spelled HOLLYWOODLAND, was built for $21,000.

1924

Walt Disney created his first cartoon, *Alice's Wonderland*.

1925

Ben-Hur, which cost a record-setting $3.95 million to produce, included a segment featuring rows of bare-breasted flower girls dancing in a pageant procession as they tossed flowers to the crowd lining the street.

The first in-flight movie, a black-and-white silent film titled *The Lost World*, was shown in a WWI converted bomber during a 30-minute flight near London.

1926

Leading man John Barrymore starred in *Don Juan* with Mary Astor and Estelle Taylor, a film that included 127 kisses.

continued

Timeline . . . *(continued)*

1927

Popular vaudevillian Al Jolson marked the end of the silent movie era when he spoke the line: "Wait a minute. Wait a minute. You ain't heard nothing yet!" in *The Jazz Singer*.

A sound-on-film system called Movietone was developed in which the sound track was placed onto the actual film next to the picture frames, rather than on a separate synchronized disc, as in Vitaphone.

Motion picture film became standardized at 24 frames per second.

The Hays Office issued a memorandum, "Don'ts and Be Carefuls," a code of decency telling the studios 11 taboos to avoid, including profanity, "licentious or suggestive nudity," illegal traffic in drugs, any inference of sex perversion, white slavery, miscegenation, sex hygiene and venereal diseases, scenes of actual childbirth, children's sex organs, ridicule of the clergy, and willful offense to any nation, race or creed.

Paramount released a film titled *It* featuring sexy starlet Clara Bow as a lingerie salesgirl, who soon became known as the "It Girl."

1928

Walt Disney introduced *Galloping Gaucho* and *Steamboat Willie*, the first cartoons with sound.

The Academy Awards were awarded for the first time; *Wings* won Best Picture.

"Movies Foster Crime, Canon Chase Charges," *The New York Times*, January 2, 1928:

The motion picture screen for the past 25 years has been a school of crime, according to Canon William S. Chase, who took the affirmative in a debate at the Ingersoll Forum, 113 West Fifty-seventh Street, last night on "Should There Be Federal Supervision of Motion Pictures?" Dr. Wolf Adler upheld the negative.

"Did you notice that in his account of his dreadful crime, Hickman said it was his habit to see motion pictures daily?" Canon Chase asked.

He said the movies were a menace to the children of the world, and to the furtherance of world peace. By representing American life in a false light, he charged that motion pictures aroused the antagonism of other countries and created much ill feeling by portraying foreigners as villains and Americans as heroes.

Because moving pictures are run by interests with the sole purpose of making money, he urged that the government supervise the movies so as to further the best moral and political interests of the public.

Dr. Adler said he had no admiration at all for movies, but he did not believe there should be censorship or supervision, because all censorship was bad.

"If you start censoring motion pictures, you will soon begin regulating literature, the stage and every other activity of life," he said. "The movies do not influence morals for the worst. They merely reflect morals as they are by showing the realities of life. If they are immoral, they are an effect of immorality, not a cause. Federal control will not be of any use because it cannot abolish things as they are."

If the movies have tended to foster warlike tendencies, he continued, it is because they are used by every nation as propaganda against other nations.

Popular Movies:

1927		1928	
The Jazz Singer	Camille	The Last Command	Street Angel
Wings	The Way of All Flesh	The Racket	The Singing Fool
Napoleon	Love	The Crowd	The Mysterious Lady
The King of Kings	The Unknown	Sadie Thompson	The Circus
Flesh and the Devil	The General	Steamboat Willie	The Docks of New York
The Night of Love			

The movies constitute much of the education of many.... Shall this (movie industry) education produce graduates of the type of the 14-year-old murderers, of the Leopold-Loeb super-intellectuals criminal breed, of the flapper who is a potential mother and may reproduce more of the same, of the foreigner, the fool and the traitor who consider the Eighteenth Amendment a joke and laugh at the Stars and Stripes?

—Harriett Pritchard, director of the WCTU Department of Purity in Literature and Art, 1925

We believe mechanically perfect, artistically beautiful, morally clean motion pictures are one of the best-known means of preserving and transmitting to future generations the best ideals and institutions of our generation. We believe the best in the life of any people presented by the silver screen to the whole people will popularize that best....The motion picture industry through constant production of the worst has failed to transmit the best. We believe federal regulation is required to change the situation.

—Speech by Maude M. Aldrich of Oregon, chairperson of the National Woman's Christian Temperance Union's Department of Motion Pictures, November 21, 1928

Judge humor magazine, August 19, 1925:

And now they say a thing is "Catzy!" meaning marvelous, wonderful, etc. Where do these expressions come from, anyway? It's obvious "Catzy" descended from "The Cat's Meow," but what massive brain originated that—and why? Maybe the bird that names Pullman cars started all these expressions.

"Film Men Attack Morality Drives," *The New York Times*, January 28, 1928:

Various suggestions to improve the motion picture and means to overcome the exhibitor's difficulties in obtaining desirable films were discussed yesterday at the fourth annual Conference of the National Board of Review of Motion Pictures at the Waldorf. Delegates representing Better Film Committees condemned morality drives and the like and urged intelligent selection of pictures as opposed to the methods of reform groups.

Discussing a community plan to encourage the high type of motion picture, Professor Leroy E. Bowman of the Department of Social Science at Columbia [said] that the best pictures "can be evolved only through intelligent selection by the interested public and not through censorship, moralism or monopoly. It is the plan of common effort and of common sense as opposed to the narrow, moralistic and monopolistic plans that have been proposed in various quarters."

Professor Bowman praised the National Board of Review as the only extensive agency in the country on which reliance can be placed to express the interest and wishes of the public "because it approaches the problem from a natural, human point of view without bureaucratic censorship."

"The only thing the matter with movies is the audience," Ida Clyde Clarke, lecturer and author, told the delegates.

"The American public is tabloid-minded and has the tabloid soul," she said. "It wants a stimulant for its atrophied or undeveloped emotions and prefers to take it undiluted and unrefined."

Dr. Horace M. Kallen of the New School for Social Research traced the history of censorship, the psychological foundation of which, he said, is based on the three emotions—"fear, greed and a sense of shame."

Morality drives, he declared, originate in the emotions of persons who feel certain that the evils they would correct will not hurt them but might have a harmful influence on others.

Dr. Kallen warned the audience "to make sure that the vague and uncertain rules laid down are not used as instruments of competitive oppression within the industry.

"Certain types of prohibitions," he said, "have been recently adopted by the picture industry which involve affecting the sense of shame with respect to sex. It is necessary to make sure that there is not some psychopathic influence in the work of censorship within the industry."

Countries we have long characterized as 'heathen' have taken active steps against American movies. Even Turkey has forbidden children under 15 years of age to attend movies 'to protect young Turks from the demoralizing effects of American-made films.' The infidel nation is aroused to save its children from the Christian nation. . . . Will Hays said in a recent speech in Berlin 'the worldwide distribution of films fills an important part in making people in different lands understand each other,' but Sir Hesketh Bell (former Governor of Uganda) says, "Nothing has done more to destroy the prestige of the white man among the colored races than these deplorable pictures."

—Helen A. Miller, New York State Director of Motion Pictures, 1926

1929 NEWS FEATURE

"Beware Big City's Glamouring Lure to Seek Fortune Mid Madding Crowd's Ignoble Strife," Editorial, *Comfort*, Augusta, Maine, October 1929:

Much has been talked as well as published in print deprecating the increasing drift of population in this country from the farms and small towns to the great cities because of its detrimental effect on the moral, social, and material welfare of our people. But teaching and preaching to the public on this injurious phase of our national development have utterly failed to check the movement, and the continuous large influx of men and women, especially those of the younger generation, seeking to better their condition by migrating to the big cities swells the host of unemployed and adds to the burden of supporting the destitute at public expense or by private charity in these overcrowded communities. Caring for these accessions of jobless adventurers has long been a serious problem for the cities, and has become more acute with the increase of moving pictures and more extensive circulation of fiction presenting exaggerated portrayals of the opportunities for successful careers in the big city, and of the thrill of metropolitan life.

The distressful consequences of the in-rush of fortune-seekers to New York have attained such proportions that last year the Welfare Commission of that city broadcast a warning that a single person "cannot live independently and decently in New York on less than $25 a week" and that the metropolis is not a good place to be "without a job, friends, relatives, or a bank account." The warning also asserts that of the thousands, who in the course of a year come to New York, intent on abiding and gaining a livelihood there, the majority "soon find themselves in an environment so depressing or demoralizing as to affect their lives or character permanently, and of these the world hears little." As the woeful, repulsive facts on which the warning is based are devoid of romantic or sentimental interest, they are not featured in the moving pictures, nor in current fiction.

In commenting on the Welfare Commission's warning, the *Washington Post* said: "a recent advertisement for the services of a boy brought a thousand youngsters to the door of the employer. The plight of the middle-aged seeker after employment was emphasized all during the winter. The difficulty of approaching the desks of busy men is known to every applicant for work. The lure of the city will, however, continue. Once the lure has seized a victim, a cure is almost impossible, and the shining success of those who have gone and conquered will be remembered longer than any warning which may be broadcast.

1930–1939

Few Americans escaped the devastating impact of the most severe depression in the nation's history. Economic paralysis gripped the country: banks failed; railroads became insolent; factories closed; unemployment shot upward and Americans took to the road looking for work, stability and something to believe in. Farmers defied court-ordered evictions; mothers desperate to feed their families staged food riots; school attendance was back to five months. Fewer couples chose marriage, fewer still had children in this austere environment.

By 1934, one in every four farms had been sold for taxes and 5,000 banks had closed their doors, eradicating in seconds the lifetime savings of millions of Americans, rich and poor. In some circles the American depression was viewed as the fulfillment of Marxist prophecy—the inevitable demise of capitalism. President Franklin D. Roosevelt thought otherwise. Backed by his New Deal promises and a focus on the "forgotten man," the president produced a swirl of government programs designed to lift the country out of its paralytic gloom.

Roosevelt's early social experiments were characterized by relief, recovery and reform. Believing that the expansion of the United States economy was temporarily over, Roosevelt paid attention to better distribution of resources and planned production. The Civilian Conservation Corps (CCC), for example, put

250,000 jobless young men to work in the forests for $1.00 a day. By 1935, government deficit spending was spurring economic change. By 1937, total manufacturing output exceeded that of 1929; unfortunately, prices and wages rose too quickly and the economy dipped again in 1937, driven by inflation fears and restriction on bank lending. Nonetheless, many roads, bridges, public buildings, dams and trees became part of the landscape thanks to federally employed workers. The Federal Theatre Project, for example, employed 1,300 people during the period, reaching 25 million attendees with more than 1,200 productions. Despite progress, 10 million workers were still unemployed in 1938 and farm prices lagged behind manufacturing progress. Full recovery would not occur until the United States mobilized for World War II.

While the nation suffered from economic blows, the West was being whipped by nature. Gigantic billowing clouds of dust up to 10,000 feet high swept across the parched Western Plains throughout the '30s. Sometimes the blows came with lightning and booming thunder, but often they were described as being "eerily silent, blackening everything in their path." All human activity halted. Planes were grounded. Buses and trains stalled, unable to race clouds that could move at speeds of more than 100 miles per hour. On the morning of May 9, 1934, the wind began to blow up the topsoil of Montana and Wyoming, and soon some 350 million tons were sweeping eastward. By later afternoon, 12 million tons had been deposited in Chicago. By noon the next day, Buffalo, New York was dark with dust. Even the Atlantic Ocean was no barrier. Ships 300 miles out to sea found dust on their decks. During the remainder of 1935, there were more than 40 dust storms that reduced visibility to less than one mile. There were 68 more storms in 1936, 72 in 1937, and 61 in 1938. On the High Plains, 10,000 houses were simply abandoned, and nine million acres of farm turned back to nature. Banks offered mortgaged properties for as little as $25 for 160 acres and found no takers.

The people of the 1930s excelled in escape. Radio matured as a mass medium, creating stars such as Jack Benny, Bob Hope, and Fibber McGee and Molly. For a time it seemed that every child was copying the catch phrase of radio's Walter Winchell, "Good evening, Mr. and Mrs. America, and all the ships at sea," or pretending to be Jack Benny when shouting "Now, cut that out!" Soap operas captured large followings and sales of magazines like *Screenland* and *True Story* skyrocketed. Each edition of *True Confessions* sold 7.5 million copies. Nationwide, movie theaters prospered as 90 million Americans attended the "talkies" every week, finding comfort in the uplifting excitement of movies and movie stars. Big bands made swing the king of the decade, while jazz came into its own. And the social experiment known as Prohibition died in December 1933, when the Twenty-first Amendment swept away the restrictions against alcohol ushered in more than a decade earlier.

Attendance at professional athletic events declined during the decade, but softball became more popular than ever and golf began its drive to become a national passion as private courses went public. Millions listened to boxing on radio, especially the exploits of the "Brown Bomber," Joe Louis. As average people coped with the difficult times, they married later, had fewer children, and divorced less. Extended families often lived under one roof; opportunities for women and minorities were particularly limited. Survival, not affluence, was often the practical goal of the family. A disillusioned nation, which had worshipped the power of business, looked instead toward a more caring government.

During the decade, United Airlines hired its first airline stewardess to allay passengers' fears of flying. The circulation of *Reader's Digest* climbed from 250,000 to eight million before the decade ended and *Esquire,* the first magazine for men, was launched. The early days of the decade gave birth to Hostess Twinkies, Bird's Eye frozen vegetables, windshield wipers, photoflash bulbs, and pinball machines. By the time the Depression and the 1930s drew to a close, Zippo lighters, Frito's corn chips, talking books for the blind, beer in cans, and the Richter scale for measuring earthquakes had all been introduced. Despite the ever-increasing role of the automobile in the mid-1930s, Americans still spent $1,000 a day on buggy whips.

1932 PROFILE

CIVIL RIGHTS: THE SCOTTSBORO CASE

Convinced of the Scottsboro boys' innocence, Penelope Vertrees decided to help fund their defense, but when her maid came to her with an unusual request, Penelope was of two minds.

Life at Home

- Penelope Vertrees was delighted with herself the first time she wrote a check to help the Scottsboro boys.
- Significantly, it was the tenth anniversary of her husband's death when she used his money—$100—to support the Negroes of Scottsboro, Alabama, for the first time.
- She knew without equivocation that Henry would never have approved; in fact, he would have been so furious his face would have turned beet red.
- Giving money at church was one thing, he would have said; supporting causes you didn't know anything about was another kettle of fish.
- Being a 62-year-old widow was lonely at times, but it sure had its benefits.
- Penelope's involvement with the Scottsboro boys started a year earlier because her maid Lucinda's cousin was the mother of one of the boys accused of raping two white women in Alabama.
- Lucinda had been working for Penelope since they were both teenagers, so when Lucinda lingered at the dining room door after bringing in a bowl of breakfast grits, Penelope knew something was on her mind.
- After being invited to speak up, Lucinda told the story of the nine black youths who had been arrested and tried in Scottsboro, Alabama, for raping two white hobo women on a train.
- Four of the accused were from Chattanooga, Tennessee, including Lucinda's cousin's son.

Penelope Vertrees quietly supported the Scottsboro boys.

Nine black youths were arrested in Scottsboro, Arizona, for raping two white women.

- The trouble had started on March 25, 1931, when the Chattanooga-to-Memphis freight train was stopped in Paint Rock, Alabama, by a sheriff's posse investigating a fight between white and black youths on the train.
- In all, nine Negro youths aged 14 to 20 were removed from the train, even though several were not involved in the fight and most of the hobo travelers did not know each other.
- As they were taken from the train, two white women, Victoria Price and Ruby Bates, accused the men of rape.
- Physical evidence of a rape was scanty, and the reputation of both women tawdry at best.
- On March 31, a grand jury indicted the nine for rape, based on the women's testimony.
- Trials for the boys took place almost immediately to thwart efforts to lynch them.
- Of the six members of the Jackson County, Alabama bar appointed to defend the boys, only the aging Milo Moody and Chattanooga attorney Stephen Roddy spoke for the Scottsboro boys at the trial.
- Stephen R. Roddy was retained by Chattanooga's Interdenominational Colored Ministers' Alliance.
- When they learned four of the boys were from Chattanooga, the Alliance decided to become involved, raising $50.08 and approaching Stephen Roddy about taking the case.
- The Chattanooga attorney agreed to defend the nine for $120.
- The grand jury formally indicted the nine boys on March 31, and trial was set for April 6.
- In Scottsboro, the first Monday of each month was known as "Fair Day," and people from as far away as 50 miles came to town to meet friends, attend county court trials, sell produce and buy supplies.
- On this first Monday, several thousand people pushed their way past the National Guard picket lines, who had been ordered by the governor to maintain order.

- Rooftops became crowded as people climbed up for a better view of the courthouse.
- Stories circulated about the proper way to punish black youths who took liberties with white women.
- In the courtroom, attorney Stephen Roddy had already been drinking.
- He informed the judge that he was not there as counsel for the defense, but was a representative for interested parties.
- He would not clearly define his position, except to say that he had not prepared for the case.
- When Milo Moody stepped up and agreed to help Roddy, the case was able to proceed on schedule.
- Roddy's petition for a change of venue was quickly dismissed, and defendants Clarence Norris and Charley Weems were tried together.
- The first trial lasted a day and a half, and within an hour of their case going to the jury, defendant Haywood Patterson went on trial.
- In the middle of Patterson's trial, the first jury returned a verdict of guilty and sentenced Norris and Weems to death.
- The crowd's roar of approval was heard by the Patterson jury.
- The trial of Haywood Patterson took the afternoon of April 7 and the morning of April 8.
- The jury went into deliberations by 11:00 a.m.
- They reached a decision within 25 minutes, but by that time the trial of Ozie Powell, Willie Roberson, Andy Wright, Eugene Williams, and Olen Montgomery was already underway.
- Haywood Patterson was also found guilty and sentenced to death.
- The crowd controlled its response to this verdict under threat from the judge.

Victoria Price, one of the two accusers, on the witness stand.

- The third case went to the jury at 4:20 p.m.
- Roy Wright was only 14 years old, and under Alabama law could only be tried in juvenile court.
- Solicitor H. G. Bailey offered Wright life imprisonment in return for a guilty plea in an effort to complete the trials quickly.
- Roddy would not agree, as a guilty plea would prevent an appeal.
- On Thursday morning, the fourth day of trials, the five were declared guilty and given the death sentence.
- Although the state had asked the jury for life imprisonment for Roy Wright, seven of the jurors insisted on the death penalty.
- None of the jurors would budge, and Judge Hawkins declared a mistrial.
- In just three days, all of the boys except Roy Wright were convicted and sentenced to death.
- Penelope listened, read the news accounts, kept her own counsel and became a supporter of the Scottsboro boys.
- Someone had to help them gain their freedom through the courts; besides, all the mass meetings in places like New York and Chicago were doing nothing but stirring up bad feelings throughout the South.

- The Scottsboro boys were innocent and did not deserve to be executed, but that didn't mean that women didn't need protection from the lustful ways of men of all colors and shades.

Life at Work

- For the past year, Penelope Vertrees had quietly but proudly supported the cause of the Scottsboro boys, so when her maid asked to talk this time, Penelope assumed more money was needed.
- Recently, she had celebrated with Lucinda the November announcement that the U.S. Supreme Court had reversed the convictions of the Scottsboro boys.
- The high court ruled that Alabama had failed to provide adequate assistance of counsel as required by the due process clause of the Fourteenth Amendment.
- New trials were to be scheduled, she knew, and trials meant lawyers and lawyers equaled money.
- Even before the ruling and the need for another trial, Alabama's schools were on the edge of bankruptcy and capable of opening for only a few months.
- An expensive trial under the national spotlight would only exacerbate the problem.
- Besides, the people of Alabama were getting pretty tired of outsiders coming into the state telling them how to treat their Negroes and run their courts.
- Several deputies and scores of tenant farmers had been shot in race incidents stirred up by outside agitators; more trouble could be coming, and Penelope was unsure how she felt about that.
- As a member of both the Daughters of the American Revolution and the Colonial Dames, she did have a reputation to maintain.
- But this time Lucinda wanted more than money.
- She wanted Penelope to open her home to visitors from the North who were working on the defense of the Scottsboro boys.
- In a clear, quiet voice, Lucinda asked her to turn her home into a wayside motel for people doing research for the trial.
- The very idea was shocking.
- Although her financial support was well known in the black community of Chattanooga, no one on the altar guild of her church dreamed that she had been helping the Scottsboro boys for more than a year.
- Part of the strategy at the next trial was to insist that some Negroes be allowed on the jury.
- She had never seen a colored man serve on a jury and was unsure of how he might handle himself.
- Then, Penelope realized how much courage the request had required: no maid would even think she could determine the social calendar for the lady of the house.
- But now that a new trial was scheduled, there was no telling who might show up at the house.
- After the first trials, both the Central Committee of the Communist Party of the U.S. and the National Association for the Advancement of Colored People fought for control in the case.
- The more conservative NAACP had tried to remain uninvolved, not wanting to be associated with the incident unless they were sure the boys were innocent.
- The Communist Party, on the other hand, got involved as soon as convictions were issued and began a telegram campaign to court officials.

THEY MUST BE FREED!

NINE INNOCENT LIVES FACE INSTANT MURDER

Judge Callaghan, member of Klu Klux Klan, has just denied a new trial to Heywood Patterson and Clarence Norris, two of the Scottsboro boys. Callaghan fiendishly orders that new briefs be filed by March 3rd.

By this move, he seeks to make it impossible for I. L. D. attorneys to file new briefs. This will enable him to have the Scottsboro boys executed by March 5th.

BUT HE WILL NOT SUCCEED!

The united protests of all workers, professionals and all sincere Scottsboro defenders will stop this bloody murder!

ATTEND THIS

SCOTTSBORO MASS MEETING

FRIDAY, MARCH 2, 8 p. m.
I. W. O. HALL, 415 LENOX AVENUE

NEW YORK DISTRICT INTERNATIONAL LABOR DEFENSE, 870 Broadway
HARLEM SECTION INTERNATIONAL LABOR DEFENSE, 326 Lenox Avenue

TEAR THIS OFF AND MAIL AT ONCE TO GOVERNOR MILLER

- -

Governor Miller,
Montgomery, Alabama.

Scottsboro boys innocent of any crime. Demand their immediate, unconditional release.

Signed *William Barfield*
Address *59 W. 128th St.*

- The Communist Party believed the Negroes' problems were another phase of the capitalistic class exploitation.
- They felt that destruction of the existing economic order was the only way to solve the problem.
- The battle for power between the two groups made Penelope dizzy and more than occasionally suspicious about how her money was being spent.
- But she knew that the ministers who comprised the Interdenominational Colored Ministers' Alliance were honorable men who had the best interests of their race at heart.
- Lucinda reassured her of that often.

Life in the Community: Scottsboro, Alabama

- Scottsboro had a population of 3,500, a central waterworks system, a sewage plant that served the white sections of town, and two hosiery mills that employed 850 people.
- The seat of the largely agrarian Jackson County, Scottsboro served as the trade center for the surrounding farms.
- Along with the rest of the Tennessee Valley, Jackson County was hit hard by the crash of 1929, and was suffering from two years of drought.
- Farmers were planting less cotton and concentrating efforts on subsistence crops, leaving less money to spend in town.
- They were equally distressed by the widespread publicity and negative images projected on the community by out-of-state press reports about the Scottsboro case.
- Huge rallies, which attracted thousands, had been staged in major cities across the nation and as far away as Berlin, where the inflamed crowd engaged in rock throwing.
- Equally distressing was the willingness of the mothers of the Scottsboro boys to tour the country whipping up racial unrest and raising money for the International Labor Defense.
- They had even heard that when the supply of mothers was inadequate, substitutes were found.
- And they hated the Communist-backed efforts to brand the convictions of the Scottsboro boys as an attempt by the white ruling classes to inflict "willful, cold-blooded and deliberate murder."
- These same rallies often resulted in petition drives and telegram campaigns for justice.
- The Scottsboro rallies had even spawned calls for other forms of freedom.
- The International Labor Defense used the upcoming trials as a springboard in nearby Birmingham to discuss freedom of speech for Negroes, repeal of vagrancy laws, abolition of the chain gang, elimination of poll taxes and an increase in welfare appropriations.

Free the Nine Scottsboro Boys!

Dear Fellow Worker

We, nine Negro boys, of Scottsboro, has been saved from the electric chair once more. We was saved because you and all the working-people heeded our cry to save us. You and all the working-people of the world followed the International Labor Defense to save us.

We boys is innocent. They framed us up down here only because we is children of working people, and because our skins is black. For that they want to send us to the electric chair. But our lives is innocent. They got no right to send us to the electric chair. But they will if you give them the chance.

Now even the Supreme Court has to give us a new trial. But the boss men down here in Kilby prison, they sure still aiming to burn us. We'll get you next time the prison guards tell us. Only the I.L.D can save us. They saved us so far. We ask all working people, black and white, to help the I.L.D save us. Don't let them kill us. We innocent boys. Only they want to kill us cause our skins is black and cause we is poor. Help the I.L.D. save us.

RESOLVED: We, Negro and white workers of the United States, demand the immediate and unconditional release of these innocent Negro working class boys. They have been framed-up and sentenced to death in an attempt to split the growing unity of the white and Negro workers. They have been sentenced to die because they represent a nation of enslaved Negro workers and poor farmers in the South, struggling for freedom. Their fight is our fight. As long as the Negro masses are doubly exploited, jim-crowed, lynched, the white workers will suffer from the great division in their workingclass ranks. The fight to free the Scottsboro boys is the fight of the whole working class. "The 9 Negro Scottsboro boys must be freed!"

"Help the I. L. D. Save Us!"

NAME	ADDRESS
Imolee Gordon	11th St + East Spruce Ext.
Mrs. Mary Helen Gordon	11th St + East Spruce Ext.
Fatima New 23 St	Price McKinney
J. T. Simms	R. 7. Box 152
Alice E. Simms	R 7 Box 152
Gladys Hall	
Mrs. Elnora Grable	808 S. 2 St
Miss Fanny Thompson	808 S 4 St.
John A. Hall	101 No Front St.
John Mierys	Yakima
Mike Mierys	Yakima
Ed Mierys	Wapato
John Finks	Wapato
Ed Funk	Brownstown
J. F. Fink	Brownstown

HISTORICAL SNAPSHOT
1932

- As wages dropped and unemployment rose, thousands of indigent nomads roamed from state to state looking for work
- The FBI publicized a list of "Public Enemies"
- The Zippo lighter, the Mounds candy bar, Fritos corn chips and Skippy peanut butter all made their first appearance
- Mobster Al Capone, convicted of income tax evasion, entered the federal penitentiary in Atlanta
- President Herbert Hoover reduced his own salary by 20 percent in response to the Depression
- Congress changed the name "Porto Rico" to "Puerto Rico"
- Over 10,000 war veterans marched on Washington, DC, demanding to be paid their bonuses for service in World War I
- The Dow Jones Industrial Average fell to 41.89, only one point above where the average began in 1896
- Amelia Earhart became the first woman to fly nonstop across the United States, traveling from Los Angeles to Newark, New Jersey, in just over 19 hours
- Book publications included William Faulkner's *Light in August,* Pearl S. Buck's *The Good Earth,* Erskine Caldwell's *Tobacco Road* and Aldous Huxley's *Brave New World*
- Gandhi began a hunger strike against the treatment of Untouchables in India
- The discovery of the male hormone testosterone stimulated interest in animal gonad transplants
- Iraq became independent after a hundred years of direct foreign rule
- Cole Porter's musical *The Gay Divorcee* premiered in New York City
- The Committee on Cost of Medical Care recommended socialized medicine in the United States
- German physicist Albert Einstein was granted a visa, making it possible for him to travel to the United States
- Fred Astaire and Ginger Rogers made *Flying Down to Rio* their first movie together
- Radio City Music Hall opened in New York City
- A new rule in basketball required that the ball be brought over the mid-court line in 10 seconds
- The Glass-Steagall Act was passed, giving the Federal Reserve the right to expand credit in order to increase money circulation and separating banks from brokerage houses
- The infant son of Charles and Anne Lindbergh was kidnapped and later found dead; a handwritten note left at the scene demanded a $50,000 ransom
- The executive committee of the Daughters of the American Revolution voted to exclude blacks from appearing at Constitution Hall

Selected Prices, 1932

Baby's Rubber Pants, Three Pairs $0.22
Camera, Kodak $20.00
Coal, per Half Ton $4.00
Electric Iron $1.00
Hair Cut, Barber Shop $0.20
Motor Oil, Gallon $0.49
Rug, 9' x 12' $14.95
Sewing Machine $19.95
Shotgun, Double Barrel $36.98
Towels, Six $0.65

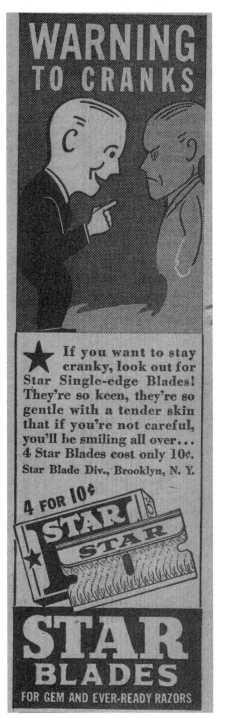

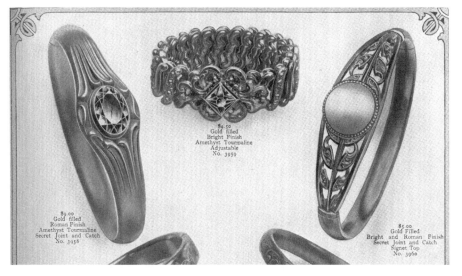

Gold-filled rings, $4.50 to $9.00

Scottsboro Boys Timeline

1931

March 25

The Scottsboro boys were arrested and charged with assault; rape charges were added against all nine boys based on the accusations made by Victoria Price and Ruby Bates.

March 26

The Alabama National Guard was called out to prevent the lynching of the nine at Scottsboro jail.

March 30

The grand jury indicted all the Scottsboro boys for rape.

April 6

Trials began before Judge A. E. Hawkins.

April 7

Clarence Norris, Charles Weems, Haywood Patterson, Olen Montgomery, Ozie Powell, Willie Robertson, Eugene Williams and Andy Wright were tried, convicted and sentenced to death; the trial of Roy Wright ended in a mistrial when some jurors held out for the death penalty even though the prosecution asked for life imprisonment.

June

Executions were halted pending an appeal to the Alabama Supreme Court.

April-December

The NAACP and the Communist-backed International Labor Defense fought for control of the appeal.

The Scottsboro boys and their attorney.

continued

Timeline . . . *(continued)*

1932
January
Attorneys argued their appeal motions before the Alabama Supreme Court.

The NAACP withdrew from the case.

Ruby Bates denied in a letter to a friend that she was raped by the Scottsboro boys.

March
The Alabama Supreme Court affirmed the conviction of seven of the Scottsboro boys; the conviction of 14-year-old Roy Wright was reversed because he was a juvenile.

May
The U.S. Supreme Court agreed to review the Scottsboro convictions.

November
The U.S. Supreme Court reversed the convictions of the Scottsboro boys because Alabama failed to provide adequate counsel as required by the Fourteenth Amendment; a new trial was ordered.

Ruby Bates retracted her testimony against the Scottsboro boys, and led a parade of 3,000 before the White House to appeal for their freedom.

"Protest at Executions, Speakers Here Say Eight Negroes in Alabama Were 'Railroaded,'"
The New York Times, June 29, 1931:

Three thousand Negroes crowded yesterday afternoon into Salem Methodist Episcopal Church, at 129th Street and Seventh Avenue, to protest the execution, scheduled for July 10, in Scottsboro, Ala., of eight Negroes, all minors, for attacks on two white girls.

The speakers were Walter White, secretary of the Association for the Advancement of Colored People; William Pickens, field secretary of the association, and Bishop R. C. Lawson of the Pentecostal Church of Harlem, who presided.

White and Pickens, who went to Alabama to investigate, declared that the defendants, ranging in age from 14 to 20, were "railroaded." Only one attorney of six in the town of Scottsboro dared to accept the task of defending the youths, Pickens said, because Scottsboro, normally 1,400 in population, was thronged with a crowd of 10,000 during the trial.

The speakers deprecated the efforts of Communists on behalf of the condemned boys, saying they were harming the case more than helping it. Communists broke up a similar protest meeting recently in Chicago, Pickens said. Ten patrolmen were on duty at the church to prevent interference.

Anyone who tries to take an impartial attitude towards the conduct of the Scottsboro case is immediately branded a communist and a nigger-lover.

—Rabbi Benjamin Goldstein, who was given the
option to sever all connection with the
Scottsboro case or resign from Temple Beth Or,
Montgomery, Alabama.
Goldstein resigned.

"Negro Pastors Assail Labor Defense Body, Red Propaganda Is Real Aim of Scottsboro Moves, Chattanooga Alliance Charges," *The New York Times,* **May 24, 1931:**

CHATTANOOGA, Tenn.—The City Interdenominational Ministers' Alliance of Negro Divines today broadcast a denunciation for the international labor defense for its activity on behalf of eight Negro youths under death sentence for a purported attack on two white girl hobos aboard a freight train near Scottsboro, Ala.

The statement of the ministers said the labor defense interest is "mainly for the purpose of drawing Negroes of the South into the Communist organization, and if the movement is successful it will tear the South asunder and destroy the peace and harmony existing for many years."

"13 Are Sentenced in Scottsboro Row, Each Gets $100 Fine or 60 Days in Jail for March on Capitol in Protest to High Court," *The New York Times,* **November 11, 1932:**

WASHINGTON—Judge Isaac R. Hitt in police court today sentenced 13 participants in the Capitol Monday prior to the Supreme Court's decision in the Scottsboro case to a $100 fine or 60 days in jail.

The charge against all 13 was illegal parading and in six cases assaulting policemen.

THEY MUST NOT DIE!

Against Race Discrimination!

"Crisis Threatens Alabama Schools, Shortage of Funds Has Closed 85 Percent, with Remainder on Part Time," *The New York Times*, April 21, 1933:

MONTGOMERY, Ala.—The State of Alabama is confronted with a financial crisis which threatens the very life of its free public schools. With 85 percent of its elementary schools closed already, the people of the state are facing the prospect of utter collapse of their educational system or, at best, a drastic curtailment of its functions.

This is a serious prospect for any state. It is especially so for Alabama, which has the fifth largest number of illiterates in the United States and which is struggling to keep a respectable number of pupils in its classrooms beyond the lower grades of grammar school. Yet three and a half years of economic depression have brought its school system, geared as it was to a $28 million operating fund in 1929, to a point where it must continue to function, if at all, on less than half that amount unless new revenues are found in sources yet untapped. . . .

Discussing the situation in an interview with *The New York Times* correspondent today, Dr. A. F. Harmon, State Superintendent of Education, made no attempt to disguise or minimize the gravity of the conditions threatening his department and the 5,688 schools over which it exercises supervisory control.

"As far as education is concerned," said Dr. Harmon, "we are facing the worst situation that has confronted us since the Reconstruction period. . . .

"Our school system is in the throes of an agony induced by the statewide, nationwide and worldwide financial panic. The shafts of light which have begun to shine through the nation's financial clouds have not reached the doors of the schools of this state. The sacrifices made by teachers, though great, have not been sufficient, nor can they ever be sufficient, to carry through the complete school program without help."

[The Scottsboro case is] a nauseating struggle between the Communist group and Negro society, not so much that justice may be done as that selfish interests may be advanced through the capitalization of the episode.

—George Fort Milton, chairman of the Southern Commission on the Study of Lynching, 1931

"Orders Widen Fight for Negro's Rights, Conference Adopts Margold Plan to Begin 100 Cases in South Against Discrimination," *The New York Times*, May 21, 1932:

WASHINGTON—A legal campaign planned by Nathan R. Margold of New York to defend Negroes against every form of discrimination was adopted here today by the National Association for the Advancement of Colored People.

Dr. Robert R. Moton, head of Tuskegee Institute, endorsed the plan as one likely to obtain for Negroes "a reasonable certainty of justice nowhere assured to them at present in this country." The plan is to be carried out under the direction of Mr. Margold.

The plan involves bringing simultaneously more than 100 cases in as many communities to test the right of states or of individuals "to infringe" on the social as well as the civic rights of Negroes.

"We plan a flood of litigation in all of the Southern states," he said, "asserting the right of the Negro to equality of treatment, and striking at the heart of the situation by challenging the principle of segregation which is the backbone of the whole Negro problem.

"In the case of schools, the segregation issue will be the legal weapon employed to secure equality in the form of more and better schools for Negro children.

"Jim Crow laws will be the subject of direct attack on a new front. . . ."

The Scottsboro case was cited by Dr. Moton as an instance in which Negroes had been condemned on testimony which, he asserted, would have led to the acquittal of white men.

1933 Profile

Property Rights: Taking Charge of the Land

During the Great Depression, with banks foreclosing on farm mortgages at a rate of 20,000 per month, Jim Brown was determined to use the system to keep his friend from losing his farm.

Life at Home

- As tradition and work schedules dictated, all the farmers drove to Villisca, Iowa, on Saturday night to buy supplies for the coming week.
- By 7 p.m., with the sun already set, the town square was crowded with some 80 cars carrying close to 200 farmers, but few were shopping.
- Most Saturdays, the town talk was about rain or the lack of it, the rising cost of seed, the beauty of a tractor engine, or the burden of property taxes.
- Because most of the men were conservative to the core, disobeying the law was against their upbringing and nature.
- So it was with a dry mouth that Jim Brown told the men, many older than his father, that, come Tuesday morning at 9 a.m., he would be the only person bidding at Phil Long's farm foreclosure sale.
- This land had been in the Long family for five generations, through good times and bad, Jim reminded the crowd.
- Phil's father Hank had done favors for every farmer in the county, whether it was lending a hand at harvest time or hauling fertilizer when someone's truck broke down.

The Long family was positioned to lose their farm through bank foreclosure.

- After he died suddenly, his son Phil began to run the farm.
- The bank was not going take it away through foreclosure—not if Jim could help his neighbor and friend.
- No one could have predicted that the farm depression would linger for so long.
- Phil Long, his young wife and three scrawny children were not the only farm family being threatened with a bank mortgage foreclosure.
- Nearly every farmer in Iowa had been upset with his banker at some point in the past, when he restricted credit the farmer needed to buy seed or lectured him about money management—as though the banker had actually worked an honest day in his entire life.
- But since the depression had set in, farmers were fighting for the very soil that defined their lives.
- And the many promises made by newly inaugurated President Franklin Roosevelt weren't going to erase their debt or give them a fair price for their wheat anytime soon.
- For most, the farm depression started a decade earlier and only got worse when city workers got the same illness three years prior.
- Political power for the farmer, however, had begun to fade in the 1850s, when the manufacturing interests and financiers snared a firm grip on Washington policy.
- Then came tariff laws, unreasonable railroad rates and bank control of farm money; farm power, once so dominant, simply drained away.
- Farm mortgage debt now represented 8 percent of total farm expenses—double the burden of farmers in 1920.
- Worse yet, taxes on farm property absorbed 11 percent of gross farm income.
- It was enough to make many farmers at least listen to the Bolsheviks' crazy talk about everyone being equal under communism.
- Even in farm-rich Iowa, only a quarter of the people still farmed for a living; for many years young people had been seduced by city ways, electrical appliances, churches with organs and movies with sound.
- But the time for worry-talk was over; Jim Brown understood that he was surrounded by men of principle who would make sure he was the only bidder at the auction.
- This was not the first time farmers had declared that enough was enough.
- Two years earlier when the depression was not considered great at all, the first signs of farm revolt were ignited in Henryetta, Oklahoma.
- There, 200 starving men, women and children, led by a clergyman, raided 16 grocery and provision stores for food.
- Since then, Northwest dairymen had gone on strike; in Portland, Oregon, the strike included a five-day blockade of all highways leading to the city in order to halt all milk trucks.
- Closer to home, farmers surrounding Sioux City, Iowa, stopped all traffic leading to the city for a month.
- The plan was to withhold farm products until prices rose above the cost of production.
- Hay bales and telephone poles were used to barricade routes into the city; cars with business in Sioux City were allowed to pass; trucks hauling food—especially milk—were turned back or their cargo forcibly dumped into ditches.
- The price paid for most farm products had been cut in half between 1920 and 1930, then halved again in the last three years.
- In North Dakota, the Farmers' Union asked the governor for a farm debt moratorium, and in dozens of communities, farmers united for the sole purpose of blocking foreclosure sales through mob action.

Rising production costs and decreasing prices for farmed goods resulted in 47 percent of farmers no longer owning the land they tilled.

- Jim had even heard that a group of Oklahoma farmers hauled a World War I cannon from the town square to a farm where a forced sale was scheduled.
- The mere presence of the intimidating field-piece frightened the sheriff into calling off the forced sale.
- But Jim wanted to avoid violence so he would have the opportunity to buy back his friend's farm and then return it to him.

Hank Long did favors for every farmer in the county, from lending a hand at harvest time to helping haul products when the neighbor's truck broke down.

Life at Work

- The bank-sponsored foreclosure sale at Phil Long's farm was scheduled for 9 a.m., a late morning time for farmers accustomed to rising by 5 a.m.
- The yard of the farm, churned black in a previous thaw, was frozen in ruts and holes.
- The weather-bleached stalls of corn, combed and broken, stood ghostly in the pale, chilly air.
- Included in the farm buildings on the Long property were a machine shed, chicken houses, pig houses, corncribs, barn, silo and farmhouse.
- Despite hard times, the farm was well kept; there was nothing rundown about it.
- Most of the 300 farmers were middle-aged and dressed in workaday overalls, sagging sweaters and mud-stained boots.
- Jim Brown shared the tension of most of the farmers, who huddled together and talked quietly in their slow, concrete manner.
- The sheriff's paper said that the Long family had failed to pay interest due on a $2,000 mortgage.
- There was no disputing that fact; nor was there a question that Phil Long would pay if he could.
- Everyone knew that the interest and debt were three times harder to satisfy now as when the mortgage was given.
- They also knew that Phil had offered the bank $56.00 against his debt—all the money he had—but the community-based farmer's bank, which was fighting for its own survival, had refused the offer.
- So the men agreed that they would bid back $56.00 to the bank during the auction.
- Fair was fair.
- After all, their own property might soon be endangered by defaults.
- And none of them ever wanted to see in the eyes of their own families the hollow look so prominent in the face of Phil's wife.
- Attending the auction to help the Long family was the first time in a long time that they stopped being haunted by helplessness and actually felt like men.
- The bank representative stood off to one side with his attorney and auctioneer.
- The banker himself, who had been so free with his loans and advice, had sent someone else to do his dirty work.
- The auctioneer sensed that this was not to be an ordinary auction.
- He was well aware that tear-gas bombs had been required to break up a farmer's riot near Council Bluffs.
- He also knew that some frustrated farmers were now willing to display their feelings with small ropes arranged into a noose, so he was more than a little startled when the farmers surrounded him on the way to the barn.
- They simply wanted reassurance that no household goods would be put up for sale.
- He agreed to that condition and then mounted a wagon and began the sale.
- The first item offered was the Long children's favorite mare, led by Phil Long himself.
- To cover his embarrassment, Phil spent considerable time comforting the horse by smoothing her mane.

Phil Long's wife comforted the children's favorite mare during the live-stock auction.

- Everyone was surprised that the auctioneer offered livestock first; normally, machinery was auctioned first.
- The auctioneer broke the silence with his lively, fast-paced call for a bid of at least $15.
- The mare was 16 years old and sound except for a wire cut and a blue eye.
- The auctioneer, accustomed to the opening bid being difficult, this day struggled to give the proceedings an air of normality.
- Finally, Jim bid $2.00 for the mare.
- Immediately the auctioneer called for more bids, quick to remind the 300 men gathered that the mare was worth 20 times that much.
- He was met by a prearranged silence.
- The auctioneer continued his work, called for more bids and then finally gave in.
- When three more horses were offered, Jim was the only bidder.
- The machinery was next: a hay rack, a wagon, two plows, a binder, rake, mower, disc harrow, cultivator, and pulverizer were sold for anywhere from $0.10 to $1.00.
- Jim kept a running total of his bids so that his total would not exceed $56.00.
- The bank received what Phil could afford; Phil's livelihood was saved.
- After the sale, the bank representative was livid, his attorney stunned, the farmers giddy, although most hid their excitement.

Farm familes anguished over losing multi-generational homes.

- Many had loans due to the same bank and had no desire to attract undue attention.
- But that night at a hastily called gathering at the church, a festive air invaded the Sunday School room as the farmers, their wives and children gathered to celebrate.
- Nothing like this had ever occurred before in Villisca.
- Some wanted to debate the ethics of their united civil disobedience, others wanted to shout just to relieve tension, and the children were more than willing to run about in groups, thrilled by the unexpected gathering and its jubilant atmosphere.
- Jim rose to speak and thank his fellow farmers but was drowned out by cheers; no one doubted that the bank would be looking for the first opportunity to cancel his loans.

Life in the Community: Villisca, Iowa

- Villisca, Iowa, was awash in farm discontent in 1933.
- Only 16 percent of farm households earned incomes above the national median of $1,500; more than half had an annual income of less than $1,000.
- Wheat and corn prices didn't cover the cost of production.
- Located in the southwest corner of the state, Villisca was settled by German and Irish immigrants, pleased by both the quality of the soil and the independent spirit of the region.
- Unwanted notoriety was visited upon the community in 1912 when eight people were murdered in a single house, permanently disrupting the residents' sense of security.

- Three people were convicted of the crimes, and although doubts lingered concerning their guilt, the area enjoyed remarkable prosperity in the years leading to World War I and its immediate aftermath.
- But by 1933, the cost of production was exceeding the price offered at market; debt and taxes were rising, while farm crop prices were falling.
- Not joiners by nature, hundreds of farmers became members of the Farmers' Holiday Association, whose goals included fair pricing for farm crops.
- Thanks to 10-cent corn to pay 75-cent debts, 30 percent of all Iowa farms had been lost to their original owners in the last seven years.
- As a result, 47 percent of farmers were no longer owners of the land they tilled.
- Landlords who were successful in removing a tenant often faced a labor boycott; few wanted to till the soil of repossessed land.
- Farmers who defied the community and moved onto repossessed land discovered that no trucks would haul their crops, and neighbors refused to assist with community tasks such as silage.
- Agricultural income was down 60 percent in the last four years.
- Nationally, banks were foreclosing on farm mortgages at a rate of 20,000 per month.
- Unrest was palpable.
- The president of the conservative Farm Bureau Federation testified before a U.S. Senate agriculture committee, "Unless something is done for the American farmer, we will have a revolution in the countryside within 12 months."
- Dozens of farm proposals reverberated through Congress, ranging from debt cancellation and subsidized exports, to direct payments to farmers who agreed not to produce certain crops.
- Farmers were not alone in their troubles.
- Five thousand banks nationally had failed between the time of the stock market crash in October 1929 and March 1933.
- Several states and 1,300 municipalities, whose real estate values and tax base had disappeared overnight, first defaulted on their creditors, then cut back on services and reduced payrolls dramatically.
- Chicago was forced to pay its teachers in tax warrants, followed in 1933 by no payments at all.
- The gross national product was cut in half between 1929 and 1933.
- A few industries such as shoe and cigarette manufacturing proved themselves to be depression-proof, but they were the rare exceptions.
- Car production declined 65 percent between 1929 and 1933; iron and steel production dropped 60 percent.
- Residential construction shriveled to less than one-fifth of its pre-depression volume, a down shift that reverberated through lumber camps, steel mills, appliance companies, roofing contractors and electrical firms.
- Across America, unemployment was so high in 1931 that 100,000 American workers applied for jobs in the emerging promised land known as the Soviet Union.
- By 1933, 400,000 Mexican Americans returned to Mexico, some voluntarily, others through organized persuasion.

HISTORICAL SNAPSHOT
1933

- The first episode of *The Lone Ranger* radio program was broadcast
- The first singing telegram was introduced by the Postal Telegram Company in New York
- President-elect Franklin Roosevelt escaped an assassination attempt in Miami that claimed the life of Chicago Mayor Anton J. Cermak
- *Newsweek* and *Esquire* magazines were first published
- Ground was broken for the Golden Gate Bridge in San Francisco
- The U.S. Congress passed the Twenty-first Amendment to repeal the Eighteenth Amendment, which outlawed the sale of alcohol
- The movie *King Kong* premiered featuring Fay Wray
- Franklin D. Roosevelt was inaugurated to his first term as president; in pledging to lead the country out of the Great Depression, he said, "We have nothing to fear but fear itself"
- At the start of his administration, Roosevelt ordered a four-day bank holiday in order to stop large amounts of money from being withdrawn from the banks
- In German parliamentary elections, the Nazi Party won 44 percent of the vote, enabling it to join with Nationalists to gain a slender majority in the Reichstag
- The board game Monopoly was introduced
- Adolph Hitler seized power in Germany; the Nazis ordered a ban on all Jews in businesses, professions, and schools
- Congress authorized the Civilian Conservation Corps to relieve rampant unemployment, which exceeded 25 percent
- The United States went off the gold standard
- Gandhi began a hunger strike to protest British oppression in India
- The Tennessee Valley Authority Act was created
- The first drive-in movie theater opened, in Camden, New Jersey
- Aviator Wiley Post completed the first solo flight around the world in seven days, 18 and three-quarter hours
- Albert Einstein fled Hitler's Germany and emigrated to the United States
- Pennsylvania voted to legalize Sunday sports
- The first of the great dust storms of the 1930s hit North Dakota
- Workers staged the first sit-down strike against Hormel meat packers in Austin, Minnesota
- Jack Kirkland's *Tobacco Road* premiered in New York City
- The ban on James Joyce's book *Ulysses* was lifted
- The Pope condemned the massive Nazi sterilization of Jews

Selected Prices, 1933

Automobile, Reo Motor Car $795.00
Candy Bar, Hershey's Almond $0.05
Ice Box $18.75
Knickers, Boy's $0.77
Movie Ticket, Adult $0.25
Moving Picture Camera/Projector $13.75
Sanitary Napkins, Kotex, Dozen $0.85
Waffle Iron, Westinghouse $7.95
Washing Machine $57.95
Wristwatch, Lady Elgin $25.00

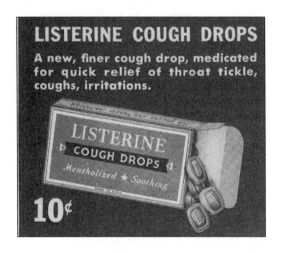

Agricultural Timeline

1840

Farmers made up 69 percent of the labor force.

Factory-made agricultural machinery increased the farmers' need for borrowing and encouraged commercial farming.

1841

The Preemption Act gave squatters first rights to buy land.

The first practical grain drill was patented.

1842

The first grain elevator was constructed in Buffalo, New York.

1844

A practical mowing machine was patented.

1845-55

The potato famine in Ireland and the German Revolution of 1848 greatly increased immigration to America.

1849

Pre-mixed chemical fertilizers were first sold commercially.

1850

Farmers made up 64 percent of the labor force and owned an average of 203 acres each.

Successful farming on the prairies began.

Ninety labor hours were required to produce 100 bushels of corn using two and a half acres with a walking plow, harrow, and hand planting.

1850-70

The expanded market demand for crops accelerated the adoption of improved technology, which increased farm production.

1854

A self-governing windmill was perfected.

1856

The two-horse straddle-row cultivator was patented.

1860

Farmers comprised 58 percent of the labor force; the average farm covered 199 acres.

1862-75

Hand power was replaced by horse power, triggering a major American agricultural revolution.

1865-75

Gang plows and sulky plows came into use.

1866-77

The cattle boom accelerated settlement of the Great Plains, igniting range wars between farmers and ranchers.

1868

Steam-powered tractors were tested.

continued

Timeline ... *(continued)*

1869

Spring-tooth harrow or seedbed preparation began.

1870

Farmers made up 53 percent of the labor force; the average farm was 153 acres.

Illinois, Iowa, and Ohio were the chief wheat states.

Foot-and-mouth disease was first reported in the United States.

Deep-well drilling became widely used.

Grain silos gained popularity.

1874

Grasshopper plagues erupted in the West.

Glidden barbed wire was patented, which allowed the fencing of rangeland and ended the era of unrestricted, open-range grazing.

1882

Bordeau mixture fungicide became popular in the United States.

Texas became the largest producer of cotton.

1884

Horse-drawn combines gained use in wheat areas of the Pacific coast.

1886-87

Blizzards, following drought and overgrazing, devastated the northern Great Plains cattle industry.

1889

The Bureau of Animal Industry discovered the carrier of tick fever.

1890-95

Cream separators became widely used.

1890s

Agriculture became increasingly mechanized and commercialized.

1890

Thirty-five to 40 labor hours were required to produce 100 bushels of corn on two and a half acres with a two-bottom gang plow, disc and peg-tooth harrow, and two-row planter.

Forty to 50 labor hours were required to produce 100 bushels (five acres) of wheat with a gang plow, seeder, harrow, binder, thresher, wagons, and horses.

1892

The boll weevil crossed the Rio Grande and began to spread north and east.

1899

An improved method of anthrax inoculation was developed.

1900

Farmers made up 38 percent of the labor force; the average farm comprised 147 acres.

Turkey red wheat was gaining importance as a commercial crop.

Experimental work on breeding disease-resistant varieties of plants began.

continued

Timeline . . . *(continued)*

1903

An effective hog cholera serum was developed.

1904

A serious stem-rust epidemic affected the wheat harvest.

1910

Farmers made up 31 percent of the labor force; the average farm was 138 acres.

Large open-geared gas tractors came into use.

1911-17

The immigration of agricultural workers from Mexico accelerated.

1915-20

Enclosed gears were developed for the farm tractor.

1918

Small prairie-type combines with auxiliary engines were introduced.

1920

Farmers made up 27 percent of the labor force; the average farm covered 148 acres.

1920-40

Expanded use of mechanized power increased farm production and credit needs.

1926

The cotton-stripper was developed for the High Plains.

1926

A successful light tractor was developed.

1930

Farmers comprised 21 percent of the labor force; the average farm was 157 acres.

All-purpose, rubber-tired tractors with complementary machinery came into wide use.

The use of hybrid-seed corn became common in the Corn Belt.

One farmer supplied 9.8 persons in the United States and abroad.

Fifteen to 20 labor hours were required to produce 100 bushels of corn on two and a half acres of land with a two-bottom gang plow, seven-foot tandem disc, four-section harrow, and two-row planters, cultivators, and pickers.

The New York Times, February 12, 1933:

What the people who live in the midst of these alarums and excursions . . . see is not Red revolution, not an organized movement to defraud creditors, but a desperate effort to preserve the existing property status from wreckage. In spite of cow-testing wars, farm strikes, highway picketing, and interference with tax and mortgage foreclosure sales, the general level of respect for law and its orderly process remains high.

Before the depression. I wore the pants in this family, and rightly so. During the depression, I lost something. Maybe you call it self-respect, but in losing it I also lost the respect of my children, and I am losing my wife.

—Jobless father to interviewer, 1933

I am a farmer. . . . Last Spring I thought you really intended to do something for this country. Now I have given it all up. Henceforward I am swearing eternal vengeance on the financial barons and will do every single thing I can to bring about communism.

—Indiana farmer to newly elected president Franklin D. Roosevelt, October 16, 1933

The plains are beautiful, but, oh, the terrible, crushing drabness of life here. And the suffering, for both people and animals. . . . Most of the farm buildings haven't been painted in God only knows how long! If I had to live here, I think I'd just quietly call it a day and commit suicide. . . . The people up here . . . are in a daze. A sort of nameless dread hangs over the place.

—Letter from Lorena Hickok to Eleanor Roosevelt, October 1933, while inspecting economic conditions in North Dakota

THE FORGOTTEN FARMER

REPUBLICAN PROMISES 1928

They all ran after the farmer's wife, the farmer and the farm hands with soothing syrup for agricultural complaints.

REPUBLICAN QUACK REMEDIES 1932

THE HAWLEY-SMOOT TARIFF. It has bankrupted the farmer by causing other nations to match our tariff walls so that he cannot sell his surplus crops abroad, and it raises his cost of living at home.

The HOOVER FARM BOARD. Its wasteful scheme of buying and storing crops for future sale has cost $500,000,000 and sent wheat prices to their low levels through fear the Government might "dump" its holdings.

The Farmers' Plight Today

The farmer's average yearly earnings are $730; of all other workers, $1,415.

The 22 percent of farm population get only 7 percent of the national income, less than half as much as in 1920.

Farm values have fallen over $22,000,000,000 since 1920.

Farm mortgages have reached a peak of over $10,000,000,000.

Farm taxes have risen from an average of $100 in 1914 to $266 in 1932.

Farm products are worth about half as much as in 1929.

Roosevelt Restores Rural Hope

HIS IMMEDIATE PRACTICAL PROGRAM

Repeal of the Farm Board provisions that compel government speculation in crops.

An emergency, self-supporting plan of tariff protection whereby the farmer would get roughly the world price for staple surplus products sold abroad, and for those sold at home the world price plus the amount of a tariff benefit equal to the reasonable tariff benefit given to industrial products.

Saving farm homes by reducing excessive interest on farm mortgages.

Strengthening of the farm cooperative movement.

HIS FAR REACHING GOALS

A re-organized Department of Agriculture of more help to farmers.

National cooperation in lightening local tax burdens.

National aid to states in planning the use of land more wisely and transferring sterile soil from farming to forestry.

HIS RECORD AS GOVENOR OF NEW YORK

His interest in farm problems in New York, fifth agricultural state, led to the creation of a state Agricultural Advisory Commission. As a result of its soil survey showing that 20% of cultivated land should be put to other uses, he stimulated a remarkable reforestration program through which the state is turning worthless farms into a sound investment in timber supply, watershed protection and people's playgrounds.

His efforts have secured cheaper and more electric service for farmers.

His leadership has caused a revision in rural taxation methods, giving the poorer districts more state aid for roads and schools.

Bring Back Better Times to Farmers

Vote for ROOSEVELT and GARNER

Issued by Democratic National Campaign Committee
Hotel Biltmore—New York City

"A Heavy Hand Will Make Crime Unpopular and Unprofitable," Editorial, *Comfort Magazine*, June 1932:

Speaking of economy in government, how can we justify the expense of caring for the convicted criminal all the rest of his natural life? Courts do not condemn a person to death or to life imprisonment as a punishment for crime. A life sentence is given only when it is considered dangerous to allow the convicted person to associate with law-abiding people again. In any case where a life sentence might be applied with justice, capital punishment should be employed.

It sounds very heartless, we admit, to talk of saving dollars at the expense of human life, but society must protect itself and it owes nothing to the criminal who is at war against it. If you owned a horse which turned outlaw, which never would be safe to use again or allow it to have its liberty, you would not think of penning it up in a stall and carrying feed and water to it until it should die a natural death. Why should you be more sentimental about the person convicted of murder or some other crime which has been thought deserving of a maximum sentence? Perhaps there is a place for sentiment in dealing with law violators who may possibly be made over into good citizens. A person who steals may see the error of his ways, but the person who is in line for a life sentence is an outlaw against society. He never will be anything but an outlaw. If he gains his liberty, he will again be a menace. Why should you pay for his board and lodging for 25 or 30 years, waiting for him to die? It will be cheaper, more humane, and a great deal safer to get him buried as soon as possible.

"Television Apparatus Given Final Trial for Public Debut," by C. E. Butterfield, *The Raleigh Times* (NC), April 11, 1931:

Possibilities of studio television are to be investigated when New York gets on the air with its first combined sight and sound broadcasts.

Program plans are not complete, but the intention is to put on illustrated news items, stock reports, illustrated talks, drama, dancing lessons, vaudeville artists, costumed singers, and other types of entertainment suitable for sight as well as sound.

Following somewhat in the footsteps of Chicago, where "talking movies" of studio presentations have been on the air for some time via WMAQ and WIBO and their associated short-wave television stations, the metropolitan area thus will have a chance to tune in for visual and aural entertainment coming from the same studio. . . .

A broadcasting station, WGBS on 254 meters, is to deliver the sound parts of the program, while WXCR, Jenkins experimental television transmitter on 147.5 meters, will deliver the sight. Two receivers will be necessary to bring in the synchronized programs, a broadcast set for sound and a short-wave receiver for television.

"Children in Gainful Occupations," Editorial, *Needlecraft* magazine, March 1935:

No one who has ever seen a child made prematurely old and careworn by the unrelenting taskmaster, hard work, can fail to sympathize with the efforts which have been put forth from time to time in an attempt to limit the age at which children may be employed in gainful occupations. In his recent message to Congress, President Roosevelt commended upon child labor, stating it had been "for the moment outlawed" under the various codes of fair competition. For years the question of an amendment to our constitution restricting the labor of children has been agitated. A way back in June 1924, this amendment was first proposed and it has been ratified by 20 states. The resolution reads: "The Congress shall have power to limit, regulate, and prohibit the labor of persons under 18 years of age."

Much controversy has been waged over the advisability of ratifying this amendment. Its foes point out that it involves a question which should be determined by each state individually; that climatic conditions have much to do with the age at which young people should be permitted to go to work; and that there is danger in permitting to Congress power to absolutely control the life of young people throughout the nation, where conditions vary so decidedly in the various sections of the country. . . .

The American Farm Bureau Federation has been, until recently, opposed to the child labor amendment, but of late they have reversed their opinion, and are now lined up with the advocates of the amendment . . . and they are now calling upon the state federations of 28 states to make the passage of the amendment their chief legislative objective this winter.

You and I will probably be called upon later to vote to either ratify or defeat this resolution, so it is not too soon to be thinking the matter over. . . . In any event, we can all undoubtedly agree that every child has an inalienable right to leisure, wholesome recreation, opportunity for education, and freedom from adult cares while he is growing, and before he has reached his maturity. It is not only for his welfare but for the future welfare of the nation in which he lives that this should be possible. That is a consideration we should not overlook.

1937 Profile

Prohibition: The Fight to Make America Liquor-Free

A stalwart fundamentalist Christian without compromise or apology, Zachary Junger was the national voice of prohibition, preaching in churches and on the radio against the dangers of sinful alcohol.

Life at Home

- Zachary Junger was born in 1900, the third child of Nathan and Nannie Junger.
- Family lore recorded that his birth occurred in a dugout in the forks of the Tongue River three miles west of Paducah, Texas.
- Later in life, his sworn enemies, mostly the pro-liquor crowd, claimed that Zach was born on the dark side of the moon, weaned on dill pickle, and fed crabapples and green persimmons.
- For his part, Zach enjoyed saying that when the doctor held him by his ankles and spanked him to make him cry, he opened his lungs and mouth wide and found no reason to close them since.
- On nationwide radio broadcasts, where he was promoted as "the voice of temperance," he announced, "I have been protesting evil treatment from that day to this."
- His father deserted the family two months after he was born, so Zach's early years were spent in the home of his grandparents.
- West Texas was ranch country then, composed mostly of cattle, coyotes, prairie dogs, rattlesnakes, horned frogs and dog owls.
- His mother took in washing to earn their keep.
- At the age of four, while on a trip with his aunt, Zach fell in love with a little cigar box cart and took it home with him as though it were his.

Zachary Junger preached in churches and on the radio against the dangers of sinful alcohol.

- When his theft was discovered, he had to return the toy and confess that he was a sinner and a sneak or get whipped "until his hide won't hold shucks."
- It was a seminal event that forever removed his temptation to steal anything, including the reputation of another.
- Yet poverty was constant in his youth.
- To help the family make ends meet, he and his siblings often walked the right-of-way of the railroad tracks in search of lumps of coal that had fallen from the railroad engines.
- Zach and his brother also picked up and delivered clothing for their mother to wash.
- The wolf was not just at the door, Zach liked to say; it lived in every room of the house.
- Through it all, his mother continued to believe in God, read her Bible daily, and regularly attend a primitive Baptist church.
- She sang hymns while she worked: "There Is a Great Day Coming" or "The Home Over There" or "When I Can Read My Title Clear."
- When Zach was nine, he got a job before and after school helping a local blind businessman who sold insurance and handled real estate.
- For $1.25 a week, Zach would lead the blind man from his home to his office each morning and back every evening, fetch his firewood, and run errands.
- In 1910, when his father returned from his wanderings, Zach's parents remarried and relocated, employing a covered wagon to take them to eastern Oklahoma near the Muddy Boggy River outside the town of Soper.
- There, as a 12-year-old, Zach learned to worked "like a grown-up," driving two yoke of oxen to haul logs or hewing ties for sale to the railroad.
- School and church disappeared from his life.
- The family moved frequently, living in shacks or tents.
- At age 18, Zach rejoined the church and began his lifelong crusade to rid the world of alcohol.
- By then, the family had moved to Red River country and settled on a farm six miles north of Detroit, Texas.
- There, he and a young woman he favored attended a little country church each week, preaching once a month, and a prayer meeting every Sunday night.
- His girl had made her intentions clear: "If you don't intend to go to Sunday School and church and prayer meeting with me, you may as well take your hat and go home."
- Heeding the church teachings, Zach was then willing to challenge the common practice of harvesting crops seven days a week, which violated the commandment to keep the Sabbath day holy.
- Shortly thereafter he was called to preach.
- Fortified with only a second-grade education, Zachary Junger—a big, strong, awkward farm boy—went back to school "so green" he said, "I had to keep walking to keep from taking root and growing."
- By 1920 he had progressed sufficiently to attend Simmons College, where he also worked odd jobs to pay bills and tuition.
- "We had beans and cornbread for dinner and at night we had cornbread and beans," he would tell his radio listeners; "If a doctor had tested our blood in those days, he would have found it at least 98 percent bean juice."
- While still in school, he took a pastorate call to Cuthbert, Texas, where once a month he led Sunday School and performed the preaching, the singing, and the sweeping up after; sometimes he was even paid.

- In 1926, the First Baptist Church of Weatherford, Texas, extended a call to him as he was completing his degree in Bible study.
- There he was introduced to the pre-millennial view of the second coming.
- He earned a master's degree from Brown University, along with a healthy disdain for modern theories that ridiculed the authority of the Bible or made fun of people who believed in the blood atonement, the bodily resurrection, and the second coming.

Life at Work

- Zachary Junger found a spiritual home in Stamford, Texas, where he took his wife, child, and newly printed master's degree.
- With the First Baptist Church as his base, Zach fought "sin inside the church and outside it," opposing gambling, drinking, dancing, Sunday picture shows, and civic corruption of all kinds.
- He also discovered the power of radio preaching, especially when the topic was liquor.
- He even opened his own unlicensed radio station, taking great care to only allow his broadcast signal to be heard in Texas so an interstate radio license would not be required.
- His temperance work began in earnest in 1928 when Al Smith ran for president, promising to repeal the Eighteenth Amendment, which established national prohibition.
- When the women of the Parker County Women's Christian Temperance Union, known as the WCTU, asked him to speak about the 1928 presidential campaign, he worked hard on his text, which was published in the local newspaper.
- Soon after he read his talk on the air, speaking requests arrived from all corners of the state.
- The talk was even published as a pamphlet for national distribution.
- On election day, Democrat Al Smith was defeated by a wide margin, but by 1932, national pro-drink leaders had branded the effort to eliminate alcohol consumption "a failure."
- That same year, Zach was called to a parish in Western Pennsylvania where the anti-drinking sentiment was strong and the range of the local radio station wide.
- Immediately, he went to work to stop the passage of the Twenty-first Amendment to the Constitution, designed to nullify the passage of the Eighteenth Amendment.
- This time, he had a new tool with which to fight the devil-drink.
- The Twentieth Amendment, which had given women the right to vote, also gave them the power to stop the "wets" in their tracks if right-thinking women exercised their power at the ballot box.
- Using a public address system mounted on his car, Zach drove all across the western part of Pennsylvania preaching for prohibition and against sinful drunkenness.
- He spoke on public streets, in public parks, and on courthouse lawns.
- Every time the wets would stick their heads up, he liked to say, he would shoot at them to keep them off balance.
- A favorite target was the illegal liquor dives established in the north of the town, just across the county line.
- Using his influence as a radio personality, he had the illegal liquor joints closed.
- The city fathers and business leaders quickly appointed a committee to ask Zach to quiet down; the city was getting a black eye, they warned.
- One pro-booze politician threatened to blow Zach's brains out.
- "Good prophets were put here to lead, not follow," he told himself. "They should be the creators of public opinion."

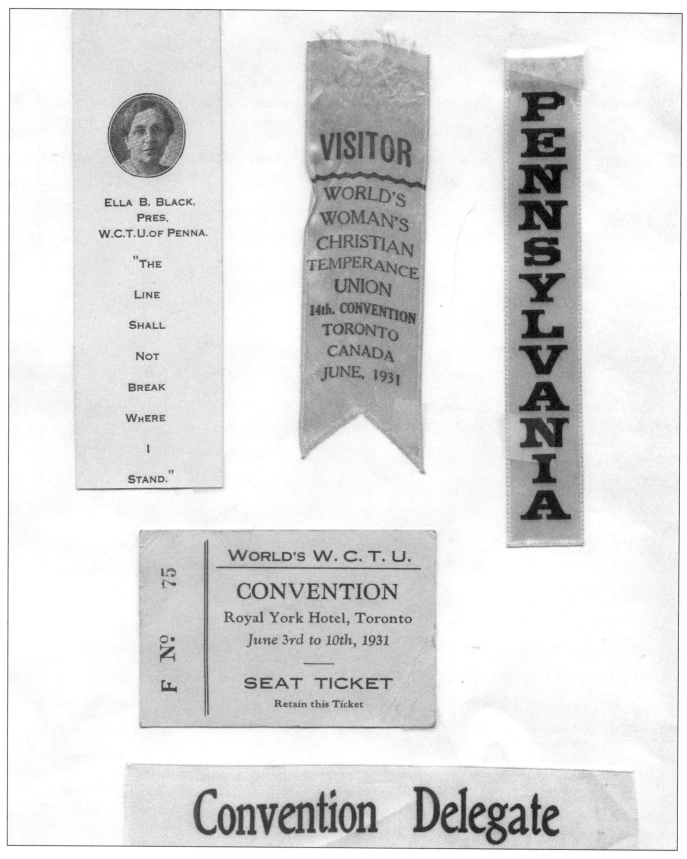

Zachary spoke at the Women's Christian Temperance Union, whose members worked hard against the evils of alcohol.

- Denounced as a troublemaker and a "political parson," Zach persisted, even when the church leadership declared that the liquor fight was a losing cause and should be avoided in the pulpit.
- With that, he abandoned the pulpit and took to the radio in earnest.
- Within a month, he was allowed two 15-minute broadcasts each day to tell the people—especially women—all the reasons that liquor should not be allowed back through the front door.
- His radio talks highlighted the ways that liquor unleashed domestic violence, infidelity, unemployment and poverty.
- He preached that the current failure of prohibition was not an endorsement of liquor, but the work of the devil.
- And he prayed with his radio audience that politicians would reject the proposed Twenty-first Amendment to the Constitution—the first reversal of an amendment in history—so that America could remain dry forever.
- But when the passing of the Twenty-first Amendment allowed the wets to drink openly, Zach's time on the radio was curtailed—until he received a call from Mexico.
- There, a group of right-thinking Americans had established a radio station with a strong, unregulated signal that could reach deep into the heartland of America, using a class 1-a clear channel station, licensed by the Mexican Government according to the Havana Radio Treaty.
- That allowed Zach to become the national voice of temperance to a nation that thought the prohibition issue had been settled.
- During winter months the signal reached most of the United States, Cuba, parts of South America and as far west as Hawaii.
- Mail poured in from all over the world.
- Based on the level of donations, many in the United States were not convinced the fight was over, especially as bars sprang up on neighborhood corners and crime grew worse.
- Four years after America had, according to Zach, erred in its voting, drinking was once again officially condoned and immorality was on the rise.
- If the Eighteenth Amendment was a simple failure, the Twenty-first Amendment was a disaster.
- Talk of another prohibition amendment was in the air, with many counties approving the local option of halting alcohol sales in their communities.
- That meant that someone needed to step forward and lead the crusade.
- On the strength of his radio popularity, Zach embarked on the speaking circuit, tearing the hide off John Barleycorn at every stop.

Life in the United States during Prohibition
- Passage of the Eighteenth Amendment followed years of work, initiated before the Civil War.
- The advocates of temperance and prohibition waged a lengthy 80-year campaign to ban alcohol, raising high expectations for this "Noble Experiment."
- Supporters predicted that alcohol's banishment would lead to the eradication of poverty and vice.
- The prohibition movement achieved initial successes at the local and state levels, particularly in rural Southern and Western states.

President's Message

"WHAT DO YOU KNOW?"

Dear Comrades:

"What do you know?" "How much do you know?" These are questions asked recently by Ruth Cameron. This writer then discussed our thinking.

A daily newspaper that comes to our home carries each day a short quiz called "Horse Sense." I usually take time to check this to see if I do or do not see the ordinary things of life. Do I walk with my eyes open or half open? Do I think or day-dream?

It has been surprising to me how many ordinary questions I miss.

I wonder if this is not true regarding our knowledge of what the liquor traffic is, and what it is doing?

Do people realize that in Pennsylvania a licensee who accepts food, clothing, articles of any kind, in payment for liquor, is breaking the law?

The law states that liquor shall be sold for *cash*. Those who sell on time, and then cash relief or pay checks to pay for drinks already consumed are also breaking the law.

Do our taxpayers realize what it costs our state, in maintenance of institutions, to license liquor?

Do our Christian men and women know the amount spent for liquor in Pennsylvania last year?

Do they realize the increase in sales in 1939 over 1938?

Does the average automobile driver realize what one drink may mean to his driving?

Captain James Killip's $7,000 "Safety School on Wheels" is a scientific wonder. Your State President had the privilege, at the Tampa Fair, of testing her coördination, to prove whether she is or is not capable of driving a car.

"He that hath ears to hear, let him hear." May we take time to listen, especially to the words spoken to us in God's word.

"Give therefore thy servant an understanding heart." Solomon's request should be my request today.

What do I know? Not much.

Can I be helpful with what knowledge I have? Yes, if I am willing.

Yours for Pennsylvania homes,

ELLA B. BLACK,
State President.

- By the early twentieth century, prohibition was a national movement, widely supported by the emerging middle class eager to help control the working, immigrant class.
- But it was only after the U.S. entry into the Great War that prohibitionists were able to secure enactment of national legislation.
- In 1918, Congress passed the Eighteenth Amendment to the Constitution, prohibiting the manufacture, transportation and sale of alcoholic beverages.
- Forty-six of the 48 states ratified the Amendment the next year.
- America officially went dry on January 16, 1920, the day the Volstead Act enforcing the Eighteenth Amendment went into effect.
- For the next 14 years, enormous time, money and manpower would be devoted to the enforcement of prohibition in what became an impossible task.
- Soon, such terms as "bootlegger," "bathtub gin," and "speakeasy" became household words.
- Gangs of hoodlums wielded immense power as they trafficked in alcohol.
- The U.S. Treasury Department's new Prohibition Agents made over 500,000 arrests during prohibition.

- Alcohol consumption, which dropped by half during the first few years of prohibition, ended the 1920s at near pre-prohibition levels.
- "Rum fleets" filled with liquor from Europe appeared off the Atlantic coast.
- Some nights, more than a dozen ships at a time would lie at anchor just outside U.S. territorial waters, while smaller boats made the run to safe harbors in Boston, New York or Charleston, South Carolina.
- The Canadian border was a sieve through which liquor easily flowed.
- Clandestine distilleries grew like mushrooms in the cities and the countryside.
- Alcohol was served at the White House during Harding's administration (1921-1923).
- Alliances between politicians and gangsters formed to serve the public's desire for alcohol.
- By 1926, it was apparent that the "Noble Experiment" was not working.
- Polls indicated the majority of Americans favored repeal of the Eighteenth Amendment.
- No Constitutional amendment had ever been repealed.
- By the early 1930s, most Americans viewed prohibition as a failure.
- Banning the sale and consumption of alcohol had not brought the widespread social benefits—sobriety, fewer crimes, and less poverty—that its supporters had promised.
- Instead, violent crime during the period grew tremendously, with homicide rates increasing by 78 percent.
- Organized crime thrived on prohibition's illegal liquor trade, especially in big cities like Chicago and New York.
- Even more troubling, hundreds of thousands, if not millions, of normally law-abiding Americans eagerly flouted the law.
- On February 20, 1933, Congress proposed the Twenty-first Amendment to the Constitution repealing the Eighteenth Amendment.
- On December 5, Utah became the thirty-sixth state to vote for ratification, assuring acceptance of the Twenty-first Amendment.
- Prohibition was dead in the minds of most on the national level.
- On the local level, 5,000 political units—cities, counties and states—voted to go dry by the end of 1937.

HISTORICAL SNAPSHOT
1937

- In Flint, Michigan, a sit-down strike against General Motors ended after 44 days, with the company agreeing to recognize the United Automobile Workers Union
- DuPont research chemist Wallace H. Carothers received a patent for nylon
- A six-foot-tall concrete statue of the cartoon character Popeye was unveiled during the Second Annual Spinach Festival in Crystal City, Texas
- Jack S. Liebowitz and Harry Donenfeld published their first issue of *Detective Comics*, later known as *DC Comics*
- Leon Trotsky called for the overthrow of Soviet leader Josef Stalin
- The radio show *Lorenzo Jones* starring Karl Swenson was first aired
- German planes sent to Spain by Adolf Hitler to help fascist General Francisco Franco overthrow the communist Popular Front regime attacked the Basque town of Guernica, killing as many as 1,650 Basque civilians and injuring 900
- The first U.S. Social Security checks were distributed
- President Franklin Roosevelt signed an act of neutrality, keeping the United States out of World War II
- Margaret Mitchell won a Pulitzer Prize for her novel *Gone with the Wind*
- The *Hindenburg* burst into flames and crashed to the ground, killing 36, as it attempted to dock with a mooring mast at Lakehurst Naval Air Station in New Jersey
- New York City's Lincoln Tunnel opened to traffic
- Actress Mae West performed a skit featuring Adam and Eve that got her banned from NBC Radio
- The first Santa Claus Training School opened in Albion, New York
- President Franklin Roosevelt dedicated the WPA-constructed Timberline Lodge in Mt. Hood National Forest
- The U.S. House of Representatives passed the Marijuana Tax Act stipulating that pot could not be sold without a license and that no licenses would be issued
- The Pullman Company formally recognized the Brotherhood of Sleeping Car Porters
- Ernest Hemingway's novel *To Have and Have Not* was published
- German Chancellor Adolf Hitler told his military advisors of his intentions of going to war
- NBC formed the first full-sized symphony orchestra exclusively for radio broadcasting for Arturo Toscanini
- The U.S. congressional session was air-conditioned for the first time

Selected Prices, 1937

Airline Fare, Los Angeles to New York	$149.95
Automobile, Plymouth Sedan	$685.00
Baby Carriage	$12.98
Bicycle	$43.95
Cocktail Glasses and Shaker	$0.79
Cow Milker	$42.50
Kitchen Range	$76.95
Movie Camera	$49.50
Shotgun	$30.00
Tire, Goodyear	$18.75

"Repeal Clover Has Withered," by the Radio Evangel, *The National Voice*, March 10, 1938:

It was the repeal of the dry laws that was to emancipate America from the economic dumps. It was going to help balance the budget for one thing; but it has, if anything, unbalanced the budget a whole lot worse than it was—during prohibition. Oh, we were going to be in clover just as soon as we got that terrible prohibition of legalized booze out of the way. Oh, yea!

And all we've gotten out of it is multiplied headaches, more relief, more misery, more hell, more lawlessness, more crime, more broken homes, more divorces, more sin, more whoopee. YES, and we were going to have liquor minus what they called the "old saloon." And what have we got? Well, we've got so many saloons now it would make Bathhouse John, Hinky, Dink and Joe Schmitzelheimer dizzy to try to count them. True, they have "dolled them up" to make them look like "what they ain't," but the sickening smell of booze clings to the taverns and inns just as it used to cling to the "old saloons." True, the lady bartender may have improved the atmosphere to some extent, but tell us, has it improved the thousands of girls that have been turned into bartenders?

The following statistics are from the *Christian Herald*, and should be of interest to our readers:

"We drank 15 gallons of liquor per capita in the U.S. in 1937. That means a liquor bill of about $5 billion.

"Out of the $5 billion, the government collected $0.12 on the dollar: a good stiff tax. But it wasn't enough; last year the government ran a deficit of $2,707,347,110.60!

"Taxes have not been reduced; they have been increased. Relief has remained practically stationary. The budget has not been balanced. The gross public debt has reached the highest point in the nation's history.

"Add to that the cost of enforcing repeal, which is about the same cost of enforcing prohibition: $13 million. Add also this: A billion dollars a year was diverted, during prohibition, to legitimate business channels; the relegalized traffic, in a 54-month period since 1932, has taken away from this legitimate business some $12,417,790,860. Add to that another $4 billion in costs of liquor-bred accidents, crime, destitution, disease and inefficiency. Add to that . . .

"You add it. I'm tired."

The Temperance Army Song, 1890s

Now the temp'rance army's marching,
With the Christian's armor on;
Love our motto, Christian Captain,
Prohibition is our song!

Chorus:
Yes, the temp'rance army's marching,
And will march forevermore,
And our triumph shall be sounded,
Round the world from shore to shore,
Marching on, marching on forevermore,
And our triumph shall be sounded,
Round the world from shore to shore.

Now the temp'rance army's marching,
Firm and steady in our tread;
See! the mothers they are leading,
Marching boldly at the head.

Chorus

Now the temp'rance army's marching,
Wives and Sisters in the throng;
Shouting, "Total Prohibition,"
As we bravely march along.

"The Curse of Strong Drink," *The Booze Buster* by Sam Morris, 1943:

Strong drink caused Noah to commit the first sin following the flood.

Strong drink caused Lot to become the father of his own daughters' children.

Strong drink debauched and killed Nabal, the son of famous old Caleb.

Strong drink played a part in the story of David's sins of adultery and murder.

Strong drink was employed by Absolom when he killed his half-brother Amnon.

Strong drink caused the defeat of the Amalekites by David.

Strong drink led to the murder of Elah, King of Israel, by Zimri, who took the throne.

Strong drink caused the defeat of Ben-hadah by wicked old Ahab.

Strong drink caused the death of Belshazzar and the defeat and overthrow of mighty Babylon by Darius the Mede.

Strong drink is depicted in Proverbs as the instrument of the harlot when she wishes to entice men.

"Howdy, Neighbor"

SAM MORRIS
"The Voice of Temperance"
SAN ANTONIO, TEXAS

Too many people weep and wail about the awful booze conditions around them but never open their mouths in public against those conditions, and they never help the WCTU, the Anti-Saloon League, or the Prohibition Party. They vote for wet Parties and candidates, they trade where booze is sold, and they keep quiet "because they don't want to stir up trouble." They are dry in the mouth but wet every other way. They are prohibition scarecrows.

—Sam Morris, radio broadcast

"Prohibition Accomplishments," *The Henry Bulletin*, Virginia, June 17, 1932:

Booze is now news. Selling liquor, drinking liquor and even getting drunk was an everyday occurrence prior to prohibition and consequently not treated as news.

It has raised the price above the means of many wage earners.

Those who would drink lack confidence in the stuff that is sold; therefore, thousands who would drink frequently, now drink with caution or not at all.

Sales are restricted to those who sanction or are supposed to sanction bootlegging.

Booze no longer seeks the man. Man must seek the booze. The best locations on Main Street and the most conspicuous advertising spaces are no longer monopolized by liquor dealers.

Uncle Sam has dissolved partnership with the traffickers in hootch and no longer stamps with legality the sale of death-dealing, soul-damning, intoxicating liquor.

"Hoover Favors Change in Prohibition and an Attack on Depression," *The Washington Post*, August 11, 1932:

President Hoover declared tonight, in accepting renomination to the presidency, that he believed a change in national prohibition is necessary "to remedy present evils" that have grown up under it.

As to the economic situation, he spoke of new plans looking into a movement "from defense to a powerful attack upon the depression," an assertion that was said in high quarters to embrace the carrying out of his recently enunciated nine-point program as well as other propositions not ready for announcement.

I would rather chase a hummingbird all over the field and never get in 10 feet of him than to chase a hornet three feet and grab him. Brother, when you vote for wet politicians you get stung every time.

No politician can serve humanity and the liquor traffic at the same time. If the dry voters would oppose politicians who are wet, and refuse to wear wet party colors, we could lick the booze business to a frazzle.

—Sam Morris, radio broadcast, 1937

Pennsylvania Youth's Temperance Council, 27th Annual Convention and Leadership Training School, 1937:

The purpose of the Youth's Temperance Council is to unite the Young People of the community, state and nation in a Christian Citizenship program, to build for total abstinence for the individual and sobriety for the nation.

PLEDGE

I promise, by the help of God, never to drink alcoholic liquors; never to use tobacco in any of its forms, and to use every means to fulfill the command: Keep thyself pure.

"Based upon a Lie and Cannot Endure," from an address by Dr. Stephen Leacock, Professor of Economics, McGill University, Montreal. Reprinted from *The Minute Man; 1932:*

I am honestly and sincerely opposed to prohibition as a matter of principle. I think the movement is the worst national development that has come to us in half a century. It is my candid belief that the adoption of prohibition in the United States is the worst disaster that has fallen upon the republic since its organization. If it could last, it would undermine the foundations of the government itself. If it could last, it would in time bring down the strongest political fabric into anarchy and dissolution.

But prohibition cannot last, neither here nor there nor anywhere, because it is based upon a lie. And a lie cannot endure. Prohibition declares it to be a crime to drink beer. And it is not a crime. The common sense of every honest man tells him that it is not a crime to drink a glass of beer. All the Legislatures that ever sat cannot make it so. You can make your statutes as cruel and sharp as you like. You may multiply your spies and informers; you may throw wide the doors of your penitentiaries, and you still cannot make it a crime; and the sharper and harder your law, the more public sense and public feeling will revolt against it.

Let those who have organized the legislative tyranny of prohibition look well to what is bound to follow. They are putting down their trust in coercion, in the jail, in the whip, and the scourge. They are done with the moral appeal. They are finished with persuasion. They want, however, authority. They want to say "Thou Shalt" and "Thou Shalt Not," and when they say it, to be obeyed under the fear of the criminal law. And the time must come when they and their law must go down together. If there is a moral issue involved in this present contest, it is the moral issue of the spirit of human freedom struggling against bondage.

I lay stress on this aspect of liberty because that is what is at stake. The prohibitionist tries here to mislead you. He wants to fool you into

A PHILOSOPHY

For an Approach To and a Study Of

THE ALCOHOL (DRINK) PROBLEM

COMPILED

by Estelle Bozeman

WITH THE

MORAL and RELIGIOUS PHASE

by Dr. A. C. Ivy

Distinguished Professor of Physiology and Head, Department of Clinical Science University of Illinois, Chicago

THE FINDINGS of the many teachers who have attended the National WCTU Seminars and Summer School Classes on materials, methods, and techniques for presenting the factual reasons for total abstinence to children are summarized in this pamphlet.

THE FINDINGS are based on the serious and careful study and evaluation of information derived from more than 100 years of experience and from the results of at least 70 years of research in scientific laboratories.

THE GENESIS OF THE PROBLEM

THE TRAFFIC in alcoholic drinks exists to promote the sale of the product: (1) the consumer of which is never bettered in any way and usually is impaired in health, morals, efficiency, and wealth; and (2) the promoters of which must continually seek new and younger customers to replace the habitues who, on the average, have thirteen years less than normal life expectancy. Thus the youth of our country become the victims. *(Consider what would be the ultimate end of a nation in which there were unrestricted freedom for this traffic, and in which alcoholism were steadily increasing.)*

1

continued

"Based upon a Lie and Cannot Endure," ... *(continued)*

thinking that it is an administrative question, or a medical question, or a political question of the right of the majority to rule. It is none of these things. The prohibitionist, I say, would try to deceive you into thinking that the question at issue is a medical question, that it turns upon the goodness or badness of beer from a purely digestive standpoint. It is not so. Beer may be good or may be bad. My own candid opinion, reached after 51 years of reflection, is that there is nothing like it. But even if I knew it were as bad as the excessive use of tea or coffee, I still would strongly oppose criminal law to prohibit its consumption.

But the plain truth is that beer is just an ordinary beverage. You cannot make it criminal if you try. The attempt is silly. Common sense revolts at it. Some people like beer and some don't. Some people find that it agrees with them and others do not. It belongs in the same class with cucumbers. And the attempt to make the consumption of beer criminal is as silly and as futile as if you passed a law to send a man to jail for eating cucumber salad.

I lay stress upon this word "criminal," because I think it needs to be stressed. I doubt whether the people realize that the Volstead Act and such like statutes are criminal laws. What they propose is virtually to send all people to jail who dare to drink beer, and to send them again and again for each new offense, to break them into compliance as people were once broken upon the wheel.

The thing is monstrous. It is the most brutal invasion of the province of liberty attempted within a century. It cannot succeed. It must fail as all tyranny has failed. But it is sad to think of the deplorable havoc it is destined to make in its course; of the way in which it undermines the respect for the law, the way in which it breaks from the splendid traditions of freedom upon which, till this thing came, we had built up the commonwealth.

There is a spirit that you cannot break by the simple vote of a majority. The individual man, when he stands upon his plain right, will not down. His house is his castle and his life is own.

What service and obedience he owes to those in authority he renders as he should. But when authority passes into tyranny and law into oppression, then his obedience ends. He stands, if need be, alone and single-handed against the law, but behind him as his inspiration he has a thousand years of the tradition of individual liberty. There is a spirit in him that kings have never conquered, that parliaments have never compelled, that the scourge has never beaten out, and that the fire has never consumed.

What is happening to America? Law, divorced from the support of the individual conscience, is breaking down. A vast wave of crime is sweeping over the continent. And the reason is not far to seek. Prohibition is the most fruitful mother of crime that ever spawned its progeny upon the world.

Note well what has happened. Before the prohibitionists had their way and before hysteria, fanaticism, and mistaken desire for righteousness placed them in power, there was no more frequent argument, no greater mainstay of their cause than the plea that prohibition would lessen crime. See what has happened. It needs no statistics to prove the awful and appalling wave of crime upon this continent. The world stands horrified. In the streets of New York and Chicago human life is no longer safe. Organized robbery is everywhere and murder has its daily price and hire.

The reason is clear. The rising generation of today see all about them a form of criminal law called prohibition. They see it everywhere broken. They see it broken by many of the most respected people of the community. They know that it can only be maintained at all by the most brutal, most stringent, and most repulsive of methods. They see employed in its service the vilest of human creatures, the paid informer—the man that lacks even the honor that prevails among thieves—the man who carries down through the ages the part of Judas Iscariot. This they see and upon this they act. The law has become something to be despised, to be broken or evaded at will, the source of adventure

continued

"Based upon a Lie and Cannot Endure," . . . *(continued)*

or of profit, but no longer based upon the plain teaching of right and wrong.

Can you blame any youth if he grows up with a confused sense as to obedience to the law? He knows that the most conspicuous and the most discussed law on your statute book is a sham and a lie. He knows that it is broken everywhere. He knows that the methods used in its enforcement are often despicable. And he knows that there are enlisted in its service some of the most contemptible characters that walk the earth—the spies and informers that are the ears and the tongue of prohibition.

As between the paid informer, coaxing his victim to betrayal, and the criminal, out and out, fighting the law, which do you prefer? Which is, for such good as still lingers in him, the better man? I say it straight, the criminal.

That is the spectacle you are giving to your young men. What, think you, will be the result? You have broken with liberty, you have done with the morality of Jesus Christ that relied ever upon the moving spirit, you have seized the sword to smite off the ear of your opponents—force and power and the tyrant's brutal delight in coercion, that is what the prohibitionist has chosen.

The sharper the tyranny the quicker the cure. A government and a code of law based upon a lie shall sooner or later be dashed to pieces against the impregnable power of truth.

And the end will be destruction. It may be in a year, or in 10, or in a generation. But of the end there is no doubt.

Membership dues receipts from the WCTU.

1939 News Feature

F. W. Lilly interviewed by Works Progress Administration (WPA) writer Mary S. Venable, _Talk about Trouble: A New Deal Portrait of Americans in the Depression_, recorded June 3, 1939:

It was not the blacksmith in our alley of whom Goldsmith wrote, "a mighty man is he," for this one is tall, sparely built and frail in appearance. By irony of nomenclature his name is that of the white flower, the emblem of purity. In spite of his years, he swings his hammer with ease and hearty action. And says to his patrons who come to this shop in preference to the one other the town affords, "You can get it this evening," referring to the job brought in.

He comes from the Scotch settlement near Lexington, Virginia; "out in the country near Brownsburg," he was born. His father died when he was 10 years of age, [and left] five children and a widow. Leaving the fifth grade to go to work on the neighboring farms at $0.25 per day, Mr. Lilly "got no more schooling." At that time a man got $0.50 on a farm (excepting for wheat harvesting; then he got $1.00) but $0.25 was the regular wages for a boy. Pork was $0.08 per pound, and they had a good garden and cows, pigs, and chickens, so the family "made it all right."

His father had been a blacksmith. So as soon as the son reached maturity he went to Brownsburg and learned the trade from M. B. Cash, working in his shop in that large farming district. "You know what that is," he says, and to refresh one's memory he mentions the tragedy of Henry Walker. "They moved away from there after that. Had a big farm. The McClung brothers bought it after he got killed." BANG goes the anvil as he talks, and with such regularity that one cannot stop him to ask who it was that moved. The din is so great and he takes for granted that this local episode will ever live in the memory of man. "It is a good farm, one of the best around Brownsburg.

"If you come to think of it, all we get is out of the earth," philosophizes the smith. "Human beings live off its vegetables, grain, meat. It was put here for us to get our food from, but nobody wants to pay the farmer what his work is worth. And so BANG, the young—BANG—farmer won't work—BANG, BANG; he just scratches around with some of these new-fangled machines." BANG, SZZZZZZ goes the heated piece into the tub of water; SZZZZZZ, another picked out of the dust where it has been cooling, SZZZZZZ, SZZZZZZ, another and another. He is tempering and sharpening his set of cold chisels, 10 or more, for the day's work. "You can't find a farmer who wants to do good ploughing and work for a whole day like used to be. When you come to think of how he sees other folks gettin' rich quick, I dunno as you can blame him.

"Not long ago I was in a butcher's shop here and a farmer from up at Barbers come in and asks the butcher, says he, 'I've got a young beef dressed out here. What will you give me for it?' The butcher says, 'Seven cents on foot is the best we can pay out.' 'I can't [afford] that. It's cost me more than that,' says the farmer. After he left I says to the butcher where I had come to buy my meat, 'I want a cheap piece—say brisket, or maybe a soup bone—a bone with some meat on it, I mean. What's your *cheapest* meat wuth?' 'FOURTEEN cents,' says he. I says, 'That's your *cheapest,* double what you offered that farmer for his best meat and all? What would you make off the best, three or four times that? And here you send to Chicago and pay freight on meat what's been dead two years or mebbe more, nobody knows how long. And this here good meat, raised in this county, you won't give the farmer a decent price for. That's what's the matter. You butchers want the Chicago stockyards and the railroads to eat us up with their profits. And you COULD furnish us good, healthy meat to eat, if you would.'

"He said he had to buy where he could get it regular, that the farmers 'round here would sell in the spring and fall, and there wouldn't be any to buy between their seasons. I told him that could be managed if the farmers were sure they could sell. There could be a slaughterhouse set up and regular killin' done, like used to be. There's Slaughter Pen Hollow, got its name from the slaughterhouse what was there. But the small man is not trying to help the small man. He wants to buy from the rich fellow in Chicago. Maybe buy back the beef sold from *here,* payin' freight both ways."

A young fellow brings a long steel rod in the door and slams it down on top of a lot of debris. It is a half-inch rod to be cut: "Four eye-bolts six inches long, and five, four inches long, a two-inch hook on the end of the four-inch. When can I get it?" "Alleghany Mill?" "Umph-hum." "This evening, about fo'."

Picking up the conversation together with his small hammer, Mr. Lilly bends over the anvil, while his helper seems to be an automatic part of the cooperative plan, losing no fraction of a second when comes the instant to strike or to lift with pincers the glowing metal from the bed of coals. Mr. Lilly decries the get-rich-quick idea of business today. "It used to be [if] a merchant was making 20 percent profit he was satisfied, and if he made a lot of money, he did it by years of putting by a reasonable profit on his goods. Same way with a miller. D'ever hear of a rich miller in the old times? Well, now they got to get three pieces for grindin' and get rich in a year or so. They don't leave nothin' for the other man, the customer or the farmer raisin' his wheat. They don't divide like they used to do.

"So the farmer gets to catchin' on and he wants to go up in prices. I don't blame him, for he's held the short end a hundred years. But this is what I want to know: 'WHO'S GOIN' TO FEED THE NATION?' We gotter eat. Look at these po' people all around here, out on these mountains. They got what they raise, but some ain't got no land to raise wheat on. They got to BUY flour. And there's sugar and coffee and store stuff. They ain't got enough clothes to go to school, let alone Sunday School!

"AND THE WOMEN'S CLUBS PLANTIN' TREES and makin' gardens, with naked and hungry chillun scattered all around 'um. Trees cost from two and a half dollars to fifteen, and when did those same women pay out that much for clothes for po' chillun? The young boys and girls are no 'count. Those off a farm won't handle a spade. And if they stay on the farm they won't raise enough to feed theirselves. They want six or eight dollars a day and they don't know eight-cents'-worth a day.

"My wife hired a scrub woman, a young one, the other day. She knew she come to work, but when my wife told her to mop the floor, d'yer think she'd do it? No sir, said she couldn't spile *her* han's. There was red nail polish on 'um! And she *didn't* mop the floor. The girls can't sew, can't cook, don't do no washin', and all they kin do is to buy dresses—which ain't got no cloth in 'um—at the store, and pay six times what they are worth. They can't make a biscuit fitten to eat and they don't want to learn how. I feel sorry for the boys that get 'um for wives!"

While the iconoclast is taking in more work and memorizing the dimensions for same, it is unusual to hear nothing said of pay, costs, or any mention of money. The patrons say, "You cut one for me last year about this time." Thus, they return. Perhaps the smith "leaves some for the other fellow," in naming his prices.

This shop was an old stable. The door is on the alley which parallels the river. A century ago these lots were in deeds mentioned as "ice-house-lots," when ice was cut off the river and brought up by pulleys. But since the mill polluted the river, no ice has been cut off it. The square below the shop is a "court," in which modern cottages face the river and the rear of the houses across the alley have beautiful gardens to look upon. But this sole remaining stable is unsightly. Its windows lost their sashes about a quarter-century ago and the cracks in the side walls (of broad planks) permit the smoke to escape. Not all of it, as the faces of the two men show.

The helper is from Botetourt County. He is a huge man with arms like barrels. His neck and shoulders bring to mind the marvelous perfection of the created body when "Tubal-cain was a whetter [an instructor] of every artificer in brass and iron" (Genesis 4:22). From a heart in-size-proportioned, he speaks of the flu epidemic during the World War era.

"I was using my truck for an ambulance to bring the sick from the country round about. Up at Barber [Barbour] found five, a woman and four children. They didn't have no sleepin' clothes and they were lyin' on straw with no ticks. Just straw! We brought 'um to the schoolhouse here what was turned into a hospital then. I helped all through that flu epidemic, and worked with the sick carryin' them in and out, and I never took the flu. A lot of folks did, what nursed them."

The hearth or forge is in the center of the shop. It is high off the floor on legs, a heavy molded iron square about forty inches, each dimension. The hand bellows is at one corner and a pipe runs underneath the hearth admitting the draft in the center. On one side of the room is a rack of horseshoes of various sizes. Across, on the opposite side, is a rack of tools: nippers, buck saws, rip saws, wrenches, braces, and some scraps of discarded parts. Near the anvil is a bench of files, pliers, and hammer, black with the dust of the morning. In the back of the room is a long table running its breadth. The vise is "handy" and several tins of oil are on the shelf underneath. An old water cooler lies on its side, top yawning, spigot bent. The anvil weighs 350 pounds, the helper states, and it was bought at the auction of the old furnace when it was dismantled. This chime of the anvil is as melodious as, presumably, it was when its furnace works paid to the workers of the county $80,000 per month. "Those were great days," this man smiles at the recollection.

Mr. Lilly says he has had no work on the old handmade iron since coming to this county, but that in Rockbridge in his early days, "there were a lot of *kittles* and so on," brought to him to work on. "And them pots made cookin' taste good. The cabbage cooked in 'um was yellow, not sickly-lookin' white like that today cooked in granite or aluminum. This aluminum gives no flavor to anything. Dunno why 'tis, but them old iron pots my mother used to cook in for us chillun made everythin' taste good."

On Memorial Day he would have liked to have gone to Rockbridge to the graves of two infants of his sleeping there, he mentions with a depth of feeling and a low-pitched voice. His other children are grown and married. Only he and his wife are left to provide for, and he says he makes a "good living," has nothing to complain of and, with a grin, "I have a fine boss. I like him." His helper seems to be of the same opinion.

Between the clank, clank of the anvil, under the rolling clouds of smoke, with rivulet tobacco amber from the corner of his mouth, an added smudge on his nose, he returns to his regrets of Memorial Day. "I have a truck. We could have gone if we had had the *tins* to put in it (licenses). A fellow has to cover up his car with tins before he dares run it these days. Dunno when I'll be able to get mine. I need the truck, too.

"I could borrow a horse but the trip would take two days and horse feed. I couldn't lose the time." He claims there "are a lot of horses around this part of the country. A lot of men owe me for shoein' 'um. I could have got some of their horses but I didn't." He says he goes out to the country twice a year to shoe horses, goes to the farms. The owners prefer that to bringing the horses to him in town. He has a scheduled route "when fryers get grown" or late in the fall "when cider is runnin' from the presses." In the one county, he states, he has the names of 120 farmers whose horses he keeps shod.

When Mr. Lilly worked at the paper mill as a mechanic, he got $0.80 per hour. He counted a 10-hour day and was pleased with his boss and his pay. He is still very indignant over losing out because of his age. "What's left for men 45 years old? Knock 'um in the head and get rid of 'um. No place in the work that took them years and years to get experience in. Experience that benefits the company. 'Bout the time a man has got some judgment from experience in his line, out he goes! They threw me out at 45. I was hale and hearty. You see me now, well, that was 25 years gone! They had a physical examination and you put your age down. Out I went! The boy who took my place didn't know NOTHIN'. He didn't know 'nuff to be safe to the fellows he was workin' beside. But he was YOUNG and it'd be a long time before he got to be 60, the pension age. Well, an old man can't DIE. You got to eat." Perspiration streams from his brow as he adds another smudge to his nose, and hits a knothole in the plank of the walk across the back door with a well-directed stream of tobacco juice. The log chain is finished. Cut to required lengths without any pencil note of dimensions or name in the ledger.

Mr. Lilly says he is too tired to go anywhere when he leaves the shop. He never walks down to the city playground and does not read. He lives over Grime's Market. His wife missed her flowers and he would like some grass to "loaf on after the sun goes down," but "what are you gonna do when rents are what they are?" He is not at all interested in the election for Town Council or mayor because his vote "would not be counted." All that he wants to vote on is the reduction of taxes. "Taxes is eatin' the country up," he thinks.

The times have passed, the blacksmith of today says, when a man can make a lot of money as he did when wheel tires wore out on the rocky roads and had to be replaced every year. Good ones were of tempered metal and sold for $6.00 or more. If a man failed to pay the blacksmith's bill, his wheels would probably fall down before the next year. So collections were better than today, [when] a man can get in his car and extend his limit of credit geographically to a wide radius. "But I cut the bad ones off my list. If they don't pay, they needn't come back," Mr. Lilly states decisively.

He is proud of his work. Just close to where his forge is today, what was practically "the same stand, for it's been a smith's shop next to the bridge for 140 years, Aaron Clarke shod the cavalry for General Jackson. Here is the bill." He takes from his folder a grimy sheet which is a receipt from the Provost Marshall in 1863 for mending muskets and bayonets and shoeing horses for Capt. (Stonewall) Jackson's cavalry. "They must have stopped on their way to the skirmish at McDowell, either on their way there or on the way back. I must look up the date of that skirmish and find out," Mr. Lilly remarks as he carefully folds the scrap of yellow paper and replaces it in a worn folder.

A listener questions if that shop where the cavalry stopped was not on the east side of Bridge Street; Mr. Lilly's is on the west. He says, "It was hereabouts, anyway. And my shop is the only one around now."

1940–1949

The all-encompassing World War II both dominated the lives of all Americans and served as a national cauldron for mixing people, attitudes and relationships. Women went to work by the millions and gained confidence in their skills. Southern blacks lived and worked outside the daily tyranny of segregation. War-battered immigrants once again found America a welcoming society, while Japanese Americans were forced into refugee camps. Women were encouraged to enter college or even consider becoming doctors. The military talked about desegregating its units and labor unions sensed that power was finally within the grasp of the working man. Children and adults alike joined conservation drives, suffered when tragic telegrams arrived, and learned to eat what the ration tickets made available.

People from every social stratum either signed up for the military or went to work supplying the military machine. Even children, eager to do their share, collected scrap metal and helped plant the victory gardens that symbolized America's willingness to do anything to defeat the "bullies." In addition, large amounts of money and food were sent abroad as Americans observed meatless Tuesdays, gas rationing and other shortages to help the starving children of Europe.

Business worked in partnership with government; strikes were reduced, but key New Deal labor concessions were expanded, including a 40-hour week and time and a half for overtime. As manufacturing demands increased, the labor pool shrank, and wages and union membership rose. Unemployment, which stood as high as 14 percent in 1940, all but disappeared. By 1944, the U.S. was producing twice the total war output of the Axis powers combined. The wartime demand for production workers rose more rapidly than for skilled workers, reducing the wage gap between the two to the lowest level in the twentieth century.

From 1940 to 1945, the gross national product more than doubled, from $100 billion to $211 billion, despite rationing and the unavailability of many consumer goods such as cars, gasoline, and washing machines. Interest rates remained low, and the upward pressure on prices remained high, yet from 1943 to the end of the war, the cost of living rose less than 1.5 percent. Following the war, as controls were removed, inflation peaked in 1948; union demands for high wages accelerated. Between 1945 and 1952, confident Americans—and their growing families—increased consumer credit by 800 percent.

To fight inflation, government agencies regulated wages, prices, and the kind of jobs people could take. The Office of Price Administration was entrusted with the complicated task of setting price ceilings for almost all consumer goods and distribution ration books for items in short supply. The Selective Service and the War Manpower Commission largely determined who would serve in the military, whose work was vital to the war effort, and when a worker could transfer from one job to another. When the war ended and regulations were lifted, workers demanded higher wages; the relations between labor and management became strained. Massive strikes and inflation followed in the closing days of the decade and many consumer goods were easier to find on the black market than on the store shelves until America retooled for a peacetime economy.

The decade of the 1940s made America a world power and Americans more worldly. Millions served overseas; millions more listened to broadcasts concerning the war in London, Rome, and Tokyo. Newsreels brought the war home to moviegoers, who numbered in the millions. The war effort also redistributed the population and the demand for labor; the Pacific Coast gained wealth and power, and the South was able to supply its people with much-needed war jobs and provide blacks with opportunities previously closed to them. Women entered the work force in unprecedented numbers, reaching 18 million. The net cash income of the American farmer soared 400 percent.

But the second World War extracted a price. Those who experienced combat entered a nightmarish world. Both sides possessed far greater firepower than ever before, and within those units actually fighting the enemy, the incidence of death was high, sometimes one in three. In all, the United States lost 405,000 men and women to combat deaths; many suffered in the war's final year, when the American army spearheaded the assault against Germany and Japan. The cost in dollars was $350 billion. But the cost was not only in American lives. Following Germany's unconditional surrender on May 4, 1945, Japan continued fighting. To prevent the loss of thousands of American lives defeating the Japanese, President Truman dropped atomic bombs on the Japanese cities of Hiroshima and Nagasaki, ending the war and ushering in the threat of "the bomb" as a key element of the Cold War during the 1950s and 1960s.

Throughout the war, soldiers from all corners of the nation fought side by side and refined nationalism and what it meant to America though this government-imposed mixing process. The newfound identity of the American GIs was further cemented by the vivid descriptions of war correspondent Ernie Pyle, who spend considerable time talking and living with the average soldier to present a "worm's eye view" of war. Yet, despite the closeness many men and women developed toward their fellow soldiers, spawning a wider view of the world, discrimination continued. African-American servicemen were excluded from the marines, the Coast Guard and the Army Corps. The regular army accepted blacks into the military—700,000 in all—only on a segregated basis. Only in the closing years of the decade would President Harry Truman lead the way toward a more integrated American by integrating the military.

Sports attendance in the 1940s soared beyond the record levels of the 1920s; in football the T-formation moved in prominence; Joe DiMaggio, Ted Williams, and Stan Musial dominated baseball before and after the war, and Jackie Robinson became the first black in organized baseball. In 1946, Dr. Benjamin Spock's work, *Common Sense Baby and Child Care*, was published to guide newcomers in the booming business of raising babies.

1943 Profile

Civil Rights: Internment of 110,000 Japanese Americans

George Fossey, a missionary's son who grew up immersed in Japanese culture, did everything he could to help Japanese Americans upon their removal to internment camps during World War II.

Life at Home

- The son of a missionary, George Fossey grew up in Japan, where he lived until his teens.
- Diabetes forced his father's retirement in 1936 and his subsequent return to the West Coast of the United States.
- Upon retirement, George's father established a farm outside Seattle, Washington, and hired dozens of Japanese Americans to help him manage the land and to teach him the fine art of Japanese furniture making.
- George grew up speaking Japanese, playing Japanese games and eating Japanese food.
- Location and the large number of Japanese students at the University of Washington drove his decision to attend college there, where his major was political science, specializing in Asian affairs.
- George was a first semester junior when the events of Pearl Harbor on December 7, 1941, changed everything.
- Within hours, all Japanese Americans were under suspicion, even those who had been born and raised in the United States.
- Use of the slang phrases "yellow peril" and "Jap menace" became patriotic and acceptable.
- Japanese Americans who had lived as neighbors for decades quickly fell under the rubric of "the enemy."

George Fossey worked to help Japanese Americans sent to internment camps during World War II.

- Immediately demands were bruited for the removal of over 110,000 Japanese Americans from the West Coast and for their internment in "relocation centers" away from the coast.
- George hoped the hysteria would pass, especially when people realized that many of the Japanese under suspicion were American citizens.
- He suspected that much of the outcry was not motivated by legitimate security needs, but by anti-Japanese sentiment that had been festering for decades.
- But with America under attack and the Pacific war going badly, there was little time for polite debate; the prevailing attitude was that the Japanese must be removed from the vulnerable West Coast to points inland, voluntarily or by force.
- In the midst of the war frenzy, George and his father looked for help and found little support for the Japanese.
- The few allies they encountered were men and women like them who had developed close ties to Japanese Americans, both the first-generation Issei and the second-generation Nisei.
- Many of them considered calls for Japanese internment equivalent to the attitude of the Nazis toward the German Jews.
- George believed that victory in World War II would be flawed, at best, if the United States did not treat non-whites as equal allies in the fight against fascism at home and abroad.
- But most of his appeals fell on deaf ears.
- The wholesale internment of Japanese American citizens was the climax of a long history of racism on the West Coast directed against Asian immigrants.
- Discrimination against the Chinese in the mid-1800s resulted in both the federal Chinese Exclusion Act of 1882 and the massacre of 28 Chinese miners in Wyoming in 1885 at the hands of white miners fearful of labor competition.
- Japanese immigration increased after the virtual cutoff of Chinese immigrants, and cries of another "yellow peril" soon followed.
  - Only the protests of the Japanese government and the intervention of President Theodore Roosevelt prevented the segregation of Japanese American students in the San Francisco school system in 1906.
  - The California legislature weighed in with a 1913 law preventing ownership of land by "aliens ineligible for citizenship" intended to undermine the successful farms of the hard-working Japanese immigrants.
  - One U.S. senator from California ran for re-election on the slogan, "Keep California white."
  - This attitude became enshrined in federal policy in the 1922 U.S. Supreme Court ruling that Japanese immigrants could not become naturalized American citizens, and then in the 1924 law that largely halted immigration from Japan altogether.
  - Most of the Japanese immigrants settled in California, Washington and Oregon.
  - Issei found abundant labor opportunities in lumber mills, agriculture and salmon canneries.
  - Eventually, the Japanese labor force could be found in the inland states of Wyoming, Utah and Colorado where they helped construct railroads, mine coal and harvest sugar beets.

The Japanese labor force helped construct railroads, mine coal and harvest sugar beets.

Attack on Pearl Harbor.

- The devastating Sunday morning attack on Pearl Harbor reignited a fear of all things Japanese.
- Within days Japanese businessmen, farmers and bankers were rounded up and questioned, and their homes searched.
- The *Seattle Post-Intelligencer* published an unfounded story claiming that enemy aliens were setting arrow-shaped grass fires to help direct the Japanese air assault on Seattle.
- George's white farmer neighbors were openly hostile to the Japanese, and many happily admitted they were tired of the competition.
- *Life* magazine published an article entitled, "How to Tell the Japs from the Chinese."
- In mid-February 1942, West Coast military commander General John DeWitt formally requested the removal of all Japanese Americans from his command zone.
- DeWitt claimed that the enemy of the United States was not the Japanese government but "the Japanese race."
- "Along the vital Pacific Coast over 112,000 potential enemies of Japanese extraction are at large today," he said.
- Franklin Roosevelt's Executive Order 9066, issued on February 19, 1942, legalized the calls for removal and authorized the military to detain and expel any individuals from West Coast military zones.
- Implementation of the executive order eventually led to the expulsion of about 110,000 Japanese Americans, two-thirds of them U.S. citizens, from their West Coast homes.
- Most were given only a few days to sell their homes, cars and valuables; most lost their jobs and businesses.
- Japanese Americans were forced to go first to makeshift assembly centers on the outskirts of the major West Coast cities and then to hastily built relocation camps in remote areas of several Western states.
- Japanese Americans from the Seattle area, for example, were sent first to a converted fairground about 30 miles south of the city, in Puyallup, and then to the Minidoka camp in south-central Idaho almost a thousand miles away.
- The assembly centers featured primitive accommodations and unsanitary conditions and were under direct military control, while the relocation camps were generally in inhospitable mountainous or desert areas and were supervised by the newly organized War Relocation Authority.
- Many Western states vehemently protested the "dumping" of Japanese Americans within their borders and provided few resources for their care.

Japanese Americans were forced to live in primitive accommodations under direct military control.

Life at Work

- Within weeks of the Pearl Harbor attack, Americans were turning the depression-riddled country into a production machine.

- Work, sacrifice and unity against a common enemy were suddenly symbols of patriotism.
- Women across the nation baked cookies for care packages, children gathered scrap metal, and many made watching for the Jap Menace a popular pastime.
- George Fossey had become disheartened before the Tolan Committee of the U.S. House of Representatives announced that it would take testimony in four West Coast cities.
- Finally, an opportunity to prevent this injustice, George and his father thought.
- So when the committee arrived in Seattle, the faculty and students at the University of Washington were mobilized to oppose mass removal.
- Sociology Department Chair Jesse F. Steiner compared the mass evacuation of U.S. citizens to "the treatment of minorities by the totalitarian governments in Europe and Asia."
- Students Curtis Aller and Hildur Coon challenged the widely held belief that Japanese Americans could never assimilate.
- The 250 Nisei on campus were, above all, Americans, they testified, and very much involved in campus life.
- Evacuation would destroy the loyalty of the Japanese American community.
- The campus newspaper strongly denounced prejudice against African Americans and Japanese Americans in wartime, saying, "If segregation of our citizenry by racial groups persists, democracy is doomed."
- The article blamed business leaders out to make money and the American Legion's misguided flag-waving, not real security needs, for demands for removal of Japanese Americans.
- But despite George's best efforts, many students were reluctant to champion the rights of America's newest enemy.
- The newspapers daily reported stories concerning "Jap" propaganda campaigns, Japanese victories in the Pacific islands and fiery, anti-Japanese political speeches.

George championed the rights of Japanese Americans among faculty and students at the University of Washington.

- His father became embroiled in a dispute off campus when mothers in a Seattle PTA demanded 27 young Japanese American women be ousted from their jobs as public school secretaries.
- Despite his internal anger, George's father gently suggested that one of the reasons "we were fighting Hitler was because of his persecution of peoples not strictly German."
- On campus, 1,000 University of Washington students signed a petition opposing the mistreatment of the secretaries, who had resigned as a group to avoid further controversy.
- Letters supporting the Japanese secretaries appeared in the *Seattle Post-Intelligencer* and challenged the military necessity of firing secretaries who had access to little more information than the tardy and absence reports of elementary school children.
- But when it became clear that the Tolan Committee was only for show, George and his father joined a committee of deans, professors and students on the Seattle campus to assist exiled Nisei students' transition to the camps.
- George was proud of UW President L. P. Sieg, who protected activist professors when calls for their dismissal grew loud.
- President Sieg also allowed Nisei students who would have graduated in 1942 to receive their degrees despite being unable to complete their final quarter of classes, and personally traveled to the internment camps to bestow their degrees.
- Eventually, George abandoned the public arena and focused on his friends, fellow students and workers from the family farm, who had lost nearly all their possessions in the evacuation.
- Once a week he wrote letters of encouragement, convinced the evacuation orders would be lifted soon.
- He worked with volunteers at the local American Friends Service Committee to ease the blow of evacuation by helping to arrange the safe storage of possessions owned by the Japanese, leasing of their lands and operations of their abandoned stores and businesses.
- He also helped care for elderly Japanese Americans left behind in hospitals.

Life in the Community: Seattle, Washington

- Nearly everyone in Seattle, Washington, was impacted by the mass movement of Japanese Americans to the internment camps, called "concentration camps" by some.
- The principal of one Seattle elementary school told an assembly that regardless of where their parents came from, all the children in the school were Americans, and then had to watch the children leave with their parents.
- When the order came for Japanese Americans to leave Seattle in April 1942, Ella Evanson, a seventh and eighth grade teacher, asked her students to write about their feelings.
- Correspondence continued between these white students in Seattle and the Nisei in the Assembly Center in Puyallup, Washington, for several years.
- Evanson herself sent books, magazines and other materials to her former pupils.
- She also worked on their behalf in other ways, at one point writing a character reference for the Issei father of one of her best students, who had been detained by the FBI as an "enemy alien."
- Another Seattle teacher, Lila Foltz, kept up a four-year correspondence with the family of one of her former pupils while they were interned at Tule Lake, and sent Christmas gifts and necessities for the children.
- George and his father made trips to the camp, 700 miles away, and brought news from home, personal belongings from storage, and gifts from friends.

- But as 1942 drew to an end, the mental strain of the uprooted Japanese Americans began to show in the faces of the Nisei group, despite small victories.
- George and his father brought the impounded automobile of one family who had arranged to move East, making it possible for them to leave the camp.
- Both father and son came to believe that America's 20-year policy of restricting Japanese immigration was directly linked to the Japanese attack on America's Pacific fleet at Pearl Harbor.
- This view shrank George's circle of friends, many of whom were aghast that anyone would suggest that America was responsible for the surprise attack.
- Several women refused to date a "Jap-radical."
- George's father was unfazed by the criticism and challenged groups to go beyond the boundaries of race and class to embrace all of humanity, including the unemployed, the exploited, the Negro and the Asian.

Japan's war minister Tojo.

HISTORICAL SNAPSHOT
1943

- President Franklin D. Roosevelt flew to Morocco for a top-secret meeting with British Prime Minister Winston Churchill; no U.S. president had previously flown while in office because the Secret Service regarded flying as too dangerous
- Frankfurters were replaced by Victory Sausages, a mix of meat and soy meal
- Work was completed on the Pentagon, headquarters of the U.S. Department of Defense
- A wartime ban on the sale of pre-sliced bread in the United States went into effect, aimed at reducing bakeries' demand for metal replacement parts
- The Battle of Stalingrad ended as small groups of German soldiers of the Sixth Army surrendered to the victorious Red Army forces
- Duke Ellington led the debut of *Black, Brown and Beige* at Carnegie Hall in a Russian War Relief effort headed by Harriet Moore, a Communist sympathizer
- The American 442nd Regimental Combat Team, made up almost entirely of Japanese Americans, was authorized
- Shoe rationing began, limiting each purchaser to three pairs for the year
- German tanks and two infantry battalions broke the Allied line and took Kasserine Pass in North Africa
- The battleship *USS Iowa*, the first in the navy's 45,000-ton class, was commissioned
- German women demonstrated outside a Berlin community center where their Jewish husbands and children had been rounded up for deportation to Auschwitz; 1,200 men and children were released a week later
- Berlin was bombarded by the RAF with 900 tons of bombs
- Japanese forces and American troops fought for five days in Bougainville
- Aaron Copland's *Fanfare for the Common Man* and Rodgers and Hammerstein's *Oklahoma!* both opened on Broadway
- Rationing of meat, butter and cheese began
- Japanese Admiral Isoroku Yamamoto, the mastermind of the attack on Pearl Harbor, was shot down by American P-38 fighters
- In Warsaw, Poland, young Jews staged a futile uprising against the Nazis
- President Roosevelt announced that several of the captured Doolittle pilots were executed by the Japanese
- U.S. troops invaded Attu in the Aleutian Islands to expel the Japanese
- British Prime Minister Winston Churchill pledged his country's full support in the war against Japan
- Norman Rockwell's painting *Rosie the Riveter* appeared on the cover of *The Saturday Evening Post*
- The Allies began bombing Germany around the clock

ROCK HILL PRINTING & FINISHING COMPANY

THIS IS NO TIME FOR FOOLING! STICK TO YOUR JOB.

ROCK HILL PRINTING & FINISHING COMPANY

KICK IN AND HELP KICK HITLER OUT!

WORK WILL WIN

THE MAJORITY OF YOUR WORK IS FOR THE GOVERNMENT.

DYE DEPT. EMPLOYEES YOUR WORK HERE IS IMPORTANT TO YOUR GOVERNMENT

You turn out this Raincoat Material  → To Make These Coats For Our Soldiers

 →

You turn out this Comfort Material → To Make these Comforts For Our Soldiers

 →

ATTENTION DYE DEPT EMPLOYEES!
KNOW WHAT YOU ARE DOING FOR OUR COUNTRY!
YOU ARE PRODUCING GOODS FOR 14 MILLION HANDKERCHIEFS ENOUGH FOR 2 EACH FOR AN ARMY OF 7 MILLION MEN!
YOU ARE PRODUCING GOODS FOR 6 MILLION SHORTS FOR OUR ARMY.
YOU ARE PRODUCING CAMOUFLAGE GOODS FOR NETTING HEAD PIECES FOR OUR MARINES IN JUNGLE COUNTRIES ENOUGH FOR 1¼ MILLION FIGHTING MARINES
YOU ARE PRODUCING GOODS FOR COMFORTERS ENOUGH TO SUPPLY 150,000 SOLDIERS OR 10 DIVISIONS. THESE FIGHTING MEN ARE DEPENDING UPON YOU!
R.H. P & F. PRODUCTS FIGHT ON EVERY FRONT!

Selected Prices, 1943

Bourbon, Fifth $3.80
Brassiere $1.00
Bunk Bed $10.98
Coffee Percolator $2.95
Fountain Pen $15.00
Golf Clubs, Set of Five Irons $12.95
Hotel Room, Times Square $6.00
Laundry Tub $9.85
Opera Ticket $2.00
Record Albums, Four 12" LPs $4.72

THE COMMODORE

One of the world's great hotels, The Commodore is a landmark to visitors to New York . . . . an institution to New Yorkers. Its four magnificent restaurants are noted for superb food. Its famous function rooms seat from 35 to 2500 persons. In its twenty-seven stories The Commodore contains 2000 large outside rooms, all with private bath . . . . shops of every type . . . . a city within a city. Its many services are staffed by an intelligent, highly trained personnel. The Commodore is . . . .

NEW YORK'S BEST LOCATED HOTEL

. . . . Right at Grand Central Terminal . . . . just across 42nd Street from the Airlines Terminal . . . . within a few minutes of theatres, smart shops, museums . . . . with direct entrances to express subway services to Greater New York . . . . Noted, too, for its friendly hospitality . . . . its real economy.

SINGLE ROOMS from $3

THE **COMMODORE**
MARTIN SWEENY, President
RIGHT AT GRAND CENTRAL AND AIRLINES TERMINALS

WHAT SECRETARIES REALLY THINK . . .

29% longer lasting flavor in Beech-Nut Gum, tests with 615 secretaries show

IN 26 CITIES throughout the country, 615 secretaries tested peppermint chewing gum. They reported that Beech-Nut's peppermint flavor lasted, on an average, 29% longer than the peppermint flavor of all the other brands tested. In addition, 2 out of 3 said that they preferred the peppermint flavor of Beech-Nut to that of the other brands. When *you* buy chewing gum, get the *yellow* package of Beech-Nut. *It's delicious.* Discover how long and how much you enjoy its better, stronger peppermint flavor.

An independent consumer research organization made the tests*

615 secretaries in 26 cities were tested. Various brands of peppermint chewing gum were bought in local stores and re-wrapped in *plain* wrappers. Each secretary was given two different brands

(Beech-Nut and one other), asked to report how long she thought the flavor of each stick lasted and which stick tasted better. Beech-Nut was thus tested against all the other brands.

Name on request.

They said:
more minutes of flavor

BEECH-NUT GUM
Always Refreshing!

Japanese American Timeline

1912
Japanese Americans owned 12,726 acres of farmland in California.

1913
The California Alien Land Law prohibited all Asian immigrants from owning land or property, but permitted three-year leases.

1920
The California Alien Land Law prohibited leasing land to "aliens ineligible for citizenship."

1925
Alien land laws were passed in Washington, Arizona, Oregon, Idaho, Nebraska, Texas, Kansas, Louisiana, Montana, New Mexico, Minnesota and Missouri.

1922
The U.S. Supreme Court reaffirmed that Asian immigrants were not eligible for naturalization.

1935
Congress passed an act making aliens eligible for citizenship if they had served in the U.S. armed forces between April 6, 1917, and November 11, 1918.

1939
U.S. law enforcement and military intelligence began compiling lists of dangerous enemy aliens and citizens.

1940
The U.S. Census recorded 126,947 Japanese Americans; 62.7 percent were citizens by birth.

1941
The Hawaiian National Guard was federalized.

The Japanese Language School at the Presidio of San Francisco was formed.

Japan bombed Pearl Harbor; the U.S. entered World War II.

A blanket presidential warrant authorized the FBI to arrest "dangerous enemy aliens," including German, Italian and Japanese nationals; 737 Japanese Americans were arrested the first day.

By December 11 the FBI had detained 1,370 Japanese Americans classified as "dangerous enemy aliens."

All enemy aliens in California, Oregon, Washington, Montana, Idaho, Utah and Nevada were ordered to surrender contraband.

1942
Japanese American selective service registrants were classified IV-C, or enemy aliens.

Active military Japanese American soldiers were discharged or assigned to "kitchen police."

Congressman Leland Ford of California demanded that all Japanese Americans be removed from the West Coast.

United States Attorney General Francis Biddle established zones where German, Italian and Japanese aliens were forbidden.

California Attorney General Earl Warren called Japanese Californians the "Achilles heel of the entire civilian defense effort."

continued

Timeline . . . (continued)

1942

The U.S. Army established 12 "areas in which enemy aliens were restricted by a 9 p.m. to 6 a.m. curfew, allowed to travel only to and from work, and not more than five miles from their homes."

The West Coast congressional delegation requested that the president remove "all persons of Japanese lineage . . . aliens and citizens alike, from the strategic areas of California, Oregon and Washington."

President Roosevelt signed Executive Order 9066 authorizing the secretary of war to define military areas "from which any or all persons may be excluded as deemed necessary or desirable."

The Quakers Society of Friends and the American Civil Liberties Union objected to the order.

Japanese American residents of Terminal Island, San Pedro, California, were given 48 hours to settle their affairs and leave.

The House Committee on Un-American Activities released its 300-page report detailing thousands of charges against Japanese Americans.

General DeWitt issued Public Proclamation No. 1, creating military areas in Washington, Oregon, California and parts of Arizona, and declaring the right to remove German, Italian and Japanese aliens and anyone of "Japanese ancestry" living in Military Areas No. 1 and 2 should it become necessary.

Roosevelt created the War Relocation Authority (WRA) responsible for the removal of designated persons from the restricted areas.

Manzanar, the first American concentration camp, opened.

Alien and non-alien persons of Japanese ancestry were given one week to leave Bainbridge Island near Seattle.

Governors and representatives of Nevada, Idaho, Oregon, Utah, Montana, New Mexico, Wyoming, Washington and Arizona refused to accept Japanese American evacuees; Colorado Governor Ralph Carr was the only one to offer cooperation.

The removal of 110,000 Japanese Americans from the military area was completed.

Eight thousand Japanese detainees worked to save the crop harvest in various Western states.

When unrest and strikes occurred at Manzanar, military police fired into the crowd, killing two protesters and wounding at least 10 more.

1943

Over 2,500 Japanese volunteered for military service; restrictions on Nisei service were removed.

California Governor Earl Warren signed a prohibition on granting commercial fishing licenses to alien Japanese.

Tule Lake internment camp was designated as a "segregation" facility for dissidents.

Secretary of War Henry Stimson announced plans to form an all-Japanese American combat team to be made up of volunteers from both the mainland and Hawaii.

First Lady Eleanor Roosevelt toured the Gila River internment camp in Arizona.

The Supreme Court ruled that a curfew may be imposed against a group of American citizens based solely on ancestry.

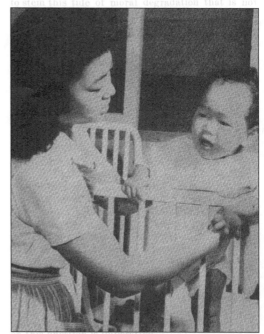

"War Relocation Authority," *Britannica, Book of the Year*, 1944:

Established by executive order of the president March 18, 1942, the War Relocation Authority was set up primarily to provide for the 110,000 people of Japanese ancestry who were evacuated by military order from the Pacific Coast region in the spring and summer of 1942. The agency's prime objective was to relocate as many of these evacuated persons as possible on farms and cities outside the restricted West Coast zone. While resettlement went forward, the WRA maintained the evacuated people in barracks cities known as relocation centres, and provided them with food, shelter, medical care, work opportunities and standard education for the children.

Relocation of the evacuated people out of these centres into normal communities began on a significant scale in the early months of 1943 and continued at an average rate of 400 departures a week throughout the summer. By the end of 1943, more than 16,000 former residents of the centres had resettled across the country, and during the year 8,500 went west out of the centres on seasonal agricultural jobs.

War Relocation Centers attempted to relocate Japanese Americans to farms and cities outside the restricted zone.

We should share in such ways as our limited resources permit in breaking the force of this calamity which has come upon the Japanese population.

—Clarence Pickett, executive director,
American Friends Service Committee,
March 1942

Future historians will record this evacuation—this violation of citizenship rights—as one of the blackest blots on American history; as the time that democracy came the nearest of being wrecked.

—Rev. Emery Andrews, a Baptist minister
and former missionary to Japan, 1943

National columnist Henry McLemor, Hearst Newspapers, December 1941:

Everywhere that the Japanese have attacked to date, the Japanese population has risen to aid the attackers. Pearl Harbor. Manila. What is there to make the Government believe the same wouldn't be true in California? Does it feel that the lovely California climate has changed them and that thousands of Japanese who live in the boundaries of this state are all staunch and true Americans?

I am for the immediate removal of every Japanese on the West Coast to a point deep in the interior. Herd 'em up, pack 'em off, and give 'em the inside room in the badlands.

Let 'em be pinched, hurt, hungry, and dead up against it. Personally, I hate Japanese. And that goes for all of them.

Let's quit worrying about hurting the enemy's feelings and start doing it.

We were ordered by the local army command to evacuate within 30 days. My father sold everything in the house for $21.00. Each of us carried a suitcase with all of our worldly possessions.
—Japanese American evacuee Robert Ichikawa, 1942

"A Letter Written by a Young Japanese," George E. Taylor, *The Atlantic Monthly*, May 1942:

Tonight as I sit here and type at my portable placed on a card table that is used for almost everything under the sun, the thought comes to me that I ought to portray an actual evening at home in an overcrowded apartment. I consider mine an overcrowded apartment, for in it there are seven of us. At the present moment my wife is trying in vain to put our four-month-old baby girl to sleep. She is pacing the length of the 20' by 25' room with the baby in her arms, but the baby continues to cry. My elderly male cousin is lying prone on his bed in one corner of the apartment and trying hard to concentrate on the front page of a three-day-old newspaper, but I am certain that it is only with difficulty that he is reading the paper, for he is constantly casting glances toward my wife and the wailing baby. My middle-aged female cousin is also lying prone on her bed, which is located in the center of the room alongside the bed of her 10-year-old daughter who is still very much full of pep and energy despite a strenuous day of play outdoors. The young daughter is keeping herself busy between making a necklace of melon seeds and calling everyone's attention to the little minnows that some of her little boy friends caught for her during the day in the nearby creek. My mother-in-law was puttering around for a while with her sewing, but she must have tired of it, for I now note that she has gone outside and is carrying on a conversation with one of the neighbors on our front "porch." The thing that strikes me just at this particular moment is this: How long can we keep up this strain that is brought about by the lack of privacy?

WARTIME CIVIL CONTROL ADMINISTRATION
Induction and Reception Center Division
PUYALLUP, WASHINGTON

August 6, 1942

INSTRUCTIONS FOR MOVEMENT OF ADVANCE CREW

Evacuee members of the advance crew will be allowed a maximum of 150 pounds per person on baggage. Baggage should be limited to necessities only. Hand luggage taken into the coach is not included in the 150 pounds baggage limitation.

Saturday afternoon, August 8th, all baggage excepting hand luggage will be ready for loading on trucks in each area. All baggage from Area "D" will be taken by the evacuee to the Area "D" Headquarters location and will be loaded on trucks at that place. Baggage from Areas "B" and "C" will be picked up by Operations and taken to Area "D" Headquarters loading point. Baggage in Area "A" will be loaded on trucks at Pitcher's Field.

All baggage (not hand luggage) shall be tagged, showing the name of the evacuee, the family number, and the number of pieces, for example 1 of 4, 2 of 4, etc. Hand luggage will not be tagged nor loaded with the baggage.

If an evacuee has baggage in excess of the limit allowed, it should be boxed or crated, or securely tied in bundles and left in care of a responsible person in the section. These articles should also be tagged, showing the family name, number and number of pieces. Such items will be shipped at a later date. For your information the War Relocation Authority, within a reasonable time after arrival of evacuees at Relocation Projects, will arrange to have household and personal effects of evacuees now in storage outside Assembly Centers, shipped to the Relocation Project.

All Government property charged against the evacuee which includes beds, mattresses, ticks, and blankets will be checked on Saturday afternoon, August 8th by area. Beds, mattresses, ticks, and blankets shall be left in apartments after evacuation on Sunday morning and will be picked up and removed to the warehouse after the movement has been completed. All property not accounted for shall be charged against the evacuee's account. IT IS IMPERATIVE THAT BAGGAGE SHOULD BE HELD TO A MINIMUM AS INFORMATION RECEIVED INDICATES THAT ONLY ONE BAGGAGE CAR WILL BE AVAILABLE FOR THIS ENTRAINMENT.

[Signed E. S. Parmeter]

"*Get 'em into the Blue*"
...off the production line...into the sky

Above illustration—Largest single delivery of airplanes to U. S. Army Air Corps. 31 Vultee BT-13 planes in mass formation over Vultee Field, California.

MATERIALS...parts...supplies stream into Vultee plants from every point of the compass. Out the factory doors flows a steady stream of completed airplanes...ready to fly for defense.

Back of every operation, permeating the entire Vultee organization, there's a primary production objective best expressed in the simple phrase: "Get 'em into the Blue"...into the Blue for the U. S. Army Air Corps and the foreign democracies.

Early in 1941, Vultee becomes one of the first aircraft manufacturers to complete its current expansion program, representing an increase in plant area of 1300%. Decentralization of manufacturing facilities into 3 complete divisions together with other innovations will enable Vultee to multiply deliveries 10 times during this year.

Stinson Aircraft, a division of Vultee is now in production on a new commercial plane for 1941. Write Stinson for complete information.

VULTEE AIRCRAFT, INC.
VULTEE FIELD, CALIFORNIA • NASHVILLE, TENNESSEE
STINSON AIRCRAFT
WAYNE, MICHIGAN

Vultee Stinson

Letter from James Y. Sakamoto of the Emergency Defense Council Seattle Chapter of the Japanese American Citizens League, March 23, 1942:

Mr. President:

We, the American Citizens of Japanese parentage in these United States, have taken seriously your various statements on the Four Freedoms. Our parent generation, too, has taken comfort from those assertions. They have not enjoyed the rights of citizenship in this country. For that reason they are at this time particularly open to accusation and suspicion.

We were reassured when war broke out and heard your directions as to the treatment to be accorded aliens of enemy countries. We felt those were commands upon all American citizens to pull together for a common objective. Even when the clamor against us was raised by a national organization whose patriotic motives undoubtedly seemed about to threaten our very lives, we trusted in your protection.

The picture has changed since then. Evacuation has now become a certainty for all of us, non-citizen and citizen alike. We citizens have been singled out for treatment that has hitherto not been meted out to any American. Though the medicine was bitter, we have attempted to obey without criticism, and to swallow it.

We were prepared to go where we might be sent, to be uprooted permanently from the homes we have known since childhood. Our parents before us had in many instances built up the only homes we knew. They had given us an American education and in some thousands of instances sent us gladly into the service of our country. They, too, were to accompany us. We thought it would simply be a matter of transfer to another locality in which we might carry on, under a cloud indeed, but demonstrating our loyalty nonetheless, by obeying a humiliating and distasteful command.

We are still so minded. We shall obey willingly. We shall continue to trust you and to give our allegiance to the ideals you enunciate.

In the working out of the details of evacuation, we have noticed an insistence upon the necessity for speed in going to places not designated by anyone. We are willing to go, glad to escape from even the possibility of ever being accused of even being present in the area where sabotage might conceivably take place.

Under the circumstances prevailing, we have been so completely discredited by the American people at large that it is impossible for us to appear anywhere without giving rise to some hysterically false assumption that we are engaged in some nefarious design against a country that is as much ours as it is that of our fellow citizens. So marked is this that had we any intention such as we are popularly credited with, the easiest manner in which it might be accomplished would be for us to simply pick up and spread our unwanted presence over the American map and so precipitate, under Army decree, that complete disruption of the war effort.

Our people have not been unconscious of the extent to which our country has been dependent upon them for the production of certain articles of food in areas now filled with Army installations and all lines of war work. Certainly, had they any mind to sabotage, they could have done so no more completely than by ceasing to produce the food upon which so much of the war effort depended.

Mr. President, we have protested our loyalty in the past. We have not been believed. We are willing to assume the burden of continuing to demonstrate it under all but impossible conditions. We would be deeply grateful if you would point it out to our fellow citizens that we are not traitors to our country as the above facts, in our opinion, amply demonstrate.

Restore our good name to us that our soldiers of Japanese ancestry need no longer hang their heads in shame as their hearts secretly bleed in anxiety over the whereabouts of their parents and loved ones possibly stranded penniless in some desert of the Southwest, or begging their bread in the streets of some strange place. Give to us some refuge in the heart of the country far removed from even the suspicion or possibility to do harm. We

continued

Letter from James Y. Sakamoto . . . *(continued)*

have helped to feed the nation in the past. Let us continue to do so now that it is needed the more. Only let us do so freely and not under that compulsion made notorious in an enemy country. We do not have to be driven to work for a country in which we believe for ideals more precious than our life-blood.

We know there have been dissident elements among us, often unknown to ourselves. We know that some of the customs brought from abroad do lay some members of our parents open to suspicion even yet. We, like our fellow citizens, have complete confidence in the all-seeing eye of the Federal Bureau of Investigation. We have seconded their efforts when told what it was they were searching for and we shall continue to do so.

We hope to find in the hearts of those like ours some understanding of our problems and some surcease from the burdens that oppress us. We have confidence that you yourself may present our case to them as a demonstration here of sincerity toward the promises you have made to the world.

Trusting that you will give us your sympathetic assistance and with the greatest hope for your continued good health, I am, my dear Mr. President,

Faithfully yours,
James Y. Sakamoto

Letters to teacher Elizabeth Willis from a former Japanese American student living in Internment Camp Harmony, Puyallup, Washington:

May 14, 1942
Dear Mrs. Willis,

Sorry that I didn't write to you sooner but we were busy getting settled. We arrived here (Camp Harmony) on Friday afternoon May 8 and there were many to greet us. They were the people who came before us and they helped us to get settled.

The camp is divided into four areas, Area A, B, C, and D. The areas are then subdivided into sections. My house number is A-6-46, that is, Area A section 6 apartment 46.

The barracks with their rooms were not what I expected them to be, but they are comfortable enough. It is a framework of wood with shiplap over it. The walls between the rooms don't quite reach the ceiling and if one talks loudly he can be heard at the other end of the barracks. In each room there is a wood stove which takes care of the heating problem, for in the morning and night it gets quite cold. Although the living quarters are close, one can live comfortably.

We've hung curtains and drapes, made our own furniture and have tried to make our room as much as possible like home. Everything is a little crude but it's all right, for a little crudeness fits into the picture. It's a place for old clothes and boots because when it rains the streets get muddy and when it becomes hot, you eat a lot of dust, so the boys say.

There are six mess halls and when it's time to eat, we line up outside. By the time the doors open there is a very long line, so the early birds eat first. The food is all right but I think I could stand a little more, and as always, it could be better.

continued

Letters to teacher Elizabeth Willis . . . *(continued)*

You ought to see some of the signs they have by the doors. Some of them are very funny and would give you a laugh. There was one which was very well suited to the place, "Knot Inn." It's very well suited because the boards have many knots and sometimes they fall out and leave gaping holes.

The place is entirely surrounded by a barbed wire fence and soldiers watch on towers and march back and forth along the fence. Sometimes we talk to them and they are friendly. I don't mind them watching me and I believe that the others don't mind either. Everyone seems to be contented and have adapted themselves to the change even though many things are lacking.

Right now I would rather be in school and be with all my friends. Well, I have to hit the hay now and when I say hay I mean hay, for the mattresses we have are filled with hay.

A pupil,
Eiji Murata

P.S. I wanted to say good-bye but just didn't get around to it. Thanks for all you've done.

July 7, 1942
Dear Mrs. Willis

It's been quite some time since I've written you. Sorry that I didn't write sooner but I've had a down and out feeling with a cold for the past week. On top of that it's been so hot that it was uncomfortable to stay inside and write. A cold in the summer is very hard to get rid of.

We've had to clean out our rooms and mop them. Our straw or hay mattresses had to be refilled and what a time the hay fever victims had. The day was very hot and it felt like an oven inside because the roofs are made of black tar paper which absorbs a great deal of heat.

I hope you are enjoying yourself at Agate Point. It must be wonderful to go swimming in the cold salt water and then to lie on the warm sand. How I wish I could do that! I hear you are having good weather and so are we, but lately it's been too hot and we can't do anything to avoid the heat except sit in the shade of the barracks which isn't very good.

My journal was just getting started when I forgot about it. I'm pretty far behind now and don't feel up to writing it. As you said it may be important to historians if it is good enough, but it's quite a job and pretty hard to keep it up in these conditions.

What I wouldn't give to be back in Seattle next September to continue my studies at Garfield. Many of the boys say this too. Some of them who were not good students and didn't like school even say this. It is my belief that everyone here would like to go back to their normal life.

But recently I've read quite a bit about taking away the U.S. citizenship of the American-born Japanese and to deport them after the war. The Native Sons and Daughters of the Golden West are trying to do this, and from what I read they are in dead earnest. Our citizenship is very dear to us and I hope this thing never occurs.

Until I write again I remain,

A pupil,
Eiji Murata

"Would Bar All Asiatics," *The New York Times*, September 20, 1920:

SAN FRANCISCO, Cal.—"I do not wish to see this nation commit suicide," said Samuel Shortridge, Republican candidate for United States senator. "I am a nationalist and not an internationalist, and I am, have been and always will be firmly against the League of Nations. It is not because I am afraid to fight. Personally I should be the first to fight for America and the last to surrender her independence. From the beginning of time the Monroe Doctrine has been enough for me, and I am still willing to let it lead me wheresoever I may go.

"Furthermore, I am a protective tariff man, a protectionist first, last and always. I wish my country to be industrially and commercially independent. If we entangle ourselves in foreign alliances we are subjecting this country to a national suicide. No real American wishes to commit this outrage, and we all would be willing to fight if civilization were again at stake.

"I am a firm believer in Senator—or should I say President?—Harding's statement in regard to the Pacific Coast. The Golden Gate must not swing open to admit the refuge of Oriental countries. The thought of it appalls the calmest mind and disturbs the stoutest heart. Twenty years ago, as represented by the Chinese, was acute. As then, so since and now, I am opposed to Asiatic immigration to California. And by this I mean the Hindus, Chinese and Japanese."

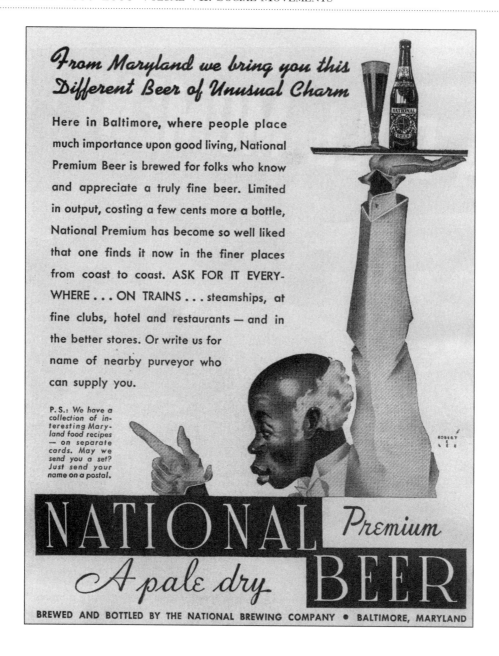

1946 Profile

Civil Rights: Desegregating the Military

John William Gibson was so frustrated by the racial discrimination in the U.S. Navy that he met with the battalion commander to obtain an appointment to air the grievances of the Black troops.

Life at Home

- As war and rumors of war grew more pronounced in 1940, most African Americans were deeply skeptical of American participation.
- John William Gibson was an exception to the rule.
- He had grown up hearing tales of World War I told by his uncle, Pink Beam, who had been stationed in France.
- Uncle Pink had served in one of the few Black units to actually see combat, so his stories included tales of both glorious battles and widespread acceptance of the Black doughboys in France.
- Uncle Pink had shared drinks with French civilians, earned the respect of White soldiers who would never have spoken to him in America, and shared the appreciation of the French people as they showered praise on Black and White soldiers without discrimination.
- "The military may be the ticket to helping the White man and the colored man live together, but not in my lifetime," Uncle Pink told J.W., as John William was known. "Maybe in your lifetime, but not in mine."
- After a few drinks and out of J.W.'s earshot, Uncle Pink would describe the mistreatment, violence and intolerance committed against the colored troops after they returned home from the Great War.
- "It wears a man out to fight for his life in France, only to fight again at home," Uncle Pink told his friends in North Carolina.
- J.W. followed the campaign for the desegregation of the military through articles in the *Pittsburgh Courier,* the most widely circulated Black newspaper in the country.

John William Gibson was frustrated by the racial discrimination in the Navy.

John's Uncle Pink served in one of the few Black units to see combat.

- Since 1937 the *Courier* had been running a campaign to end segregation in the armed forces.
- This effort became more focused in 1941, when Labor leader A. Philip Randolph organized a Negro march on Washington to demand equal participation in the military.
- President Franklin D. Roosevelt resented the tactic of a staged protest in front of the White House.
- Randolph was summoned to the White House and asked to call off the march.
- In the absence of a firm commitment from Roosevelt to end job discrimination in the defense industries and the military, Randolph refused to stop the march, which would include thousands of Blacks.
- Days before the scheduled protest, Roosevelt signed order 8802, decreeing "there shall be no discrimination in the employment of workers in the defense industries or in government because of race, creed, color or national origin."
- Even though the order did not mention the desegregation of the military, Randolph called off the protest march, for which he was widely criticized.
- After the attack on Pearl Harbor in December 1941, the *Pittsburgh Courier* stepped up its efforts for desegregation by launching the "Double V for Victory" campaign.
- One "V" signified victory over fascism in Europe and Asia, and the other "V" was for victory over Jim Crow in America.
- The *Courier* also provided J.W. with news of race riots at Ft. Oswego, fighting at Camp Davis, discrimination at Fort Devens; Jim Crow conditions at Camps Blanding and Lee; stabbings at Fort Huachuca, killings at Fort Bragg, and an edict "not to shake a nigger hand" at Camp Upton.
- Undeterred and thoroughly convinced that Uncle Pink was right about the potential of the military to end discrimination, J.W. decided in 1942 to enlist in the Navy Seabees, a recently formed construction arm of the navy, one of the segregated branches in the military.
- J.W. was especially qualified; since he was 10 years old, he had worked alongside his father, a carpenter and mason.
- After graduation from high school, J.W. attended the North Carolina Agricultural and Technical Institute in Greensboro for two years, majoring in construction management.
- And he was eager to make an impact on the all-encompassing war effort.
- The need for a militarized naval construction force was paramount after the Japanese attack on Pearl Harbor and the U.S. entry into the war.
- Judge William H. Hastie was appointed civilian aide to the Secretary of War to help integrate Blacks into the defense program.
- It was a difficult assignment; the military was wrestling with the festering wound of Black discrimination while also preparing for war.

- Rear Admiral Ben Moreell requested authorization to activate, organize and man navy construction units on December 28, 1941, just three weeks after the Japanese attack.
- Admiral Moreell looked first for men already trained in construction.
- In July, 1942, 24-year-old John William received orders to report to Camp Allen in Norfolk, Virginia, to begin boot camp training.
- There, J.W. completed the three-week Seabee training course that emphasized military discipline and the use of light arms.
- Most of the first Seabee recruits were experienced in construction; nearly all were volunteers, not draftees.
- The average age of the early recruits was 37.
- These were men who had helped to build Boulder Dam, the national highways and New York's skyscrapers.
- Most were able to quickly adopt the civilian construction skills to military needs.
- All were ready to do their patriotic duty by building a new naval base in Puerto Rico; the new base had been planned on so large a scale it was nicknamed "The Pearl Harbor of the Caribbean."

Life at Work

- After boot camp, John William Gibson of Eden, North Carolina, was assigned to Roosevelt Roads, Puerto Rico, which was slated for a massive expansion by the navy.
- Initial reports indicated that the base would rival the size and scope of the badly damaged facility at Pearl Harbor, Hawaii.
- There, the construction battalion, the fundamental unit of the Seabee organization, comprised four companies that included the necessary construction skills required for any job, plus a headquarters company composed of medical and dental professionals, administrative personnel, storekeepers, cooks and other specialty personnel.
- The standard battalion complement was 32 officers and 1,073 men.
- Construction man Gibson was assigned to Charlie Company, Third Platoon, First Squad.
- Most of the other Black soldiers also were assigned to "C" Company, which was composed of builders and steelworkers.
- Most of C Company's assignments, however, involved painting and general labor such as mixing mortar or staging materials.
- J.W. became especially frustrated that the colored troops always got the low-skilled, dirty jobs, while less experienced White sailors got the plum assignments.
- He became aware that Company C Blacks were not given the opportunity to rate as equipment operators, construction mechanics, construction electricians, utilities men or engineering aides jobs for which J.W.'s experience and education qualified him.
- Also, when his leadership skills were needed, the task always involved labor details, concrete pours or painting details.
- Nevertheless, J.W. decided that he and his peers would be the best labor force available and make themselves indispensable.
- Excellence, not complaining, would most impress the White officers who looked down on Negro soldiers.
- In Puerto Rico, J.W. found it difficult to follow the experiences of other Black soldiers after the military declared newspapers such as the *Pittsburgh Courier* contraband, so J.W. and his fellow Seabees relied on stateside relatives to secretly send the *Courier* via care packages.

John's parents in North Carolina.

- Race mixing in military camps resulted in fights and other types of violence during the war.
- The alleged beating of the wife of a Black soldier by a White military policeman sparked a race riot at Camp Stewart, Georgia, in which one White MP was killed and four others wounded.
- False rumors of race riots resulted in the death of one Negro soldier, and one White soldier was critically wounded when fights between Black and White soldiers erupted en route from Fort Bliss to El Paso, Texas.
- Sparking even deeper resentment was the treatment accorded German prisoners of war incarcerated in the South.
- Much to the exasperation of Black soldiers, German prisoners were allowed to dine with the White civilian population on trains while Black soldiers were told to eat behind a Jim Crow curtain.
- The NAACP issued posters attacking the Red Cross' segregated blood drives, citing scientific evidence that the composition of Black and White plasma was the same.
- But the nature of segregation came home to J.W. when he convinced his fellow Seabees that Jim Crow must go in Puerto Rico.
- To ease racial tensions, the military began calling for the elimination of Jim Crow discrimination on military bases to include the desegregation of transportation and recreational facilities.
- All these issues came to a head one afternoon, when two dozen Black soldiers became furious after a fight broke out resulting from a mix-up in segregated scheduled ball field practice time.
- For the Black soldiers of C Company, it was the last straw.
- First J.W. listened to their anger, mixed with years of earned bitterness.
- He allowed the men to scream and rage themselves into exhaustion.
- Only after every man had taken the time to tell the others how segregation had held him back did J.W. explain his plan.
- First they would list all their grievances on a single piece of paper.
- Any man could put a complaint on the list; only a unanimous vote could take it off the list.
- The list of concerns would be held to 12 items that a delegation could present to the battalion commander.
- The Seabees worked hard on the list, arguing, demanding and cajoling to get their personal grievances included in it.
- The complaints involved equal opportunity in military promotions, construction projects and the post exchange; the list also called for equal treatment on liberty buses and the removal of restrictions on which beaches that Black soldiers could use and when.
- Only when the list was complete did J.W. meet with the battalion commander to obtain an appointment, which was granted two days hence.
- The in-person meeting was designed to be off the record and respectful.
- In all, 16 men agreed to meet with the commander; J.W. was designated as their leader.
- Then, on the day of the meeting, an emergency arose; J.W. was ordered to stand the watch of a shipmate who had broken his arm in an accident.
- The group voted to go without him.
- As disciplined soldiers who had thought through the issues, they went to meet the battalion commander.
- Two military police stood on each side of the commander as the 15 members of C Company made the presentation that J.W. had prepared.

- They began with the concept that the military could lead the nation in fighting Jim Crow traditions by awarding Negro soldiers the dignity they deserved.
- Then they respectfully listed their requests.
- The men were nervous.
- The commander sat in stony silence, as usual, until the end.
- All of the Negro soldiers believed that speaking off the record to the commander was the proper path.
- They were wrong.
- When the last man had spoken, the commander rose to his feet and barked, "How dare you bring a mob to demand anything? Being a Seabee is not enough, so now you expect to be treated White. Lock these men up. I will not have race riots on my watch."
- All 15 men were escorted from the commander's office, arrested for insubordination and court-martialed.
- They were all dishonorably discharged and sent back to the states.
- When his fellow soldiers were disciplined, J.W. stepped forward to receive his punishment, but was told to return to duty.
- One miserable year later, 34-year-old J.W. was honorably discharged, more than ready to rejoin civilian life.
- His dream was to marry Volia Wilkerson, an elementary school teacher who had faithfully written him letters during the war years.
- By 1946, he was one of 1.2 million African Americans who had served their country, battling for freedom across the globe.
- He was disillusioned and angry.
- But J.W. quickly discovered that returning Black soldiers were more defiant and less willing to accept Jim Crow thinking from civilians who had not gone to war.
- On February 12, 1946, Sgt. Isaac Woodward, a decorated Pacific veteran, was blinded in a struggle after being arrested for sitting with a White soldier on a bus returning the men home from Camp Gordon, Georgia.
- Woodward's offense was demanding that the bus driver "talk to me like a man."
- Black veteran John Jones was beaten to death by a group of White men in Louisiana; a dispute over a radio in Columbia, Tennessee, between a White army veteran and a Black navy veteran resulted in the mobilization of 500 National Guardsmen to calm the race riot.

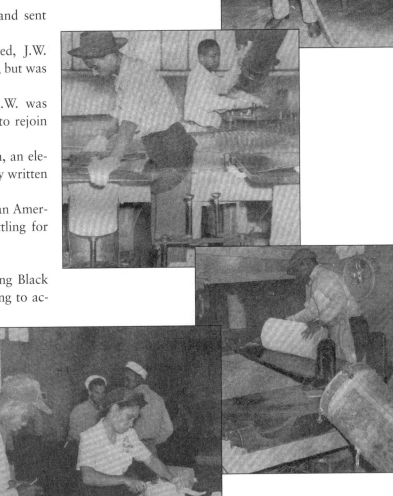

Most Black soldiers were assigned to Company C, which meant painting and low-skilled construction jobs.

Life in the Community: Roosevelt Roads Naval Station, Puerto Rico

- Roosevelt Roads Naval Station was located in the eastern part of Puerto Rico in the town of Ceiba, about 50 miles from San Juan.
- It was named for then assistant secretary of the Navy Franklin D. Roosevelt, who conceived the idea in 1919 on a surveying trip.
- He envisioned it as one of the largest naval facilities in the world.
- The station was first commissioned as a U.S. naval operations base in 1943, designed to become the keystone of the Caribbean Defense System with a well-protected anchorage, a major air station and an industrial establishment capable of supporting 60 percent of the Atlantic fleet under wartime conditions.
- There was even talk that if the British Empire ever fell to Axis powers, Roosevelt Roads would become the new operating base for the British fleet.
- But by 1943, it was clear that with Allied operations focusing on Europe and the Pacific, a major defense hub on the island would be unnecessary.
- Construction on the base was halted in 1944 and Naval Operating Base Roosevelt Roads was put in a maintenance status with a public works officer, a detachment of Seabees and a large civilian workforce.

Historical Snapshot
1946

- Weight Watchers was formed
- Popular music of the day included: "Oh, What It Seemed to Be" by the Frankie Carle Orchestra with Marjorie Hughes; "Personality" by Johnny Mercer; "Day by Day" by Frank Sinatra; and "Guitar Polka" by Al Dexter
- In Japan, 28 former leaders were indicted in Tokyo as war criminals
- The first packages from the relief agency CARE (Cooperative for American Remittances to Europe) arrived in Europe, at Le Havre, France
- The musical *Annie Get Your Gun* opened on Broadway starring Ethel Merman
- A patent was filed for the hydrogen bomb
- The United States Supreme Court struck down Virginia's segregation statute on interstate buses
- The United States exploded a 20-kiloton atomic bomb near Bikini Atoll in the Marshall Islands in the Pacific Ocean
- The Philippines, which had officially become a territory of the United States in 1902, gained its independence on July 4
- The bikini bathing suit made its debut during a fashion show in Paris
- In Japan, Emperor Hirohito publicly rejected the notion that the emperor was a living god and that the Japanese were superior to other races
- The first General Assembly of the United Nations convened in London
- The United Mine Workers rejoined the American Federation of Labor
- The Electronic Numerical Integrator and Calculator (ENIAC), was unveiled at the University of Pennsylvania; the machine took up an entire room, weighed 30 tons and used more than 18,000 vacuum tubes to perform functions such as counting to 5,000 in one second
- The Republican Party took control of the Senate and the House in mid-term elections
- Walt Disney's *Song of the South* was released
- The first artificial snow was produced from a natural cloud at Mt. Greylock, Massachusetts
- Lillian Hellman's play *Another Part of the Forest* premiered in New York City
- The Supreme Court granted Oregon Indians land payment rights from the U.S. government
- President Harry Truman created the Committee on Civil Rights by Executive Order
- The United Nations International Children's Emergency Fund (UNICEF) was established
- The United Nations General Assembly voted to establish the U.N. headquarters in New York City
- The film *It's a Wonderful Life,* starring James Stewart and Donna Reed, premiered

Selected Prices, 1946

Automobile, Mercury Convertible $2,209.00
Girdle $6.95
Hair Dryer $9.95
Handkerchiefs $0.69
House, Five-Room, North Carolina $5,700.00
Movie Ticket $1.00
Night Cream, Noxema $0.59
Pepsi-Cola, Bottle $0.05
Television, General Electric $189.95
Whiskey, Fifth $3.98

African American Military Timeline

1917

The United States entered World War I and declared war on Germany.

After Congress passed the Selective Service Act, about 700,000 Black men volunteered for the draft on the first day; over two million ultimately registered.

The Central Committee of Negro College Men organized at Howard University furnished over 1,500 names in response to an army requirement for 200 college-educated Blacks to be trained as officers.

Army senior leaders publicly expressed doubts about enlisting large numbers of Blacks because they believed Blacks could not fight and were concerned about possible subversion by an "oppressed minority."

Congress authorized 14 training camps for White officer candidates but none for African Americans; after Black protests the U.S. Army established the first all-Black officer training school at Fort Des Moines, Iowa.

The first American troop ship dispatched to France included over 400 Black stevedores and longshoremen; by the end of the war 50,000 African Americans in the U.S. Army were employed as laborers in French ports.

Racial tension involving U.S. servicemen flared into a major riot in Texas where Black troops were assigned to Camp Logan to guard the construction of a training facility, resulting in the death of 16 Whites, including five policemen.

1918

Racial violence was sparked in Manhattanville, Kansas, by a local theater's refusal to admit a Black sergeant, a type of discrimination prohibited by state law.

The all-Black Ninety-second ("Buffalo") Division arrived in France, then moved to the front; despite individual acts of heroism, army leaders maintained that the division did not perform well under combat conditions.

An editorial in the National Association for the Advancement of Colored People (NAACP) publication, *Crisis*, urged Black Americans to put the war effort before their own needs by "closing ranks" with White Americans in support of the fighting in France.

The French liaison to the American Expeditionary Force (AEF) headquarters advised French officers to keep their distance from any Black officers, to give only moderate praise to Black troops, and to keep Black troops and White French women apart.

German propaganda leaflets dropped on African American troops encouraged desertion: "To carry a gun in this service is not an honor but a shame. Throw it away and come over to the German lines. You will find friends who will help you."

Over 367,000 African American soldiers served in this conflict, 1,400 of whom were commissioned officers.

Most Blacks were placed in noncombat services of supply units which provided labor.

Approximately 100,000 African Americans went to France during World War I; despite the American restriction on the use of Blacks in combat units, about 40,000 African Americans fought in the war.

The 369th (or "Harlem Hellfighters") was the first Allied regiment to reach the Rhine River during the final offensive against Germany.

Members of the 370th Infantry Regiment won 21 American Distinguished Service Crosses and 68 French Croix de Guerre during WWI.

The Army Nurses Corps accepted 18 Black nurses on an experimental basis following the influenza epidemic.

The White 369th Infantry Regiment was honored in a grand parade down New York City's Fifth Avenue, while most Black units were ignored.

In St. Joseph, Missouri, Black veterans refused to march at the back of a victory parade.

continued

Two officers in the Aleutians gossip over their clothesline on wash day. All men are obliged to do their own laundry on this particular island.

KEEP IT CLEAN!

Saturday night happens, no matter where.
Maybe it takes scheming, but Americans
get their baths, and keep clothes clean.

French, Italian and German salvage went into this washing machine which was designed and built by members of 12th AF Service Command stationed in Sicily.

This outdoor bath and laundry has a personalized touch. And from the unwelcome signs about the place one gathers that the GI hopes to keep it that way.

No Roman bath for Cpl. Howard F. Evans, with a bomb squadron in southern Italy, but a very serviceable tub made from that highly adaptable article, the oil drum.

Timeline . . . *(continued)*

1919

During the summer following the Armistice of November 1918, racial violence spawned serious riots in Texas, Nebraska, Illinois, and Washington, DC.

Ten veterans were among the 75 African Americans lynched by White mobs.

The American Legion, a veterans' organization, allowed Black veterans to join, but only in segregated posts.

1925

An Army War College study reported that African Americans would never be fit to serve as military pilots.

1932

The U.S. Navy allowed African Americans to enlist, lifting the restriction in place since the end of WWI that excluded Blacks from serving in the navy.

1936

Black cadet Benjamin O. Davis, Jr., graduated from West Point, after enduring four years of "silencing."

1939

The Committee for the Participation of Negroes in National Defense was formed and successfully helped to get nondiscrimination clauses inserted into the Selective Service Act passed in September 1940.

Congress passed the Civilian Pilot Training Act to create a pool of trained aviators in the event of war; seven different institutions enrolled Blacks for flight training, but the Army Air Corps continued to exclude African American pilots.

Britain and France declared war after Germany invaded Poland, while President Franklin D. Roosevelt announced American neutrality in a fireside chat.

1940

President Roosevelt signed the Selective Training and Service Act, the first peacetime draft in U.S. history; the act contained an anti-discrimination clause and established a 10 percent quota system to ensure integration.

Segregation of troops remained official U.S. Army policy throughout World War II.

Black leaders met with the Secretary of the Navy to present a seven-point program for the mobilization of African Americans that included demands for flight training, the admission of Black women into military nursing units, and desegregation of the armed forces.

The War Department established a quota for enlisting Blacks based on a percentage of their numbers in the general population.

Judge William H. Hastie, dean of the Howard University Law School, assumed the position of civilian aide to the Secretary of War in Matters of Black Rights.

1941

The U.S. Army activated the 366th Infantry Regiment, the first all-Black Regular Army unit officered by African Americans only.

WE WANT ROOSEVELT

continued

Timeline . . . (continued)

1941

Labor and civil rights leader A. Philip Randolph, president of the Brotherhood of Sleeping Car Porters, proposed a massive March on Washington in July 1941 to protest unfair labor practices in the defense industry and the military's discrimination against African Americans.

Secretary of War Henry L. Stimson formally approved the establishment of the flight training program at Tuskegee Institute.

The U.S. Army established the 78th Tank Battalion, the first Black armor unit.

President Roosevelt issued Executive Order 8802, which reiterated the federal government's previously stated policy of nondiscrimination in war industry employment in keeping with a promise made to A. Philip Randolph if he would call off his planned "March on Washington."

The Army opened its integrated officers' candidate schools, although Black officers were not allowed to command White troops.

The U.S. Army Air Corps began training African American pilots at the Tuskegee Institute in Alabama.

Black leaders launched the "Double V" campaign, and urged African Americans to support the war effort as a way to fight racism abroad.

The U.S. Army activated the 93rd Infantry at Fort Huachuca, Arizona, the first Black division formed during World War II.

Black newspapers that ran articles strongly criticizing segregation and discrimination in the armed forces had trouble obtaining newsprint until they softened their stance; the U.S. Justice Department threatened to charge 20 editors with sedition.

1942

Approximately 1,800 Blacks sat on draft boards in the United States.

President Roosevelt ordered the U.S. Navy and U.S. Marine Corps to enlist African Americans into their regular military units.

The U.S. Coast Guard recruited its first 150 Black volunteers.

The 761st Tank Battalion was activated at Camp Claiborne, Louisiana, with six White officers, 30 Black officers, and 676 enlisted men.

The U.S. Navy began accepting Black inductees from the Selective Service Board for the first time.

About 167,000 Blacks served in the U.S. Navy in WWII; 123,000 of these men served overseas, and almost 12,500 African Americans served in the Seabees, as the navy's construction battalions were called.

The U.S. Marine Corps began admitting African American recruits for the first time in 167 years; of the 19,168 Blacks who served in the Marine Corps during the war, 12,738 served overseas.

1943

The First Marine Depot was the first Black USMC unit to be sent overseas in World War II.

Judge William H. Hastie resigned his position as civilian aide to the Secretary of War because of continuing discrimination and segregation in the armed forces.

The Women's Marine Corps was created, the only WWII-era women's auxiliary that did not admit any African Americans.

The federal government barred all war contractors from discriminating on the basis of race.

continued

Timeline . . . (continued)

1943

African Americans reported White hostility to their presence in war plants, including a race riot in Detroit, Michigan, in which 25 African Americans and nine Whites were killed.

1944

The percentage of African Americans employed in war production rose from less than 3 percent in 1942 to over 8 percent.

The War Department prohibited racial discrimination in recreational and transportation facilities on all U.S. Army posts.

American film director Frank Capra produced *The Negro Soldier,* the first U.S. Army training film to favorably depict African American servicemen.

The percentage of Black soldiers in the U.S. Army peaked at 8.74 percent.

The U.S. Army's racial policies became an important issue during this year's presidential campaign; Black leaders continued to criticize the army's restricted use of Black troops in combat.

The U.S. Navy commissioned 13 African Americans as its first Black officers.

The U.S. Army Air Corps' all-Black 332nd Fighter Group, also known as the Tuskegee Airmen, first saw combat.

The *USS Mason,* a destroyer escort, was the first naval warship with a predominantly Black crew and at least one Black officer.

The first African American Marines to be decorated by the Second Marine Division—Staff Sergeant Timerlate Kirven and Corporal Samuel J. Love, Sr.—won purple hearts for wounds received in the assault on Saipan.

Army Lieutenant John Roosevelt Robinson, one of the 761st "Black Panther" Tank Battalion's few Black officers, refused orders to sit in the back of a military bus at Fort Hood, Texas; he was court-martialed, but acquitted because the order was a violation of war.

During fighting along the Gothic line in Italy, the 92nd Infantry Division lost momentum and was forced into a disorderly retreat; the division commander and his staff used racist remarks to explain the division's initial combat failure.

The WAVES accepted its first 72 Black women, two of whom became officers.

The U.S. Army integrated Black volunteers with White troops to fight during the "Battle of the Bulge," the Germans' last desperate counteroffensive to break through in the Ardennes forest in Belgium; it was the first and only example of an integrated army fighting force in WWII.

1945

The U.S. Navy eliminated all of its segregated stations and schools.

continued

Timeline . . . *(continued)*

1945

Colonel Benjamin O. Davis, Jr., taking command of the 477th Composite Group of Godman Field, Kentucky, was the first African American to command a military base in the United States and the first to command a U.S. Army Air Force installation.

The National Association of Colored Nurses forced the U.S. Army Nurse Corps to drop its racial restrictions on qualified nurses.

The first and only Black WACs assigned to overseas duty were the 800 women of the 6888th Central Postal Directory Battalion.

The "Black Panthers" helped to breach the Siegfried Line in Germany.

Members of the "Tuskegee Airmen" from the 477th Bombadier Squadron "mutinied" in protest against a discriminatory policy; a group of 104 African American Army Air Corps officers was arrested after entering the officers' club at Freemen Field, Indiana, which was closed to non-Whites.

Wesley A. Brown received an appointment to the U.S. Naval Academy at Annapolis, Maryland, and became the first African American to graduate and earn his commission from the academy four years later.

At the end of WWII, 695,000 African Americans were in the U.S. Army.

MEN WANTED: UNCLE SAM ISSUES CALL FOR EXPERTS

The Army needs men skilled in almost every profession, business, and trade. Whatever your job is, if you are extra good at it, you may be wanted. Here are some of the posts now being filled:

PROFESSIONS	WHERE SERVICES ARE REQUIRED
ENGINEERS AND PRODUCTION MEN	Electrical engineers in Signal Corps and other branches (urgent). Mechanical engineers in Ordnance Department and other branches. Metallurgists and metallurgical engineers in several branches. Some sanitation and public-utility engineers. Probably some draftsmen, inspectors, supervisors, foremen, and other skilled men for production, especially metal fabrication, and maintenance work.
CHEMISTS	Chemical engineers and chemists in Chemical Warfare Service and other branches.
COMMUNICATIONS MEN	Radio, telephone, and telegraph engineers, and others in Signal Corps and other technical branches. Radio maintenance men and telephone and telegraph operators (heavy demand).
TRANSPORTATION MEN	Railroad traffic and operating executives and other experts in various branches (urgent). Air-transport executives and other air experts in Air Corps and other branches (urgent). Experienced truck-fleet operation and maintenance men in Quartermaster Corps (urgent). Some water-borne transportation men.
BUSINESS MEN, BANKERS, AND LAWYERS	Personnel, office, and finance executives, and clerical supervisors in administrative posts in ground and air forces. Some economists, foreign and domestic-trade specialists, and lawyers. Wholesale and retail executives, especially with food, textile, and clothing experience, in Quartermaster Corps. Men with retail and chain-store experience as post-exchange officers.
ACCOUNTANTS	Accountants, auditors, and statisticians in several branches.
WAREHOUSEMEN	Experienced men for Army depots.
MISCELLANEOUS	Many men for censorship work—those speaking a foreign language especially valuable.

ARMY SPECIALIST CORPS PAY RATES

OFFICERS		ENLISTED SPECIALISTS	
Colonel	$6,500	Specialist, 1st Class (master sergeant)	$2,900
Lieutenant Colonel	5,600	Specialist, 2nd Class (technical sergeant)	2,600
Major	4,600	Specialist, 3rd Class (staff sergeant)	2,300
Captain	3,500-3,800	Specialist, 4th Class (sergeant)	2,000
First Lieutenant	3,200	Specialist, 5th Class (corporal)	1,800
Second Lieutenant	2,600-2,900		

Crisis, edited by W.E.B. Dubois, December 1940:

This is no fight merely to wear a uniform [but a] struggle for status, a struggle to take democracy off of parchment and give it life.

Letters to the Editor, *Yank*, 1944:

Dear Yank:

Here is a question each Negro soldier is asking. What is the Negro soldier fighting for? On whose team are we playing? Myself and eight other soldiers were on our way from Camp Claiborne, Louisiana, to the hospital here at Fort Huachuca. We had to lay over until the next day for our train. On the next day we could not purchase a cup of coffee at any of the lunchrooms around here. As you know, Old Man Jim Crow rules. The only place where we could be served was at the lunchroom at the railroad station but, of course, we had to go into the kitchen. But that's not all; 11:30 a.m. about two dozen German prisoners of war, with two American guards, came to the station. They entered the lunchroom, sat at the tables, had their meals served, talked, smoked, in fact had quite a swell time. I stood on the outside looking in, and I could not help but ask myself these questions: Are these men sworn enemies of this country? Are they not taught to hate and destroy all democratic governments? Are we not American soldiers, sworn to fight for and die if need be for this our country? Then why are they treated better than we are? Why are we pushed around like cattle? If we are fighting for the same thing, if we are to die for our country, then why does the government allow such things to go on? Some of the boys are saying you will not print this letter. I'm saying that you will. . . .

—Cpl. Rupert Trimmingham, Fort Huachuca, Arizona, April 28, 1944

Dear Yank:

Just read Cpl. Rupert Trimmingham's letter titled "Democracy" in a May edition of Yank. We are White soldiers in the Burma jungles, and there are many Negro units working with us. They are doing more than their part to win this war. We are proud of the colored men here. When we are away from camp working in the jungles, we can go to any colored camp and be treated like one of their own. I think it is a disgrace that, while we are away from home doing our part to help win the war, some people back home are knocking down everything we are fighting for.

We are among many Allied nations' soldiers that are fighting here, and they marvel at how the American army, which is composed of so many nationalities and different races, gets along so well. We are ashamed to read that the German soldier, who is the sworn enemy of our country, is treated better than the soldier of our country, because of race.

Cpl. Trimmingham asked: What is a Negro fighting for? If this sort of thing continues, we the White soldiers will begin to wonder: What are we fighting for?

—Pvt. Joseph Poscucci (Italian), Burma, June 1944

"Report on the Negro Soldier," by Major Robert F. Cocklin, *Infantry Journal*, December 1946:

The relationship of White and colored people in America is too complex for discussion here, and of course, it carried over when the Negro became a soldier. Lifelong prejudices survived the expansion of the army, although the pressure of work, training and war tended to force them somewhat into the background.

The Doolittle Committee and its subsequent report have clearly indicted the reluctance of the civilian in general to accept the more disciplined life of the soldier. In this, the colored soldier in no way differed from his White countryman. But unfortunately, the rigors of military discipline were all too frequently tagged "discrimination" when they concerned the Negro soldier. In this regard, I firmly believe that a large part of the Negro press did a disservice to the members of their race. Since they provided the chief source of news about their race, Negro publications were read with avid interest by every colored soldier who could lay his hands on one. Often, these papers were handed around until they were almost worn out.

Much of the Negro press, with its sensational news stories, continually screamed that the colored soldier was being discriminated against at every turn. Obvious distortions of facts were often evident. Journalism of this type may have been good for circulation but it was definitely poor for the morale of the troops and served only to stir up unrest. . . .

Perhaps the biggest problem confronting the officers who trained the Ninety-third Division was the general inability of the colored soldier to assimilate instruction. The Army General Classification Test scores of by far the greater part of the soldiers assigned to the Ninety-third fell in the lower two of the five classified categories. This was, of course, far below the average on which the War Department had based its training plans and periods. In consequence, we simply had to slow our training programs down and simplify it as much as possible. We went through the basic training cycle three times.

Pvt. Joe Louis says_

"We're going to do our part ...and we'll win because we're on God's side"

"Get Wise: You Can Pay for Mistakes Like These with Your Life,"
by Lt. Col. George Richardson, MC, *Air Force* magazine, October 1944:

Case 1: Some people should never be given a knife. They're bound to hurt themselves. Take the GI in Italy, for instance. Instead of plunging his issue knife into a German belly, he sent it into his own. Not intentionally, of course. He wasn't committing hara-kiri. He was merely trying to make a hole in some leather. Placing the butt of the knife on the table, he pressed the leather against the point. Darned if that knife didn't go right through the leather and into the soldier's abdominal wall. To repair the damage, a surgical unit required an hour—one hour of valuable time which could have been used for men wounded in action.

Case II: Perhaps the four officers, who were riding a jeep in Normandy, couldn't read. It's hard to believe they would be foolish enough to disregard the sign which in plain English warned: "Shoulders are not free of mines." The quartet was traveling a rural road, when for some reason they decided to turn back. The driver swung out on the shoulder of the road and all that settled to earth after the explosion was dust. The grave registration men are still looking for the dog tags.

Case III: The ground crewman was a good-looking, 19-year-old kid. But he isn't good-looking any more, because he didn't use his head. He decided to make a cigarette lighter from a 20 mm shell, figuring the gadget would be a nice souvenir. After removing the projectile, he found the wadding was packed tightly. Picking at it with his knife didn't seem to do much good, so he lightly tapped the base of the shell. Sometime later, he woke up in a field hospital. He couldn't see, and his hands and ear hurt him. He didn't realize immediately that both eyes had been blinded by casing fragments, that both hands and part of one ear were gone, and that his face would always carry blue scars from the shower of exploding powder particles. He knows all about it now. He knows also that fooling with ammunition is dangerous. But he got wise too late.

BIG WORDS DON' MEAN NOTHIN' WEN A NIGGUH USE 'EM ---- EN DEY DON' MEAN MUCH, NO TIME!

ANOTHER REMARK BY HAMBONE
Ef'n I evuh does git rich I gwine buy sump'n' on de credit 'en den make 'em wait fuh dey money jes' long es I please!

Soldier
Sailor
Marine

1" SQUARES

1947 Profile

Refugee Rights: Helping Polish Jews

Edward Sienkiewicz, a Polish clothing manufacturer living in Portland, Maine, felt an obligation to help Poland's Jewish community in any way he could after the devastation brought to that country during World War II.

Life at Home

- Edward Sienkiewicz had been successful most of his life, fulfilling the dreams of his refugee grandparents who came from Poland at the turn of the century.
- So when his neighbor Hannah proposed over dinner that he contribute to the American Jewish Joint Distribution Committee or JDC, he quickly decided that it was time for him to do more.
- The Second World War had ended and a broad spectrum of newspapers and magazines were reporting widespread hunger and disease in Europe.
- The recovery work from six long years of Nazi domination was just getting underway in places like his grandparents' native Poland.
- Before the outbreak of World War II, more than 3.3 million Jews lived in Poland, the second-largest Jewish community in the world.
- Only 11 percent—370,000—had survived the terror of the Nazi regime.
- Jewish merchants first emigrated to Poland in the eleventh century CE.
- The country served as a safe haven for Jewish immigrants during the thirteenth-century Crusades.
- By the mid-sixteenth century, 80 percent of the world's Jews lived in Poland.
- In 1897, 14 percent of Polish citizens were Jewish, about the time Edward's grandparents, along with their teenage daughter, emigrated to America.
- Jewish oppression flared up anew after Poland became a sovereign state following World War I, resulting in the deaths of nearly all of Edward's extended family who had not left Poland.

Edward Sienkiewicz felt obligated to help Poland's Jewish community after the devastation of World War II.

- Following emigration, Edward's grandparents and mother never returned to their traditional homeland, although his grandfather clung to the Yiddish language as though it were a precious jewel.
- Prior to World War II, Edward was immersed in life as a clothing manufacturer who could scarcely find Poland on a map.
- With factories in Maine, Maryland and North Carolina, he had enough to do simply keeping up with business.
- But as the war progressed, he became obsessed by information detailing the systematic annihilation of the Jewish culture in Europe.
- After the tragedy of the war, he felt called to raise enough money to bring hope to his people in Poland.
- Surely now was the time to share the many blessings showered upon his family.
- His youngest daughter Polly felt the same way; his wife and two oldest children were simply pleased that the war was over and rationing was coming to an end.
- The destruction of the Jewish culture began almost immediately following the German invasion of Poland in September 1939.
- The invading German military killed 20,000 Jews in Poland and bombed 50,000 Jewish-owned factories, workshops and stores in 120 Jewish communities.
- In the first months of occupation, several hundred synagogues were destroyed.
- Jews were prohibited from owning bank accounts and were fired from their jobs in textile and leather factories.
- Merchants were required to display a Star of David outside their businesses.
- To provide land for Germans, Jews were uprooted from the Polish countryside and forced to live in a handful of cities, creating ghettos.
- In the summer of 1942, the Nazis began the systematic liquidation of the Jewish enclaves; within 18 months most were empty.
- Germany's genocidal plans became clear to Edward during the ghetto uprising in Warsaw, the city of his mother's birth.
- Following the deportation of 300,000 Warsaw Jews to concentration camps in late 1942, the Warsaw uprising alerted the world to the wholesale destruction underway.
- For more than a month the Polish underground fought the Germans for control of the Warsaw ghetto before the German army was forced to attack the civilian uprising with greater ferocity.
- The uprising was put down, but for the rest of the Allied world Warsaw became a symbol of courage and resistance.
- Over 85 percent of Polish Jewry perished in the Holocaust.
- Many survivors fled to Romania and Germany, hoping to be part of the proposed state of Israel.
- Those who remained were subjected to anti-Semitic pogroms, creating additional emigration; of the approximately 100,000 Jews left in Poland by 1947, many were sick and most were poor and in need of outside assistance.

Life at Work

- Before he donated a dime, Edward carefully researched the background of the American Jewish Joint Distribution Committee, or JDC.
- Founded in 1914 shortly after the outbreak of World War I in Europe, the JDC became the primary communal agency for overseas relief and rehabilitation and raised $16 million for relief efforts.

- Following the Great War, the JDC sent convoys of food, clothing, medicine and supplies to Jewish communities devastated by war and the subsequent persecution and pogroms.
- Once the immediate needs of the Jewish community had been met, the Committee helped build hospitals, provided medical equipment, and sent hundreds of American doctors to war-torn Europe.
- During the 1930s, the JDC publicized the plight of Jews overseas and managed to obtain sizable contributions for overseas relief.
- Despite the Great Depression, contributions to the JDC actually increased as American Jews became increasingly aware of the dangers and hardships facing their European counterparts.
- Between 1929 and 1939, the Committee raised and spent almost $25 million on relief.
- Until the United States entered World War II in December 1941, the JDC sent food and money by various means to Poland, Lithuania, and other German-occupied countries.
- It also helped central European Jews find asylum in various parts of the world, including the United States.
- After America entered the war against Germany, the JDC could no longer operate legally inside German-controlled countries.
- The Committee helped rescue Jews in Hungary in 1944 by providing funds to support children's shelters and helping to fund the rescue operations of diplomats such as Raoul Wallenberg and Carl Lutz.
- During World War II, between 1939 and 1945, it raised more than $70 million.
- Now that the war was over, the need was even greater.
- The JDC needed $200 million for refugee aid, and Edward wanted to be a leader in the effort.
- The first time he spoke about the JDC following a dinner hosted in his own home, Edward was awkward and stilted, but passionate.
- His inexperience as a fundraiser was outweighed by his enthusiasm; even his wife was impressed, especially after the pledges from the 30 guests totaled nearly $26,000.
- Many of his friends were astonished by his energy and knowledge.
- He told them how the JDC had worked with large numbers of Polish refugees forced to leave their homeland.
- He described how 15 million people had been displaced by war, many of whom had no homes left.
- Within months of Germany's surrender in May 1945, the Allies repatriated to their home countries more than six million displaced persons.
- Most Jews who had survived concentration camps or had been in hiding were unable or unwilling to return to eastern Europe because of postwar anti-Semitism and the destruction of their communities during the Holocaust.
- Many of those who did return feared for their lives.
- In Poland, locals initiated several violent pogroms.
- The worst occurred in Kielce in 1946, when 42 Jews, all survivors of the Holocaust, were killed.
- In 1947, while America was alive with hope and energy, Poland was still filled with refugees.
- America, whose economy had been jumpstarted by the war, had an obligation to help the impoverished Jews of Europe, Edward insisted.
- By the time of his tenth or eleventh talk, he was conversant concerning the medical needs of Europe's Jews and described how the JDC was helping to support 85 medical institutions in Poland, including the shipment of a complete 500-bed hospital into the country.

- In Romania, the JDC had created 16 medical institutions, including eight hospitals with a total capacity of 900 beds, maternity homes accommodating 3,840 patients, and first aid stations and clinics which treated more than 10,000 patients each month.

  - Seven hospitals with 1,000 beds were supported by the JDC in Hungary.
  - At the same time, the Committee helped nearly 60,000 Jewish children and young people—many of whom had been locked out of school during the Nazi occupation—continue their education.
  - Edward also spoke of the need for vocational training, not only for its economic advantage, but also for the therapeutic value inherent in it.
  - With great emphasis, he would tell how nearly 42,000 men and women were enrolled in training "in preparation for a life of economic independence."
  - By the time he stood before his twenty-fifth audience, he talked about the need to help Jews to come to America.
  - Already 9,000 Jews had come to the United States with JDC assistance.

In 1947, Poland was still filled with refugees.

Life in the Community: Poland

- At Yalta, in February 1945, the victorious Allies assigned Poland to the Russian zone of influence in postwar Europe.
- To most Poles the meaning was clear; Poland had been betrayed by the agreement and was destined to fall under Stalin's Communist regime.
- The United States and England had bargained away one of the first countries invaded by Germany to reward Russia for its efforts during the war.
- During World War II, six million civilians, or 22 percent, of the total population died.
- About half of the dead were Polish Christians and 50 percent were Polish Jews.
- Approximately 5,384,000, or 89.9 percent, of Polish war losses were the victims of prisons, death camps, raids, executions, annihilation of ghettos, epidemics, starvation, excessive work and ill treatment.
- Virtually every family had someone who had been tortured or imprisoned in the concentration camps.
- The results of war included one million war orphans and over half a million invalids.
- Poland lost 38 percent of its national assets.
- Many Poles could not return to the country for which they had fought because they belonged to the "wrong" political group.
- Others were arrested, tortured and imprisoned by the Soviet authorities for belonging to the Home Army.
- Although "victors," Poles were not allowed to partake in victory celebrations.
- Through the process of war and negotiated peace, the Poles exchanged one master for another.

Historical Snapshot
1947

- Congressional proceedings were televised for the first time
- Great Britain nationalized its coal mines
- The Voice of America began broadcasting to the Soviet Union
- Edwin H. Land introduced the Polaroid Land camera, capable of producing a black-and-white photograph in 60 seconds
- President Harry Truman outlined the Truman Doctrine of economic aid to nations threatened by Communism, particularly Greece and Turkey
- *The Best Years of Our Lives* won the Academy Award for best picture
- Congress proposed limiting the presidency to two terms
- Jackie Robinson broke the color barrier in major league baseball
- Presidential confidant Bernard M. Baruch said in a speech, "Let us not be deceived—we are today in the midst of a cold war"
- A camera lens that provided zoom effects was demonstrated
- The House Un-American Activities Committee (HUAC) convened in Hollywood to hunt for Communists in the film industry
- The B.F. Goodrich Company of Akron, Ohio, developed the tubeless tire
- Congress overrode a presidential veto to approve the Taft-Hartley Act that prohibited the use of union funds for political purposes, outlawed the closed shop, and empowered the government to serve injunctions against strikes likely to cripple the nation's economy
- Secretary of State George C. Marshall called for a European Recovery Program supported by American aid that came to be called the Marshall Plan
- Sugar rationing ended
- President Harry Truman signed the National Security Act, creating the Department of Defense, the National Security Council, the Central Intelligence Agency (CIA), and the Joint Chiefs of Staff
- India gained independence after some 200 years of British rule
- Americans were asked to have meatless Tuesdays and Fridays to help stockpile grain, normally used for feeding cattle, for the starving people in Europe
- *Meet the Press* made its television debut on NBC
- The U.N. General Assembly passed a resolution calling for the partitioning of Palestine between Arabs and Jews

Selected Prices, 1947

Automobile, Jaguar Sedan	$4,600.00
Adding Machine	$120.00
Baby Swing	$1.85
Carpet Sweeper, Electric	$19.95
Cuff Links, 14 Karat Gold	$47.50
Food Chopper	$2.98
Mink Coat	$1,650.00
Movie Ticket	$1.00
Sofa Bed	$79.88
Television, General Electric	$189.95
Tie, Silk	$3.50

Timeline of Jewish Oppression by the Nazis

1933

Adolf Hitler was named chancellor of Germany by President Hindenburg.

The German Reichstag was burned in an act of arson; Hindenburg agreed to let Hitler use emergency powers, and civil rights were suspended in Germany.

The Reichstag passed a law that permitted Hitler to rule by decree for the next four years.

Joseph Goebbels, Minister for Propaganda and Public Enlightenment, began urging that the German press characterize Jews as a "cancer" within Germany.

Nazi storm troopers began intimidating shoppers to boycott Jewish-owned businesses; Jews were removed from civil service jobs and a quota system was established that limited the number of Jewish students in German schools and universities.

Books by Jewish writers, socialist writers and others who were condemned as "subversive" or "decadent" were burned in public bonfires.

The citizenship of Jews from Poland and other eastern European countries was revoked if they had emigrated to Germany after 1918.

Germany concluded an agreement with Zionist officials, which allowed Jews to emigrate to Palestine with more assets; the German press encouraged Jews to take advantage of this and leave.

Jewish writers, musicians, conductors and artisans were stripped of their positions.

Homeless, alcoholic and unemployed people were sent to concentration camps.

1934

Following the death of President Hindenburg, Hitler became both chancellor and president of the nation; the German military and all public officials in Germany were forced to swear an oath of personal loyalty to Adolf Hitler.

Jews were prohibited from having health insurance.

1935

Jews were excluded from serving in the military.

Sterilization laws allowed the state to mandate abortions for women who were deemed "eugenically unfit."

German citizenship was restricted to those of German or kindred blood.

Marriage and sexual relations between Jews and non-Jews was prohibited.

All Jews in the German civil service, including military veterans, were dismissed from their jobs.

1936

Persecutions of the Jews were reduced as Germany prepared to host the Olympic Games at Berlin.

1937

The Buchenwald concentration camp was completed and opened.

Himmler issued a decree that permitted the arrest and detention of any "asocial" person, meaning Jews and other "undesirables."

1938

Jews were required to register with the state all their major assets.

Representatives of 32 nations met to discuss ways to help the growing number of Jewish refugees in Europe and the rest of the world; only the Dominican Republic offered to take in a sizable number of Jews.

continued

Timeline . . . *(continued)*

1938

The Jewish synagogue in Munich was destroyed.

The passports of all Austrian and German Jews had to be stamped with a large red letter "J."

All Jewish men in Germany were required to add the middle name "Israel" to their names, and all women had to add "Sara" to their names.

Jews were prohibited from practicing law or medicine in Germany.

Fifteen thousand "stateless" Jews in Germany were expelled and driven across the Polish border.

Jewish children were forbidden to attend non-Jewish German schools.

After a Jewish student in Paris killed a German diplomat, some 30,000 Jews were arrested and detained in concentration camps.

1939

Hitler said in a speech to the Reichstag that a new war would lead to the "annihilation of the Jewish race in Europe."

German troops occupied the remainder of the Czech state.

Jews in Bohemia and Moravia were arrested and placed in concentration camps.

Ravensbruck concentration camp was completed and opened for women prisoners.

Germany invaded Poland.

Britain and France declared war on Germany.

Five special German units were told to "decapitate" Polish leadership by killing teachers, writers, intellectuals and anyone who could organize opposition to the Nazi conquest of Poland; tens of thousands of Poles were shot by these units.

German troops began rounding up Polish Jews from the various towns and villages for the purpose of placing them into segregated ghettos.

Jews were forced to begin building concentration camps in Poland; thousands died from exposure.

1940

The Auschwitz concentration camp opened in Poland.

The Warsaw Ghetto in Poland was sealed off by the German army with around 400,000 Jews inside.

U.S. soldiers examining the famous German "tiger" tank.

continued

Timeline . . . *(continued)*

1941

Germany attacked the Soviet Union; special German units killed 90,000 Jews in Russia.

Jews in Germany were ordered to begin wearing the Yellow Star, thus making them easier to identify.

A Nazi death camp was opened at Chelmno, Poland.

1942

Special German units executed several hundred thousand Jews in Latvia, Estonia, Lithuania and the Ukraine.

German military leaders determined that shooting so many individuals was, "psychologically an immense burden to bear" and began conducting experiments in mass executions with the use of gas.

The mass gassing of Jews began at Auschwitz-Birkenau.

1943

Jews resisted deportation in the Warsaw Ghetto Uprising, resulting in a month-long battle.

With the Russians advancing from the east, many death camps were closed and evidence destroyed.

1944

Hungarian Jews numbering 440,000 were transported to Auschwitz.

1945

Many remaining German concentration camps were closed and evidence of their existence destroyed.

Faced with impending defeat, Hitler committed suicide.

Germany surrendered and the war in Europe ended.

Surviving Nazi leaders were put on trial at Nuremberg.

1946

With the help of the American Jewish Joint Distribution Committee, 27,000 Jews left Europe for homes in Palestine, the United States and other areas.

1947

The British stopped the ship *Exodus 1947* at the port of Haifa, Israel, and sent the 4,500 Holocaust survivors on board back to Germany.

The United Nations General Assembly voted to partition Palestine into two new states, one Jewish and the other Arab.

BATTLEGROUNDS OF EUROPE

R.R. Network Centers and Significant R.R.

Fortifications

French Naval Bases

Italian Naval Bases

Major Industrial Areas

Scale

0   50   100   200   300 mi.

NORTH SEA

Midlands

ENGLAND

London

THE NETHERLANDS

Area Dutch can flood

Meuse R.

Albert Canal

BELGIUM (Flanders)

Ruhr

PARIS BASIN

Paris

Verdun

Lorraine Gateway

SOUTH

Rhine

Danube

Belfort Gap

Tours

Poitou

SWITZERLAND

Lyon

Rhone

PO VALLEY

Milan

Turin

Bordeaux

AQUITANIAN BASIN

Genoa

La Spezia

Bilbao

SPANISH PLATEAU

Roncesvailles

Toulouse

Ebro

Marseille

Toulon

CORSICA

Ajaccio

La Maddalena

PORTUGAL

Madrid

Barcelona

SARDINIA

TYRR

Lisbon

BALEARIC IS.

Cagliari

Gibraltar

SP. MOROCCO

Mers-el-Kebir

Algiers

Bizerte

Casablanca

ALGERIA

TUNISIA

"We CANNOT Afford Another Prolonged War," by Harold Ickes, *Read,* May 1946:

We may have peacetime conscription. We may retain a tremendous peacetime navy. But the plain fact is that we cannot afford another prolonged war in 20 or 30 years.

Not that we haven't the men, not that we haven't the will to fight again if we have to, not that we haven't the cash—we just haven't got the oil, copper, the zinc, and the mercury, which are so vital to the machine and munitions of modern warfare.

The prodigal harvest of minerals that we have reaped to win this war has bankrupted some of our most vital mineral resources. We no longer deserve to be listed with Russia and the British Empire as one of the "Have" nations of the world. We should be listed with the "Have Nots" such as Germany and Japan.

The overwhelming significance of this change from a "Have" to a "Have Not" nation lies in these facts: without mineral resources, the United States could never have built the ships, the planes, and the guns which have made us the greatest military power in the world. We could never have been more than an agricultural country. We could never have been able to support, at a standard of living that is the envy of the world, the 135 million people now living within our borders.

Does this change in status mean that we are about to become a pushover for other countries, that our standard of living will be greatly reduced, that we shall all become farmers, and "horse-and-buggy" farmers at that? This, in fact, is the future that we are now carving out for our grandchildren and our great-grandchildren by our do-nothing policy.

It should be burned into our consciousness that we do not have an inexhaustible supply of minerals—the sinew that makes this country mighty. Our minerals are exhaustible and irreplaceable. Unlike wheat and corn, new crops of minerals do not appear from year to year.

Further, the faster we grow in industrial strength and military potency, the more rapidly we dissipate our mineral resources—the very basis of our military and industrial power.

To prevent the decline of the United States as a major military and industrial power, and to maintain our high standard of living, we must take immediate positive action to increase our known mineral resources.

We must begin at once

To stockpile minerals.

To explore our country more extensively than ever before.

To hunt for better methods of recovering metals from scrap.

To have access, in common with other peacefully disposed nations, to minerals in lands that have been conquered in the recent war, for from now on we shall be increasingly dependent upon imports for our minerals.

"Inflation as It Really Is," *The Emporia Gazette*, May 1946:

Here are some of the things that can happen under a runaway monetary inflation:

When the inflation of Germany's paper currency was raging in 1923, one author received a royalty check on his writings, only to find that it could not buy the smallest postage stamp. To replace a pair of shoe laces cost more than the shoes had cost. To repair a broken window cost more than the house had originally cost. A new pair of shoes cost more than the whole shoe store had originally cost. Beggars contemptuously tossed million-mark notes into the gutter. A mortgage was paid off with a postage stamp.

Foreign money and articles of daily use were the real treasures. An American $10 bill would buy a house. Some German boys who found a misplaced box of soap lived like kings by selling a cake each day. A gold coin, raked out from antiques, brought bushels of newly printed money, more than a man could carry. The inflation ruined Germany's middle class and prepared the way for the dictatorship of Hitler.

"Recorded Books after the War," *Predictions of Things to Come*, February-March 1943:

After the war, one will be able to go to a lending library and obtain a 2×5 spool, much like a spool of cotton, on which is wound a hair-thin steel wire. On this wire the text of a book has been magnetically transcribed. This thin wire, when put into a machine, will read the book to you. Eight hours of transcription goes on one spool. This device has been developed by Marvin Camras, a lad only two years out of college. His invention has recently been patented by the Armour Research Foundation in Chicago. The invention also may be used for the transcription of court proceedings and business dictation.

"Things You Can Look Forward to Having," *Predictions of Things to Come*, February-March 1943:

Longer and wider bathtubs of plastic, like small swimming pools, which will not stain or chip.

Plastic refrigerators, having small compartments so you won't air out the whole refrigerator when you reach for the cream. Such an arrangement should save electricity and do away with wear and tear on your refrigerator motor.

"Crystal" furniture in lovely colors of transparent plastics. You may have a real blue room in your postwar house.

These are the predictions of Mr. J. Earl Simonds, leading research chemist of Plastics Industries Technical Institute.

"Famine and Pestilence Ahead, In the relief and rehabilitation of suffering Europe, America will win the peace, as it will win the war," by Leo Lania and Barthold Fles, *Predictions of Things to Come,* February-March 1943:

On the day when the war is over, "the unconquerable fortress," as Hitler calls Europe under his mailed fist, will fall. The German front will collapse. But it will be more than a military collapse, more than the collapse of a system. What follows will be complete chaos, with "Every man for himself" as the order of the day. Soldiers will desert, disorder will be rampant everywhere. German soldiers in the east will seize cars and trains in which to return home, but in other parts of the Reich and the occupied territories, bands of German officers and soldiers will form to continue the war on their own initiative. The dammed resentment of the oppressed nations is certain to overflow. Civil war will break out. All Europe will become a battlefield; the oppressed nations fighting the Germans, the army against the Elite Guard, workers against Nazis, frontline troops against home regiments.

Overnight the United Nations will find themselves faced with a gigantic problem. For some time past, the groundwork has been laid for its solution. But the difficulties are enormous—at first glance they seem all but insoluble.

Immediately after the war, the armies of the United Nations will advance and occupy the most important and strategic cities and centers in Europe. The Allies will take over the work of policing the continent. They will have to replace the authority of the state, for that authority will be lacking everywhere.

But that is only the start. The disarmament of the various warring elements, the pacification of the continent, will not prove the most difficult thing to accomplish. There is a still more dangerous enemy; and even tanks will prove powerless against him.

The enemy is hunger. Its most dangerous ally is typhus. A terrible epidemic will break out and threaten to annihilate central Europe. . . .

With the collapse of the German war machine, typhus and tuberculosis will take the offensive. The plagues of the Middle Ages will again stalk across the whole European continent with a ferocity they have not evinced for centuries. Disease will prove to be the chief product of Hitler's so-called "New Order." Starvation, due to the Nazi looting of the foodstuffs from the occupied countries, is the cause. Germany's policy of deliberately concentrating large groups of people into small areas, such as ghettos, will aid its dissemination. . . .

It will be up to America and the other United Nations to supply all that. To send a sufficiency of food—of meat and milk and flour and coal and vitamins—to Europe, is of itself an immense undertaking. But it won't be enough. Doctors and nurses will have to be mobilized, and mobile hospitals and bath houses established in all cities and centers of traffic.

Anything that Hoover had done after World War I will be child's play compared to the task that America has to accomplish after this war—not only in the interest of Europe, but in the interest of the entire world, including America itself. For pestilence does not stop at oceans.

Auschwitz Survivor, Solomon Radasy, www.holocaustsurvivors.org:

My mother and my older sister were killed in the last week of January 1941. The year 1941 was a cold winter with a lot of snow. One morning the SD [Sicherheitsdienst des Reichsfuehrers-SS] and the Jewish police caught me in the street. I was forced to work with a lot of other people clearing snow from the railroad tracks. Our job was to keep the trains running.

When I returned to the ghetto I found out that my mother and older sister had been killed. The Germans demanded that the Judenrat [Jewish Council] collect gold and furs from the people in the ghetto. When they asked my mother for jewelry and furs, she said she had none. So they shot her and my older sister, too.

My father was killed in April 1942. He went to buy bread from the children who were smuggling food into the ghetto. The children brought bread, potatoes and cabbages across the wall into the Warsaw ghetto. A Jewish policeman pointed out my father to a German and told him that he saw my father take a bread from a boy at the wall. The German shot my father in the back.

The deportations started on July 22, 1942. My other two sisters and two brothers went to Treblinka. After that I never saw anybody from my family again. . . .

On May 1, 1943, I was shot in the right ankle. The bullet went through the meat and not the bone, so I did not lose my leg. I was taken to the Umschlagplatz [the place where the Jews had to assemble to board the trains which transported them to the death camp at Treblinka]. The Treblinka extermination camp could only take 10,000 people a day. In our group we were 20,000. They cut off half of our train and sent it to Majdanek concentration camp. Majdanek was another death camp.

At Majdanek they took our clothes and gave us striped shirts, pants and wooden shoes. I was sent to Barracks 21. As I lay in my bed, an older man asked me how I was. He said, "I can help you." He had been a doctor in Paris. He took a little pocket knife and operated on me. To this day I do not understand how he could have kept a knife in the camp. There were no medicines or bandages. He said, "I have no medication, you have to help yourself. When you urinate use some of the urine as an antiseptic on your wound."

We had to walk three kilometers to work. I had to hold myself up straight without limping and walk out of the gate of the camp. I was scared. If I limped, they would take me out of line. At Majdanek they hung you for any little thing. I did not know how I would make it. God must have helped me and, I was lucky.

We stood at the appell in our wooden shoes. Then when we got out of the gate we had to take off our wooden shoes and tie them over our shoulders with a piece of string. We had to walk to work barefoot. There were little stones on the road that cut into your skin and blood was running from the feet of many people. The work was dirty field work. After a few days some people could not take it anymore, and they fell down in the road. If they could not get up, they were shot where they lay. After work we had to carry the bodies back. If 1,000 went out to work, 1,000 had to come back. . . .

In my nine weeks at Majdanek I had not changed my shirt or washed myself. We were eaten up with lice, and many of us were swollen from hunger. When we got off the train, we saw that we had arrived at Auschwitz. There was a selection and some of us were machine gunned in a field there. They did not take them to the gas chambers.

I was taken to get a number tattooed on my arm. I got Number 128232. The separate numbers add up to 18. In the Hebrew language the letters of the alphabet stand for numbers. The letters which stand for the number 18 spell out the Hebrew word "Chai," which means life. After I was tattooed, I was given a potato.

I was first sent to the camp at Buna. After I got out of quarantine, I was put to work building railroad tracks. The Capo there was a murderer. I am short, and he would put a short man together with a tall man to carry 20-foot lengths of iron. The tall man I worked with had to bend his knees.

continued

Auschwitz Survivor, Solomon Radasy . . . *(continued)*

One time I fell down and could not get up. The Capo started screaming and beating me, and he pulled me aside. There was a selection, and we had to take off our clothes and stand naked the whole night. The next morning a truck with a red cross came, and they pushed us into it, one on top of the other. We thought that they were going to take us to the gas chambers.

Instead, we were taken to the Auschwitz I camp. A Polish man came out of a building, and he asked us to call out our numbers. I said, "128232." He looked at a paper and asked my name. I said, "Szlama Radosinski," which is my name in Polish and doesn't sound like a Jewish name. He asked me where I was from. "Warsaw," I said. How long was I there? "I was raised there," I said.

He started to cuss me like I never heard before in my life. He pulled me out of the line and put me in a corner. He said, "Stay here." He brought me a piece of blanket to cover myself with. I was freezing, so he brought me inside the barracks.

I lay down. I did not know what was happening or what to think. A young guy came up to me and said, "I know you." I asked him, "Who are you?" He said his name was Erlich and that he knew me from Majdanek.

I asked him what this place was. He said it was the hospital barracks, Block 20. He told me, "It is very bad here. Dr. Mengele comes two times a week to make selections. But this is Tuesday and he will not come again this week. I will let you know what is going to happen." I had not eaten since Monday. He gave me a bread.

Erlich had been there five weeks. He had come from Majdanek to Auschwitz the same day as I did. Two of the doctors at the hospital knew his grandfather, who had been their rabbi in Cracow. They had hidden him from Dr. Mengele. Those doctors had tried to help hide Jewish people in Cracow. When the SS came, they killed the Jews they hid and took the doctors to Auschwitz.

On Thursday Erlich came to me and said, "You have to get out of here." I said, "What am I going to do—jump from the second floor window?" In the afternoon he came again and said, "You have to get out of here, or after tomorrow you are going to be dead." About an hour later a man came in and sat at a table. He asked, "Who wants to go to work?" The Poles in the hospital were not worried about going to work. Why should they go to work when they were getting packages from the Red Cross and having enough to eat?

I had to get this work. The man at the table asked me my number and then he cussed me out. I begged him, "I want to go out. I have friends outside. Please let me out." He gave me a piece of paper that said Block 6.

I walked to Block 6, and I showed the paper. The man there said, "I cannot let you in until 9 o'clock at night." I stayed there until the men returned from work. One man asked me, "You are new here; where are you from and what did you do?" I said, "I am from Warsaw and I was a furrier." He asked me where I lived, and I told him. He asked me if I knew a certain man's name and I said, "Yes, he is a furrier, too, and he lives in such and such street."

One of the men said, "I don't believe you; what is this man called? He has a nickname." I said, "This man has a little piece of skin hanging down by his left ear, and they call him 'tsutsik' (Yiddish for nipple)." When I said this, they started to help me. They brought me a big piece of bread and some cold soup.

They asked me where I was going to work, and I showed them the piece of paper. They said, "Oh, no! You will not make it over eight or 10 days in that job." The job was to work in a coal mine. "The longest anyone lives in that job is two weeks. After that they go to the crematorium." I was scared. My number was registered as working there. I said, "If I do not go there, then I am going to be hanged next to the kitchen, and the prisoners are going to walk by me."

They said, "Don't worry." One guy calls another guy and says, "Go fix this!" They went to the Capo with the piece of paper. This Capo was a murderer. He had a green triangle. The Germans opened up the jails and they made the prisoners our bosses. Some of the boys worked in Canada. When the transports came they

continued

Auschwitz Survivor, Solomon Radasy . . . *(continued)*

separated the valuables. They risked their lives to smuggle out gold and other things. Every day they brought this Capo cigarettes or salami, so he said, "Yes."

The next morning they woke me up and they took me with them. They put me in the middle of the line and we walked together out of the gate. They told me that as soon as we get out of the gate, I would be safe because over 6,000 prisoners walk out of the gate every day and nobody knows who is who.

There was a beautiful orchestra playing by the gate. They would not let me go to the other job. I stayed with them until the last minute when Auschwitz was liquidated. They helped me out with little pieces of bread and a little soup.

One day the boys asked me if I could make a cap for the Capo, and they brought me some striped material. I took a piece of string to take a measurement. I asked them for some thread and a needle, and I made the cap in about two hours. For stiffness I took some paper from a cement bag and doubled the material at the top. The Capo liked the cap. I was his guy from then on, and he never beat me the whole time.

I was working for over a year with the boys at the same job, digging sand. Ten of us worked in the sand mine. There was a little guy from Breslau that we made our supervisor. He stood on top, and we were 20 feet down below. Every day we loaded up a wagon with the sand and pushed it 16 kilometers. That was two trips of four kilometers one way and four kilometers coming back—over 10 miles a day.

Twice a day we carried sand to Birkenau to cover the ashes of the dead. The sand was to cover the ashes that came from the crematoria. I did this for more than a year.

The ovens were on one side of the crematoria, and the ashes came out this side. The other side was where the gas chamber was. The Sonderkommando took the ashes out of the ovens. There were big holes for the ashes and we covered the ashes with sand.

I saw when the transports came. I saw the people who were going in, who to the right and who to the left. I saw who was going to the gas chambers. I saw the people going to the real showers, and I saw the people going to the gas. In August and September of 1944 I saw them throw living children into the crematorium. They would grab them by an arm and a leg and throw them in.

1947 NEWS FEATURE

"Hold Fast! Ye Southern Textile Workers"
From a pamphlet by J. K. Smith, 1947:
Chapter 2: We Are Learning

For the first few years of Roosevelt's administration, I, like thousands of other textile workers, looked upon him as a savior of the working class of people. But now, as the Bible says, "We see face to face." Roosevelt might have meant well and probably thought he was doing what was right, but it is also possible for him to be blinded the same as ordinary men. After all, you can't read men's hearts. No one but God can do that.

Some of the highest-ranking union labor leaders had been Roosevelt's friends and advisors for years, and our present condition has been planned for NO SHORT TIME.

It is true that some of the things that grew out of the New Deal and its administration are useful and a benefit to mankind, but these are not worth the fact that our country is now in the hands of the Communist. When it gets to the place that the late Sidney Hillman and now Pototsky, Russian Communists, have to tell a nation as great as America, who it can run for vice president, things are in bad shape. The Constitution says that, "The Government is of the people, by the people, and for the people." We elect them by voting. That may be true, but look who says, "who" can run. It seems that puppet rulers are back in style, even in a democracy.

The greatest vote in our country comes from us working people, and it seems that we have been blinded to true facts for the past few years.

Labor's progress in the last decade has been slow but sure, and regardless of who our president was or is, there is still going to be progress. The progress we want, though, is not toward Communism, but toward an ultimate goal of perfection to ideals and a greater democracy.

As I understand it, each individual in America has the same opportunity of equality and the chance to climb as high as his or her ambition will permit them. If we, as individuals, fail to do this, we have no one to blame but ourselves. There is a place at the top of the ladder for everyone who has the energy and ambition to climb there. The trouble with us is that we are satisfied with too little of that thing called Knowledge. We are too satisfied to be like the fellow next door to us.

There is in our South the opportunity for everyone to educate himself and choose any profession which he might be successful in.

We Southern textile workers are a different class of people from other localities, and we should realize that fact before it is too late. We are born and reared in the same community, and very few of us have a desire to go anyplace else, or get into a different work. The percentage is very, very small. There is hardly a village in our Southern textile area where you can go and talk about someone, to someone else, unless you are talking about their relatives. We are reared together and intermarry, and the majority do marry before we can make up our minds what we want to do or be. Cousins and double-first cousins are very numerous, and aunts and uncles are no end.

We Southern textile workers do not give this much thought because we have everything we need right in our community, and we live, work, and play together and are happy and content. As I have said before, we take care of our own and we have been very fortunate in having men at the head of our plants who are interested in the welfare of their people. Good old Southern men of good stock, and who believe in living and let live.

I would say that 99 percent of our supervisors are men that have risen from the ranks of our Southern textile workers, and many of them are from our textile families, who prepared themselves in our colleges and universities. They were reared among us and know our problems, and our way of life; therefore our grievances are few.

There are also other men from our Southern textile workers who have prepared themselves for other fields, and there is a great demand for others of their type at the present. The reason is that these Southern men are reared in the South and our principles are different from those of other sections. The environment and atmosphere are different, and they are reared where true religion and a feeling for their neighbors flourishes. We do not feel that "we must do to the other fellow before he does to us," but "do unto your neighbor as ye would have him do unto you."

We want to keep our South like that and by God's help, and with all our Southern textile people of character, and love of their South, working together, we can do that.

These Communist and labor leaders have taken advantage of the working people by slowly but surely gaining a foothold in our government, and putting enough money into our Democratic party to hold a margin of influence and control, whereby they can use our government for their own needs and accomplishments. James (Jimmy) Byrnes, not being endorsed for vice president, is a good example of that.

Look at the drive of the C.I.O. and the A.F.L. in the South. Those Communist-loving traitors can pass through our textile plants and distribute and organize all they please and what can be done about it? Nothing. I sincerely believe and think it a sacrilege for us to even let one near our plants. They defile what we Southern textile workers hold dear and sacred when they even talk to or distribute their foul and Communist literature among us. Wake up, Southern textile workers, before it is everlastingly too late. Do you want your wife, son or daughter working side by side and intermingling with negroes? Again, I say, read the Creed of the C.I.O. Regardless of race, creed, or color. Do you want a country like Russia? Do you love that church where you have worshipped so long and faithfully? Do you want to be separated from your loved ones and sent wherever one of these Communists tells you to work? That's their creed and contract. Some of you people who are classed as Southern textile workers, and have been instrumental in helping pass out their filthy literature and propaganda, should get down on your knees and beg God to have mercy on your souls for even listening to a C.I.O. member talk. It is contrary to all of God's word and laws. Ask your minister and preacher, the man you have confidence in. Don't take my or anyone else's word for it. Do you have a family, loved ones whom you hold in the highest esteem? If you do, please, for God's sake, think of their future and the future of America. Let's not give up those ideals and traditions that our forefathers fought and died for, to make this a free country. Let's live our lives according to God's plan and hold fast to that which is dear and precious, and right will triumph. If it pleases God, I would pray that my children and your children have the same chance to grow up in a world like the one you and I grew up in. Free from Communism, let theirs be the chance to worship a true and living God.

Are we going to throw in our lot with Satan and his Communist group, or shall we look to God for leadership and guidance in our hour of need? Each individual must ask himself that question and no one else can answer for him. It is we Southern Textile Workers to whom I am talking, you who have the capacity for friendship which you enjoy; you who have the privilege to do as you please. You who have the chance to uphold a sinful and ungodly nation. Shall we bring crowns or crosses to the children of our Southern Textile workers?

1950–1959

The consequences of World War II were everywhere in the decade of the 1950s: a population eagerly on the move, industries infused with energy and confidence, plans for interstate highways, hydroelectric dams to power America, a plethora of new national brands made for Americans. Optimism was rampant. Women tended to marry at an earlier age and bear children in their twenties. As the decade progressed, much of America's energy was focused on family and the potential of children. Television programs that educated and toys that expanded creativity were in vogue. Family travel was considered a necessity and college a definite possibility. Health insurance was common and everyone knew someone who owned a television set. America was on a roll. It manufactured half of the world's products, 57 percent of the steel, 43 percent of the electricity, and 62 percent of the oil. As a result of World War II, the economies of Europe and Asia lay in ruins, while America's industrial structure was untouched and well oiled to supply the needs of a war-weary world.

In addition, the war year's high employment and optimism spurred the longest sustained period of peacetime prosperity in the nation's history. A decade full of employment and pent-up desire produced demands for all types of consumer goods. Businesses of all sizes prospered. Rapidly swelling families, new suburban homes, television, and most of all, big, powerful, shiny automobiles symbolized the hopes of the era. During the 1950s, an average of seven million cars and trucks were sold annually. By 1952, two thirds of all families owned a television set; home freezers and high-fidelity stereo phonographs were considered necessities. Specialized markets developed to meet the demand of consumers such as amateur photographers, pet lovers, and backpackers. At the same time, shopping malls, supermarkets, and credit cards emerged as important economic forces.

This economic prosperity also ushered in conservative politics and social conformity. Tidy lawns, "proper" suburban homes with "neat and trim" interiors were certainly "in" throughout the decade as Americans adjusted to the post-war years. Properly buttoned-down attitudes concerning sexual mores brought stern undergarments for women like bonded girdles and stiff, pointed, or padded bras to confine the body. The planned community of Levittown, New York, mandated that grass be cut at least once a week and laundry washed on specific days. A virtual revival of Victorian respectability and domesticity reigned; divorce rates and female college attendance fell while birth rates and the sale of Bibles rose. Corporate America promoted the benefits of respectable men in gray flannel suits whose wives remained at home to tend house and raise children. Suburban life included ladies' club memberships, chauffeuring children to piano and ballet classes and lots of a newly marketed product known as tranquilizers, the sales of which were astounding.

The average wage earner benefited more from the booming industrial system than at any time in American history. The 40-hour workweek became standard in manufacturing. In offices many workers were becoming accustomed to a 35-hour week. Health benefits for workers become more common and paid vacations were standard in most industries. In 1950, 25 percent of American wives worked outside the home; by the end of the decade the number had risen to 40 percent. Communications technology, expanding roads, inexpensive airline tickets, and an unbounded spirit meant that people and commerce were no longer prisoners of distance. Unfortunately, up to one-third of the population lived below the government's poverty level, largely overlooked in the midst of prosperity.

The Civil Rights Movement was propelled by two momentous events in the 1950s. The first was a decree on May 17, 1954, by the U.S. Supreme Court which ruled "that in the field of public education the doctrine of 'separate but equal' has no place. Separate educational facilities are inherently unequal." The message was electric but the pace was slow. Few schools would be integrated for another decade. The second event established the place of the Civil Rights Movement. On December 1, 1955, African-American activist Rosa Parks declined to vacate the white-only front section of the Montgomery, Alabama, bus, leading to her arrest and a citywide bus boycott by blacks. Their spokesman became Martin Luther King, Jr., the 26-year-old pastor of the Dexter Avenue Baptist Church. The yearlong boycott was the first step toward the passage of the Civil Rights Act of 1964.

America's youths were enchanted by the TV adventures of *Leave It to Beaver*, westerns, and *Father Knows Best*, allowing them to accumulate more time watching television during the week (at least 27 hours) than attending school. TV dinners were invented; felt skirts with sequined poodle appliqués were worn; Elvis Presley was worshipped and the new phenomena of *Playboy* and Mickey Spillane fiction were created only to be read behind closed doors. The ever-glowing eye of television killed the "March of Time" newsreels after 16 years at the movies. Sexual jargon such as "first base" and "home run" entered the language. Learned-When-Sleeping machines appeared, along with Smokey the Bear, Sony tape recorders, adjustable shower heads, *Mad Comics*, newspaper vending machines, Levi's faded blue denims, pocket-size transistor radios and transparent plastic bags for clothing. Ultimately, the real stars of the era were the Salk and Sabin vaccines, which vanquished the siege of polio.

1954 Profile

Censorship: Banning Comic Books

Working and raising a son on her own after her husband died in World War II was difficult enough for Ann O'Conner without having to worry about the dangers of her child reading lurid, violent comic books.

Life at Home

- Ann O'Conner of the Bronx, New York, was obsessed with one dream: a better life for her and her family.
- Most of those dreams revolved around her only son, Jonathan, and her plans for his attending college.
- Education was the key to a good life, and she knew that she could not allow comic books to get in the way, no matter how much her teenaged son protested.
- After all, she had seen in a national magazine the scientific evidence that excessive comic book reading was directly linked to juvenile delinquency.
- It was hard enough to raise a son alone in a major city without the corrupting influence of innocent-appearing adventure comic books.
- Jonathan's father had died in World War II without ever meeting his son and namesake.
- He died in 1943 when the truck he was driving crashed on a wet English rural road.
- Ann and Jonathan had dated for two years, fashioning luxurious plans for the future, before hastily getting married only weeks before his deployment to Europe.
- After his death, Ann raised her son with the help of her father and mother, Karl and Mary Pagel, in their tiny apartment.
- Mary Pagel often watched Jonathan while Ann worked during the day or evenings as a waitress at a local diner.

Ann O'Connor worried about the effect of comic books on her son.

Jonathan's father was killed in WW II.

- The Bronx was full of activity and the restaurants were often busy, but Ann's tips rarely provided enough money to raise a child with college in his future.
- On her down days she was reminded that no one in her family had graduated from high school, much less college.
- Her father worked in the shipyards of New York as a loader while her mother stayed at home to raise children.
- But mother and daughter were united in the dreams for Jonathan by faith; Ann and her family were practicing Catholics and attended church in the Bronx at Blessed Sacrament on Sundays and holy days.
- The most treasured items in the home were the family Bible and a crucifix Karl Pagel had brought from Germany when he emigrated in 1913.
- Ann loved to hold the Bible, but because it was in Latin, she could only read the most familiar phrases.
- At Blessed Sacrament Elementary School, Jonathan was an exceptional student.
- One of the nuns informed Ann about the opportunities at Regis High School in the Upper East Side of Manhattan.
- Regis High School was a tuition-free high school founded in 1914 by the Society of Jesus, also known as the Jesuits.
- The high school accepted eighth-grade Catholic boys with an "A" average regardless of their family income.
- Ann couldn't believe her good fortune.
- After a lot of tutoring and hard work, Jonathan was accepted into Regis High School.
- In the spring of his sophomore year in 1954, however, Jonathan's grades began to slip.
- One of his teachers, who reported that Jonathan enjoyed reading *Batman* and *Superman* comic books, was sure the books were influencing his academics.
- The news alarmed Ann.
- The detrimental effects of comic books were in the news; the U.S. Senate judiciary subcommittee was even holding hearings on the role of comic books in the rise of juvenile delinquency.
- Reports from educational experts warned that the publications, especially those that emphasized crime fighting and horror, were having criminal effects on children.
- The comic book industry scoffed at the claims that mere comic books could turn children into "little monsters."
- Ann's worst suspicions were reaffirmed in May when she read that month's *Reader's Digest.*
- Inside the monthly magazine was an excerpt from a book entitled *Seduction of the Innocent* by Dr. Fredric Wertham, whose studies indicated that comic books contributed to delinquency in children through the picture stories of unabashed violence and sex.
- According to Dr. Wertham's research, juvenile delinquency had increased about 20 percent since 1947.
- The books also illustrated "foreign-looking" people as villains, which belied American efforts to persuade the world that race hatred was not a staple of American life.
- The article disturbed Ann, who immediately feared that these books may corrupt her son and jeopardize his future.
- As a result, she banned comics from her home, over Jonathan's protests.
- Then she discovered he was visiting his friends' homes to read the books.

Jonathan was a Grade A student when he started high school.

Life at Work

- Ann O'Conner knew the only way to save her son was to organize.
- First, she voiced her concerns to the mothers in the neighborhood and then to the women of the church.
- She explained that comic books led to burglary, violence, gangs, and eventually drugs.
- Then she proposed that everyone ban comic book reading in her home.
- Ann also managed to convince the women to clean up the neighborhood with protests at the local newsstands that sold the vile content.
- That day, as a group, they visited one corner newsstand to protest the horror comics on display.
- During the boisterous exchange, the owner told the women that he had to buy the horror comics to acquire the better-selling comic books and family magazines.
- This was known as "tie-in sales" and helped sell the lesser-quality comics and magazines.
- Many of the comic book companies and distributors required the vendors to accept the delivered bundles, regardless of content.
- Ann purchased a couple of the comic books and personally examined what her son was reading.
- She was shocked that for $0.10 her son could see the horrible drawings found in books with titles such as *Tomb of Horror*.
- Just as disturbing, one of the books she bought advertised knives and air rifles.
- Dr. Wertham had indicated in his book that some comic books advertised knives that were easy to throw for only $1.98.

- The comics made Ann more determined to take her concerns to several more newsstands in her neighborhood.
- Most of the workers thought she was crazy and said they could not do anything about the deliveries.
- Frustrated by the excuses, she knew she needed to do more.
- Ann thought it best to protest by writing letters to her congressmen, local newsstand owners and the Newsdealers Association.
- She even recruited a few of her friends and neighbors to write letters as well.
- Ann's mother Mary decided to stay out of the protest because she did not want to draw attention to herself or cause any trouble.
- Some of Ann's neighbors were active in women's clubs in New York which were also protesting the sale of violent comic books.
- Ann wrote letters after a full day of work as a waitress.
- Jonathan thought his mother went a little overboard, creating too much commotion over grades and reading *Batman*.
- That summer, Ann's efforts were rewarded.
- The newspaper reported that the Newsdealers Association of Greater New York would refuse to handle "lewd, horror or indecent magazines that may fall into the hands of juveniles."
- It was a small victory in her crusade.
- Later in June, the Kable News Company, a distributor of comics, reported to the Senate that the reformers were going too far and were attempting to "destroy the imagination of American kids," and that if all the comics were removed from New York, one would have "more juvenile delinquency."
- During the Senate subcommittee hearings, reformers attacked many of the distributors, the comic book companies and their supporters for influencing delinquency.
- They commented that comic book covers showing human heads boiling in vats were in poor taste and books that teach methods in crime to juveniles were irresistible.
- Horror and crime comics were big business, with annual sales in the millions.
- Ann O'Conner thought that greed was the motivating reason in the industry and that federal legislation was important to prevent the spread of indecency to children.
- One of the publishers of the horror comics, William Gaines of the Entertaining Comic Group, told the subcommittee that juvenile delinquency "is a product of the real environment in which the child lives, and not of the fiction he reads."
- By July, New York State law went into effect banning "tie-in" sales of magazines to newsdealers; New Jersey and Idaho passed similar measures.
- Ann and her friends thought the tide was turning and hoped federal law would help the cause, especially with tie-in sales.

Life in the Community: Bronx, New York

- The U.S. Senate hearings, which created much national and international attention, also got big play in the O'Conner household in the Bronx.
- One day, Jonathan was presented with a news story that said the Canadian courts had linked two homicides by teenaged killers to the reading of crime comics.

- A few days later, he was told that British Prime Minster Winston Churchill had announced that he planned to read a handful of horror comics to weigh the need for a possible ban.
- After the U.S. Senate hearings, legislators indicated that it would not be likely that federal law would ban tie-in sales of horror comics packaged with family magazines.
- Instead, the congressmen hoped to see more local action and public pressure.
- The senators pressured the comic book industry to enforce a code of good taste.
- But Ann and her friends did not believe that the industry code would do any good.
- During a July annual meeting, the General Federation of Women's Clubs declared a campaign against juvenile delinquency.
- The Federation compiled a list of current objectionable comics and sent them to all the other clubs so that they could protest.
- The Federation listed 36 comics "very objectionable," 122 "objectionable" and 158 as "on objections."
- Ann tried to acquire this list but was not a member of any women's organization; her job left her no time to devote to a women's group.
- However, she continued to communicate with her state and local representatives on the issue.
- Included in her letters were lists of the comics that she thought should be banned from newsstands, such as *True Crime, Two-Fisted Tales* and *Crypt of Terror*.
- Nationwide, women were campaigning to stop the objectionable materials.
- New York even held a special Joint Legislative Committee one weekend to discuss legislation barring the "glamorizing of brutality and sadism in publications" available to minors.
- Representatives from Governor Thomas Dewey's office also attended the meeting.
- After the committee meetings, Ann received a letter from her state senator thanking her for her interest in this important issue and telling her that he was working to find a solution.
- Ann's mother Mary was proud of her daughter's hard work and recognition by an important statesmen.

Charles Murphy was the censor of the Comic Book Association.

- Mary wanted to frame the letter.
- Ann's father insisted that she not bother with the frame; it was only a form letter drafted by the senator's staff.
- Regardless, the letter reinforced that Ann's efforts were part of the greater good of society, especially the youth, and were a step in protecting her son and the children of other families.
- In September, the comics industry formed a new self-regulatory group and planned to develop a code to protect the children from questionable content.
- The organization, called the Comic Magazine Association of America, was formed with 90 percent participation of the comic industry.
- The industry selected New York City Magistrate Charles F. Murphy as the official "censor" of the organization.
- The Comic Magazine Association provided Magistrate Murphy with a $100,000 budget for the job and a two-year contractual commitment to develop and enforce a comic book code.
- Upon his appointment, Murphy received numerous letters from legislators and citizens throughout the nation.

- Ann sent Charles Murphy a letter every single week with a list of books that should be banned and examples of comic issues that contained poor content.
- With all the protest, the Comic Magazine Association developed its code by the end of 1954, when a vast majority of the crime and horror comics disappeared from the newsstands.
- Ann saw what had occurred over the past several months as a victory for women.
- During an afternoon discussion with a group of her friends over coffee, the topic turned to another issue that might lead to juvenile delinquency: the influence of television.

The Comic Book Association was based in New York City.

HISTORICAL SNAPSHOT
1954

- After the televised Senate Army-McCarthy hearings ended, the Senate voted 67-22 to censure Senator Joseph R. McCarthy, R-Wisconsin, for "conduct that tends to bring the Senate into dishonor and disrepute"
- Medical student Roger Bannister broke the four-minute mile barrier during a track meet in Oxford, England, finishing in 3 minutes 59.4 seconds
- The Battle of Dien Bien Phu in Vietnam ended after 55 days with Vietnamese insurgents overrunning French forces, which led to the creation of North Vietnam led by Ho Chi Minh and an anti-Communist regime in South Vietnam under Ngo Dinh Diem
- The musical play *The Pajama Game* opened on Broadway
- The Supreme Court unanimously ruled for school integration in *Brown vs. Board of Education* of Topeka, Kansas
- President Eisenhower signed an order adding the words "under God" to the Pledge of Allegiance
- Food rationing ended in Great Britain almost nine years after the end of World War II
- Elvis Presley's first commercial recording session, a performance of "That's All Right (Mama)," took place at Sun Records in Memphis, Tennessee
- The first mass inoculation of children against polio with the Salk vaccine began
- Howard Hughes paid $23.5 million for the RKO motion picture company
- The Miss America pageant made its network TV debut on ABC
- Walt Disney's television program, *Disneyland,* premiered on ABC
- Ellis Island closed after processing more than 20 million immigrants since opening in New York Harbor
- Popular movies included *White Christmas, The Caine Mutiny* and *Rear Window*
- The Iwo Jima Memorial was dedicated in Arlington, Virginia
- Chevrolet introduced the V8 engine
- The U.S. Armed Forces ended racial segregation
- The film *Godzilla, King of the Monsters* was released
- The FORTRAN computer program was used for the first time
- Puerto Rican nationalists fired gunshots from the gallery of the House of Representatives, wounding five congressmen
- First Lady Mamie Eisenhower christened *Nautilus,* the nation's first atomic-powered submarine
- Boeing unveiled the "707," the first commercially successful jet aircraft
- A team of doctors at Harvard Medical School successfully completed the first kidney transplant operation
- *On the Waterfront* won the Academy Award for Best Picture; actor Marlon Brando won the Best Actor award for his leading role in the film
- The most popular TV Shows were *I Love Lucy, The Jackie Gleason Show* and *Dragnet*

Selected Prices, 1954

Automobiles

Chevrolet, 150 Series Sedan $1,696.50

Packard, Clipper $2,638.00

Tires, Firestone, Each . . . .$10.95-$11.95

Clothing

Man's Suit, Dacron $60.00

Man's Shirt, Sport . . . .$1.49-$2.49

Woman's Skirt, Tailored . . . .$3.00-$14.00

Woman's Dress, Cotton-Orlon $8.98

Woman's Sweater, Cashmere . . . . . .$10.38-$22.98

Woman's Handbags . . . .$5.32-$16.67

Boy's Jacket or Slacks $3.95

Girl's Playsuits . . . .$1.99-$2.99

Food

Bacon, Pound $0.87

Bananas, Two Pounds $0.25

Beans, Baked, Van Camp's, Two No. 2 Cans $0.29

Beef, Sirloin Steak, Pound $0.61

Bread, White, 16-Ounce Loaf $0.15

Kellogg's Rice Krispies, 9.5-Ounce Pkg. $0.26

Chicken, Frying, Pound $0.29

Chocolate, Whitman's Sampler, Pound $2.25

Coffee, Ehlers, Instant, Two-Ounce Jar $0.59

Cookies, Sunshine Hydrox, 12-Ounce Pkg. $0.35

Corn, Frozen, Birdseye, Two Pkgs. $0.29

Crackers, Ritz, Pound $0.39

Crisco, Can $0.33

Fish, Flounder Fillet, Pound $0.65

Ham, Pound $0.79

Margarine, Good Luck Brand, Pound $0.30

Mayonnaise, Kraft Miracle Whip, Quart $0.47

Milk, Borden's, Quart $0.22

Onions, Texas, Three Pounds $0.19

Oranges, Florida, Five Pounds $0.39

Peanut Butter, Skippy, 14 Ounces $0.37

Potatoes, New, Five Pounds $0.29

Soda, C & C, Three 12-Ounce Cans $0.29

Tea, White Rose, 48 Count $0.55

Tuna, Chicken of the Sea, 6.5 Ounces $0.38

TV Dinner, Swanson's Turkey $0.89

continued

Selected Prices, 1954 *(continued)*

Garden Equipment
Grass Seed, Five Pounds . . . . $5.45-$7.15
Hose, Plastic, 50 Feet $1.99
Lawn Mower, Hand $7.99
Lawn Mower, Gas . . . . $61.70-$99.95
Picnic Table Set, Redwood $22.00
Rake, Metal, 20 Inches, ... $0.79
Rose Bushes, Three, ... $2.00
Household Goods
Air Conditioner, Philco, Window Unit, ... $199.00
Ammonia, Parsons, Quart, ... $0.22
Bedspread, Chenille, ... $3.97-$9.98
Cleanser, Old Dutch, Two 14-Ounce Cans, ... $0.23
Clothes Washer and Dryer
    General Electric . . . . $449.90-$529.00
Cookware, Revereware, 11-Piece Set, ... $39.95
Dinnerware Set, 136 Pieces, ... $29.73
Ironing Board $9.99
Laundry Soap, Cheer, ... $0.30
Range, Sears, Gas, ... $99.00
Refrigerator, Kelvinator, 12 Cubic Feet, ... $329.95
Reynolds Wrap, 12″ Width, 25′ Roll, ... $0.45
Sheets, Cannon, ... $1.87
Sterling Silver Service, Eight Settings, ... $89.95
Vacuum Cleaner, ... $24.95-$59.95

continued

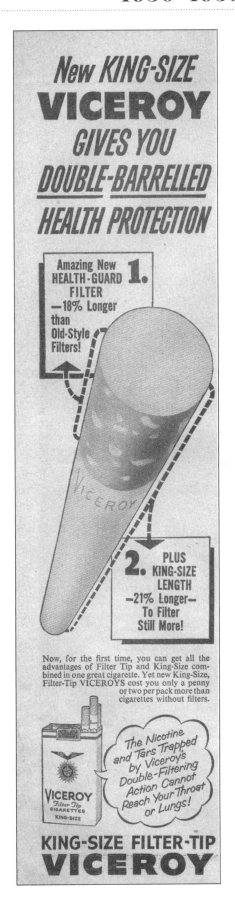

Selected Prices, 1954 *(continued)*

Personal Care and Health

Bandaids, Johnson & Johnson $0.33

Shaving Cream, Mennen $0.79

Soap, Ivory, Three Cakes $0.25

Tissues, Four Packets $0.19

Toilet Paper, Three Rolls $0.29

Toothpaste, Pepsodent, Two Tubes $0.69

Recreation and Amusements

Badminton Set, Sears $3.69

Baseball Glove, J.C. Higgens $4.44

Bicycle, Sears, 14 Inches $19.95

Bus Trip, Greyhound, NYC

    Washington DC, Round Trip $8.65

Camera Film, Three Rolls $1.00

Fishing Rod Set $10.88

Golf Balls, Three $1.25

Radio, Zenith, Portable $39.95

Roller Skates, Sears $1.99

Sewing Machine, Necchi $98.95

Swing Set, 10-Ply Steel $28.88

Television, B&W, 21 Inches, ...$149.95

Mahogany Cabinet

Television, Color, RCA Victor $1,000.00

Theatre/Movie Ticket $1.00

CAFE-BAR MARTINIQUE

TYPICAL BEDROOM

"Not So Horrible," Commentary, *The New York Times*, September 19, 1954:

In New York last April, a Senate judiciary subcommittee on juvenile delinquency held hearings for two days on crime and horror comics. The sociologist and experts could not agree. Some held that only those children already "disturbed" mentally and emotionally were harmed by horror comics. Others argued that they were harmful primarily to normal children, and did not greatly affect morbid children already "wrapped in their own fantasies...."

Last Wednesday, the newly formed Comics Magazine Association of America announced that it had appointed an official censor—New York Magistrate Charles F. Murphy, who has been active in combating juvenile delinquency. Mr. Murphy said he had accepted the job on condition that member publishers take crime and horror comics off the list. Two days before Mr. Murphy's appointment, Mr. Gaines called a press conference to announce that he was substituting a "clean, clean line" since that "seems to be what the American parents want."

"Real Curb Sought for Delinquency, Erick H. Erikson Deplores Tendency to Make Comics and TV 'Scapegoats,'" Murray Illson, *The New York Times*, October 3, 1954:

There is too much "scapegoating" on the subject of juvenile delinquency and not enough careful search for the real causes, an authority on adolescent psychology said today.

Erik H. Erikson, senior staff member of the Austen Riggs Center here, asserted that there was an unfortunate and increasing tendency to blame without adequate evidence such media as comic books, television, movies and all the graphic representations of violence.

He declared that these could not be dismissed as harmless, but the evidence as to the precise role they played in the world of atom bombs and total war had not been gathered. . . .

"When people get worked up," Mr. Erikson said, "they often look for something or someone to blame. That makes them feel better but it doesn't mean they have found the cause.

"They fool themselves into believing they have an immediate cure, with no evidence whatever that it will work now or has worked in the past, because usually this 'remedy' is an old one that never really worked. This misleads everybody and helps to retard responsible efforts to solve the problem."

"Druggists to Curb Comics," *The New York Times*, October 1, 1954:

Drugstore members of the Upstate Pharmaceutical Council will not handle comic books detrimental to youthful minds, it was announced today by the council at its annual meeting. . . . Members of the council unanimously approved the campaign by the New York State Pharmaceutical Association. . . .

The New York Times, October 14, 1954:

The American Legion Auxiliary announced today a nation-wide "Operation Book-swap" to give children a chance to trade crime and horror comics for good books.

"GOTTA PATROL A PLANET, DAD!"

I'D SAY you're equipped for the assignment, Son. With that modern gadget you'll handle any emergency, and your mission will be successful.

Emergencies in *bushess*, such as accidents on the job also require special "equipment." They call for workmen's compensation insurance placed with a reliable organization that assures quick, sympathetic service.

Hardware Mutuals rank among the leaders in promptness of paying workmen's compensation claims. This promptness helps speed recovery by relieving financial worry. With the help of Hardware Mutuals loss prevention specialists, employers can eliminate hazards *before* they cause accidents.

Among other benefits of Hardware Mutuals *policy back of the policy* is friendly, nationwide, day-and-night service. More than $110,000,000 in dividend savings have been returned to policyholders.

For all the facts, simply *call Western Union, ask for Operator 25,* and say you'd like the name and address of your nearest Hardware Mutuals representative.

Insurance for your AUTOMOBILE...HOME...BUSINESS

Hardware Mutuals.

Stevens Point, Wisconsin · Offices Coast to Coast

HARDWARE MUTUAL CASUALTY COMPANY · HARDWARE DEALERS MUTUAL FIRE INSURANCE COMPANY

"Clubs War on Books by Newsstand Lists," *The New York Times,* October 20, 1954:

Club women in various parts of the country are waging war against crime and sex "comic" books by simple and direct methods, the president of the General Federation of Women's Clubs said yesterday.

Mrs. Theodore S. Chapman described how committees from the clubs, sometimes jointly with other civic-minded groups, drew up lists of undesirable "comics" and then informed newsstands that they should not be carried.

"We tell them we are trying to protect our children, and authorities have convinced us that our committees have great influence," she reported.

The federation, Mrs. Chapman added, is carrying out its campaign under a youth conservation committee that distributes a "blueprint" of action to federation members. . . .

"Jersey School Unit Urges 'Comic' Curb," *The New York Times,* October 23, 1954:

The New Jersey Congress of Parents and Teachers called today on the State Legislature to ban the publication and distribution of so-called comic books, pictures, films and similar media carrying indecent, obscene and crime material.

The action was taken in a resolution adopted by the more than 2,000 delegates attending the fifty-fourth annual meeting. . . .

In the . . . resolution, the delegates called on the United States Congress "to take action against the showing of television programs on crime, sex and horror stories detrimental to the health, moral character and spiritual development of our youth." A copy was ordered sent to the Senate subcommittee presently engaged in investigating such TV programs.

The Standards of the Comic Code Authority as Originally Adopted
(Excerpts)

CODE FOR EDITORIAL MATTER
General Standards

1. Crimes shall never be presented in such a way as to create sympathy for the criminal, to promote distrust of the forces of law and justice, or to inspire others with a desire to imitate criminals.
2. No comics shall explicitly present the unique details and methods of a crime.
3. Policemen, judges, government officials and respected institutions shall never be presented in such a way as to create disrespect for established authority.

continued

The Standards of the Comic Code Authority as Originally Adopted . . . *(continued)*

CODE FOR EDITORIAL MATTER
General Standards

4. If crime is depicted it shall be as a sordid and unpleasant activity.

5. Criminals shall not be presented so as to be rendered glamorous or to occupy a position which creates a desire for emulation.

6. In every instance good shall triumph over evil and the criminal punished for his misdeeds.

7. Scenes of excessive violence shall be prohibited. Scenes of brutal torture, excessive and unnecessary knife and gun play, physical agony, gory and gruesome crime shall be eliminated.

8. No unique or unusual methods of concealing weapons shall be shown.

9. Instances of law enforcement officers dying as a result of a criminal's activities should be discouraged.

10. The crime of kidnapping shall never be portrayed in any detail, nor shall any profit accrue to the abductor or kidnapper. The criminal or the kidnapper must be punished in every case.

11. The letter of the word "crime" on a comics magazine cover shall never be appreciably greater in dimension than the other words contained in the title. The word "crime" shall never appear alone on a cover.

12. Restraint in the use of the word "crime" in titles or subtitles shall be exercised.

General Standards

1. No comic magazine shall use the word horror or terror in its title.

2. All scenes of horror, excessive bloodshed, gory or gruesome crimes, depravity, lust, sadism, masochism shall not be permitted.

3. All lurid, unsavory, gruesome illustrations shall be eliminated.

4. Inclusion of stories dealing with evil shall be used or shall be published only where the intent is to illustrate a moral issue and in no case shall evil be presented alluringly nor so as to injure the sensibilities of the reader.

5. Scenes dealing with, or instruments associated with walking dead, torture, vampires and vampirism, ghouls, cannibalism and werewolfism are prohibited.

Dialogue

1. Profanity, obscenity, smut, vulgarity, or words or symbols which have acquired undesirable meanings are forbidden.

2. Special precautions to avoid references to physical afflictions or deformities shall be taken.

3. Although slang and colloquialisms are acceptable, excessive use should be discouraged and wherever possible good grammar shall be employed.

Marriage and Sex

1. Divorce shall not be treated humorously nor represented as desirable.

2. Illicit sex relations are neither to be hinted at nor portrayed. Violent love scenes as well as sexual abnormalities are unacceptable.

3. Respect for parents, the moral code, and for honorable behavior shall be fostered. A sympathetic understanding of the problems of love is not a license for morbid distortion.

4. The treatment of love-romance stories shall emphasize the value of the home and the sanctity of marriage.

5. Passion or romantic interest shall never be treated in such a way as to stimulate the lower and baser emotions.

6. Seduction and rape shall never be shown or suggested.

7. Sex perversion or any inference to same is strictly forbidden.

"No Harm in Horror, Comics Issuer Says," Peter Kihss, *The New York Times*, April 22, 1954:

A comic-book publisher, who boasted he was the first in the country to publish "horror comics," told a Senate subcommittee yesterday that he believed no healthy, normal child ever had been "ruined" by a comic book. A child's personality is set before he reaches reading age, the publisher contended.

William Gaines, president of the Entertaining Comics Group, which prints two million comic books a month with a gross sale of $80,000 and a net profit of $4,000, said that he opposed any censorship and recognized only a limit of "good taste."

He was asked by Senator Estes Kefauver, Democrat of Tennessee, if he considered in "good taste" the cover of his Shock SuspenStories, which depicted an axe-wielding man holding aloft the severed head of a blond women. Mr. Gaines replied:

"Yes, I do—for the cover of a horror comic. I think it would be in bad taste if he were holding the head a little higher so the neck would show with the blood dripping from it."

"You've got blood dripping from the mouth," Senator Kefauver pointed out, softly. . . .

"Comic Books—Blueprints for Delinquency" *Reader's Digest*, May 1954:

Year by year, the statistics of crime are becoming more terrifying. In the first six months of 1953 the number of crimes committed in the nation's cities was 33.4 percent above the 1937-1939 average. Even more ominous is the fact that most of the increase has been in crimes of violence—aggravated assault, negligent manslaughter, murder and rape. (The number of rape cases has risen by approximately 80 percent.)

At the same time, the average age of the nation's criminals has been falling steadily; juvenile delinquency has become a major menace. Nor are the teenagers merely vandals and petty thieves. More and more they are going in the big-time crime. They carry guns, and they're even quicker than the adult criminals to kill.

What has caused this situation? The most important factor, criminologists believe, is the unrest that has gripped the world since 1939. The two wars had an unsettling effect on the nation's social structure, and particularly on the home and on youth. Moreover, they have led to a weakening of public and private morality and, among teenagers, to a feeling of "tomorrow we die."

Once the great majority of youngsters who got into trouble with the law came from poor homes. Now, increasingly, we find juvenile gangsterism in well-to-do neighborhoods. Only recently New York City police picked up a 17-year-old second offender charged with assaulting and robbing women at knife point. He was the son of a respected author who lives in as swanky a neighborhood as New York can boast.

Criminologists believe that only a stiffening of the moral fabric of the nation and a spiritual renaissance can halt the steady increase in crime. Police can catch the criminals, and penal institutions can hold them, but they can't begin to deal with the real problem—the fact that society keeps creating criminals at a fearsome rate.

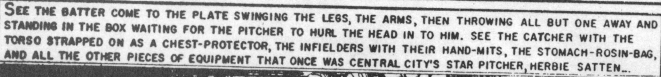

Seduction of the Innocent, Fredric Wertham, M.D., Rinehart & Co., New York, 1954:

In 1946 crime comics represented only about one-tenth of all comic books. By 1949 crime comics had increased to one-half the total output, and by 1953 formed the vast majority. The so-called "good" comics—sports, animal stories, Disney comics—today make up no more than one-fifth of the whole. . . .

One comic book bears the legend, "We hope that within these pages the youth of America will learn to know crime for what it really is: a dead-end road of fools and tears." Inside, a criminal terrorizes a farm family, makes advances to the farmer's wife, beats the farmer, kidnaps the little boy as a hostage. "I'll knock yer teeth out!!" he snarls as he beats the child. In the end the criminal evades the law by shooting himself, like a hero. The story has 97 pictures of the criminal winning, and only for his violent end—a ratio of 97 parts of "crime" to one of "does not pay". . . .

Lurid advertisements, interspersed among the comics, are veritable invitations to delinquency. Pictures of air pistols, a "genuine .22 rifle" accompany sequences showing how the guns may be used to threaten people. An ad for a switchblade knife shows how to hold it, "with your thumb on the button." Another, for a telescope, points out that you can look into "neighbors' homes," and the illustration shows a half-nude girl. Still others offer secret creams for girls with small busts, and patent medicines to develop "virility". . . .

Many comic books describe how to set fires, by methods too various to enumerate. In some stories fire-setting is related just as a detail; in other stories such as "The Arson Racket" the lesson is more systematic. There are other sidelights, like how to break windows so you cannot be found out; all this highlighted by the philosophy of the character who says: "From now on—I'm making dough the easy way—with a gun! Only SAPS work!" That lesson, incidentally, is true of crime comics as a whole: glamour for crime, contempt for work. . . .

1956 Profile

Environmental Movement: Preserving the National Parks System

Tom Baldwin, a geology professor in Utah, was dedicated to keeping the Western lands of the United States pristine and the national parks from being ruined by the building of dams.

Life at Home

- Tom Baldwin fell in love for the first time when he was nine years old.
- His first love was a rock—actually, the huge rock formations in his native Wyoming.
- As he came of age, he explored on horseback the geologic mosaic laid before him in Utah, Colorado and Wyoming—a veritable showcase of geologic history, replete with ancient petroglyphs on the canyon walls.
- He also cherished the writing of Western naturalist John Muir, who campaigned for the preservation of natural places.
- Nearly everyone else believed that environmental beauty was always trumped by economic necessity.
- As early as 1908, Muir wrote an article entitled "A High Price to Pay for Water" for *Century* magazine concerning plans by the City of San Francisco to use portions of Yosemite National Park for its water supply.
- Although everyone expected that Tom, a certified loner with a scientific bent, would choose geology to study in college, most were surprised that he stayed long enough to get his Ph.D. so that he could teach in high school and college.
- Few had ever heard him say more than a few words at a time unless the subject was rocks, and fewer still could envision this confirmed bachelor lecturing for an entire class period.
- Now 42, Tom had been working at a small college in Utah for six years when he was confronted by the possibility of a dam forever changing the landscape of Yampa Canyon.

Tom Baldwin's mission was preserving the Western wilderness.

- Utah had experienced astonishing economic growth since the beginning of World War II.
- The war alone had created 50,000 jobs, which spurred new demand for cheap electricity to support the burgeoning industrial infrastructure of a region desperate to grow prosperous.
- Damming the rivers was on the wish list of every aspiring politician.
- Since the late 1930s, economic forces had targeted the Colorado River as an unexploited resource capable of saving dozens of drought-ridden farm communities in New Mexico, Utah, Colorado and Wyoming.
- Western farming was often a precarious occupation at best; droughts and dust storms could tip the balance toward disaster.
- And it was not unusual for ranchers, farmers and communities in four different states to represent competing interests and needs for the water flowing through their regions.
- Especially in economically depressed areas, the construction of dams to regulate water, irrigate dry lands, attract tourists and generate electricity—like the TVA miracle in Appalachia or the Hoover Dam in Nevada—was viewed as an obvious solution.
- After all, the history of Western development revolved around the construction of railroads in advance of population.
- Constructing dams to fuel twentieth-century Western growth was a logical next step.
- But not for Tom, who had grown up loving the scenic beauty of the Western lands.
- With the help of two friends, he constructed his own home on a rock ledge in a style that emphasized the landscape, not the house.

Tom's house was built on a rock ledge.

- Every day he was reminded of his Western heritage by a gallery of framed pictures, including one featuring his grandmother and her sisters standing outside a primitive prairie hut they had built.
- So when he told the Wilderness Society that he was willing to assist in preserving the natural beauty of Dinosaur National Monument, he was fully committed, never dreaming that the fight would last six years and serve to unify conservation groups across the nation.

Tom's grandmother and her sisters built a primitive hut to live in.

Life at Work

- Tom Baldwin first became aware of the Echo Park Dam controversy at Dinosaur National Monument in 1950 shortly after a friend in the Department of the Interior told him about a clash with the Bureau of Reclamation.
- Echo Park Dam, planned for the Green River to generate power and create a recreational lake, would have flooded the Echo Park Valley inside Dinosaur National Monument on the Utah-Colorado border.
- The Department of the Interior was looking to protect the integrity of the national parks, while the Bureau of Reclamation wanted to develop America economically by using the country's resources, including parts of the parks system.
- The water and power vote of the West insisted that a prosperous America demanded that its natural resources not be locked away, but fully exploited.
- Besides, people argued, few had been able to visit Echo Park in Dinosaur National Monument because of poor roads and swift water; the greater good would be served with hydroelectricity and a glittering, manmade lake.
- At first, Tom was unsure of how he could best participate in a project this big.
- He tried lecturing in Utah and Colorado about the beauty of the sacred place, but few were interested in protecting something they had never seen.
- To counter this problem, he started taking colored slides of the sheer cliffs and dazzling landscapes of Echo Park.
- This sparked interest, but not passion; after each talk his all-volunteer army of budding conservationists would express enthusiasm, and then go about their lives.
- After three years of crusading, Tom figured he needed another tactic; "I seem to be shoveling the same snow over and over again," he told friends.
- This was especially true of the issue of whether the dam at Echo Park would damage the ancient bone fossils for which Dinosaur National Monument was named.
- *Time* magazine derisively called opponents of Echo Park Dam "professional nature lovers."
- Tom even asked himself whether a remote and virtually unknown national monument with a misleading name was the place to mount a preservation battle.

Tom's photos illustrated the dazzling landscapes.

- Clearly, the canyons of the Green and Yampa Rivers—tributaries of the Colorado River—possessed undeniable beauty, but Dinosaur National Monument hardly had the kind of name recognition of Yellowstone.
- But when Western big business branded the preservation effort "Eastern elitism" populated by "armchair birdwatchers," Tom knew that as a native of Wyoming, he had a job to do.
- "I can stay in the saddle a little longer," he told himself.
- In the summer of 1953, he found the answer.
- While acting as a rafting guide on the Yampa River in hopes of exposing more people to this special place, he met a family determined to capture their vacation trip with an 8-mm film camera.
- The children giggled and waved a lot, the pictures occasionally went totally out of focus, but the breathtaking images captured by the $200 Wollensak 53 handheld camera were unmistakable.
- The Wollensak was capable of wide angle, normal and telephoto shots that made it possible to record the vastness of the canyons without losing the intimacy of a trek down the rivers, all on one reel.
- Within months, Tom became an expert cameraman and even purchased the equipment needed to splice the film, remove blurry sections and then set the trip to music with a portable phonograph he purchased.
- A film about the beauty of Echo Park came at the right time.
- Hesitation was in the air.
- The total cost of placing multiple dams on the tributaries to the Colorado River had diminished the Eisenhower Administration's desire to create new deficits, especially in the wake of the expensive Korean war.
- Besides, conservation had been able to call into question for the first time the economic justifications used by the Bureau of Reclamation.
- Additionally, the post-World War II generation had fallen in love with recreational traveling.
- This expansive, adventuresome spirit included the exploration of remote places and the kayaking of rivers in collapsible boats known as folboats.
- As the public relations battle raged from the hallowed halls of Washington to the echoing canyons of Utah, the conservationists developed their main approaches.

- First was the need to promote the beauty of Echo Park and the canyons of Dinosaur National Monument.
- Pictures, films, magazine articles and rafting tours formed the core of this strategy.
- Second was the forging of partnerships between conservationists and other political forces opposed to all or some of the damming of the Colorado River.
- This produced unlikely allies such as the U.S. Army Corps of Engineers, California businesses that feared that their use of the Colorado could be compromised, and Midwestern politicians who did not want the agricultural competition that the new dams could produce.
- The coalition then made conservationists vulnerable to attacks by the *Denver Post* as selling out to California water interests.
- Tom's colleagues questioned his motives and loyalties.

- He responded to his critics by reminding them that the development of the Colorado River was a national issue.
- "The expense of Colorado dam development will be borne by the American taxpayer and its beauty will be lost to all Americans no matter where they currently live."
- And he carefully noted who his friends were when the chips were down.
- But as the campaign moved into its fifth year, Tom came to appreciate the power of numbers.
- When the Wilderness Society was able to calculate the taxpayers' cost of the Colorado River projects, conservationists and critics alike had a field day.
- The cost of producing hydroelectricity was higher than standard, while the bill for irrigated land topped $124,000 per acre.
- For months, the cost-benefit analysis for water, power, beauty, birds and preservation was endlessly debated in Congress by committees and subcommittees.
- Along the way, the leaders of the Echo Park campaign picked up the support of Senators Hubert Humphrey and John Kennedy, who both spoke against the project.
- Several times, Tom was asked to speak in Washington, but he always declined.
- He was convinced his Western accent would be laughed at back East; he knew his place and it was west of the Mississippi River.
- On the day President Eisenhower signed a presidential order prohibiting dams in any part of the national park system, Tom was alone hiking well-known paths in Dinosaur National Monument.

Rafting tours were popular and brought attention to the natural beauty of the Colorado River.

Life in the Community: Dinosaur National Monument, Utah and Colorado

- In prehistoric times, the canyons of Dinosaur National Monument were inhabited by the Fremont people and later by the Ute.
- Few Europeans settled in the rocky cliff, but the discovery of dinosaur bones attracted considerable attention from archeologists and museums, particularly the Carnegie.
- On the strength of those discoveries, Dinosaur National Monument was created in 1915 with a caveat that included the possibility of dams and power plants within the preserve.
- Despite ambitious plans, most of the roads and the scale of the envisioned dinosaur museum were never realized.
- By 1950, the Echo Park Dam appeared a foregone conclusion to many.
- Among the monument's supporters was Frederick Law Olmsted, Jr., the nation's foremost landscape architect, who warned that the loss of "scenic and inspirational values obtainable by the public" at the monument would be "catastrophically great."
- Olmsted urged the Department of the Interior to choose an alternative site, but his pleas were ignored.
- That's when grassroots conservation groups joined the fight and refused to back down.
- In July 1950, an article by Bernard DeVoto informed over four million *Harper's* readers of the potential impact of a dam at Echo Park.
- DeVoto pleaded his case around the question of public ownership.
- Soon, others joined the fight.
- Californians protested that their water was being diverted.

- Easterners declared themselves unwilling to pay taxes for Western water projects.
- Then, in 1952, David Brower became president of the Sierra Club and made the preservation of Dinosaur his personal crusade.
- River trips were promoted, scenic films were created and lectures given nationally.
- Brower then asked New York publisher Alfred A. Knopf to publish *This Is Dinosaur,* a collection of essays by notable wilderness advocates intended to show what would be lost through the damming of Echo Park.
- Each member of Congress was sent a copy of the book, with a special brochure about the monument sewn into the binding.
- The battle for Dinosaur National Monument was even featured in the 1954 movie, *The Long, Long Trailer,* starring Lucille Ball and Desi Arnaz, when Lucy declared her favorite souvenir to be a very, very large rock from Dinosaur National Monument.
- Western opposition, Eastern protests, a coalition of conservation groups and too high a cost eventually doomed the dam.
- In November 1955, Secretary of the Interior Douglas McKay announced that Echo Park would be removed from the Upper Colorado River project.
- In March, both Houses approved three water storage sites—Flaming Gorge, Utah; Glen Canyon in Northern Arizona; and Navajo, New Mexico—but excluded Echo Park.
- The Park Service quickly took advantage of Dinosaur's national fame to push for a visitor center.
- The Park Service chose to construct a monumental modernist building that demonstrated its commitment to the "protection and use" of Dinosaur National Monument.

Historical Snapshot
1956

- Dynamite exploded on the porch of Martin Luther King's home
- Elvis Presley's "Hound Dog"/"Don't Be Cruel" was the nation's number one single for a record 11 weeks
- The U.S. banned the launching of weather balloons because of Soviet complaints
- The Montgomery, Alabama bus boycott sparked hundreds of arrests that included that of Martin Luther King
- *My Fair Lady* starring Julie Andrews and Rex Harrison opened on Broadway
- Union workers struck the Westinghouse Electric Corporation for 156 days
- The soap operas *As the World Turns* and *The Edge of Night* premiered on CBS television
- Ampex Corporation introduced a commercial videotape recorder
- Popular music ranged from "(You've Got) The Magic Touch" by the Platters to Harry Belafonte's album *Calypso*
- America dropped a thermonuclear bomb from a plane onto Bikini Atoll
- President Dwight Eisenhower signed the Agriculture Act that created a "soil bank" plan to reduce surpluses
- Jerry Lewis and Dean Martin stopped working together after 16 movies
- The United States Federal Highway Act authorized a 42,500-mile network, largely financed by the federal government, linking major urban centers
- Egyptian Premier Gamal Abdel Nasser nationalized the Suez Canal to provide revenue for the construction of the Aswan Dam
- America established a Middle-East Emergency Committee to assure Western Europe of oil supplies if the Suez crisis interrupted shipments
- Adlai E. Stevenson was nominated for president at the Democratic National Convention in Chicago
- The Tennessee National Guardsmen halted rioters protesting the admission of 12 African Americans to schools in Clinton
- Elvis Presley made his first appearance on *The Ed Sullivan Show*
- The first prefrontal lobotomy was performed
- Dr. Albert Sabin created the oral polio vaccine
- Don Larsen pitched a perfect game for the New York Yankees in the World Series
- A revolt in Hungary was crushed by Soviet troops
- *The Huntley-Brinkley Report* with Chet Huntley and David Brinkley premiered as NBC's nightly television newscast, replacing *The Camel News Caravan*
- *The Wizard of Oz* was first televised
- The Eisenhower-Nixon Republican ticket won the presidential election

Selected Prices, 1956

Ballet Ticket, Royal Danish Ballet $7.50
Bicycle $64.95
Cigars, 20 . . . .$0.35
Guitar, Spanish $27.50
Hotel Room, Ritz-Carlton, Boston, per Night $9.00
Rifle, Remington $15.40
Soft Drink, Lucky Pop Fizz Tablets, 150 . . . .$1.00
Toy Truck $3.50
Vodka, Smirnoff, Fifth $5.23
Women's Stockings $1.65

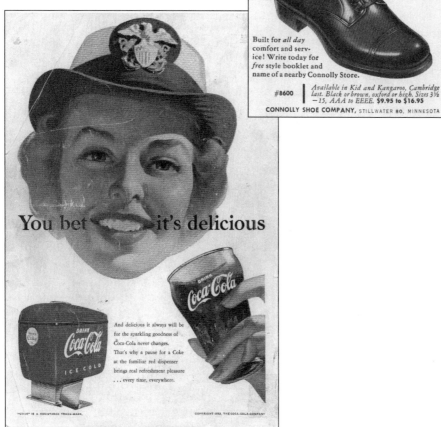

Dinosaur National Monument Timeline

1909

Paleontologist Earl Douglass discovered an amazing deposit of fossilized dinosaur bones in the remote and arid northeastern corner of Utah that yielded many museum-quality full skeletons.

1915

Based on the discoveries, President Woodrow Wilson proclaimed Dinosaur a national monument encompassing 80 acres.

1924

Paleontologist Earl Douglass envisioned a museum exhibit and visitor center to house the discoveries.

Congress defeated a bill designed to properly display the discoveries at Dinosaur National Monument.

1925

Further excavation was halted until the bones could be properly protected after most of the site had been explored by the Carnegie Museum and others.

1930

The American Museum of Natural History in New York bargained with the Park Service for rights to fossilized remains in exchange for developing a public exhibit.

1936

Using state and federal relief project labor, a temporary structure for the paleontologists that served as a museum was constructed.

1937

Preliminary designs for a museum were produced through the collaboration of the American Museum of Natural History and the Park Service.

1938

The Dinosaur National Monument was enlarged from 80 acres to 325 square miles, bringing attention and financial support to the area.

1944

The Park Service produced two alternatives for museums in the Quarry area.

1951

Plans were approved for a utilitarian structure resembling a warehouse or farm building.

1956

The Park Service announced that $615,000 would be allocated for improvements at Dinosaur, including roads, a new $275,000 visitor center, employee housing, and water and sewer facilities.

"Water for Utah," Water and Power Board Records, 1948:

It would indeed be poor and short-sighted policy to restrict potential development of hydroelectric power sources in the State to such industries which can now be envisioned as a definite potential of establishment. It must be remembered that new industries cannot wait for power supplies to be developed when all other factors are favorable. Thus, new power capacity and transmission systems must be built well in advance of actual market definition. This principle is well recognized in other parts of the United States, particularly in the West.

"This Is Dinosaur," by Devereux Butcher, *National Parks Magazine,* October-December, 1950:

Dinosaur National Monument, in the writer's opinion, is second to no other area of the national park and monument system in its magnificence of scenic grandeur, and its unique scenery is duplicated nowhere else in the system.

"Shall We Let Them Ruin Our National Parks?" Bernard DeVoto, *Saturday Evening Post,* July 22, 1950:

Echo Park Dam would back water so far that throughout the whole extent of Lodore Canyon the Green River, the tempestuous, pulse-stirring river of John Wesley Powell, would become a mere millpond. The same would happen to Yampa Canyon. Throughout both canyons the deep artificial lakes would engulf the magnificent scenery, would reduce by from a fifth to a third the height of the precipitous walls, and would fearfully degrade the great vistas. Echo Park and its magnificent rock formations would be submerged. Dinosaur National Monument as a scenic spectacle would cease to exist.

Editorial, *Denver Post,* July 22, 1950:

There are "those who want to maintain the West as a colony so that nature lovers from east of the Allegheny can come out every five or 10 years to sniff the clean air. Despite the "desecration" of Dinosaur Monument, there's still plenty of scenery left for all America.

"The West's Most Fabulous Highway," Claire Noall, *Deseret News Magazine,* Salt Lake City, Utah, June 10, 1951:

A million dollars for 30 miles of highway to reach a town of 217 people sounds fantastic, not just in regard to the money spent or the emancipation of the last packhorse-mail-route town in the United States—but in beauty.

Boulder would still be isolated in winter were it not for the amazing highway. In summer the town can be reached from Wayne County (on the north) via a narrow precipitous dirt road over Boulder Mountain. Between Escalante (30 miles southwest) and Boulder lies the romantic Hell's Backbone dirt road. But the Boulder Mountain road reaches an altitude of nearly 11,000 feet. Hell's Backbone strikes out at about 9,000. Both are closed in winter. Calf Creek, the most gloriously beautiful of the three, remains open all winter.

Prior to 1935, the way into Boulder from Escalante was by packhorse or mule back, over the Death Hollow trail if you took the shortcut. If you wanted to play safe, you might take the much longer but easier trail over the backbone. In winter, however, it was mighty cold in Hell and the Death Hollow trail was the best bet, though one's mule might slide off the narrow path down a rocky descent towards the infernal pit.

The Calf Creek turnpike has banished the use of both pack trails as a necessity. Hand-built by the CCC [Civilian Conservation Corps] boys, it has made the drive between Escalante and Boulder one of the most spectacularly beautiful in the whole United States. Yet how few people are aware of this treat in scenic novelties!

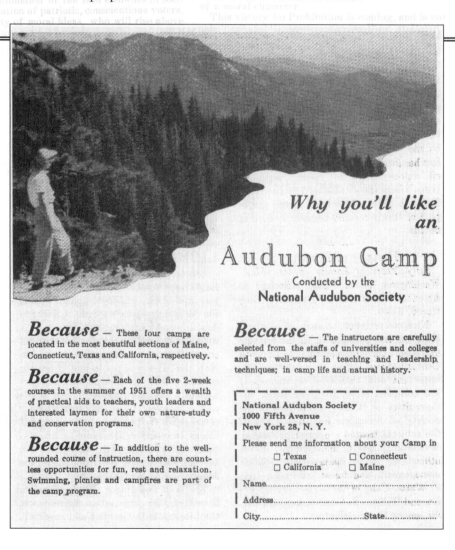

Why you'll like an

Audubon Camp
Conducted by the National Audubon Society

Because — These four camps are located in the most beautiful sections of Maine, Connecticut, Texas and California, respectively.

Because — Each of the five 2-week courses in the summer of 1951 offers a wealth of practical aids to teachers, youth leaders and interested laymen for their own nature-study and conservation programs.

Because — In addition to the well-rounded course of instruction, there are countless opportunities for fun, rest and relaxation. Swimming, picnics and campfires are part of the camp program.

Because — The instructors are carefully selected from the staffs of universities and colleges and are well-versed in teaching and leadership techniques; in camp life and natural history.

National Audubon Society
1000 Fifth Avenue
New York 28, N. Y.

Please send me information about your Camp in
☐ Texas   ☐ Connecticut
☐ California   ☐ Maine

Name..

Address...

City...State................

1956 NEWS FEATURE

DESEGREGATION WILL FAIL, Speech by the Rev. Leon C. Burns of Columbia, Tennessee, February 19, 1956:

In discussing this subject tonight it is not our purpose to add to the already high state of unrest and fear existing here in the South over the segregation problem. We simply wish to study this problem in the light of all that has developed in the 21 months since the Supreme Court handed down its decision on desegregation in the schools of the South.

I have no desire to favor either the White or the Colored race in this discussion, but I do sincerely desire to look at this question with common sense and reason in the hope that I will be able to help both races do all they can to preserve America. Few people seem to realize that the trouble caused over this question is undoubtedly the effort of alien powers to divide and destroy America.

Let it be understood that I am appealing to the honest, sincere, and patriotic American of both races, not the radical fringe of either race. I am convinced that the majority of the colored people, especially in the South, want what is best for America. They know, as we all know, that if the American way of life is not preserved, the last vestige of human freedom and liberty will perish from the earth.

Since, in 1933, Franklin Roosevelt forced us to recognize Soviet Russia, the Communist Party has tried with ever increasing zeal to create strife between the Negroes and Whites of the South; not because they cared about the freedoms of the Negro, but simply because they saw an opportunity to stir racial hatred in America. In 1935, the Communist Party published a pamphlet called "The Negroes in a Soviet America." This pamphlet was reviewed and exposed in a full-length article which appeared in the *Nashville Banner* on July 31, 1945. The Communist plan, as revealed by a carefully drawn map, was to take over the South and create what they called a "Black Belt" which swung across the South from Texas to Maryland to Virginia. The idea was to form in this "Black Belt" a "Soviet Negro Republic," which was to form a federation with the Soviet Union. This plan was accepted by the Southern Conference for Human Welfare, a Communist-front organization. The Negroes of the South were too intelligent and too patriotic to fall for such a scheme.

The Communists, however, have not ceased in their efforts to destroy America by creating race hatred in the South. They have done this by poisoning the minds of Northern Negroes and sending them into the South to stir hatred in the hearts of their own people. A few isolated events have been seized upon by Northern newspapers, played up and twisted out of all proportions, in an effort to make the rest of the country believe that the honest and sincere Negro of the South is in revolt, but those of us in the South know this is not the case. It is my sincere prayer that the Southern Negro is still too intelligent and too patriotic to fall for this effort of a foreign power to destroy America.

It is now a matter of record that the so-called race riot which occurred here in Columbia several years ago was seized upon by every Communist and Communist-front organization in the country in an effort to create trouble in the South.

The most successful effort of the Communist has been to encourage the creation of the National Association for the Advancement of Colored People (NAACP). This organization denies that it is Communist, but it has followed the Communist Party Line in every detail. It is no accident that the *Daily Worker*, the official Communist paper in America, has often announced the plans of the NAACP before these plans were announced by the Association itself. Walter White, Executive Secretary of the NAACP, has repeatedly stated that it was his organization that finally forced the Supreme Court decision of May 17, 1954. . . .

The Negro in the South has made greater progress in the past 50 years than any race of people since the beginning of time. This desegregation decision will not just temporarily halt this progress, but will set it back 100 years. In my lifetime I have seen the Southern Negro grow in the respect and admiration of the White people. When I came to Columbia just 15 years ago, you would never see a Negro mentioned in the daily paper unless he happened to get caught stealing a chicken, but long before the Supreme Court decision, news reports of civic and social activities of Negroes of our community, along with their pictures, were appearing in the paper. Negroes were taking part in Red Cross drives and in other civic movements. This has been going on all over the South for many years. Every Negro that has shown talent and the desire to get ahead has been given every possible encouragement and opportunity, opportunities seldom granted even to White people. Negro musicians, writers, doctors, statesmen, and athletes or businessmen have never gone unpraised or unrespected, but now that we are forced by un-American influences to bow before a decision that we know was not made in the interest of the Negro, the progress made by the Negro of the South in the past 50 years will be lost.

Common sense and a little knowledge of human nature should teach us that forced desegregation is wrong, and is not in the interest of either the White or Colored race. We should remember that all racial problems are deep-seated. They are not born in a day, but are the result of customs, characteristics, and environments that have accumulated through hundreds of years. You do not change such customs by handing down a decree. You do not unite the hearts and minds of a people by simply passing a law which says they shall be united. Neither can you make people equal by simply passing a law which says they shall be equal. Equality is a thing which must take place in the minds and souls of men, and can never be forced upon any man; it must be the growth of mutual understanding, respect and confidence. When this takes place among men, no law is needed to make them equal, and until this does take place, there can be no equality.

It is human nature to seek the companionship of those of our own race and class. The Negro is happy among his own people, and to try to force him into a society that is not prepared to receive him is the most inhuman thing you could do. To force a Negro child to attend school where Whites greatly outnumber Negroes is the most unkind deed you could practice on the child. Can you realize what may happen to the mind and heart of a

Negro child when he's forced into a group where he may not be wanted and may constantly be reminded of this fact? It is grossly inhuman to make children the victim of such cruel circumstances. It will not be surprising if these children turn into criminals of the worst sort in their rebellion against a society that was not ready to accept them.

There is not the slightest doubt in my mind that the Negro would have gradually worked his way into the life and economy of the South, and hence would have brought a gradual end to segregation if he had been allowed to do so, but under forced desegregation it is extremely doubtful that he ever will. It is impossible to visualize the economic pressure, social injustices, suffering and misery that may be brought upon the Negro of the South, not by honest God-fearing people, but by those who care nothing for a human soul—White or Negro. It is sad indeed when the honest and sincere people of two races are made to suffer, and the peace and harmony of America threatened, by a small group of Communistically influenced individuals. It is sadder still when this same group—bent upon the destruction of America—is allowed to interpret our Constitution and make our laws. The present members of the Supreme Court of the United States should dress themselves in sackcloth and ashes, and bow their heads in shame.

If we are able to avoid conflict, you may rest assured that there will develop a sort of passive resistance to the Negro in the South, as there is already in the North. This sort of thing can become more permanently detrimental to the Negro than open war. However it turns out, the Negro will be the one to suffer most; there is no way to escape it.

Before closing this talk, let me try to answer one question about the South. People of the North seem unable to understand the attitude of the Southerner toward the Negro. They are constantly asking, "Why do you Southerners feel as you do?" They fail to understand that the feeling of the Southerner toward the Negro is not one of hate or of superiority. The Southerner's feeling is a part of his heritage, born of many things, over many years. The worship of a cow by the people of India is to us a foolish thing, but to the people of India it is something very real, and very powerful. Who would think of trying to convert the people of India by suddenly killing all of their cows? The same is true with regard to the Southerner. His attitude toward the Negro may seem foolish to the rest of the world, but to him it is very real, and very important. Is anyone so foolish as to think the federal government can convert the Southerner from his way of thinking by simply handing down a decree which demands that he make this change within a few months? The Supreme Court seems to think this can be done. How could any sane person be so thoughtless?

Having been reared in the South, I have worked with Negroes all of my life. I know their problems and sincerely believe I am as well qualified to speak for them as any White man should be. The honest and sincere Negro of the South is a peace-loving soul. He wants no trouble with White people, nor does he wish to impose himself upon anybody. He simply wants the right to live and be happy, and to make a place for himself in the world, not as a White man, nor as a cross-breed, but as a Negro.

In closing, let me sound a solemn warning to those of you who are members of the Negro race. Those groups in America now claiming to fight your battle of freedom are Communistic. They care no more for you than they would for a dog trotting down the street. They see in you a chance to foster the godless doctrine of Communism and the destruction of America. I would appeal to you not to be carried away by these sowers of discord and strife, but to think soberly and prayerfully on any question that involves your relationship with other races.

To the White people of the South, may I urge that you not allow prejudice and hatred to rule your thinking, but remember that God will solve our every problem if we but give Him a chance.

I would be unworthy of the patience with which you have listened to me if I did not offer some solution to our racial problem. In this respect I have but four suggestions to make. They are:

1. Reverse by act of Congress the Supreme Court decision of May 17, 1954.
2. Allow the Southern States to work out their own racial problems to the best interest of both races, thus allowing each State to maintain the dignity of self-government, and each individual—Black or White, to maintain the dignity of free men.
3. An intensified program of education among the Negroes of the South, supplying them with educational advantages second to none.
4. A thorough investigation of the NAACP by the Federal Bureau of Investigation.

1959 Profile

Worker Rights: The New York Hospital Workers Strike

Walking the picket line was part of the job for Nidia Fernandez, as she tried to better the situation for workers through recognition of their union by New York City hospitals.

Life at Home

- Nidia Fernandez was born in 1930 in Paterson, the second-largest city in New Jersey.
- She was the second child and only daughter of Juan Fernandez and Alicia Juarez.
- Her mother's parents were born in New Jersey; her father's parents had immigrated to America from Puerto Rico.
- When Nidia was a toddler, her parents divorced and she moved to New York City with her mother and two brothers.
- As a single parent during the Great Depression, her mother struggled.
- To support the family, she worked at a cannery at night and as a waitress during the day; her father helped watch the children.
- Nidia enjoyed a close relationship with her grandfather, who called her "seven tongues" because she always talked so much.
- During the 1940s and the onset of the war economy, her family's financial situation improved.
- Nidia's mother remarried and became the owner of a restaurant and hotel visited by Japanese, Chinese, Jews, Filipinos, and Puerto Ricans.
- At age 16, Nidia dropped out of school to work.
- She and her mother were often at odds, mostly about the boys with whom Nidia associated.
- Nidia began spending more time with her biological father, who still lived in Paterson.

Nidia Fernandez led her hospital co-workers to better working conditions.

Nidia with her mother, brother and step-father.

- From him she learned to cherish the role unions played in helping workers gain their rights.
- In 1913 Paterson was the site of a major labor strike initiated by 800 broad silk weavers; they were soon joined by the ribbon weavers and the dry house workers.
- The strike eventually affected 300 mill and dye houses, which employed 24,000 workers.
- Their demands included wage increases, the establishment of an eight-hour workday, and abolition of the four-loom system in broad cloth that required workers to service multiple looms.
- More than 2,000 workers allowed themselves to be arrested, flooding the jails and disrupting the courts.
- But after several months of bitter picketing, the English-speaking and better-paid workers returned to work, breaking the back of the strike.
- The experience taught Nidia that unions were the only way workers could gain the strength to demand a fair share, but only if they were well organized.
- She was shocked that most unions had been reluctant to accept women workers like herself.
- During the war years, the increased number of women in the nation's shops and factories posed a major problem for America's unions, many of which barred female members.
- But the gender restrictions fell quickly under the pace of World War II production demands.
- Both the government and women workers applied pressure to open the doors of the unions.
- The International Association of Machinists; the Molders and Foundry Workers; the Iron Shipbuilders and Helpers; and the Carpenters and Joiners admitted women soon after the attack on Pearl Harbor.
- In the fall of 1942, the intransigent International Brotherhood of Boilermakers admitted women to its membership for the first time in its 62-year history.
- By 1944, 11 national unions reported more than 40,000 women members.
- By the war's end, nearly all AFL and CIO unions had accepted women, although many local unions remained opposed to their admission.
- But the doors of many unions remained closed to women of color, including most blacks and Puerto Ricans.
- In 1948, Nidia took a job in a New York cafeteria, convinced that worker solidarity and clear demands would win the day.
- The prosperous economy of post-World War II America was creating many new jobs, but most of the best-paying jobs were going to men.
- After three months on her first job, Nidia demanded equal pay with men and bathroom break privileges.
- She was promptly fired as a troublemaker.

Life at Work

- In the winter of 1958, when Nidia Fernandez was approached about her participation in a new hospital worker's union, she asked a lot of questions.
- Twenty-nine, divorced and the mother of two, she was more cautious about where she spoke out these days.

- She had been a nursing assistant for three years at Mount Sinai Hospital in New York City; work was steady and predictable, although the pay was poor.
- Nonprofit or voluntary hospitals claimed that they generated so few revenues, they should not be expected to pay competitive wages.
- "A hospital is not an economic, industrial unit," declared Dr. Martin Steinberg, director of Mount Sinai. "It is a social unit. . . . Human Life should not be a pawn in jousting for economic gain or power."
- Most of the larger unions already had passed on proposals to organize legions of hospital workers, most of whom were black and Puerto Rican women.
- But Union Local 1199 had a long history of uniting diverse groups.
- Founded in 1932 by progressive pharmacists and clerks, 1199 and its leaders were guided by the slogan "An injury to one is an injury to all."
- Originally part of the Pharmacist Union of Greater New York, by 1936 it had become Local 1199, Retail Employees Union, a part of the Retail, Wholesale & Department Store Union, attached to the American Federation of Labor.
- As early as 1937, the predominantly Jewish union won a campaign in Harlem for the hiring of African American pharmacists using a seven-week strike.
- In 1958, when 1199 undertook a campaign to organize New York City's voluntary hospital workers, most traditional labor leaders marked it for failure.
- The workers, most of whom were women who did not like working together, earned about $32.00 a week with few or no benefits.
- Many were too poor to manage the economic stress of a protracted strike.
- All voluntary hospitals were exempt from labor laws because they were charitable organizations, another mark against a successful strike.
- The modest 5,000-member 1199 accepted the challenge almost by accident.
- A black porter at the Montefiore Hospital happened to compare his wages and conditions with those of a relative who worked as a porter in a Bronx pharmacy.
- The unrepresented hospital porter was being paid $36.00 for a 44-hour week, while the drugstore porter, who worked for a 1199-unionized pharmacy, was earning $72.00 for 40 hours.
- In addition, the unionized employee was covered by an employer-financed pension plan and health and welfare protection.
- Disturbed by the difference, the Montefiore porter assembled a group of co-workers and went to the 1199 for support.
- The union assigned Elliott Godoff, who was formerly with the teamsters, to organize the workers; Theodore Mitchell, a black drugstore porter, was named to assist.
- Their goal was to organize bedpan emptiers, dietary aides and laundry room workers, most of whom were underrepresented Latin American, black or Puerto Rican women, in New York City's hospitals.
- Within three months, 600 of the 800 workers had joined the union.
- The average wages were $34.00 to $38.00 a week for most; laboratory technicians received $50.00 to $55.00.
- The union invited the hospital to negotiate wages, benefits and union representation.
- The hospital declined, stating clearly and accurately that employees of voluntary hospitals were excluded from labor legislation protection.

Hospital workers met with union leaders.

- Petitions, telegrams and several meetings failed to move the hospital trustees.
- Even a much-sought-after union endorsement in *The New York Times* failed to persuade hospital administrators.
- The dam broke when, in December 1958, Montefiore workers voted overwhelmingly for 1199.
- Mount Sinai workers got into the act on March 6, 1959, when 800 workers boycotted the cafeteria in a lunch-hour demonstration.
- The workers, including Nidia, demanded that the hospital recognize the union.
- The hospital administrators issued a letter to employees that said that higher wages could only be created by higher hospital income and that the hospital was working with the city, insurers and other sources to get more money.
- Concerning strike threats, the letter asked, "Strike against whom? Our patients, sick people, children needing immediate medical care?"
- Mount Sinai's rank and file rejected the administration's arguments and voted, along with the employees of five other nonprofit hospitals, to walk out.
- In all, 3,500 workers, including elevator operators, orderlies, nursing aides, kitchen workers and other housekeeping employees, exchanged their jobs for the picket line.

Life in the Community: New York, New York

- When the New York hospital workers strike began, Nidia had no savings; she had been living paycheck to paycheck since her divorce five years earlier.
- Every morning of the strike she dressed carefully and joined her fellow strikers on the picket line.
- She was proud to walk the line every morning and yell at the strike-breaking scabs who had picked a pitiful paycheck over union solidarity.
- Nidia's sign declared, "Mount Sinai workers can't live on $32.00 a week. ON STRIKE. Please help us win."
- She was even proud that the newspapers described the picketers as "a bedraggled army"; at least they were standing for something.
- And she was invigorated when the same newspapers pointed out that the strikes made New York City's hospital workers the first employees in private, nonprofit hospitals in the nation to unionize.
- She never dreamed that the strike would last so long and attract national attention.
- For its part, the union leadership decried the "shameful working conditions" that "threaten the health of the infants and children of these workers . . . and breed juvenile delinquency, crime and violence."
- The Greater New York Hospital Association countered, "This is not a strike, but revolution against law and order."
- As far as Nidia was concerned, the secret weapon was the national attention the strike was attracting, thanks to its links with the civil rights movement.
- Starting in 1956, the union had solicited membership funds to support the Montgomery, Alabama bus boycott.
- As a result the union established a friendship with Dr. Martin Luther King, Jr., leader of the boycott.
- To rally public support, Local 1199 lined up backing from civil rights leaders like Dr. King, Bayard Rustin, A. Philip Randolph, and many elected officials and editorial writers.

- Dr. King, who described 1199 as his "favorite union," called the fight to raise wages for the $30.00-a-week workers a civil rights struggle.

- But links to Dr. King were only one of the workers' strengths.

- The hospital workers' strike also captured the attention of the traditional labor leaders.

- New York City Central Labor Council President Harry Van Arsdale saw the strike as a means of uniting the labor movement in the city.

- First, he participated in the marathon negotiating sessions with the hospital; then, he led 700 unionists in joining the picketers at Beth Israel Hospital.

- Nidia had been told repeatedly that the labor leaders themselves never walked the line; now she knew this strike would be successful.

- The bitter fight for recognition lasted 46 days; the poor, undereducated workers had not been broken as the men downtown on both sides of the issue had predicted.

- But in the end the union was not recognized, despite a New York judge's accusation that the hospital management's refusal to recognize the union was an "echo of the nineteenth century."

- Management only agreed to arbitration.

- The final agreement guaranteed "no discrimination against any employee because he joins a union"; a minimum wage of $1.00 an hour; wage increases of $5.00 a week; a 40-hour week; time and a half for overtime; seniority rules; job grades; and rate changes.

Dr. Martin Luther King's family supported his alliance with the hospital worker's union.

HISTORICAL SNAPSHOT
1959

- Alaska and Hawaii were admitted to the Union as the forty-ninth and fiftieth states
- American Airlines entered the jet age with the first scheduled transcontinental flight of a Boeing 707 from Los Angeles to New York for $301.00
- Arlington and Norfolk, Virginia, peacefully desegregated their public schools
- A plane crash claimed the lives of rock-and-roll stars Buddy Holly, Ritchie Valens and J. P. "The Big Bopper" Richardson
- The United States successfully test-fired a Titan intercontinental ballistic missile from Cape Canaveral
- The U.S. launched its first weather station, *Vanguard II*, into space
- The FCC applied the equal time rule to TV newscasts of political candidates
- Miles Davis recorded the album *Kind of Blue* with John Coltrane, Cannonball Adderly, Philley Joe Jones, Paul Chambers and Bill Evans
- The Barbie doll was unveiled at the American Toy Fair in New York City by the Mattel Toy Company for $3.00
- The *USS Skate* became the first submarine to surface at the North Pole
- NASA announced the selection of America's first seven astronauts for the Mercury program: Scott Carpenter, Gordon Cooper, John Glenn, Gus Grissom, Wally Schirra, Alan Shepard and Donald Slayton
- "The Battle Of New Orleans" by Johnny Horton peaked at number one on the pop singles chart and stayed there for six weeks
- Congress authorized food stamps for poor Americans
- The first telephone cable linking Europe and the United States was laid
- Television's *The Twilight Zone*, *The Untouchables*, *Rawhide* and *Bonanza* all premiered
- The Guggenheim Museum, designed by Frank Lloyd Wright, opened in New York City
- The Rodgers and Hammerstein musical *The Sound of Music* opened on Broadway
- The film *Ben-Hur*, starring Charlton Heston, had its world premiere in New York
- The first color photograph of Earth was received from outer space

DAVID MERRICK presents

"SETS BROADWAY ABLAZE"
—Life

MARY **URE** KENNETH **HAIGH**

LOOK BACK IN ANGER

MAIL ORDERS FILLED. Evgs.: $5.75, 4.80, 3.60, 2.90, 2.30, 1.75. Mats. Wed. & Sat.: $4.30, 3.60, 2.90, 2:30, 1.75.
LYCEUM THEATRE, 149 W. 45 St. N.Y.C.

LIMITED ENGAGEMENT
by arrangement with
The English Stage Co. and L.O.P. Ltd.
LAURENCE **OLIVIER**
in a new play

THE ENTERTAINER

MAIL ORDERS FILLED. Evgs.: Orch. $7.50; Balc. $6.90, 4.80, 3.60, 2.90. Mats. Wed. & Sat.: Orch. $4.80; Balc. $4.30, 3.60, 2.90, 2.00.

ROYALE THEATRE, 242 W. 45 St. N.Y.C.

"THE SEASON'S MOST SUCCESSFUL MUSICAL COMEDY PUT ON TO ENTERTAIN THE PUBLIC."
—ATKINSON, TIMES

LENA HORNE
RICARDO MONTALBAN

Jamaica

BROADWAY'S NEW MUSICAL HIT!
MAIL ORDERS FILLED. Evgs.: $8.35, 6.90, 5.20, 4.30, 3.60, 3.00, 2.50. Mats. Wed. & Sat.: $4.80, 4.30, 3.60, 3.00, 2.50, 2.00.
IMPERIAL THEATRE, 249 W. 45 St. N.Y.C.

"AS FUNNY AS ANYTHING YOU WILL SEE THIS SEASON"
—Gibbs, New Yorker

Peter Ustinov

ROMANOFF AND JULIET
the new comedy hit

MAIL ORDERS FILLED. Mon. thru Fri. Evgs.: $5.75, 4.80, 4.30, 3.60, 2.50. Sat. Evgs.: $6.25, 4.80, 4.30, 3.60, 2.50. Mats. Wed. & Sat.: $4.10, 3.60, 2.90, 2.30.
PLYMOUTH THEATRE, 236 W. 45 St. N.Y.C.

Selected Prices, 1959

Automobile, Ford Thunderbird $4,222.00
Candygram, Western Union, Pound $2.95
Chandelier, Crystal $425.00
Child's Jeans $1.64
Hamburger, Burger King Whopper $0.37
Lawn Sprinkler $16.95
Movie Projector $89.95
Scotch, Chivas Regal, Fifth $8.06
Stereo $129.95
Transistor Pocket Radio, Zenith $75.00

Labor Timeline

1910

A bomb destroyed a portion of the Llewellyn Ironworks in Los Angeles, where a bitter strike was in progress.

1911

The Supreme Court ordered the AFL to cease its promotion of a boycott against the Bucks Stove and Range Company.

The Triangle Shirtwaist Company fire in New York City resulted in the death of 147 people, mostly women and young girls working in sweatshop conditions.

1912

Women and children were beaten by police during a textile strike in Lawrence, Massachusetts.

The National Guard was called out against striking West Virginia coal miners.

1913

Police shot three maritime workers during a strike against the United Fruit Company in New Orleans.

1914

The Ford Motor Company raised its basic wage from $2.40 for a nine-hour day to $5.00 for an eight-hour day.

Five men, two women and 12 children died in the "Ludlow Massacre" when company guards attempted to break a strike at Colorado's Ludlow Mine Field.

A Western Federation of Miners strike was crushed by the militia in Butte, Montana.

1915

Labor leader Joe Hill was arrested in Salt Lake City on murder charges and executed 21 months later despite worldwide protests and two attempts to intervene by President Woodrow Wilson.

Twenty rioting strikers were shot by factory guards in Roosevelt, New Jersey.

The Supreme Court upheld "yellow dog" contracts, which forbade membership in labor unions.

1916

A bomb set off during a "Preparedness Day" parade in San Francisco killed 10 and resulted in the conviction of Thomas J. Mooney, a labor organizer, and Warren K. Billings, a shoe worker.

Riots erupted during a strike at Everett Mills, Everett, Washington; local police watched and refused to intervene, resulting in the death of seven workers.

Federal employees won the right to receive worker's compensation insurance.

1917

Vigilantes forced 1,185 striking copper miners in Bisbee, Arizona, into manure-laden boxcars and "deported" them to the New Mexico desert.

The Supreme Court approved the Eight-Hour Act under the threat of a national railway strike.

Industrial Workers of the World (IWW) organizer Frank Little was lynched in Butte, Montana.

Federal agents raided the IWW headquarters in 48 cities.

1919

United Mine Worker organizer Fannie Sellins was gunned down by company guards in Brackenridge, Pennsylvania.

Looting and violence erupted in Boston after 1,117 Boston policemen declared a work stoppage to gain union representation.

continued

Timeline . . . *(continued)*

1919

Three hundred fifty thousand steel workers walked off their jobs to demand union recognition.

IWW organizer Wesley Everest was lynched after a Centralia, Washington IWW hall was attacked by Legionnaires.

Approximately 250 "anarchists," "communists," and "labor agitators" were deported to Russia, marking the beginning of the so-called "Red Scare."

1920

The U.S. Bureau of Investigation began carrying out the nationwide Palmer Raids, seizing labor leaders and literature to discourage labor activity.

Seven management detectives and two coal miners were killed in the Battle of Matewan in West Virginia.

1922

Violence resulted in the deaths of 36 people during a coal miners' strike in Herrin, Illinois.

1924

Congress approved a child labor amendment to the U.S. Constitution; only 28 of the necessary 36 states ratified it.

1925

Two company houses occupied by non-union coal miners were blown up by labor "racketeers" during a strike against the Glendale Gas and Coal Company in Wheeling, West Virginia.

1926

Textile workers fought with police in Passaic, New Jersey, during a year-long strike.

1930

Labor racketeers shot and killed contractor William Healy, with whom the Chicago Marble Setters Union had been having difficulties.

One hundred farm workers were arrested for their unionizing activities in Imperial Valley, California.

1931

Vigilantes attacked striking miners in Harlan County, Kentucky.

1932

Police killed striking workers at Ford's Dearborn, Michigan plant.

1933

Eighteen thousand cotton workers went on strike in Pixley, California.

1934

During the Electric Auto-Lite Strike in Toledo, Ohio, two strikers were killed and over 200 wounded by National Guardsmen.

Police stormed striking truck drivers in Minneapolis who were attempting to prevent truck movement in the market area.

A strike in Woonsocket, Rhode Island, directed at obtaining a minimum wage for textile workers, resulted in over 420,000 workers striking nationwide.

1935

The Committee for Industrial Organization (CIO) was formed to expand industrial unionism.

1937

General Motors recognized the United Auto Workers Union following a sit-down strike.

continued

Timeline . . . *(continued)*

1937
Police killed 10 and wounded 30 during the "Memorial Day Massacre" at the Republic Steel plant in Chicago.

1938
The Wages and Hours Act was passed, banning child labor and setting the 40-hour work week.

1939
The Supreme Court ruled that sit-down strikes were illegal.

1941
Henry Ford recognized the United Auto Workers.

The AFL agreed that there would be no strikes in defense-related industry plants for the duration of the war.

1944
President Franklin D. Roosevelt ordered the army to seize the executive offices of Montgomery Ward and Company after the corporation failed to comply with a National War Labor Board directive regarding union shops.

1946
Packinghouse workers nationwide went on strike.

Four hundred thousand mine workers struck.

The U.S. Navy seized oil refineries to break a 20-state postwar strike.

1947
The Taft-Hartley Labor Act, curbing strikes, was vetoed by President Harry Truman but overridden by Congress.

1948
Labor leader Walter Reuther was shot and seriously wounded by would-be assassins.

1950
President Truman ordered the U.S. Army to seize all the nation's railroads to prevent a general strike.

1952
President Truman ordered the U.S. Army to seize the nation's steel mills to avert a strike; the order was later ruled to be illegal by the Supreme Court.

1955
The two largest labor organizations in the U.S. merged to form the AFL-CIO, with a membership estimated at 15 million.

1956
Columnist Victor Riesel, a crusader against labor racketeers, was blinded when a hired assailant threw sulfuric acid in his face.

1959
The Landrum-Griffin Act passed, restricting union activity.

The Taft-Hartley Act was invoked by the Supreme Court to break a steel strike.

Fairest of the Fairlane 500's . . . the Town Victoria

Low-cost way to live like royalty

Could be you under that hat. You could be lord and master of this long, low dream of a car.

Because it's a Ford you can *live* like a king in a king-size cruiser without paying a princely price.

And live like a king you will. There's a royal welcome waiting for you even before you step inside. Solid-fitting rear doors have Automatic Doorman hinges that make door clos-

ing practically effortless. The way they close behind you—with a bank vault's precision—merely echoes the quiet quality that is Ford's.

You settle into Ford's sofalike seat with a deep new respect for the magicians who designed this luxury car.

You just signal for power. And var-r-room! Your Ford V-8 moves out front with all the ease and grace of a gazelle. There's power galore in

Ford's new Silver Anniversary V-8's and Mileage Maker Six.

And ride? Ford engineers did it again. This luxury item stems from a whole new "Inner Ford" that nobody thought could happen in such a low-priced car.

So pamper yourself. Action Test a '57 Ford at your Ford Dealer's. You'll love the new kind of life you lead in this new kind of Ford.

The new fine car at half the fine car price

The person who is unorganized because of a racial bar or discrimination of any kind is a threat to the conditions of those who are organized. Anyone who is underpaid, who has substandard conditions, threatens the situation of those in unions.

—AFL President George Meany, 1955

Men make history and not the other way around. In periods where there is no leadership, society stands still. Progress occurs when courageous, skillful leaders seize the opportunity to change things for the better.

—Former President Harry S. Truman, 1959

"Victims of Charity," Dan Wakefield, *Nation*, March 14, 1959:

A Negro lady from the nurses' aides' department spoke up to say: "We're doing pretty good in our department, but a lotta people are afraid—they think they're gonna be fired. And some of the nurses told the girls they shouldn't join a union because then the hospital would be like a 'business.' "

The others hooted, and one voice raised above the rest to say, "It's all right for the nurses to talk; they get plenty and they don't want us to get it."

A lady from the kitchen staff raised her hand and reported that "the ladies in the cafeteria say they get paid mostly by tips and the union can't help them. One of the supervisors said the union can't help us, we'll still have to work no matter what the union does. Well, all I know is when I see those people making $32.00 a week, I'm ready to join anything."

A.H. Raskin, *The New York Times*, May 29, 1959:

They seem determined to carry on indefinitely. THEY say they are tired of being "philanthropists" subsidizing the hospitals with their labor. One girl picketer said: "Whenever we feel disheartened, we can always take out the stub of our last paycheck and get new heart for picketing." She pulled out her own and showed that it came to $27.00 in weekly take-home. . . .

Financial hardship has been a part of their life so long that the prospect of higher pay is less of a goal for many than the pivotal issue of union recognition. They feel for the first time that they "belong" and this groping for human dignity through group recognition is more important than more cash.

"6-Hospital Strike Delayed 2 Weeks, Union Bars Walkout Today After Hospitals Agree to Consider Fact Finding," Ralph Katz, *The New York Times*, April 22, 1959:

A strike of nonprofessional employees at six voluntary hospitals, scheduled for 6 a.m. today, was deferred last night for two weeks. The union agreed to put off action while the hospital boards of trustees considered a fact-finding formula.

The development was announced by Mayor Wagner at 11 p.m. after a series of conferences at City Hall with union and management representatives. Earlier it appeared the strike was inevitable.

Talks had begun at 10 a.m. yesterday. By 8 p.m. it appeared that Local 1199 of the Retail Drug Employees Union would proceed with plans to call out its membership among the hospitals' 4,550 nonprofessional employees. The union claims 3,450 of the workers as members.

At issue is the union demand for recognition as collective-bargaining agent. The two-week delay was offered, the Mayor said, because five of the six hospitals are Jewish institutions. The Jewish High Holy Days of Passover begin at sundown tonight.

1960–1969

The decade of the sixties made quite a reputation for itself through rebellion and protest. No aspect of American society escaped this social upheaval entirely unscathed. The decade included tragic assassinations, momentous social legislation for African Americans, remarkable space achievements, the awakening of a Native American rights movement and some of the nation's largest antiwar protests in its history. Music, hairstyles, the willingness of people to speak out would all be transformed. It was the beginning of the Beatles and the tragic end of the nonviolent phase of the civil rights movement. While the nation's "silent majority" slapped "Love it or Leave it" (it, being America) bumper stickers on their cars, thousands of highly vocal, well-educated middle class citizens carried signs in the streets to loudly protest America's involvement in Vietnam. It was truly a time of wrenching conflict in search of social change.

From 1960 to 1964, the economy expanded; unemployment was low and disposable income for music, vacations, art or simply having fun grew rapidly. Internationally, the power of the United States was immense. Congress gave the young President John F Kennedy the defense and space-related programs Americans wanted, but few of the welfare programs he proposed. Then, inflation arrived, along with the Vietnam War. Between 1950 and 1965, inflation soared from an annual average of less than two percent (ranging from six percent to 14 percent a year) to a budget-popping average of 9.5 percent. Upper class investors, once content with the consistency and stability of banks, sought better returns in the stock market and real estate.

The Cold War become hotter during conflicts over Cuba and Berlin in the early 1960s. Fears over the international spread of communism led to America's intervention in a foreign conflict that would become a defining event of the decade: Vietnam. Military involvement in this small Asian country grew from advisory status to full-scale war. By 1968, Vietnam had become a national obsession leading to President Lyndon Johnson's decision not to run for another term and fueling not only debate over our role in Vietnam, but more inflation and division nationally. The anti-war movement grew rapidly. Anti-war marches, which had drawn but a few thousand in 1965, grew in size until millions of marchers filled the streets of New York, San Francisco, and Washington, DC, only a few years later. By spring 1970, students on 448 college campuses made ROTC voluntary or abolished it.

The struggle to bring economic equality to blacks during the period produced massive spending for school integration. By 1963, the peaceful phase of the Civil Rights movement was ending; street violence, assassinations, and bombings defined the period. In 1967, 41 cities experienced major disturbances. At the same time, charismatic labor organizer Caesar Chavez's United Farm Workers led a Civil Rights-style movement for Mexican-Americans, gaining national support which challenged the growers of the West with a five-year agricultural strike.

As a sign of increasing affluence and changing times, American consumers bought 73 percent fewer potatoes and 2.5 percent more fish, poultry, and meat and 50 percent more citrus products and tomatoes than in 1940. California passed New York as the most populous state. Factory workers earned more than $100 week, their highest wages in history. From 1960 to 1965, the amount of money spent for prescription drugs to lose weight doubled, while the per capital consumption of processed potato chips rose from 6.3 pounds in 1958 to 14.2 pounds eight years later. In 1960, approximately 40 percent of American adult women had paying jobs; 30 years later, the number would grow to 57.5 percent. Their emergence into the work force would transform marriage, child rearing, and the economy. In 1960, women were also liberated by the FDA's approval of the birth-control pill, giving both women and men a degree of control over their bodies that had never existed before.

During the decade, anti-establishment sentiments grew: men's hair was longer and wilder, beards and mustaches became popular, women's skirts rose to mid-thigh, and bras were discarded. Hippies advocated alternative lifestyles, drug use increased, especially marijuana and LSD; the Beatles, the Rolling Stones, Jimi Hendrix, and Janis Joplin became popular music figures; college campuses became major sites for demonstrations against the war and for Civil Rights. The Supreme Court prohibited school prayer, assured legal counsel to the poor, limited censorship of sexual material, and increased the rights of the accused.

Extraordinary space achievements also marked the decade. Ten years after President Kennedy announced he would place a man on the moon, 600 million people around the world watched as Neil Armstrong gingerly lowered his left foot into the soft dust of the moon's surface. In a tumultuous time of division and conflict, the landing was one of America's greatest triumphs and an exhilarating demonstration of American genius. Its cost was $25 billion and set the stage for 10 other men to walk on the surface of the moon during the next three years.

The 1960s saw the birth of Enovid 10, the first oral contraceptive (cost $.055 each), the start of Berry Gordy's Motown Records, felt-tip pens, Diet-Rite cola, Polaroid color film, Weight Watchers, and Automated Teller Machines. It's the decade when lyrics began appearing on record albums, Jackie and Aristotle Onassis reportedly spent $20 million during their first year together, and the Gay Liberation Front participated in the Hiroshima Day March—the first homosexual participation as a separate constituency in a peace march.

1965 Profile

Civil Rights: Selma, Alabama, Awakens America

Roy Stokes was awakened suddenly to the injustices of racial segregation after a trip he made to visit his friend in Selma, Alabama, where he first witnessed the anger of Black people marching and protesting in the streets.

Life at Home

- Roy Stokes was born in Asheville, North Carolina, and grew up in rural Enka, North Carolina, a mill town 12 miles from Asheville.
- Enka was named for and dominated by the American Enka Company, a rayon-producing firm.
- Most of the people in the area either worked the land or worked in the mill.
- Roy's father had a medical practice; they lived on "the Gross property," still identified by locals according to the previous owner's name.
- Like most of the South, Enka was largely a racially segregated area.
- Despite the 1954 call by the U.S. Supreme Court to integrate America's schools, Enka still operated "separate but equal" schools based on race.
- No African American students attended Roy's school, so he had experienced very little contact with the Black community.
- Occasionally, racial jokes and fearful stories were told about Valley Street, the Black community in downtown Asheville.
- One story revolved around a man who often drove down Valley Street in a Volkswagen yelling racial slurs at Blacks crossing the street.
- After weeks of harassment, several dozen African Americans appeared, stopped the car and turned over the Volkswagen.
- Roy's best friend Melvin, whose family had lived in a trailer near the farm, moved the previous year to a little town in Alabama called Selma.
- So when Melvin wrote him a letter and invited him to visit over the summer, Roy made plans to take the Greyhound bus from Asheville to Selma.

Roy Stokes had little contact with the Black community growing up.

Many people in Enka traditionally worked the land.

- Roy had no idea he was about to be an accidental spectator to what the civil rights movement called "Freedom Summer."
- Freedom Summer sought to educate and register Black voters for the November 1964 presidential elections.
- While most of the focus was on Mississippi, Alabama was experiencing a level of unrest in the summer of 1964.

Life at School

- Roy Stokes knew little about the American Civil Rights Movement, but what he had heard was mostly negative—that the Communists were involved, and that the movement was mostly caused by outside agitators who wanted to cause trouble.

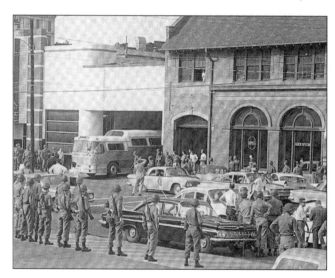

Roy witnessed Black protesters in Selma.

- Blacks would get equality, people insisted, if they would just be patient, but now was not the time for the integration the races.
- With no African American friends, he had virtually no other point of view.
- Besides, his plans involved visiting his best friend, not participating in changing the fundamental power and social structure of the South.
- His perspective began to change immediately after he got off the bus in Selma.
- Angry people were marching and protesting in the streets as Melvin's father came to pick him up at the bus station.
- The tension in the bus station was palpable.
- Melvin's father was angry about the protests.
- He used the "n" word and a lot of very angry remarks on the events happening in Selma.
- But Roy was ready to enjoy this visit.

Freedom Summer, 1964, brought tension to Birmingham.

- The boys quickly lapsed into conversation about old times and mutual friends.
- Melvin's father even took the teens to Birmingham, Alabama, where they saw the Iron Man statue.
- Even there, Roy was confronted by the tension revolving around Freedom Summer and the battle for civil rights.
- From an observation platform beneath the Iron Man, he could see the streets of Birmingham below, and watched protests and demonstrations going on.
- He overheard comments in Birmingham about court rulings, marching, voter rights, and about Northerners coming into the area and stirring up trouble.
- There was also discussion of the bombing of the Baptist church that had occurred the year before and had resulted in the deaths of four Black girls.
- When he left Selma, he was somewhat relieved to be returning to North Carolina, but was stirred by what he had witnessed.
- There was an unfairness to the system of racial segregation that always called upon the Blacks to be patient while Whites moved along with their lives.
- On his fifteenth birthday, Roy asked his dad why the world seemed so unfair.
- "Change is difficult for everyone," his father explained. "Why, even the colored ministers are fearful that demanding too much too quickly will cause a violent backlash."
- Roy heard his father's caution, but he also remembered the obvious frustration on the faces of the demonstrators.
- When he watched some demonstrators on television get beaten with Billy clubs, he knew the angry protestors had waited long enough.
- So, deciding to be an expert in the rights of man, including the right to vote and the right to get good jobs, he began to read about the issues.
- He read newspapers voraciously, studied history books and asked questions of his teachers.
- Nothing he heard or read gave him a full sense of understanding; the scene was changing too quickly.
- Enlightenment arrived by accident; Roy met other teens who were witnessing disturbing racial violence on television.
- They met, they talked, they felt giddy, they felt frustration.

- So they spoke to a young English teacher from Winthrop College in Rock Hill, South Carolina, about helping them sort out the issues.
- They met in her modest apartment after school and discussed e. e. cummings, T. S. Elliott and race in America.
- The weekly gatherings had been underway most of the fall semester when trouble arose.
- The teacher was accused of improperly entertaining students in her home, spreading radical ideas and behaving in a way that was unbecoming of a teacher.
- Roy's young teacher-friend was promptly fired and told not to return for the spring semester.
- Only then did he understand the anger he had seen in the faces of the Selma demonstrators.

Life in the Community: Selma, Alabama

- Selma, Alabama, was a small town of about 30,000 people where only one percent of eligible Blacks were registered to vote.
- Many Blacks had been raised to believe that voting was "White folks' business."
- Registering to vote wasn't easy; the registrar's office was only open twice a month, and the registrars often came in late, took long lunch breaks, and went home early.
- Besides, most Blacks failed the required test for registration, no matter how much education they possessed.
- Even Black school teachers were told they had flunked the test and were refused a registration certificate.
- In addition, attempts by Blacks to register were often met with strong resistance.
- When the Student Nonviolent Coordinating Committee (SNCC) organized a "Freedom Day" on October 7, 1963, a local photographer, under orders from the sheriff, took pictures of the 250 Blacks who lined up to register to vote.

Blacks lined up to register to vote.

- The photographer then asked all of them what their employers would think when he showed them the pictures.
- During the same registration drive, the police beat SNCC workers who tried to bring food and water to those in line.
- That same year, a group of Selma community activists formed the "Dallas County Improvement Association" with the goals of increased access to jobs, voter registration for Blacks, and having "White" and "Colored" signs removed from public buildings.
- But their efforts were largely ignored by the traditional leadership of the community.
- So after winning the Nobel Peace Prize in December 1964, Martin Luther King, Jr., and the Southern Christian Leadership Conference (SCLC) decided to focus on Selma.
- When Mayor Joseph Smitherman heard of King's plans, he urged Sheriff Jim Clark not to use violence against the civil rights leader.
- Smitherman had just been elected on a promise to bring industry to the town, and he did not want the negative publicity violence could bring.
- However, the sheriff was difficult to control.
- At one peaceful SCLC protest, the much-respected community leader Amelia Boynton was arrested.
- Pictures of the violent arrest by club-wielding Sheriff Clark ran in *The New York Times* and the *Washington Post*.
- A few days later, over 100 school teachers marched on the courthouse to protest Boynton's arrest, giving local credibility to the movement.
- Black school teachers held an elite position in the community and traditionally did not march for fear of retaliation from the White school board.
- The teachers' march also destroyed local claims that the Blacks were too ignorant to be voters.
- Then students, inspired by their teachers and by the arrest of King, began to protest as well.
- When a group of about 200 teenagers refused to move from the courthouse on February 10, 1965, Sheriff Clark led them on a "forced march" that left some vomiting from exhaustion.
- Even White citizens who had never championed equal rights called for more control of Clark.
- About the same time, a night march in nearby Marion resulted in rumors that protestors would break James Orange, an SCLC field secretary, out of jail.
- At the conclusion of the march, police and state troopers attacked the 200 marchers.
- Blacks were beaten at random.
- They didn't have to be marching; they simply had to be Black.
- Twenty people were hospitalized; Jimmie Lee Jackson, a Black Vietnam veteran, was shot and killed as he attempted to protect his mother.
- To symbolically take Jimmy Lee Jackson's body from Selma to the state capital in Montgomery, a march from Selma to Montgomery, 54 miles away, was planned for Sunday, March 7.

Martin Luther King in Selma.

Violence erupted during the march.

- As marchers crossed the Edmund Pettus Bridge in Selma, they were met by police and state troopers with orders from Alabama Governor George Wallace to stop the march.

- They told the marchers, "It would be detrimental to your safety to continue this march. You are ordered to disperse, go home or to your church. This march will not continue."

- When the protesters did not move, the law enforcement officers fired tear gas into the crowd and severely beat protesters.

- The police forced the marchers to return to the church.

- That night, TV stations interrupted their normal programming to show clips of the violence at Selma.

- ABC interrupted the showing of a film about Nazi war crimes, *Judgment at Nuremberg,* to feature the violence in Selma, Alabama.

- Then, a White minister from Boston, in Selma to support Martin Luther King's civil rights march, was clubbed to death outside the Silver Moon Café, attracting even more national attention.

- A week later a federal judge ruled that the state could not block the march from Selma to Montgomery; President Lyndon Johnson federalized the Alabama National Guard to give protection to the marchers.

- On March 21, 14 days after Bloody Sunday, the marchers crossed over the Edmund Pettus Bridge and marched for five days.

- The march was 25,000 people strong when it arrived in Montgomery, the birthing point for the civil rights movement that had started 10 years earlier with the bus boycott.

- King told his audience, "However difficult the moment, however frustrating the hour, it will not be long, because truth crushed to the earth will rise again. . . . How long? Not long. Because mine eyes have seen the glory of the coming of the Lord."

HISTORICAL SNAPSHOT
1965

- The Council on Religion and the Homosexual launched a gay Mardi Gras Ball in San Francisco that was raided by police
- In his State of the Union address, President Lyndon Johnson outlined the goals of his "Great Society" that included an attack on diseases, a doubling of the war on poverty, greater enforcement of the Civil Rights Law, immigration law reform and greater support of education
- Eighteen were arrested in Mississippi for the murder of three civil rights workers
- In Selma, Alabama, Reverend Martin Luther King, Jr. and 770 of his followers were arrested on their civil rights march in protest of voter discrimination
- President Johnson ordered the bombing of North Vietnam known as "Rolling Thunder" and authorized commanders in Vietnam to commit U.S. ground forces to combat
- Fourteen Vietnam War protesters were arrested for blocking U.N. doors in New York
- The *Ranger 8* spacecraft crashed on the moon after sending back 7,000 photos of the lunar surface
- Former Black Muslim leader El-Hajj Malik El-Shabazz, known as Malcolm X, was shot to death in front of 400 people in New York by assassins identified as Black Muslims
- Julie Andrews starred in the film adaptation of the popular Broadway hit, *The Sound of Music*
- Neil Simon's play *The Odd Couple*, starring Walter Matthau as Oscar Madison and Art Carney as Felix Unger, opened on Broadway
- The Rev. James J. Reeb, a White minister from Boston, died after Whites beat him during civil rights disturbances in Selma, Alabama
- President Johnson called for new legislation to guarantee every American's right to vote
- President Johnson ordered 4,000 troops to protect the Selma-Montgomery civil rights marchers
- The United States launched the *Early Bird* communications satellite
- Sixteen-year-old Lawrence Wallace Bradford, Jr. was appointed by New York Republican Jacob Javits to be the first Black page of the U.S. Senate
- The U.S. Army and Marines invaded the Dominican Republic to stop a civil war
- The Rolling Stones recorded "Satisfaction"
- Astronaut Edward White became the first American to "walk" in space during the flight of *Gemini 4*
- The American space probe *Mariner 4* flew by Mars and sent back 22 photographs of the planet
- The Medicare bill was signed into law
- President Johnson signed the Voting Rights Act of 1965, which outlawed the literacy test for voting eligibility in the South

MISSING CALL FBI

THE FBI IS SEEKING INFORMATION CONCERNING THE DISAPPEARANCE AT PHILADELPHIA, MISSISSIPPI, OF THESE THREE INDIVIDUALS ON JUNE 21, 1964. EXTENSIVE INVESTIGATION IS BEING CONDUCTED TO LOCATE GOODMAN, CHANEY, AND SCHWERNER, WHO ARE DESCRIBED AS FOLLOWS:

ANDREW GOODMAN

JAMES EARL CHANEY

MICHAEL HENRY SCHWERNER

	ANDREW GOODMAN	JAMES EARL CHANEY	MICHAEL HENRY SCHWERNER
RACE:	White	Negro	White
SEX:	Male	Male	Male
DOB:	November 23, 1943	May 30, 1943	November 6, 1939
POB:	New York City	Meridian, Mississippi	New York City
AGE:	20 years	21 years	24 years
HEIGHT:	5'10"	5'7"	5'9" to 5'10"
WEIGHT:	150 pounds	135 to 140 pounds	170 to 180 pounds
HAIR:	Dark brown; wavy	Black	Brown
EYES:	Brown	Brown	Light blue
TEETH:		Good; none missing	
SCARS AND MARKS:		1 inch cut scar 2 inches above left ear.	Pock mark center of forehead, slight scar on bridge of nose, appendectomy scar, broken leg scar.

SHOULD YOU HAVE OR IN THE FUTURE RECEIVE ANY INFORMATION CONCERNING THE WHEREABOUTS OF THESE INDIVIDUALS, YOU ARE REQUESTED TO NOTIFY ME OR THE NEAREST OFFICE OF THE FBI. TELEPHONE NUMBER IS LISTED BELOW.

Selected Prices, 1965

Air Conditioner, 8,000 btu	$189.95
Baby Stroller, Two-Seater	$29.95
Beer, Schlitz, Six-Pack	$0.99
Camera, Polaroid Color Pack	$50.00
Coffee, Folger's, Two Pounds	$1.27
Electric Toothbrush	$12.50
Hair Spray	$0.47
Rider Tractor	$352.95
Rod and Reel	$15.49
Tape Player, 8-Track	$67.95

Our heaviest (12.5-oz.) thickset cotton corduroy, slacks-tailored

$377

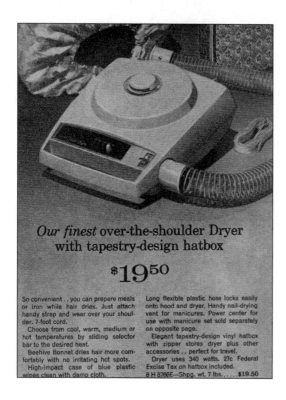

Our finest over-the-shoulder Dryer with tapestry-design hatbox

$19⁵⁰

So convenient . . you can prepare meals or iron while hair dries. Just attach handy strap and wear over your shoulder. 7-foot cord.

Choose from cool, warm, medium or hot temperatures by sliding selector bar to the desired heat.

Beehive Bonnet dries hair more comfortably with no irritating hot spots.

High-impact case of blue plastic wipes clean with damp cloth.

Long flexible plastic hose locks easily onto hood and dryer. Handy nail-drying vent for manicures. Power center for use with manicure set sold separately on opposite page.

Elegant tapestry-design vinyl hatbox with zipper stores dryer plus other accessories . . perfect for travel.

Dryer uses 340 watts. 27c Federal Excise Tax on hatbox included.

8 H 8766E—Shpg. wt. 7 lbs. $19.50

$109⁸⁸*
standard pica or elite

Even at this low price, our Constellation has a 12-inch carriage and other premium features

Office-size 12-inch carriage lets you put in a sheet of 8½x11-inch paper *sideways* for charts and tables . . takes a full-size envelope with room to spare. 88-character keyboard has !, ¢, =, and +. A flick of your finger sets margins.

Adjust key tension to suit your touch. Page-Gage tells space left from 2½ in. to end of page. Removable roller makes cleaning easy. 12-inch erasing table. Finished in handsome willow green. Sturdy steel frame and tough— yet light—die-cast aluminum body. Carrying case is vinyl-covered steel. Guaranteed 5 yrs. (see page 934). Freight (rail or truck) or express.

3 H 52004N—Standard pica
Shipping weight 21 pounds. *$6 monthly* . . . .
3 H 52005N—Standard elite
. . . . Cash $109.88*

3 H 52006N
Artistic script
3 H 52007N
Presidential pica
3 H 52008N
Futura
Shipping weight 21 pounds. *$6.50 monthly* . . . . Cash $114.88*

Civil Rights Timeline

1921

Race riots in Tulsa, Oklahoma, resulted in approximately 150 people killed, 800 injured, and 10,000 homeless.

1931

The Scottsboro Boys, nine African American boys accused of raping two White women, were arrested.

1940

The Supreme Court freed three Black men who were coerced into confessing to a murder.

1941

President Franklin Delano Roosevelt issued Executive Order 8802, the "Fair Employment Act."

1944

The United Negro College Fund was incorporated.

1947

Jackie Robinson became the first Black player in professional baseball.

1948

Hubert Humphrey spoke in favor of American civil rights at the Democratic National Convention.

President Harry S. Truman issued Executive Order 9981 ending segregation in the armed forces.

1950

In *McLaurin v. Oklahoma State Regents* the Supreme Court ruled that a public institution of higher learning cannot provide different treatment to students solely because of their race.

In *Sweatt v. Painter* the Supreme Court ruled that a "separate-but-equal" Texas law school was unequal.

1951

High school students in Farmville, Virginia, went on strike; the case *Davis v. County School Board of Prince Edward County* was heard by the Supreme Court in 1954 as part of *Brown v. Board of Education of Topeka, Kansas.*

1952

Briggs v. Elliott: after a district court ordered separate but equal school facilities in South Carolina, the Supreme Court agreed to hear the case as part of *Brown v. Board of Education.*

1954

The Supreme Court unanimously ruled in *Brown v. Board of Education* that segregation in public schools was unconstitutional.

The Supreme Court decided in *Hernandez v. Texas* that Mexican Americans and all other racial groups in the United States were entitled to equal protection under the Fourteenth Amendment to the U.S. Constitution.

1955

President Dwight D. Eisenhower signed Executive Order 10590, establishing the President's Committee on Government Policy to enforce a nondiscrimination policy in federal employment.

Fourteen-year-old Chicagoan Emmett Till was kidnapped, brutally beaten, shot, and dumped in the Tallahatchie River for allegedly whistling at a White woman in Mississippi.

NAACP member Rosa Parks refused to give up her seat at the front of a bus to a White passenger, sparking a bus boycott which lasted more than a year.

continued

Timeline . . . (continued)

1957

Martin Luther King, Charles K. Steele and Fred L. Shuttlesworth established the Southern Christian Leadership Conference (SCLC), of which King was president.

In Little Rock, Arkansas, nine Black students were blocked from entering a school on the orders of Governor Orval Faubus; President Dwight Eisenhower ordered federal troops to intervene on behalf of the students.

The Civil Rights Act of 1957 was signed.

1958

The Supreme Court awarded the NAACP the right to continue operating in Alabama under *NAACP v. Alabama*.

1960

Four Black students from North Carolina Agricultural and Technical College began a sit-in at a segregated Woolworth's lunch counter, sparking a national movement to integrate parks, swimming pools, theaters, libraries, and other public facilities.

The Student Nonviolent Coordinating Committee (SNCC) was founded at Shaw University, providing young Blacks with a place in the civil rights movement.

The Civil Rights Act of 1960 was signed.

1961

The Congress of Racial Equality (CORE) began sending student volunteers on bus trips to test the implementation of laws prohibiting segregation in interstate travel facilities; a mob in Alabama set the riders' bus on fire.

James Meredith became the first Black student to enroll at the University of Mississippi; President John Kennedy was forced to send 5,000 federal troops to control the rioting.

1963

Martin Luther King was arrested and jailed during anti-segregation protests in Birmingham, Alabama, where he wrote his "Letter from Birmingham Jail," arguing that individuals have the moral duty to disobey unjust laws.

During civil rights protests in Birmingham, Alabama, Commissioner of Public Safety Eugene "Bull" Connor used fire hoses and police dogs on Black demonstrators; the images of brutality were televised and published widely.

Mississippi's NAACP field secretary Medgar Evers was murdered outside his home.

About 200,000 people gathered for the March on Washington, where Martin Luther King delivered his "I Have a Dream" speech.

Four young girls were killed when a bomb exploded at the Sixteenth Street Baptist church in Birmingham, Alabama, a popular location for civil rights meetings.

continued

Timeline . . . *(continued)*

1964

The Twenty-fourth Amendment abolished the poll tax.

The Council of Federated Organizations (COFO), a network of civil rights groups that included CORE and SNCC, launched a massive effort to register Black voters.

President Johnson signed the Civil Rights Act of 1964, the most sweeping civil rights legislation since Reconstruction.

The bodies of three civil-rights workers—two White, one Black—were found in an earthen dam in Mississippi.

1965

Malcolm X, Black nationalist and founder of the Organization of Afro-American Unity, was shot to death in New York.

Congress passed the Voting Rights Act of 1965, making it easier for Southern Blacks to register to vote; literacy tests and other requirements were made illegal.

Race riots erupted in a Black section of Los Angeles.

Asserting that civil rights laws alone were not enough to remedy a history of discrimination, President Lyndon Johnson enforced affirmative action in hiring for the first time.

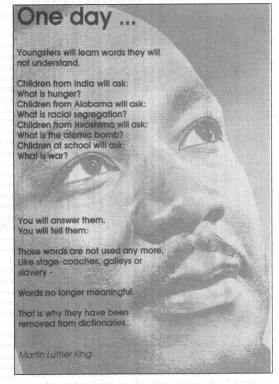

One day ...

Youngsters will learn words they will not understand.

Children from India will ask:
What is hunger?
Children from Alabama will ask:
What is racial segregation?
Children from Hiroshima will ask:
What is the atomic bomb?
Children at school will ask:
What is war?

You will answer them.
You will tell them:

Those words are not used any more,
Like stage-coaches, galleys or slavery -

Words no longer meaningful.

That is why they have been removed from dictionaries.

Martin Luther King

First I heard the shouts, then the shots. I had never heard a gun fire before, so I thought they were shooting the people. Then we saw the tear gas and the horses trampling people. And we ran.

—Joanne Bland describing Bloody Sunday, 1965

LOVE LIFE STOP THE VIOLENCE

Song of civil rights marchers as they entered Montgomery, Alabama, 1964:

Keep your eyes on the prize, hold on, hold on.
I've never been to heaven, but I think I'm right,
You won't find George Wallace anywhere in sight. . . .

We are willing to be beaten for democracy!
—SCLC Rev. C. T. Vivian to Selma Sheriff Jim Clark

"Strongest Rights Law Signed by President," *Roanoke (Virginia) Times*, July 3, 1964:

President Johnson signed the strongest civil rights law in nearly a century Thursday night, only three hours after Congress approved it amid cheers, and called on Americans to "eliminate the last vestiges of injustice in America."

In a historic ceremony in the East Room of the White House, Johnson pledged himself to "faithful execution" of the statute and announced immediate steps to insure its enforcement.

Johnson delivered a conciliatory statement to the nation, by radio and television, to more than 200 lawmakers, civil rights leaders, and government officials on the spot who helped bring the sweeping legislation to enactment.

"We have come now to a kind of testing," Johnson said slowly and solemnly. "We must not fail. Let us close the springs of racial poison. Let us pray for wise and understanding hearts. Let us lay aside irrelevant differences and make our nation whole. Let us hasten that day when our unbounded spirit will be free to do the great works ordained for this nation by the just and wise God who is the Father of all."

Then dignitaries clustered around him, each to claim one of the 72 pens with which he put his signature to the bill delivered from the Capitol with extraordinary speed after the 289-126 House vote which ended long and bitter congressional debate.

He appealed for voluntary compliance and predicted it will be given "because most Americans are law-abiding citizens who want to do what is right."

In what was clearly an effort to calm the indignation of many Southerners and refute the objections of those who have denounced the measure as an invasion of states' rights, Johnson told the country: "It provides for the national authority to step in only when others cannot and will not do the job.

"I urge every public official, every religious leader, every business and professional man, every housewife—I urge every American—to join in this effort to bring justice and hope to all our people and peace to our land. . . ."

Although the founding fathers guaranteed all Americans the blessings of liberty, Johnson said, "millions are being deprived of those blessings not because of their own failures, but because of the color of their skin.

"The reasons are deeply imbedded in history and tradition and the nature of man. We can understand—without rancor or hatred—how this happened," he went on. "But it cannot continue. Our Constitution, the foundation of our republic, forbids it. The principles of our freedom forbid it. Morality forbids it. And the law I will sign tonight forbids it."

Johnson emphasized that the measure received the bipartisan support of more than two-thirds of the members of both House and Senate including "an overwhelming majority of Republicans as well as Democrats.

"It does not restrict the freedom of any American, so long as he respects the rights of others," he said, adding: "It does say that those who are equal before God shall now also be equal in the polling booths, in classrooms, in the factories, and in hotels, restaurants, movie theaters, and other places that provide service to the public."

Only an hour's debate preceded the House vote, and most speakers sounded the familiar themes that have been echoing through the House and Senate since last June. But one member produced a major surprise—a Georgia Democrat who supported the bill.

Rep. Charles L. Weltner of Atlanta, who voted against a similar bill when it passed the House last February, drew cheers and applause from the bill's supporters when he announced he was changing his vote.

"I would urge that we at home now move on to the unfinished task of building a new South. We must not remain forever bound to another lost cause," he said.

The Southern leaders of the opposition showed no weakening in their last fruitless opposition to the bill, however.

Rep. Howard W. Smith, (Democrat, Virginia), said it would loose upon the South "a second invasion of carpet-baggers." He predicted violence, bitterness and bloodshed would inevitably follow enactment of the bill, and ended his speech, "God save the United States of America."

At times history and fate meet at a single time in a single place to shape a turning point in man's unending search for freedom. So it was at Lexington and Concord. So it was a century ago at Appomattox. So it was last week in Selma, Alabama. There is no Negro problem. There is no Southern problem. There is no Northern problem. There is only an American problem. Many of the issues of civil rights are very complex and most difficult. But about this there can and should be no argument. Every American citizen must have the right to vote. . . . Yet the harsh fact is that in many places in this country men and women are kept from voting simply because they are Negroes. . . . No law that we now have on the books...can insure the right to vote when local officials are determined to deny it. . . . There is no Constitutional issue here. The command of the Constitution is plain. There is no moral issue. It is wrong—deadly wrong—to deny any of your fellow Americans the right to vote in this country. There is no issue of States' rights or National rights. There is only the struggle for human rights.

—President Lyndon B. Johnson, 1965

Selma, Alabama high school Black student Bettie Mae Fikes and her involvement in the Movement in 1965:

I didn't have a clue what was going on around me in the adult world. I could only deal with what I was seeing from my own eyes, and I knew, I could tell there was something wrong; I just didn't know what. My mother, being a gospel singer, we traveled a lot, and traveling you get a chance to see different areas. It seemed like in each state the people lived differently, which I didn't understand. I still did not know that there was an issue between Black and White in Selma, because the White community, as far as I was concerned, were friendly to us, my godfather was a White man. . . .

When I got back to Selma, I didn't go right into the arms of the civil rights struggle, but I knew something was going on; I just didn't know what. And when my uncle and all of them would get together and talk about surrounding areas and things that were happening with the Blacks, that kind of scared me, because they were also talking about war. So I was just looking for another war or something to break out. I believe they were talking about 1925, and the soup lines, and things like that.

Around in the early sixties, I just needed an avenue to get out of the house to keep from going to church so much. This fellow here, Mr. Bonner, and my other dear friend Cle, was telling us about SNCC. And they got all of their friends that they knew involved. I was one of the friends they got involved. When it hit, it was like something that—you went to bed, like tonight, and you woke up the next day with a new world order.

All of a sudden these people are coming to town and they're talking about voters' rights. I didn't even know that was happening—that our parents didn't have the right to vote. There were a few Black people that were registered, mostly in Selma. Lowndes County and all these [surrounding] counties were unregistered. So these are the things that brought me into the Movement. . . .

The first meeting was very tense, it was at night, we had never had a mass meeting before. We didn't know what a mass meeting was. There was a lot of singing, a lot of praise to Mr. Boynton, a lot of discussion of the need to organize, to challenge the segregation laws, the apartheid laws, but most importantly, the need to register people to vote. And it was energizing, and it motivated everyone, particularly the students, to get involved in the Movement and to really try to get Black people registered to vote.

1966 Profile

Censorship: Banning the Beatles

Teenager Diana-Jane Richburg's love affair with the Beatles had its ups and downs; when she heard John Lennon's remark about the Beatles being more popular than Jesus, her adoration turned to outrage, and then, uncertainty.

Life at Home

- Diana-Jane Richburg was named after her mother's two singing sisters.
- Diana-Jane grew up loving all kinds of music: Christmas, country, gospel and rock.
- When she turned 15, her father, owner of the second-largest car dealership in Birmingham, Alabama, took her on a father-daughter trip to New York City.
- It was her first plane trip, her first Broadway play, her first subway ride and her first exposure to a new musical group from England known as the Beatles.
- Diana-Jane returned to Birmingham with tales of tall buildings, rude cab drivers, and the music of John, Paul, George and Ringo.
- The already popular Diana-Jane drew an instant crowd in January 1964 when she showed off a recording of "Please Please Me" she'd gotten in New York.
- Even the school's biggest skeptics took notice when the Beatles appeared on *The Ed Sullivan Show* February 9 and sang five songs, including "All My Loving," "She Loves You" and "I Saw Her Standing There."
- In all, 11 girls gathered in the Richburgs' living room that Sunday night to see the Beatles perform on television, while across the nation, approximately 71 million Americans witnessed the launch of Beatlemania.
- No major crimes were reported in New York City during the hour the show was broadcast.
- Mrs. Richburg had trouble seeing what all the fuss was about and why everyone kept screaming so loudly they couldn't hear the music.
- Yet, it was hard to miss in all that screaming the physical and sexual energy the music unleashed.

Diana-Jane Richburg fell in love with the Beatles at age 15.

Diana was a popular student.

- Mr. Richburg was greatly amused that his little trip to New York City had yielded such big dividends: a deliriously happy teenager.
- When the Beatles returned for a second *Ed Sullivan* appearance one week later, two dozen girls crowded the Richburg home.
- Then, for the Beatles' third *Ed Sullivan* appearance on February 23, Diana-Jane's father installed three television sets in the showroom of his automobile dealership and told his daughter to invite the whole school.
- Hundreds came dressed to the nines, most with special permission from their parents since they would be out after nine o'clock on a school night.
- Diana-Jane was in seventh heaven; *her band* was sweeping the nation!
- She loved them all, especially Paul McCartney.

Life at School

- Diana-Jane Richburg was at the lake in her bathing suit when she first heard the news in the summer of 1966.
- John Lennon had said publicly that the Beatles were more popular than Jesus.
- At first Diana-Jane laughed and told friends, "They probably are."
- Then, slowly, the significance of what Lennon had said sank in.
- No one should say they were more popular than Jesus, she thought.
- She even discussed Lennon's comment with her mother.
- When disc jockeys Tommy Charles and Doug Layton suggested on WAQY—known locally as WHACKY radio—that Birmingham boycott the Beatles, Diana-Jane was a convert.
- The controversy had been initiated months earlier, on March 4, 1966, when the *Evening Standard* in England published an interview between Maureen Cleave and John Lennon entitled "How Does a Beatle Live?"
- In the course of the article, Lennon was quoted as saying: "Christianity will go. It will vanish and shrink. I needn't argue about that. I'm right and I will be proved right. We're more popular than Jesus now. I don't know which will go first—rock 'n' roll or Christianity. Jesus was all right but his disciples were thick and ordinary. It's them twisting it that ruins it for me."
- The British public took little notice of the comment.
- Four months later an American teen magazine called *Datebook* published Lennon's statement without reprinting the original article, and featured it as part of a cover story called "The Ten Adults You Dig/Hate the Most."
- The American reaction was instantaneous.
- Radio stations across the country, especially in the South and the Midwest, stopped playing Beatles records.
- Death threats poured in directed against John and the other Beatles as well.
- Bonfires appeared with Beatles pictures and albums providing the fuel.
- Beatles spokesmen repeatedly attempted to explain that "John was certainly not comparing the Beatles with Christ. He was simply observing that so weak was the state of Christianity that the Beatles were, to many people, better known. He was deploring, rather than approving, this."
- However, it did no good.
- In Cleveland, the Reverend Thurman H. Babbs threatened to excommunicate any member of his congregation who listened to the Beatles.
- In the South, the Ku Klux Klan burned the Beatles in effigy and nailed Beatles albums to burning crosses.

Diana and her classmates.

- In Birmingham, Diana-Jane took a leadership role in organizing the protest.
- The initial plan to burn a pile of Beatles records was shelved when the city refused to issue a fire permit.
- But that did not stop several grocery stores from setting up collection points for Beatles records and memorabilia so that they could be crushed.
- Diana-Jane gathered her entire Beatles collection, except for the 45 she got of "Please Please Me" that glorious weekend in New York City.
- She then organized the junior class to publicize the drop-off locations advertised by WAQY.
- Fourteen drop-off locations around the city were established; Birmingham would show the world the Beatles couldn't get away with this.

Life in the Community: Birmingham, Alabama
- When Diana-Jane Richburg arrived at the first Ban the Beatles drop-off location, she immediately became nervous; only a handful of albums were there.
- A driver since she was 14 years old, Diana-Jane had borrowed one of her father's model cars for an inspection tour of the drop-off locations and talked two of her friends into coming along.
- At the second location, there were even fewer records, but at the third site a crowd was gathered.
- From a distance she counted a dozen people in the parking lot unloading albums.
- Diana-Jane was just on the edge of a cheer when she realized most of the fellow protesters were young—junior high young—without a popular one in the bunch.
- Surely, Alabama's largest city, with a population of 275,000, could do better than this.
- Long known as the "Pittsburgh of the South," Birmingham was a heavily industrialized city that had experienced its share of civil rights protests.

- Diana-Jane's friends were equally taken aback and immediately began to discuss who really listened to WAQY anyway.
- Besides, with school not starting for another month, organizing the student leaders was going to be hard.
- Worldwide, the reaction continued.
- On the eve of the Beatles' North American tour in August, John Lennon held a press conference in Chicago at which he attempted to make amends.
- The Ku Klux Klan tried, unsuccessfully, to stop the Beatles concert when it arrived in Memphis.
- KLUE, a radio station in Texas, organized another Beatles bonfire.
- The Vatican said, "the protest the remark raised showed that some subjects must not be dealt with lightly and in a profane way, not even in the world of beatniks."
- Three radio stations in Spain and one in Holland banned the airing of Beatles records.
- In South Africa, Piet Myer of the South African Broadcasting Corporation justified his decision to bar Beatles albums by saying, "The Beatles' arrogance has passed the ultimate limit of decency. It is clowning no longer."

HISTORICAL SNAPSHOT
1966

- Cigarette packs in the United States began carrying warning signs saying cigarette smoking was harmful to human health
- The court case *Miranda v. Arizona* required law enforcement officers to inform defendants of their rights, including the right to remain silent and the right to an attorney
- Medicare was created to help the elderly with the high cost of medical care
- The National Organization for Women was founded "to bring about equality for all women"
- Hewlett-Packard introduced its first computer, the HP 2116A
- The novel *Valley of the Dolls* by Jacqueline Susann sold over 20 million copies
- Xerox introduced the Magnafax Telecopier capable of transmitting a single-page letter in six minutes
- In Oakland, California, Bobby Seale and Huey Newton co-founded the Black Panthers, which promoted the use of violence as self-defense
- Martin Luther King, Jr. took a stand against the Vietnam War, fearing it was sapping resources from domestic social programs
- The Student Nonviolent Coordinating Committee (SNCC) ejected its historical strategy of non-violence to embrace a doctrine of "Black Power"
- Soviet *Luna 9* became the first spacecraft to soft-land on the moon
- The U.S. *Lunar Orbiter 1* entered the moon's orbit and took the first picture of Earth from there
- U.S. troop strength in Vietnam grew from 200,000 in January to 400,000 by December
- The Cultural Revolution began in China
- President Lyndon Johnson signed the Freedom of Information Act
- Racial riots erupted in Watts (Los Angeles), Omaha, Cleveland, Chicago and Atlanta
- Twenty-five thousand anti-Vietnam War demonstrators marched in New York City
- Fuel injection for cars was invented
- Popular books included *In Cold Blood* by Truman Capote and *Games People Play* by Eric Berne
- Popular music included "These Boots Were Made for Walking" by Nancy Sinatra, "The Sound of Silence" by Simon and Garfunkel, "Ballad of the Green Berets" by Barry Sadler, and "Monday, Monday" by the Mamas and the Papas
- *Star Trek, Batman, The Avengers, That Girl* and *Mission Impossible* premiered on television

Selected Prices, 1966

Acne Medicine, Clearasil	$0.98
After Shave, English Leather	$2.00
BB Gun	$12.98
Car Seat	$6.95
Cullottes	$8.00
Dance Concert, per Couple	$4.50
Drive-in Movie, per Car	$1.50
Hair Cream, Brylcreem	$0.59
Phonograph, Hi-Fi	$29.95
Tuition, Augusta Military Academy, Year	$1,300.00

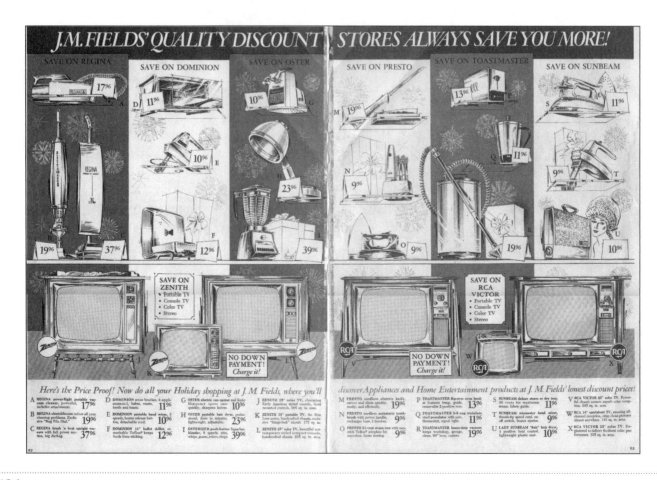

1966 Beatles Timeline

January 21

George Harrison married Patricia Anne Boyd.

February 21

The single "Nowhere Man" was released by Capitol Records.

March 4

Journalist Maureen Cleave of the *Evening Standard* interviewed John Lennon and asked a question concerning Church and God.

April 6

The Beatles began recording *Revolver* at Abbey Road studios.

May 27

The single "Paperback Writer" was released.

June 6

The Beatles appeared on *The Ed Sullivan Show.*

June 14

The "butcher cover" for the *Yesterday . . . and Today* album, which depicted the Beatles dressed up in white smocks amidst decapitated baby dolls, was pulled.

June 15

Yesterday . . . and Today was released.

July 4

After the Beatles performed before 50,000 fans at Manila's National Football Stadium, reports were circulated that the president of Manila was insulted by the Beatles' failure to show up at his children's party; as a result, the Beatles were kicked and punched as they left Manila.

July 29

Lennon's "We're more popular than Jesus" comment appeared in *Datebook.*

August 2

A ban on playing Beatles records began in Birmingham, Alabama; by August 6, 30 radio stations had removed all Beatles records from airplay.

August 6

Beatles manager Brian Epstein held a press conference in New York for damage control over John Lennon's "anti-Christ" remarks.

August 8

The *Revolver* album was released.

The singles "Yellow Submarine" and "Eleanor Rigby" were released.

August 11

John Lennon met with the American press to explain what he had meant by his "We're more popular than Jesus" remark.

continued

Timeline . . . *(continued)*

August 12

The North American Beatles tour began in Chicago.

August 29

The Beatles held their final U.S. performance in San Francisco's Candlestick Park.

September 19

John Lennon flew to Spain to star in the movie *How I Won the War*, in which he played the part of Private Gripweed.

September 20

George Harrison went to India to study the sitar with Ravi Shankar.

October 17

The Amazing Beatles was released.

November 6

John Lennon visited the Indica Gallery in London where he met Yoko Ono displaying her art.

November 24

The Beatles began recording *Sgt. Pepper's Lonely Hearts Club Band*.

December 16

The Beatles Fourth Christmas Record, *PANTOMIME: EVERYWHERE IT'S CHRISTMAS*, was issued to fan club members.

We'd done about 1,400 live shows and I certainly felt this was it.

It was nice to be popular, but when you saw the size of it, it was ridiculous, and it felt dangerous because everybody was out of hand. Even the cops were out of line. . . . It was a very strange feeling. For a year or so I'd been saying, "Let's not do this anymore." And then it played itself out, so that by 1966 everybody was feeling, "We've got to stop this." I don't know exactly where in 1966, but obviously after the Philippines we thought, "Hey, we've got to pack this in."

—George Harrison after the Beatles' last American concert in Candlestick Park

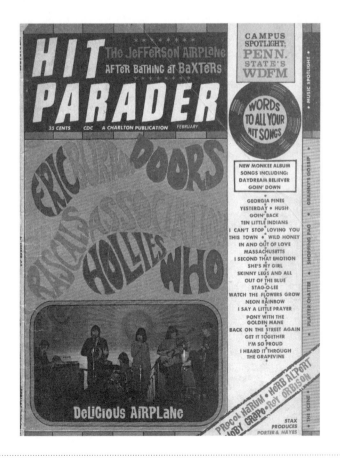

"Fan Rallies to Defense of Beatles," *Martinsville (Virginia) Bulletin,* August 26, 1966:

Editor, The Bulletin:

I hope this letter will help many people to realize the truth about the Beatles. They didn't really make that statement to be bragging. They were actually complaining. Many disc jockeys have led us to believe that the Beatles said they were better than Jesus, but they said they were more popular than Jesus.

This is true. The Beatles are more popular than Jesus and so are the Supremes, Rolling Stones, rock 'n' roll music, money, parties, liquor and almost anything else you can think of. If you don't believe me, let me give you some examples: (1). If most people were given a choice of going to church or to a party, game, the movies, etc., I'm sure they would pick the latter. (2). A person would spend $500 to better his social image but it is hardly likely that he'd give $500 to the church. (3). Many people would sit down and read paperback books for hours but would they read a Bible for that long? (4). You could ask a person plenty of questions about Viet Nam, rock 'n' roll music, etc., and he could answer every one of them, but how many questions could he answer about the Bible? Very few, if any.

John Lennon was really disgusted because the state of Christianity is so weak that nobody worships God as they are supposed to. Let's face it. Most people only go to church because they feel it's their duty. Even when a parent gives his child a quarter to put in Sunday School, he'll only put in a dime and spend the rest for candy.

This sudden banning of the Beatles is just a mass misunderstanding led mostly by disc jockeys who were too dense and thick-headed to analyze the statement. Even when the person that got the statement from the Beatles contradicted the disc jockeys' interpretation and the Beatles' manager himself appeared to the nation on CBS news and gave John's true intentions in making the statement they (the disc jockeys and others who banned them) were still too obstinate to recognize the truth in the Beatles' statement.

I don't think banning was right because the Beatles are the best thing that's happened to the rock 'n' roll industry. They've opened up new trends as well as built up the economy of both the U.S. and Britain. They've written many beautiful songs which have been performed by stars like Frank Sinatra, Andy Williams and the Hollywood Strings. They are a model which all American teenagers would do well to copy. The Beatles started in the cellars of Liverpool and rose to the top—even to play at the London Palladium and a command performance for the Queen of England, who gave them medals of honor.

By copying the Beatles many would-be juvenile delinquents of England have now formed groups of their own. The Beatles are four nice, mannerable, clean-cut lads who were brought up by strict parents who taught them to love and respect God.

Many people who banned the Beatles really didn't like them at first and thought this was a good way to get rid of them. And many others took the statement at face value without a second thought to what Mr. Lennon meant. Therefore, some people are violating one of the cornerstones of the American Democracy by condemning a person without hearing both sides of the issue. These record stores that banned the Beatles couldn't care a fig about what the Beatles said; they're just hoping to cash in on the publicity.

Some adults want to get rid of the Beatles because they hate rock 'n' roll music. They're always knocking rock 'n' roll and expect teenagers to regress to the musical styles they enjoyed as teens, such as Benny Goodman and Lawrence Welk.

There are many rock 'n' roll groups far worse than the Beatles. So why pick on the Beatles? They always look neat and clean on stage and many other groups look sloppy with hair falling to the shoulders and stupid-looking clothes on.

If these would-be savers of the U.S. and Christianity would spend more time with problems which really affect teens such as the sale of dope, sex out of wedlock and the dropout rate, they would then be really helping to raise the standards of America and what we Americans really stand for.

Signed,
Beatle Fan Forever

"Beatle Squabble Called Publicity Stunt," *Martinsville (Virginia) Bulletin*, August 9, 1966:

Editor, The Bulletin:

Ban the Beatles, Yea! Yea! Yea! Kick the mopheads out in the name of Christianity! That's the cry of a segment of the broadcasting industry who would like you to believe they are banning the Beatles to preserve the purity of the airwaves. Not so, gentle friends. Why do the very people who promoted the Beatles and other off-key singers now seek to destroy the giant they created? Ostensibly, because of a magazine article quoting Beatle John Lennon as saying his group is more popular than Jesus. But quite obviously this Ban-The-Beatles movement is simply the latest gimmick devised by publicity hungry broadcasters to gain a larger share of the shallow thinking audience.

If, indeed, there was a real interest in the good quality and high moral standards of the material presented on these stations, there would be no reason for banning the world's Number One singing foursome. Without these stations' exposure, they would never have gained their status as national heroes. And without the broadcasters' help, many other screamers who call themselves entertainers would be missing from the so-called top-40 and top-100 music charts.

Our new breed of public-spirited announcers thinks nothing of following a Ban-The-Beatles announcement with the wails of a narcotics addict or the mumblings of one whose mind is so numb from alcohol that he can't utter an intelligible word.

I say if radio stations are going to set themselves up as judges of an artist's morals, they should also sit in judgment of his talent. If this ever happens, we can expect scores of recording stars who claim to be entertainers to be taken off the air.

Some stations use the democratic approach in their Ban-The-Beatles publicity stunt. After quoting John Lennon as saying the Beatles are more popular than Jesus, they invite their teenage audience to call the station and vote to ban or not to ban. While the calls come in, the turntables are spinning, and the screams and moans of the Beatles' contemporaries fill the airwaves! It's ironic that while the Beatles are being voted out, other record stars whose morals are probably no better and whose talent certainly is no better, are being rewarded.

A disc jockey who is truly interested in providing wholesome, high-quality entertainment should use a little discretion in selecting all the records he plays. After all, as just about any radio personality will tell you, without him, the Beatles could not have made it to the top. John Lennon of the Beatles may think they're more popular than Jesus. It seems to me those who continue to promote the Beatles or their brand of entertainment think themselves more popular than God.

A Disgusted Reader

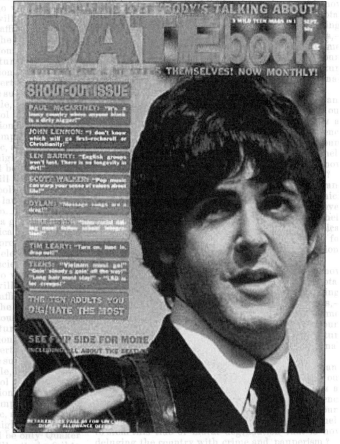

If I had said that television is more popular than Jesus, I might have got away with it. It's a fact, in reference to England, we meant more to kids than Jesus did, or religion at that time. I wasn't knocking it or putting it down. I was just saying it, as a fact and it's true, more for England than here. I'm not saying we're better or greater or comparing us with Jesus Christ as a person or God as a thing, or whatever it is, you know, I just said what I said and it was wrong, or was taken wrong, and now it's all this!

—John Lennon

NOTES FROM TH FIRST YE

YORK RADICAL WOMEN
BROADWAY, ROOM 412
NEW YORK CITY 10003

JUNE 1968
$ .50 TO WO
$1.00 TO ME

1968 NEWS FEATURE

**"Woman as Child—Notes from a Meeting by Jennifer Gardner,
Notes from the First Year," New York Radical Women, 1968:**

The Radical Women of New York, formed for discussion and action on the subject of women's oppression and liberation, has adopted the following outline for its consideration over the next few months: Woman as Child; Woman as Adolescent; Woman as Student; Woman as Single Woman; Woman as Worker; Woman as Head of Household; Woman as Wife; Woman as Mother; Woman as Aged; Woman in Male Power Structure; Woman in Capitalism; Woman in Socialism, Woman in the Revolution. There have been four crucial questions raised in each of the discussions: Woman as Sexual Object; Economic Dependence/Independence of Woman; Female Inferiority: Male Propagation-Female Internalization; In Whose Interest Is Woman's Oppressions? The following is a summary of ideas raised at a group meeting during the first discussion of Woman as Child.

The group began by considering prenatal prejudices—that is, concepts and preferences parents may have about the sex of their children even before the children are born. In a discussion of reasons many parents would prefer to have a male child, especially for their first, several feelings and myths emerged. Among them were:

1. A "royal" image and tradition of the male child as the continuation of the family line and name. This is closely connected to the fact that:

2. Both men and women are prejudiced against women, think men more interesting, exciting and real; and feel that a family of women is weak, dull and somehow unimportant.

3. A woman who regards the lot of women as hard might fear to bring another sufferer into the world.

4. Girls, as they grow older, require more care than boys, and remain dependent longer on their parents. This feeling is of course based partly on the very real advantages men have as wage earners. But the group was interested in why the feeling persists even in families where a daughter would not, theoretically, be more of an economic liability than a son.

5. A boy should be the oldest sibling—the second head of the family.

6. A daughter may appear as a sexual competitor to her mother in a Freudian sense.

Some parents, probably not many, would prefer a girl. A woman might feel that she knows women better than men and would therefore feel closer to a daughter than to a son. A man might fear that he would eventually end up competing with a son in one way or another, and would therefore like to have a daughter and avoid this complication. (The assumption here, of course, is that women are naturally subordinate to and supportive of men so that the parent-child relationship between father and daughter could remain relatively unchanged even as the daughter became an adult.)

Still another reason some parents would prefer a daughter to a son is the prevailing assumption that little girls are easier to take care of than little boys; that they are more docile, more verbal, less aggressive, less active and generally less trouble than boys. Since the existence of innate temperamental differences between boys and girls is difficult to prove, in view of their differential treatment at an early age, the group began to examine some environmental influences on girls which might account both for parental expectations and for the eventual realization of these expectations.

In general, certain kinds of behavior are systematically discouraged in girls that may be tolerated or even encouraged in boys. One such type of behavior is the overt expression of hostility and aggression. Because anger and hostility seem to be important feelings in children (not to mention adults) and their expression an important aspect of self-expression, the more severe curbing of aggressive behavior in little girls is actually a suppression of their sense of self. One possible result of this suppression may be the development of more covert expressions of hostility (bitchiness) and, perhaps, more verbal expression in general.

Little girls are further inhibited by being encouraged, more than boys to keep themselves clean and quiet. Their concept of themselves as doers and explorers is thus diminished, preparing them for later roles as spectators and sexual objects.

In boys, boisterous and even eccentric behavior can be tolerated as expressions of manliness and individuality, while girls tend to gain approval more by looking pretty and by conforming to certain adult standards of deportment. This may make girls less confident in themselves and create in them a greater need for outside approval at an early age. Because their aggressive, explorative and adventurous tendencies have been more severely suppressed (that is, these certain aspects of self have been rejected), their sense of their own worth is subverted, and they must rely more heavily on others to help reestablish it.

The question of how these "others" come primarily to mean men is probably a good one for discussion of woman as adolescent.

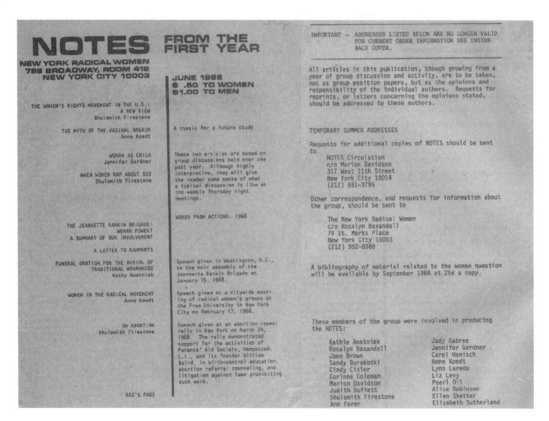

1969 Profile

American Indian Activism: Fishing Rights

Harry Smallboy was frustrated that a nation obsessed with civil rights for Negroes was still ignoring the legitimate claims of the Native Americans, so he decided to throw in his lot with other Indians fighting for fishing rights in Washington State.

Life at Home

- Harry Smallboy was sick to death with being called chief, red, injun and Tonto.
- He was particularly bored with having little boys with cowboy pistols shooting at him while shouting, "Bang, bang, you're dead. Fall down."
- Long ago, he ceased to think any of this was funny.
- The abuse was particularly bad when Hollywood was displaying its latest version of America's Western past.
- Twenty-nine years old and a native of Los Angeles, California, Harry was convinced that it was time for Indians on the West Coast to fight for their rightful place in the economy.
- He was galvanized by the takeover of the abandoned Alcatraz Island in San Francisco Bay by Indians claiming the abandoned prison as surplus federal property.
- For the first time, he realized that the actions of a handful of courageous persons could speak for thousands of people unable to voice their frustration.
- Approximately 800,000 American Indians lived in the United States with about 450,000 residing in or connected to reservations.

Harry Smallboy fought for Native American fishing rights.

Hollywood's depiction of Native Americans.

- The vast majority lived west of the Mississippi River; the Navajo Reservation in parts of Arizona, New Mexico and Utah was the nation's largest in the country, with 120,000 people occupying an area the size of West Virginia.
- The majority of reservation Indians claimed incomes below the poverty level of $4,000, with the average reservation income being $2,600.
- Seventy-five percent of all reservation homes were substandard; 50 percent were dilapidated beyond repair.
- Only half of all reservation homes had indoor sanitation facilities.
- Urban-based Indians like Harry earned an average of $4,500, thanks to better opportunities and often more education.
- The incomes of urban Indians and black males were nearly the same.
- Harry claimed a public high school diploma and one bewildering year of college.
- That level of education earned him a job in a warehouse stacking boxes and lots of red-man-sneaky-Indian-HOW jokes from his coworkers.
- Most of the time, Harry said little, only correcting others when they referred to him as being part Indian; he preferred to think of himself as an Indian who was part white.
- His mother's grandmother was enormously proud that her father was white and said so frequently.
- Harry believed that the press of racism convinced her that her white side was superior to her red side.
- Despite being raised in an urban environment like Los Angeles, Harry identified strongly with his Indian heritage and felt the role of his people was being swept away in the name of progress.

- Less than 10 percent earned their living from agriculture; less than five percent were employed in crafts.
- Vocational agriculture was removed from the curricula of federal Indian schools in the 1950s.
- And in Washington State where Harry's people originated, the Indians were losing the right to fish for salmon, all because the white man had overused, polluted and dammed the rivers.
- Purely on impulse, he quit work and drove to Washington to join a "fish-in" protest, even though he had never seen a salmon in the wild and didn't really like to fish.

Traditional crafts helped sustain Indian communities.

Harry's grandmother was proud of her White heritage.

Life at Work

- The fishing-rights dispute in Washington State had dragged on for 15 years without resolution.
- To Harry Smallboy, the issues were clear.
- Prior to the arrival of the white man, his people—the original inhabitants of Washington State's coastal waters—had been among the wealthiest native Americans, thanks to salmon fishing.
- Fishing was central to their survival and was specifically protected in the various treaties signed by his ancestors—treaties that were written to last for as long as "the grass grows and the sun comes up in the east and sets in the west."
- But for nearly 100 years the rights of his ancestors had been under assault.
- The Puyallup now owned only 33 acres of land, the Nisqually claimed two acres, the Snohomish 16 acres, and the 300-member Muckleshoot tribe to whom Harry belonged shared a reservation of a quarter of an acre.
- Deprived of their land, tribal members were forced to fish off the reservation.
- The various treaties declared this to be within their rights, although fish and game officials said otherwise.

Fishing was central to the Native Americans in Washington State.

- For most of the 1960s, state officials had been dragging Indians into court challenging their right to fish for salmon and steelhead trout.
- One year earlier, another round of litigation started when the state confiscated the boats and gear of two dozen people.

Fishing-rights protest.

- Going to court proudly dressed as Muckleshoot Indians had become a way of life for his people.
- The Washington Indians were generally the losers—until they produced pictures of an incident in which the fish and game officials used Billy clubs to pummel the protestors and then kicked and punched the women and children.
- But injustices continued, especially when the treaties of the Indians conflicted with the desires of wealthy sport fishermen determined to land a steelhead trout.
- The state even launched a nationwide advertising campaign using the slogan, "Come to Washington, a sportsman's wonderland," as if the state had decreed the steelhead trout a "white man's fish."
- Once in Washington, Harry heard jokes about the steelhead swimming to America with the *Mayflower*.
- Mostly, he heard resentment from fishermen disgusted with the concept that they needed the white man's permission to fish, hunt or gather nuts.
- One man shouted in anger, "The white man didn't plant the trees, bring the deer or raise the fish, but he wants to give me—a Puyallup—permission to use the land, the air, the water."
- Another man who had volunteered to join the next "fish-in/arrest" was a Vietnam veteran, back from his third tour of duty; he had already been arrested twice for illegal fishing and was prepared to be arrested again.
- They then talked of demonstrations, road blockades, and land takeovers as ways to express Indian outrage over injustice, poverty and white dominance.

Tribal fishing was being squeezed out by White commercial fishing.

- The legacy of being born Indian in America was dismal: an average life span of 40 due to disease, alcoholism and malnutrition; an infant mortality rate more than twice the national average; an unemployment rate 10 times the national average; the highest teen suicide rate in America, and liver disease from alcoholism five times higher than that of the white population.
- They laughed about the white reaction to Native American protests that mocked Thanksgiving and Columbus Day holidays, and lowered their voices in case the police had them under surveillance.
- But voices grew tense when it came time to stage another fish-in and risk arrest.
- Harry hung close to the Vietnam vet as he gathered up nets and fishing tackle.
- The time had arrived for Harry Smallboy—Muckleshoot Indian—to make his stand for his people.

Life in the Community: Puget Sound, Washington

- In the 1700s, the indigenous inhabitants of Puget Sound spoke numerous languages and did not have one name for themselves or for people outside the region.
- Gradually, they began to lump all traders into two categories: "King George men" or "Bostons."
- After the Americans established control of the area, "Bostons" served to identify all immigrants.
- In a similar fashion, "Indians" was used to identify a native Washington State population as diverse and changeable as "Bostons."
- At the time the fishing rights treaties were signed in 1853, white settlers had little interest in salmon fishing.
- The protection of fishing rights was explicitly demanded by native leadership because salmon fishing was central to their way of life.
- Non-Indian commercial fishing began to grow after the first salmon cannery appeared on the Columbia River in the 1870s.
- By the turn of the century, tribal fishing was being squeezed out by white commercial fishing at the mouth of the river.
- As commercial mechanization increased, Indian salmon harvests fell.
- But salmon fishing and its related activities continued to be at the heart of the Puget Sound Indian culture, even after the building of large-scale hydro-power plants reduced salmon runs in the 1930s and 1940s.
- Then, in the 1950s, as dams and pollution further decreased the salmon runs, Washington State game authorities began to require tribal fishers to observe state conservation laws, not ancient treaties.
- The Muckleshoot, Puyallup and Nisqually asserted their treaty fishing rights and continued to fish.

- Then, in January 1961, James Starr and Louis Starr, Jr., both from the Muckleshoot tribe, and Leonard Wayne, a Puyallup, were arrested for fishing on the Green River, but the court found they were fishing legally according to fishing rights.
- Washington State then started a sustained drive to end Indian treaty fishing rights any way possible, including abolishing the tribes.
- This was especially true after the Washington State Supreme Court decided in December 1963 that the state did not have the power to regulate Indian fishing for conservation purposes.
- The first fish-in as an act of political protest occurred January 1, 1964.
- This was followed by a fish-in featuring actor Marlon Brando, who was arrested, attracting huge media attention.
- Native fishermen were also arrested, received jail terms, and then went back to the river to fish and be arrested again.
- In 1964, the courts ruled that the Muckleshoot Indians were not a tribe, because no one had signed that way in the 1855 Point Elliot Treaty.
- In 1965, a county judge ruled the Puyallup Indians were no longer a tribe because they had lost their land.
- The protests and fish-in events continued.
- In 1966, black activist Dick Gregory was arrested and sentenced to 40 days in jail: "If more people went to jail for rights, fewer would go for wrongs."
- Battles between the tribal members and state fish and game officers became media events.
- The native Americans would assert their right to fish and state officials would confiscate Indian fishing boats and gear—all in front of television cameras.
- The Native American movement was electrified.

HISTORICAL SNAPSHOT
1969

- Lorraine Hansberry's *To Be Young, Gifted and Black* premiered in New York City
- Thirty thousand copies of the John Lennon/Yoko Ono album, *Two Virgins*, were confiscated by police in Newark, New Jersey, because the nude photo of John and Yoko on the cover violated pornography laws
- Newly elected President Richard Nixon said in his inaugural address, "The greatest honor history can bestow is the title of peacemaker. This honor now beckons America"
- President Nixon approved the bombing of Cambodia
- A Los Angeles court convicted Robert Kennedy assassin Sirhan Sirhan
- Mickey Mantle of the New York Yankees announced his retirement from baseball
- James Earl Ray pleaded guilty to the murder of Dr. Martin Luther King, Jr. in Memphis, Tennessee, and was sentenced to 99 years in prison
- Levi's began to sell bell-bottomed jeans
- The Supreme Court unanimously struck down laws prohibiting private possession of obscene material
- Eighty armed, militant black students at Cornell University took over Willard Straight Hall and demanded a black studies program and total amnesty for their actions
- American troop levels in Vietnam peaked at 543,000; over 33,000 had been killed
- Walt Disney World construction began in Florida
- The musical review *Oh! Calcutta!* opened in New York
- Warren E. Burger was sworn in as chief justice of the United States
- Patrons at the Stonewall Inn, a gay bar in New York City's Greenwich Village, clashed with police; the incident was considered the birth of the gay rights movement
- A car driven by Senator Edward M. Kennedy (Democrat-Massachusetts) plunged off a bridge on Chappaquiddick Island near Martha's Vineyard; his passenger, 28-year-old Mary Jo Kopechne, died
- Astronaut Neil Armstrong took "One small step for man, one giant leap for mankind" after he and Edwin "Buzz" Aldrin made the first successful landing of a manned vehicle on the moon
- The U.S. space probe *Mariner 7* flew by Mars, sending back photographs and scientific data
- Four hundred thousand young people gathered at Max Yasgur's dairy farm in the Bethel hamlet of White Lake, New York, for the Woodstock music festival
- Ho Chi Minh, the leader of North Vietnam, died at age 79
- The Food and Drug Administration issued a report calling birth control pills safe
- *Marcus Welby, MD* and *The Brady Bunch* both premiered on ABC-TV
- Peace demonstrators staged activities across the country, including a candlelight march around the White House, as part of a moratorium against the Vietnam War
- The federal government banned artificial sweeteners known as cyclamates

Selected Prices, 1969

Artificial Fingernails, Set of 10	$0.49
Ballet Ticket, New York City Ballet	$4.95
Blender, Proctor	$13.49
Bunk Bed	$69.95
Child's Sundress	$12.00
Dishwasher	$207.95
Encyclopedia, 12 Volumes	$59.00
Slide Projector	$60.00
Tape Recorder, Four-Track, with Speakers	$198.95
Television, Magnavox	$650.00

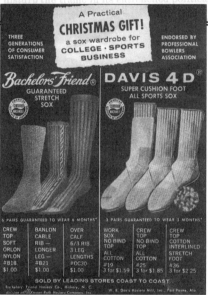

Timeline of American Indian Activism

1961

The National Indian Youth Council was organized to encourage greater self-sufficiency and autonomy.

1964

The Survival of American Indians formed to stage "fish-ins" to preserve off-reservation fishing rights in Washington State.

The Sioux made their first landing at the vacated Alcatraz prison, during which five Sioux Indians claimed the island under the Fort Laramie 1868 Sioux Treaty enabling Sioux Indians to take possession of surplus federal land.

1966

Senator George McGovern introduced a resolution highlighting the increased desire of Indian people to participate in decisions concerning their people and property.

1968

United Native Americans was founded in the San Francisco Bay Area to promote self-determination through Indian control of Indian affairs at every level.

The American Indian Movement was founded in Minneapolis to protect the city's Native American community from police abuse and to create job training and housing and education programs.

Mohawk Indians formed a blockade at the Cornwall International Bridge between the U.S. and Canada to protest U.S. restrictions on Native peoples' free movement between the two countries.

Congress passed the Indian Civil Rights Act, which required states to obtain tribal consent prior to extending any legal jurisdiction over an Indian reservation.

1969

The American Indian Center in San Francisco burned down; the loss of the center focused Indian attention on taking over Alcatraz for use as a new facility.

The 19-month occupation of Alcatraz began when a diverse group of about 90 Indians took over the abandoned island property.

Members of the American Indian Movement arrived at Alcatraz and gathered ideas about confrontational activism and land seizure as tools to confront the federal government's Indian policies.

F. 53—Alcatraz Island, San Francisco, Calif.

Copr. H. H. Tammen Co.

The right of taking fish, at all usual and accustomed grounds and stations, is further secured to said Indians, in common with all citizens of the Territory and of erecting temporary houses for the purpose of curing, together with the privilege of hunting and gathering roots and berries on open and unclaimed lands. Provided, however that they shall not take shell-fish from any beds staked or cultivated by citizens.

—Fishing-rights treaty between Territorial Governor Isaac Stevens and Western Washington tribes, 1854

MAVERICK

THE WEST

TRUE STORIES OF THE OLD WEST

MAY 1967　　　　PDC　　　　35¢

URLING C. COE– Adventures of a Range Doctor

JESSE JAMES– King of the Bandits

INKPADUTA– The Scarlet Point

OF SQUAWS AND SQUAWMEN

TALES OF PARADISE, ARIZONA

And when the last Red Man shall have perished, and the memory of my tribe shall have become a myth among the White Men, these shores will swarm with the invisible dead of my tribe, and when your children think themselves alone in the field, the store, the shop, upon the highway, or in the silence of the pathless woods, they will not be alone. . . . At night when the streets of your cities and villages are silent and you think them deserted, they will throng with the returning hosts that once filled and still love this beautiful land. The White Man will never be alone.

—Chief Sealth at the Medicine Creek Treaty ceremony, 1854

Our Indians seem to us very much like white people.

—Federal agent for the Puyallup Reservation, 1889

"CONSERVATION, Reprieve for the Redwoods," *Time*, September 27, 1968:

The giant redwood tree, which grows only in the foggy climes of Northern California and Oregon, is one of the world's oldest and largest plants. Yet it is more than a plant and more than a relic. With huge trunks soaring hundreds of feet into the sky, a forest of *Sequoia sempervirens* is a life unto itself, binding a despoiled planet to its pristine past. As California naturalist Duncan McDuffie said: "To enter a grove of redwoods is to step within the portals of a cathedral more beautiful and more serene than any erected by the hands of man."

For 50 years, conservationists have been fighting a losing battle to save the redwoods. Their mahogany-hued, durable lumber (it virtually defies dry rot) is highly prized for its structural and decorative uses. To date, the battle has gone to the chainsaw. Where there were once two million acres of virgin redwoods, only 250,000 stand today. Last week, as Congress sent to President Johnson a bill establishing the nation's first Redwood National Forest, the conservationists won a significant victory. . . .

Much of the credit for saving the redwoods belongs to the California-based Sierra Club and San Francisco's Save-the-Redwoods League, which was founded 50 years ago. Creation of the park comes none too soon. At the present rate of logging, the virgin stands of redwoods would last only another 20 years, a mere second in the lives of trees that were swaying in the Pacific breeze when Christ was born.

The Washington State Court ruling concerning fishing rights, 1916:

The premise of Indian sovereignty we reject. The treaty is not to be interpreted in that light. At no time did our ancestors in getting title to this continent ever regard the aborigines as other than mere occupants, and incompetent occupants, of the soil. Any title that could be had from them was always disdained . . . only that title was esteemed that came from white men.

The Indian was a child, and a dangerous child of nature to be both protected and restrained. In his nomadic life he was to be left, so long as civilization did not demand his region. When it did demand that region, he was to be allotted a more confined area with permanent subsistence.

These arrangements were but the announcement of our benevolence which, notwithstanding our frequent frailties, has been continuously displayed. Neither Rome nor sagacious Britain ever dealt more liberally with their subject races than we with these savage tribes, whom it was generally tempting and always easy to destroy and whom we have so often permitted to squander vast areas of fertile land before our eyes.

AT SPARROWS POINT, near Baltimore, high-efficiency venturi scrubbers backed up by water cyclones and thickeners are recovering better than 99% of the fine fume particles from the Basic Oxygen Furnaces. Left photo shows how the fumes would pour from the stacks if the control system had not been installed. Right photo shows the stacks when the scrubbers are in operation.

HERE'S HOW WE REDUCE AIR POLLUTION

Bethlehem Steel has invested $120-million in pollution-control equipment in the last 20 years. And we expect to spend many more millions in the years ahead to equip our plants with systems that will equal or exceed government requirements.

Our objective is quite simple. We want to be a good neighbor wherever we operate. And our efforts to keep the environment clean is one way we do our part.

BETHLEHEM STEEL

AT LOS ANGELES the "baghouse" dust-collecting system is one of our recent contributions to Southern California's anti-smog campaign. Left photo shows how the smoke would pour out if there were no control system. Right view shows the same building when the baghouse is in operation. This system removes about 120 tons of dust every week.

Invading Alcatraz, by Adam Fortunate Eagle, from Native American testimony by Peter Nabokov:

We set out from San Leando, my family and I, with our tribal outfits packed, and with $24 in beads and colored cloth arranged in a wooden bowl for the symbolic purchase of Alcatraz Island from the government. With a feel of optimism we were soon on the Nimitz Freeway driving for Fisherman's Wharf in San Francisco, and Pier 39.

The weather on Sunday morning, November 9, 1969, was beautiful and calm. This was a pretty strange thing we were doing. Indian people, twentieth-century urban Indians, gathering in tribal councils, student organizations, clubs, and families, and joined by concerned individuals from all over the Bay Area, with the intention of launching an attack on a bastion of the United States government. Instead of horses and bows and arrows of another era, we were riding in Fords and Chevys, armed only with our Proclamation but determined to bring about a change in federal policy affecting our people. . . .

At Fisherman's Wharf, we parked and joined a growing group of Indian students. When I learned that our scheduled boat was nowhere around I suggested that we stall while I looked for another. Richard Oakes went to the end of the pier to read our Proclamation, with Indians and television crews in tow, while I looked around. Then I noticed this beautiful three-masted barque that looked like it had come right out of the pages of maritime history. Its name was the *Monte Cristo,* and its owner, who, with tight pants and ruffled shirt looked like Errol Flynn, was Ronald Craig.

When I approached, he said, "Hey, I'm curious—what's going on over there with all those Indians?" I explained the fix we were in, pointing out the media contingent that had come to cover the landing. "I'll take you," he said, "on condition we get permission from the Coast Guard and that we carry no more than 50 people. The boat rides deep because of the keel. And I can't land on the Alcatraz dock. We'll circle a couple of times, a sort of sight-seeing tour to get your message across, OK?"

After he counted to make sure we were only 50, he fired off the little cannon on the bow. Here were Indians sailing on an old vessel to seek a new way of life for their people. I thought of the *Mayflower* and its crew of Pilgrims who landed on our shores. The history books say they were seeking new freedoms for themselves and their children which were denied in their homeland. Never mind that Plymouth Rock already belonged to someone else. What concerned them was their own fate, their own hopes. Now, 350 years later, its original citizens, to focus national attention on their struggle to regain those same basic rights, were making landfall on another rock.

1970–1979

With the Vietnam War still raging, interest in the environment rising and America's troubled cities deteriorating, the turbulent legacy of the 1960s flowed into the 1970s. Racial unrest rampaged through the public schools, and books, movies, and magazines tested American mores, while protests against the Vietnam War continued. Mix in a volatile economy that caused the cost of living to spiral and the result was an America stripped of its ability to dominate the world economy. A scandal-plagued president was driven from office, and another found his presidency—and the nation—held hostage by Iran. Gas prices skyrocketed when Arab oil producers declared an embargo on oil shipments to the United States, setting off shortages and gas rationing for the first time in 30 years. The sale of automobiles plummeted, unemployment and inflation nearly doubled, and the buying power of Americans fell dramatically.

The economy, handicapped by the devaluation of the dollar and inflation, did not fully recover for more than a decade, while the fast-growing economies of Japan and western Europe, especially West Germany, mounted direct competitive challenges to American manufacturers. The value of imported manufactured goods skyrocketed from 14 percent of U.S. domestic production in 1970 to 40 percent in 1979. The inflationary cycle of recession returned in 1979 to disrupt markets, throw thousands out of work and prompt massive downsizing of companies—awakening many once-secure workers to the reality of the changing economic market. A symbol of the era was the pending bankruptcy of Chrysler Corporation whose cars were so outmoded and plants so inefficient they could not compete against Japanese imports. The federal government was forced to extend loan guarantees to the company to prevent bankruptcy and the loss of thousands of jobs.

The appointment of Paul Volcker as the chairman of the Federal Reserve Board late in the decade gave the economy the distasteful medicine it needed. To cope with inflation, Volcker slammed on the economic brakes, restricted growth of the money supply, and curbed inflation. As a result, he pushed interest rates to nearly 20 percent—their highest level since the Civil War. Almost immediately the sale of automobiles and expensive items stopped. The decade was also marred by the deep divisions caused by the Vietnam War. For more than 10 years the war had been fought on two fronts: at home and abroad. As a result, U.S. policy makers conducted the war with one eye always focused on national opinion. When it ended, the Vietnam War had been the longest war in American history, having cost $118 billion and resulted in 56,000 dead, 300,000 wounded, and the loss of American prestige abroad.

The decade was a time not only of movements, but also of moving. In the 1970s, the shift of manufacturing facilities to the South from New England and the Midwest accelerated. The Sunbelt became the new darling of corporate America. By the late 1970s, the South, including Texas, had gained more than a million manufacturing jobs, while the Northeast and Midwest lost nearly two million. Rural North Carolina had the highest percentage of manufacturing of any state in the nation, along with the lowest blue-collar wages and the lowest unionization rate in the country. The Northeast lost more than traditional manufacturing jobs.

The largest and most striking of all the social actions of the early 1970s was the Women's Liberation Movement; it fundamentally reshaped American society. Since the 1950s, a small group of well-placed American women had attempted to convince Congress and the courts to bring about equality between the sexes. By the 1972, the National Organization for Women (NOW) multiplied in size, the first issue of *Ms. Magazine* sold out in a week, and women began demanding economic equality, the legalization of abortion, and the improvement of women's role in society. "All authority in our society is being challenged," said a Department of Health, Education and Welfare report. "Professional athletes challenge owners, journalists challenge editors, consumers challenge manufacturers . . . and young blue-collar workers, who have grown up in an environment in which equality is called for in all institutions, are demanding the same rights and expressing the same values as university graduates."

The decade also included the flowering of the National Welfare Rights Organization (NWRO), founded in 1966, which resulted in millions of urban poor demanding additional rights. The environmental movement gained recognition and momentum during the decade starting with the first Earth Day celebration in 1970 and the subsequent passage of the federal Clean Air and Clean Water acts. And the growing opposition to the use of nuclear power peaked after near calamity at Three Mile Island in Pennsylvania in 1979. As the formal barriers to racial equality came down, racist attitudes became unacceptable and the black middle class began to grow. By 1972, half of all Southern black children sat in integrated classrooms, and about one-third of all black families had risen economically into the ranks of the middle class.

The changes recorded for the decade included a doubling in the amount of garbage created per capita from 2.5 pounds to five pounds. California created a no-fault divorce law, Massachusetts introduces no-fault insurance, and health food sales reached $ 3 billion. By mid-decade, the so-called typical nuclear family, with working father, housewife, and two children, represented only seven percent of the population and the family size was falling. The average family size was 3.4 persons compared with 4.3 in 1920.

1970 PROFILE

ENVIRONMENTAL MOVEMENT: THE FIRST EARTH DAY

Miles Feimster, a teenager from Martinsville, Virginia, didn't consider himself an environmentalist, but he did like the idea of honoring the natural world by setting aside one day in its honor.

Life at Home

- Miles Feimster was part of a furniture family from a furniture town in the heart of a furniture manufacturing region.
- He grew up in company-provided housing, substandard in many ways but extremely affordable: the rent was $8.00 a month.
- His father prided himself on being financially conservative; the family was permitted one window fan to battle the sometimes brutal summer heat of Southside Virginia.
- The monthly electric bill averaged $15.00 a month.
- Although the family was the proud owner of an electric range, the wood-burning "warm morning" cook stove was still used in the fall, winter and spring.
- Indoor plumbing had not yet arrived at the company housing in Martinsville, Virginia; therefore, the family outhouse was located on a hillside away from Indian Spring, the family's source of clean water for drinking, bathing and clothes washing.
- For washing clothes, the family relied upon a Maytag wringer washer.
- The water was heated in a galvanized steel tub placed over a fire pit; rinsing was done in the larger tub filled with cool, clean water.
- Both tubs were filled by carrying water from the spring in a 36-gallon aluminum bucket.
- The outhouse received a biannual Red Devil lye treatment to combat odor and disease.

Miles Feimster supported Earth Day.

Miles grew up in housing provided by the furniture company his father worked for.

- Every third year it was relocated, with precautions taken to integrate the abandoned latrine safely back into the landscape.
- Because the home was surrounded by streams on three sides, the family re-ditched every spring to insure proper drainage and reduce the mosquito breeding areas.
- To augment the family's food supply and hold down costs, Miles raised bantam chickens for meat and eggs.
- Miles's young siblings, Allie, 14, and Hanson, 10, were entrusted with the job of selling surplus eggs to a neighbor.
- In addition, the family raised a Yorkshire hog each year that was located in a pen as far away from the house and water supply as possible.
- The family garden included tomatoes, corn, beans, potatoes, onions and greens.
- Miles's mother Addie's specialty was canning the crops at harvest; she also put up peaches, apples, jams and preserves for the coming winter.

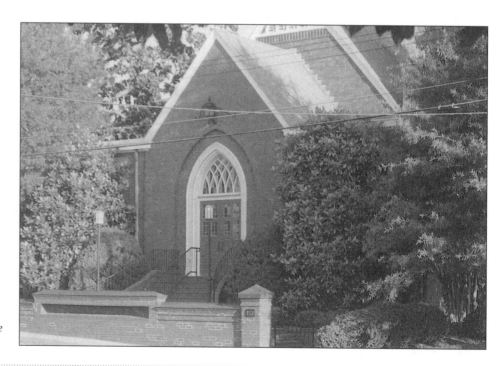

The church community was important to the Martinsville community.

- During the summer growing season, Addie Feimster enjoyed quilting, for which she had earned a highly esteemed reputation within the black and white communities of Martinsville.
- A Feimster quilt would fetch $30.00.
- Miles's favorite season was spring, which brought the opening of trout season on the Smith River.
- The rapidly moving river signaled new hope and opportunity.
- It was also the place where he began to understand the impact of man and his pollution on nature.
- At times, heavy industrial pollution gave the tender trout a metallic taste that diminished the joy of trout fishing and eating.
- But trout fishing was a cherished tradition in the Feimster household that improved the family table in all seasons.
- Miles Feimster's father, Nate, was a renowned local fisherman with many citation awards to prove his fish stories.
- He often credited his Cherokee heritage for his love of the wilds and his adeptness as a hunter.
- Every year he took down at least two deer, which were usually given to the local needy.
- Addie Feimster would not touch her husband's deer kills.

Miles's mother and sister.

Life at Work

- Eighteen-year-old Miles Feimster's participation in Earth Day, 1970, was ignited by a friend and classmate, Jan Lawless.
- Like Miles, she had grown up near the Smith River, playing along its banks and tributaries.
- It was she who had suggested that they participate in the Earth Day parade and teach-in at the local community college.
- Maybe this was a way to get people interested in the quality of the local air and water, Miles figured.
- He knew from experience that raw sewage was still pumped into the river in some places; on occasion the river changed color because of industrial discharges.
- And every teenager from the industrial areas of the town had seen the smokestack clouds rise and felt the resulting falling ash rainfall.
- Cleaning up the environment was not an abstract, theoretical concept for Miles.
- First, though, he would need approval to attend.
- Both his mother and grandmother wanted a promise that Earth Day was not going to be the type of protest in which a black teenager could be arrested, hosed or beaten.
- They had seen enough of that kind of protest.
- Miles's father and grandfather took for granted that something would go wrong.
- It was their nature to be cautious, especially with Miles pledging to ask hard questions about the very factories that supported the family.
- Pollution or not, the factories fed the community.
- Even though all wages were frozen by presidential mandate, to harness inflation, if a man could work 70 hours a week, that was prosperity.
- After Miles made the commitment to participate in the Earth Day environmental teach-in, he and his friend Jan were consumed by the possibilities.
- Most of their free time was spent in helping to prepare for the event scheduled for April 22, 1970.

Young Miles at home.

Jan encouraged Miles to participate in Earth Day.

- The date was part of a national campaign to raise awareness of environmental and conservationist issues.
- Significantly, the date was chosen by U.S. Senator Gaylord Nelson, a Democrat from Wisconsin, and Representative Paul R. McCloskey, a Republican from California.
- Environmental Teach-in Incorporated, a student-run organization, had been formed to coordinate the national campaign.
- Its goals and charter were clear and non-confrontational: organized by students with the approval of school authorities and political leaders, Earth Day sought to mobilize support for anti-pollution measures.
- Activities were created at more than 800 colleges and 2,000 high schools in every section of the nation.
- Even some of the nation's military bases, still on high alert because of the Vietnam War, elected to participate.
- In Martinsville, Virginia, biology instructor James M. McIntosh was named the local coordinator for Earth Day at Patrick Henry Community College.
- The announced topics for discussion included "What Is Pollution?," "What Is Being Done about It?," and "What Can the Individual Do to Help?"
- To kick off the teach-in, an Anti-Pollution Parade was scheduled for the afternoon of April 18, four days before Earth Day.
- Miles and Jan were eager to do their part.
- The parade was led by a hay wagon loaded with examples of pollutants, followed by students wearing gas masks and others carrying pollution protest signs.
- Jan and Miles both wore gas masks, which were hot.
- He was the only black teen in the parade and stayed toward the middle of the protest march in case the police decided to interrupt the proceedings.
- When the march ended, the 100 high school and college students who had participated were invigorated with the possibilities for change.
- To participate in the teach-in, which ran from 1:30 to 6:30 p.m. on Wednesday, April 22, Miles and Jan had to skip their afternoon high school classes—something they had never done before.

Local schools held Earth Day programs.

- The Earth Day protest had a high air of respectability—a far cry from the rag-tag anti-Vietnam War protests shown so prominently and so often on the nightly news.
- Virginia Assistant Attorney General Gerald Bailes was the keynote speaker, expounding on legal enforcement and pollution; local pediatrician Dr. John French spoke on the medical effects of pollution.
- Also included were speakers from the state Air Pollution Board and the Bureau of Solid Waste and Vector Control.
- For Miles, the impact of the day of protest began to sink in when he realized that he and Jan were part of a national movement, aimed directly at the burgeoning environmental crisis in the United States.
- At Martinsville High School, two students condemned pollution by carrying signs and riding a tricycle before school to illustrate the effect of automobiles on the environment.
- As part of the Earth Day festivities at Patrick Henry Community College, an automobile engine was laid to rest before the start of the various anti-pollution seminars and speeches on the environment.
- Martinsville City Manager Tom Noland participated on a panel representing private citizens' groups, industry and government agencies, and others concerning the effect of pollution on the area.
- Miles and Jan stayed to the end, enthralled by the possibilities for change and the opportunities ahead.

Faculty from the community college coordinated local events.

Earth Day Around the United States

- To celebrate the kick-off of Earth Day, Virginia Governor Linwood Holton signed a statement designating a Virginia "Improved Environment Week."
- Senator William Spong, Jr., an early advocate of the anti-pollution cause, spoke at a program sponsored by the Department of Environmental Sciences at the University of Virginia in Charlottesville.
- At the College of William and Mary in Williamsburg, Virginia, Dr. William Sirl, a California research physicist and a member of the Sierra Club, spoke on the "value of the wilderness."
- Nationally, 10 million public school children participated in teach-in programs.
- In New York City, cars were banned on Fifth Avenue while a picnic was held.
- In Louisville, Kentucky, 1,500 students crowded into a concourse at Atherton High School to illustrate the problems of overpopulation.
- Nationwide, students rode horses, roller skates and skateboards rather than cars or buses.
- While speaking at the University of California, Berkeley, Senator Gaylord Nelson, who had originated the Earth Day idea, proposed national policies on land use, herbicides and pesticides, national standards for air and water pollution, and a ban on oil drilling.
- New Jersey Governor William Cahill signed a bill creating a state Department of Environmental Protection.

- New York Governor Nelson Rockefeller signed a bill coordinating anti-pollution and conservation activities.
- Maryland Governor Marvin Mandel signed 21 bills and joint legislative resolutions dealing with the environment.
- During a speech in Philadelphia, Pennsylvania, Senator Edmond Muskie of Maine called for an environmental resolution against pollution.
- New York City Mayor John V. Lindsey rode an electric-powered car to his appointments that day, and told a Union Square rally, "There is a simple question: do we want to live or die?"
- In Washington, DC, Senator Bayh of Indiana called for a national environmental control agency to "conquer pollution as we have conquered space."
- Not all congressional speakers were received warmly: New York Senator Charles E. Goodell was greeted at a New York University by leaflets calling his speech "the biggest source of air pollution."
- Despite the participation of millions, arrests were few: in Boston a group protesting the air pollution of supersonic transport planes blocked the ticket counter at Logan International Airport, resulting in 13 arrests.
- While much of the nation observed Earth Day reverently, the Daughters of the American Revolution branded the environmental movement "distorted and exaggerated."

HISTORICAL SNAPSHOT
1970

- Woodstock, New York farmers sued Max Yasgur for $35,000 for damages caused by the Woodstock rock festival
- The Boeing 747 made its maiden voyage
- Diana Ross and the Supremes performed their last concert together, at the Frontier Hotel in Las Vegas
- President Nixon nominated G. Harrold Carswell to the Supreme Court, but the nomination was defeated because of controversy over Carswell's past racial views
- General Motors redesigned its automobiles to run on unleaded fuel
- The Chicago Seven defendants were found innocent of conspiring to incite riots at the 1968 Democratic National Convention
- A nuclear non-proliferation treaty went into effect, ratified by 43 nations
- The National Mobilization Committee to End the War in Vietnam organized a trip to Hanoi to meet with the prime minister of North Vietnam
- President Nixon signed a measure banning cigarette advertising on radio and television
- *Apollo 13* was crippled on the way to the moon, preventing a planned moon landing
- President Nixon announced to a national television audience that the United States was sending troops into Cambodia "to win the just peace that we desire," sparking widespread anti-war protests
- National Guardsmen fired at anti-war protestors at Kent State University, killing four and wounding 11 others, spawning campus protests nationwide
- The Beatles' film *Let It Be* premiered
- Two black students at Jackson State University in Mississippi were killed when police opened fire during student protests
- One hundred thousand people demonstrated in New York's Wall Street district in support of U.S. policy in Vietnam and Cambodia
- The federal government shut off power and fresh water supplies from the American Indians who had claimed Alcatraz Island
- Kenneth A. Gibson of Newark, New Jersey, became the first black person to win a mayoral election in a major Northeast city
- The Twenty-sixth Amendment, which lowered the voting age from 21 to 18, was signed into law
- The U.S. Senate voted overwhelmingly to repeal the Gulf of Tonkin resolution
- Heavyweight boxing champion Muhammed Ali's refusal of induction into the U.S. Army was heard by the Supreme Court
- Casey Kasem's *American Top 40* debuted on Los Angeles radio
- Gary Trudeau's comic strip *Doonesbury* first appeared
- The U.N. General Assembly accepted membership of the People's Republic of China
- The U.S. Senate voted to give 48,000 acres of New Mexico back to the Taos Indians
- The World Trade Center Towers in New York City were completed
- *Hello, Dolly!* closed at the St. James Theater on Broadway after a run of 2,844 performances

Selected Prices, 1970

Biofeedback Monitor Kit	$125.50
Camera, Kodak Pocket	$28.00
Hair Spray, Adorn	$1.09
Hotel Room, Sheraton, New York City	$22.00
Mattress, Queen Size, Two Pieces	$399.95
Microwave Oven, Radarange	$450.00
Pressure Cooker	$18.99
Record Album, Simon & Garfunkel's *Bridge Over Troubled Water*	$5.98
Telephone, Western Electric	$6.95
Wheelbarrow	$34.95

Environment Timeline

1898

Cornell became the first college to offer a program in forestry.

The U.S. Rivers and Harbors Act banned the pollution of navigable waters.

1902

The U.S. Bureau of Reclamation was established.

1903

The nation's first wildlife refuge was formed when President Theodore Roosevelt protected Pelican Island, Florida, from hunters decimating the island's bird population.

1905

The United States Forest Service was established within the Department of Agriculture to manage forest reserves.

1908

The Grand Canyon in Arizona was set aside as a national monument.

President Theodore Roosevelt hosted the first Governors' Conference on Conservation to inventory America's natural resources.

Chlorination was first used extensively at U.S. water treatment plants.

1911

Canada, Japan, Russia, and the United States signed a treaty to limit the annual harvest of northern fur seals.

The Weeks Act appropriated $9 million to purchase six million acres of land in the eastern United States for the purpose of establishing national forests.

1913

President Woodrow Wilson approved a plan to dam the Hetch Hetchy Valley to serve as a reservoir for the city of San Francisco.

1914

Martha, the last passenger pigeon, died in the Cincinnati Zoo and became a symbol of species extinction.

1915

Dinosaur National Monument was established in Colorado.

1916

The National Park Service and the National Park System were established to conserve scenery, wildlife and "historic objects" for future generations.

1917

President Woodrow Wilson created Alaska's Mount McKinley National Park.

1918

The Save-the-Redwoods League was created.

The hunting of migratory bird species was restricted by a treaty between the U.S. and Canada.

continued

Timeline . . . (continued)

1919

Congress established the Grand Canyon National Park in Arizona.

1920

The U.S. Mineral Leasing Act regulated mining on federal lands.

1922

The Izaak Walton League was established as a nonprofit research and advocacy organization.

1924

Naturalist Aldo Leopold secured the designation of Gila National Forest in New Mexico as America's first extensive wilderness area.

1928

The Boulder Canyon Project (Hoover Dam) was authorized to bring irrigation, electric power and flood control systems to the Western United States.

1930

Chlorofluorocarbons (CFCs) were hailed as safe refrigerants because of their nontoxic and non-combustible properties.

1933

The Tennessee Valley Authority was created lo develop the Tennessee River for flood control, navigation, electric power, agriculture and forestry.

1935

Aldo Leopold, Robert Marshall, Benton MacKaye, Robert Sterling Yard and others joined to form the Wilderness Society.

1947

Everglades National Park was established in Florida.

Effigy Mounds National Monument was established in Iowa.

1956

Congress passed the Colorado River Storage Project Bill halting dam construction within any national park or monument.

1961

Investigators in the U.S. Adirondacks confirmed that acid rain was killing some animal species living in and around the lakes.

1962

Silent Spring by Rachel Carson exposed the dangers of pesticides.

The Padre Island National Seashore was established in Texas.

continued

Timeline . . . (continued)

1963

Congress passed the first Clean Air Act.

1964

Congress passed the Wilderness Act, setting up the National Wilderness Preservation System.

1965

Congress passed the Solid Waste Disposal Act, the first major solid waste legislation.

1966

Congress passed the Rare and Endangered Species Act.

1967

Scientists predicted that increased amounts of carbon dioxide in the atmosphere would lead to global warming.

The bald eagle, California condor, whooping crane, gray wolf, and grizzly bear were placed on the Endangered Species List.

Congress passed the Air Quality Act.

1968

Congress passed the Wild and Scenic Rivers Act, identifying areas of scenic beauty for preservation and recreation.

President Lyndon Johnson signed the Central Arizona Project into law, protecting the Colorado River from damming.

North Cascades National Park was established in Washington State.

Redwoods National Park was established in California.

1970

An estimated 20 million people participated in the first Earth Day demonstrations and activities across the country.

The National Environmental Policy Act was signed into law, which required an analysis of the environmental impacts of federal actions.

The U.S. Environmental Protection Agency began operations.

American and peregrine falcons were placed on the Endangered Species List.

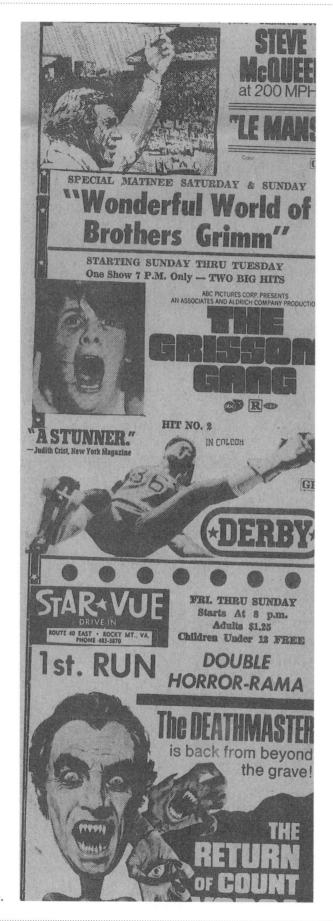

At the movies in 1970.

"How the First Earth Day Came About," Speech by Senator Gaylord Nelson, founder of Earth Day, 1993:

What was the purpose of Earth Day? How did it start? These are the questions I am most frequently asked.

Actually, the idea for Earth Day evolved over a period of seven years starting in 1962. For several years, it had been troubling me that the state of our environment was simply a non-issue in the politics of the country. Finally, in November 1962, an idea occurred to me that was, I thought, a virtual cinch to put the environment into the political "limelight" once and for all. The idea was to persuade President Kennedy to give visibility to this issue by going on a national conservation tour. I flew to Washington to discuss the proposal with Attorney General Robert Kennedy, who liked the idea. So did the president. The president began his five-day, 11-state conservation tour in September 1963. For many reasons, the tour did not succeed in putting the issue onto the national political agenda. However, it was the germ of the idea that ultimately flowered into Earth Day.

I continued to speak on environmental issues to a variety of audiences in some 25 states. All across the country, evidence of environmental degradation was appearing everywhere, and everyone noticed except the political establishment. The environmental issue simply was not to be found on the nation's political agenda. The people were concerned, but the politicians were not.

After President Kennedy's tour, I still hoped for some idea that would thrust the environment into the political mainstream. Six years would pass before the idea that became Earth Day occurred to me while on a conservation speaking tour out West in the summer of 1969. At the time, anti-Vietnam War demonstrations, called "teach-ins," had spread to college campuses all across the nation. Suddenly, the idea occurred to me: why not organize a huge grassroots protest over what was happening to our environment?

I was satisfied that if we could tap into the environmental concerns of the general public and infuse the student anti-war energy into the environmental cause, we could generate a demonstration that would force this issue onto the political agenda. It was a big gamble, but worth a try. Reporting on the astonishing proliferation of environmental events:

"Rising concern about the environmental crisis is sweeping the nation's campuses with an intensity that may be on its way to eclipsing student discontent over the war in Vietnam . . . a national day of observance of environmental problems . . . is being planned for next spring . . . when a nationwide environmental 'teach-in' . . . coordinated from the office of Senator Gaylord Nelson is planned. . . ."

It was obvious that we were headed for a spectacular success on Earth Day. It was also obvious that grassroots activities had ballooned beyond the capacity of my U.S. Senate office staff to keep up with the telephone calls, paperwork, inquiries, etc. In mid-January, three months before Earth Day, John Gardner, founder of Common Cause, provided temporary space for a Washington, DC headquarters. I staffed the office with college students and selected Denis Hayes as coordinator of activities.

Earth Day worked because of the spontaneous response at the grassroots level. We had neither the time nor resources to organize 20 million demonstrators and the thousands of schools and local communities that participated. That was the remarkable thing about Earth Day. It organized itself.

"Sky Spies to Watch Pollution," *Martinsville Bulletin* (Virginia), March 3, 1970:

Air and water pollution can be monitored effectively and traced to the source by survey satellites being developed by the United States, researchers reported today.

Two teams of researchers who are testing camera and sensor systems for the satellites, the first of which will be launched in March 1972, made their report to an Earth Conference. . . .

The application with the broadest current user interest is detecting elements of water pollution, tracing them to their source, and measuring the dispersion and concentration of the pollutants.

To illustrate, the MIT-NASA team showed a picture of Massachusetts Bay, near Salem, and identified a plume-like image as the flow from a combined sanitary and storm sewer and a smaller plume as a surface slick created by a power plant coolant.

"Pollution Clean-up of Nation Will Take Time, Experts Warn," by Alton Blakeslee, *Martinsville Bulletin*, March 19, 1970:

The galloping popular campaign to clean up the nation's polluted environment won't witness some magical quick fix.

And that is worrying some experts in pollution control.

They are concerned that enthusiasm will fade when the drive to clean up air, water and land runs into inevitable practical realities, even if given all the goodwill in the world to do the job.

Disappointment and fading interest could deflate the pressures to do what is really required—a continuing commitment and motivation to raise the money, to pass and enforce the laws, to develop technology and to do all the work first to halt and then correct manmade insults to the environment. And then to keep improving antipollution controls as population expands.

As one reality, take a river basin which is being polluted by raw sewage from a number of towns.

By popular demand, even law, all towns are asked to halt their pollution, right now. People along other rivers make similar demands.

But would there be enough engineers to make the essential surveys, then to plan and design the sewage treatment plants, or would there be enough skilled construction firms—given contracts for the lowest bid—to build all the plants for all the towns and cities at the same time?

The point is raised by Reinholt W. Thieme, a deputy assistant secretary of the Interior, not in terms of suggesting any slowdown, but merely to point out that some cities might have to wait their turn to complete the clean-up of the entire river.

Seventy percent of the solid particles contaminating urban air have not been identified, and even if we had limitless resources we could not formulate really effective control programs because we know so little about the origin, nature and effects of most air pollutants.

—Dr. Rene Dubos of Rockefeller University

"Conservationists Disappointed," *Martinsville Bulletin*, April 2, 1970:

Conservationists have expressed disappointment at President Nixon's failure to appoint a clearly qualified environmentalist as undersecretary of the Interior.

But they withheld judgment on Nixon's choice of multimillionaire Fred J. Russell, an unknown in the field of environment and resources, to succeed the highly respected Russell E. Train, the No. 2 job at Interior.

In a sense, some prominent conservation spokesmen said, the calm greeting of Russell amounts to a vote of confidence in Interior Secretary Hickel.

"Leaded Gasoline Fights Critics as Anti-Pollution Drive Grows," *Martinsville Bulletin*, March 17, 1970:

The automobile industry is urging the petroleum industry to get the lead out—literally—to help clean up the nation's air. The lead is tetraethyl lead, which has been used in gasoline since its anti-knock qualities were discovered by Thomas Midgley, Jr. in 1921.

The petroleum people say they will be happy to supply unleaded gasoline any time Detroit mass-produces engines that can use it. The automakers say they will start building the engines as soon as the oil men give them the specifications of the fuel.

Now a third interested party has gotten into the act.

J. L. Kimberley, executive vice president of the Lead Industries Association, claims that no studies have shown any health hazard to the public from the lead in gasoline. Not only that, we don't know what health hazards might result from widespread use of unleaded gasoline, he says.

1971 Profile

The Peace Movement: Vietnam Veterans Against the War

After two tours of duty in Vietnam, James Delucca joined the Vietnam Veterans Against the War to protest war crimes that were taking place as a result of American policies and to assist Vietnam veterans in gaining the rights and privileges awarded to other vets.

Life at Home

- James Delucca was conceived in a 1,200-square-foot home 30 miles north of Philadelphia, in a moment of enthusiasm shortly after World War II ended.
- The first-born son of a World War II veteran, James was often told how blessed he was to have clothes on his back and food on the table.
- His father worked as a warehouse manager for a company that manufactured air conditioner systems; James's mother was an elementary school teacher.
- The family was very patriotic and felt it was their duty to display an American flag on their front doorstep every day.
- When the forecast called for rain, James's father would make him take down and properly fold the flag with him.
- He was taught never to let the flag touch the ground or to show disrespect for the people who fought for the freedoms that they enjoyed.
- James was consumed with playing war with his friends, who pretended to be American heroes fighting against the evil Germans or the Japanese devils.
- All the while, James's father stayed on alert, positive that soon a nuclear attack would end the world as he knew it.
- He even worked with the neighbors to build a bomb shelter stocked with canned goods and water, just to be safe.
- The economy was growing rapidly in postwar America, with people buying automobiles, televisions and, of course, air conditioning systems.

James Deluca: Vietnam vet turned anti-war protester.

James was an infantry soldier.

- The gross national product grew from 200 million in 1940 to over 500 million by 1960, giving rise to an expanding middle class in America.
- As James got older, his father often said, "There is no greater honor than to die for your country."
- James also learned about Communism and the devastating effect it could have if it spread throughout the world.
- His Catholic priest told the congregation it was a good thing to kill Communists.
- James wanted to be a hero like his father.
- In 1965, with high school winding down and the Vietnam War escalating, James enlisted in the army.
- Many of his friends did not believe that the United States belonged in the war, especially in a country no one could find on a map.
- James's father lectured him about weak, unpatriotic people; when America called, his father said, a patriot responded.
- James responded with two tours of duty in the jungles of Vietnam.

Life at Work

- During his first tour, James Delucca was an infantry soldier.
- War was wet, bewildering, exciting, and depressing.
- Within weeks of arrival, he participated in a night-patrol firefight that haunted his dreams for months.
- Almost a third of the men in his unit had been killed or wounded within the first six months.
- James witnessed ambushes, torture and death until he was almost numb to its reality.
- There was no time to be a patriot; in Vietnam it was either fight or die.
- He could never explain why he signed up for a second tour; maybe fighting was all he knew.
- The second time he was in-country, sleeping was impossible, especially when it rained.
- By late 1967, the fighting grew more intense, the strategy of fighting more inexplicable, dissatisfaction with the war more pronounced.
- One day, he said out loud, "This is pointless."
- At that moment, he was ready to see the end of a war that turned kids into killers.
- James was shot twice in his left leg in March of 1968.
- He almost bled to death because both bullets hit his upper thigh.
- He was moved to a military hospital and sent back to the states after recovering from his injury.
- When he returned, he saw that there was almost as much conflict in the states as there had been in Vietnam; thousands of middle class Americans were demonstrating against the war he had been fighting.
- However, his father was still a proud patriot.
- Feeling nothing like the person who had left his family and friends after high school, James moved to New York City.

In Vietnam, it was either fight or die.

- He applied for and received a job with a furniture store in uptown Manhattan and became an assistant manager after only eight months.
- As he looked for a way to become involved in the peace movement, he saw anti-war demonstrators passing his store one day carrying a banner that read "Vietnam Veterans Against the War."
- James was intrigued.
- Over the next couple of months he followed the progress of these veterans from a distance as they participated in debates and attracted coverage in *The New York Times*.
- People were actually listening to what they had to say.

Protesting the war became a full time job for James.

- Intrigued by their message, James officially joined the Vietnam Veterans Against the War in October of 1969 and was immediately asked to help active-duty soldiers understand their alternatives to war.
- But when he participated in his first full-scale demonstration behind the banner of VVAW, he was able to give full-throated expression to his frustration.
- James finally felt like he was part of something he could believe in.
- In September 1970, he was one of the first vets to sign up for a march that retraced the trip of George Washington's Revolutionary rag-tag army to reach Valley Forge.
- Dramatically enough, the march was called RAW for Rapid American Withdrawal.
- The purpose was to give Americans a feel for the types of conditions that their soldiers were experiencing.
- The Rapid American Withdrawal march had the potential to teach people—even his father—the absolute horrors of the war in Vietnam.
- For weeks James and other veterans posted flyers all over New York City designed to shock: "Help Us To End This War Before They Turn Your Son Into A Butcher!"
- The march was directed at middle America; the VVAW wanted President Nixon's "silent majority" to experience the war.
- In all, 150 veterans joined Operation RAW for the 86-mile march from Morristown, New Jersey, to Valley Forge State Park.
- Finally, veterans who had served in the jungles of Vietnam could expose the horrible conditions there as well as the war crimes.
- On the day of the march, all of the veterans dressed in army fatigue and those who received purple hearts wrapped a red-stained gauze armband around one of their arms.
- They all carried toy M16 rifles.
- Most had long hair, beards and a look of determination; James thought them a fearsome group.
- During the march the veterans acted out a number of powerful scenes, assisted by professional actors, who often portrayed captured Viet Cong soldiers or terrified civilians.
- Whenever the march arrived at a town, the vets chained the terrified actors together as Vietnam hostages and screamed and pushed the actors to the ground.

photo by Lana Reeves.

- The marchers then fired their toy weapons at fleeing civilian actors or simulated the torture interrogation of a suspected Viet Cong prisoner.
- No ears were cut off during the brutal questioning, but they came close, James observed.
- At times, the veterans mixed the past and present so powerfully that the actors were truly terrified; Americans witnessing the guerilla theater were horrified and confused by what they saw.
- The press was mystified by the display of street theater.
- Some felt that these demonstrations were idiotic and pointless; others claimed they demonstrated how bad the conditions in Vietnam really were.
- Hundreds of people followed the march with cameras documenting the entire event; 1,500 greeted the VVAW when they reached Valley Forge Park.
- No matter how the public felt about the protest, James knew the VVAW was being heard and making a strong national impact.
- James then quit his job to help organize the Winter Soldier Investigation in 1971.
- His father was scandalized and told James he would not be welcome at the annual Thanksgiving gathering.
- The Winter Soldiers Investigation intended to gather testimonies of war crimes that were taking place as a result of American war policies.
- It was time to lay the blame for atrocities at the feet of those who made policy, not the soldiers who carried them out.

"Are you hiding a Viet Cong in there?"

Life in the Community: New York City

- Vietnam Veterans Against the War was founded by six Vietnam war veterans after they marched together with over 400,000 other protesters in the April 15, 1967 Spring Mobilization to End the War anti-war demonstration.
- After talking to members of the Veterans for Peace group at that march, the veterans discovered there was no organization representing Vietnam veterans.
- Their purpose was to give voice to the growing opposition among returning servicemen to the decade-long war in Indochina.
- VVAW also took up the struggle for the rights and needs of veterans.
- In 1970, they started the first discussion groups to deal with traumatic after-effects of war.
- They were instrumental in exposing the harmful health effects of exposure to chemical defoliants such as Agent Orange.
- They also exposed the neglect of many disabled vets in VA hospitals and helped draft legislation to improve educational benefits and create job programs.

HISTORICAL SNAPSHOT
1971

- Ohio agreed to pay $675,000 to relatives of Kent State victims
- *Masterpiece Theatre* premiered on PBS with host Alistair Cooke
- The situation comedy *All in the Family*, with Carroll O'Connor as Archie Bunker, began on CBS TV
- A federal grand jury indicted Rev. Philip Berrigan and five others on charges of plotting to kidnap Henry Kissinger
- The 1964 Gulf of Tonkin resolution, which amounted to a declaration of war against Vietnam, was repealed by Congress
- Charles Manson and three women followers were convicted in Los Angeles of murder in the 1969 slayings of seven people, including actress Sharon Tate
- OPEC decided to set oil prices without consulting buyers
- Two *Apollo 14* astronauts walked on the moon
- The U.S. Capitol building was bombed in protest of U.S. involvement in Laos
- Senator Edward Kennedy estimated that 25,000 Vietnamese civilians had been killed in the previous year
- Army Lt. William L. Calley, Jr. was convicted of murdering at least 22 Vietnamese civilians in the My Lai massacre
- President Nixon pledged a withdrawal of 100,000 more men from Vietnam by December
- The U.S. Supreme Court upheld the use of busing to achieve racial desegregation in schools
- Anti-war protesters calling themselves the Mayday Tribe began four days of demonstrations in Washington aimed at shutting down the nation's capital
- President Nixon ordered John Haldeman to do more wiretapping and political espionage against the Democrats
- The U.S. Occupational Safety and Health Administration (OSHA) was created
- Federal marshals, FBI agents and special forces swarmed Alcatraz Island and removed the Native American occupiers: five women, four children and six unarmed men
- *The New York Times* published the Pentagon Papers, leaked to it by Daniel Ellsberg
- "It's Too Late" by Carole King peaked at #1 on the pop singles chart and stayed there for five weeks
- The United States Supreme Court overturned the draft evasion conviction of boxer Muhammad Ali
- The Twenty-sixth Amendment to the Constitution was ratified, lowering the minimum voting age from 21 to 18
- The United States turned over complete responsibility of the Demilitarized Zone to South Vietnamese units
- President Nixon announced he would visit the People's Republic of China to seek a "normalization of relations"

Selected Prices, 1971

Apartment, NYC, Two-Bedroom, Month	$475.00
Coloring Book	$0.10
Condoms, Nine	$3.00
Jeans, Lady Wrangler	$15.00
Jewel Case, Gucci	$99.00
Pipe	$3.95
Potter's Wheel	$55.00
Puppy, Husky	$150.00
Slide Rule	$2.95
Wok	$17.50

You'll thank Live-Ins for making it with Cotton, at a time like this.

For the sporting life, indoors or out, 83% of American men want comfort first in clothing.* Cotton is comfortable because it breathes. Live-Ins™ wisely makes these sports minded match ups in Cone Mills' denim look 100% cotton chambray. If you're into the sporting season, get into the proper uniform.

That way, you'll feel good, whether you take anything home or not. Left, western jacket, $14; jeans, $11. Right, shirt jacket, $14; pants, $12. Tops, S, M, L, XL, pants, 26-38 S, M, L, XL. Denim blue or faded blue. Live-Ins at all fine stores.

*National Clothing Study by Opinion Research Corp.

1370 AVE. OF THE AMERICAS, NEW YORK, N.Y. 10019 • LOS ANGELES • RALEIGH • DALLAS • WASHINGTON   COTTON INCORPORATED

The extraordinary gift. Crowning jewel of the master craftsmen.

There are occasions when only the extraordinary will do. That is the time to give a solid sterling "Silver Imperial" or 14K gold-filled Sheaffer "Imperial Sovereign". Majestic masterpieces from the world's foremost penmaker. Luxuriantly crafted from clip to inlaid point. Single and gift sets from $17.50 to $75.00.

SHEAFFER.
the proud craftsmen

SHEAFFER, WORLD-WIDE, A textron COMPANY

8 cars. $4,385.

The Audi
It's a lot of cars for the money.

Suggested retail price East Coast P.O.E. for 100LS $4,385. Leatherette upholstery optional, at extra cost. West Coast P.O.E. slightly higher. Local taxes and other dealer delivery charges, if any, additional.

Vietnam War Timeline

1950

The United States sent the first shipload of arms aid to pro-French Vietnam.

1954

The Viet Minh overran the French fortress at Dien Bien Phu.

1955

The first U.S. advisers to South Vietnam were sent to train the South Vietnamese Army.

1956

President Dwight Eisenhower said the French were "involved in a hopelessly losing war in Indochina."

1961

President John Kennedy ordered 100 "special forces" troops to South Vietnam.

1962

President Kennedy ordered a build-up of American troops in Thailand to counter Communist attacks in Laos.

1963

South Vietnamese President Diem and his brother were assassinated outside of Saigon.

1964

The U.S. military contingent in Vietnam increased by 5,000 to total 21,000.

U.S. Navy destroyers *Maddox* and *C. Turner Joy* were reportedly attacked by North Vietnamese torpedo boats in the Gulf of Tonkin.

Congress approved the Gulf of Tonkin resolution affirming "all necessary measures to repel any armed attack against the forces of the United States."

The U.S. declined an offer of secret peace talks with North Vietnam.

1965

A guerilla assault against the military barracks at Pleiku left eight Americans dead; President Johnson ordered a retaliatory air strike against North Vietnam known as Operation Rolling Thunder.

Alice Herz set herself on fire in Detroit shortly after President Johnson announced major troop increases and the bombing of North Vietnam.

Hanoi restated a peace proposal.

Quaker Norman Morrison set himself on fire and died outside Secretary of Defense Robert McNamara's Pentagon office.

Congress appropriated $2.4 billion for the Vietnam war effort.

1966

The U.S. dropped 600,000 tons of bombs on North Vietnam.

Bombing began around Haiphong and Hanoi, North Vietnam.

1967

Nguyen Van Thieu was elected president of South Vietnam.

Congressman "Tip" O'Neill broke publicly with President Johnson and opposed continuation of the Vietnam War.

continued

Timeline ... *(continued)*

1968

The Communists launched the Tet Offensive, including attacks on nearly all 44 of the capitals of South Vietnam's provinces.

The My Lai Massacre occurred in Quang Ngai province.

President Johnson announced he would not seek re-election and ordered a bombing halt.

Draftees accounted for 38 percent of all American troops in Vietnam; over 12 percent of the draftees were college graduates.

1969

Expanded peace talks opened in Paris with representatives of the U.S., South Vietnam, North Vietnam, and the National Liberation Front (NLF).

President Richard Nixon proposed an "8-point Peace Plan."

President Nixon talked of a "Vietnamization" program to prepare the South Vietnamese to take over the U.S. combat role.

An estimated one million Americans across the United States participated in anti-war demonstrations, protest rallies and peace vigils.

President Nixon said he planned the withdrawal of all U.S. troops on a secret timetable.

Congress gave the president the authority to institute the "draft lottery" system aimed at inducting 19-year-olds.

Chief U.S. negotiator Henry Cabot Lodge and his deputy resigned, expressing pessimism concerning the course of the negotiations.

President Nixon announced the reduction of another 50,000 troops by mid-April 1970.

A presidential commission recommended the institution of an all-volunteer army and elimination of the draft.

1970

News of increased U.S. involvement in Laos and Cambodia surfaced.

President Nixon announced the withdrawal of another 150,000 troops over the next 12 months to lower troop strength to 284,000.

President Nixon issued an Executive Order that ended all occupational deferments and most paternity deferments.

U.S. forces invaded Cambodia, causing widespread war protests.

Four Kent State college students were shot to death by Ohio National Guardsmen during an anti-war protest, spawning protests nationwide.

A peaceful anti-war rally held in Washington, DC, was attended by about 80,000 people including 10 members of Congress.

The McGovern-Hatfield Amendment, providing for the withdrawal of all American troops by December 31, 1971, was defeated by the Senate.

continued

Timeline . . . *(continued)*

1971

President Nixon signed a bill repealing the Gulf of Tonkin resolution. The army began a campaign to intercept and confiscate personal mail containing anti-war material sent to soldiers in Vietnam.

A two-year extension of the draft passed the Congress; 48 percent of manpower for the army were draftees or "draft motivated."

Vietnam Veterans Against the War, numbering 2,300, came to Washington, DC, to participate in Dewey Canyon III, "a military incursion into the country of Congress"; many threw away their military medals and ribbons at the foot of the statue of Chief Justice John Marshall.

Ten days of protests by a group calling themselves the "Mayday Tribe" included attempted work stoppages at several federal offices in Washington, DC.

Approximately 10,000 anti-war protestors were arrested in Washington, DC.

The Pentagon Papers were published.

U.S. troop levels dropped to 156,800.

The U.S. heavily bombed military installations in North Vietnam.

"For They Are All Honorable Men," by Jan Barry, WIN Peace and Freedom through Nonviolent Action, March 15, 1971:

They came from Texas and Alabama, New York and California, Kansas and Montana. They wore jeans and business suits, afros and crew cuts, field jackets and love beads. They were all Vietnam veterans who had come to Detroit, Michigan, to testify to first-hand knowledge of American crimes in Indochina.

These were the obverse of Tom Paine's "summer soldiers and sunshine patriots." In Vietnam, they had been sergeants, lance corporals, captains, and in at least two cases, majors. They were the true heirs of the men who endured the long, bitter winter at Valley Forge. These were the veterans of Vietnam who, in the face of public apathy and indifference, and official hostility and harassment, refused to forget.

Appropriately, the Detroit war crimes hearings, organized by the Vietnam Veterans Against the War, a national organization of 5,000 members, were called the Winter Soldier Investigation. For these were, truly, the "winter soldiers" of the war in Vietnam.

A dozen at a time, division after division, each group spanning the six years American combat forces have been in Vietnam, they walked onto the public stage hour after hour for three full days (January 31-February 2) and presented their eyewitness accounts of prisoners tortured and killed, civilians intimidated and shot, villages bombarded and burned, borders illegally and secretly crossed, indiscriminate defoliation and bombing and artillery daily and nightly used, massacres large and small. . . .

Altogether, about 100 Vietnam veterans, from 1962 to the present, testified at the three-day hearings in Detroit's downtown Howard Johnson's Motor Lodge. Another 400-500 Vietnam veterans from all over the continental United States and Canada came and listened, added their support and conducted non-stop organizing meetings in the hallways and nearby rooms.

Much of the testimony was gruesomely familiar to even casual followers of the court-martial of Lt. William Calley. What was new was the evidence presented that the same grisly "incidents" permeated the experiences of men who had served in Vietnam in every year, in every major unit, in every region of Vietnam. One woman or child killed here, 30 killed there, a half-dozen somewhere else, 50 another day, in another place.

The pattern of daily, or near-daily American war atrocities year on end was too stark, and too thickly-woven, to be soon forgotten by those hundreds of Detroit and Canadian citizens who came to hear, 500 at a time, these men who so obviously had been there. Dozens of sober, concerned, middle-income and often middle-aged Detroiters had to be turned away for lack of room. The doubters were conspicuously hushed and few. . . .

Yet it remained by and large a hostile press. The liberal, mostly Eastern-establishment papers imposed a near-blackout on the hearings, while the conservative, mostly Midwestern press reveled in retorts such as "alleged veterans," and "so-called hearings," and other hackneyed tricks of the put-down trade.

President Nixon's Speech on "Vietnamization," November 3, 1969:

Let us all understand that the question before us is not whether some Americans are for peace and some Americans are against peace. The question at issue is not whether Johnson's war becomes Nixon's war.

The great question is: How can we win America's peace?

Well, let us turn now to the fundamental issue. Why and how did the United States become involved in Vietnam in the first place?

Fifteen years ago North Vietnam, with the logistical support of Communist China and the Soviet Union, launched a campaign to impose a Communist government on South Vietnam by instigating and supporting a revolution.

In response to the request of the Government of South Vietnam, President Eisenhower sent economic aid and military equipment to assist the people of South Vietnam in their efforts to prevent a Communist takeover. Seven years ago, President Kennedy sent 16,000 military personnel to Vietnam as combat advisers. Four years ago, President Johnson sent American combat forces to South Vietnam.

Now, many believe that President Johnson's decision to send American combat forces to South Vietnam was wrong. And many others, I among them, have been strongly critical of the way the war has been conducted. But the question facing us today is: Now that we are in the war, what is the best way to end it?

In January I could only conclude that the precipitate withdrawal of American forces from Vietnam would be a disaster not only for South Vietnam but for the United States and for the cause of peace. For the South Vietnamese, our precipitate withdrawal would inevitably allow the Communists to repeat the massacres which followed their takeover in the North 15 years before. They then murdered more than 50,000 people and hundreds of thousands more died in slave labor camps. We saw a prelude of what would happen in South Vietnam when the Communists entered the city of Hue last year. During their brief rule there, there was a bloody reign of terror in which 3,000 civilians were clubbed, shot to death, and buried in mass graves.

With the sudden collapse of our support, these atrocities of Hue would become the nightmare of the entire nation and particularly for the million and a half Catholic refugees who fled to South Vietnam when the Communists took over in the North.

For the United States, this first defeat in our nation's history would result in a collapse of confidence in American leadership, not only in Asia but throughout the world.

Three American Presidents have recognized the great stakes involved in Vietnam and understood what had to be done. . . .

The defense of freedom is everybody's business, not just America's business. And it is particularly the responsibility of the people whose freedom is threatened. In the previous administration, we Americanized the war in Vietnam. In this administration, we are Vietnamizing the search for peace.

The policy of the previous administration not only resulted in our assuming the primary responsibility for fighting the war, but even more significantly did not adequately stress the goal of strengthening the South Vietnamese so that they could defend themselves when we left.

The Vietnamization plan was launched following Secretary Laird's visit to Vietnam in March. Under the plan, I ordered first a substantial increase in the training and equipment of South Vietnamese forces.

After five years of Americans going into Vietnam, we are finally bringing men home. By December 15, over 60,000 men will have been withdrawn from South Vietnam, including 20 percent of all of our combat forces.

The South Vietnamese have continued to gain in strength. As a result they have been able to take over combat responsibilities from our American troops.

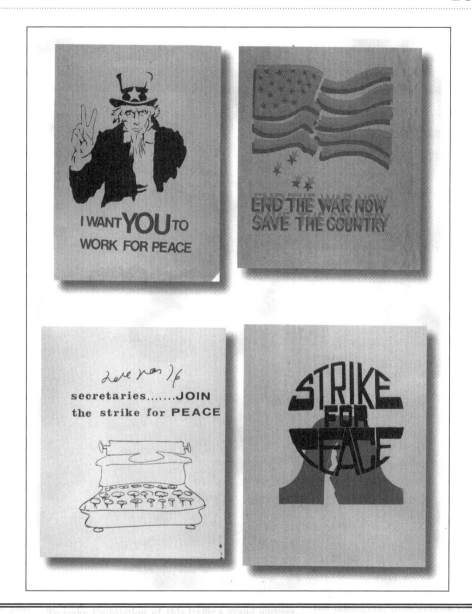

"California Reservists Speak Out Against War," WIN Peace and Freedom through Nonviolent Action, December 15, 1970:

In two separate actions, Northern California military Reservists recently demonstrated their opposition to the war.

On October 31, a contingent of Army, Marine and Coast Guard Reservists marched in a peace parade through downtown San Francisco.

The same week, 16 Marine Reservists in Marin County, just north of San Francisco, bought an advertisement in a local newspaper. Their ad supported a county ballot proposition calling for withdrawal of U.S. troops from all of Southeast Asia.

The Marines were all enlisted men of M Co., 23rd Marine Regiment, San Rafael. A Marine Corps spokesman made vague threats to the press that the men would be punished for their actions, but so far the Marine Corps has apparently been unable to find any regulation it can use against them.

wín

FEBRUARY 15, '71   30¢

enough is f-cking enough
end
the
war
now!!

"March 14 Draft Card Turn-in in Chicago," WIN Peace and Freedom through Nonviolent Action, May 1, 1970:

March 14, CADRE and War Tax Resistance prematurely ushered in Antidraft Week with a lively demonstration and draft card turn-in at the Fed. l Building. Twenty-three cards and 14 IRS forms were collected with the approval of some 200 people, mostly young men. It was like a resurgence of the Resistance movement, but with some differences. One sign read: "Give Peace a Chance/They Didn't Take It/ It's Rip-off Time." Another poster, headed "This Is A Low Sulfur Emission," showed a fellow burning a draft card with much black smoke. There were quite a few high school students so that even CADRE stalwarts began to look like the Old Guard.

One after the other, about a dozen young men gave their reasons before [throwing the] draft cards into a red can with the white omega:

"A draft card to me is the emblem the Jews had to wear in Germany . . . . Right on to revolution!"

"I find freedom in subverting illegitimate authority."

"These laws are stupid. I'm just getting rid of it [draft card]."

"I'm free; I'm unhooked again."

Setting one afire with a lighter: "I hope this smoke goes toward Heaven."

"That little piece of paper, that means nothing. Just like a high school diploma."

Ripping up his 2-S: "It's a symbol of white middle class privilege. I don't dig it anymore."

"Roger Priest Trailed by Agents," WIN Peace and Freedom through Nonviolent Action, September 1969:

Roger Priest, journalist seaman apprentice in the navy who edits an anti-war newsletter and who willed his service-connected life insurance to the War Resistance League, has been followed by as many as 25 naval intelligence agents during the past four months.

This was revealed in navy testimony at a two-day hearing July 22 and 23 to determine whether Priest should be court-martialed.

R. B. Howard, Jr., a special investigator for the naval intelligence service, testified how he wrote Priest under an assumed name to obtain copies of the newsletter and then retrieved his letter from Priest's wastebasket with the cooperation of the Washington Sanitation Department which made a "special pickup" of trash from Priest's apartment house.

Throughout the hearing, the navy concentrated on proving that Priest publishes the newsletter, a fact which he not only does not deny, but boasts.

INTERFAITH REPORTER

an
the Lord;

d
e

e water
t its roots

r
es,

JUNE 17, 1971

"WALK" TRIAL COMPLETED

1971 News Feature

Interfaith Reporter, **published by the San Fernando Valley Interfaith Council, June 17, 1971:**

Angela Davis Legal Defense Fund Furor Described

Presbyterian churches across the Valley and the nation are reverberating in response to the allocation of $10,000 by the Council on Church and Race (COCAR) to the Angela Davis Defense Fund. Valley Interfaith Council member Dick Bunce gives this background information: "At last year's General Assembly, the Council on Church and Race was instructed to establish the Emergency Fund for Legal Aid, a fund budgeted for the amount of $100,000 per year. The purpose of the fund is to provide financial help to people of color who are incarcerated and cannot afford the cost of bail or the cost of hiring defense counsel adequate for a fair trial. The Session of the Presbyterian Church in Marin County and the Ethnic Church Affairs Office of the synod of Golden Gate became convinced that Angela Davis was in particular need of an adequately financed defense in light of the negative publicity that surrounds her case. COCAR responded last March with the disbursement of $10,000 for the Angela Davis Defense Fund.

The Reverend Elder Hawkins, a former moderator of the General Assembly, co-chairman of COCAR, and a black person himself, explained the action . . . saying that equal justice is an inalienable right of all Americans, which means being assumed innocent until proven guilty. Mr. Hawkins and other Council spokesmen reminded the Assembly that in our society, even a person who is a black militant and a member of the Communist Party has a right to a fair trial when charged with a crime. Mr. Hawkins stated his strong hope that her political affiliation would not be used to confuse the issue, and that it would be understood that COCAR was acting in support of a fair trial and not of Miss Davis's personal views.

In the ensuing debate . . . some argued that many poor blacks and other minority people need the money far more than Angela Davis. The COCAR response was that the Angela Davis Defense Fund was not overflowing, but that money necessary to maintain a team of pre-trial lawyers was being expended as fast as it was coming in. Elder G. E. Bushnell said, "I can tell you as a practicing trial lawyer that

Angela Davis

without full preparation there is no opportunity to bring the proper issues to court." A black commissioner said, "Angela Davis is the exception to the miracle, the miracle being that there is anyone who is black who has not lost confidence in the American system. We who are black see ourselves in Angela Davis. We believe she should have a fair trial. Angela Davis may very well be guilty, but it is not for us to judge."

Elder Jackson Peters said the Angela Davis trial is a political spectacle, and opposed church involvement in it. The Rev. Bryce Little said that he had served the church in Indonesia, and urged commissioners to realize that the need for the Church to support a fair trial for Miss Davis is as important for the Church overseas as it is crucial here.

Many churches in the Valley have protested the allocation. The Session of Dick Bunce's church (Pasadena Presbyterian) defeated a resolution to censure the COCAR action, and supported a resolution affirming the Presbyterian connectional system. (This system allows for a disagreement between decision-making bodies.)

Meanwhile, six prominent black clergymen have promised to repay the Church the $10,000 "as an affirmation that the cause of justice and liberation will triumph." Mrs. Ralph M. Stair, new moderator of the United Presbyterian Church, U.S.A., has said that she is "glad for the generous gift and the love it brings," and sad because "once again the blacks have found it necessary to make the first move of love and reconciliation. Once again" she added, "they have shown trust of us when we are in the midst of denying their definition of mission."

VIC Board Members Endorse Campaign to Halt War

Most of the Valley Interfaith Council members have endorsed individually the following resolution:

"We, the undersigned, members of the Board of Directors of the Valley Interfaith Council, join wholeheartedly with representatives of 24 religious groups who are presently engaged in a "Set the Date Now" campaign to halt the war in Indochina. The cost in blood and treasure for the nations involved is more than the world can bear—600,000 Vietnamese slaughtered, more than two million refugees, in excess of 50,000 American deaths on the "battlefield," a $150 billion expenditure of U.S. funds. Whatever might have been the intent of our initial involvement, there is no moral justification for prolonging this tragic conflict. Nearly every religious group affiliated with the Valley Interfaith Council has made a positive statement condemning the continuance of this conflict and has urged the end of it no later than December of this year. We urge our members and the concerned citizens in our Valley to do all in their power to achieve this goal. We also urge each local religious institution to make its own declaration of concern known where it will have the greatest effect. The urgency of this cannot be overstated.

We call upon the president and Congress to set the date now to withdraw and end all direct and indirect military involvement in Indochina by December 31, 1971, so that an immediate ceasefire can stop the death and destruction; all prisoners can be set free; domestic priorities can be met; the youth of America can have new hope.

Community Heard at Earthquake Hearings

"I would like to ask why there were no Spanish-speaking government personnel in the San Fernando barrio right after the earthquake? And why, if there is to be discrimination in disaster response, was the barrio community (one of the hardest hit) not closely surveyed by the Office of Emergency Preparedness until four months after the earthquake?" These were the words of Mrs. Sylvia Shaw, field worker for VIC's Earthquake Response Committee, to the Senate Public Works Committee last Friday.

One would think that to change the focus of the hearings from roads, bridges, dams, and earthquake prediction to people's problems, one would have to write a lengthy speech and have political power. Not so! Mrs. Shaw helped to bring about this change by asking the right question at just the right moment.

Originally, the hearings had been set with little publicity and few grassroots persons on the agenda. But Sen. Tunney (Democrat-California) gave the floor to the community for 15 minutes the last part of the day Thursday. This proved so fruitful that on Friday, Sen. Bayh (Democrat-Indiana) opened the hearing in the middle of the day for almost an hour, at which time Mrs. Shaw managed to speak. By Saturday, at the Santa Rosa Church, so many community persons from the barrio spoke that the entire agenda changed.

1977 Profile

Refugee Rights: Caring for the Boat People

Born in Peking, China, to parents running a YMCA, Harry Johnson made use of his government service experience to assist Vietnamese refugees arriving in Hong Kong.

Life at Home

- After a lifetime of government service, Harry Johnson was tackling a challenge he found impossible to resist: assisting refugees.
- At first, he provided aid to those fleeing the turbulent world of Communist China, but in 1977 the harbor of Hong Kong became a center for thousands of Vietnamese "boat people" seeking food, shelter and an opportunity to relocate to America.
- It was a consuming task, and Harry had never been happier.
- After three decades of managing information about the changing face of China, he was grappling daily with the economic realities of helping refugees.
- Harry was born in Peking, China, in 1919 while his parents were in language school in training for the job of running a YMCA in China.
- His father had been appointed general secretary for the YMCA in Nanchang, where Harry grew up.
- The first trip to the United States was a year-long sojourn in 1924 that included a coast-to-coast automobile trip.
- At age five Harry was introduced to running water, flush toilets and electric lights aboard the ship that brought the family to Seattle.
- Following fad and fashion, the family camped their way across America, often following roads so rough they could barely claim that name.
- In China, the family lived in a two-story brick house in Nanchang that offered no plumbing and few amenities.
- Most of Harry's friends were American except for the children of servants.
- He spent little time at the YMCA, which served the Chinese with services such as English and Bible classes and vocational courses such as stone block lithography or complex wood chest carving.

Harry Johnson assisted Vietnamese refugees in Hong Kong.

The American Embassy in Nanking.

- Summers in China were spent at the mountain resort of Kuling, an enclave of foreign residents of China, established by a New Zealand missionary and made available to Americans and others.
- School was provided by American missions and home schooling that followed the Calvert System in Baltimore, a program that was created for Americans living overseas, offering books, study guides and tests in a single package.
- The stock market crash of 1929 ultimately forced the reduction of the YMCA's support of its program in China.
- Most of the 150 American workers there had to be released; fortunately, the Chinese staff had been properly trained and continued the work.
- Back in the U.S., when Harry entered the seventh grade in La Jolla, California, it was only his second year of formal education.
- When Harry's dad asked the boys if they wanted to return to China, both said yes, despite the conveniences of American life.
- They returned to China, and after high school, Harry entered college at Yenching University in Peking.
- His second year was spent at Occidental College in Los Angeles, California, where he felt like a misfit.
- His fellow students were so parochial that they rarely thought beyond, "Will I get a date on Saturday?" or "Will the Oxy team win this weekend?"
- His inability to acclimate drove him to transfer to the University of California at Berkeley.
- There he joined a co-op housing organization which controlled costs by doing much of their own work, such as waiting tables or policing the grounds.
- Room and board was $23.00 per month.
- This became his introduction to blue collar workers and people who promoted the concept of worker unionization.
- By his senior year, Harry was vice president of the house and head of entertainment.
- Discussion forums included a program on the war raging in Europe and America's role in early 1941.
- The panel included speakers from the American Legion, the Socialist Workers Party, and the local Communist Party, which initially refused to be on the same program with the Socialists and the Christian pacifists.
- In the discussion, the speaker from the American Legion nearly caused a riot by insisting, "We will soon get into this war and you will be the first to sign up."
- After the Japanese attack on Pearl Harbor, Harry enlisted in the Navy and was assigned to Japanese language school.

Life in Hong Kong.

- In January 1943, he was assigned as a translator at the Pearl Harbor-based Joint Intelligence Center.
- There he translated captured Japanese documents, including soldiers' diaries and inscriptions on maps, and provided intelligence to the Pacific theater.
- He also organized the creation of a gazetteer of Japanese place names arranged by Chinese characters—much needed, as all Japanese gazetteers were arranged phonetically.
- After the war, Harry joined the Office of Naval Intelligence and 18 months later was assigned to the Naval Attaché's office at the American Embassy in Nanking, China.
- During that tour, Harry and his growing family were caught up in the Communist takeover of Nanking and for six months were their "guests" under constant threat of imprisonment.
- On their second daughter's first birthday, the family was allowed to board a ship to America.
- The next assignment was in the Pentagon.

Life in Nanking.

Life at Work

- For some time, Harry had understood that he was incompatible with the military mind.
- As early as the 1950s, Harry had been lambasted by his naval superiors at the Pentagon for suggesting that the Chinese Communists had viewed America's massing of troops along the Yalu River as an offensive act that helped trigger China's role in the Korean War.
- If only America had maintained communications, the always-wary and often-attacked Chinese might have responded to America's show of military might differently, he told them.
- The advice of the China expert was not well received; he was labeled a sympathizer and a Communist.
- Convinced by the experience that he was better suited to preserving world peace than planning the next war, Harry jumped at the opportunity to serve as a China expert at the State Department.
- From 1951 to 1974, he was with the State Department and served two four-year terms as a consul in Hong Kong while in the Foreign Service.
- At age 55 and retired from government service, Harry was ready for another challenge when he was asked to return to Hong Kong, this time for the International Rescue Committee, or IRC.
- He and his family had previously been stationed in Hong Kong from 1956 to 1961, then from 1965 to 1969.
- In 1974, Hong Kong felt like home.
- With headquarters 12,000 miles away, Harry enjoyed relative autonomy.
- His job, as IRC Hong Kong office director, was to run five-day nurseries and assist the Chinese nationals who had escaped the Communist mainland by fleeing to the island of Hong Kong, which had been a British colony since 1842.

Hong Kong Hotel

- Then the Vietnam War officially ended in 1975, and the tide of refugees coming to Hong Kong began to change from predominately Chinese to Vietnamese.
- Within two years, what began as a trickle in 1975 became a flood, taxing the capacity of the available housing, sewage system and patience of the Hong Kong government.
- At first the refugees, many of whom had braved days at sea on rickety boats, were housed at warehouses at the docks while the governmental red tape was untangled.
- Then, practically overnight, Harry and the IRC were told to find housing for 800 desperate refugees, which quickly became 7,000 Vietnamese boat people.
- Quickly, the IRC transformed two buildings of 90 apartments each into dwellings for thousands.
- The apartments had been constructed as military officer housing before World War II and had been largely abandoned since then.
- Harry was consumed by the task of feeding, housing and processing the needy.
- Most had faced oppression for years and trusted few.
- The Hong Kong government supplied food; the Lutheran World Relief helped the people complete immigration applications, and the IRC attempted to keep pace with the boat people escaping Southeast Asia.
- In the aftermath of the Vietnam War, the homeless Vietnamese were people adrift, suffering through the trauma of war, the fall of South Vietnam, threats, relocations, re-education, escape, leaky ships, foreign languages, lots of paperwork, few personal documents, fewer connections to Hong Kong and strong desires to reach America.
- And in the center of the chaos was Harry, charged with untangling the bureaucracy, calming the people, securing aid, moving refugees in and out, dealing with the Hong Kong government, and paying a staff.

Life in the Community: Southeast Asia

- After the war in Vietnam ended on April 30, 1975, over 130,000 Vietnamese left the country in the final moments of that war.
- Of these, some 65,000 Vietnamese military and government officials and Vietnamese employees of the United States and their families were considered "at risk" and were evacuated directly by the U.S. military; another 65,000 got out on their own in military aircraft, ships and boats.
- Most were taken first to Guam and then resettled in the United States.
- The last two Americans to die in that war were lost late when their CH-46 evacuation helicopter crashed at sea near the *USS Hancock*, one of the navy ships receiving refugees; they were en route back to the mainland to collect more refugees.
- The United States thought that this initial wave would comprise all the Vietnamese war-related refugees needing sanctuary in the United States.
- In fact, this evacuation was merely the beginning.
- In the end, some three million people left their homes in the former French Indochinese colonies of Vietnam, Laos, and Cambodia, including 1.75 million Vietnamese land refugees and boat people.

A total of 7,000 Vietnamese boatpeople arrived in Hong Kong.

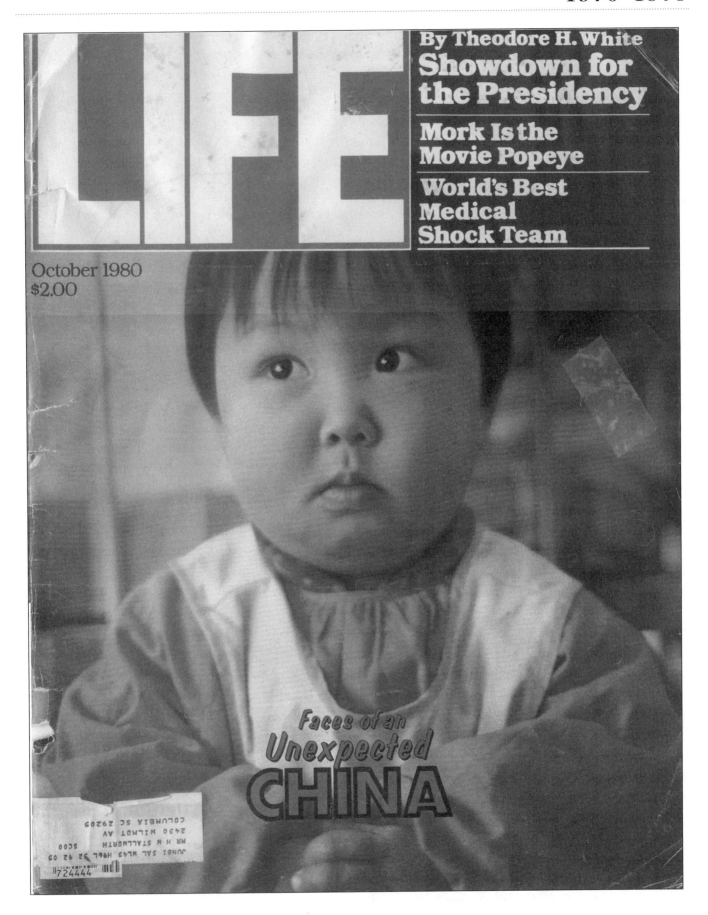

LIFE

October 1980
$2.00

By Theodore H. White
Showdown for the Presidency

Mork Is the Movie Popeye

World's Best Medical Shock Team

Faces of an Unexpected **CHINA**

JUNIOR BANK CLERK (MALE)

REQUIRED BY A FOREIGN BANK IN CENTRAL

Form 5 graduate.   Age 18-21.
Good knowledge of English and typing essential. No experience required.

Apply in own handwriting to Box 3917, "S. C. M. Post," quoting following items together with one photo, copies of school records for the last year:—

1. Name both in English and Chinese.
2. Birth date and place.
3. Present address and telephone.
4. Family status: names, ages, occupations etc.
5. Education.
6. Qualification.
7. Language ability.
8. Typing ability.
9. Expected salary.
10. References.

Applicants not interviewed by April 15, 1969 should consider their applications unsuccessful.

Hong Kong news, this page and next.

- In the years immediately following 1975, only a small trickle of Vietnamese left on boats heading for destinations throughout the area: Malaysia, Thailand, Indonesia, Hong Kong, and the Philippines.
- But by 1977, the trickle had become a torrent.
- The exodus of those getting out of Vietnam was linked to the new policies pursued by Vietnam's unified revolutionary government.
- By the end of 1977, more than 15,600 Vietnamese had landed on the shores of Southeast Asian countries and Hong Kong.
- Refugee officials and diplomats commonly called them "the boat people."
- A few were indeed fishermen, but most were city folk who knew nothing of the ocean or its dangers.
- Nobody knew how many had drowned or been murdered by pirates.
- But more than two years after the fall of Saigon, they kept coming, and in increasing numbers.
- Some ran the gauntlet of the pirates to the Thai coast where the Thais, their camps already full of Cambodians and Laotians, were beginning to turn them away.
- Some looked toward Singapore, which was not the refugee haven for which they had hoped.
- And some headed for the Philippines or Hong Kong.
- The refugees' stories had a sameness that could be summed up in the word "incompatibility," and reflected the Communists' demands that the South Vietnamese middle class learn to love their new role as agricultural laborers.
- Some spent months in detention camps, knowing that sooner or later they would be taken to a re-education camp.

- None of the Southeast Asian countries was prepared to let more than a handful stay permanently.
- And the American quota of 15,000 for Indochinese refugees fell far short of the total of 80,000 in camps in Thailand alone.
- Most governments felt that the continuing departure of refugees from Indochina was an American problem resulting from the Vietnam War, and did not want to consider letting these refugees stay in their countries.
- They didn't even want to call them "refugees," using instead the phrases "displaced persons" and "illegal immigrants."
- Most of the countries in the area had somewhat stable but historically delicate "balanced" multiethnic societies.
- They feared that the arrival and permanent resettlement of Vietnamese, especially ethnically Chinese Vietnamese, could upset that balance.
- The Hong Kong Chinese believed their British Crown colony to be a "three-legged stool," with one leg in Beijing, another in London, and the third in Hong Kong.

- This fragile tripod arrangement officially began on January 20, 1841, when Britain's China Trade Superintendent annexed Hong Kong Island on his own volition to obtain trade concessions, to recover compensation for thousands of chests of British opium confiscated earlier at Canton, and to redeem a bent British pride.
- Six days later, Commodore Sir J. Gordon Bremer led a British naval force onto Possession Point for the ritual planting of Her Majesty's flag.
- The annexation was instantly unpopular in both London and Beijing, but remained in place.

Save the tower

AT this time, when so much of Hongkong's historic heritage is falling victim to the wreckers' hammers in the name of progress, a strong plea should be made for the preservation of one of the few remaining reminders of our past.

The Kowloon-Canton Railway is already in the process of moving from its Tsimshatsui terminal to a new site. Within a fairly short time, the present station premises will become redundant, leaving it prey to the redevelopers.

Few will miss the station itself—but could not the tower be saved? If possible, with the building's colonnaded facade.

Kowloon just wouldn't be the same without it, and the cross-harbour view would be missing a colourful landmark if it was demolished.

True, very little can be said for its architectural merit — if anything, it is a bit of a monstrosity, really — but it does have an old-fashioned charm, the quiet dignity of an ageing dowager, and a resilience and indifference to change that is a constant joy in this age of turmoil.

It has an individuality and character unmatched by the hulking glass and concrete piles that line our streets with monotonous uniformity, and to many new arrivals it has been a warm and friendly beacon of hope, a symbol of safety at a long journey's end.

When the planners get down to apportioning the vacated station site (and they already have their predatory eyes on it) it is to be hoped that aesthetic needs will not take second place to merely practical considerations.

There are those who will see the site as perfect for a badly-needed expanded bus terminal—but the terminal would be only marginally less convenient for commuters if it was sited further along Salisbury Road.

This would leave the ferry concourse area free for a much-needed beautification programme, providing freer pedestrian and motor traffic movement.

The station tower could easily become the central motif for a harbour-side park, surrounded by trees and gardens. Perhaps the present public concourse section could be converted into a sound shell for band concerts and other open air performances.

With the Cricket Club doomed, little more than the Hongkong Club, the Central post office and the Tsimshatsui station remain in the older areas of the Colony as links with the past. And the post office is due to go soon.

The KCR clock tower ought to be retained and preserved as a reminder of that past which Hongkong is rapidly outgrowing and forgetting.

HISTORICAL SNAPSHOT
1977

- Steven Jobs and Steve Wozniak founded the Apple Computer Company and produced the first pre-assembled, mass-produced personal computer
- Anti-French demonstrations took place in Israel after Paris released Abu Daoud, responsible for the 1972 Munich massacre of Israeli athletes
- President Gerald Ford pardoned Iva Toguri D'Aquino (Tokyo Rose), an American who had made wartime broadcasts for Japan
- President Jimmy Carter urged 65 degrees as the maximum thermostat temperature for heating homes to ease the energy crisis
- President Carter pardoned almost all Vietnam War draft evaders as long as they had not been involved in violent acts
- The TV miniseries *Roots*, based on the Alex Haley novel, ran for eight nights on ABC
- The Vatican reaffirmed the Roman Catholic Church's ban on female priests
- The U.S. Army announced that it had conducted 239 open-air tests of germ warfare
- A dozen armed Hanafi Muslims invaded three buildings in Washington DC, killing one person and taking more than 130 hostages
- The U.S. Senate followed the example of the House by adopting a stringent code of ethics requiring full financial disclosure and limits on outside income
- An estimated 20,000 to 30,000 American homes had computers
- The ban on women attending West Point was lifted
- The musical play *Annie* opened on Broadway
- Americans with physical disabilities began staging protests at federal buildings in San Francisco, Los Angeles, and Washington, DC
- President Carter directed Congress to make a one-year study of the probable changes in the world's population, natural resources and environment through the end of the century
- The trans-Alaska oil pipeline was completed after three years of work
- Larry Ellison and Robert Miner founded Oracle Corporation in Belmont, California, after they persuaded the CIA to let them pick up a lapsed contract for a special database program
- The Supreme Court struck down state laws and bar association rules that had prohibited lawyers from advertising their fees for routine services
- President Carter announced his opposition to the B-1 bomber
- In China, Deng Xiaoping was named vice premier
- The Department of Energy was established
- Elvis Presley died at Graceland Mansion in Memphis, Tennessee
- The United States launched *Voyager 2*, an unmanned spacecraft carrying a 12-inch copper phonograph record containing greetings in dozens of languages, samples of music and sounds of nature
- The first wave of Southeast Asian "boat people" arrived in San Francisco under a new U.S. resettlement program

Selected Prices, 1977

Airfare, TWA, New York-San Francisco	$252.00
Bean Bag Chair	$37.95
Casserole, Metal	$58.00
CB Radio	$39.88
Cradle	$34.99
Ice Bucket	$80.00
Massage Shower Head	$26.95
Men's Jeans	$13.00
Theater Ticket, *A Chorus Line*	$17.50
Women's "Earth" Shoes	$23.50

International Rescue Committee Timeline

1933

The American branch of the European-based International Relief Association (IRA) was founded at the suggestion of Albert Einstein to assist Germans suffering under Hitler; refugees from Mussolini's Italy and Franco's Spain were later assisted.

1940

The Emergency Rescue Committee (ERC) formed to aid European refugees trapped in Vichy France; over 2,000 political, cultural, union and academic leaders were rescued in 13 months.

1942

The IRA and ERC joined forces under the name International Relief and Rescue Committee, later shortened to the International Rescue Committee (IRC).

1946

The IRC, at the end of World War II, initiated emergency relief programs, established hospitals and children's centers, and started refugee resettlement efforts in Europe.

After the descent of the Iron Curtain in 1946, the IRC initiated a resettlement program for East European refugees, which continued until the end of the Cold War.

1950

The IRC intensified its aid in Europe with Project Berlin, providing food to the people of West Berlin amid increased Soviet oppression.

1954

In South Vietnam, the IRC began a program to aid one million refugees following defeat of the French by the North Vietnamese; the program was expanded to include resettlement for Indochinese refugees from Vietnam, Laos and Cambodia.

1956

The IRC began resettlement and relief programs for Hungarian refugees after the revolution was crushed by Soviet forces.

1960

An IRC resettlement program began for Cuban refugees fleeing the Castro dictatorship and for Haitian refugees escaping the Duvalier regime.

1962

IRC operations were extended to Africa when 200,000 Angolans fled to Zaire; the IRC also provided aid to Chinese fleeing to Hong Kong from the mainland.

1971

The IRC provided extensive support, especially medical, health, child care and schooling, for the 10 million East Pakistani refugees fleeing to India.

The IRC began the resettlement of Asian nationals persecuted and expelled from Uganda by dictator Idi Amin.

continued

Timeline . . . *(continued)*

1975

Chilean refugees were assisted by the IRC in their efforts to win asylum in the U.S.

President Gerald Ford signed the Indochina Migration and Refugee Act, which admitted 130,000 Southeast Asian refugees into the United States.

1976

The IRC began emergency relief, medical, educational and self-help programs for Indochinese refugees fleeing to Thailand, later to include thousands from Burma.

In Vietnam, the Fourth Party Congress began the mass relocation of people and forced collectivization of agriculture, creating economic chaos.

1977

The IRC organized the Citizens Commission on Indochinese Refugees and served as a leading advocate of people fleeing from Vietnam, Cambodia and Laos.

The "second wave" of Vietnamese refugees began with thousands fleeing the country every month.

International Rescue Committee, Hong Kong, Annual Report for 1977:

The patterns for operations during 1976 of the International Rescue Committee in Hong Kong continued in 1977. Our immigration assistance caseload remained at about the same level, although we assisted over three times as many refugees from Vietnam as in the previous year. Relatively few came to be housed in our hostel or for financial assistance. Of the refugees who are getting into Hong Kong from China, many had relatives or friends who took them in and assisted them so that they did not need agency assistance. The plight of Chinese refugees in Hong Kong was made easier by a generally healthy economy which created a steady demand for unskilled labor. . . .

The numbers of Vietnamese refugees getting to Hong Kong by boat increased from 191 in 1976 to 1,001 in 1977. IRC became further involved with assisting these refugees with their immigration to other countries, primarily to the United States, and also equipped with warm clothing some of those going to cold climates. . . .

RESETTLEMENT ABROAD

IRC in Hong Kong helps refugees apply for immigration to the United States. Normally, refugees are assisted in applying under the seventh—or special refugee—preference of the Immigration and Nationality Act, which provides for "conditional entry" to the United States. After two years in this status, the refugee can become a permanent resident alien. If the refugee meets the requirements for immigration under the regular provisions of the Immigration and Nationality Act, rather than under the seventh preference, he is usually urged to apply this way, as he will thus become a permanent resident on arrival in the United States. An Indochina Parole Program was established before the end of the year, under which special numbers were allocated to Indochina refugees to permit them to enter the United States outside the regular visa process. . . .

Our seventh preference caseload of 1,728 was slightly below our figures in 1976, possibly because we were devoting more time to Vietnamese refugees than before. We assisted 196 cases (342 persons) from Vietnam, of which 146 cases (265 persons) were boat people. We also helped about 50 percent more cases than in 1976 with applications for immigrant visas.

continued

International Rescue Committee . . . *(continued)*

VIETNAMESE REFUGEES

During the year the pattern of Vietnamese refugees being picked up in the South China Sea and brought to Hong Kong in ships began to change as the refugees learned that they could make it all the way in their own boats, particularly if they departed from Danang, which is about the closest point. The numbers who started out and did not make it is unknown, but some observers believe that only about half survive. Many of the boats which successfully got to Hong Kong have not been very seaworthy and that they made it at all has been a miracle.

During the first three months of the year, no Vietnamese refugees got to Hong Kong by sea. After that there was an undulating flow, with no arrivals in November. . . .

On arrival, immigration authorities sought a guarantee from the regional representative in Kuala Lumpur of the United Nations High Commissioner for Refugees (UNHCR) that he would care for the refugees and seek countries of ultimate asylum. With this assurance, the refugees were landed. ICEM [Inter-Governmental Committee for European Migration] then found hotel space for the refugees, interviewed them, and assigned them to one of four voluntary agencies who prepared immigration applications for them. In the case of those going to the United States, which was the destination for most of them, the applications were sent by the local agencies to corresponding agencies in New York to seek sponsorships. IRC accepted responsibility for resettlement of over half of the Vietnamese refugees who got to Hong Kong during 1977. After the application had been processed by the American Consulate General and INS [Immigration and Naturalization Service], and the refugees had been approved for immigration, ICEM arranged transportation. Where travel loans were required, which was so in most cases, the voluntary agencies prepared the loan documents. Refugees from Hong Kong were also accepted by France and Australia. A few were permitted to remain in Hong Kong.

IRC was able to purchase warm clothing for some of the refugees going to cold climates. Funds for these purchases were transmitted by the Hong Kong Christian Council from a fund sent by the Norwegian Churches. We also assisted a family to whom a baby was born in Hong Kong with money donated by the Ladies' Guild of St. Joseph's Church.

Letter written to friends by Harry Allen in Nanking, China, July 9, 1949:

Our current isolation here in Nanking has increased our natural propensity for not writing letters, so now that we have a chance to get some mail out, we have decided to do it this way. . . . We trust you will not take offense, but will be grateful for any word at all from us.

Earlier this year we had orders to report to Washington by 1 July, but a series of events has insured that we not only are in Nanking now, but have little hope of leaving for some time to come. The first event was a curtailment of U.S. government transports calling at Shanghai, which was followed by the Communist "liberation" of Nanking. We were pretty much cut off from the rest of the world until Shanghai also capitulated, and then before the Communists became sufficiently organized in that city to grant exit visas to foreigners, the port was denied to shipping first by the fear that the Nationalist navy had mined the mouth of the Yangtze, and later by illegal "port closures," also imposed by the KMT (Kuomintang or Nationalist Government). Now it looks as if we might be here at least over the summer. So far we have been lucky, as the summer is a good month late in starting, and to date we have had only about two uncomfortable days and nights. . . .

We have, perhaps, been exposed to danger here in Nanking, and if Nationalists make good their leaflet-raid threat of last Sunday to bomb us day and night, we may yet be in for some excitement, but to date we have survived without even a close call. Our worst day was 23 April, shortly after the Communists made their initial crossings of the Yangtze, both east and west of here. My driver met me in the morning with the disquieting news that all police had been withdrawn from the city the night before. On my way to work I passed a police station and later a middle school which had been taken over for some time by the military police. Both were deserted

continued

Nanking countryside.

Letter written to friends by Harry Allen . . . *(continued)*

by their former occupants, and were being systematically dismantled by the local populace. At the police station an old woman was hammering out the clapboard walls with a brick. Even young children were cooperating in carrying away parts of the windows, flooring, whole doors, and any scraps of wood that they could get their hands on. At the middle school, all windows and door frames and even the upstairs flooring were removed. In one building, in which the second story was of Quonset hut construction, only the lower brick walls and the ribs of the Quonset remained. I later found out that this same thing was going on at practically every precinct station and gendarmerie in the city, as well as the home of the acting President Li, the mayor, and several other high KMT officials who had fled the city in the night. The main thoroughfares were lined with people streaming south. Most were troops, who, lucky for us, were minding their own business of getting out of town before the Communists arrived. They had their military gear and in addition many had household furnishings and sometimes their families piled on rickshaws, peddicabs, two-wheeled carts, horse carriages, taxis, busses, and trucks or any other kind of vehicle they could commandeer. Outside the city to the north we could see a large column of smoke rising from the railroad station. As I found on later inspection, not the loading platforms and marshalling yards, but the waiting room and ticket offices of the most modern station in China had been set on fire by the departing KMT, an act of wanton destruction. . . .

As the morning wore on, and as the people exhausted the possibilities for looting unoccupied buildings, and as they came to understand the implications of the absence of police, and as they began to feel the lack of security in the general situation and to fear for their future food supply, they began to turn their attention to rice shops. Before noon every rice shop in the city had been broken into. We had invited a friend who lived in the south part of the city to lunch that day, but he had phoned to say that he did not dare come unless we came in our car to pick him up. As we drove through the streets we could see people standing in front of their shops in groups of three or four. They had scared looks on their faces. All of a sudden, someone threw the first brick at a rice-shop door, and as if they were guided by a single mind, all the scared people as far as the eye could see started running toward that rice shop, only now all signs of fear had gone and printed on their faces was only the desire to get their share. By mid-morning a civil committee which had partly been appointed by the departing authorities . . . began to restore order. They had a small supply of rifles which were apparently issued to volunteers, many of whom appeared to be teenagers glorying in their first big responsibility. In front of one rice shop two such youngsters were keeping strict discipline. The looters were cued up waiting their turn each to take only one bag of flour (60 pounds). To remind them not to step out of line, an early transgressor lay motionless by the curb, victim of the new authority.

Harry's neighborhood in Nanking, above and right.

The City of Nanchang, China, by Harry Allen, 1991:

Nanchang was a walled city, as were most provincial capitals, and this gave it a cohesiveness as well as a feeling of history. It was an old city, and presumably the wall was centuries old. It was in many places 20 or more feet high and faced with brick on both sides with the outer wall crenellated the entire length. The top of the wall was wide enough to form a road around the city which could be used to move troops to the point of an alien attack. The several gates had three or four storied towers over them with the traditional curved-up cornered roofs. These provided quarters for the garrisons guarding the gates when the city was threatened. At each gate, there was a double wall leaving a rectangular area outside the main gate. The outer gate was in one of the side walls so that if artillery was used to penetrate the outer gate, it could not be brought to bear on the inner gate....

Nanchang had several lakes, interconnected by canals which were crossed by camel-backed ridges. At one time we lived in a house overlooking one of the lakes.... The lakes were regularly fished by men who would row their sampans down one side of the lake while one of them beat on the deckboards with the intent of driving the fish to the other side of the lake. Then they would take their boats to the other side and drop their nets. Another economic activity was the digging of lotus roots. The lakes were not very deep, which made it possible for the lotus to grow and for men (and women) to walk out in the water up to their shoulders pushing floating wooden tubs. They carried poles fitted with hooked knives, and when they found a tubular lotus root at their feet, they would cut it loose and put their "harvest" in the tubs....

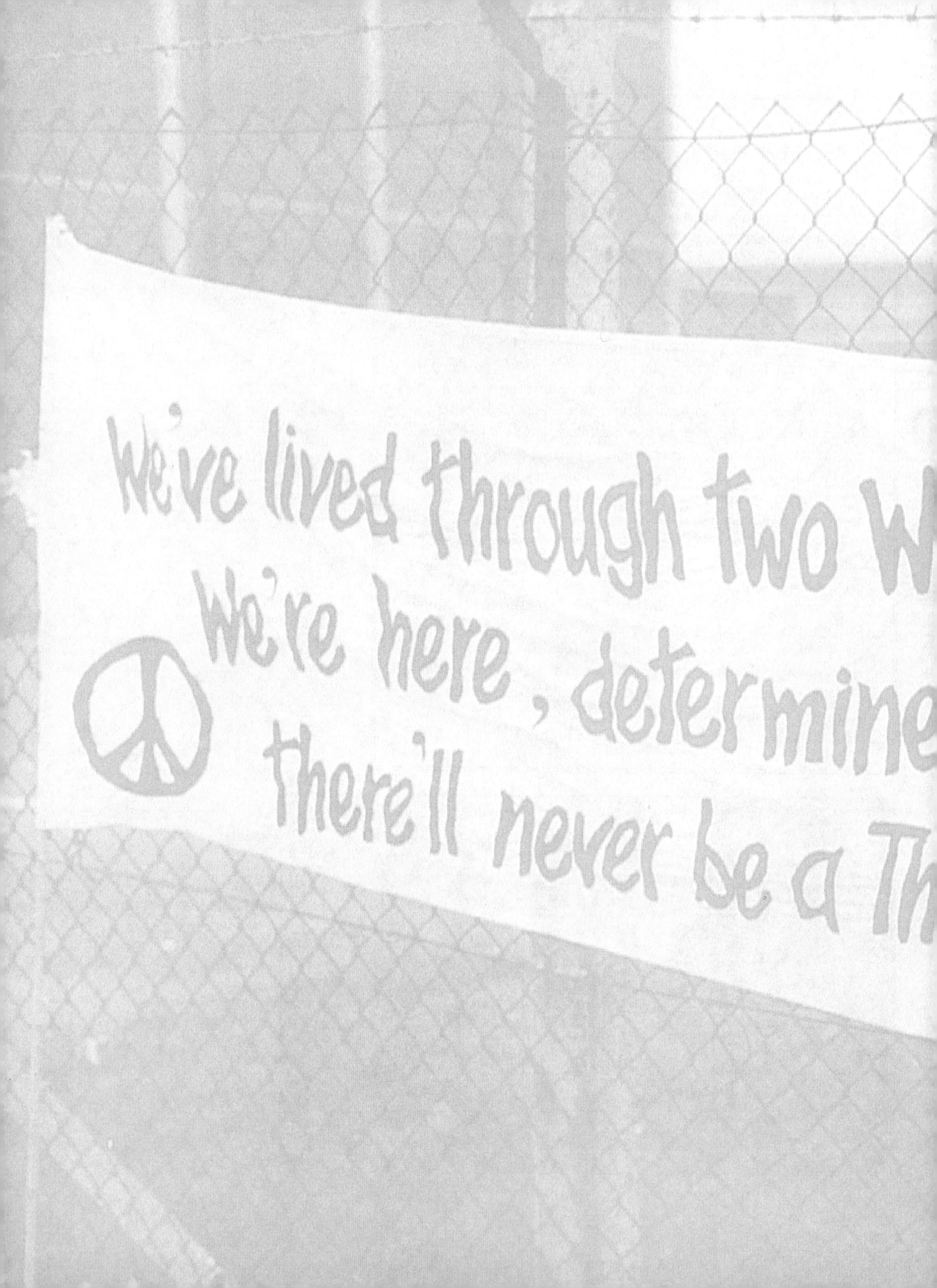

We've lived through two W
We're here, determine
there'll never be a Th

1980–1989

The decade of the 1980s suffered an unpropitious beginning. Interest rates and the rate of inflation reached a staggering 18 percent. Unemployment was rising. America was in its deepest depression since the Great Depression of the 1930s. The two-career family became the norm; more than half of all married woman and 90 percent of female college graduates worked outside the home. This economic instability paired with the rising number of women in the workforce injected new energy into the movement for social change. America loudly questioned the role of nuclear weapons in world affairs, grappled with the abortion question and furiously wrestled with the conflicting needs of the economy and Mother Nature. By the end of the decade, thanks in part to the productivity gain proved by computers and new technology, more Americans entered the rarified atmosphere of the millionaire and felt better off than they had in a decade.

Convinced that inflation was the primary enemy of long-term economic growth, the Federal Reserve Board brought the economy to a standstill in the early days of the decade. It was a shock treatment that worked. By 1984, the tight money policies of the government, stabilizing world oil prices, and labor's declining bargaining power brought inflation to four percent, the lowest level since 1967. Despite the pain it caused, the plan to strangle inflation succeeded; Americans not only prospered, but many believed it was their right to be successful. The decade came to be symbolized by self-indulgence.

At the same time, defense and deficit spending roared into high gear, the economy continued to grow, and the stock market rocketed to record levels (the Dow Jones Industrial Average tripled from 1,000 in 1980 to nearly 3,000 a decade later). In the center of recovery was Mr. Optimism, President Ronald Reagan. During his presidential campaign he promised a "morning in America" and during eight years, his good nature helped transform the national mood. The Reagan era, which spanned most of the 1980s, fostered a new conservative agenda of good feeling. During the presidential election against incumbent President Jimmy Carter, Reagan joked, "A recession is when your neighbor loses his job. A depression is when you lose yours. And recovery is when Jimmy Carter loses his."

The economic wave of the 1980s was also driven by globalization, improvements in technology, and willingness of consumers to assume higher and higher levels of personal debt. By the 1980s, the two-career family became the norm. Forty-two percent of all American workers were female, and more than half of all married women and 90 percent of female college graduates worked outside the home. Yet, their median wage was 60 percent of that of men. The rapid rise of women in the labor force, which had been accelerating since the 1960s, brought great social change, affecting married life, child rearing, family income, office culture, and the growth of the national economy.

The rising economy brought greater control of personal lives; homeownership accelerated, choices seemed limitless, debt grew, and divorce became commonplace. The collapse of communism at the end of the 1980s brought an end to the old world order and set the stage for a realignment of power. America was regarded as the strongest nation in the world and the only real superpower, thanks to its economic strength. As democracy swept across eastern Europe, the U.S. economy began to feel the impact of a "peace dividend" generated by a reduced military budget and a desire by corporations to participate in global markets—including Russian and China. Globalization was having another impact. At the end of World War II, the U.S. economy accounted for almost 50 percent of the global economic product; by 1987, the U.S. share was less than 25 percent as American companies moved plants offshore and countries such as Japan emerged as major competitors. This need for a global reach inspired several rounds of corporate mergers as companies searched for efficiency, market share, new products, or emerging technology to survive in the rapidly shifting business environment.

The 1980s were the age of the conservative Yuppie. Business schools, investment banks, and Wall Street firms overflowed with eager baby boomers who placed gourmet cuisine, health clubs, supersneakers, suspenders, wine spritzers, high-performance autos, and sushi high on their agendas. Low-fat yogurt, high-fiber cereals and Jane Fonda workout books symbolized much of the decade. As self-indulgence rose, concerns about the environment, including nuclear waste, acid rain, and the greenhouse effect declined. Homelessness increased and racial tensions fostered a renewed call for a more caring government. During the decade, genetic engineering came of age, including early attempts at transplantation and gene mapping. Personal computers, which were transforming America, were still in their infancy.

The sexual revolution, undaunted by a conservative prescription of chastity, ran head-on into a powerful adversary during the 1980s with the discovery and spread of AIDS, a frequently fatal, sexually transmitted disease. The right of women to have an abortion, confirmed by the Supreme Court in 1973, was hotly contested during the decade as politicians fought over both the actual moment of conception and the right of a woman to control her body. Cocaine also made its reappearance, bringing drug addiction and a rapid increase in violent crime. The Center on Addiction and Substance Abuse at Columbia University found alcohol and drug abuse implicated in three-fourths of all murders, rapes, child molestations, and deaths of babies suffering from parental neglect.

For the first time in history, the Naval Academy's graduating class included women, digital clocks and cordless telephones appeared, and 24-hour-a-day news coverage captivated television viewers. Compact disks began replacing records, Smurf and E.T. paraphernalia were everywhere, New York became the first state to require seat belts, Pillsbury introduced microwave pizza, and Playtex used live lingerie models in "Cross Your Heart" bra ads. The Supreme Court ruled that states may require all-male private clubs to admit women, and 50,000 gathered at Graceland on the tenth anniversary of Elvis Presley's death.

ve lived through two World Wars We're here, determined there'll never be a Third !

1983 PROFILE

NUCLEAR-FREEZE MOVEMENT: ANTI-NUCLEAR WEAPONS

The daughter of Vietnam War protestors, Anna Delgado first became involved in the Anti-Nuclear Weapons Movement through her activity in rallies held to put a freeze on the growth of nuclear weapon stockpiles.

Life at Home

- Though only 21 years old, Anna Delgado had spent the last two years actively working for the nuclear freeze movement—an effort to stop the development of weapons that could potentially destroy the world's population.
- As a result, she had seen the inside of a jail for the first time, had long political talks with her parents and found a cause she felt was worth fighting for.
- Throughout the Cold War, the United States had been competing with the Soviet Union to develop thousands of Intercontinental Ballistic Missiles, or ICBMs, capable of delivering nuclear warheads across the world.
- This growth in potential nuclear destruction disturbed Anna, and she vehemently disagreed with the media's assertion that the growth of nuclear weapons was a method for peace.
- The United States was currently promoting new weapons to maintain the peace, such as the MX missile and the Space Defense Initiative.
- The MX missile would allow the United States to send 10 nuclear warheads in one missile halfway around the world with deadly accuracy.
- The Space Defense Initiative—a satellite system that would destroy incoming missiles attacking America—was nicknamed "Star Wars" and attacked by critics as unlikely to succeed.

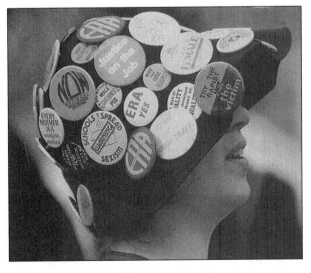

Anna Delgado worked for the nuclear freeze movement.

- This was in addition to the thousands of Minuteman missiles already in place and prepared to be launched at targets around the world in the event of a nuclear attack.
- While attending the University of Pennsylvania, Anna first got involved in the nuclear movement by participating in several rallies intended to persuade the U.S. and other governments to freeze the number of nuclear weapons.
- Finding the time to participate in protests was a challenge—her obligations to her college coursework in elementary education and her part-time job left little time to be involved in the movement.
- But by attending the protests, she discovered a strong connection to what her parents believed in and the need to thwart the growing war establishment.
- Both her mother and father had protested the Vietnam War, especially after her older brother went "missing in action" in 1972.
- She vividly remembered attending anti-war rallies with her mother a decade earlier.
- Regretfully, it did nothing to help bring her brother back home.
- At nuclear weapons rallies, Anna carried one of her two protest picket signs designed by her father: "End the Arms Race NOW!" and "Women for Peace."
- Anna saw this movement as a "New Abolitionist Movement" and was proud of being part of a national effort.
- This concept was reinforced when she read a *Rolling Stone Magazine* article on the subject in March.
- At the protest rallies off-campus in the city, Anna was one of the youngest protesters; the vast majority were working professionals 10 or 20 years older, often with families.
- Also at these rallies were religious people, especially those with Christian backgrounds, who viewed the development of nuclear weapons as immoral.
- Some of the older protestors had worked to elect politicians in Congress who would support a bilateral freeze of nuclear weapons with the Russians and stop the proliferation of nuclear devices, weapons, and generating plants, all nicknamed "nukes."

- During the prior year's elections, these activists worked nationwide to support candidates in 45 election races in the House of Representatives on this issue.
- Pro-freeze candidates won 36 of the races.
- Over 1,500 different peace groups across the country were backing the freeze.
- Yet the majority of Americans still believed that the best way to be safe from Communist domination was to build the biggest weapons.
- At the rallies Anna attended in Philadelphia, she was often confronted by supporters of the government's nuclear arms policy, who called her a "dupe of the Kremlin."
- They insisted that the American Pro-Freeze rallies were hurting the United States' effort to negotiate with the Soviets.
- They were also called "freezeniks," along with other references of being communists and traitors to America.
- During one of the protests, an older woman told Anna about a women-only protest at the Seneca Army Depot in New York planned for the summer.
- The summer protest was called the Women's Encampment for a Future of Peace and Justice and would operate from July 4 to Labor Day.

- Through the summer, the encampment would condemn the nuclear weapons the U.S government was storing on-site, including the Pershing cruise missiles for shipment to Western Europe.
- The location was also chosen for its close proximity to Seneca Falls, where the first women's rights convention occurred in 1848.
- Anna knew immediately that she wanted to participate.
- With help from friends, she arranged to sublease her apartment during the summer and saved money to cover expenses for six weeks.
- Anna packed her Ford Pinto with camping gear, her "comfy" sleeping pillow, her protest signs, several changes of clothes, three milk gallon jugs of water, four cartons of Virginia Slims cigarettes and three grocery bags full of rice, beans and canned vegetables.
- By the end of June, Anna left her parents' home in Columbia, Maryland, and traveled to Romulus, New York—the location of the women's encampment.

Life at Work

- When Anna Delgado arrived in Romulus, New York, at the Women's Encampment for a Future of Peace and Justice, the grounds were already full of women from all over the United States.
- Many saw this protest as a way to protect their families from nuclear war, but others supported a range of feminist and peace issues.
- Some believed that women-centered protests enabled the world to see women as the caretakers of the world and of families.
- All women were encouraged to volunteer for many duties; Anna decided to help prepare the vegetarian meals for the attendees during her stay.
- The opening day of protest on July 4 was full of excitement and debate.
- One early controversy was whether to accept an American flag from a local community leader for the women to fly on the encampment property.
- Many of the women were conflicted because the American flag held mixed symbols of militaristic nationalism and of benevolence.

- Some felt that an international peace camp should not fly any nation's flag.
- The women decided not to fly the flag, but to permit the women to create their own flags the size of a pillowcase to hang on a clothesline.
- The local community did not receive the decision favorably.
- Anna was thrilled with the first day's activities, which started with approximately 500 women gathered to pledge their allegiance to the earth, for the life it provides and for peace and beauty for all.
- Later she and the others followed a Buddhist woman beating her drum while they walked slowly, chanting "All we are saying is give peace a chance."
- As the women marched past the Seneca Army Depot gate, they planted two rose bushes—one red, one white—as symbols of life.
- Later, the women lined up holding up their hands in a triangular shape known as a "yoni," or ancient goddess symbol, which became the sign of the women's resistance to the Depot.

- Four local veterans planted little American flags by the two rose bushes outside the depot, saluted and walked away.
- The opening day's protest was peaceful and viewed as a successful beginning.
- Peaceful protest continued daily at the Seneca Army Depot with other symbols that showed the strength of women.

- Women formed in circles or webs—both signs of unification, strength, and the world's connectivity.
- The interconnected web was painted on a number of the structures around the camp.
- In another symbolic act, the protestors tied onto the Army Depot's fence possessions they did not want to lose in the event of a nuclear war.
- Items included photos of families and children.
- Anna tied a number of webs to the fence with photos of her parents, her friends and the family dog.
- She wanted to put her missing brother's photo on the fence, but she was afraid of losing one of her few remaining mementos of him.
- Anna shared her grief of losing her brother in Vietnam with some of the friends she made at camp; they encouraged her to hold on to the photo until he was found.
- Over the next couple of weeks of protests, hundreds of women arrived to condemn the nuclear weapons on the base.
- Over time, the women expanded their civil disobedience by climbing over the Seneca Army Depot's fence to protest.
- Anna was a bit hesitant at first to participate in this aggressive form of protest.
- The women who climbed over were arrested by military police and detained on the post, fingerprinted, photographed and given letters barring them from re-entering the property.
- Anna climbed over the fence one hot summer morning.
- Immediately she was arrested by a military police sergeant and handcuffed while chanting "Peaceful women wanting peace."
- After a couple of hours of military arrest, Anna was fingerprinted and awarded her "bar letter" prohibiting her from re-entering the site.
- Anna was excited and immediately went to a pay phone to call her parents about the arrest, receiving her bar letter and the good she was doing for the world.
- They were happy for her but cautioned her not to do anything that would hurt her professionally in the long run.
- After the call, she jumped up and down with glee.
- She now had documented proof that her protests were impacting the military, and it further validated her efforts in the Freeze Movement.

Life in the Community: Seneca, New York

- Local residents in the Seneca, New York area had issues with the women protesters.
- Some tried to welcome the women but received little community support.
- Residents were also concerned about the added cost and attention the protest brought to the community and feared that it might cause the closure of the military base.
- Anna and the women did not want the base to close, but to be used for something peaceful to the community.
- Regardless of how often the protesters communicated this message, the residents were worried that jobs would be lost.
- Times had been tough and didn't need to get tougher.
- Also, the community was shocked by the broad feminist nature of the protests, which ranged from nuclear weapons to sexuality, religion and the concerns of oppressed women.
- A large number of the residents were simply offended by the alternative lifestyles the women were supporting and viewed the protest as un-American.
- Anna often spent time discussing these concerns with the other women: Would the locals come to see their point of view or should the women attempt to improve relations with the local community?
- Most in the discussion agreed that there was little that could be done to improve the situation.
- The community's wariness exploded during a planned 15-mile feminist walk from Seneca Falls to the Peace Camp on Saturday, July 30.
- The women communicated this planned march to local officials along the route, including the town of Waterloo near the women's encampment.
- On that Saturday, when Anna and hundreds of women entered Waterloo, they wore white bibs printed with historically important women's names, such as Elizabeth Cady Stanton and Susan B. Anthony.
- At the Waterloo Bridge, they encountered 300 local residents waving American flags with a 20-foot banner in front saying, "Many Men and Women Have Earned the Right for Anyone to Protest in America. Respect Them, Our Flag, and Our Country."
- Some of the local residents were holding American flags or cardboard signs that said, "Go Home," "We're Proud to Be Americans," and "Pinko Lesbians, Go Home."
- They were also chanting "America" and screaming at the women, "Go home" and "Go protest in Russia."
- The local citizens' counter-protest blocked traffic and the flow of the women marchers for a period of time.
- Local law enforcement was fearful of a riot at the bridge.
- Anna was concerned; she had never seen so much anger and hatred from those who opposed her.
- Instead of trying to cross the bridge, the women decided to stop and sit in the road.
- Many of the women were becoming angry at the comments and expletives coming from the bridge.
- Within a short time, both sides were yelling at each other.
- The moment became extremely frightening when a man with a rifle approached the women.
- Fortunately the police apprehended the man and arrested him immediately.
- After two hours of tension between the two groups, the officers instructed the women to leave and return to the encampment.
- The women refused because the local citizens, not the women, were illegally blocking the road.

- The police disagreed.
- A number of the women, including Anna, held their ground until the police dragged them away and arrested them.
- As each was hauled away, the local citizens cheered and encouraged the police.
- The authorities charged 53 women from the encampment for disorderly conduct at the bridge.
- The only local resident arrested was the man with the rifle.
- Because there was little space in the sheriff's department jail, a makeshift jail was established at a school away from Waterloo in Seneca County.
- It was stuffy, confusing and maddening.
- The women supported each other during the next several days while in prison at the school.
- Anna thought about calling her parents for help, but the other women convinced her that she had done nothing wrong and should go free.
- Each day when she thought she should call, she decided to wait one more day.
- She even thought of trying to escape as two women did while imprisoned at the school.
- After several days, the local authorities dropped all charges on the women.
- While Anna was under arrest, approximately 2,000 women protested at the Seneca Army Depot.
- Over 200 were arrested for peacefully trespassing onto the federal property.
- Upon returning to the women's encampment, Anna heard rumors that the locals may cause further harm to the women.
- Rumors of bombings or burnings were bruited for a couple of days.
- With all the excitement and stress over the past several weeks, Anna's time at the camp came to an end.
- She decided to head home and prepare for her final year at the University of Pennsylvania and the next confrontation with the military establishment.

HISTORICAL SNAPSHOT
1983

- The musical *Annie* was performed for the last time after 2,377 shows in New York City
- President Ronald Reagan proclaimed 1983 "The Year of the Bible"
- A special commission report of the U.S. Congress was critical of the practice of Japanese internment during World War II
- IBM released the IBM PC XT
- President Reagan called the Soviet Union an "evil empire" and made his initial proposal to develop technology to intercept enemy missiles called the Strategic Defense Initiative, dubbed "Star Wars"
- The first non-American Disney theme park opened in Japan as Tokyo Disneyland
- The U.S Embassy in Beirut was bombed, killing 63 people
- Maine schoolgirl Samantha Smith was invited to visit the Soviet Union by its leader Yuri Andropov after he read her letter in which she expressed fears about nuclear war
- *Stern* magazine published the "Hitler Diaries," which were later found to be forgeries
- *Pioneer 10* became the first manmade object to leave the solar system
- Sally Ride was first American woman in space on the space shuttle *Challenger*
- A Soviet jet fighter shot down Korean Air Flight 007, killing all 269 passengers and crew on board, when the commercial aircraft entered Soviet airspace
- Soviet military officer Stanislav Petrov averted a worldwide nuclear war by refusing to believe that the United States had launched missiles against the USSR, despite the indications given by his computerized early warning systems
- A suicide truck-bombing destroyed the United States Marine Corps barracks at Beirut International Airport, killing 241 U.S. servicemen
- The United States invaded Grenada
- President Reagan signed a bill creating a federal holiday to honor civil rights leader Martin Luther King, Jr.
- McDonald's introduced the chicken McNugget
- Popular films included *Star*

I'D RATHER BE PLAYING SCRABBLE.® Brand Crossword Game

America's Favorite Crossword Game

SCRABBLE® is the registered trademark of Selchow & Righter Co., Bay Shore, NY. for its line of word games and entertainment services

Selected Prices, 1983

Apartment, Chicago, Two Bedroom, Month	$489.00
Attaché Case, Leather	$89.99
Car Stereo, Sanyo	$179.99
Golf Clubs, Wilson, 11-Piece	$219.99
Men's Leather Driving Gloves	$17.00
Skateboard	$59.99
Sofa, 80-Inch, Fabric	$1,495.00
Video Disc Player	$539.00
Video Tape, Maxell	$13.49
Wristwatch, Rolex	$2,725.00

Nuclear Weapons Protest Timeline

1957

The Committee for a SANE Nuclear Policy was founded and published an advertisement in *The New York Times*.

1958

The USSR announced a unilateral halt to atmospheric nuclear tests; the United States responded with a one-year testing moratorium.

The National Student Council for a SANE Nuclear Policy was organized.

1960

A SANE rally in Madison Square Garden, New York, attracted 20,000 to hear Eleanor Roosevelt, Norman Cousins, Norman Thomas, A. Philip Randolph, Walter Reuther, and Harry Belafonte call for an end to the arms race.

1961

SANE hosted an eight-day, 109-mile march from McGuire Air Force Base in New Jersey to U.N. Plaza attended by 25,000 to petition President Kennedy to maintain a moratorium on testing in the atmosphere.

The arms race intensified as the Soviet Union resumed atmospheric testing of nuclear weapons; the United States resumed underground testing.

1962

The U.S. conducted above-ground testing of nuclear weapons.

After photographs showed Soviet missile bases under construction in Cuba, the United States established an air and sea blockade of Cuba and threatened to invade unless the bases were dismantled.

Dr. Spock was recruited as a national sponsor of the SANE pro-freeze movement.

Graphic Artists for SANE was organized, including Jules Feiffer, Ben Shahn, and Edward Sorel.

1963

President John F. Kennedy signed the Limited Test Ban Treaty in which Britain, the Soviet Union, and the United States agreed to outlaw nuclear weapons tests in the atmosphere, underwater and in outer space.

1964

China detonated its first atomic weapon.

1966

The first French atomic bomb was tested at Muruoa Atoll.

The U.S. Minuteman ICBM (intercontinental ballistic missile) entered service.

1967

The Outer Space Treaty banned nuclear weapons from being placed on any celestial body, or in orbit around Earth.

The Treaty of Tlatelolco created a Latin America nuclear-weapons-free zone.

China detonated its first hydrogen bomb.

1968

France tested its first hydrogen bomb at Fangataufa Atoll in the South Pacific.

1969

SANE produced ads attacking anti-ballistic missiles (ABMs): "From the people who brought you Vietnam."

President Richard M. Nixon announced plans to deploy a missile defense system called "Safeguard" to protect U.S. ICBM fields from attack.

continued

Timeline . . . *(continued)*

1969

Preliminary Strategic Arms Limitation Treaty (SALT) talks took place in Helsinki, Finland.

1970

The U.S. deployed the first missile with multiple independently targetable re-entry vehicles (MIRVs).

1971

The first Poseidon submarine-launched ballistic missiles were introduced by the U.S.

1972

President Nixon and General Secretary Leonid Brezhnev signed the Anti-Ballistic Missile (ABM) Treaty, the Strategic Arms Limitation Treaty (SALT) and the Interim Agreement on Strategic Offensive Arms in Moscow.

SALT II treaty negotiations began.

1974

India tested a low-yield nuclear device under the Rajasthan desert.

The Threshold Test Ban Treaty (TTBT), which limited nuclear test explosions to under 150 kilotons, was signed in Moscow.

President Gerald Ford and General Secretary Brezhnev signed the Vladivostok Accord, agreeing to limit the number of strategic launchers and MIRV launchers.

1976

President Ford and General Secretary Brezhnev signed the Underground Nuclear Explosions for Peaceful Purposes (PNE) Treaty.

1977

The United States successfully tested a neutron bomb, whose lethal effects come from the radiation damage caused by the neutrons it emits.

Peace groups launched a national Campaign to Stop the B1 Bomber by restricting congressional allocations.

1978

The United States cancelled development of the neutron bomb.

1979

The Three Mile Island nuclear power plant near Harrisburg, Pennsylvania, suffered a partial core meltdown.

The SALT II Treaty was signed in Vienna, Austria.

A mysterious flash detected by a U.S. satellite was determined to be from a clandestine nuclear explosion by South Africa.

Peace groups began a national STOP-MX Missile Campaign.

1980

The first of many nuclear freeze resolutions were approved in western Massachusetts.

A referendum against MX missiles was approved in Nevada.

1981

Israeli aircraft destroyed Iraq's Osirak reactor, thought to be producing materials for an Iraqi nuclear device.

President Reagan unveiled plans for a record $200 billion military budget funded through cutbacks in social programs.

The Nuclear Weapons Freeze Campaign was founded in D.C.

continued

"Women Plan Arms Protest Upstate," Suzanne Daley, *The New York Times*, June 27, 1983:

Romulus, NY June 24—Beside a small farm on Route 96 here in the Finger Lakes Region, a sign says: Women's Encampment for a Future of Peace & Justice"....

A group of women bought the 52-acre farm in May and hopes to attract hundreds of women here this summer to use the farm's fields as a camping ground and assembly area for antinuclear demonstrations.

Adjoining the land is the target of the protest—the Seneca Army Depot, an 11,000-acre ammunitions storage site that is widely assumed to contain nuclear weapons. The Army will not comment on this....

The prospect of such a protest has set the Army to building fences, hiring extra caviling guards and holding meetings to ease the concerns of workers. It has also caused a great deal of anxiety in this town of about 2,000 residents....

Mr. Zajac [Town Supervisor] who thinks the women "have a beautiful dream but have bitten off more than they can chew," says he has many concerns. They range from the town's limited water supply to its lack of a police force to having only one judge....

"We aren't equipped to deal with this," Mr Zajac went on. "The women say: 'We're not trying to bother you. Our beef is with the federal government.' But they've already caused a hardship with all the worrying. They say that by the end of the summer we'll all be great friends but if that happens, I'll sit in this office and eat my hat."

Like the commander of the Army Depot and the sheriff, Mr. Zajac says he feels frustrated because the women maintain they have no leader and are sometimes vague in describing what they plan to do.

"Nothing is clear," said Mr. Zajac, "They don't know, so we don't know how many people will show up. We aren't so much worried about them, although I want to tell you that the prospect of breaking up 300 mothers is awesome—but what about the others who will be attracted to this sort of thing. Maybe motorcycle gangs—who knows?"....

One of the three paid workers at the farm, Barbara Reale, 23 years old, who studied economics at Cornell University and has since worked for several peace organizations, said the farm would have campsites ready to accommodate about 350 people. Some fields will be kept available to handle any overflow attendance....

The encampment, said Miss Reale, is being sponsored by a large assortment of individual women and women's groups. Contributors, she said, include such groups as the American Friends Service Committee, a Quaker pacifist group; the New England War Tax Resistance; Church Women United; Nuclear Weapons Facilities Network; the Rochester Peace and Justice Education Center; and the Women's International League for Peace and Freedom....

Several of the women on the farm cite instances of people who have been friendly to them—a bar down the road gave a refrigerator, some local women have brought pies or homemade bread. But there are people in town who are angry that their way of life may be changed this summer.

"They aren't going to do anything but raise our taxes," said Milly Todd.... "We are going to have to pay for more protection for them and for ourselves. I don't think they have any idea what they are doing to a small town. We don't even dare go away on our summer vacation. If people are coming in here by the droves, who knows what will happen?"

No War Toys

"200 Protesters Seized by M.P.s at Army Depot, 1,900 Women in a Rally Against Nuclear Arms," *The New York Times*, August 2, 1983:

ROMULUS, N.Y., Aug 1 (AP)—Military policemen arrested more than 200 women this afternoon as about 1,900 women protesting nuclear arms rallied at the Seneca Army Depot.

The protesters were jeered by more than 200 flag-waving counter-demonstrators, mostly local residents, who chanted, "Go Home."

With an Army helicopter overhead, the military policemen spread razor-sharp wire along 200 yards of fence to prevent the women from climbing it. But many of the women climbed over the fence into the arms of military policemen and were arrested.

"The message we are giving is that we are peace-loving women," said Connie McKenna, a spokesman for the protesters. She said the women had wanted to plant trees, gardens and rose bushes inside the depot. Some of the women have been spending the summer at the Women's Encampment for a Future of Peace and Justice, near the depot in the Finger Lakes region.

Planners for the rally said it was called to demand a halt in the United States plans to deploy Pershing 2 and Cruise missiles later this year. The demonstrators believe that the base is an arsenal for nuclear weapons. The Army refuses to confirm or deny the presence of nuclear weapons at the Seneca Army Depot or any other site.

The Seneca County Sheriff's Department was being assisted in handling the demonstration by 100 sheriff's deputies from nearby counties.

Reagan's Case Against the Freeze, Excerpts from a speech by President Ronald Reagan to the Los Angeles World Affairs Council on March 31, 1983:

The freeze concept is dangerous for many reasons. It would preserve today's high, unequal and unstable levels of nuclear forces and, by so doing, reduce Soviet incentives to negotiate for real reductions.

It would pull the rug out from under our negotiators in Geneva, as they have testified.

After all, why should the Soviets negotiate if they've already achieved a freeze in a position of advantage to them?

Also, some think a freeze would be easy to agree on, but it raises enormously complicated problems of what is to be frozen, how it is to be achieved, and verified. Attempting to negotiate these critical details would only divert us from the goal of negotiating reductions for who knows how long.

The freeze proposal would also make a lot more sense if a similar movement against nuclear weapons were putting similar pressures on Soviet leaders in Moscow.

As former Secretary of Defense Harold Brown has pointed out: The effect of the freeze "is to put pressure on the United States, but not on the Soviet Union."

Finally, the freeze would reward the Soviets for their 15-year buildup while locking us to our existing equipment, which in many cases is obsolete and badly in need of modernization. Three-quarters of the Soviet strategic warheads are on delivery systems five years old or less. Three-quarters of the American strategic warheads are on delivery systems 15 years old or older. The time comes when everything wears out. The trouble is it comes a lot sooner for us than for them. And, under a freeze, we couldn't do anything about it.

"Circle of Fire," based upon a song by Linda Hirschorn, sung by the Women's Encampment for a Future of Peace and Justice:

Chorus

Circle for survival, circle for the right
Not to disappear into the everlasting night
Circle for survival, circle for the right
Not to disappear into the everlasting night

Circle all the bases, circle day and night
Enclose them in a wall of sacred strength and sight
Let the people see them for what they really are
Let the people know they threaten our home star

Chorus

Circle all the strip mines, circle day and night
Circle all the people, lend them all our might
Circle all the rapists, the men and their machines
Circle all the ones who take away our dreams

Chorus

Circle all the pueblos, keep them safe from harm
Circle native people with hearts and minds and arms
They're fighting for their homelands, what little they have left
It's up to us to help them rectify the theft

Chorus

The circle is our weapon, the circle is our tool
The circle is our heartspace, the circle is our school
The circle is our kiva, the circle is our truth
The circle is our power against the ones who rule

Chorus

1983 News Feature

"Charity Begins with the Homeless," by Loudon Wainwright,
Life, **January 1983:**

There used to be a homeless man who lived just off the sidewalk near my office in a recess about the size of a two-drawer filing cabinet. I came to think of him as Mr. Bearded Grayface, and on his most manic days he would venture out into the heavily trafficked street carrying a pair of drumsticks. Then bending over at the waist with his legs apart and perfectly straight at the knees, he would beat out a tattoo over and over on the surface of the road. Graceful as a matador he stood there, tattered trousers rolled up so his pale and grimy calves were exposed, now and then weaving to a new position while the cabs and buses whirled dangerously around him. On some occasions I would pass him as he lay sleeping through rain or snow in his snug concrete cave; often he was simply standing there drinking coffee or chewing on a roll. For a while he had a friend, a beefy woman even more ragged than he, and they took turns sleeping in the protected space. Sometimes we looked at each other, Mr. Bearded Grayface and I, two men of an age who worked the same street, but we never spoke. Others, I have heard, stopped and gave him money, but I would pass him by, shame nipping at my heels.

I haven't seen him for many months now, perhaps a year or more, and I've begun to think he's dead. But the fact about modern America that he represents—that there are a lot of people like him out there who never belly up to the banquet of the good life—is more dramatically apparent with each passing day. The numbers of the homeless, estimated now to be between 500,000 and two million people nationwide, are growing. Cities all over the country are reporting increased pressure for additional facilities for men and women who simply don't have a place to sleep. Public shelters in New York provide for nearly 5,000 each night. Informed Chicago sources guess that there are 25,000 homeless wandering around town every day, double the number from 1981. In Houston, where about 3,000 beds are available for the needy, hundreds of applicants are turned away nightly for lack of space.

There are changes, too, in the makeup of the homeless population. Many, of course, are those pitiful chronic dropouts from life in the U.S., the derelicts and drifters, the alcoholics, the ex-cons, the former mental patients whose numbers have risen sharply with the release from hospitals in many states of all but the most severely ill. Yet, as the director of one New York public shelter told me, blacks, formerly a minority among the homeless, are now in the majority in several places. Also, the average age of this impoverished population is steadily dropping, and substantial numbers of the destitute are under 30.

Both these factors suggest that the current economic situation is making devastating contributions to the stats of homelessness in America. Jobs would have kept a lot of these people out of the shelters. "These are working people," says one shelter director in Denver, where the homeless have quadrupled in the last year. Many are the "new poor," prideful and increasingly embittered people whose well-managed lives have been shattered by the loss of jobs and the ability to pay for adequate food and shelter for themselves and their families. They are everywhere, particularly in the Southwest and West, where they are drawn by the mild climate and by the mistaken impression that jobs are more plentiful.

The problem, in fact, threatens to get so big that many relatively comfortable citizens might have to start rethinking their notions about the meaning of charity. The practice of lending a hand to one's less fortunate fellows has been common to civilizations since the beginning of recorded history. The major religions, of course, have made charity a requirement of the spiritual life—and in some cases, a ticket to heaven. When religious organizations took over the administration of charity, those individuals who offered their alms or paid their tithes could relax and feel that their obligations were being satisfied.

With the rise of the welfare states and the diminution of Church influence over daily life, governments accepted the bulk of the charitable load as an obligation of the enlightened society. And the private person wound up still further from the people he paid his taxes to help. Now, with governments at all levels claiming to be broke, the need is growing for renewed charity on the part of those of us who prefer to keep ourselves at checkbook's length—at least—from the suffering of others.

Yet the private urge to keep the whole tacky problem at a safe remove is very powerful. A lot of people are truly repelled by the needy. Perhaps they remind us most poignantly of the fact that the good life is precarious. There, but for the. . . . Then, too, as one urban priest told me: "People who want to help often feel paralyzed by the magnitude of the problem"; for whatever reasons, raw uncharitability shows up in various ways again and again. Residents of a number of New York communities have squawked furiously—and effectively—to keep the city from setting up shelters in their neighborhoods. Politicians in Phoenix struck a blow against the hungry late last year by passing an ordinance that makes it an offense for people to take food out of garbage containers.

Still, there are impressive signs of rising consciousness. The newly reelected governor of Colorado, Richard Lamm, asked people to make contributions to the needy instead of giving him an inaugural ball. And with the Red Cross, he has set up a donation system to which one Wyoming farmer has given 500,000 pounds of potatoes. In one unlikely alliance, General Motors and the United Automobile Workers are going to manage a national food drive paid for by employee contributions and $2 million in matching funds put up by the company. A Chicago man and his wife spent four months remodeling a former convent where they now house up to 26 homeless people, including two pregnant teenagers and a family of five.

The private effort to help in New York includes an alliance called Partnership for the Homeless, through which small groups of men and women are housed overnight by various Manhattan churches and synagogues. At the church basement I visited, the "guests" arrived about 10 in the evening and, with some volunteer workers from the parish, immediately began setting up cots and mattresses for the night. The 10 men, who had been fed and offered clean clothing at a larger center earlier (and screened as well so that volunteers would not have to deal with some of the more volatile cases), gathered around a table, drank coffee and talked quietly or watched television until 11 when the lights would be turned out. A sort of relief was palpable in the warm room.

I asked one of the volunteers, an anesthesiologist in a big hospital who stops by to help most every night, why she was there. "I got tired of looking at these guys sitting on grates," she said. "I do it for my conscience." I asked the same question of a young accountant who, with his wife, would stay overnight in the shelter with the men and then get them ready to leave the next morning at seven. He looked at me with friendly surprise. "It has to be done," he said. "You can't just walk by." Charity, as Paul told the Corinthians, is not puffed up.

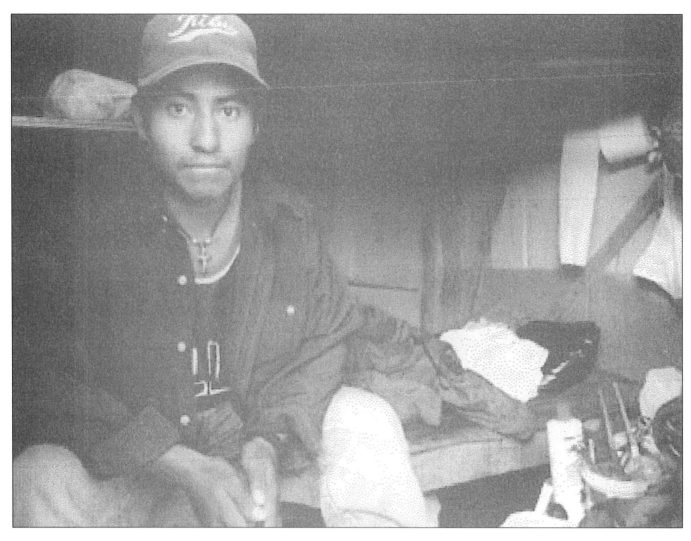

In 1983, the homeless estimate was 500,000 to 2 million people nationwide.

1988 Profile

Animal Conservation: Spotted Owls vs. Timbering

Jake Szmanda worked in the timber industry at a time when environmentalists, on behalf of the northern spotted owl, threatened to destroy his livelihood, while he felt there was room enough for both people and animals in the woods.

Life at Home

- Jake Szmanda grew up in the tiny town of Lakeview, located in the southeast corner of Oregon and nestled against the Willamette National Forest—the source of 86 million feet of board lumber a year.
- Jake's father Larry worked in the timber industry, first for a major company and then as an independent contractor running his own crew.
- As a project manager, Larry supervised much of the on-site logging work, while Jake's older sister, Mary, worked as an administrative assistant.
- The family shared a love for nature and respected the wood products that supported them financially.
- Jake's grandfather even built their house from trees he had cut, boarded, dried and nailed.
- The cabin was given to Jake's parents as a wedding present; Jake was always told that the house was part of his legacy and should never leave the family.
- Jake grew up in the woods and loved to track rabbits, identify snakes and recite excited tales about grizzly bears he spotted.
- He was taught that there was room enough for man and animals in the woods if they showed each other some respect.
- Early on, Jake learned that working with timber was demanding, requiring 11- to 12-hour days of hard physical labor.
- As a boy he was taught how to fell a tree to an exact spot using either an axe or a saw.

Jake Szmanda fought for the right to work in the timber industry.

Jake's grandfather built their house from trees he had cut, boarded, dried and nailed.

- Jake's father was proud of his profession; wood from the Willamette forests was shipped across the entire United States and used for homes, businesses, furniture and many other things which were "vital to the American way of life," Larry frequently said.
- But not everyone felt that way.
- A new species of human beings who called themselves environmentalists wanted a say in how the national forests were managed.
- Of particular concern were recent studies that determined that the old-growth trees that brought a premium price were also home to northern spotted owls, a rare, nocturnal species uniquely dependent on the Northwest's virgin forests.
- The centuries-old trees were the primary nesting ground for the northern spotted owls, which were declining in population as the old-growth forests were harvested.
- Concentrated for the most part in 12 national forests on the western slope of the Cascades, these giant evergreen stands of spruce, hemlock and Douglas fir—some taller than a 30-story building—once covered an estimated 19 million acres.
- Scientists said that only 2.5 million to 3.5 million acres of old-growth timber remained and were disappearing at the rate of 67,000 acres a year.
- About 900,000 acres were permanently protected in parks or wilderness areas.
- But the weapon that environmentalists wanted to wield against loggers was the Endangered Species Act, which protected birds and animals that were in danger of becoming scarce or extinct.
- Larry said that the definition of an environmentalist was a "city dweller with a new pair of hiking boots in his closet."
- But he secretly knew his industry was in a death struggle over the future of the Northwest's dwindling ancient forests, a mountainous, fog-shrouded realm that stretched from northern California to British Columbia.

Jake's family shared a love for nature.

- He also knew that the power enjoyed by the wood products industry was changing as Americans got their nature knowledge from the Discovery Channel and Disney.
- When Jake graduated high school in 1984, he planned to attend community college.
- Then, unexpectedly, his girlfriend Holly told him that she was pregnant.
- They married, Jake dropped out of college and joined his father in the Oregon forest, where work was steady and the pay excellent.
- But tensions were already building between the logging industry and environmental groups.

- Demonstrations and petitions against logging became more common.
- Logging roads were blockaded and loggers threatened; some radical environmentalists began driving metal railroad spikes into the uncut trees to make harvesting more dangerous and less profitable.
- Jake's father called them all "tree huggers" and said they were a passing fad.
- One day, Jake's sister came to the work site extremely upset.
- She said that there were news cameras and demonstrators outside her office: city people, every one of them.
- The next day it was all over the papers: the demonstrators wanted to stop logging in the Willamette.
- The northern spotted owls were now more important than the livelihood of loggers.

Life at Work

- Jake Szmanda and his family quickly learned that the northern spotted owl controversy would not go away.
- With another mouth to feed, Jake was haunted by the phantom owl as he tried to sleep.
- He needed to work steadily, not when the government said it was okay.
- Besides, everyone in logging agreed the compromise offered by the United States Forest Service was a giveaway to the eco-freaks who wouldn't know a spotted owl from a mockingbird.
- The plan called for the protection of 314,000 to 690,000 acres of national forest and would cost the timber industry $28 million to $32 million a year.
- The agency considered a number of alternatives, ranging from no formal measures to protect the owl to a complete ban on timber production in existing owl habitats.
- Then, the Reagan Administration declared that America's resources should be used, not hidden away; besides, new fast-growing trees could be planted in their place.
- It was great to have the president on your side, Larry said, but he was concerned about the future.
- After years of saying, "Don't worry," Larry had changed his tune to "We're now the ones who are endangered."
- Larry and Jake agreed that if the spotted owl gained federal protection under the Endangered Species Act, their livelihoods were doomed.
- After a lifetime of ignoring newspapers and magazines, Jake became a reader.
- And he was appalled to see loggers branded as wasteful despoilers of the land; clear cutting was an effective land management tool.
- The environmentalists clearly knew little about the economics or the dangers of harvesting the wood products Americans were eager to buy, but they knew everything about running their mouths and crying to Congress.
- Activists had petitioned Congress to declare the northern spotted owl an endangered species, which would forbid the logging industry to destroy any part of the forest that the owls might inhabit.
- The people in the logging industry were enraged.
- Small towns all over the Pacific Northwest, many of which were dependent on logging, were in turmoil.
- Jake was caught right in the middle of the crossfire.
- Without logging he, his father, and his sister would be out of a job with no qualifications to do anything else.

The Northern Spotted Owl

- Larry's solution was to cut as much timber as he could before the restrictions were put in place; Jake and Holly decided to take on the environmentalists by using the media.
- Jake told Holly, "Our kids are a lot cuter than any spotted owl; someone has to say that timbering is about people's lives."
- "Besides," Holly said, "it isn't an all-or-nothing situation. We may not have as many spotted owls if we keep cutting, but they won't disappear."
- To get his first interview, Jake approached a TV reporter and told him he had something to say.
- The interview, which took place right in front of a bunch of sign-waving city kids, lasted three full minutes.
- That night, Holly, Larry and Mary were thrilled to hear him say, "The environmental community would have you believe that the last of the old growth is on a logging truck heading for the mill, and that's not the case. It's time for some truth-telling and a lot less yelling." And then the camera swung over to the demonstrators.
- For the second interview, Holly dressed the two boys in bib overalls and held them on her lap while Jake talked about his love of the woods, including the spotted owl, a bird he had only seen twice.
- After that, TV stations from San Francisco to Boston couldn't wait to interview the cute family who thought there was room enough in the woods for both birds and people.
- But it quickly stopped being fun.
- Wood product executives—whose hands had never held a chainsaw—started telling him what to say, what to do and how to dress the kids.
- Eco-demonstrators hurled a stuffed owl at his oldest son and yelled "bird-killer" in his four-year-old's face.

- And business was drying up.
- With the changing regulations and uncertainty, the little guy was getting squeezed out by the more sophisticated corporations with lobbyists in Washington.
- Owl or no owl, some days there was no wood to cut.
- Small mills were closing up and small towns suffering.
- So Jake started talking about hard times and unemployment checks during the TV interviews, and the requests to speak stopped coming.
- He just wasn't cute anymore.

Life in the Community: Willamette National Forest, Oregon
- Nowhere were competing pressures of environment versus economy more acute than in the 1.7-million-acre Willamette National Forest, which sprawled across Oregon's western Cascades.
- Like many national forests in the Northwest, the Willamette remained largely undisturbed until the postwar building boom.
- About 500,000 acres of old growth remained in the Willamette, and 90,000 of that was permanently protected as designated wilderness.
- But many environmentalists felt that more of the old-growth forests should have been set aside to save the spotted owl.
- Scientists estimated that a single pair of the 15-inch-tall nocturnal birds required about 4,000 acres of old-growth forest to ensure an adequate food supply.

Willamette National Forest

- Biologists said that the bird's population, currently at about 3,000 pairs, was declining at the rate of 1 to 2 percent a year.
- Meanwhile, forest managers in the Willamette were obligated to provide timber at the levels specified by Congress and thus found themselves at odds with their own biologists.
- Spotted owls and environmentalists notwithstanding, timber accounted for 85 percent of the Willamette's management budget.
- Besides, the Reagan Administration was urging the Forest Service to accelerate the liquidation of the old trees in these virgin stands and replace them with faster-growing young stock.
- The approach reflected the goal of the Reagan Administration to greatly increase the production of timber, as well as oil, minerals and other commodities from the national forests.
- Under the plan, more economic activity could be generated from federal lands by turning over their resources to private industry as quickly as possible.
- The National Forest system had been created by the Forest Reserve Act of 1891.
- Based in part on the recommendations of Gifford Pinchot, the nation's first chief forester, the law was intended to prevent the reckless pillaging of the nation's forests.
- Reflecting Pinchot's views, the forests were to first serve the purpose of watershed protection, and then to assure "a continuous supply of timber for the use and necessities of the United States."
- The role of the forests was gradually broadened through such laws as the Multiple Use-Sustained Yield Act of 1960 and the National Forest Management Act of 1976, which required the forests to serve a broad spectrum of purposes, including wildlife protection and recreation.

HISTORICAL SNAPSHOT
1988

- The Supreme Court ruled that public school officials had broad powers to censor school newspapers, school plays and other "school-sponsored expressive activities"
- The Andrew Lloyd Webber musical *Phantom of the Opera* opened on Broadway
- When the board of trustees at Gallaudet University in Washington, D.C., a liberal arts college for the deaf, selected a hearing woman to be school president, outraged students shut down the campus and forced the selection of a deaf president
- Congress overrode President Ronald Reagan's veto of the Civil Rights Restoration Act and restored jurisdiction over Title IX issues in athletic programs to the Office for Civil Rights
- Former national security aides Oliver L. North and John M. Poindexter and two businessmen were indicted in the Iran-Contra affair
- The novel *Beloved* by Toni Morrison was awarded the Pulitzer Prize for fiction, while the *Charlotte Observer* (NC) won the prize for public service for its coverage of the Praise the Lord scandal
- The first McDonald's behind the Iron Curtain opened in Belgrade, Yugoslavia
- *The Last Emperor* won best picture at the 60th Annual Academy Awards ceremony; Cher won best actress for *Moonstruck,* while Michael Douglas won best actor for *Wall Street*
- The U.S. Patent and Trademark Office issued a patent to Harvard University for a genetically engineered mouse, the first patent granted for an animal life form
- The Soviet army pulled out of Afghanistan after nine years of fighting
- A federal ban on smoking during domestic airline flights of two hours or less went into effect
- Microsoft surpassed Lotus to become the number one computer software vendor
- Hong Kong announced a clampdown on "boat people," saying newly arriving Vietnamese refugees would be incarcerated and returned to Vietnam if they could not prove that they had fled religious or political persecution
- The Supreme Court unanimously upheld a New York City law making it illegal for private clubs to exclude women and minorities
- U.N. Secretary-General Javier Perez de Cuellar announced a ceasefire between Iran and Iraq
- President Reagan signed the Civil Liberties Act, a measure providing $20,000 payments to Japanese-Americans interned by the U.S. government during World War II
- The controversial movie *The Last Temptation of Christ,* directed by Martin Scorsese, premiered despite objections by some Christian groups
- Thousands of civil rights marchers gathered in Washington, D.C., for the 25th anniversary of Martin Luther King's "I Have a Dream" speech
- The TV sitcom *Roseanne* premiered

Selected Prices, 1988

Compact Disc Player, Technics	$229.95
Compact Disc	$11.95
Computer Game	$149.00
Computer, Apple IIGS	$795.00
Disposable Diaper, Pampers, Each	$0.21
Floppy Disks, 5¼″, per Box	$9.95
Perfume, Jovan Andron, per Ounce	$2,750.00
Scanner	$299.99
Television Satellite Dish	$1,995.00
Woman's Tibetan Lamb Jacket	$399.00

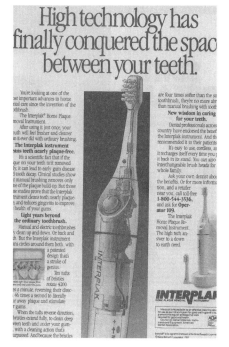

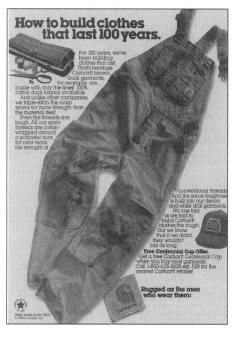

Forestry Timeline

1891

Congress passed the Forest Reserve Act, the legislative foundation for the National Forest system.

1892

The Sierra Club was founded with John Muir as the organization's first president.

1893

President Benjamin Harrison set aside 13 million acres of forest reserves.

1905

Control of the national forest system was transferred to the U.S. Department of Agriculture Forest Service.

The National Association of Audubon Societies for the Protection of Wild Birds and Animals was founded in New York, officially uniting the numerous state groups.

1905–1907

President Theodore Roosevelt set aside more than 180 million acres of land for wildlife refuges and national parks.

1907

Western ranching and mining interests called for the ceding of public lands to the states and restriction of national forests.

1916

The National Park Service was founded as a division of the U.S. Department of the Interior.

1919

The National Parks Association was founded.

1930

Dutch elm disease was first discovered in Cleveland, Ohio.

Late 1940s

After World War II, Americans flocked to the suburbs, accelerating deforestation around cities.

1950s and 1960s

Dutch elm disease devastated America's urban forests.

1970

The first Earth Day was celebrated on April 22.

1973

The Endangered Species Act was passed through Congress.

1986

Congress ordered the Forest Service to increase the sale of timber on public lands.

The Reagan Administration cut funds for urban forestry and other ecology programs.

"Dispute Flares over Harvest of Pristine National Forests," by Philip Shabecoff, *The New York Times*, January 12, 1985:

McKENZIE BRIDGE, Ore.—This is the forest primeval. But whether it should remain that way is a matter of intense dispute between the Reagan Administration, which wants to speed the harvest of virgin timber from the National Forests, and conservationists who seek an emphasis on recreation and protecting wildlife.

Here in the heart of the Willamette National Forest there are still large remnants of the "old growth" conifer forests that covered much of the Pacific Northwest until the beginning of this century.

Ancient Douglas firs, shaggy barked and draped with moss, tower hundreds of feet over a forest floor now carpeted with the thin layer of snow that has managed to penetrate the tangle of thick branches high overhead.

Under a policy pressed by John B. Crowell, who is departing after four years as Assistant Secretary of Agriculture in charge of national forests, the Forest Service would accelerate "liquidation" of the old trees in these virgin stands and replace them with faster-growing young stock.

Seeking to Increase Output

Mr. Crowell's approach to the old forests reflects the goal, stated when he was nominated by President Reagan four years ago, of greatly increasing the production of timber, as well as oil, minerals and other commodities from the national forests. He said at the outset that it would be possible to double or even triple the harvest of wood from the national forests. Last year's harvest was 10.5 billion board-feet; the historical high in 1973 was 12.4 billion board-feet.

That goal was a key element of the Reagan Administration's basic policy of generating more economic activity from federal lands by turning over their resources to private industry as quickly as possible.

Mr. Crowell's ambitions for the forests have not been realized. Although the "allowable cut" from the national forests has been raised substantially, timber production from the forests is still at about the levels reached in the Carter Administration.

Mr. Crowell said the nation would need more timber from the national forests as the pace of home building picked up. "We accomplished nothing in increasing the cut because the market was so lousy and interest rates were too high," he said in a recent interview. But the Administration's efforts to speed the timber harvest have aroused concern and protests among conservation groups and others who have asserted that the Administration has managed the forests primarily for the benefit of the forest products industry, in defiance of its legislative mandate to assure that they serve "multiple uses"

In Bed with Timber Industry

"Our impression is that the Forest Service is in bed with the timber industry and has frozen out conservationists," Peter Coppleman, of the Wilderness Society, said at a recent symposium on the national forests held in San Francisco.

Spokesmen for the wood and paper industry, however, praised the Administration's efforts to make the national forests more productive and described the complaints of the conservation groups as part of an effort to "lock up" all undeveloped federal forest land as untouchable wilderness.

Officials of the National Forest Products Association, a leading trade group, said this Administration's principal impact on the industry had not stemmed from its national forest policies but from its fiscal and monetary policies. These policies, they said, generated high interest rates that discouraged home building and increased the value of the dollar, which made timber from Canada more attractive. Max Peterson, chief of the Forest Service, said recently that "everybody wants a bigger piece of the pie," but that the Forest Service "is not in anybody's corner."

JARED GOEGELINE: 12-year-old Junior High Student; Hunter; 50,000th Junior Member of the National Rifle Association.

"My first gun was a BB gun I shot at a hay bale in our backyard. I was ten years old when I first shot a firearm. I haven't done much competitive shooting, but once I shot at a target in a turkey shoot and won a seven-pound ham. It's challenging to see how good a shot you are.

"I thought I should be a member of the NRA because everybody in my family is. So my Dad signed me up. I can go to shooting competitions and read interesting stories about hunting in InSights magazine. I like how they teach you to clean your gun and handle it safely. That's real important.

"Young people who like to shoot might want to become NRA Junior Members. It's fun and you can call the people at the NRA to get involved in all kinds of fun things." **I'm the NRA.**

Each year NRA certified instructors teach hundreds of thousands of young people safe gun handling and basic marksmanship skills. If you would like to join the NRA and want more information about our programs and benefits, write G. Ray Arnett, Executive Vice President, P.O. Box 37484, Dept. JG-13, Washington, D.C. 20013.

Paid for by members of the National Rifle Association of America. Copyright 1985.

"Forest Service Backs a Plan to Protect Owls in Northwest,"
The New York Times, August 10, 1986:

The United States Forest Service has urged a compromise between environmentalists and the timber industry that would preserve hundreds of thousands of acres in the Pacific Northwest to protect the northern spotted owl.

The spotted owl is not on the endangered species list, but Bob Nelson, a Forest Service official, estimated that logging in Oregon and Washington had caused a 50 percent reduction in the number of spotted owls.

The plan would protect from 314,000 to 690,000 acres of national forest and would cost the timber industry $28 million to $32 million a year, said J. Lamar Beasley, deputy chief for national forest systems.

Before settling on the proposal announced Thursday, the agency considered a number of alternatives, ranging from no formal measures to protect the owl to a complete ban on timber production in existing owl habitats, said Max Peterson, chief of the Forest Service.

WOODWORKING GUIDE

CUT AND DRIED

Working with wood is a joint venture between you
and the material. Learn to get along.

From an economic standpoint, those trees are doing nothing but standing there rotting. We could get more value
by cutting them down and growing a new crop.

—John B. Crowell, Assistant Secretary of Agriculture, 1985

1989 Profile

Reproductive Rights: Operation Rescue

Charles Coughlin Myers, an anti-abortion protester, was convinced that America was perched on a new era of greatness that would bring quality values back into the mainstream.

Life at Home

- Charles Coughlin Myers knew in his heart that, thanks to the leadership of President Ronald Reagan, the horrors of the New Deal era were being wiped out, Communism was on the verge of collapse, and AIDS was punishing the homosexuals and drug abusers for their deviant ways.
- The crowning achievement would be the abolishment of abortion in the United States.
- Now, with the election of President Reagan's handpicked successor, George Bush, America was destined to complete the work already begun.
- Charles's greatest disappointment in this quest was the refusal of the United States Senate to confirm Robert H. Bork for the Supreme Court in 1987.
- Judge Bork would have revolutionized the thinking of the court if the liberals had not ambushed him by mailings, fervent lobbying, scare rhetoric and television ads.
- Charles was also convinced the liberal press finally could see the sea change underway and was running scared.
- That's why it had demonized Judge Bork and frightened the voters into thinking that he was a monster who would sterilize women, bring back the poll tax and eliminate condoms.

Charles Myers was an anti-abortion protester.

Anti-abortion activists often preached from street corners to get their message out.

- The day the Senate refused to recognize the brilliance of Judge Bork was the day Charles understood that America was engaged in a civil war over its future moral framework.
- And he knew it was a wake-up call to stand on the front lines to defend America from decay.
- Born in 1946, Charles Coughlin Myers was proud that his parents had named him after the 1930s crusading Roman Catholic priest Father Charles Coughlin, who had used his radio broadcasts to challenge immorality, the bank cartel that was ruining the country, and America's first elected dictator, Franklin D. Roosevelt.
- It took courage to swim upstream against public opinion then, and the same was true today.
- That's why two years earlier, Charles resigned from his job as a software designer to become a full-time protestor with one goal: to stop government-approved murder of the unborn.
- Easy access to abortions had encouraged sexual relations by the unmarried and a decline in morality, Charles believed.
- He fully understood that the purpose of sex was the propagation of children and had fostered that belief throughout his 18-year marriage.
- During his first year as a professional protester, or as Charles preferred, "Pioneer for God," his wife and four children had traveled with him from march to demonstration to abortion clinic confrontation.
- The palpable tension and boisterous condemnation of women seeking abortions upset the children.
- Now they stayed in the New York apartment overlooking Central Park with their mother and attended school regularly again.
- Charles tried to visit at least once a month, no matter how busy he was.

Life at Work

- Charles Coughlin Myers appreciated that his father had been supportive of his beliefs; in fact, he even died at the right time.
- Just as boredom was setting in at work and his desire to reclaim the goodness of America at its peak, Charles's father had suddenly died of a massive heart attack, leaving behind a multimillion-dollar estate.
- That meant that Charles was unbound from the earthly need to provide for his family and freed to fight the iniquity unleashed in 1973 when the U.S. Supreme Court ruled in *Roe v Wade* that abortions could be performed legally nationwide.
- But Charles believed that, thanks to the Reagan "Era of Righteousness," restrictions on abortions were coming back step by step.
- After years of writing letters and talking to friends, he first decided to act during a protest condemning the opening of a gynecologist's office in Manhattan.
- Charles brought the entire family to the event, part of a week-long effort by a young organization known as Operation Rescue, the members of which believed that direct confrontation was essential for meaningful change.
- Charles's day began at 6 a.m., when the demonstrators assembled in the lobby of the Times Square Hotel on West 43rd Street, where many were staying.
- Groups of people held hands and prayed, and then left for the subway.
- They were told to follow guides who held American flags and were the only ones to know the route or destination.

- Charles was jubilant when he arrived at the protest and joined the others.
- Boisterously but peacefully, they sat on the sidewalk and street, praying and chanting before the office of the gynecologist at 154 East 85th Street, where they had been told abortions were performed.
- Across the street, supporters of abortion rights, including representatives of the National Organization for Women and the National Abortion Rights Action League, chanted, too.
- No one tried to enter the small residential building that housed the doctor's office because access was blocked.
- A few patients stood on the sidelines and then left, while medical personnel were blocked from going to work.
- That's when the arrests began in an orderly and peaceful manner.
- Charles had never been arrested before and was unsure whether to be proud or ashamed.

Watching anti-abortion protests.

- Their leader, Operation Rescue founder Randall A. Terry of Binghamton, New York, told the press, "Our goal is to completely close down abortion facilities for an entire day, and each day we will target another one."
- He told *The New York Times* that he had been planning the events for a year and a half.
- "We are simply producing the social tensions that bring about political change," he said.
- "Everyone here is committed to being arrested."
- During the three-hour protest, 503 demonstrators were taken into custody, bused to the Police Academy on East 20th Street, charged with disorderly conduct and released.
- Charles fully realized that too much energy had been concentrated on changing laws through the courts and legislatures; Operation Rescue wanted to save babies right now in the most direct way possible—by keeping women out of abortion centers.
- Minutes after being released from jail, Charles signed up for the protest in Chicago, where he learned the value of graphic pictures to shock women into keeping their babies.
- Women seeking abortions needed to face the visual consequences of their actions, Charles had come to understand.
- Several abortion-seekers turned away from his sign during the Chicago demonstration, but one woman actually threw up on the sidewalk when he showed her a picture of an aborted baby.
- It may have been his proudest moment in Chicago.
- From there Charles traveled the country at his own expense, fighting for the rights of the unborn.
- Quickly he learned that the press could not be trusted and refused to talk to them.
- In Atlanta, during the Democratic National Convention that year, the various protest groups had to take turns demonstrating in a two-acre area of parking lots that the city had set aside for that purpose.

- But Operation Rescue commanded headlines after 134 hymn-singing opponents of abortion blocked access to a medical clinic by lying across the steps in front of the door.
- Thirty-one of the anti-abortion demonstrators, including Charles, got further publicity for their cause when they refused to disclose their identities to police.
- Operation Rescue wanted to overcrowd the prison system by refusing to give their real names to police, thus making them ineligible for bond.
- For 40 days the protesters from New York, California, Virginia and Illinois sang and prayed behind bars.
- At the same time in Chicago, the police were unable to take two of the protesters into custody because they locked themselves to a bar attached to a concrete block, while in Pennsylvania, 74 activists were found guilty of trespassing outside a women's health clinic in Paoli.
- On New Year's Day, 1989, Charles was more optimistic than ever about the future of the right to life movement.
- The arrest Charles relished the most was the day he was handcuffed as a leader of the movement, while his children watched.
- For months his wife had been saying that he was setting a poor example for the children.
- Now it was his time to shine.
- That day police arrested 685 abortion opponents for demonstrating outside a Manhattan abortion clinic for the second consecutive day.
- Many of the protesters had stopped traffic and blocked sidewalks, but it was Charles's idea to chain 12 people, just like disciples, together in a line.
- Charles then swallowed the key to the locking system securing the chain and dared the police to make them stop blocking the doors of the Margaret Sanger Center, operated by Planned Parenthood.
- The protests defied an injunction issued by a Manhattan federal judge that forbade Operation Rescue from obstructing access to abortion clinics in the city.
- Charles's delight with the blocking maneuver turned to elation when the police shouted, "Take him first; he's their leader."
- And it was all said right in front of his children: a great day indeed.

Charles' children watched their father's arrests.

Life in the Community: New York City

- Until the Supreme Court ruled on *Roe v Wade*, each state had set its own laws concerning abortions and conditions under which they could be performed.
- New York State had the most liberal abortion access laws in the nation.
- So anti-abortion leaders began preparing early for the day when the Supreme Court ruling that legalized abortion was overturned and the issue returned to the states.

- Charles Coughlin Myers expected that some time during George Bush's Administration, the great evil of abortion would be halted.
- He believed that President Bush would shift the Supreme Court away from the 1973 *Roe v. Wade* decision through wise, conservative appointments, now that three of the Justices who had joined in the ruling were in their eighties.
- Sixteen years earlier, the Supreme Court had declared that a woman's right must be weighed against the fetus's growing potential for life.
- Therefore, the court reasoned, the state's interest in protecting life increased as the fetus grew.
- Accordingly, the decision was left up to a woman and her doctor whether to continue a pregnancy, at least during the first trimester.

Heavily-populated New York had liberal abortion access laws.

- States were allowed to impose some limitation on abortion in the second trimester, and allowed stronger limitation in the third.
- Polls indicated that a substantial majority of Americans believed strongly in a woman's right to an abortion, although anti-abortion groups contended that their support was growing rapidly.
- "I think there is a definite movement away from abortion now, as more people come to believe that it is not acceptable for mothers to murder their babies," according to Joseph Scheidler, executive director of the Chicago-based Pro-Life Action League.
- "We have whole groups of ex-abortionists coming and telling us how persuasive we've been.
- "And since the Democratic convention, there have been 10,000 arrests in anti-abortion demonstrations. That's a lot of people putting their bodies on the line."
- According to figures provided by Congress, half of all pregnancies in America were unintended and half of these unintended pregnancies ended in abortion.
- Nearly half of the unintended pregnancies were the result of a contraceptive failure.
- Nationwide, doctors performed 1.6 million abortions annually.

Historical Snapshot
1989

- Surgeon General C. Everett Koop told President Ronald Reagan he would not issue a report on the health risks of abortion

- *42nd Street* closed on Broadway after 3,486 performances

- Bowing to public outrage, Congress voted to kill their scheduled 51 percent pay increase

- Reverend Barbara C. Harris became the first woman consecrated as a bishop in the Episcopal Church

- Iran's Ayatollah Khomeini called on Muslims to kill Salman Rushdie, author of *The Satanic Verses,* a novel Khomeini condemned as blasphemous

- Union Carbide agreed to pay $470 million to the government of India in a court-ordered settlement of the 1984 Bhopal gas leak disaster

- Time Inc. and Warner Communications Inc. announced a deal to merge into the world's largest media and entertainment conglomerate

- Some 2,500 veterans and supporters marched at the Art Institute of Chicago to demand the removal of an American flag placed on the floor as part of a student's exhibit

- The Bush Administration announced a ban on imports of semiautomatic assault rifles

- The supertanker *Exxon Valdez* ran into Bligh Reef in Alaska's Prince William Sound and spilled 11 million gallons of crude oil

- The movie *Rain Man* won the Academy Award for best picture

- *The Heidi Chronicles* by Wendy Wasserstein won the Pulitzer Prize for drama; the *Anchorage Daily News* won the public service award for its reports on alcoholism and suicide among native Alaskans

- The first versions of HTML that launched the Web appeared

- Former White House aide Oliver North was convicted of shredding documents and two other crimes stemming from the Iran-Contra affair

- The FBI's promotion system was found to have systematically discriminated against its Hispanic employees in both advancements and assignments

- The Danish parliament allowed legal marriage among homosexuals

- The U.S. Senate rejected a proposed constitutional amendment barring desecration of the American flag

- The Chinese military launched a savage assault on the demonstrators in Tiananmen Square, killing an unknown number and crushing dissent in China

- Iranian leader Ayatollah Khomeini died

- Hungary proclaimed itself a republic and declared an end to Communist rule

- The United States sent troops into Panama to topple the government of General Manuel Noriega

- Romania's hard-line Communist ruler, Nicolae Ceausescu, was ousted in a popular uprising

Selected Prices, 1989

Baby's Car Seat	$54.99
Beer, Michelob, Case	$9.95
Bicycle Helmet	$19.99
Car Phone, Metrocom	$995.00
Carving Set, Ebony Handles, Set of Four	$675.00
Coffee Maker, Mr. Coffee	$36.00
Condo, One Bedroom, New York City	$225,000
Entertainment Center	$699.00
Radar Detector, FuzzBuster	$69.00
Television, 41-Inch Widescreen	$1,995.00

Reproductive Rights Timeline

1942

The Birth Control Federation of America, Inc., changed its name to Planned Parenthood Federation of America, Inc.

1959

The American Law Institute proposed a model penal code for state abortion laws.

1960

The Food and Drug Administration approved the use of oral contraceptives.

1965

The U.S. Supreme Court found unconstitutional the Connecticut law prohibiting birth control for married couples.

1967

Colorado allowed abortion in cases of permanent mental or physical disability of either the child or mother or in cases of rape or incest.

1970

New York allowed abortion on demand up to the twenty-fourth week of pregnancy.

Congress enacted Title X of the Public Health Service Act, which provided funds for family planning services, education and research.

1971

The U.S. Supreme Court upheld a District of Columbia law permitting abortion only to preserve a woman's life or "health" to include "psychological and physical well-being."

1972

The U.S. Supreme Court struck down a Massachusetts statute that barred distribution of contraceptives to unmarried people.

Thirteen states permitted limited access to abortions in cases of permanent mental or physical disability or cases of rape; four states allowed abortion on demand.

1973

The U.S. Supreme Court ruled in *Roe v. Wade* that a "right of privacy" encompassed a right to an abortion, making abortion legal nationwide.

1974

The first March for Life rally was held in Washington, D.C., on the anniversary of the *Roe v. Wade* decision.

1975

The first Human Life Amendment was introduced in the U.S. Senate.

1976

The Supreme Court struck down a Missouri law that obliged a married woman seeking an abortion to obtain her husband's consent.

The manslaughter conviction of Doctor Kenneth Edelin was overturned by the Massachusetts Superior Judicial Court, which ruled that legal abortions are manslaughter only if the baby was living outside the mother's body.

Congress barred the use of federal Medicaid funds to provide abortions to poor women, restricting abortion access.

continued

Timeline . . . *(continued)*

1977

Mission Possible was launched by the Minnesota Citizens Concerned for Life to develop state right to life groups, primarily in the Southeastern United States.

The first reported arson was committed at an abortion clinic, in St. Paul, Minnesota, and the first known bombing of an abortion clinic happened in Cincinnati, Ohio.

The U.S. Supreme Court ruled that federal and state governments were under no obligation to fund abortion in public assistance programs, even if childbirth expenses were paid for indigent women and even if the abortion was deemed to be "medically necessary."

1979

Dr. Bernard Nathanson, the National Abortion Rights Action League cofounder, published *Aborting America*.

1980

Republican pro-life candidates Ronald Reagan and George Bush defeated President Jimmy Carter and Vice President Walter Mondale.

1981

The U.S. Supreme Court approved a Utah law that required a doctor to notify the parents of a minor girl who was still living at home when an abortion was scheduled.

1983

The U.S. Supreme Court struck down state laws requiring waiting periods for women seeking abortions and that abortions performed after the first trimester be done in a hospital.

The U.S. Senate rejected the Eagleton-Hatch Amendment, that declared "a right to an abortion is not secured by the Constitution."

The U.S. Congress barred the use of federal employees' health benefits programs to pay for abortions, except to protect the life of the mother.

1984

The Reagan Administration announced the "Mexico City Policy," which denied funds to foreign organizations that "perform or actively promote abortion as a method of family planning in other nations."

1986

In *Thornburgh v. American College of Obstetricians and Gynecologists*, the U.S. Supreme Court struck down state laws mandating a waiting period for women seeking abortions.

The Senate confirmed President Reagan's promotion of Associate Justice William Rehnquist to chief justice of the Supreme Court; Antonin Scalia was confirmed to replace Rehnquist as an associate justice.

1987

President Reagan restricted the use of Title X funds and appointed a federal task force to encourage adoption as an alternative to abortion.

The nomination of pro-life Judge Robert Bork to the U.S. Supreme Court was rejected by the U.S. Senate.

1988

The Reagan Administration issued a moratorium on new federally funded fetal tissue transplant research.

The French government approved the licensing of RU-486; the U.S. Food and Drug Administration banned the importation of RU-486 for personal use.

continued

Timeline . . . *(continued)*

1988

The U.S. Senate barred the District of Columbia from paying for abortions or performing abortions in its city-operated hospital.

1989

A reported 300,000 Pro-Choice supporters rallied in Washington, D.C.

The U.S. Supreme Court found that the Constitution does not require the government to make public facilities such as hospitals available for use in performing abortions.

The Freedom of Choice Act was introduced for the first time in Congress.

President George Bush vetoed a foreign aid appropriations bill that would have restored funding to an organization that played a key role in China's coercive population-control program.

Ronald Reagan was Charles Myers' hero.

"Why Abortion Is Genocide," by Gregg Cunningham, Brochure, "The Center for Bio-Ethical Reform":

Rationale for the Genocide Awareness Project (GAP): As part of its Genocide Awareness Project, The Center for Bio-Ethical Reform exhibits large photo murals comparing aborted babies with Jewish Holocaust victims, African Americans killed in racist lynching, Native Americans exterminated by the U.S. Army, etc. Our purpose is to illustrate the conceptual similarities which exist between abortion and more widely recognized forms of genocide. This is important because perpetrators of genocide always call it something else and the word "abortion" has, therefore, lost most of its meaning.

Genocide as Indescribable Evil: Visual depictions of abortion are indispensable to the restoration of that meaning because abortion represents an evil so inexpressible that words fail us when we attempt to describe its horror. Abortion will continue to be trivialized as "the lesser of two evils," or perhaps even "a necessary evil," as long as it is allowed to remain an invisible abstraction. Pictures make it impossible for anyone with a shred of intellectual honesty to maintain the pretense that "it's not a baby" and "abortion is not an act of violence." Pictures also make clear to people of conscience the fact that abortion is an evil whose magnitude is comparable to that of any crime against humanity. Educators invariably use shocking imagery to teach about genocide and we insist on the right to do the same.

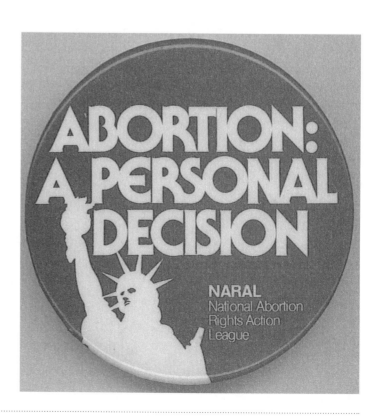

"685 Are Arrested Opposing Abortion," by Constance L. Hays, *The New York Times*, January 15, 1989:

The police arrested 685 abortion opponents yesterday demonstrating outside Manhattan abortion clinics for the second consecutive day. Many of the protesters had stopped traffic, blocked sidewalks and, in one case, chained themselves together, the police said.

By late last night, charges against 215 of the protesters had been dropped, said a police spokesman, Sgt. Edward Burns. Another 269 people, who refused to identify themselves to police, were scheduled to be arraigned on charges of disorderly conduct, criminal trespass or resisting arrest. In addition, 151 people received summonses for disorderly conduct and 60 others were issued desk-appearance tickets, the sergeant said.

The protesters defied an injunction issued by a Manhattan federal judge last week forbidding members of a right-to-life group called Operation Rescue from obstructing access to abortion clinics in the city. A counter protest in favor of the right to choose abortion was held outside St. Patrick's Cathedral last evening by about 100 people. They said they were protesting John Cardinal O'Connor's support for Operation Rescue.

Almost half of the anti-abortion protesters arrested were attempting to block the doors of the Margaret Sanger Center, operated by Planned Parenthood at 380 Second Avenue near East 21st Street. A total of 350 people were arrested after a crowd of about 500 stopped traffic near the clinic for about two hours in the morning.

A Planned Parenthood manager, Barbara Clayton, told the Associated Press that police officers and barricades prevented the protesters from reaching the building, and that staff members escorted patients inside.

Copyright 1989. Reprinted by permission of The New York Times, New York, NY

We're following God's law, and that's more important than man's law.

—Philadelphia nurse Peg Roach, who was arrested and jailed as an Operation Rescue demonstrator

---

If you believe abortion is murder you must act like it is murder.

—Operation Rescue credo

We as a nation are doomed to a severe chastening from the hand of God. Abortion is the symbol of our decline, the slaughter of the most innocent. What kind of justice is it, when 10 of us are fined $450,000 for trying to stop the murder of innocent babies, while the homosexuals who entered St. Patrick's Cathedral and disrupted Mass are fined $100 each? I'll tell you, if we were homosexual, we'd be treated a lot better in the courts.

—Randall Terry, founder of Operation Rescue, 1990

"Rallies for Abortion Rights Span Nation," by Robin Toner, *The New York Times*, November 13, 1989:

Tens of thousands of people rallied in the nation's capital today on behalf of abortion rights, celebrating recent political victories and vowing to redouble their efforts in battles to come.

They gathered at the steps of the Lincoln Memorial under a warm sun to hear one politician after another pledge commitment to their cause and to roar their disapproval of a president on the other side.

"Do you get the message, George Bush?" asked Representative Don Edwards, Democrat of California, as the crowd cheered just a few blocks from the White House.

"Together, we will show the president and the nation that pro-choice is a winning issue," said Representative Nita M. Lowey, Democrat of Westchester County. [Senator Bob] Packwood, fearful for G.O.P. President Bush, who has vetoed two major spending bills in recent weeks because they would expand public financing of abortion, was at Camp David today and had no comment on the rally. But today's demonstrations, in Washington and in cities across the country, capped a troublesome week for many Republicans who fear that their party's and their president's identification with the anti-abortion movement will prove politically costly.

"Unless our party changes its position, we're going to lose more elections," Senator Bob Packwood, Republican, of Oregon, said in a brief interview at the rally. He is a longtime supporter of abortion rights.

In Los Angeles, the Rev. Jesse Jackson told a cheering throng that women were not "puppets of the Court" and that God gave them the right to choose. "We are creatures of a Creator who endowed us with choice," he said. "In our society, women are burdened with choices, and they must have the freedom to choose a response to those burdens."

The police estimated the crowd in Los Angeles at 20,000.

In Washington Molly Yard, president of the National Organization for Women, declared, "This will be the issue of 1990."

1990–2006

The economy limped into the 1990s under the gloom of recession, but quickly exploded into the Era of Possibilities. This robust economy empowered and emboldened the nation's traditionally less well off. The ranks of the African American middle class swelled; women filled half of all seats at the nation's law and medical schools, and Hispanic workers immigrated in droves to chase the dream of economic prosperity in a foreign land. America's disabled gained new rights and more respect, and America's Christian fundamentalists found their political voice. And as wealth grew, the possibilities flourished. Colleges became overcrowded, while the buying power and media attention paid to America's youth exploded. Personal computers, fully capable of competing with television and its rapidly expanding array of specialized channels, became a fixture in millions of homes. The 1990s were characterized by steady growth, low inflation, low unemployment and dramatic gains in technology-based productivity. The resulting expansion was particularly meaningful to computer companies and the emerging concept known as the Internet—a technology that would revolutionize business, media, consumer buying and interpersonal relations in the opening years of the twenty-first century.

As the 1990s opened, America was struggling with a ballooning national debt and the economic hangover of the savings and loan industry. Media headlines were dominated by stories of rising drug use, crime, racial tensions and the increase of personal bankruptcies. Family values became a political touchstone. Guided by Federal Reserve Chair Alan Greenspan's focus on inflationary controls and a declining deficit, the U.S. economy soared, producing its best economic indicators in three decades. By the end of the 1990s the stock market was posting record returns, job creation was at a 10-year high and businesses were desperately searching for qualified workers in a technologically savvy world. As a result, the 1990s gave birth to $150 tennis shoes, condom boutiques, pre-ripped jeans, digital cameras, DVD players, and 7.7-ounce cellular telephones. The decade was also a time of debate, much of it powered by 24-hour programming on television channels and the resurgence of talk radio. American publicly debated limits on abortion, tougher criminal enforcement, the role of affirmative action, bilingual education, food safety and Internet child pornography.

History will record that the new century began in the United States on September 11, 2001, when four American commercial airliners were hijacked and used as weapons of terror. After the tragedies at the World Trade Center in New York; Shanksville, Pennsylvania; and the Pentagon in Washington, DC, Americans felt vulnerable to a foreign invasion for the first time in decades. America's response to the attacks was to dispatch U.S. forces around the world in a "War on Terror." The fist stop was Afghanistan, where a new brand of terrorist group known as al-Qaeda had planned and executed the attacks under the protection of the country's Taliban rulers. America's technologically superior weaponry was impressively displayed as the Afghan government was quickly overthrown, although capturing al-Qaeda leader Osama bin Laden and stabilizing a new government proved more vexing. With the shell-shocked economy in overall decline and the national debt increasing at a record pace, the United States rapidly shifted from Afghanistan to Iraq. Despite vocal opposition from traditional allies such as Germany and France, President George W. Bush launched Operation Iraqi freedom with the goal of eliminating the regime of Saddam Hussein and his cache of weapons of mass destruction. The invasion resulted in worldwide demonstrations, including some of America's largest protest marches since the Vietnam War. As in the invasion of Afghanistan, the U.S. achieved a rapid military victory, but struggled to secure the peace. When no weapons of mass destruction were found, soldiers continued fighting while an internal, religious civil war erupted; support for the war waned and vocal protest increased.

Despite the cost of the war, the falling value of the dollar and record high oil prices, the American economy began to recover by 2004. Unemployment declined, new home purchases continued to surge, and the full potential of previous computer innovation and investment impacted businesses large and small. Men and women of all ages began to buy and sell their products on the Internet. Ebay created the world's largest yard sale; Amazon demonstrated, despite sneering critics, that it could be the bookstore to the world; and we all learned to Google, whether to find the exact wording of a Shakespearian sonnet or the menu at Sarah's Pizza Parlor two blocks away. At the same time, globalization took on a new meaning and political import as jobs—thanks to computerization—moved to India, China or the Philippines, where college-educated workers were both cheap and eager. American manufacturing companies that once were the centerpiece of their community's economy closed their U.S. factories to become distributors of furniture made in China, lawn mowers made in Mexico or skirts from Peru. The resulting structural change that pitted global profits and innovation against aging textile workers unable to support their families resulted in a renewed emphasis in America on education and innovation. If the U.S. was to maintain its economic dominance, the pundits said, innovative ideas and research would lead the way.

Professional women, who for decades had struggled to rise past the glass ceiling in their companies, began to find bigger opportunities in the 2000s. Significantly, the promotion of a woman to a top slot in a Fortune 500 company ceased to make headlines. Some top female CEOs even began to boldly discuss the need for more balance in the workplace. Yet, surveys done at mid-decade showed that more Americans were working longer hours than ever before to satisfy the increasing demands of the marketplace and their own desire for more plentiful material goods. In some urban markets the average home sales price passed $400,000; average credit card debt continued to rise and the price of an average new car, with typical extras, passed $20,000.

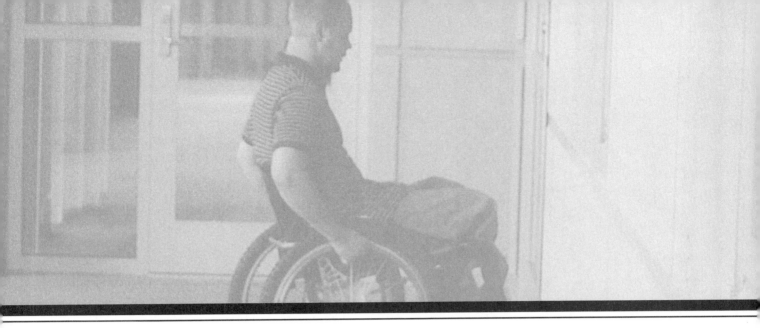

1992 PROFILE

RIGHTS OF THE HANDICAPPED: THE DISABILITY ACT

Jordan Mitchell, a high school football jock, saw his whole world change when his car accident left him paralyzed from the waist down.

Life at Home

- Jordan Mitchell, the second of two children, was born on March 1, 1972, while his father was completing an internship at the University of Colorado Medical School.
- His mother taught math at a local middle school to help out financially.
- They did not have much money during the early years of Jordan's life.
- His father had recently received a Ph.D. in biochemistry and was hoping to work his way up the scientific research ladder.
- After a few years in Colorado, Jordan's father finished his postdoctoral training and was soon offered his first job in Baltimore, Maryland, at the prestigious Johns Hopkins Medical Center.
- The job allowed the family to move into their first home in a residential neighborhood.
- Jordan and his family lived there until he was five, when Wake Forest Medical University offered Jordan's father a position at the Medical Center in Winston-Salem, North Carolina, close to Jordan's extended family.
- As he grew, Jordan developed a passion for playing sports: baseball, soccer, basketball and football—he loved the competition.
- The sport that captured his focus was football, especially as a running back.
- Jordan enjoyed scoring touchdowns, but loved to run people over even more.
- The second year he played, the coaches switched him to linebacker, which allowed him to use what he had learned on offense to read the developing play on defense and then react.
- By the time Jordan reached high school, he had narrowed the number of sports he participated in down to one: football.

Jordan Mitchell refocused his energy from football to rights for the disabled.

Jordan was a top player on his HS team.

- His goal was to become a starter on the varsity team by the time he was a junior, even though he was undersized for a linebacker at just 5'11" and only 185 pounds.
- Relying on instincts and quickness, Jordan was soon one of the top players on the team and one of the most feared linebackers in the conference.
- When Jordan's team lost in the second round of the state playoffs his junior year, the team's rising seniors vowed to win a state championship.
- The next season got off to a terrific start with only one loss during the regular season and no defeats in their conference for the third straight year.
- When it was playoff time, Jordan and his teammates were thrilled to be the number one seed and breezed through the opening rounds.
- The state semifinal contest promised to be tremendous: Jordan's Mount Tabor Spartans against perennial powerhouse West Charlotte.
- On the day of the game, the team was scheduled to report to the gym at 3 o'clock.
- It was a messy day.
- Rain poured hard on this Friday after Thanksgiving, and Jordan was anxious to report, anxious to play, anxious to do well.
- On the way to the gym, Jordan lost control of his Honda Accord going around a turn.
- That was the last thing he could remember.
- Everything that happened during the next two weeks was a blur.
- Between the shock and the powerful painkillers, it became hard to sort things out.
- He could remember parts of the ambulance ride to the hospital as well as talking to his girlfriend when he first arrived, but little else.
- The Spartans won the game that night for Jordan but lost a week later in the championship.
- During those two weeks, family members, teammates, and friends streamed in and out of his hospital room.
- The intensive care nurses said they had never seen so many people come to visit one person.
- The doctors told Jordan's parents that he had sustained a number of serious injuries, all of which would heal except for one.
- Jordan had broken his back in the accident and was paralyzed from the waist down.
- A week after his wreck, he had surgery to place five metal rods down his spinal cord.
- One morning, Jordan woke up and everything that had taken place suddenly seemed all too real.
- He was devastated, and scared about his future.
- When Jordan had recovered from his internal injuries, he was moved to the Shepherd Center, a top spinal cord rehabilitation facility in Atlanta, Georgia.
- There, Jordan began to learn the basics of living in a dramatically different body.
- The first step was simply to sit up straight.
- The interrupted blood flow in his body caused him to pass out every time he sat up.
- It took three weeks before he was finally sitting up for extended periods of time.
- Jordan felt like a newborn all over again; he could not control his bowels or bladder and was reduced to wearing a diaper.
- The muscles for which Jordan had worked so hard were gone; he lost 30 pounds in a little under a month.

- There was still no movement or sensation in his legs, but Jordan promised himself that he would do his best with what he still had.
- He learned how to transfer himself from his bed to a wheelchair.
- This was his first step toward independence, but certainly not his last.
- He lifted weights to regain some of his upper body strength.
- He learned how to get in and out of a car from his wheelchair, how to take a shower, and how to manage his bowels and bladder.
- The rehab experience proved to be extremely beneficial.
- While most patients needed three to four months to finish, Jordan took two.
- However, although he was ready physically, he was not mentally prepared to go out into a social environment.
- The first month was a learning experience.
- Accustomed to being the big "jock," he felt his self-confidence evaporate and struggled to look people in the face.
- While visiting a friend who lived in an older house, Jordan discovered that he could not even fit through the bathroom door.
- For the first time, he wondered how anyone could have built a house without thinking about the needs of someone in a wheelchair.
- Jordan decided to inform himself.
- He had never thought about wheelchair barriers before, almost as if they did not exist.
- He remembered hearing about the Americans with Disabilities Act (ADA) that was passed in 1990 but was unclear of the details.
- The main objective of the ADA was to provide equal rights for disabled people to include job opportunities, Social Security benefits, building regulations, and health care.
- Jordan was amazed at the fact that it took until 1990 for a law like this to be passed, and wondered how disabled people had functioned before.

Life at School

- Although it had been over a year since the Americans with Disabilities Act was passed, the process of making facilities accessible to all was just starting.
- Private employers were required to make accommodations for future disabled employees.
- Public buildings were given 12 months to comply with accessibility regulations.
- Change was coming, but in baby steps.
- Jordan Mitchell graduated high school in 1991 by completing his remaining classes at home.
- He applied for and was accepted to a major university.
- During orientation Jordan felt out of place.
- Surrounded by people he did not know, he was unsure how to ask others for help.
- As they toured the campus, Jordan struggled to get up many of the hills.
- Because a number of buildings had no ramps, he could not even enter some parts of his own school.
- Before the start of the first semester, Jordan met with the school's disability office, still in its infancy.
- The staff handed Jordan a generic letter for his professors that explained that he might arrive late for class and may need special bathroom privileges.

It took time for Jordan to feel comfortable at his university.

- On the first day of classes, Jordan was up early to make sure he got to class on time.
- As he rolled on to the main campus, a feeling of anxiety crashed over him.
- Jordan noticed people looked at him differently.
- Some were looks of curiosity; most seemed to be looks of sympathy.
- By the time Jordan made it to class, he was physically and emotionally worn out.
- He tried to concentrate on class work but found it hard to think about anything except how uncomfortable he was with his new life.

- As weeks progressed, so did Jordan.
- He learned campus shortcuts and which buildings provided quality access points; he even began to hold his head up a little more when he rolled, as a show of confidence.
- Jordan lived in an on-campus apartment with two of his friends from high school.
- It was important to live with people around whom he felt comfortable; living independently and being a paraplegic were challenges in and of themselves.
- Laundry was the toughest thing to do alone.
- Because his bladder still leaked on occasion in his sleep, Jordan had much more laundry than a normal college student would.
- It hurt his back to try to reach far enough into the washing machine to retrieve his clothes; it was the same with the dryer.

Jordan learned about his rights on campus and off.

- After about a month of struggling, Jordan finally hired a laundry pick-up service to do his laundry every week for $30.00.
- He felt as if he had control of something for the first time since his accident.
- As late summer turned to fall, Jordan was excited about attending a university football game.
- He missed his favorite sport and could not wait to watch his new team perform.
- Jordan went to the ticket office intent on obtaining some of the best seats in the stadium that were accessible to the handicapped.
- The people there explained that good handicap access seats were limited: there was not yet a way for a wheelchair to get down to the lowest level near the field.
- He could only get a seat at the top of the deck.
- Jordan was infuriated but did not want to draw attention to himself until he had at least gone to the game to check the seats out.
- He and his father, who came with him to the game, were impressed by how close the handicap parking spots were to the stadium.
- The seats turned out to be terrible.

- Jordan was not close enough even to feel part of the game.
- He could not help but laugh and say that he would have been better off watching the game on TV.
- Afterwards, Jordan went to the library to do some further research on the Americans with Disabilities Act of 1990.
- If the disabled had rights, it was time he learned what they were.
- He found that under Section 302, Article IV states that no individual can be discriminated against on the basis of disability in the full and equal employment of public goods, services, facilities, advantages or accommodations that are not equally afforded to other individuals.
- He also learned that public places of entertainment and sporting events were definitely included.

- All public buildings were supposed to comply within 12 months of the act being passed.
- It had been 16 months and the stadium was clearly not up to par.
- This meant that if able-bodied people could purchase a ticket to sit in the front row, then so should someone in a wheelchair.
- So Jordan printed this information out and took it to the disability office on campus.
- They seemed impressed by his initiative and insistence and promised to present this information to the dean of the school.
- After a week the office finally called to say that the dean was concerned about the situation and had been totally unaware that this was a problem.
- He promised to inquire with the city as well as the North Carolina Department of Labor in Raleigh to see what could be done.

Handicap seating was far removed from the action.

- The next month, Jordan checked by the office weekly to see if the school had made any progress.
- He also attended the games and continued to sit in the upper deck.
- Six weeks after he first asked about the situation, his persistence was rewarded.
- Jordan received a personal call from the dean of students telling him that because the team's stadium was owned by the city, it was responsible for fixing the problem.
- A decision had been made to install an elevator as well as make room for 20 new handicap seats in the lower deck.
- All the changes were completed for the start of the 1992 football season.
- By then Jordan had adjusted to his new life: he drove to school using hand controls affixed to a regular car, did all his own laundry, and held his head up high.
- Most of all, on Saturdays when he sat in the lower deck, he felt responsible for having done something positive.

The Americans with Disabilities Act

- The Americans with Disabilities Act, or ADA, was termed the most comprehensive federal civil rights statute protecting the rights of people with disabilities.
- It affected access to employment; state and local government programs and services; access to places of public accommodation such as businesses, transportation, and nonprofit service providers; and telecommunications.
- The scope of the ADA in addressing the barriers faced by people with disabilities was very broad.
- Advocates insisted that the Americans with Disabilities Act protections paralleled those that had previously been established by the federal government for women and racial, ethnic and religious minorities.
- Critics predicted that accommodating America's 54 million citizens with disabilities would bankrupt the economy.
- A critical aspect to the ADA's ability to bring about change was the practice of designing products, buildings, public spaces and programs to be usable by the greatest number of people.

- The Act helped create a society where curb cuts, ramps, lifts on buses, and other access designs are increasingly common.
- In the process, curb cuts designed for wheelchair users were also used by delivery people, people with baby carriages, and people on skateboards and roller blades.
- When the ADA was before Congress, members predicted a flood of lawsuits that would bankrupt or at least overburden business.
- One congressional leader characterized the ADA a "disaster" benefiting only "gold diggers" filing frivolous lawsuits.
- But adoption was less expensive than the doomsayers predicted.
- Many businesses found that compliance was often as easy as raising or lowering a desk, installing a ramp, or modifying a dress code.
- One survey found that three-quarters of all changes cost less than $100.

The school library was difficult to maneuver.

HISTORICAL SNAPSHOT
1992

- The Food and Drug Administration called on surgeons to stop using silicone gel breast implants because of safety questions
- Japan apologized for forcing tens of thousands of Korean women to serve as sex slaves for Japanese soldiers during World War II
- Mideast peace talks continued in Washington, with Israel and Jordan holding their first formal negotiations
- President George H. W. Bush proposed tax breaks and business incentives to revive the economy, and announced dramatic cuts in the U.S. nuclear arsenal
- The U.S. Coast Guard shipped home 250 more Haitian refugees from the Guantanamo Bay Naval Base in Cuba, a day after repatriating a shipload of about 150 Haitians
- The 100th episode of *Cops* aired on the Fox network
- Natalie Cole won seven awards at the 34th Annual Grammys, including best album for *Unforgettable*
- The Supreme Court ruled prison guards who use unnecessary force against inmates may be violating the Constitution's ban on cruel and unusual punishment even if they inflict no serious injuries
- The U.N. Security Council stood firm in its demand that Iraq comply totally with Gulf War ceasefire resolutions
- The Supreme Court upheld Pennsylvania's restrictive abortion law but also reaffirmed a woman's basic right to an abortion
- McDonald's opened its first fast-food restaurant in the Chinese capital of Beijing
- The Ms. Foundation began its "Take Our Daughters to Work Day"
- For the first time in 74 years, worshippers celebrated the Russian Orthodox Easter in Moscow
- The U.S. Agriculture Department unveiled a pyramid-shaped recommended-diet chart that had cost nearly $1 million to develop
- Deadly rioting that killed 55 and injured 2,300 erupted in Los Angeles after a jury acquitted four Los Angeles police officers of state charges in the videotaped beating of Rodney King
- The Supreme Court ruled criminal defendants may not use race as a basis for excluding potential jurors from their trials
- The motion picture *Batman Returns* opened with the first weekend box office revenues of $47.7 million
- The Supreme Court strengthened its 30-year ban on officially sponsored worship in public schools, prohibiting prayer as a part of graduation ceremonies
- President Bush vetoed the so-called "motor-voter" registration bill
- The Senate voted to sharply restrict U.S. testing of nuclear weapons
- The Mall of America, the biggest shopping mall in the country, opened in Bloomington, Minnesota

Selected Prices, 1992

Backpack, Leather	$29.95
Camcorder, RCA	$699.00
CD/Cassette Player, Sony	$166.00
Exercise Bicycle	$249.99
Luggage, Garment Bag, American Tourister	$39.96
Men's Tennis Shoes, Converse	$24.00
Pager, Motorola, per Month	$7.95
Pistol, Smith & Wesson, .38 Caliber	$309.00
VCR, JVC	$399.00
Women's Polo Shirt	$18.00

Americans with Disabilities Timeline

1817

The American School for the Deaf was founded in Hartford, Connecticut, the first school for disabled children anywhere in the United States.

1848

The Perkins Institution in Boston, Massachusetts, became the first residential institution for people with mental retardation.

1864

The Columbia Institution for the Deaf and Dumb and Blind was authorized by the U.S. Congress to grant college degrees.

1927

The Supreme Court decision ruled that forced sterilization of people with disabilities was not a violation of their constitutional rights; nationally, 27 states began wholesale sterilization of "undesirables."

1935

The League for the Physically Handicapped in New York City was formed to protest discrimination by the Works Progress Administration.

The Social Security Act established federally funded old-age benefits and funds to states for assistance to blind individuals and disabled children.

1943

The LaFollette-Barden Vocational Rehabilitation Act added physical rehabilitation to the goals of federally funded vocational rehabilitation programs and provided funding for certain health care services.

1945

President Harry Truman created an annual national "Employ the Handicapped Week."

1948

The National Paraplegia Foundation, founded by members of the Paralyzed Veterans of America as the civilian arm of their growing movement, began advocating for disability rights.

1956

Social Security Amendments created the Social Security Disability Insurance program for disabled workers aged 50 to 64.

1961

President John Kennedy appointed a special President's Panel on Mental Retardation.

1963

The Mental Retardation Facilities and Community Health Centers Construction Act authorized federal grants for the construction of public and private nonprofit community mental health centers.

1965

Medicare and Medicaid were established providing federally subsidized health care to disabled and elderly Americans covered by the Social Security program.

continued

Timeline . . . *(continued)*

1968

The Architectural Barriers Act prohibited architectural barriers in all federally owned or leased buildings.

1973

The Rehabilitation Act prohibited discrimination in federal programs and services and all other programs or services receiving federal funds.

1974

A suit filed in Pennsylvania on behalf of the residents of the Pennhurst State School and Hospital became a precedent in the battle for de-institutionalization of the mentally handicapped.

1975

The Individuals with Disabilities Education Act required free, appropriate public education in the least restrictive setting.

1977

Demonstrations by disability advocates took place in 10 American cities after Joseph Califano, U.S. Secretary of Health, Education and Welfare, refused to sign meaningful regulations.

1978

The American Disabled for Public Transit staged a year-long civil disobedience campaign to force the Denver, Colorado Transit Authority to purchase wheelchair lift-equipped buses.

1981–1984

Disability Rights advocates generated more than 40,000 cards and letters to Congress to halt attempts by the Reagan Administration to amend regulations implementing the Rehabilitation Act of 1973 and the Education for All Handicapped Children Act of 1975.

The Reagan Administration terminated the Social Security benefits of hundreds of thousands of disabled recipients.

1985

The Mental Illness Bill of Rights Act required states to provide protection and advocacy services for people with psychological disabilities.

1986

Toward Independence, a report of the National Council on the Handicapped, outlined the legal status of Americans with disabilities and documented the existence of discrimination.

1988

The Air Carrier Access Act prohibited airlines from refusing to serve people simply because they were disabled and from charging people with disabilities more than non-disabled travelers for airfare.

1990

The Americans with Disabilities Act provided comprehensive civil rights protection for people with disabilities; it mandated that local, state and federal governments and programs be accessible, and that businesses with more than 15 employees make "reasonable accommodations" for disabled workers.

"Don't Blame Disabled for the Delay in Building Public Toilets," Letter to the Editor, *The New York Times*, June 3, 1991:

To the Editor:

"In New York, Few Public Toilets and Many Rules" (news article, May 21) makes people with disabilities who suffer the indignities of inaccessible housing, transportation and public accommodations, and rampant discrimination the scapegoat for New York City's inability to build public toilets.

It is hard to imagine that you would entertain a discussion of whether or not any other minority group should be allowed access to a public toilet, one of the hard-won battles of the civil rights movement. People with disabilities have a right to use toilets and any other facilities like anyone else. And for the city's Art Commission to think accessible construction may be "unattractive" and therefore objectionable is outrageous.

The solution is simple:

- Follow the handicap access laws.
- Follow the procurement laws to find a company willing to build accessible, and attractive, toilets.
- Follow the public access laws and do not charge a fee for the toilets. The toilets are primarily intended for the indigent, and charging a quarter will hardly deter vandalism.

I am troubled by your general implication that compliance with the handicap access laws is "why it is so hard to get things done in New York." As the hours of congressional testimony that preceded passage of the Americans with Disabilities Act bear out, handicap access is easily achievable, is not unaesthetic and is not inordinately costly.

—Ruth Lowenkron, Staff Attorney, New York Lawyers
for the Public Interest Disability Law Center, New York

The ADA guaranteed the same rights for all Americans.

Disability, like race and gender, is a natural and normal part of the human experience that in no way diminishes a person's right to live a normal life and participate in mainstream activities.

—Professor Robert Silverstein of George Washington University

"As the Labor Pool Dwindles, Doors Open for the Disabled," by Kathleen Teltsch, *The New York Times*, June 22, 1989:

For millions of Americans with disabilities, the country's shrinking labor pool of qualified workers is opening up new job opportunities.

Since a 1975 federal law required public schools to open their classrooms to the handicapped as fully as possible, more and more disabled Americans have been striving to translate their educational gains into economic gains. Aided by advances in technology that help them do jobs that were once impossible, they have been trying to move into the mainstream work force, away from reliance on government aid, family support and jobs in sheltered workshops.

"These kids are graduating now, a new generation educated to live in a competitive world," said Pat Wright, the Washington director of the Disability Rights Education and Defense Fund of Berkeley, California. "There is no question they expect to work, and it does not dawn on them that society has a mind-set to think of them as different or as dependents."

Their job prospects will be enhanced if Congress approves legislation that would extend to private industry existing provisions prohibiting federal agencies and federal contractors from discriminating against the handicapped in hiring and promotions.

A major provision of this sweeping package of civil rights measures would prohibit a private employer of 15 or more workers from discriminating against a qualified job applicant or worker because of a handicap. . . .

The bill already makes some provisions to ease the business burden, including the exemption of small businesses. It also requires employers to make "reasonable accommodations" for the disabled, unless it would result in an undue burden on the employer. Employers already have the right to inquire about medical conditions that might limit a person's performance in a specific job. Advocates for the rights of the 43 million Americans with physical or mental impairment, while generally encouraged, maintain that there is a long way to go. . . . Their ranks include those with sensory impairment, like the deaf or blind, and those who use wheelchairs and otherwise have limited mobility. Federal regulations also protect those with disabilities that cannot be readily observed, like epilepsy, diabetes, cancer and heart disease as well as recovering alcoholics and people with AIDS.

The improving job prospects for the handicapped, a group that grows as an estimated 500,000 Americans become disabled each year, were a recurring theme at a recent New York conference that brought together advocacy groups, scores of the disabled and leaders of philanthropic organizations, which are showing an increasing interest in the issue.

Copyright 1989. Reprinted by permission of The New York Times, New York, NY

No otherwise qualified handicapped individual in the United States, shall, solely by reason of his handicap, be excluded from the participation in, be denied the benefits of, or be subjected to discrimination under any program or activity receiving federal financial assistance.

—The Rehabilitation Act of 1973, Section 504

Letting every employee have an identical opportunity to use a restroom located up a flight of stairs may be "identical" treatment, but it is hardly equal treatment for a worker who uses a wheelchair.

—Professor Robert Burgdorf, Jr., one of the drafters of the original bill that became the Americans with Disabilities Act, 1990

1996 Profile

Worker Rights: The Immigrants' Strike

Once Airto Escavedo left war-torn Guatemala for America to make a better life for his family, he found himself in the midst of another battle—for better working conditions in the North Carolina poultry processing plant where he was employed.

Life at Home

- Twenty-five-year-old Airto Escavedo grew up in the midst of war in Guatemala.
- Like most indigenous Guatemalans, Airto was of Mayan descent and traced his bloodline and language back to the ancient "corn people."
- He was the son of Soledad and Flora Escavedo, successful garlic farmers in Aguacatan.
- There, commercial agriculture was the main industry; crops consisted of tomatoes, onions, and especially garlic, which was the chief export to foreign markets.
- Perched between mountain ridges, Aguacatan had historically been a busy farming and commercial center because of its well-irrigated valley location.
- Size as well as its proximity to the provincial capital contributed to its prosperity.
- But Soledad's failing health and the disastrous effects of the war had all but eliminated the family business.
- For nearly 30 years, the Western Hemisphere's longest-running guerilla war between the armed left and the military-dominated government had ravaged Guatemala's economy in a Cold War conflict.
- The war had claimed an estimated 200,000 casualties in dead and disappeared; some 600 indigenous communities were eliminated by government-sponsored attacks, according to a United Nations Truth Commission.
- It was against this backdrop of economic stagnation that men like Airto Escavedo prepared to leave their homeland in the late 1980s, seeking the means in America to support their families.
- And Airto believed he possessed an advantage—an education.

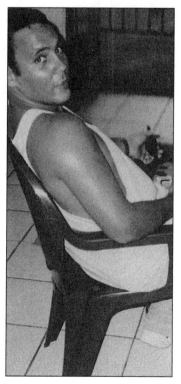

Airto Escavedo left Guatemala for a better life in the U.S.

Looking for work in Guatemala.

- Education was more easily available in Aguacatan because of the efforts of Henry and Lucille McArthur.
- The McArthurs were Canadian-born missionaries, linguistic scholars and Wycliffe Bible translators, who did much to promote literacy and education among the Aguacatan people by cross-translating indigenous languages and Spanish.
- Through their efforts, thousands of children were enrolled in primary schools and more than 500 attended secondary schools.
- Newly married with a child on the way, Airto knew that he must leave Guatemala if he was to support his family.
- For prospective émigrés like Airto, survival in America would depend on locating job prospects, arranging transportation, successfully crossing the border, finding housing, actually getting a job, and then learning the ropes at work and outside work.
- To travel to the United States, it cost up to $3,000, which he borrowed from his parents.
- Airto walked, paid for van rides, and rode a bus through Mexico before crossing into the United States by way of Arizona.
- Upon arrival in the U.S., Airto worked in agriculture and construction until he was advised by a family friend and fellow Aguacateco Francisco Fuentes of the opportunity for work at a poultry processing plant known as Case Farms.
- Airto was told that Case Farms was located in the more familiar mountain surroundings of Morganton, North Carolina, offered inside work, and steady pay.

Typical Guatemalan hut.

- It was such a popular designation for Mayans that a regular van service from Indiantown, Florida, to Morganton had been established.
- Case Farms even rented public housing for its Guatemalan labor and provided bicycles as transportation to work.
- Fuentes charged Airto $20.00 for the trip and $30.00 as a referral fee for a job at the plant.
- Fuentes claimed to have transported over 300 workers to Morganton by the time Airto arrived in 1993.
- It was rumored that Fuentes received up to $50.00 from Case Farms for each worker he procured.

Life at Work

- Airto Escavedo's goal as an employee of Case Farms in Morganton, North Carolina, was simple: to make enough money to return to his pueblo and be with his family and community in Guatemala.
- By 1993, Airto was becoming familiar with his new surroundings.
- He noted three major differences between American life and what he had previously known.
- One, he discovered the meaning of the weekend; two, he opened a bank account; and three, television became a part of his daily routine.
- Airto lived in a single male household with six other Aguacateco men in their twenties and thirties, who took turns cooking and cleaning for themselves.
- Eighty percent of Aguacateco male workers were married, but few had been able to bring their wives along.

- But the large Mayan population in Morganton meant he could routinely eat traditional foods, such as corn tortillas and beans, and use natural cures for minor ills.
- Upon arrival in Morganton, Airto started work in the "live bird" area of Case Farms, where workers pulled live, struggling birds from crates and hung them on hooks by their feet.
- He was paid $6.35 an hour, which was less than he had been promised.
- He found that work in a poultry plant, even under the best conditions, presented a demanding and unpleasant routine.
- His education concerning poultry processing and illegal immigrant labor started almost immediately upon arrival.
- The poultry industry provided the lowest pay in the food industry.

The Case Farms plant.

- Poultry plants were known for unreported accident claims: carpal tunnel syndrome was ranked the third-highest complaint among U.S. industries.
- One out of every six employees in the poultry industry suffered a work-related illness or injury every year, according to the U.S. Department of Labor.
- For employers, immigrant workers were a valuable commodity, who filled hard-to-hire-for jobs at a low price.
- The first large-scale labor eruption at the Case Farms plant occurred in May 1993, just months before Airto arrived.
- Approximately 100 workers stood up in the plant cafeteria and refused to return to work unless the company addressed a list of grievances.
- The list included unpaid hours, unauthorized company deductions for safety equipment like smocks and gloves, the lack of bathroom breaks, poor working materials and inadequate pay.
- The plant manager summoned local police and 52 workers were charged with trespassing.
- Following mediation by lawyers from the local legal services office and state labor board officials, the workers agreed to return to work and the company dropped all legal charges.
- The disruption was also one of the reasons that Airto was able to get a job so easily: troublemakers were being moved out.
- But by early 1995, he was tired of handling chickens, angry with management, and nowhere close to having enough money to return to Guatemala.
- He desperately missed his wife and child.
- Airto's first confrontation with management occurred on May 11, 1995.
- By this time, of the 500 people employed at the Case Farms processing plant, 80 percent were Spanish-speaking, and of those, 80 to 90 percent were Guatemalan.
- The work protest began in Airto's "live bird" area.
- By prior agreement, everyone stopped work when a supervisor denied a bathroom break requested by one of the men.
- Once the workers had management's attention, three men were designated to approach the manager with their grievances: the arbitrary control of bathroom breaks, increasingly stressful line speed, deductions for safety equipment, and consistently low wages.

Scenes of Case Farm, above and below.

- Instead of giving the three young men a hearing, the manager had them arrested for trespassing.
- A plant-wide shutdown then began, immediately followed by a workers' rally outside the plant gates.
- The strike lasted 11 days.
- Following threats by the company to replace them, the workers returned to their jobs, having succeeded in getting a real response from the company and bringing the Mayan workers into contact with the American trade unions.
- As the strike proceeded through its first week, the chief organizer for the Laborers' International Union of North America arrived in Morganton.
- He was awestruck by the fact that the workers had organized this strike and demonstration with no help from any sort of institution except the church and a legal aid attorney in Morganton.
- He was also amazed that the workers self-organized so that the first union-organizing meeting could be translated into seven or eight dialects required by the Mayan workers.
- At meetings on the property of Francisco Fuentes, and later at St. Charles Catholic church, the movement gathered strength.
- The workers were ready to fight even if the company took their jobs and evicted them from their apartments.
- On July 12, 1995, after a heated campaign, the employees voted 238-183 to form a union and be represented by the Laborers' International Union of North America.
- The vote by the workers made the Case facility the only unionized chicken plant in the state.
- Nationally, the story of the Case Farms workers became a cause célèbre in labor circles.
- Union leaders saw it as a potential breakthrough in their drive to organize the low-wage poultry industry, which employed more than 21,000 people in North Carolina, many of them immigrants.
- But big victories took time.
- The national union win rate in National Labor Relations Board elections was less than 40 percent, a figure that dropped even further in "right to work" states like North Carolina.
- At the national level, fewer than 20 percent of private sector workers who attempted to organize were able to gain representation under a union contract.

- Airto had been told that even after winning an organizing drive, the Case Farms workers might not get serious consideration of their desire to bargain for a union contract—and they didn't.
- The company's lawyers filed a variety of appeals.
- By delaying union recognition and serious contract bargaining, the company wanted to take advantage of worker turnover, fatigue, demoralization and the dwindling union organizing budget.
- In the 1990s, an estimated one-third of the workplaces where workers voted for a union never achieved a first contract.
- And Airto could only wait so long.
- He was not prepared to spend another Christmas without his family, and be too poor to send presents and be a good father.

- By February 1996, he had given up and journeyed back to Guatemala as poultry workers from North Carolina joined national religious and labor activists in demanding a "code of ethics" for an industry they branded as unsafe, unsanitary and inhumane.

Life in the Community: Morganton, North Carolina

- Prior to the arrival of the Maya in Morganton, North Carolina, the area had absorbed two extraordinary immigrant colonies in the past century.
- At the beginning of the 1900s, several hundred French-speaking Waldensians arrived in Burke County and settled in a nearby community named Valdesa.
- Beginning in the late 1970s, 500 Laotian Hmong refugee families settled in Morganton with help from area churches and the federal government.
- The gradual migration of hundreds of Mayan immigrants was largely ignored.
- The community of Morganton and the Guatemalan workers at Case Farms occupied different worlds.
- So the workers used a self-created community to protect themselves and find comfort.
- Airto enrolled in a successful all-Hispanic soccer league, organized by town of origin.
- Religious life was directed with the establishment of two additional Hispanic evangelic churches.
- But the average Morganton resident did not welcome the new arrivals with open arms.
- They seemed to feel that eventually the newcomers would just disappear.
- Mayor Mel Cohen judged that the Mayan migration had a more negative than positive effect on Morganton.
- Cohen's observation was based on five points.
- First, the immigrants' inability to understand the language.
- Second, their inability to adhere to the local quality of life.
- Third, they sent most of their money back to Guatemala and did not spend it locally.
- Fourth, their lack of respect for community property.
- Fifth, their willingness to live in substandard habitation.
- The immigrants, for their part, held a residual distrust for anyone in uniform because of their experience with corrupt police and military in their own country.
- As the Mayan population grew, they became the victims of neglect more than hostility.
- Banished to the margins of town life, the Mayan presence took more than a decade to appear in the annual Morganton Historic Festival.
- Yet a small band of citizens helped to ease the migrants' acclimation.
- As early as 1992, National Red Cross agencies hired a Spanish-speaking teacher to direct Project Amigo, an outreach program, which provided the new Guatemalan community with health care and other services.
- Unquestionably, the center for Guatemalan socialization was St. Charles Catholic church.

HISTORICAL SNAPSHOT
1996

- The U.S. banned the manufacture of freon because of its effect on the ozone layer
- Iraqi leader Saddam Hussein decreed economic austerity measures to cope with soaring inflation and widespread shortages caused by U.N. sanctions
- President Bill Clinton and Monica Lewinsky, a White House intern, engaged in a series of sexual encounters at the White House
- The U.S. Army disclosed that it had 30,000 tons of chemical weapons stored in Utah, Alabama, Maryland, Kentucky, Indiana, Arkansas, Colorado and Oregon
- Sheik Omar Abdel-Rahman and nine followers were handed long prison sentences for plotting to blow up New York-area landmarks
- France detonated its sixth and most powerful nuclear bomb
- New protease-blocking drugs were shown to be effective in combating AIDS
- Twenty-four church fires were reported, 17 of them involving largely African American congregations
- Congress voted overwhelmingly to rewrite the 61-year-old Communications Act, freeing the exploding television, telephone and home computer industries to jump into each other's fields
- World chess champion Garry Kasparov beat IBM supercomputer "Deep Blue," winning a six-game match in Philadelphia
- The Space Telescope Science Institute announced that photographs from the Hubble Space Telescope confirmed the existence of a "black hole" equal to the mass of two billion suns
- Alanis Morissette's *Jagged Little Pill* won best rock album and album of the year at the Grammy Awards
- Dr. Jack Kevorkian was acquitted of assisted suicide for helping two suffering patients kill themselves
- Liggett became the first tobacco company to acknowledge that cigarettes are addictive and cause cancer
- The first of the Nixon White House tapes concerning Watergate were released
- Nevada's governor designated a 98-mile stretch of Route 375 the Extraterrestrial Highway
- The Senate passed an immigration bill to tighten border controls, make it tougher for illegal immigrants to get U.S. jobs, and curtail legal immigrants' access to social services
- The nation's 16,000 public companies were required to file their financial reports electronically with the Securities and Exchange Commission
- Guatemala's leftist guerrillas and the government signed an accord to end 35 years of civil war
- The federal government set aside 3.9 million acres of land in California, Oregon and Washington state for the endangered marbled murrelet

Selected Prices, 1996

Breadmaker	$100.00
Deodorant, Secret	$1.50
Food Processor, Cuisinart	$139.00
Fur Coat, Russian Sable	$7,995.00
Olive Oil, 23 Ounces	$32.00
Rollerblades	$34.97
Television, Digital Home Theater	$10,000
Vegetable Slicer	$45.00
Videotape, *The Lion King*	$29.97
Whirlpool Tub	$1,660.00

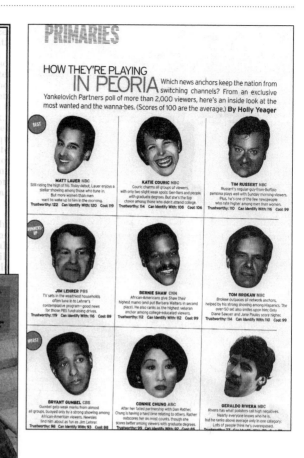

Immigrant Labor Timeline

1941

The Fair Employment Practices Act was passed to eliminate discrimination in employment.

1943

Prompted by the labor shortage in World War II, the U.S. government made an agreement with the Mexican government to supply temporary workers, known as *braceros,* for American agricultural work.

The so-called "Zoot Suit" riots took place in southern California, where hundreds of soldiers roamed Hispanic neighborhoods beating up Mexican American young men who were wearing zoot suits.

1945

The War Brides Act authorized the limited admission into the U.S. of the wives and children of military men without regard to quotas.

1948

The Displaced Persons Act permitted the immigration of 202,000 Europeans displaced as a result of political or racial persecution.

1950

Congress upgraded Puerto Rico's political status from protectorate to commonwealth.

1954

The Supreme Court recognized Hispanics as a separate class of people suffering profound discrimination, paving the way for Hispanic Americans to use legal means to attack all types of discrimination.

1954–1958

Operation Wetback, a government effort to locate and deport undocumented workers, resulted in the deportation of 3.8 million persons of Mexican descent.

1960s

Young Mexican Americans created a new identity for themselves known as the Chicano Movement.

1962

The United Farm Workers Organizing Committee in California began as an independent organization led by César Chávez.

1964

Congress enacted the Civil Rights Act of 1964, which prohibited discrimination on the basis of gender, creed, race or ethnic background.

1965

Amendments to the Immigration and Nationality Act abolished the nation-origin quotas and established an annual limitation of 170,000 visas for immigrants in the Eastern Hemisphere.

The end of the *bracero* program forced many Mexicans to return to Mexico, with many settling near the U.S. border.

When Fidel Castro allowed Cubans to leave the island nation if they had relatives in the United States, several hundred thousand emigrated to Florida.

continued

Timeline . . . *(continued)*

1968

Chicano student organizations sprang up throughout the nation, as did barrio groups such as the Brown Berets.

Immigration was limited to 120,000 persons annually from the Western Hemisphere.

1970

A Chicano Moratorium to protest the Vietnam War was organized in Los Angeles to draw attention to the disproportionately high number of Chicano casualties in that war.

1974

Congress passed the Equal Educational Opportunity Act that made bilingual public education available to Hispanic youth.

1970s–1980s

The rise in politically motivated violence in Central America spurred a massive increase in undocumented immigration to the United States.

1977

The Immigration and Naturalization Service (INS) apprehended more than one million undocumented workers.

An amendment to the Immigration and Nationality Act abolished separate quotas for the Western and Eastern Hemispheres, changing the quota to 290,000 immigrants worldwide annually with a maximum of 20,000 from any one country.

1980

The Refugees Act reduced the worldwide quota to 270,000 immigrants.

More than 125,000 Cuban "Marielito" refugees migrated to the United States.

1980s

The rate of immigration approached the levels of the early 1900s as 6.3 million immigrants were granted permanent residence; Hispanic immigrants continued to account for more than 40 percent of the total.

1986

After more than a decade of debate, Congress enacted the Immigration Reform and Control Act which gave legal status to applicants who had been in the United States illegally since January 1, 1982.

1990

The Immigration Act of 1990 set an annual ceiling of 700,000 immigrants per year to enter the U.S. for the next three years and an annual ceiling of 675,000 per year for every year thereafter.

1994

The North American Free Trade Agreement (NAFTA) took effect to eliminate all tariffs among trading partners Canada, Mexico, and the United States within 15 years from this date.

Californians passed Proposition 187, which banned undocumented immigrants from receiving public education and public benefits such as welfare and subsidized health care, except in emergency situations.

1996

The Illegal Immigration Reform and Immigrant Responsibility Act made it easier to deport aliens attempting to enter the U.S. without proper documents.

"Immigrant Poultry Workers' Struggle for Respect Draws National Attention," by Craig Whitlock, *The News and Observer* (Raleigh, NC), November 30, 1996:

MORGANTON—Faced with a shortage of local workers willing to tolerate the unpleasant conditions at its chicken-processing plant, Case Farms Inc. of Morganton decided to look southward.

In the early 1990s, the poultry producer dispatched 15-passenger vans to recruit migrant workers in Florida and spread the word in Texas and California that jobs were plentiful at its factory in the North Carolina foothills.

Case Farms was especially eager to hire Guatemalan immigrants. Company executives decline to say why, but others suggest it was rooted in a perception that the Guatemalans were hardworking and docile—unlikely to complain, join a union or balk at the messy task of butchering chickens.

Today, business is booming at Case Farms. About 90 percent of its 550 factory workers are Latinos, a huge majority of them from Guatemala. The company's labor strategy, however, has backfired. Upset with what they see as oppressive treatment and a lack of respect, the workers have voted to join the Laborers' International Union of North America and have engaged in a series of strikes and protests to force Case Farms to the bargaining table. So far, the company has refused.

But the dispute has put pressure on Case Farms and the rest of the state's fast-growing poultry industry, which has come to depend on immigrant labor and, until now, has successfully fought off union organization campaigns in North Carolina.

This week, U.S. Labor Secretary Robert Reich announced that the federal government would investigate working conditions in poultry plants nationwide, with an emphasis on North Carolina and Arkansas, where chicken producers predominate. Reich said his decision was prompted in part by publicity about the Case Farms conflict.

The story of Case Farms, however, is more than a labor dispute. It also is an illustration of how simple corporate decisions can unleash economic and cultural forces that collide in unexpected ways.

For instance, Case Farms' hiring practices have forced the city of Morganton to absorb an influx of newcomers that is straining services and fueling resentment.

The same perplexing issue is surfacing all over the state, but especially in small towns and rural areas, as thousands of immigrants move north to fill low-wage farm and factory jobs that local people don't want.

Chris Scott, executive director of the AFL-CIO in North Carolina, describes the Case Farms organizing effort as "one of the major labor struggles in the country.

"The main problem with these kinds of workers is that they are extremely vulnerable," he says. "Some of them may not have gotten Jesse Helms to stamp their passport on the way in. They may not want to rock the boat that much."

Last Straw, First Strike

In January 1995, Carlos Salido was working construction jobs near West Palm Beach, Fla., when a man made him a tempting offer. A chicken plant in North Carolina was hiring workers. Salido could earn $7.50 an hour, the man said, and have the opportunity to work as many as 70 hours a week.

continued

"Immigrant Poultry Workers' Struggle for Respect Draws National Attention" . . . *(continued)*

Salido accepted. The labor recruiter drove Salido and three other job-seekers on a 700-mile trip north to a place they had never heard of before: Morganton, a town of 16,000 people 50 miles east of Asheville.

Case Farms paid the recruiter $50.00 for each worker he brought, then put Salido and the others right to work. With no formal training, Salido began on the "whole bird" line, where he sliced off chickens' feet.

He also spent time in the "live hang" department, where the job required him to grab live chickens and shackle them to steel hooks, at a rate of several birds a minute. The work was hard—the chickens would scratch and claw—and it paid less than advertised, a maximum of $6.35 an hour.

"The lines were flying by and the work was so repetitive," said Salido, a native of Guatemala who was later fired by Case and now works full-time for the Laborers as an organizer. "It was cold. It sucked."

Supervisors also imposed strict rules on the factory floor, which was chilled to a temperature of 45 degrees to keep the meat from spoiling. Workers were permitted three bathroom breaks a day and had to pay for their own hairnets, gloves and rubber boots.

One day in May 1995, three workers tried to seek out the plant manager to complain about the working conditions. After being ignored, they defiantly refused to return to the butchering line. The company fired them on the spot and had them arrested for trespassing.

The arrests caused a stir among co-workers who thought their colleagues had been treated unfairly. The next Monday, 300 people walked off the job in protest and went on strike for three days.

Union Gains a Toehold

News of the strike spread quickly and reached the Laborers' Union, which had been trying without success to organize workers at two Perdue Farms poultry plants in Lewiston-Woodville and Robersonville, both in northeastern North Carolina.

The Laborers immediately sent staff members to Morganton to see if they could build support for a union. Some workers at Case proved enthusiastic, and an election was held two months later. Despite stiff opposition from the company, employees voted 238 to 183 in favor of the union.

"It wasn't like you had to spend time talking to each of them to convince them," said Patrick Moran, a Laborers organizer currently assigned to Morganton. "They were definitely ready to run."

It was the first time workers at a chicken plant in North Carolina had voted to unionize, despite numerous attempts. The only other poultry plant in the state with a union is a House of Raeford turkey plant in Hoke County.

Labor organizers have spent several years targeting the state's $2 billion poultry industry, which employs more than 21,000 people, according to the N.C. Poultry Federation. Only three states produce more chickens each year than North Carolina, which sent 570 million birds to market last year.

Poultry processing is also one of the state's most hazardous occupations. Wages are low, and the injury rate is high. The state's worst workplace disaster occurred at a chicken plant—the Imperial Food Products factory in Hamlet, where 25 people died in a 1991 fire.

Even so, unions have had little success organizing poultry workers in North Carolina, which has long been unfriendly territory for unions. Like many Southern states, it has right-to-work laws, which prohibit labor agreements that require workers to join a union. The state's overall workforce is the second-least unionized in the nation.

As a result, unions see the Case Farms labor conflict as a potential breakthrough, a reason to redouble efforts at other chicken plants in the state.

"Case Farms is no different from other places," said Jackie Nowell, a UFCW official. "Conditions in poultry plants across North Carolina are deplorable. And if people in the general public knew what was going on, they'd be horrified. . . ."

continued

"Immigrant Poultry Workers' Struggle for Respect Draws National Attention" . . . *(continued)*

Long, Hard Path to Progress

Huehuetenango (Way-way-tuh-nang-go) is a rural province in western Guatemala, bordering Mexico. About 800,000 people live there; some are of Hispanic origin, some are Native Americans, and many are a mixture of both. Just about everybody is poor.

Hundreds of people originally from Huehuetenango now work for Case Farms. Most already have U.S. work permits from previous jobs in border states such as Texas and California. But some have come to North Carolina illegally.

The company is reluctant to talk about how its Guatemalan labor pipeline started. But John Vail, executive director of Catawba Valley Legal Services, a group that provides legal aid to the poor, traces it to a telephone call he received in late 1990 or early 1991 from a Catholic nun in Immokalee, Fla.

The nun wanted to know if employees were about to go on strike at the Case Farms plant in Morganton. Company officials had come to south Florida and were aggressively recruiting Guatemalan farm laborers from the sugarcane fields, and the nun was concerned that the workers were being imported as potential strike-breakers.

"They said they were asking for Guatemalans, because Guatemalans were known to be especially docile," Vail recalled.

The company's first Guatemalan recruits soon were followed by friends and relatives from Huehuetenango, many of whom were already working in the United States. While most of them arrived in Morganton eager to work, they have not always proven to be docile.

In addition to the May 1995 walkout, the workers went on strike for two weeks in August. They've also organized a small number of other brief work stoppages, some lasting no more than a few minutes.

Workers and union officials insist that wages aren't a major complaint. Many say they are more concerned about the safety hazards presented by the constantly moving knives and hooks. Most say they simply want Case Farms to hold them in higher regard.

"I want to see respect," said Sergio Matheu, 21, who has worked in the plant for two years. "I want to see justice in the way they treat people and talk to people."

Juan Montes, a Mexican who came to Morganton last year after working for a decade in San Diego, said that although Case refuses to bargain, the presence of the union clearly has had an effect.

The assembly line has been slowed, reducing the risk of injury. The floor, once caked with chicken blood and grease, is cleaner these days. And wages have risen slightly, from $6.35 an hour to $6.85.

"We may be Guatemalans and Mexicans, but we are humans, too, and we deserve respect," said Montes, who expects to take his oath of citizenship next month and settle permanently in Morganton with his wife and two daughters. . . . .

Reprinted by permission of The News & Observer of Raleigh, North Carolina

ALLAS, Ga.—The horns of the Paulding County High School marching band blew the last note of the national anthem, and there was lence. Then one voice, then another, then thousands.

Soon, the chorus dominated the modest stadium—asking this day for their daily bread, forgiving those who trespass against them, eking to be led not into temptation but delivered from evil.

This recitation of "The Lord's Prayer" was simple but fundamentally defiant. Fans here compared themselves to Christian soldiers, ghting to save religion's place in schools before the courts strip it away.

The scene is being repeated on Friday nights, in varying forms but with an identical message, on the South's most hallowed battle-rounds—its football fields.

"People understand we are a religious nation," said the Rev. Curtis Turner, who brought his Baptist congregation from half a me-opolis away to pass out copies of the prayer before Paulding County's game with arch-rival East Paulding. "It shouldn't be confined. Vhat if we confine it? They'll do it like a smoking ban."

2000 PROFILE

PRAYER IN PUBLIC SCHOOLS: PRAYER AT A FOOTBALL GAME

Rita Willis found herself embroiled in a school prayer debate when a dozen teens gathered at her home after a football game at which a student had led the crowd in reciting the "Lord's Prayer."

Life at Home

- At 51 years old, Rita Willis was sure she was well past her rebel stage.
- Of course, when she went to law school in the early 1970s, she was considered a token female admission and a rebel of sorts.
- After all, the world seemed firmly convinced that only men were capable of coping with the rough-and-tumble world of "the law."
- "The law" appeared to rank above religion, presidential edicts, congressional mandates and the traditions of local practice.
- So, as she sat through the intoxicating world of constitutional law, she dreamed of fighting for the civil rights of the downtrodden and oppressed.
- Reality arrived quickly when she clerked for the first time at a major law firm where she was the lowest member of a very tall totem pole.
- Twelve-hour days of arcane research regarding commercial transactions hardly squared with her law school visions of glory.
- So after law school, marriage, and the birth of a child, Rita looked for an area of the law that balanced her love of legal precision and the tempo of her family.
- Real estate was booming in Macon, Georgia, as was the need for real estate lawyers.
- Real estate law paid reasonably well, was flexible enough to accommodate three very active children, and overall, it was an area of the law that was not festooned with conflict and controversy.
- Apparently, conflict was reserved for her personal life.

Real estate lawyer Rita Willis took a stand against prayer in school.

Prayer at a football game ignited a five-year court battle.

- Comfortable as a partner in one of Macon, Georgia's most respected law firms, Rita discovered that controversy could be thrust on anyone, at any age.
- And as a lifelong Episcopalian and choir member, she was shocked to discover that tackling the issue of school prayer would result in accusations that challenged her Christianity.

Life at Work

- The issue of prayer at school officially arose more than five years earlier when a student chaplain delivered a prayer over the public address system before a home varsity football game.
- Rita was at the game with her husband to support her youngest daughter, a cheerleader on the varsity squad.
- She stood with the rest, listened passively to the prayer delivered by a student, held her hand over her heart for the playing of the national anthem and cheered the team as they roared onto the field.
- The rhythm and pattern had been unchanged for 30 years.
- Only later, when a dozen teens gathered at Rita's home after the game, did she come face to face with the inequity of public prayer.
- An argument broke out about that evening's prayer.
- A junior girl of the Muslim faith said she didn't think it right for everyone in the entire stadium to be asked to pray to "Jesus Christ our Lord" for protection and guidance.
- The boys quickly told her to "shut up or go back home," which made the her cry, and made the other girls mad enough to berate the boys.
- Rita stepped in just as the disagreement reached a fevered pitch.
- Since 1962, she told them, the Supreme Court had consistently ruled that "Congress shall make no law respecting an establishment of religion."
- The Founding Fathers intended that no act of government—including laws governing public schools—should favor any one religion over others.
- That's hard to do, she said, because once someone mentioned God, Jesus, or anything even remotely "Biblical," he or she immediately pushed the constitutional envelope by "favoring" one practice of religion over all others.

- It may very well be that the only way not to favor one religion over others was not to favor any religion at all—a path now being chosen by many public schools already.
- The room was silent.
- "Shouldn't the majority rule?" her daughter asked to break the awkward silence.
- Rita knew that public opinion polls showed that a majority of people disagreed with the Supreme Court's religion-in-schools rulings and she told them so.
- Then she added, "While it's fine to disagree with them, it is not really fair to blame the Court for making them."
- The rulings were based on the way the Justices interpreted the First Amendment to the Constitution.

- The First Amendment spelled out America's guiding principles regarding religion, speech, press, assembly, and petition.
- Basically, it protected all Americans' right to worship as they wanted, to say what they wanted, to publish what they wanted, to gather in groups, and to make their concerns known to the government.
- It also prohibited the government from identifying with a particular religion, effectively separating church and state.
- Had the Supreme Court not been asked to interpret the Establishment Clause by private citizens, including some members of the clergy, they never would have done so.
- The Establishment Clause stated that Congress "shall make no law respecting an establishment of religion."
- "But," said Rita, "when you say, 'the majority rules,' does that include the majority that kept women out of law schools or medical schools or that said it was right for black people to ride in the back of the bus?"
- This time the room erupted into a flurry of questions and a few accusations of "Commie liberal talk."
- That's when Rita climbed out on the fragile limb that would support her life for the next five years.
- "Perhaps the most important job of the Supreme Court is to see to it that the will of the majority is never unfairly or hurtfully forced on the minority, and, that's a good thing because you never know when the minority might be you."
- All weekend she brooded over the conflict and what she had said.
- Her daughter seemed impressed with what had taken place.
- But Rita was unsure whether her daughter agreed with her comments or was simply pleased to see the boisterous boys shut down so effectively.
- When Monday arrived, Rita knew she had to act on her comments, so she made an appointment with the high school principal, a newcomer to Macon who might be sensitive to the needs of the students.
- In 1992, the Supreme Court had barred clergy-led prayers at graduation ceremonies, but there appeared to be unclear guidance about student-led prayer at football games.
- Her intent was to express her concerns and relate the weekend's events.
- But despite her best efforts, the first meeting went poorly.
- Early in the conversation, she casually mentioned the name of her law partner, and the principal immediately summoned his secretary to witness the remainder of the conversation.
- The second meeting involved the superintendent, the third a school district lawyer and the fourth was convened before the school board in open session.
- By the time she arrived home from the school board meeting, she was famous—or infamous.
- The 11 o'clock television news led with the word, "Prayer condemned as illegal by local attorney," beside an unflattering picture of Rita.
- The phone rang all night with calls that were mostly ugly and from people she didn't know.
- She attempted to take a low profile, but her timing was terrible.
- In Texas a case was brought by Mormon and Catholic students concerning the banning of prayer at football games.
- Nationally, school prayer became a hot topic once again.

Rita's daughter seemed impressed by her mother's stand.

- No matter what she said or how framed her answers, every media outlet in the South portrayed her as a godless spokeswoman for the Devil who wanted to rip prayer from the mouths of America's youth.
- During the lawsuit's five-year journey through the courts, Rita was vilified.
- After a time, the viciousness of the verbal assaults only served to remind her that the Constitution belonged to everyone, especially the Muslim girl who was verbally attacked by the boys that Friday night.
- In the intervening five years, her youngest daughter graduated from high school and college, her oldest daughter married and gave her a grandson, while her lawyer son took a job in Atlanta.
- Rita continually prayed for guidance and even joined a contemplative prayer group that gave her a measure of peace.
- And she began to explore the economic inequality of her community as a volunteer server at a local soup kitchen.
- By the time the courts ruled on the Texas prayer case, Rita was at peace with herself.
- But she could not keep from smiling at the results: the Supreme Court had ruled in favor of protecting the rights of America's minorities.

Life in the Community: Santa Fe, Texas

- In 1995 two families filed a lawsuit against the Santa Fe, Texas school district over prayer in school.
- Unlike that of Rita, the identity of the two families who filed the lawsuit, one Catholic and one Mormon, was sealed by the courts.
- Their lawsuit alleged that the school district's policy of allowing students to lead prayers at home football games violated the First Amendment by creating a religious atmosphere, and a lower court agreed in principle.
- A federal appeals court ruled that student-led prayers that were not limited to one specific religion and did not attempt to create converts were allowed at graduations, but banned before football games which the court said were not serious enough to be "solemnized with prayer."
- The school district responded to the lower court ruling by implementing strict guidelines banning pre-game prayer, and warned senior Marian Ward, elected by fellow students to deliver religious messages before football games, that she would be disciplined if she prayed.
- Ward's family filed suit in September, arguing that the guidelines violated her free speech rights.
- A U.S. district court judge agreed that the guidelines the school had written were unconstitutional and ruled that the school could not censor Ward's speech.
- So it was up to the Supreme Court to sort out all of the lower court rulings and make a decision.
- In the summer of 2000, the U.S. Supreme Court ruled 6-3 that public schools could allow student-led prayer before high school football games.
- The central question was whether allowing prayer violated the First Amendment's Establishment Clause, which stated that Congress "shall make no law respecting an establishment of religion."
- "We recognize the important role that public worship plays in many communities, as well as the sincere desire to include public prayer as a part of various occasions so as to mark those occasions' significance," Justice John Paul Stevens wrote for the majority.

- "But such religious activity in public schools, as elsewhere, must comport with the First Amendment," he added.
- The 4,000-student southern Texas school district, until 1995, had a policy in which students elected student council chaplains to deliver prayers over the public address system before the start of high school football games.
- While the lower courts were considering the legal challenge, the school district adopted a new policy under which student-led prayer was permitted but not mandated.
- Students were asked to vote on whether to allow prayers and to vote again to select the person to deliver them.
- A lower court retooled that policy to allow only non-sectarian, non-proselytizing prayer.
- An appeals court found the modified policy constitutionally invalid and the nation's highest court agreed with the appeals court, rejecting the argument that the pre-football prayer was an example of "private speech" because the students, not school officials, decided the prayer matter.

HISTORICAL SNAPSHOT
2000

- The arrival of the year 2000 failed to produce the predicted terrorist attacks, Y2K meltdowns or mass suicides among doomsday cults
- The last new daily *Peanuts* strip by Charles Schulz ran in 2,600 newspapers
- Two Austrian banks agreed to a $40 million settlement with an estimated 1,000 Holocaust victims or their heirs for having confiscated their assets
- Time Warner agreed to be acquired by AOL in a merger valued at $162 billion
- The U.S. Supreme Court gave police broad authority to stop and question people who run at the sight of an officer
- Reports indicated that the number of Internet users in China had more than doubled over the last six months from 4 million to 8.9 million, most of them young, single men
- Nitrogen-based fertilizers were blamed for the rapid decline of the spotted frog in the Pacific Northwest
- The female-oriented TV cable channel Oxygen made its debut
- President Clinton proposed a $2 billion program to bring Internet access to low-income households
- A federal jury in Portland, Oregon, ordered abortion foes who had created "wanted" posters and a Web site listing the names and addresses of "baby butchers" to pay $107 million in damages
- Carlos Santana won eight Grammy awards, including album of the year for *Supernatural*
- Pope John Paul II begged for God's forgiveness for sins committed or condoned by Roman Catholics over the last 2,000 years, including wrongs inflicted on Jews, women and minorities
- CBS filmed the TV show *Survivor* on the Malaysian island of Pulau Tiga
- The Tribune Company bought the LA Times in a $6.5 billion merger with the Times Mirror Company
- More than 600 people set out on a five-day, 120-mile protest march to Columbia, South Carolina, to urge state lawmakers to remove the Confederate flag from the state house dome
- Judge Thomas Penfield Jackson ruled that Microsoft violated the Sherman Act by tying its Internet browser to its operating system
- The National Labor Relations Board ruled that graduate students who work as teaching assistants may organize a union
- Leaders of developing nations called for a "New Global Human Order" to spread the world's wealth and power
- In California, President Clinton created Giant Sequoia National Monument in Sequoia National Park to protect 328,000 acres of sequoias from timber harvesting
- The International Whaling Commission turned down requests from Japan and Norway to allow expanded whaling

Selected Prices, 2000

Blender, Oster	$80.00
Computer Desk	$999.00
Cordless Drill, DeWalt	$129.00
Diapers, Pampers, 40	$14.99
Digital Video Camera, Fisher	$899.99
iTunes Album	$16.99
Laser Eye Surgery, Lasik, per Eye	$599.00
Movie Ticket	$7.50
Treadmill, ProForm	$599.99
Weedwacker, Craftsman	$29.99

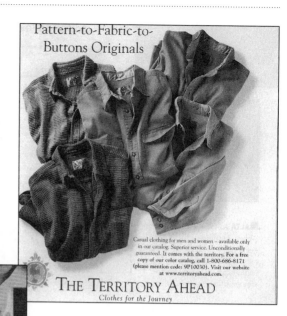

Timeline of Religion in Schools

1940

The Supreme Court ruled that a public school may require students to salute the flag and pledge allegiance even if doing so violated their religious beliefs.

1943

The Supreme Court overturned itself and ruled that no one can be forced to salute the flag or say the pledge of allegiance if it violates the individual conscience.

1948

The Supreme Court found religious instruction in public schools a violation of the Establishment Clause of the First Amendment and therefore unconstitutional.

1952

The Supreme Court ruled that release time from public school classes for religious instruction did not violate the Establishment Clause.

1962

The Supreme Court found school prayer unconstitutional.

1963

The Supreme Court ruled that Bible reading over the school intercom was unconstitutional.

The Supreme Court found forcing a child to participate in Bible reading and prayer unconstitutional.

1968

The Supreme Court ruled that states could not ban the teaching of evolution.

1980

The Supreme Court found the posting of the Ten Commandments in schools unconstitutional.

1985

The Supreme Court found that state laws enforcing a moment of silence in schools had a religious purpose and was therefore unconstitutional.

1987

The Supreme Court ruled that state law requiring equal treatment for creationism had a religious purpose and was therefore unconstitutional.

1990

The Supreme Court ruled that the Equal Access Act did not violate the First Amendment; public schools that received federal funds and maintained a "limited open forum" on school grounds after school hours could not deny equal access to student groups based upon religious, political, philosophical or other content.

1992

The Supreme Court found that prayer at public school graduation ceremonies violated the Establishment Clause and was therefore unconstitutional.

1993

The Supreme Court said that school districts could not deny churches access to school premises after hours if the district allowed the use of its building to other groups.

2000

The Supreme Court ruled that student-led prayer at a public high school athletic event violated the Establishment Clause and was unconstitutional.

"Defiant Prayers Surface on the South's Gridirons," by Erin McClam, *Atlanta Constitution*, September 23, 2000:

DALLAS, Ga.—The horns of the Paulding County High School marching band blew the last note of the national anthem, and there was silence. Then one voice, then another, then thousands.

Soon, the chorus dominated the modest stadium—asking this day for their daily bread, forgiving those who trespass against them, seeking to be led not into temptation but delivered from evil.

This recitation of "The Lord's Prayer" was simple but fundamentally defiant. Fans here compared themselves to Christian soldiers, fighting to save religion's place in schools before the courts strip it away.

The scene is being repeated on Friday nights, in varying forms but with an identical message, on the South's most hallowed battlegrounds—its football fields.

"People understand we are a religious nation," said the Rev. Curtis Turner, who brought his Baptist congregation from half a metropolis away to pass out copies of the prayer before Paulding County's game with arch-rival East Paulding. "It shouldn't be confined. What if we confine it? They'll do it like a smoking ban."

Turner's congregation, like others across the nation's Bible Belt, took offense with the Supreme Court's ruling this summer that amplified, student-led prayer approved by public school officials crosses the line in the separation of church and state.

Those leading the prayers are growing bolder every week, almost challenging the powers that be to stop them from praying.

Every Friday night this fall, Turner—who cuts an awkward figure in a dark suit and shiny necktie among football fans with pompoms and booster T-shirts—is leading his followers to a different game in metro Atlanta.

Each time, the church members pass out cards bearing "The Lord's Prayer" and encouraging fans to recite it after the national anthem. Each time, they claim they are fighting for God-fearing students who are losing their right to practice their religion in school.

"They've been intimidated," Turner said. "They're afraid to speak or pray. They think that prayer has been outlawed."

Church-state separatists argue that mass prayers in public, including school-sponsored events, infringe on the rights of religious minorities. Turner's caravanning prayers are "extremely inconsiderate," said Debbie Seagraves, executive director of Georgia's chapter of the American Civil Liberties Union.

"This is a group of people willing to stand up at a public school event, and very loudly over everyone else say, 'This is our prayer,' no matter what anybody else wants," she said.

But across the South, a region where devotion to football has been called religious itself, students and fans are bucking the high court's ruling, refusing to quiet their prayers.

In Alabama, most schools have replaced prayer with a moment of silence since the Supreme Court ruling. But Etowah County High School continues to broadcast students' prayers over the stadium public-address system.

"Number one, we think it's the right thing to do," principal David Bowman said. "And, number two, football is a contact sport where kids are apt to get hurt, and you need God on your side."

In rural South Carolina, a student body president took the press-box microphone at her school's football opener to lead fans in a pre-game prayer. In the face of a lawsuit threatened by the ACLU, other students at Batesburg-Leesville High School plan to sign up to lead prayers at future home games.

And in western Kentucky, high schools in two counties have no plans to stop holding public pre-game prayers. In another Kentucky town, a radio station broadcasting high school football is airing prayers before kickoff.

"The Christian people have rights, too," said Bob Kerrick, principal of Hancock County High School.

continued

"Defiant Prayers Surface on the South's Gridirons" . . . *(continued)*

The ACLU contends it is not opposed to private prayer in school. But huge masses reciting prayers in football stadiums are both disruptive and offensive to fans of other religions, Seagraves said.

"Suppose a group decided to stand up during 'The Lord's Prayer' and sing a rap song," she said. "Wouldn't the school consider that a disturbance? It's important we be considerate of each other's differences in society."

The Supreme Court decision does not outlaw prayer in school, by students or otherwise. But schools violate the Constitution when they advocate a "particular religious practice" by sponsoring amplified, student-led prayer.

Turner insists he is not promoting Baptism, or even Christianity, by leading the prayers in metro Atlanta. "The Lord's Prayer" is just what he knows best, he said, and members of other religions are free to pray to their gods at the same time.

Some of the pastor's followers believe the erosion of prayers in schools is responsible for the downfall of America's youth, including school shootings. They say schools bleached of religion are a sure sign of the country's moral destruction.

"Over 224 years, this has been part of our heritage. We can't rob the next generation of that," said Clint Andrews, 22, who passes out prayer cards with Turner's congregation. "They're trying to take away prayer altogether. So we're taking a stand. We're on the last straw. This is it, right here.

"Republished with permission of Atlanta Journal Constitution, from "Defiant Prayers Surface on the South's Gridirons," Erin McClam, September 23, 2000; permission conveyed through Copyright Clearance Center, Inc."

GENERATIONS OF
RESPECT

Brooks Brothers
—— Generations *of* Style ——

800.274.1815 | BrooksBrothers.com

Madison Avenue . South Coast Plaza . Americana Manhasset . Rodeo Drive . Fifth Avenue . Short Hills . Lenox Square

There is such a misrepresentation of what can and cannot be done. People say you can't pray in school. That is not true. People say you cannot read a Bible in school. That is not true. There is freedom of religion, and there is a division between religion and government.

—Dale Stuckey, chief counsel at the South Carolina
Department of Education, 1999

Remarks of Principal Jody McLoud before a Roane County High School football game, Kingston, Tennessee, on September 1, 2000:

It has always been the custom at Roane County High School football games to say a prayer and play the National Anthem to honor God and Country.

Due to a recent ruling by the Supreme Court, I am told that saying a prayer is a violation of Federal Case Law.

As I understand the law at this time, I can use this public facility to approve of sexual perversion and call it an alternate lifestyle, and if someone is offended, that's okay.

I can use it to condone sexual promiscuity by dispensing condoms and calling it safe sex. If someone is offended, that's okay.

I can even use this public facility to present the merits of killing an unborn baby as a viable means of birth control. If someone is offended, it's no problem.

I can designate a school day as Earth Day and involve students in activities to religiously worship and praise the goddess, Mother Earth, and call it ecology.

I can use literature, videos and presentations in the classroom that depict people with strong, traditional, Christian convictions as simple-minded and ignorant and call it enlightenment.

However, if anyone uses this facility to honor God and ask Him to bless this event with safety and good sportsmanship, Federal Case Law is violated. This appears to be inconsistent at best, and at worst, diabolical.

Apparently, we are to be tolerant of everything and anyone except God and His Commandments.

Nevertheless, as a school principal, I frequently ask staff and students to abide by rules that they do not necessarily agree with. For me to do otherwise would be inconsistent at best, and at worst, hypocritical. I suffer from that affliction enough unintentionally. I certainly do not need to add an intentional transgression.

For this reason, I shall render unto Caesar that which is Caesar's and refrain from praying at this time. However, if you feel inspired to honor, praise and thank God, and ask Him in the name of Jesus to bless this event, please feel free to do so. As far as I know, that's not against the law yet.

"Over 900 People Encircle School with Prayer Chain," by Stump Martin, *Chattanooga Times Free Press* (Tennessee), May 17, 1999:

Over 900 Rhea Countians "built a hedge" around Rhea County High School Sunday afternoon, seeking divine protection and a spiritual solution to the nation's problems.

It was the latest example of an increasing push to restore group prayer in public schools.

Organizers counted 950 people gathered at the high school's football stadium for prayer before being directed to join hands in a circle around the school. Billy Hall told the crowd, "We calculated it would take at least 800 to go all the way around the school; we have more than 900."

He told the group, "Your presence acknowledges the fact that the problems in this nation are not just social but spiritual. Yes, the family situation has deteriorated; yes, there is violence; yes, there are horrible things on TV. But they are symptoms, not the problem.

"We have got to acknowledge that there is a devil, and that Satan wants to get into the hearts and minds of people, especially young people. We are going to build a hedge of protection around our young people. We are going to ask the Lord to intervene in the lives of the children of this county."

Jeff Pewitt, who, with Mr. Hall, helped organize the program, told the crowd that members of their Sunday school class at New Union Baptist church near Dayton had talked about the shootings at Columbine High School in Colorado the Sunday following the tragedy. "The Lord put it on our hearts to do this."

Another example of the continuing drumbeat to restore structured prayer in public schools was on May 5 when the Hamilton County Commission sent a resolution to Tennessee's congressional delegation asking that they enact laws that would permit voluntary prayer in public schools.

The Rev. Marvin Morrison of Mission Ridge Baptist church in Rossville agreed. "For almost 200 years we had prayer in schools," he said. "During that time we became the greatest nation economically, morally and militarily that the world had ever known."

But then Madalyn Murray O'Hair, a committed atheist who founded the American Atheists in 1963, filed one of the lawsuits that prompted the United States Supreme Court to ban structured prayer in public schools.

"Almost 40 years after," asks Rev. Morrison, "where are we?

"We may be good economically. And we may be OK militarily. But we're bankrupt morally," he said.

There are strong sentiments on both sides as the argument rages: If prayer is put back in schools, whose prayer will be used?

An April 14, 1998 advertisement paid for by the American Civil Liberties Union stated: "Official prayer sessions in public school seem like a good idea to many Americans, provided they get to choose the prayer. But in such a diverse society, how can one prayer satisfy every religious belief?"

Hedy Weinberg of the Tennessee chapter of the ACLU said the same people who accuse her organization of not being religious "are the same people we're protecting by being so staunch.

"We're not against an individual student having prayer in schools before they take an exam or if there is a crisis at home. But we don't want a student standing up in math class interrupting the rest of the class.

"The minute the government decides when you pray, to whom you pray, or where you pray, we have a problem," said Ms. Weinberg. "The (U.S.) Constitution reads that you can't entangle government in promotion of religious activities."

Reprinted with permission by the Chattanooga Free Press.

2004 PROFILE

WOMEN'S RIGHTS: TITLE IX

John Walker Hall, a high school girls' basketball coach, became frustrated at the inferior practice facilities, meager transportation to away games, and even lack of uniforms suffered by his players.

Life at Home

- Hailing from Roanoke, Virginia, John Walker Hall graduated from Longwood College in Farmville, Virginia, in 1990.
- While still a student and a member of the basketball team there, he decided on a coaching career.
- In college, he met and wooed his future wife Dawn, a 6'3" center for the Longwood women's team.
- After graduation John taught and coached at several middle schools in the Roanoke, Virginia area, while Dawn worked as a pharmacist.
- John's plunge into controversy occurred after he was hired as a history teacher and girls' high school varsity basketball coach in Hemphill, West Virginia, in 2002.
- Hemphill was located in the Western Blue Ridge Mountains off I-77 in Appalachia coal mining country.
- Most of the employed citizens of Hemphill and nearby Welch were employed by either the Kingston Pocahontas Coal Company or Solvay Collieries Company.
- From the outset of his coaching stint, John was struck by the differences in the way the athletic programs were run in Hemphill in comparison to those in the Roanoke area.
- In particular, he was concerned that the girls' basketball program was consistently short-changed.
- Despite inconsistent support, he found his girls' basketball team, the Lady Hawks, was a skilled bunch.
- The Lady Hawks had won multiple district and regional championships despite their being relegated to inferior practice space at a local elementary school.

Coach John Hall fought for equality for his female basketball team.

Hemphill was in the Blue Ridge Mountains.

- The only time the girls' team used the high school gym was for games, virtually eliminating their home team advantage.
- In addition, because of the distance between the high school and elementary school gymnasium, they had to carpool, often resulting in delayed practice times.
- And, the most obvious affront of all, the girls' basketball team had to share their uniforms with the girls' track team, despite occasional scheduling overlaps.
- Sounding out his rising senior players on the issue, he discovered the prevailing attitude was, "That's the way it's always been."
- So for the first two years, he said little.
- Besides, he had six solid players returning from last year's 16-4 season and had his eyes on a state championship in 2004.
- The Halls enjoyed a good life in a comfortable house with their two girls actively involved in the youth basketball league.
- But Coach Hall couldn't shake his frustration concerning the inequities between the boys' and girls' teams.
- So he began researching Title IX, which was signed into law in 1972, specifically aimed at creating parity in education and athletics.
- Using the Web, he found detailed examples of other high schools in New Orleans and Michigan that relegated girls teams to inopportune conditions and times in order to accommodate the boys' teams.
- He became familiar with the opposing sides' arguments, including the argument that reducing male funding and increasing female funding could also be considered unequal.
- And he found the story of Coach Roderick Jackson, who lost his job for speaking up for the girls' team.
- But Coach Hall knew there was a middle path that would bring fairness to his high school; reasonable people could find reasonable solutions.

Life at Work
- John Hall could not have been happier with his team.
- The Lady Hawks were halfway through an undefeated season and the entire community was buzzing about the possibility of a state championship.
- His team's reputation for tough, smart play was drawing college recruiters from as far away as Washington State University.
- While he found the accolades rewarding, he was increasingly angry.
- Underneath the praise, he knew about the adversity his young women had to overcome daily.
- No one seemed to care that the team practiced in an elementary school gymnasium, which had 1950s-style crescent-shaped, non-regulation metal backboards.
- Instead of a customary wooden floor, they practiced on a slick metal floor with a concrete sub-floor.

- Sure that the rock-hard surface would impact his girls' knees and joints, he prayed that it would not result in a season-ending injury.
- Knowing younger women were more susceptible to anterior cruciate ligament (ACL) injuries because of their wider hips, he sometimes shortened practice to prevent injuries that might be exacerbated by the outdated practice facilities.
- John was also frustrated that his girls had to arrange carpools to away games, while the boys' team traveled by bus.
- And even though the school owned two whirlpool tubs to ease muscle injury, access was limited.
- The boys used the whirlpools after practice; John could only schedule his girls for whirlpool therapy in the early morning hours before school.
- Funding was also an issue.
- Thanks to a tradition of winning, the Lady Hawks attracted standing-room-only crowds, nearly always out-drawing the boys.
- But he was continuously told that girls' teams were money losers and not to ask for too much.
- So, by the time Coach Hall was ready to take his grievances to his superiors, he had a full head of steam.
- Having already familiarized himself with the basics of Title IX, he proceeded to learn about contemporary developments in its history.
- He learned that requiring equal access was impacting the entire educational process, not just athletics.
- He discovered that half of all law and medical students were female, as were roughly three of every four veterinary students.
- In 1972, the year Title IX was enacted, women earned 7 percent of the nation's law degrees.
- That same year, 18 percent of female high school graduates were completing at least four years of college compared to 26 percent of their male peers.
- The studies showed that in 2004, 32 years after Title IX was enacted, women were earning 57 percent of bachelor's degrees, outpacing men.
- Nationwide, in 2002 girls and women accounted for four out of every 10 high school and varsity athletes.
- But not all had changed.
- Male coaches still led 50 percent of college women's teams; few women coached men's teams.
- Coach Hall also learned that many high schools and middle schools continued to short-change girls' athletic programs.
- At the midpoint of the season, John met with the athletics director and the head football coach to lay out his concerns.
- They assured John that change was imminent and presented him with order forms for new uniforms for his team.
- Also, they agreed that the girls' team could use school transportation for away games.
- Then, after much discussion, they even ordered that the boys' and girls' teams alternate the use of the practice gymnasium and whirlpool facilities.
- That's when the trouble started.
- It was okay to give the girls equal treatment as long as it did not impact the boys.
- At first it was anonymous phone calls to his home after midnight with a single message: "Stop screwing with the boys' basketball team. Get out of our gym."
- Then came calls to his wife: "Don't think you are too big to be messed with."
- Finally, he learned that his starting five were being threatened by scrawled notes and angry outbursts in the hallways.

The Lady Hawks were a winning team.

- Obviously, challenging the system was not going to be easy.
- The showdown came just days before the regional tournament.
- Both the boys' and the girls' teams were eligible for regional tournament play; both were favored to make the state tournament.
- Both had tough opponents.
- Coach Hall was anxious to practice his team against the high-pressure defense they would face next.
- Also, college scouts from five Division I schools were scheduled to be at the game to recruit his best players.
- But the boys' team was occupying the high school gym on a day they were scheduled to be at the tiny elementary school gym and refused to leave.
- Polite requests turned to harsh words, then frustration, then shouting.
- Both teams were at the peak of anxiety over the upcoming tournament play.
- Both refused to give ground.
- Controlling his temper, Coach Hall called the athletic director to mediate.
- The athletic director was calm and clear: the boys' tournament game was more important, and yes, he had given the boys permission to use the high school facilities at this important time of the season.
- Coach Hall was stunned.
- How could he tell the girls they were second-class citizens again?
- When he broke the news, his voice was clear, breaking only once with disappointment.
- The girls' reaction was immediate; first a chorus of "no fair," followed by fervent denunciation of the boys' team, and then, resignation.
- Half of the girls then said, "It's okay coach; the little gym will do just fine."
- The other half wanted revenge, and the opportunity came quickly.
- The next day an all-school pep rally was scheduled for the two basketball teams.
- The athletic director and principal traditionally enjoyed showing the teams that the student body was behind them all the way.
- As usual, the girls' team was introduced first, as a warm-up to announcing the boys' team.
- Coach Hall spoke to a packed auditorium about the dedication, skill and teamwork his team displayed, to rousing cheers.
- He then left the stage, but the girls' team stood still and refused to exit.
- Even after the boys' team was announced, the girls' basketball team stayed in place, refusing to give ground.
- The auditorium was filled with laughter, shouting, catcalls and cascading noise when Carrie, the smallest member of the team, walked to the microphone, and told the students about the battle for practice space, and said, "We will move when we are treated equally."
- The auditorium exploded with energy.
- Then the boys' team members attempted to physically push the girls' team members off the stage, at which point the principal took back the microphone and shouted at the girls' team, "Leave the stage or be suspended."
- The student body president shouted, "You can't suspend us all," and led the students out of the auditorium, including the entire girls' team.
- When the room fell silent, only one-third of the students, mostly freshmen, remained.
- In front of that timid gathering, the principal stormed up to Coach Hall and shouted, "You will pay for this!"
- Equally frustrated, they both went outside to meet with the students.

The Origins of Title IX

- Congresswoman Edith Green of Oregon, who later was acknowledged as the mother of Title IX, began House Higher Education Style committee meetings on discrimination against women in June and July 1970.
- Over seven days, distinguished women, scholars and government officials outlined the ways in which women were left out of educational opportunities.
- State universities in John Hall's home state of Virginia had turned away thousands of qualified women since the early 1960s because of gender, not qualifications.
- The freshman class at the University of North Carolina consisted of 1,900 men and just 426 women.
- At the University of Michigan, more qualified women applied than men, so the school adjusted its requirements to keep women to less than half of the incoming class.
- Quotas at many medical and law schools limited females to just 10 students out of every 100.
- Even though most teachers from grade school through high school were women, most principals were men.
- Ms. Green's key supporters on the House Labor and Education Committee included Shirley Chisholm of New York, the first African American congresswomen, and Patsy Mink of Hawaii, the first woman of color elected to Congress, who helped write the section of Title IX that would apply to girls and women.
- Congressman Ed Koch of New York also spoke out in support of Title IX, accusing his fellow lawmakers of slow, incremental movement of rights to women.
- In the opening days of Title IX, the main thrust was directed at leveling the field in education itself.

The struggle for women athletes was decades old.

- Only later was the emphasis shifted to athletics, thanks to the efforts of former Olympic swimming champion Diane Di Palma and tennis great Billie Jean King, who trounced Bobby Riggs in the Battle of the Sexes televised tennis match.
- Billie Jean King became pivotal in transforming American attitudes about women in sports.
- Cartoonist Charles M. Shultz of *Peanuts* fame also helped through the creation of comic strip character Peppermint Patty, the epitome of the modern, competitive girl of the 1970s.
- Civil rights laws such as Title IX have historically been a powerful mechanism for effecting social change in the United States.
- Title IX of the Education Amendments of 1972 was modeled on Title VI of the Civil Rights Act of 1964 prohibiting discrimination on account of race, color and national origin.
- Title IX was followed by three other pieces of civil rights legislation: Section 504 of the Rehabilitation Act of 1973 prohibiting disability discrimination; the Age Discrimination Act of 1975; and Title II of the Americans with Disabilities Act of 1990 prohibiting disability discrimination by public entities.

HISTORICAL SNAPSHOT
2004

- Pakistani scientists admitted to giving Libya, Iran and North Korea the technology to build nuclear weapons

- The U.S. required international travelers to be fingerprinted and photographed to enter the country

- President George W. Bush proposed a plan the would allow illegal immigrants working in the United States to apply for temporary guest worker status and increase the number of green cards granted each year

- Paul O'Neill, former treasury secretary, told *60 Minutes* that the Bush Administration had been planning an attack against Iraq since the first days of Bush's presidency

- Two NASA Rovers landed on Mars and sent back spectacular images of the planet

- The Salvation Army reported that Joan Kroc, heir to the McDonald's fortune, had left the nonprofit entity $1.5 billion

- A computer worm, called MyDoom or Novarg, spread through Internet servers, infecting one in 12 e-mail messages

- Terrorists exploded at least 10 bombs on four commuter trains in Madrid, Spain, during rush hour, killing 202 people and wounding about 1,400

- The California Supreme Court ordered San Francisco to stop issuing marriage licenses to same-sex couples

- NASA reported the discovery of a distant object in our solar system that closely resembled a planet

- The American military continued to engage in fierce fighting in Iraq

- America was stunned by graphic photos of American soldiers grinning as they abused Iraqis in the Abu Ghraib prison

- The Bush Administration admitted that it failed to give the commission investigating the September 11, 2001 terrorist attacks thousands of pages of national security papers

- President Bush said in a national broadcast that to abandon Iraq would fuel anti-American sentiment around the world

- Several hundred thousand demonstrators gathered in Washington, DC, to protest the Bush Administration's policy on reproductive rights

- The popular search engine Google went public

- A federal judge in San Francisco said the Partial Birth Abortion Ban Act was unconstitutional because it lacked a medical exception to save a woman's life, and it placed an unnecessary burden on women who sought abortions

- United Nations Secretary General Kofi Annan said the war in Iraq was illegal and violated the U.N. charter

- The International Committee of the Red Cross found that military personnel used physical and psychological abuse at the Guantanamo prison in Cuba that was "tantamount to torture"

Selected Prices, 2004

Camera Flip Phone, Telos $99.00
College Tuition, Annual, St. John's College $30,570
Digital Camera, Olympus $800.00
Gas Grill, Kenmore $134.99
Handbag, Jill Stuart $175.00
Handheld Computer, Palm One $99.99
Printer, HP $178.22
Scanner, Canon $49.00
Software, Microsoft Office 2003 . . . . $349.99
Walkman, Sony $200.00

It's an engine for economic growth. This V8 engine is part of a very powerful system. Built by the team at Toyota Motor Manufacturing, Alabama, it will provide the power for one of over 100,000 Tundra trucks being manufactured at our plant in Indiana.* It's all part of our commitment to investing in the places where we do business. A commitment that has grown to include eight U.S. manufacturing facilities, research and design centers, sales and marketing operations, and a network of local suppliers and dealers. As a result, Toyota is responsible for creating more than 190,000 jobs across America, and with two new plants under construction in Texas and Tennessee, we'll continue to create opportunities for economic growth.** Local manufacturing, local investment, local jobs – it's a pretty powerful combination.

toyota.com/usa

TOYOTA

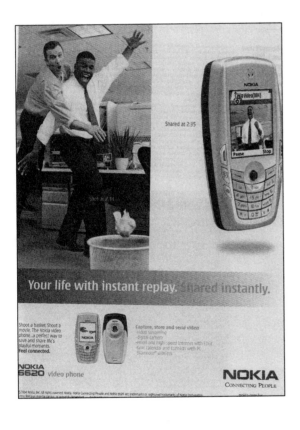

Your life with instant replay. Shared instantly.

Shoot a basket. Shoot a movie. The Nokia video phone...a perfect way to save and share life's playful moments. **Feel connected.**

Capture, store and send video

NOKIA 6620 video phone

NOKIA CONNECTING PEOPLE

DOLCE & GABBANA PARFUM

Title IX Timeline

1972

Title IX of The Educational Amendments of 1972 was signed into law by President Richard Nixon.

1973

The Association for Intercollegiate Athletics for Women (AIAW) adopted legislation to permit the first college scholarships for female athletes.

The U.S. Open was the first tennis tournament to offer equal prize money—$25,000—to men and women.

1974

The first women's professional football league began with seven teams; players earned $25.00 a game.

The Women's Sports Foundation was established by Billie Jean King.

1976

The first women's rowing and basketball competitions took place in the Olympics.

1977

Janet Guthrie became the first woman driver in the Indianapolis 500.

1978

The courts ruled that female sportswriters should have equal access to male athletes' locker rooms in the United States.

The Amateur Sports Act passed, which prohibited gender discrimination in open amateur sports in the United States.

1982

The Supreme Court ruled that Title IX covered employees, such as coaches, as well as students.

The Association for Intercollegiate Athletics for Women, which previously governed many women's collegiate sports, closed its doors and filed an unsuccessful antitrust lawsuit challenging the NCAA's authority over women's sports.

1984

Title IX was limited by the Supreme Court's ruling in *Grove City v. Bell*, which stated that only educational institutions receiving direct federal funds were affected by Title IX.

Joan Benoit Samuelson won the gold medal in the first official Olympic women's marathon.

1986

The first woman to play on an all-male professional basketball team, Lynette Woodard, debuted with the Harlem Globetrotters.

1988

The Civil Rights Restoration Act became law following a congressional override of a veto by President Ronald Reagan; the law mandated that all educational institutions that received federal money were bound by Title IX.

Judith Davidson became the first female athletic director at a Division I school—Central Connecticut State University.

continued

Timeline . . . *(continued)*

1990

Jodi Haller became the first woman to pitch in a college baseball game as a member of Pennsylvania's St. Vincent College team.

1991

Judith Sweet became the first female president of the NCAA.

The U.S. women's soccer team won the first-ever Women's World Cup.

1993

There occurred the first of nine straight sellouts for the NCAA Women's Final Four basketball championship.

1995

America3, the first all-women's team, competed in the America's Cup Race and advanced to the final round.

1996

A record number of women competed in the 1996 Olympic Games in Atlanta—close to 1,000 more than in any previous games—3,684 women as opposed to 7,059 men.

1998

Women's ice hockey made its Olympic debut in Nagano, Japan; the U.S. team won the first gold medal.

2000

The National Women's Football League (NWFL) was formed.

The women's United Soccer Association was formed, attracting investors such as Time Warner, Comcast Corporation, and Cox Communications.

No person in the United States shall, on the basis of sex, be excluded from participation in, be denied the benefits of, or be subject to discrimination under any educational programs or activity receiving federal financial assistance.

—Preamble to Title IX of the Education Amendments of 1972

"Girls' Basketball Gaining Prestige, Changes in Attitudes Spur Sport's Growth," by Tony Cooke, *The Commercial Appeal* (Memphis, Tenn.), February 27, 1995:

Don't tell Rashida Allgood there is something unladylike about being a tough, physical competitor.

She might smack you.

"Girls can be tough, too," says the scrappy Northside guard, an expert on outside shots, quick passes and diving grabs for loose balls. Allgood is part of a new generation of basketball players that is transforming the girls' game, putting hustle and muscle into a sport once regarded as the weak stepsister of the boys' game.

More experienced observers of girls' sports, the veterans of the battle for equality, agree with Allgood that girls' sports and their athletes have come far. But they also see a long road ahead.

"No question. It's a half-full, half-empty story," said Donna Lopiano, executive director of the Women's Sports Foundation, a national nonprofit educational organization. "It's nothing like it used to be. If you go back as little as 20 years ago, women weren't allowed to run long-distance races in the Olympics."

These days, with Title IX mandating gender equity in sports, there is less outright discrimination, she said, but subtle social pressures and a lack of resources still plague girls' sports.

Lesa Mears played girls' basketball 15 years ago; now she coaches at Harding Academy.

"I think there's just been a bigger push at every level for girls," said Mears. "When I was growing up, there was only one sport available for girls."

When Mears, 33, was growing up at a small Arkansas school, that sport was six-on-six basketball, played with a ball the same size as the men's ball.

Now, the ball has shrunk slightly, to a more appropriate size for a girl's smaller hand; and the game is a more exciting traditional five-on-five. But perhaps just as important, the social biases against female athletes have shrunk.

"It seemed to me like when I was growing up it wasn't feminine to be an athlete. Girls just wanted to be cheerleaders. . . . I definitely don't see that with our kids. . . . You can step on the court and be a lady and a great athlete."

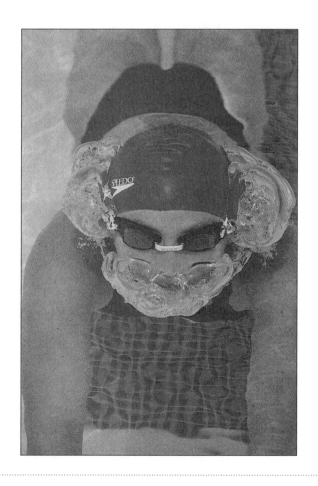

"Clarifying Title IX," Editorial, *St. Petersburg Times* (Florida), July 19, 2003:

The formal clarification the U.S. Department of Education has issued on Title IX ought to satisfy all who sought fair play for women and men in collegiate sports. But it hasn't. And those who now complain are revealing an agenda that has little to do with gender equity

The DOE letter makes two abundantly clear points about the continued enforcement of Title IX:

1. Universities do not have to prove that their sports opportunities for women are "substantially proportionate" to their numbers on campus in order to comply. They can show they have a history of advancing women's sports or that they are "fully and effectively" serving women athletes. "Each of the three prongs of the test is an equally sufficient means of complying with Title IX, and no one prong is favored over the other," the letter advises.

2. Universities are not required and not encouraged to eliminate men's teams to bring equity between genders. Says the letter: "Nothing in Title IX requires the cutting or reduction of teams in order to demonstrate compliance with Title IX, and . . . the elimination of teams is a disfavored practice."

Those two points go directly to the allegations of unfairness that have been leveled by male wrestlers, gymnasts and swimmers who say their teams were eliminated to comply with Title IX. The National Wrestling Coaches Association even sued DOE in 2001, claiming that male wrestlers were losing their scholarships because of Title IX. But U.S. District Judge Emmet Sullivan, in ruling against the wrestlers last month, reached the same conclusion as Gerald Reynolds, the U.S. assistant secretary for civil rights who wrote the advisory letter. Both say that the sports teams were dropped because of financial pressures, not gender compliance. The record bears them out.

Title IX, an amendment to the Education Act passed by Congress 31 years ago, has been hugely successful in providing educational and athletic opportunities for women. In college, the number of women playing varsity sports has increased fivefold and, in high school, 10-fold. At the same time, there has been no credible evidence that those opportunities have come at the expense of men. In fact, the number of men playing intercollegiate sports has continued to grow, albeit at a smaller rate than for women, and 53 of the universities that eliminated wrestling teams did so during a four-year period in the mid-1980s when Title IX was not enforced.

The documented trends of sports participation haven't dissuaded some male athletes from pointing the finger at their female counterparts, however. And the groups that represent them are not satisfied with a DOE letter that specifically condemns the elimination of male sports teams. When asked for his reaction, Eric Pearson, chairman of the Washington-based College Sports Council, told reporters that "the Bush Administration has completely caved in to the gender-quota advocates."

While it is likely true that the Bush Administration calculated the politics of overturning a widely embraced gender-equity measure, it can hardly be argued that the president is a quota advocate. DOE appointed a special commission to examine Title IX in part because the president expressed precisely the same concern about quotas. The course he ultimately chose was a moderate one, but its effect is the same. Under Title IX, universities are being told they need not turn to quotas; they need only serve women equitably. Sometimes the guys don't always like that.

2006 NEWS FEATURE

"Granny Power Takes on the Iraq War," by Ellen Goodman,
***The Boston Globe*, May 5, 2006:**

I went to the grannies for a booster shot of optimism. It's been that kind of week. We just passed the third anniversary of the flight-jacket photo op and its mission unaccomplished. The plunge in the president's approval ratings, down to 33 percent, hasn't translated into a howl of protest but a low-level depression. And the Official Bush Countdown Clock is barely a tick below 1,000 days.

But in Manhattan, 18 women of granny age, full of wit and wisdom, have just won a court case and sent their protest story around the world. I'll take my optimism where I can. Last fall, these women descended by foot, cane, and walker onto an armed forces recruitment center in Times Square. Inspired by groups such as the Tucson Raging Grannies, they demanded—"we insist/we enlist"—that the Army take them rather than their grandchildren. When the soldiers locked them out, 91-year-old Lillian Runyon banged on the door, singing: "If I had a hammer . . ." The women of the Granny Peace Brigade then staged a sit-down until the police, rather more gently than is their wont, took them to jail in handcuffs.

Their cry against the war's dishonorable conduct came up against the government's claim of their disorderly conduct. But on April 27, a mere whippersnapper of a judge—46 years old—declared them not guilty. Whereupon Joan Wile, lyricist and grandmother of five, promptly then told the courthouse crowd, "Listen to your granny; she knows best."

Now four of those grannies were sitting around the conference table in their lawyer's office still wearing buttons and the glow of notoriety. Wile was even brushing up the lyrics of her call-to-elder-arms: "Grandmas get offa your tush/We've got to go after Bush."

Something about the granniness of the event—though some were younger than the average senator—made the coverage read more like a lifestyle story than a gathering political storm. But then again, these protesters have a lightness of spirit that brings a message home: "Just forget your retirement pursuits/And get out your old marching boots."

Wile, 74, and Molly Klopot, 87, and Carol Husten, 74, and Vinie Burrows Harrison, "don't ask," are not amateurs in the action department. Molly's first protest as a child was for Sacco and Vanzetti. Vinie remembers the Depression Era civil rights protest in Harlem: "Don't shop where you can't work."

They didn't know each other before they got together over a shared antiwar sentiment. But now they finish each other's sentences. What do grannies have that won the attention? "Novelty." "Respect." "Authority." "Mom and apple pie."

Why are they protesting while their children and grandchildren aren't? "They're busy; we're retired," says Joan. Molly adds, "We helped the world get in the shape it's in. We have some responsibility here." And all shake heads in agreement with Vinie and Carol on the notion that they have reached a wonderful stage of life called: nothing left to lose.

You can argue that these women have an unsophisticated political solution to the war: Get out. But first read that same unsophisticated view in the journal *Foreign Policy* by retired Lieutenant General William Odom under the title: "Cut and Run? You Bet."

You can argue too that protest is futile against an administration that has left the reality-based community. But first consider what the granny movement with its loose connections across 38 groups offers those of us who turn from disapproval and confusion to passivity.

With her button reading "Love the troops/hate the war," Carol says simply, "If you're not hopeful, you're helpless." Vinie adds, "You have to stand up for something or you mean nothing." As Norman Siegel, their longtime civil rights lawyer, says with respect, they represent a generation that still believes they can make change. "They have in their experience the belief that you can challenge the government. They believe they can stop the war."

We are now in the run-up to Mother's Day, a holiday that evolved from Julia Ward Howe's antiwar crusade to Hallmark Cards' breakfast-in-bed day. The grannies are cooking up something that won't fit on a bed tray.

Before I leave, Joan rifles through the folder on her lap, stops for a moment to hand me another set of lyrics, "Grandmas, let's unite/While we are still upright." But then she pauses to quote something from a man who never got beyond 38, the Rev. Martin Luther King Jr.: "Our lives begin to end the day we become silent about things that matter."

She looks around the table at grannies against the war who are shaking their heads and adds: "I think that's our theme." A booster shot of optimism? Mission accomplished.

INDEX

Page numbers in italics indicate images

Page numbers in italics indicate images

Page numbers in italics indicate images

Page numbers in italics indicate images

Page numbers in italics indicate images

Page numbers in italics indicate images

Page numbers in italics indicate images

Page numbers in italics indicate images

Page numbers in italics indicate images

Page numbers in italics indicate images

Page numbers in italics indicate images

Page numbers in italics indicate images

Page numbers in italics indicate images

Page numbers in italics indicate images

Page numbers in italics indicate images

Page numbers in italics indicate images

Page numbers in italics indicate images

Page numbers in italics indicate images

Page numbers in italics indicate images

Also Available from Grey House Publishing
General Reference Titles

The Value of a Dollar 1600-1859, The Colonial Era to The Civil War

Following the format of the widely acclaimed, T*he Value of a Dollar, 1860-2004, The Value of a Dollar 1600-1859, The Colonial Era to The Civil War* records the actual prices of thousands of items that consumers purchased from the Colonial Era to the Civil War. Our editorial department had been flooded with requests from users of our Value of a Dollar for the same type of information, just from an earlier time period. This new volume is just the answer – with pricing data from 1600 to 1859. Arranged into five-year chapters, each 5-year chapter includes a Historical Snapshot, Consumer Expenditures, Investments, Selected Income, Income/Standard Jobs, Food Basket, Standard Prices and Miscellany. There is also a section on Trends. This informative section charts the change in price over time and provides added detail on the reasons prices changed within the time period, including industry developments, changes in consumer attitudes and important historical facts. This fascinating survey will serve a wide range of research needs and will be useful in all high school, public and academic library reference collections.

600 pages; Hardcover ISBN 1-59237-094-2, $135.00

The Value of a Dollar 1860-2004, Third Edition

A guide to practical economy, *The Value of a Dollar* records the actual prices of thousands of items that consumers purchased from the Civil War to the present, along with facts about investment options and income opportunities. This brand new Third Edition boasts a brand new addition to each five-year chapter, a section on Trends. This informative section charts the change in price over time and provides added detail on the reasons prices changed within the time period, including industry developments, changes in consumer attitudes and important historical facts. Plus, a brand new chapter for 2000-2004 has been added. Each 5-year chapter includes a Historical Snapshot, Consumer Expenditures, Investments, Selected Income, Income/Standard Jobs, Food Basket, Standard Prices and Miscellany. This interesting and useful publication will be widely used in any reference collection.

"Recommended for high school, college and public libraries." –ARBA

600 pages; Hardcover ISBN 1-59237-074-8, $135.00

Working Americans 1880-1999
Volume I: The Working Class, Volume II: The Middle Class, Volume III: The Upper Class

Each of the volumes in the *Working Americans 1880-1999* series focuses on a particular class of Americans, The Working Class, The Middle Class and The Upper Class over the last 120 years. Chapters in each volume focus on one decade and profile three to five families. Family Profiles include real data on Income & Job Descriptions, Selected Prices of the Times, Annual Income, Annual Budgets, Family Finances, Life at Work, Life at Home, Life in the Community, Working Conditions, Cost of Living, Amusements and much more. Each chapter also contains an Economic Profile with Average Wages of other Professions, a selection of Typical Pricing, Key Events & Inventions, News Profiles, Articles from Local Media and Illustrations. The *Working Americans* series captures the lifestyles of each of the classes from the last twelve decades, covers a vast array of occupations and ethnic backgrounds and travels the entire nation. These interesting and useful compilations of portraits of the American Working, Middle and Upper Classes during the last 120 years will be an important addition to any high school, public or academic library reference collection.

"These interesting, unique compilations of economic and social facts, figures and graphs will support multiple research needs. They will engage and enlighten patrons in high school, public and academic library collections." –Booklist

Volume I: The Working Class ◆ 558 pages; Hardcover ISBN 1-891482-81-5, $145.00 ◆ Volume II: The Middle Class ◆ 591 pages; Hardcover ISBN 1-891482-72-6; $145.00 ◆ Volume III: The Upper Class ◆ 567 pages; Hardcover ISBN 1-930956-38-X, $145.00

Working Americans 1880-1999 Volume IV: Their Children

This Fourth Volume in the highly successful *Working Americans 1880-1999* series focuses on American children, decade by decade from 1880 to 1999. This interesting and useful volume introduces the reader to three children in each decade, one from each of the Working, Middle and Upper classes. Like the first three volumes in the series, the individual profiles are created from interviews, diaries, statistical studies, biographies and news reports. Profiles cover a broad range of ethnic backgrounds, geographic area and lifestyles – everything from an orphan in Memphis in 1882, following the Yellow Fever epidemic of 1878 to an eleven-year-old nephew of a beer baron and owner of the New York Yankees in New York City in 1921. Chapters also contain important supplementary materials including News Features as well as information on everything from Schools to Parks, Infectious Diseases to Childhood Fears along with Entertainment, Family Life and much more to provide an informative overview of the lifestyles of children from each decade. This interesting account of what life was like for Children in the Working, Middle and Upper Classes will be a welcome addition to the reference collection of any high school, public or academic library.

600 pages; Hardcover ISBN 1-930956-35-5, $145.00

To preview any of our Directories Risk-Free for 30 days, call (800) 562-2139 or fax to (518) 789-0556

Working Americans 1880-2003 Volume V: Americans At War

Working Americans 1880-2003 Volume V: Americans At War is divided into 11 chapters, each covering a decade from 1880-2003 and examines the lives of Americans during the time of war, including declared conflicts, one-time military actions, protests, and preparations for war. Each decade includes several personal profiles, whether on the battlefield or on the homefront, that tell the stories of civilians, soldiers, and officers during the decade. The profiles examine: Life at Home; Life at Work; and Life in the Community. Each decade also includes an Economic Profile with statistical comparisons, a Historical Snapshot, News Profiles, local News Articles, and Illustrations that provide a solid historical background to the decade being examined. Profiles range widely not only geographically, but also emotionally, from that of a girl whose leg was torn off in a blast during WWI, to the boredom of being stationed in the Dakotas as the Indian Wars were drawing to a close. As in previous volumes of the *Working Americans* series, information is presented in narrative form, but hard facts and real-life situations back up each story. The basis of the profiles come from diaries, private print books, personal interviews, family histories, estate documents and magazine articles. For easy reference, *Working Americans 1880-2003 Volume V: Americans At War* includes an in-depth Subject Index. The *Working Americans* series has become an important reference for public libraries, academic libraries and high school libraries. This fifth volume will be a welcome addition to all of these types of reference collections.

600 pages; Hardcover ISBN 1-59237-024-1; $145.00
Five Volume Set (Volumes I-V), Hardcover ISBN 1-59237-034-9, $675.00

Working Americans 1880-2005 Volume VI: Women at Work

Unlike any other volume in the *Working Americans* series, this Sixth Volume, is the first to focus on a particular gender of Americans. *Volume VI: Women at Work*, traces what life was like for working women from the 1860's to the present time. Beginning with the life of a maid in 1890 and a store clerk in 1900 and ending with the life and times of the modern working women, this text captures the struggle, strengths and changing perception of the American woman at work. Each chapter focuses on one decade and profiles three to five women with real data on Income & Job Descriptions, Selected Prices of the Times, Annual Income, Annual Budgets, Family Finances, Life at Work, Life at Home, Life in the Community, Working Conditions, Cost of Living, Amusements and much more. For even broader access to the events, economics and attitude towards women throughout the past 130 years, each chapter is supplemented with News Profiles, Articles from Local Media, Illustrations, Economic Profiles, Typical Pricing, Key Events, Inventions and more. This important volume illustrates what life was like for working women over time and allows the reader to develop an understanding of the changing role of women at work. These interesting and useful compilations of portraits of women at work will be an important addition to any high school, public or academic library reference collection.

600 pages; Hardcover ISBN 1-59237-063-2; $145.00

Working Americans 1880-2005 Volume VII: Social Movements

The newest addition to the widely-successful *Working Americans* series, *Volume VII: Social Movements* explores how Americans sought and fought for change from the 1880s to the present time. Following the format of previous volumes in the Working Americans series, the text examines the lives of 34 individuals who have worked -- often behind the scenes -- to bring about change. Issues include topics as diverse as the Anti-smoking movement of 1901 to efforts by Native Americans to reassert their long lost rights. Along the way, the book will profile individuals brave enough to demand suffrage for Kansas women in 1912 or demand an end to lynching during a March on Washington in 1923. Each profile is enriched with real data on Income & Job Descriptions, Selected Prices of the Times, Annual Incomes & Budgets, Life at Work, Life at Home, Life in the Community, along with News Features, Key Events, and Illustrations. The depth of information contained in each profile allow the user to explore the private, financial and public lives of these subjects, deepening our understanding of how calls for change took place in our society. A must-purchase for the reference collections of high school libraries, public libraries and academic libraries.

600 pages; Hardcover ISBN 1-59237-101-9; $145.00
Seven Volume Set (Volumes I-VII), Hardcover ISBN 1-59237-133-7, $945.00

The Encyclopedia of Warrior Peoples & Fighting Groups

Many military groups throughout the world have excelled in their craft either by fortuitous circumstances, outstanding leadership, or intense training. This new second edition of The Encyclopedia of Warrior Peoples and Fighting Groups explores the origins and leadership of these outstanding combat forces, chronicles their conquests and accomplishments, examines the circumstances surrounding their decline or disbanding, and assesses their influence on the groups and methods of warfare that followed. This edition has been completely updated with information through 2005 and contains over 20 new entries. Readers will encounter ferocious tribes, charismatic leaders, and daring militias, from ancient times to the present, including Amazons, Buffalo Soldiers, Green Berets, Iron Brigade, Kamikazes, Peoples of the Sea, Polish Winged Hussars, Sacred Band of Thebes, Teutonic Knights, and Texas Rangers. With over 100 alphabetical entries, numerous cross-references and illustrations, a comprehensive bibliography, and index, the Encyclopedia of Warrior Peoples and Fighting Groups is a valuable resource for readers seeking insight into the bold history of distinguished fighting forces.

"This work is especially useful for high school students, undergraduates, and general readers with an interest in military history." –Library Journal

Pub. Date: May 2006; Hardcover ISBN 1-59237-116-7; $135.00

To preview any of our Directories Risk-Free for 30 days, call (800) 562-2139 or fax to (518) 789-0556

The Encyclopedia of Invasions & Conquests, From the Ancient Times to the Present

Throughout history, invasions and conquests have played a remarkable role in shaping our world and defining our boundaries, both physically and culturally. This second edition of the popular Encyclopedia of Invasions & Conquests, a comprehensive guide to over 150 invasions, conquests, battles and occupations from ancient times to the present, takes readers on a journey that includes the Roman conquest of Britain, the Portuguese colonization of Brazil, and the Iraqi invasion of Kuwait, to name a few. New articles will explore the late 20th and 21st centuries, with a specific focus on recent conflicts in Afghanistan, Kuwait, Iraq, Yugoslavia, Grenada and Chechnya. Categories of entries include countries, invasions and conquests, and individuals. In addition to covering the military aspects of invasions and conquests, entries cover some of the political, economic, and cultural aspects, for example, the effects of a conquest on the invade country's political and monetary system and in its language and religion. The entries on leaders – among them Sargon, Alexander the Great, William the Conqueror, and Adolf Hitler – deal with the people who sought to gain control, expand power, or exert religious or political influence over others through military means. Revised and updated for this second edition, entries are arranged alphabetically within historical periods. Each chapter provides a map to help readers locate key areas and geographical features, and bibliographical references appear at the end of each entry. Other useful features include cross-references, a cumulative bibliography and a comprehensive subject index. This authoritative, well-organized, lucidly written volume will prove invaluable for a variety of readers, including high school students, military historians, members of the armed forces, history buffs and hobbyists.

"Engaging writing, sensible organization, nice illustrations, interesting and obscure facts, and useful maps make this book a pleasure to read." –ARBA

Pub. Date: March 2006; Hardcover ISBN 1-59237-114-0; $135.00

Encyclopedia of Prisoners of War & Internment

This authoritative second edition provides a valuable overview of the history of prisoners of war and interned civilians, from earliest times to the present. Written by an international team of experts in the field of POW studies, this fascinating and thought-provoking volume includes entries on a wide range of subjects including the Crusades, Plains Indian Warfare, concentration camps, the two world wars, and famous POWs throughout history, as well as atrocities, escapes, and much more. Written in a clear and easily understandable style, this informative reference details over 350 entries, 30% larger than the first edition, that survey the history of prisoners of war and interned civilians from the earliest times to the present, with emphasis on the 19th and 20th centuries. Medical conditions, international law, exchanges of prisoners, organizations working on behalf of POWs, and trials associated with the treatment of captives are just some of the themes explored. Entries range from the Ardeatine Caves Massacre to Kurt Vonnegut. Entries are arranged alphabetically, plus illustrations and maps are provided for easy reference. The text also includes an introduction, bibliography, appendix of selected documents, and end-of-entry reading suggestions. This one-of-a-kind reference will be a helpful addition to the reference collections of all public libraries, high schools, and university libraries and will prove invaluable to historians and military enthusiasts.

"Thorough and detailed yet accessible to the lay reader. Of special interest to subject specialists and historians; recommended for public and academic libraries." - Library Journal

Pub. Date: March 2006; Hardcover ISBN 1-59237-120-5; $135.00

The Religious Right, A Reference Handbook

Timely and unbiased, this third edition updates and expands its examination of the religious right and its influence on our government, citizens, society, and politics. From the fight to outlaw the teaching of Darwin's theory of evolution to the struggle to outlaw abortion, the religious right is continually exerting an influence on public policy. This text explores the influence of religion on legislation and society, while examining the alignment of the religious right with the political right. A historical survey of the movement highlights the shift to "hands-on" approach to politics and the struggle to present a unified front. The coverage offers a critical historical survey of the religious right movement, focusing on its increased involvement in the political arena, attempts to forge coalitions, and notable successes and failures. The text offers complete coverage of biographies of the men and women who have advanced the cause and an up to date chronology illuminate the movement's goals, including their accomplishments and failures. This edition offers an extensive update to all sections along with several brand new entries. Two new sections complement this third edition, a chapter on legal issues and court decisions and a chapter on demographic statistics and electoral patterns. To aid in further research, The Religious Right, offers an entire section of annotated listings of print and non-print resources, as well as of organizations affiliated with the religious right, and those opposing it. Comprehensive in its scope, this work offers easy-to-read, pertinent information for those seeking to understand the religious right and its evolving role in American society. A must for libraries of all sizes, university religion departments, activists, high schools and for those interested in the evolving role of the religious right.

" Recommended for all public and academic libraries." - Library Journal

Pub. Date: November 2006; Hardcover ISBN 1-59237-113-2; $135.00

To preview any of our Directories Risk-Free for 30 days, call (800) 562-2139 or fax to (518) 789-0556

From Suffrage to the Senate, An Encyclopedia of American Women in Politics

From Suffrage to the Senate is a comprehensive and valuable compendium of biographies of leading women in U.S. politics, past and present, and an examination of the wide range of women's movements. Up to date through 2006, this dynamically illustrated reference work explores American women's path to political power and social equality from the struggle for the right to vote and the abolition of slavery to the first African American woman in the U.S. Senate and beyond. This new edition includes over 150 new entries and a brand new section on trends and demographics of women in politics. The in-depth coverage also traces the political heritage of the abolition, labor, suffrage, temperance, and reproductive rights movements. The alphabetically arranged entries include biographies of every woman from across the political spectrum who has served in the U.S. House and Senate, along with women in the Judiciary and the U.S. Cabinet and, new to this edition, biographies of activists and political consultants. Bibliographical references follow each entry. For easy reference, a handy chronology is provided detailing 150 years of women's history. This up-to-date reference will be a must-purchase for women's studies departments, high schools and public libraries and will be a handy resource for those researching the key players in women's politics, past and present.

"An engaging tool that would be useful in high school, public, and academic libraries looking for an overview of the political history of women in the US." –Booklist

Pub. Date: October 2006; Two Volume Set; Hardcover ISBN 1-59237-117-5; $195.00

An African Biographical Dictionary

This landmark second edition is the only biographical dictionary to bring together, in one volume, cultural, social and political leaders – both historical and contemporary – of the sub-Saharan region. Over 800 biographical sketches of prominent Africans, as well as foreigners who have affected the continent's history, are featured, 150 more than the previous edition. The wide spectrum of leaders includes religious figures, writers, politicians, scientists, entertainers, sports personalities and more. Access to these fascinating individuals is provided in a user-friendly format. The biographies are arranged alphabetically, cross-referenced and indexed. Entries include the country or countries in which the person was significant and the commonly accepted dates of birth and death. Each biographical sketch is chronologically written; entries for cultural personalities add an evaluation of their work. This information is followed by a selection of references often found in university and public libraries, including autobiographies and principal biographical works. Appendixes list each individual by country and by field of accomplishment – rulers, musicians, explorers, missionaries, businessmen, physicists – nearly thirty categories in all. Another convenient appendix lists heads of state since independence by country. Up-to-date and representative of African societies as a whole, An African Biographical Dictionary provides a wealth of vital information for students of African culture and is an indispensable reference guide for anyone interested in African affairs.

"An unquestionable convenience to have these concise, informative biographies gathered into one source, indexed, and analyzed by appendixes listing entrants by nation and occupational field." –Wilson Library Bulletin

Pub. Date: July 2006; Hardcover ISBN 1-59237-112-4; $125.00

American Environmental Leaders, From Colonial Times to the Present

A comprehensive and diverse award winning collection of biographies of the most important figures in American environmentalism. Few subjects arouse the passions the way the environment does. How will we feed an ever-increasing population and how can that food be made safe for consumption? Who decides how land is developed? How can environmental policies be made fair for everyone, including multiethnic groups, women, children, and the poor? American Environmental Leaders presents more than 350 biographies of men and women who have devoted their lives to studying, debating, and organizing these and other controversial issues over the last 200 years. In addition to the scientists who have analyzed how human actions affect nature, we are introduced to poets, landscape architects, presidents, painters, activists, even sanitation engineers, and others who have forever altered how we think about the environment. The easy to use A–Z format provides instant access to these fascinating individuals, and frequent cross references indicate others with whom individuals worked (and sometimes clashed). End of entry references provide users with a starting point for further research.

"Highly recommended for high school, academic, and public libraries needing environmental biographical information." –Library Journal/Starred Review

Two Volume Set; Hardcover ISBN 1-57607-385-8 $175.00

World Cultural Leaders of the Twentieth Century

An expansive two volume set that covers 450 worldwide cultural icons, World Cultural Leaders of the Twentieth Century includes each person's works, achievements, and professional careers in a thorough essay. Who was the originator of the term "documentary"? Which poet married the daughter of the famed novelist Thomas Mann in order to help her escape Nazi Germany? Which British writer served as an agent in Russia against the Bolsheviks before the 1917 revolution? These and many more questions are answered in this illuminating text. A handy two volume set that makes it easy to look up 450 worldwide cultural icons: novelists, poets, playwrights, painters, sculptors, architects, dancers, choreographers, actors, directors, filmmakers, singers, composers, and musicians. World Cultural Leaders of the Twentieth Century provides entries (many of them illustrated) covering the person's works, achievements, and professional career in a thorough essay and offers interesting facts and statistics. Entries are fully cross-referenced so that readers can learn how various individuals influenced others. A thorough general index completes the coverage.

"Fills a need for handy, concise information on a wide array of international cultural figures."-ARBA

Two Volume Set; Hardcover ISBN 1-57607-038-7 $175.00

To preview any of our Directories Risk-Free for 30 days, call (800) 562-2139 or fax to (518) 789-0556

Universal Reference Publications
Statistical & Demographic Reference Books

Profiles of New York ◆ Profiles of Florida ◆ Profiles of Texas ◆ Profiles of Illinois ◆ Profiles of Michigan ◆ Profiles of Ohio ◆ Profiles of New Jersey ◆ Profiles of Pennsylvania

Packed with over 50 pieces of data that make up a complete, user-friendly profile of each state, these directories go even further by then pulling selected data and providing it in ranking list form for even easier comparisons between the 100 largest towns and cities! The careful layout gives the user an easy-to-read snapshot of every single place and county in the state, from the biggest metropolis to the smallest unincorporated hamlet. The richness of each place or county profile is astounding in its depth, from history to weather, all packed in an easy-to-navigate, compact format. No need for piles of multiple sources with this volume on your desk. Here is a look at just a few of the data sets you'll find in each profile: History, Geography, Climate, Population, Vital Statistics, Economy, Income, Taxes, Education, Housing, Health & Environment, Public Safety, Newspapers, Transportation, Presidential Election Results, Information Contacts and Chambers of Commerce. As an added bonus, there is a section on Selected Statistics, where data from the 100 largest towns and cities is arranged into easy-to-use charts. Each of 22 different data points has its own two-page spread with the cities listed in alpha order so researchers can easily compare and rank cities. A remarkable compilation that offers overviews and insights into each corner of the state, our *Profiles of... Series* goes beyond Census statistics, beyond metro area coverage, beyond the 100 best places to live. Drawn from official census information, other government statistics and original research, you will have at your fingertips data that's available nowhere else in one single source. Data will be published on additional states in 2007 and 2008.

Profiles of New York: 800 pages; Softcover ISBN 1-59237-161-2; $149.00 ◆ Profiles of Florida: 800 pages; Softcover ISBN 1-59237-110-8; $149.00 ◆ Profiles of Texas: 800 pages; Softcover ISBN 1-59237-111-6; $149.00 ◆ Profiles of Illinois: 800 pages; Softcover ISBN 1-59237-148-5; $149.00 ◆ Profiles of Michigan: 800 pages; Softcover ISBN 1-59237-149-3; $149.00 ◆ Profiles of Ohio: 800 pages; Softcover ISBN 1-59237-175-2; $149.00 ◆ Profiles of New Jersey: 800 pages; Softcover ISBN 1-59237-209-0; $149.00 ◆ Profiles of Pennsylvania: 800 pages; Softcover ISBN 1-59237-210-4; $149.00

America's Top-Rated Cities, 2006

America's Top-Rated Cities provides current, comprehensive statistical information and other essential data in one easy-to-use source on the 100 "top" cities that have been cited as the best for business and living in the U.S. This handbook allows readers to see, at a glance, a concise social, business, economic, demographic and environmental profile of each city, including brief evaluative comments. In addition to detailed data on Cost of Living, Finances, Real Estate, Education, Major Employers, Media, Crime and Climate, city reports now include Housing Vacancies, Tax Audits, Bankruptcy, Presidential Election Results and more. This outstanding source of information will be widely used in any reference collection.

"The only source of its kind that brings together all of this information into one easy-to-use source. It will be beneficial to many business and public libraries." –ARBA

2,500 pages, 4 Volume Set; Softcover ISBN 1-59237-076-4, $195.00

America's Top-Rated Smaller Cities, 2006/07

A perfect companion to *America's Top-Rated Cities*, *America's Top-Rated Smaller Cities* provides current, comprehensive business and living profiles of smaller cities (population 25,000-99,999) that have been cited as the best for business and living in the United States. Sixty cities make up this 2004 edition of *America's Top-Rated Smaller Cities*, all are top-ranked by Population Growth, Median Income, Unemployment Rate and Crime Rate. City reports reflect the most current data available on a wide-range of statistics, including Employment & Earnings, Household Income, Unemployment Rate, Population Characteristics, Taxes, Cost of Living, Education, Health Care, Public Safety, Recreation, Media, Air & Water Quality and much more. Plus, each city report contains a Background of the City, and an Overview of the State Finances. *America's Top-Rated Smaller Cities* offers a reliable, one-stop source for statistical data that, before now, could only be found scattered in hundreds of sources. This volume is designed for a wide range of readers: individuals considering relocating a residence or business; professionals considering expanding their business or changing careers; general and market researchers; real estate consultants; human resource personnel; urban planners and investors.

"Provides current, comprehensive statistical information in one easy-to-use source... Recommended for public and academic libraries and specialized collections." –Library Journal

1,100 pages; Softcover ISBN 1-59237-135-3, $160.00

To preview any of our Directories Risk-Free for 30 days, call (800) 562-2139 or fax to (518) 789-0556

Profiles of America: Facts, Figures & Statistics for Every Populated Place in the United States

Profiles of America is the only source that pulls together, in one place, statistical, historical and descriptive information about every place in the United States in an easy-to-use format. This award winning reference set, now in its second edition, compiles statistics and data from over 20 different sources – the latest census information has been included along with more than nine brand new statistical topics. This Four-Volume Set details over 40,000 places, from the biggest metropolis to the smallest unincorporated hamlet, and provides statistical details and information on over 50 different topics including Geography, Climate, Population, Vital Statistics, Economy, Income, Taxes, Education, Housing, Health & Environment, Public Safety, Newspapers, Transportation, Presidential Election Results and Information Contacts or Chambers of Commerce. Profiles are arranged, for ease-of-use, by state and then by county. Each county begins with a County-Wide Overview and is followed by information for each Community in that particular county. The Community Profiles within the county are arranged alphabetically. *Profiles of America* is a virtual snapshot of America at your fingertips and a unique compilation of information that will be widely used in any reference collection.

A Library Journal Best Reference Book "An outstanding compilation." –Library Journal

10,000 pages; Four Volume Set; Softcover ISBN 1-891482-80-7, $595.00

The Comparative Guide to American Suburbs, 2005

The Comparative Guide to American Suburbs is a one-stop source for Statistics on the 2,000+ suburban communities surrounding the 50 largest metropolitan areas – their population characteristics, income levels, economy, school system and important data on how they compare to one another. Organized into 50 Metropolitan Area chapters, each chapter contains an overview of the Metropolitan Area, a detailed Map followed by a comprehensive Statistical Profile of each Suburban Community, including Contact Information, Physical Characteristics, Population Characteristics, Income, Economy, Unemployment Rate, Cost of Living, Education, Chambers of Commerce and more. Next, statistical data is sorted into Ranking Tables that rank the suburbs by twenty different criteria, including Population, Per Capita Income, Unemployment Rate, Crime Rate, Cost of Living and more. *The Comparative Guide to American Suburbs* is the best source for locating data on suburbs. Those looking to relocate, as well as those doing preliminary market research, will find this an invaluable timesaving resource.

"Public and academic libraries will find this compilation useful…The work draws together figures from many sources and will be especially helpful for job relocation decisions." – Booklist

1,700 pages; Softcover ISBN 1-59237-004-7, $130.00

Weather America, A Thirty-Year Summary of Statistical Weather Data and Rankings

This valuable resource provides extensive climatological data for over 4,000 National and Cooperative Weather Stations throughout the United States. *Weather America* begins with a new Major Storms section that details major storm events of the nation and a National Rankings section that details rankings for several data elements, such as Maximum Temperature and Precipitation. The main body of *Weather America* is organized into 50 state sections. Each section provides a Data Table on each Weather Station, organized alphabetically, that provides statistics on Maximum and Minimum Temperatures, Precipitation, Snowfall, Extreme Temperatures, Foggy Days, Humidity and more. State sections contain two brand new features in this edition – a City Index and a narrative Description of the climatic conditions of the state. Each section also includes a revised Map of the State that includes not only weather stations, but cities and towns.

"Best Reference Book of the Year." –Library Journal

2,013 pages; Softcover ISBN 1-891482-29-7, $175.00

The Asian Databook: Statistics for all US Counties & Cities with Over 10,000 Population

This is the first-ever resource that compiles statistics and rankings on the US Asian population. *The Asian Databook* presents over 20 statistical data points for each city and county, arranged alphabetically by state, then alphabetically by place name. Data reported for each place includes Population, Languages Spoken at Home, Foreign-Born, Educational Attainment, Income Figures, Poverty Status, Homeownership, Home Values & Rent, and more. Next, in the Rankings Section, the top 75 places are listed for each data element. These easy-to-access ranking tables allow the user to quickly determine trends and population characteristics. This kind of comparative data can not be found elsewhere, in print or on the web, in a format that's as easy-to-use or more concise. A useful resource for those searching for demographics data, career search and relocation information and also for market research. With data ranging from Ancestry to Education, *The Asian Databook* presents a useful compilation of information that will be a much-needed resource in the reference collection of any public or academic library along with the marketing collection of any company whose primary focus in on the Asian population.

1,000 pages; Softcover ISBN 1-59237-044-6 $150.00

To preview any of our Directories Risk-Free for 30 days, call (800) 562-2139 or fax to (518) 789-0556

The Hispanic Databook: Statistics for all US Counties & Cities with Over 10,000 Population

Previously published by Toucan Valley Publications, this second edition has been completely updated with figures from the latest census and has been broadly expanded to include dozens of new data elements and a brand new Rankings section. The Hispanic population in the United States has increased over 42% in the last 10 years and accounts for 12.5% of the total US population. For ease-of-use, *The Hispanic Databook* presents over 20 statistical data points for each city and county, arranged alphabetically by state, then alphabetically by place name. Data reported for each place includes Population, Languages Spoken at Home, Foreign-Born, Educational Attainment, Income Figures, Poverty Status, Homeownership, Home Values & Rent, and more. Next, in the Rankings Section, the top 75 places are listed for each data element. These easy-to-access ranking tables allow the user to quickly determine trends and population characteristics. This kind of comparative data can not be found elsewhere, in print or on the web, in a format that's as easy-to-use or more concise. A useful resource for those searching for demographics data, career search and relocation information and also for market research. With data ranging from Ancestry to Education, *The Hispanic Databook* presents a useful compilation of information that will be a much-needed resource in the reference collection of any public or academic library along with the marketing collection of any company whose primary focus in on the Hispanic population.

"This accurate, clearly presented volume of selected Hispanic demographics is recommended for large public libraries and research collections."-Library Journal

1,000 pages; Softcover ISBN 1-59237-008-X, $150.00

Ancestry in America: A Comparative Guide to Over 200 Ethnic Backgrounds

This brand new reference work pulls together thousands of comparative statistics on the Ethnic Backgrounds of all populated places in the United States with populations over 10,000. Never before has this kind of information been reported in a single volume. Section One, Statistics by Place, is made up of a list of over 200 ancestry and race categories arranged alphabetically by each of the 5,000 different places with populations over 10,000. The population number of the ancestry group in that city or town is provided along with the percent that group represents of the total population. This informative city-by-city section allows the user to quickly and easily explore the ethnic makeup of all major population bases in the United States. Section Two, Comparative Rankings, contains three tables for each ethnicity and race. In the first table, the top 150 populated places are ranked by population number for that particular ancestry group, regardless of population. In the second table, the top 150 populated places are ranked by the percent of the total population for that ancestry group. In the third table, those top 150 populated places with 10,000 population are ranked by population number for each ancestry group. These easy-to-navigate tables allow users to see ancestry population patterns and make city-by-city comparisons as well. Plus, as an added bonus with the purchase of *Ancestry in America*, a free companion CD-ROM is available that lists statistics and rankings for all of the 35,000 populated places in the United States. This brand new, information-packed resource will serve a wide-range or research requests for demographics, population characteristics, relocation information and much more. *Ancestry in America: A Comparative Guide to Over 200 Ethnic Backgrounds* will be an important acquisition to all reference collections.

"This compilation will serve a wide range of research requests for population characteristics … it offers much more detail than other sources." –Booklist

1,500 pages; Softcover ISBN 1-59237-029-2, $225.00

The American Tally: Statistics & Comparative Rankings for U.S. Cities with Populations over 10,000

This important statistical handbook compiles, all in one place, comparative statistics on all U.S. cities and towns with a 10,000+ population. *The American Tally* provides statistical details on over 4,000 cities and towns and profiles how they compare with one another in Population Characteristics, Education, Language & Immigration, Income & Employment and Housing. Each section begins with an alphabetical listing of cities by state, allowing for quick access to both the statistics and relative rankings of any city. Next, the highest and lowest cities are listed in each statistic. These important, informative lists provide quick reference to which cities are at both extremes of the spectrum for each statistic. Unlike any other reference, *The American Tally* provides quick, easy access to comparative statistics – a must-have for any reference collection.

"A solid library reference." -Bookwatch

500 pages; Softcover ISBN 1-930956-29-0, $125.00

To preview any of our Directories Risk-Free for 30 days, call (800) 562-2139 or fax to (518) 789-0556

The Grey House Handbook on Alternative Energy, 2006

This is the first ever resource to pull together information, resources and statistics for all types of Alternative Energy, including Hydro, Wind, Solar, Coal, Natural Gas and Atomic Energy sources. The Handbook begins with an informative Introduction to Alternative Energy Resources, including editorial on the history of energy, the necessity of using alternative energy, conservation and the economics of using alternative energy sources. Plus, handy charts are also included that cover uses of energy sources today; forecasts of energy sources and the availability of energy sources in the future. Next, readers will find chapters on each Type of Energy Source. Chapters begin with an Introduction to the specific energy source, History, Strengths & Drawbacks, Industrial & Residential Use and Trends. Several articles are also included for each energy source, followed by Resources, including Associations, Magazines, Trade Shows and Vendors. The Grey House Handbook on Alternative Energy also contains a informative, useful section on Statistics. These charts allow for easy location of very specific data. A handy Glossary and section on Public Energy Companies is also included for easy reference. Three indexes, Product Index, Subject Index and Entry Name Index allow the user to locate specific resources quickly and easily. As the need for alternative energy sources continues to grow, having access to these resources will become more and more important. This first edition will prove useful to the reference collections public and academic libraries.

800 pages; Softcover ISBN 1-59237-134-5; $165.00

The Environmental Resource Handbook, 2005/06

The Environmental Resource Handbook is the most up-to-date and comprehensive source for Environmental Resources and Statistics. Section I: Resources provides detailed contact information for thousands of information sources, including Associations & Organizations, Awards & Honors, Conferences, Foundations & Grants, Environmental Health, Government Agencies, National Parks & Wildlife Refuges, Publications, Research Centers, Educational Programs, Green Product Catalogs, Consultants and much more. Section II: Statistics, provides statistics and rankings on hundreds of important topics, including Children's Environmental Index, Municipal Finances, Toxic Chemicals, Recycling, Climate, Air & Water Quality and more. This kind of up-to-date environmental data, all in one place, is not available anywhere else on the market place today. This vast compilation of resources and statistics is a must-have for all public and academic libraries as well as any organization with a primary focus on the environment.

"...the intrinsic value of the information make it worth consideration by libraries with environmental collections and environmentally concerned users." –Booklist

1,000 pages; Softcover ISBN 1-59237-090-X, $155.00 ◆ Online Database $300.00

To preview any of our Directories Risk-Free for 30 days, call (800) 562-2139 or fax to (518) 789-0556

Grey House Publishing
Business Directories

The Rauch Guide to the US Adhesives & Sealants, Cosmetics & Toiletries, Ink, Paint, Plastics, Pulp & Paper and Rubber Industries

The Rauch Guides are known worldwide for their comprehensive marketing information. Acquired by Grey House Publishing in 2005, new updated and revised editions will be published throughout 2005 and 2006. Each Guide provides market facts and figures in a highly organized format, ideal for today's busy personnel, serving as ready-references for top executives as well as the industry newcomer. *The Rauch Guides* save time and money by organizing widely scattered information and providing estimates for important business decisions, some of which are available nowhere else. Each Guide is organized into several information-packed chapters. After a brief introduction, the ECONOMICS section provides data on industry shipments; long-term growth and forecasts; prices; company performance; employment, expenditures, and productivity; transportation and geographical patterns; packaging; foreign trade; and government regulations. Next, TECHNOLOGY & RAW MATERIALS provide market, technical, and raw material information for chemicals, equipment and related materials, including market size and leading suppliers, prices, end uses, and trends. PRODUCTS & MARKETS provide information for each major industry product, including market size and historical trends, leading suppliers, five-year forecasts, industry structure, and major end uses. For easy access, each *Guide* contains a chapter on INDUSTRY ACTIVITIES, ORGANIZATIONS & SOURCES OF INFORMATION with detailed information on meetings, exhibits, and trade shows, sources of statistical information, trade associations, technical and professional societies, and trade and technical periodicals. Next, the COMPANY DIRECTORY profiles major industry companies, both public and private. Generally several hundred companies are analyzed. Information includes complete contact information, web address, estimated total and domestic sales, product description, and recent mergers and acquisitions. Each Guide also contains several APPENDICES that provide a cross-reference of suppliers, subsidiaries and divisions. The Rauch Guides will prove to be an invaluable source of market information, company data, trends and forecasts that anyone in these fast-paced industries.

The Rauch Guide to the U.S. Paint Industry Softcover ISBN 1-59237-127-2 $595 ♦ The Rauch Guide to the U.S. Plastics Industry Softcover ISBN 1-59237-128-0 $595 ♦ The Rauch Guide to the U.S. Adhesives and Sealants Industry Softcover ISBN 1-59237-129-9 $595 ♦ The Rauch Guide to the U.S. Ink Industry Softcover ISBN 1-59237-126-4 $595 ♦ The Rauch Guide to the U.S. Rubber Industry Softcover ISBN 1-59237-130-2 $595 ♦ The Rauch Guide to the U.S. Pulp and Paper Industry Softcover ISBN 1-59237-131-0 $595 ♦ The Rauch Guide to the U.S. Cosmetic and Toiletries Industry Softcover ISBN 1-59237-132-9 $895

The Directory of Business Information Resources, 2007

With 100% verification, over 1,000 new listings and more than 12,000 updates, this 2007 edition of *The Directory of Business Information Resources* is the most up-to-date source for contacts in over 98 business areas – from advertising and agriculture to utilities and wholesalers. This carefully researched volume details: the Associations representing each industry; the Newsletters that keep members current; the Magazines and Journals - with their "Special Issues" - that are important to the trade, the Conventions that are "must attends," Databases, Directories and Industry Web Sites that provide access to must-have marketing resources. Includes contact names, phone & fax numbers, web sites and e-mail addresses. This one-volume resource is a gold mine of information and would be a welcome addition to any reference collection.

"This is a most useful and easy-to-use addition to any researcher's library." –The Information Professionals Institute

2,500 pages; Softcover ISBN 1-59237-146-9, $195.00 ♦ Online Database $495.00

Nations of the World, 2006 A Political, Economic and Business Handbook

This completely revised edition covers all the nations of the world in an easy-to-use, single volume. Each nation is profiled in a single chapter that includes Key Facts, Political & Economic Issues, a Country Profile and Business Information. In this fast-changing world, it is extremely important to make sure that the most up-to-date information is included in your reference collection. This edition is just the answer. Each of the 200+ country chapters have been carefully reviewed by a political expert to make sure that the text reflects the most current information on Politics, Travel Advisories, Economics and more. You'll find such vital information as a Country Map, Population Characteristics, Inflation, Agricultural Production, Foreign Debt, Political History, Foreign Policy, Regional Insecurity, Economics, Trade & Tourism, Historical Profile, Political Systems, Ethnicity, Languages, Media, Climate, Hotels, Chambers of Commerce, Banking, Travel Information and more. Five Regional Chapters follow the main text and include a Regional Map, an Introductory Article, Key Indicators and Currencies for the Region. As an added bonus, an all-inclusive CD-ROM is available as a companion to the printed text. Noted for its sophisticated, up-to-date and reliable compilation of political, economic and business information, this brand new edition will be an important acquisition to any public, academic or special library reference collection.

"A useful addition to both general reference collections and business collections." –RUSQ

1,700 pages; Print Version Only Softcover ISBN 1-59237-0079-9, $155.00

To preview any of our Directories Risk-Free for 30 days, call (800) 562-2139 or fax to (518) 789-0556

The Directory of Venture Capital & Private Equity Firms, 2006

This edition has been extensively updated and broadly expanded to offer direct access to over 2,800 Domestic and International Venture Capital Firms, including address, phone & fax numbers, e-mail addresses and web sites for both primary and branch locations. Entries include details on the firm's Mission Statement, Industry Group Preferences, Geographic Preferences, Average and Minimum Investments and Investment Criteria. You'll also find details that are available nowhere else, including the Firm's Portfolio Companies and extensive information on each of the firm's Managing Partners, such as Education, Professional Background and Directorships held, along with the Partner's E-mail Address. *The Directory of Venture Capital & Private Equity Firms* offers five important indexes: Geographic Index, Executive Name Index, Portfolio Company Index, Industry Preference Index and College & University Index. With its comprehensive coverage and detailed, extensive information on each company, *The Directory of Venture Capital & Private Equity Firms* is an important addition to any finance collection.

"The sheer number of listings, the descriptive information provided and the outstanding indexing make this directory a better value than its principal competitor, Pratt's Guide to Venture Capital Sources. Recommended for business collections in large public, academic and business libraries." –Choice

1,300 pages; Softcover ISBN 1-59237-102-7, $450.00 ◆ Online Database (includes a free copy of the directory) $889.00

The Directory of Mail Order Catalogs, 2006

Published since 1981, this updated edition features 100% verification of data and is the premier source of information on the mail order catalog industry. Details over 12,000 consumer catalog companies with 44 different product chapters from Animals to Toys & Games. Contains detailed contact information including e-mail addresses and web sites along with important business details such as employee size, years in business, sales volume, catalog size, number of catalogs mailed and more. Four indexes provide quick access to information: Catalog & Company Name Index, Geographic Index, Product Index and Web Sites Index.

"This is a godsend for those looking for information." –Reference Book Review

1,700 pages; Softcover ISBN 1-59237-103-5 $250.00 ◆ Online Database (includes a free copy of the directory) $495.00

The Directory of Business to Business Catalogs, 2006

The completely updated *Directory of Business to Business Catalogs*, provides details on over 6,000 suppliers of everything from computers to laboratory supplies… office products to office design… marketing resources to safety equipment… landscaping to maintenance suppliers… building construction and much more. Detailed entries offer mailing address, phone & fax numbers, e-mail addresses, web sites, key contacts, sales volume, employee size, catalog printing information and more. Jut about every kind of product a business needs in its day-to-day operations is covered in this carefully-researched volume. Three indexes are provided for at-a-glance access to information: Catalog & Company Name Index, Geographic Index and Web Sites Index.

"An excellent choice for libraries… wishing to supplement their business supplier resources." –Booklist

800 pages; Softcover ISBN 1-59237-105-1, $165.00 ◆ Online Database (includes a free copy of the directory) $325.00

Sports Market Place Directory, 2006

For over 20 years, this comprehensive, up-to-date directory has offered direct access to the Who, What, When & Where of the Sports Industry. With over 20,000 updates and enhancements, the *Sports Market Place Directory* is the most detailed, comprehensive and current sports business reference source available. In 1,800 information-packed pages, *Sports Market Place Directory* profiles contact information and key executives for: Single Sport Organizations, Professional Leagues, Multi-Sport Organizations, Disabled Sports, High School & Youth Sports, Military Sports, Olympic Organizations, Media, Sponsors, Sponsorship & Marketing Event Agencies, Event & Meeting Calendars, Professional Services, College Sports, Manufacturers & Retailers, Facilities and much more. *The Sports Market Place Directory* provides organization's contact information with detailed descriptions including: Key Contacts, physical, mailing, email and web addresses plus phone and fax numbers. Plus, nine important indexes make sure that you can find the information you're looking for quickly and easily: Entry Index, Single Sport Index, Media Index, Sponsor Index, Agency Index, Manufacturers Index, Brand Name Index, Facilities Index and Executive/Geographic Index. For over twenty years, *The Sports Market Place Directory* has assisted thousands of individuals in their pursuit of a career in the sports industry. Why not use "THE SOURCE" that top recruiters, headhunters and career placement centers use to find information on or about sports organizations and key hiring contacts.

1,800 pages; Softcover ISBN 1-59237-139-6, $225.00 ◆ Online Database $479.00

To preview any of our Directories Risk-Free for 30 days, call (800) 562-2139 or fax to (518) 789-0556

Thomas Food and Beverage Market Place, 2006

Thomas Food and Beverage Market Place is bigger and better than ever with thousands of new companies, thousands of updates to existing companies and two revised and enhanced product category indexes. This comprehensive directory profiles over 18,000 Food & Beverage Manufacturers, 12,000 Equipment & Supply Companies, 2,200 Transportation & Warehouse Companies, 2,000 Brokers & Wholesalers, 8,000 Importers & Exporters, 900 Industry Resources and hundreds of Mail Order Catalogs. Listings include detailed Contact Information, Sales Volumes, Key Contacts, Brand & Product Information, Packaging Details and much more. *Thomas Food and Beverage Market Place* is available as a three-volume printed set, a subscription-based Online Database via the Internet, on CD-ROM, as well as mailing lists and a licensable database.

"An essential purchase for those in the food industry but will also be useful in public libraries where needed. Much of the information will be difficult and time consuming to locate without this handy three-volume ready-reference source." –ARBA

8,500 pages, 3 Volume Set; Softcover ISBN 1-59237-096-9, $495.00 ◆ CD-ROM $695.00 ◆
CD-ROM & 3 Volume Set Combo $895.00 ◆ Online Database $695.00 ◆ Online Database & 3 Volume Set Combo, $895.00

The Grey House Homeland Security Directory, 2006

This updated edition features the latest contact information for government and private organizations involved with Homeland Security along with the latest product information and provides detailed profiles of nearly 1,000 Federal & State Organizations & Agencies and over 3,000 Officials and Key Executives involved with Homeland Security. These listings are incredibly detailed and include Mailing Address, Phone & Fax Numbers, Email Addresses & Web Sites, a complete Description of the Agency and a complete list of the Officials and Key Executives associated with the Agency. Next, *The Grey House Homeland Security Directory* provides the go-to source for Homeland Security Products & Services. This section features over 2,000 Companies that provide Consulting, Products or Services. With this Buyer's Guide at their fingertips, users can locate suppliers of everything from Training Materials to Access Controls, from Perimeter Security to BioTerrorism Countermeasures and everything in between – complete with contact information and product descriptions. A handy Product Locator Index is provided to quickly and easily locate suppliers of a particular product. Lastly, an Information Resources Section provides immediate access to contact information for hundreds of Associations, Newsletters, Magazines, Trade Shows, Databases and Directories that focus on Homeland Security. This comprehensive, information-packed resource will be a welcome tool for any company or agency that is in need of Homeland Security information and will be a necessary acquisition for the reference collection of all public libraries and large school districts.

"Compiles this information in one place and is discerning in content. A useful purchase for public and academic libraries." –Booklist

800 pages; Softcover ISBN 1-59237-084-5, $195.00 ◆ Online Database (includes a free copy of the directory) $385.00

The Grey House Transportation Security Directory & Handbook

This brand new title is the only reference of its kind that brings together current data on Transportation Security. With information on everything from Regulatory Authorities to Security Equipment, this top-flight database brings together the relevant information necessary for creating and maintaining a security plan for a wide range of transportation facilities. With this current, comprehensive directory at the ready you'll have immediate access to: Regulatory Authorities & Legislation; Information Resources; Sample Security Plans & Checklists; Contact Data for Major Airports, Seaports, Railroads, Trucking Companies and Oil Pipelines; Security Service Providers; Recommended Equipment & Product Information and more. Using the *Grey House Transportation Security Directory & Handbook*, managers will be able to quickly and easily assess their current security plans; develop contacts to create and maintain new security procedures; and source the products and services necessary to adequately maintain a secure environment. This valuable resource is a must for all Security Managers at Airports, Seaports, Railroads, Trucking Companies and Oil Pipelines.

800 pages; Softcover ISBN 1-59237-075-6, $195

To preview any of our Directories Risk-Free for 30 days, call (800) 562-2139 or fax to (518) 789-0556

The Grey House Safety & Security Directory, 2006

The Grey House Safety & Security Directory is the most comprehensive reference tool and buyer's guide for the safety and security industry. Arranged by safety topic, each chapter begins with OSHA regulations for the topic, followed by Training Articles written by top professionals in the field and Self-Inspection Checklists. Next, each topic contains Buyer's Guide sections that feature related products and services. Topics include Administration, Insurance, Loss Control & Consulting, Protective Equipment & Apparel, Noise & Vibration, Facilities Monitoring & Maintenance, Employee Health Maintenance & Ergonomics, Retail Food Services, Machine Guards, Process Guidelines & Tool Handling, Ordinary Materials Handling, Hazardous Materials Handling, Workplace Preparation & Maintenance, Electrical Lighting & Safety, Fire & Rescue and Security. The Buyer's Guide sections are carefully indexed within each topic area to ensure that you can find the supplies needed to meet OSHA's regulations. Six important indexes make finding information and product manufacturers quick and easy: Geographical Index of Manufacturers and Distributors, Company Profile Index, Brand Name Index, Product Index, Index of Web Sites and Index of Advertisers. This comprehensive, up-to-date reference will provide every tool necessary to make sure a business is in compliance with OSHA regulations and locate the products and services needed to meet those regulations.

"Presents industrial safety information for engineers, plant managers, risk managers, and construction site supervisors…" –Choice

1,500 pages, 2 Volume Set; Softcover ISBN 1-59237-104-3, $225.00

The Grey House Biometric Information Directory, 2006

The Biometric Information Directory is the only comprehensive source for current biometric industry information. This 2006 edition is the first published by Grey House. With 100% updated information, this latest edition offers a complete, current look, in both print and online form, of biometric companies and products – one of the fastest growing industries in today's economy. Detailed profiles of manufacturers of the latest biometric technology, including Finger, Voice, Face, Hand, Signature, Iris, Vein and Palm Identification systems. Data on the companies include key executives, company size and a detailed, indexed description of their product line. Plus, the Directory also includes valuable business resources, and current editorial make this edition the easiest way for the business community and consumers alike to access the largest, most current compilation of biometric industry information available on the market today. The new edition boasts increased numbers of companies, contact names and company data, with over 700 manufacturers and service providers. Information in the directory includes: Editorial on Advancements in Biometrics; Profiles of 700+ companies listed with contact information; Organizations, Trade & Educational Associations, Publications, Conferences, Trade Shows and Expositions Worldwide; Web Site Index; Biometric & Vendors Services Index by Types of Biometrics; and a Glossary of Biometric Terms. This resource will be an important source for anyone who is considering the use of a biometric product, investing in the development of biometric technology, support existing marketing and sales efforts and will be an important acquisition for the business reference collection for large public and business libraries.

800 pages; Softcover ISBN 1-59237-121-3, $225

The Grey House Performing Arts Directory, 2007

The Grey House Performing Arts Directory is the most comprehensive resource covering the Performing Arts. This important directory provides current information on over 8,500 Dance Companies, Instrumental Music Programs, Opera Companies, Choral Groups, Theater Companies, Performing Arts Series and Performing Arts Facilities. Plus, this edition now contains a brand new section on Artist Management Groups. In addition to mailing address, phone & fax numbers, e-mail addresses and web sites, dozens of other fields of available information include mission statement, key contacts, facilities, seating capacity, season, attendance and more. This directory also provides an important Information Resources section that covers hundreds of Performing Arts Associations, Magazines, Newsletters, Trade Shows, Directories, Databases and Industry Web Sites. Five indexes provide immediate access to this wealth of information: Entry Name, Executive Name, Performance Facilities, Geographic and Information Resources. *The Grey House Performing Arts Directory* pulls together thousands of Performing Arts Organizations, Facilities and Information Resources into an easy-to-use source – this kind of comprehensiveness and extensive detail is not available in any resource on the market place today.

"Immensely useful and user-friendly … recommended for public, academic and certain special library reference collections." –Booklist

1,500 pages; Softcover ISBN 1-59237-138-8, $185.00 ◆ Online Database $335.00

To preview any of our Directories Risk-Free for 30 days, call (800) 562-2139 or fax to (518) 789-0556

New York State Directory, 2006/07

The New York State Directory, published annually since 1983, is a comprehensive and easy-to-use guide to accessing public officials and private sector organizations and individuals who influence public policy in the state of New York. *The New York State Directory* includes important information on all New York state legislators and congressional representatives, including biographies and key committee assignments. It also includes staff rosters for all branches of New York state government and for federal agencies and departments that impact the state policy process. Following the state government section are 25 chapters covering policy areas from agriculture through veterans' affairs. Each chapter identifies the state, local and federal agencies and officials that formulate or implement policy. In addition, each chapter contains a roster of private sector experts and advocates who influence the policy process. The directory also offers appendices that include statewide party officials; chambers of commerce; lobbying organizations; public and private universities and colleges; television, radio and print media; and local government agencies and officials.

New York State Directory - 800 pages; Softcover ISBN 1-59237-145-0; $145.00
New York State Directory with Profiles of New York – 2 volumes; 1,600 pages; Softcover ISBN 1-59237-162-0; $225

Research Services Directory: Commercial & Corporate Research Centers

This Ninth Edition provides access to well over 8,000 independent Commercial Research Firms, Corporate Research Centers and Laboratories offering contract services for hands-on, basic or applied research. *Research Services Directory* covers the thousands of types of research companies, including Biotechnology & Pharmaceutical Developers, Consumer Product Research, Defense Contractors, Electronics & Software Engineers, Think Tanks, Forensic Investigators, Independent Commercial Laboratories, Information Brokers, Market & Survey Research Companies, Medical Diagnostic Facilities, Product Research & Development Firms and more. Each entry provides the company's name, mailing address, phone & fax numbers, key contacts, web site, e-mail address, as well as a company description and research and technical fields served. Four indexes provide immediate access to this wealth of information: Research Firms Index, Geographic Index, Personnel Name Index and Subject Index.

"An important source for organizations in need of information about laboratories, individuals and other facilities." –ARBA

1,400 pages; Softcover ISBN 1-59237-003-9, $395.00 ◆ Online Database (includes a free copy of the directory) $850.00

International Business and Trade Directories

Completely updated, the Third Edition of *International Business and Trade Directories* now contains more than 10,000 entries, over 2,000 more than the last edition, making this directory the most comprehensive resource of the worlds business and trade directories. Entries include content descriptions, price, publisher's name and address, web site and e-mail addresses, phone and fax numbers and editorial staff. Organized by industry group, and then by region, this resource puts over 10,000 industry-specific business and trade directories at the reader's fingertips. Three indexes are included for quick access to information: Geographic Index, Publisher Index and Title Index. Public, college and corporate libraries, as well as individuals and corporations seeking critical market information will want to add this directory to their marketing collection.

"Reasonably priced for a work of this type, this directory should appeal to larger academic, public and corporate libraries with an international focus." –Library Journal

1,800 pages; Softcover ISBN 1-930956-63-0, $225.00 ◆ Online Database (includes a free copy of the directory) $450.00

To preview any of our Directories Risk-Free for 30 days, call (800) 562-2139 or fax to (518) 789-0556

Sedgwick Press
Health Directories

The Complete Directory for People with Disabilities, 2007

A wealth of information, now in one comprehensive sourcebook. Completely updated, this edition contains more information than ever before, including thousands of new entries and enhancements to existing entries and thousands of additional web sites and e-mail addresses. This up-to-date directory is the most comprehensive resource available for people with disabilities, detailing Independent Living Centers, Rehabilitation Facilities, State & Federal Agencies, Associations, Support Groups, Periodicals & Books, Assistive Devices, Employment & Education Programs, Camps and Travel Groups. Each year, more libraries, schools, colleges, hospitals, rehabilitation centers and individuals add *The Complete Directory for People with Disabilities* to their collections, making sure that this information is readily available to the families, individuals and professionals who can benefit most from the amazing wealth of resources cataloged here.

"No other reference tool exists to meet the special needs of the disabled in one convenient resource for information." –Library Journal

1,200 pages; Softcover ISBN 1-59237-147-7, $165.00 ◆ Online Database $215.00 ◆ Online Database & Directory Combo $300.00

The Complete Directory for People with Chronic Illness, 2005/06

Thousands of hours of research have gone into this completely updated 2005/06 edition – several new chapters have been added along with thousands of new entries and enhancements to existing entries. Plus, each chronic illness chapter has been reviewed by an medical expert in the field. This widely-hailed directory is structured around the 90 most prevalent chronic illnesses – from Asthma to Cancer to Wilson's Disease – and provides a comprehensive overview of the support services and information resources available for people diagnosed with a chronic illness. Each chronic illness has its own chapter and contains a brief description in layman's language, followed by important resources for National & Local Organizations, State Agencies, Newsletters, Books & Periodicals, Libraries & Research Centers, Support Groups & Hotlines, Web Sites and much more. This directory is an important resource for health care professionals, the collections of hospital and health care libraries, as well as an invaluable tool for people with a chronic illness and their support network.

"A must purchase for all hospital and health care libraries and is strongly recommended for all public library reference departments." –ARBA

1,200 pages; Softcover ISBN 1-59237-081-0, $165.00 ◆ Online Database $215.00 ◆ Online Database & Directory Combo $300.00

The Grey House Rare Disorders Directory, 2006/07

This directory is the most comprehensive resource bringing together hard-to-find information on over 700 rare disorders, including rare cancers, muscular and genetic disorders, and more. This 2006/07 contains the most up-to-date information on each disorder. Written in layman's language, by physicians and faculty at Yale University School of Medicine and Yale New Haven Children's Hospital, the information in this directory is presented in a clear, understandable format, with helpful Cross-References running through the text. The Grey House Rare Disorders Directory is divided into five sections: Disorder Descriptions, Associations & Support Groups, Magazines, Journals & Periodicals, Government Agencies and Treatment Centers. Approximately 20 million, or 1 in every 12, Americans is affected with a rare disorder, so this directory serves a surprisingly wide range of the population. The Grey House Rare Disorders Directory will be an invaluable tool for the thousands of families that have been struck with a rare or "orphan" disease, who feel that they have no place to turn and will be a much-used addition to the reference collection of any public or academic library.

800 pages; Softcover ISBN 1-59237-123-X, $165.00

The Complete Learning Disabilities Directory, 2007

The Complete Learning Disabilities Directory is the most comprehensive database of Programs, Services, Curriculum Materials, Professional Meetings & Resources, Camps, Newsletters and Support Groups for teachers, students and families concerned with learning disabilities. This information-packed directory includes information about Associations & Organizations, Schools, Colleges & Testing Materials, Government Agencies, Legal Resources and much more. For quick, easy access to information, this directory contains four indexes: Entry Name Index, Subject Index and Geographic Index. With every passing year, the field of learning disabilities attracts more attention and the network of caring, committed and knowledgeable professionals grows every day. This directory is an invaluable research tool for these parents, students and professionals.

"Due to its wealth and depth of coverage, parents, teachers and others... should find this an invaluable resource." -Booklist

900 pages; Softcover ISBN 1-59237-122-1, $145.00 ◆ Online Database $195.00 ◆ Online Database & Directory Combo $280.00

To preview any of our Directories Risk-Free for 30 days, call (800) 562-2139 or fax to (518) 789-0556

The Complete Mental Health Directory, 2006/07

This is the most comprehensive resource covering the field of behavioral health, with critical information for both the layman and the mental health professional. For the layman, this directory offers understandable descriptions of 25 Mental Health Disorders as well as detailed information on Associations, Media, Support Groups and Mental Health Facilities. For the professional, *The Complete Mental Health Directory* offers critical and comprehensive information on Managed Care Organizations, Information Systems, Government Agencies and Provider Organizations. This comprehensive volume of needed information will be widely used in any reference collection.

"... the strength of this directory is that it consolidates widely dispersed information into a single volume." –Booklist

800 pages; Softcover ISBN 1-59237-124-8, $165.00 ◆ Online Database $215.00 ◆ Online & Directory Combo $300.00

Older Americans Information Directory, 2006/07

Completely updated for 2006/07, this sixth edition has been completely revised and now contains 1,000 new listings, over 8,000 updates to existing listings and over 3,000 brand new e-mail addresses and web sites. You'll find important resources for Older Americans including National, Regional, State & Local Organizations, Government Agencies, Research Centers, Libraries & Information Centers, Legal Resources, Discount Travel Information, Continuing Education Programs, Disability Aids & Assistive Devices, Health, Print Media and Electronic Media. Three indexes: Entry Index, Subject Index and Geographic Index make it easy to find just the right source of information. This comprehensive guide to resources for Older Americans will be a welcome addition to any reference collection.

"Highly recommended for academic, public, health science and consumer libraries..." –Choice

1,200 pages; Softcover ISBN 1-59237-136-1, $165.00 ◆ Online Database $215.00 ◆ Online Database & Directory Combo $300.00

The Complete Directory for Pediatric Disorders, 2007

This important directory provides parents and caregivers with information about Pediatric Conditions, Disorders, Diseases and Disabilities, including Blood Disorders, Bone & Spinal Disorders, Brain Defects & Abnormalities, Chromosomal Disorders, Congenital Heart Defects, Movement Disorders, Neuromuscular Disorders and Pediatric Tumors & Cancers. This carefully written directory offers: understandable Descriptions of 15 major bodily systems; Descriptions of more than 200 Disorders and a Resources Section, detailing National Agencies & Associations, State Associations, Online Services, Libraries & Resource Centers, Research Centers, Support Groups & Hotlines, Camps, Books and Periodicals. This resource will provide immediate access to information crucial to families and caregivers when coping with children's illnesses.

"Recommended for public and consumer health libraries." –Library Journal

1,200 pages; Softcover ISBN 1-59237-150-7 $165.00 ◆ Online Database $215.00 ◆ Online Database & Directory Combo $300.00

The Directory of Drug & Alcohol Residential Rehabilitation Facilities

This brand new directory is the first-ever resource to bring together, all in one place, data on the thousands of drug and alcohol residential rehabilitation facilities in the United States. *The Directory of Drug & Alcohol Residential Rehabilitation Facilities* covers over 1,000 facilities, with detailed contact information for each one, including mailing address, phone and fax numbers, email addresses and web sites, mission statement, type of treatment programs, cost, average length of stay, numbers of residents and counselors, accreditation, insurance plans accepted, type of environment, religious affiliation, education components and much more. It also contains a helpful chapter on General Resources that provides contact information for Associations, Print & Electronic Media, Support Groups and Conferences. Multiple indexes allow the user to pinpoint the facilities that meet very specific criteria. This time-saving tool is what so many counselors, parents and medical professionals have been asking for. *The Directory of Drug & Alcohol Residential Rehabilitation Facilities* will be a helpful tool in locating the right source for treatment for a wide range of individuals. This comprehensive directory will be an important acquisition for all reference collections: public and academic libraries, case managers, social workers, state agencies and many more.

"This is an excellent, much needed directory that fills an important gap..." –Booklist

300 pages; Softcover ISBN 1-59237-031-4, $135.00

To preview any of our Directories Risk-Free for 30 days, call (800) 562-2139 or fax to (518) 789-0556

Sedgwick Press
Education Directories

The Comparative Guide to American Elementary & Secondary Schools, 2006

The only guide of its kind, this award winning compilation offers a snapshot profile of every public school district in the United States serving 1,500 or more students – more than 5,900 districts are covered. Organized alphabetically by district within state, each chapter begins with a Statistical Overview of the state. Each district listing includes contact information (name, address, phone number and web site) plus Grades Served, the Numbers of Students and Teachers and the Number of Regular, Special Education, Alternative and Vocational Schools in the district along with statistics on Student/Classroom Teacher Ratios, Drop Out Rates, Ethnicity, the Numbers of Librarians and Guidance Counselors and District Expenditures per student. As an added bonus, *The Comparative Guide to American Elementary and Secondary Schools* provides important ranking tables, both by state and nationally, for each data element. For easy navigation through this wealth of information, this handbook contains a useful City Index that lists all districts that operate schools within a city. These important comparative statistics are necessary for anyone considering relocation or doing comparative research on their own district and would be a perfect acquisition for any public library or school district library.

"This straightforward guide is an easy way to find general information. Valuable for academic and large public library collections." –ARBA

2,400 pages; Softcover ISBN 1-59237-137-X, $125.00

Educators Resource Directory, 2005/06

Educators Resource Directory is a comprehensive resource that provides the educational professional with thousands of resources and statistical data for professional development. This directory saves hours of research time by providing immediate access to Associations & Organizations, Conferences & Trade Shows, Educational Research Centers, Employment Opportunities & Teaching Abroad, School Library Services, Scholarships, Financial Resources, Professional Consultants, Computer Software & Testing Resources and much more. Plus, this comprehensive directory also includes a section on Statistics and Rankings with over 100 tables, including statistics on Average Teacher Salaries, SAT/ACT scores, Revenues & Expenditures and more. These important statistics will allow the user to see how their school rates among others, make relocation decisions and so much more. For quick access to information, this directory contains four indexes: Entry & Publisher Index, Geographic Index, a Subject & Grade Index and Web Sites Index. *Educators Resource Directory* will be a well-used addition to the reference collection of any school district, education department or public library.

"Recommended for all collections that serve elementary and secondary school professionals." –Choice

1,000 pages; Softcover ISBN 1-59237-080-2, $145.00 ◆ Online Database $195.00 ◆ Online Database & Directory Combo $280.00

To preview any of our Directories Risk-Free for 30 days, call (800) 562-2139 or fax to (518) 789-0556

Sedgwick Press
Hospital & Health Plan Directories

The Comparative Guide to American Hospitals

This brand new title is the first ever resource to compare all of the nation's hospitals by 17 measures of quality in the treatment of heart attack, heart failure and pneumonia. This data is based on the recently announced Hospital Compare, produced by Medicare, and is available in print and in a unique and user-friendly format from Grey House Publishing, along with extra contact information from Grey House's *Directory of Hospital Personnel*. *The Comparative Guide to American Hospitals* provides a snapshot profile of each of the nations 6,000 hospitals. These informative profiles illustrate how the hospital rates in 17 important areas: Heart Attack Care (% who receive Aspirin at Arrival, Aspirin at Discharge, ACE Inhibitor for LVSD, Beta Blocker at Arrival, Beta Blocker at Discharge, Thrombolytic Agent Received, PTCA Received and Adult Smoking Cessation Advice); Heart Failure (% who receive LVF Assessment, ACE Inhibitor for LVSD, Discharge Instructions, Adult Smoking Cessation Advice); and Pneumonia (% who receive Initial Antibiotic Timing, Pneumococcal Vaccination, Oxygenation Assessment, Blood Culture Performed and Adult Smoking Cessation Advice). Each profile includes the raw percentage for that hospital, the state average, the US average and data on the top hospital. For easy access to contact information, each profile includes the hospitals address, phone and fax numbers, email and web addresses, type and accreditation along with 5 top key administrations. These profiles will allow the user to quickly identify the quality of the hospital and have the necessary information at their fingertips to make contact with that hospital. Most importantly, *The Comparative Guide to American Hospitals* provides an easy-to-use Ranking Table for each of the data elements to allow the user to quickly locate the hospitals with the best level of service. This brand new title will be a must for the reference collection at all public, medical and academic libraries.

2,500 pages; Softcover ISBN 1-59237-109-4 $175.00

The Directory of Hospital Personnel, 2006

The Directory of Hospital Personnel is the best resource you can have at your fingertips when researching or marketing a product or service to the hospital market. A "Who's Who" of the hospital universe, this directory puts you in touch with over 150,000 key decision-makers. With 100% verification of data you can rest assured that you will reach the right person with just one call. Every hospital in the U.S. is profiled, listed alphabetically by city within state. Plus, three easy-to-use, cross-referenced indexes put the facts at your fingertips faster and more easily than any other directory: Hospital Name Index, Bed Size Index and Personnel Index. *The Directory of Hospital Personnel* is the only complete source for key hospital decision-makers by name. Whether you want to define or restructure sales territories… locate hospitals with the purchasing power to accept your proposals… keep track of important contacts or colleagues… or find information on which insurance plans are accepted, *The Directory of Hospital Personnel* gives you the information you need – easily, efficiently, effectively and accurately.

"Recommended for college, university and medical libraries." –ARBA

2,500 pages; Softcover ISBN 1-59237-107-8 $275.00 ◆ Online Database $545.00 ◆ Online Database & Directory Combo, $650.00

The Directory of Health Care Group Purchasing Organizations, 2006

This comprehensive directory provides the important data you need to get in touch with over 800 Group Purchasing Organizations. By providing in-depth information on this growing market and its members, *The Directory of Health Care Group Purchasing Organizations* fills a major need for the most accurate and comprehensive information on over 800 GPOs – Mailing Address, Phone & Fax Numbers, E-mail Addresses, Key Contacts, Purchasing Agents, Group Descriptions, Membership Categorization, Standard Vendor Proposal Requirements, Membership Fees & Terms, Expanded Services, Total Member Beds & Outpatient Visits represented and more. Five Indexes provide a number of ways to locate the right GPO: Alphabetical Index, Expanded Services Index, Organization Type Index, Geographic Index and Member Institution Index. With its comprehensive and detailed information on each purchasing organization, *The Directory of Health Care Group Purchasing Organizations* is the go-to source for anyone looking to target this market.

"The information is clearly arranged and easy to access…recommended for those needing this very specialized information." –ARBA

1,000 pages; Softcover ISBN 1-59237-0091-8, $325.00 ◆ Online Database, $650.00 ◆ Online Database & Directory Combo, $750.00

To preview any of our Directories Risk-Free for 30 days, call (800) 562-2139 or fax to (518) 789-0556

The HMO/PPO Directory, 2006

The HMO/PPO Directory is a comprehensive source that provides detailed information about Health Maintenance Organizations and Preferred Provider Organizations nationwide. This comprehensive directory details more information about more managed health care organizations than ever before. Over 1,100 HMOs, PPOs and affiliated companies are listed, arranged alphabetically by state. Detailed listings include Key Contact Information, Prescription Drug Benefits, Enrollment, Geographical Areas served, Affiliated Physicians & Hospitals, Federal Qualifications, Status, Year Founded, Managed Care Partners, Employer References, Fees & Payment Information and more. Plus, five years of historical information is included related to Revenues, Net Income, Medical Loss Ratios, Membership Enrollment and Number of Patient Complaints. Five easy-to-use, cross-referenced indexes will put this vast array of information at your fingertips immediately: HMO Index, PPO Index, Other Providers Index, Personnel Index and Enrollment Index. *The HMO/PPO Directory* provides the most comprehensive information on the most companies available on the market place today.

> *"Helpful to individuals requesting certain HMO/PPO issues such as co-payment costs, subscription costs and patient complaints. Individuals concerned (or those with questions) about their insurance may find this text to be of use to them." -ARBA*

600 pages; Softcover ISBN 1-59237-100-0, $275.00 ◆ Online Database, $495.00 ◆ Online Database & Directory Combo, $600.00

The Directory of Independent Ambulatory Care Centers

This first edition of *The Directory of Independent Ambulatory Care Centers* provides access to detailed information that, before now, could only be found scattered in hundreds of different sources. This comprehensive and up-to-date directory pulls together a vast array of contact information for over 7,200 Ambulatory Surgery Centers, Ambulatory General and Urgent Care Clinics, and Diagnostic Imaging Centers that are not affiliated with a hospital or major medical center. Detailed listings include Mailing Address, Phone & Fax Numbers, E-mail and Web Site addresses, Contact Name and Phone Numbers of the Medical Director and other Key Executives and Purchasing Agents, Specialties & Services Offered, Year Founded, Numbers of Employees and Surgeons, Number of Operating Rooms, Number of Cases seen per year, Overnight Options, Contracted Services and much more. Listings are arranged by State, by Center Category and then alphabetically by Organization Name. Two indexes provide quick and easy access to this wealth of information: Entry Name Index and Specialty/Service Index. *The Directory of Independent Ambulatory Care Centers* is a must-have resource for anyone marketing a product or service to this important industry and will be an invaluable tool for those searching for a local care center that will meet their specific needs.

> *"Among the numerous hospital directories, no other provides information on independent ambulatory centers. A handy, well-organized resource that would be useful in medical center libraries and public libraries." –Choice*

986 pages; Softcover ISBN 1-930956-90-8, $185.00 ◆ Online Database, $365.00 ◆ Online Database & Directory Combo, $450.00

To preview any of our Directories Risk-Free for 30 days, call (800) 562-2139 or fax to (518) 789-0556